OXFORD PRIVATE INTERNATIONAL LAW
SERIES
GENERAL EDITOR: JAMES J FAWCETT
Professor of Law,
University of Nottingham

FORUM SHOPPING AND VENUE IN
TRANSNATIONAL LITIGATION

OXFORD PRIVATE INTERNATIONAL LAW SERIES

General Editor: James Fawcett

The aim of the series is to publish works of quality and originality in a number of important areas of private international law. The series is intended for both scholarly and practitioner readers.

ALSO IN THIS SERIES

Corporations in Private International law
STEPHAN RAMMELOO

Res Judicata, Estoppel and Foreign Judgments
PETER BARNETT

The Enforcement of Judgments in Europe
WENDY KENNETT

Claims for Contribution and Reimbursement in an
International Context
KOJI TAKAHASHI

The Hague Convention on International Child Abduction
PAUL BEAUMONT and PETER McELEAVY

Insolvency in Private International Law
IAN FLETCHER

Autonomy in International Contracts
PETER NYGH

Intellectual Property and Private International Law
JAMES J. FAWCETT and PAUL TORREMANS

Foreign Law in English Courts
RICHARD FENTIMAN

Declining Jurisdiction in Private International Law
JAMES J. FAWCETT

FORUM SHOPPING AND VENUE IN TRANSNATIONAL LITIGATION

ANDREW S BELL
BA, LLB (Syd); BCL, DPhil (Oxon)

Barrister, New South Wales
Sometime Vinerian Scholar in the
University of Oxford

With a Foreword by
Sir Anthony Mason AC, KBE
Chief Justice of Australia 1987–1995
Justice of the High Court of Australia 1972–1987

OXFORD
UNIVERSITY PRESS

OXFORD

UNIVERSITY PRESS

Great Clarendon Street, Oxford OX2 6DP

Oxford University Press is a department of the University of Oxford.
It furthers the University's objective of excellence in research, scholarship,
and education by publishing worldwide in

Oxford New York

Auckland Bangkok Buenos Aires Cape Town Chennai
Dar es Salaam Delhi Hong Kong Istanbul Karachi Kolkata
Kuala Lumpur Madrid Melbourne Mexico City Mumbai Nairobi
São Paulo Shanghai Taipei Tokyo Toronto

Oxford is a registered trade mark of Oxford University Press
in the UK and in certain other countries

Published in the United States
by Oxford University Press Inc., New York

First published 2003

British Library Cataloguing in Publication Data
Data available

Library of Congress Cataloging in Publication Data
Data available

ISBN 0-19-924818-4

1 3 5 7 9 10 8 6 4 2

Typeset in Palatino by
Cambrian Typesetters, Frimley, Surrey

Printed in Great Britain
on acid-free paper by
Biddles Ltd., Guildford and King's Lynn

Foreword

The area of law to which this monograph is directed is expanding at an astonishing rate. No doubt this is due to the tendency of forum shopping and choice of venue to lend themselves to litigation strategies and tactics as parties struggle to achieve some advantage at an early stage in commercial and maritime litigation.

The monograph examines forum shopping in its various manifestations, the inducements which sustain it, and its consequences. The author then deals with the responses to forum shopping, notably the allocation of jurisdiction by international agreement (The Brussels Convention on Jurisdiction and Judgments), European Council Regulation 44/2001, and the common law's development of the concept of the 'natural forum'. The author does not neglect the Australian mutation of the *Spiliada*[1] natural forum doctrine—the 'clearly inappropriate' forum doctrine adopted in *Voth v Manildra Flour Mills Pty Ltd*.[2] The author's preference is for *Spiliada*, a preference which is supported by arguments of policy and comity, his preference being shared by other Commonwealth jurisdictions. *Voth* and its Australian line of authority stand in lonely isolation.

Strategies to which defendants may have recourse ('reverse forum shopping') are discussed in detail, as is the role of international judicial comity. Likewise, jurisdiction and arbitration agreements are examined, mainly in the context of defendants attempting to elude the grip of agreements as to jurisdiction and modes of dispute resolution.

The work is of very high quality, reflecting both scholarship and perception. Yet unlike some other scholarly work, it is clearly written and easy to read. The examination of the problems and the legal issues is practical, policy informed, and principled. The discussion of the decided cases in many jurisdictions, including the United States, is comprehensive, indeed almost encyclopaedic. The analysis of the cases and judicial reasoning is penetrating.

This monograph will be invaluable to lawyers, not only to Commonwealth lawyers but also to American and European lawyers.

AF Mason

[1] [1987] AC 460.   [2] (1990) 171 CLR 538.

General Editor's Preface

Litigation over where to litigate has increased dramatically over the past two decades and this shows no sign of slowing down. Both plaintiffs and defendants and their legal advisers more than ever need to be aware of the importance of the venue for trial and of the strategies available to them to ensure that trial is held in their preferred forum. The term "forum shopping" is commonly used by academics and judges. But what are the incentives for this? What are the conceptual responses to forum shopping? What should they be? All of these matters have not received the attention that they merit. This is the first monograph to fill this gap and address these important matters. It is based on Dr Bell's thesis for which he obtained a D Phil at the University of Oxford. It is enriched by a decade of practical experience of transnational litigation at the Australian Bar. This provides fascinating insights into the practicalities of this type of litigation. As befits the subject matter of the book, a wide comparative approach has been adopted with detailed and comprehensive discussion of developments in many common law jurisdictions, particularly in England, Australia and the United States, and of developments in the European Union.

My predecessor as General Editor of the Oxford Private International Law Series, P B Carter QC recognised the importance of both this topic and of Dr Bell's contribution to it. I share his view that this is a work of both originality and quality and will be essential reading for both scholars and practitioners. As such, it is a valuable addition to the Oxford Private International Law Series.

James Fawcett
Nottingham
November 2002

Preface

This book began its life as a BCL thesis on the topic of anti-suit injunctions (at a time when that creature was far less developed and in vogue than it is today). The BCL thesis then grew into a doctoral work on the topic of 'Venue in Transnational Litigation: a study of the conditions for, motivations behind, and defences against forum shopping'. It responded to and sought to understand the burgeoning body of case law that was being generated by courts in the United Kingdom, Europe, the United States, South East Asia, Canada, Australia, and New Zealand in relation to disputes over the venue in which transnational proceedings should proceed—what Lord Templeman once described as 'litigation about where to litigate'.

In the decade since that doctoral work was undertaken, there has been no stemming of the tide of such litigation. If anything, it continues to grow apace and the highest appellate courts have had to grapple with many of the issues considered in this book. The case law is vast. In the last decade, practice at the commercial bar has also permitted many of my views in this area, originally formed in an academic context, to be tested in day-to-day commercial litigation. That experience has confirmed two central themes of this book, namely that venue does matter notwithstanding what might be considered to be the theoretical goal of private international law of uniformity of outcome irrespective of venue; and, secondly, that resolution of disputed questions or issues of venue often immediately precede settlement of a transnational dispute. Perspectives derived from practice have been integrated into the text as far as possible, for this book's subject matter, whilst undoubtedly interesting from an academic point of view, is fundamentally about day-to-day practice, predominantly although not exclusively in a commercial context.[1]

Such is the nature of the subject matter of this book that the *same* dispute will often give rise to litigation and decisions in multiple jurisdictions in respect of the same case (see, for example, *British Airways v Laker Airways* [1985] AC 58, *Midland Bank v Laker Airways* [1986] 1 QB 69 on the United Kingdom side, and *Laker Airways v Sabena World Airlines* 731 F2d 909 (1984), on the United

---

[1] The author should acknowledge his professional involvement in decisions of the High Court of Australia in *CSR Ltd v Cigna Insurance Australia Ltd* (1997) 189 CLR 345, *John Pfeiffer Pty Ltd v Rogerson* (2000) 203 CLR 503; *Agar v Hyde* (2000) 201 CLR 552 and *Renault v Zhang* (2002) 187 ALR 1, all of which are discussed, at times critically, in the text, as well as an indirect involvement in *Akai Pty Ltd v People's Insurance Company* (1997) 188 CLR 418 and [1998] 1 Lloyd's Rep 90. Other professional engagement of the author in matters before the Federal Court of Australia and the Supreme Court and Industrial Relations Commission of New South Wales and which are discussed in the text are noted in the reports of those cases.

States side; see also, more recently, *Akai Pty Limited v People's Insurance Company* which involved litigation up to and including the High Court of Australia (1997) 188 CLR 418, in England [1998] 1 Lloyd's Rep 90 as well as in Singapore). Such disputes are indicative of the very great complexity that can be and often is generated in a transnational dispute—complexity which may involve or require an understanding of legal, institutional and, sometimes, cultural differences in a range of forums.

Whilst this book is written from a common lawyer's perspective, and is directed principally to common lawyers, it is not a textbook on a particular country's jurisdictional rules. It seeks to reach a trans-jurisdictional audience consistent with its subject matter. It draws heavily not only on English decisions, which bestride both the jurisdictional scheme enshrined in the Brussels and Lugano Conventions and now European Council Regulation 44/2001 as well as the common law, but also upon decisions relating to jurisdiction and venue from Australia, Canada, New Zealand, Singapore, Malaysia, Hong Kong, the United States, and Europe.

My debts in writing this book are several. At an institutional level, I had the singular benefit of three years at Magdalen College, Oxford University with the support of the Rhodes Trust. In Oxford, I had the singular advantage of the supervision of Adrian Briggs whose ever-growing body of work in this field is a testament to both the depth of his knowledge and the sharpness of his insight. He has continued to be a source of ideas, friendship and great assistance, especially in volunteering to read the draft manuscript. I have also had the benefit of regular discussion and argument with senior members of the New South Wales Bar with and against whom I have been briefed to argue cases concerning forum disputes. I also acknowledge my debt of gratitude to Sir Anthony Mason, for agreeing to write the foreword to this book in his still hectic schedule.

On a personal level, I acknowledge the tremendous support and encouragement always provided to me by my parents throughout my education and beyond. I also acknowledge my colleagues in Chambers whose robust friendship makes for an excellent working environment. My final debt of gratitude is to my wife, Joanna Bird, whose friendship, love and encouragement cannot be adequately acknowledged. It is to her and our daughter that this book is dedicated.

The law in this book is stated as best known to me as at July 2002.

Andrew S Bell
11th Floor
Wentworth Chambers,
Sydney, NSW

Summary Contents

Table of Cases   xvii
Table of Legislation   xliii
Table of Conventions   xlvii
Table of Abbreviations   xlix

Chapter 1 Introduction   1
Chapter 2 Venue and the Plaintiff—The Incentives for Forum
    Shopping   23
Chapter 3 Conceptual Responses to Forum Shopping and
    Concurrent Jurisdiction   49
Chapter 4 Venue and the Defendant—Reverse Forum Shopping   133
Chapter 5 Venue by Consensus—The Role of Jurisdiction and
    Arbitration Agreements   275
Chapter 6 Conclusion   335

Index   343

Contents

Table of Cases		xvii
Table of Legislation		xliii
Table of Conventions		xlvii
Table of Abbreviations		xlix

Chapter 1 INTRODUCTION — 1.01
    I. Transnational Litigation and the Global Economy — 1.01
    II. Transnational Litigation and Concurrent Jurisdiction — 1.10
        1. 'Modern' Defendants: Ubiquitous and Vulnerable — 1.13
        2. 'Exorbitant' Jurisdiction — 1.19
        3. The Problems of Concurrent Jurisdiction — 1.26
    III. The Importance of Venue — 1.31
    IV. Venue in Transnational Litigation: Outline — 1.44

Chapter 2 VENUE AND THE PLAINTIFF—THE INCENTIVES FOR FORUM SHOPPING — 2.01
    I. Three Dimensions of Uniformity — 2.01
    II. The Significance of Procedure — 2.09
        1. The United States—A Forum Shopper's Delight — 2.14
        2. Beyond America: Further Procedural Inducements — 2.28
    III. Lack of Uniformity in Domestic Law — 2.33
    IV. Divergence in Choice of Law Rules and Practice — 2.37
    V. Conclusion — 2.58

Chapter 3 CONCEPTUAL RESPONSES TO FORUM SHOPPING AND CONCURRENT JURISDICTION — 3.01
    I. Introduction — 3.01
    II. Jurisdiction Allocated by Convention — 3.03
        1. The Jurisdictional Scheme of the Brussels Convention/Council Regulation 44/2001 — 3.13
        2. Multiple Proceedings and Council Regulation 44/2001 — 3.25
        3. Recognition and Enforcement of Judgments under Council Regulation 44/2001 — 3.45
        4. The Brussels Convention and Regulation 44/2001—A Model for Others? — 3.49

III. Common Law Regulation of Jurisdiction   3.68
    1. The Traditional Common Law Approach   3.71
    2. The 'Natural Forum'—Emergence of a Concept   3.78
    3. The Natural Forum—The Concept Considered   3.84
    4. The Natural Forum—The Concept Criticized   3.149
IV. Conclusion   3.170

Chapter 4 VENUE AND THE DEFENDANT—REVERSE FORUM SHOPPING   4.01
    I. Options for the Defendant   4.01
    II. Challenging Jurisdiction   4.12
        1. Challenging the Jurisdiction of Common Law
           Courts   4.13
        2. Constitutional Dimensions to Jurisdictional
           Challenges   4.27
    III. Staying Proceedings—*Forum Non Conveniens*   4.38
        1. *Spiliada* Applied   4.44
        2. Australian Abstention   4.67
        3. *Forum Non Conveniens* in the United States 4.74
    IV. Anti-Suit Injunctions   4.79
        1. Jurisdiction to Restrain Foreign Proceedings 4.84
        2. 'Protective' Anti-Suit Injunctions   4.125
        3. Anti-Suit Injunctions Upholding Legal Rights 4.146
        4. Restraint of Vexatious and Oppressive Foreign
           Proceedings   4.179
        5. Anti-Suit Injunctions and the Claims of Comity 4.223
    V. Negative Declaratory Proceedings   4.250
        1. The Mechanics of Negative Declaratory Relief 4.251
        2. Negative Declarations in the Common Law   4.261
        3. Negative Declarations and Council Regulation
           44/2001   4.284
    VI. Ignoring Foreign Proceedings   4.294
        1. Threats to the Strategy—I   4.295
        2. Threats to the Strategy—II   4.296
    VII. Conclusion   4.304

Chapter 5 VENUE BY CONSENSUS—THE ROLE OF JURISDICTION AND
    ARBITRATION AGREEMENTS   5.01
    I. The Nature and Importance of Jurisdiction
       and Arbitration Agreements   5.01
    II. Escaping the Bargain   5.15
        1. The Existence of the Jurisdiction
           or Arbitration Agreement   5.16
        2. Voidability of the Agreement   5.27

3. Overriding Effect of Mandatory Forum Law 5.37
4. The Agreement's Continuing Efficacy 5.49
5. The Nature of the Jurisdiction Agreement 5.54
6. Scope and Construction of the Jurisdiction
   or Arbitration Agreement 5.61
7. Discretion 5.72
8. Escape at Enforcement 5.101
III. Conclusion 5.104

Chapter 6 CONCLUSION 6.01

Index 343

Table of Cases

All references are to paragraph numbers.

(The) Abidin Daver [1984] AC 398 . . . . . . .1.17, 1.27, 3.79, 3.82, 3.83, 3.91, 3.98, 3.99, 3.100, 3.101, 3.115, 3.121, 3.126, 4.47, 4.53, 4.55, 4.56, 4.236, 5.93

Ace Insurance SA-NV v Zurich Insurance Co [2001] 1 Lloyd's Rep 618 . . . . .3.102, 4.63, 4.64, 5.54

Adams v Cape Industries plc [1990] Ch 433 . . . . .1.13, 4.303

(The) Adhiguna Meranti [1987] HKLR 904; [1988] 1 Lloyd's Rep 384 . . . . .2.48, 4.39, 4.58

(The) Adolf Warski [1976] 2 Lloyd's Rep 241 . . . . .5.13, 5.81, 5.85

Advanced Cardiovascular Systems Inc v Universal Specialties Ltd [1997] 1 NZLR 186 . . . . .5.29, 5.79

Aetna Life Insurance Co v Haworth 300 US 227 (1937) 4.267

Agar v Hyde (2000) 201 CLR 552 . . . . .1.25, 3.92, 4.12, 4.18, 4.19, 4.22

Agrafax Public Relations Ltd v United Scottish Society Inc [1995] CLC 862 . . . . .4.55

Agro Co of Canada Ltd v The Regal Scout (1983) 148 DLR (3rd) 412; [1984] 2 FC 851 . . . . .5.24, 5.38

AIG Europe SA v QBE International Insurance Ltd [2001] 2 Lloyd's Rep 268 . . . . .5.26

AIG Europe (UK) Ltd v The Ethniki [2000] 2 All ER 566 . . . . .5.26

Aiglon SA v Gau Shan Co Ltd [1992] 1 Lloyd's Rep 164 . . . . .4.286

Air Nauru v Niue Airlines Ltd [1993] 2 NZLR 632 . . . . .5.44

Airbus Industrie GIE v Patel [1999] 1 AC 199 . . . . .1.10, 3.32, 3.82, 3.147, 4.94, 4.102, 4.104, 4.113, 4.114, 4.234

Akai Pty Ltd v People's Insurance Company (1996) 185 CLR 571; (1997) 188 CLR 418; [1998] 1 Lloyd's Rep 90 . . . . .1.29, 1.42, 2.50, 2.51, 4.100, 4.140, 4.233, 4.238, 4.260, 5.07, 5.13, 5.38, 5.46, 5.79

(The) Al Battani [1993] 2 Lloyd's Rep 219 . . . . .1.37, 4.55, 4.56, 5.30, 5.81, 5.90

Al Ru Farm Pty Ltd v Hedleys Humpers Ltd [1991] ACL Rep 85 SA 1 . . . . .4.70

(The) Albaforth [1984] 2 Lloyd's Rep 91 . . . . .4.73, 4.275

Aldred v Australian Building Industries Pty Ltd (1987) 48 NTR 59 . . . . .5.82

Allen v Lloyd's of London 94 F 3d 923 (1996) 5.45, 5.79

Allendale Insurance Corp v Bull Data Systems Inc 10 F 3d 425 (7th Cir, 1993) .3.142, 4.121, 4.225, 4.237, 4.244

Allied-Signal Inc v Dome Petroleum Ltd [1989] 5 WWR 326 . . . . . . .4.201
Allstate Life Insurance Co Ltd v Australian and New Zealand Banking
    Group Ltd (1996) 64 FCR 1 . . . . .1.39, 3.140, 3.142, 4.131,
                                                                    4.134, 4.142, 4.216
(The) Amazonia [1990] 1 Lloyd's Rep 236 . . . . .2.01, 5.29, 5.52
Amchem Products Inc v Workers Compensation Board [1993]
    1 SCR 897 . . . . .1.04, 1.07, 1.11, 3.148, 3.156, 3.162, 4.39,
            4.104, 4.106, 4.116, 4.138, 4.179, 4.202, 4.224, 4.238, 4.240,
                                                4.241, 4.244, 4.245, 4.248
Amerco v Chatsworth [1977] 2 MLJ 181 . . . . .5.82
American Dredging Co v Miller 114 S Ct 981 (1994) 4.74, 4.76,
                                                                    4.78, 4.245
American Home Assurance Co v Insurance Corporation of Ireland
    603 F Supp 636 (1984) 3.31, 3.142, 4.121, 4.122, 4.209, 4.215
Amin Rasheed Corp v Kuwait Insurance [1984] AC 50 . . . . .3.145, 3.146,
                                                                    4.12, 4.55
Amoco (UK) Exploration Co Ltd v British American Offshore Ltd
    [1999] 2 Lloyd's Rep 772 . . . . .4.91, 4.239
Anderson v GH Michell & Sons Ltd (1941) 65 CLR 543 . . . . . .4.151, 5.89
(The) Andhika Samyra [1989] 1 HKLR 198 . . . . .4.58, 5.38
Andrea Merzario v Internationale Spedition Leitner Gesellschaft
    GmbH [2001] 1 Lloyd's Rep 490 . . . . .3.05, 4.293
(The) Angelic Grace [1994] 1 Lloyd's Rep 168; [1995] 1 Lloyd's
    Rep 87 . . . . .4.147, 4.157, 4.158, 4.162, 4.212,
                                                        4.223, 4.228, 5.01, 5.65
Anglo-Australian Foods Ltd v Von Planta (1988) FCR 34 . . . . .4.70
(The) Anita [1970] 2 Lloyd's Rep 265 . . . . .4.192
(The) Annefield [1971] P168 . . . . .5.25
Apple Computer Inc v Apple Corps SA [1990] 2 NZLR
    598 . . . . .3.108, 3.110, 4.100, 5.44
Apple Corps Ltd v Apple Computer Inc [1992] RPC 70 . . . . .3.108,
                                                        4.101, 4.147, 4.231
Arab Monetary Fund v Hashim, *Financial Times* 23 July
    1992 . . . . .4.128, 4.238
Arkwright Mutual Insurance Co v Bryanston Insurance Co Ltd [1990]
    2 QB 649 . . . . .3.126, 4.55, 4.64, 4.65, 4.273
Armstrong v Armstrong [1892] P98 . . . . .4.126
Asahi Metal Industry Co v Superior Court of California, Solano County
    480 US 102 (1987) 4.31, 4.68
Ash v Lloyd's Corporation (1991) 6 OR (3d) 235; (1992) 9 OR
    (3d) 755 . . . . .5.36, 5.45
Asher v Goldman Sachs and Co (21 October) 4.275
Ashville Investments v Elmer Contractors [1989] 1 QB 488 . . . . .5.65

(The) Asian Plutus [1990] 2 MLJ 449 . . . . .5.82, 5.92
Askin v Absa Bank [1999] IlPr 471 . . . . .4.53
Assicurazioni Generali SpA v Ege Sigorta A/S (31 July 2001) 5.26
Associated Newspapers Group plc v Insert Media Ltd [1988]
    1 WLR 590 . . . . .4.91
(The) Athenee (1922) 11 Ll LR 6 . . . . .5.13
(The) Atlantic Emperor (No 2)[1992] 1 Lloyd's Rep 624 . . . . .4.147,
                                                                                        4.161
(The) Atlantic Song [1983] 2 Lloyd's Rep 394 . . . . .5.53, 5.81, 5.89
(The) Atlantic Star [1974] AC 436 . . . . .1.17, 1.40, 2.05, 2.30, 2.31, 3.04,
    3.71, 3.72, 3.75, 3.77, 3.78, 3.79, 3.80, 3.81, 3.82, 3.83, 3.85, 3.86, 3.89, 3.96,
                                3.97, 3.98, 3.157, 4.04, 4.179, 4.180, 4.282
Attock Cement Ltd v Romanian Bank Foreign Trade [1989]
    1 WLR 1147 . . . . .4.14, 5.10
Australian Broadcasting Corporation v Lenah Game Meats Pty Ltd
    (2001) 185 ALR 1 . . . . .4.105
Australian Commercial Research and Development Ltd v ANZ
    McCaughan Merchant Bank Ltd [1989] 3 All ER 65 . . . . . .3.109, 3.111,
                                3.112, 3.113, 3.120, 4.99, 4.208, 4.260
Austrian Lloyd Steamship Co v Gresham Life Assurance Society Ltd
    [1903] 1 KB 249 . . . . .5.58, 5.60

Baghlaf Al Zafer v PNSC [1998] 2 Lloyd's Rep 229 . . . . .1.38, 5.37
Baghlaf Al Zafer Factory v Pakistan National Shipping Co [No 2]
    [2000] 1 Lloyd's Rep 1 . . . . .4.50, 5.37
Bailey v Welpley 4 Ir RCL 243 (1869) 4.206
Banca Carige v Banco Nacionale de Cuba [2001] 2 Lloyd's Rep
    147 . . . . .1.01
Banco Atlantico SA v The British Bank of the Middle East [1990] 2
    Lloyd's Rep 504 . . . . .2.58, 3.63, 3.160, 4.57, 4.58, 4.61
Banco Nominees Ltd v Iroquois Brands Ltd 748 F Supp 1070 (D Del,
    1990) 3.141
Bank of Africa Ltd v Cohen [1909] 2 Ch 129 . . . . .4.147
Bank of America v Bank of New York (1995) 17 ATPR 41-390,
    40, 337 . . . . .2.05, 4.209
Bank of New York v Bank of America 861 F Supp 225
    (1994) 4.142
Bank of Tokyo Ltd v Karoon (Note) [1987] AC 45 . . . . .2.15, 4.104, 4.112,
                                4.125, 4.132, 4.133, 4.143, 4.183, 4.195, 4.208, 4.238
Bankers Trust Co v Pt Jakarta International Hotels & Development
    [1999] 1 Lloyd's Rep 910 . . . . .4.147, 4.151, 5.05
Bankers' Trust International v PT Dharmala Sakti Sejahtera [1996]
    CLC 252 . . . . .4.131

Banque Paribas v Cargill International SA [1992] 1 Lloyd's
Rep 96 . . . . .4.269
Banque Paribas v Jarret [1991] ACL Rep 325 VIC 94 . . . . .4.70
Bayer AG v Winter, *The Times* 24 March 1986 .1.27
Beals v Saldanha (2001) 202 DLR (4th) 630 . . . . .4.299, 4.300
Beecham (Aust) Pty Ltd v Roque Pty Ltd (1987) 11 NSWLR 1 . . . . .4.223
(The) Benarty [1985] QB 325 . . . . .5.06, 5.40, 5.81, 5.96
Bendix Autolite Corp. v Midwesco Enterprises, Inc 108 S Ct 2218
(1988) 4.30
Benincasa v Dentalkit Srl [1997] ECR 3767 . . . . .5.76
Bent v Young (1838) 9 Sim 180 . . . . .4.86
Berezovsky v Michaels [2000] 1 WLR 1004 . . . . .1.26
Berisford plc v New Hampshire Insurance Co [1990] 2 QB 631 . . . . .4.55,
4.64, 4.65, 5.10, 5.54, 5.59, 5.91
Bier BV v Mines de Potasse D'Alsace SA, Case 21/76 [1976] ECR
1735 . . . . .2.36
(The) Biskra [1983] 2 Lloyd's Rep 59 . . . . .5.50
Bisso v Inland Waterways Corp 349 US 85 (1955) 2.55, 5.41
Blackman & Co v Oliver Davey Glass Co [1966] VR 570 . . . . .5.98
(The) Blue Wave [1982] 1 Lloyd's Rep 151 . . . . .5.23, 5.81, 5.90
BMG Trading Limited v AS McKay Ltd [1998] I L Pr 691 . . . . .5.37
Boma Navigation Ltee v The Hansa Bay [1975] FC 231 . . . . .5.82
Bond Brewing Holdings Ltd v Crawford (1989) 92 ALR 154 . . . . . . .4.223
Bonny v Society of Lloyd's 3 F 3d 156 (1993) 5.45, 5.79
Booker v Bell [1989] 1 Lloyd's Rep 516 . . . . .4.269
Borek v Answer Products Inc [2000] QSC 379 . . . . .4.26
Bouygues Offshore SA v Caspian Shipping Co (Nos 1, 3, 4 and 5)
[1998] 2 Lloyd's Rep 461 . . . . .3.89, 3.136, 4.216, 5.10, 5.94
Boys v Chaplin [1971] AC 356 . . . . .2.05, 2.39, 3.80, 3.83, 4.275
BP Exploration Co (Libya) Ltd v Hunt (No 2) [1983] 2 AC 352 . . . . .4.254
(The) Brabo [1949] AC 326 . . . . .3.145, 4.19, 4.22
Breavington v Godleman (1988) 169 CLR 41 . . . . .2.09, 4.148
Bremen v Zapata Offshore Co *see* (The) Chaparral
Brinco Mining Ltd v Federal Insurance Co 552 F Supp 1233
(DDC, 1982) 3.141
Brinkerhoff Maritime Drilling Corp v PT Airfast Services Indonesia
[1992] 2 SLR 776 . . . . .4.50
Bristol Corporation v John Aird & Co [1913] AC 241 . . . . .5.05
Britannia Steamship Insurance Association v Ausonia
Assicurazioni SpA [1984] 2 Lloyd's Rep 98 . . . . .2.58, 3.126, 4.25,
4.58, 4.61
British Aerospace plc v Dee Howard Co [1993] 1 Lloyd's Rep
368 . . . . .5.10, 5.59, 5.91, 5.92

British Airways Board v Laker Airways Ltd [1984] QB 142;
[1985] AC 58 . . . . .3.147, 4.97, 4.99, 4.102, 4.109, 4.110,
4.111, 4.113, 4.115, 4.137, 4.138, 4.146, 4.148, 4.187, 4.190, 4.194,
4.218, 4.219, 4.250, 5.44
British South Africa Co v Companhia de Moçambique [1893]
AC 602 . . . . .5.77
Bruno v Soc Citibank Ct App Versailles 1991 . . . . .4.295, 5.77
Bulk Oil (Zug) AG v Trans-Asiatic Oil Ltd SA [1973] 1 Lloyd's Rep
129 . . . . .3.130, 5.95
Burnham v Superior Court of California 110 S Ct 2105 (1990) 1.16
Bushby v Munday (1821) 5 Madd 297 (56 ER 908) 4.86
Buttes Gas & Oil Co v Hammer [1971] All ER 1025 . . . . .4.20

Caltex Singapore Pte Ltd v BP Shipping Ltd [1996] 1 Lloyd's Rep
286 . . . . .2.52, 2.56
(The) Cambridgeshire [1987] AC 460 . . . . .3.93, 3.114
Camilla Cotton Oil Co v Granadex SA [1975] 1 Lloyd's Rep 470;
[1976] 2 Lloyd's Rep 10 . . . . .3.120, 4.251, 4.252, 4.260, 4.269,
4.276, 4.283, 5.95
Canadian Commercial Bank v Carpenter (1990) 62 DLR
(4th) 734 . . . . .4.14
Canadian Filters (Harwich) Ltd v Lear-Siegher, Inc 412 F 2d 577
(1st Cir, 1969) 4.100
Canadian Home Assurance Co v Cooper (1985) 29 DLR (4th)
419 . . . . .4.147, 4.201
Cannon Manufacturing Co v Cudahy Packing Co 267 US 33
(1925) 1.13
Cannon Screen Entertainment v Handmade Films (Distributors) Ltd
(11 July 1989) 4.195, 4.201, 5.59
(The) Cap Blanco [1913] P 130 . . . . .5.02, 5.58
(The) Cap Bon [1967] 1 Lloyd's Rep 543 . . . . .4.208
Cargill v Hartford Accident & Insurance Co 531 F Supp 710 (D Minn,
1982) 3.31, 4.121, 4.215
Carnac, Re; Ex parte Simmonds (1885) QBD 308 . . . . .4.221
Carnival Cruise Lines v Shute 499 US 585 (1991) 1.06, 5.06, 5.12,
5.34, 5.88
Carob Industries Limited (In Liquidation) v Simto Pty Limited [1997]
18 WAR 1 . . . . .5.25
Carron Iron Co v Maclaren (1855) 5 HL Cas 416 . . . . .4.85
Carter Holt Harvey Timber Ltd v Pacifico Timber Importers Pty Ltd
(High Court of New Zealand, 7 December 1992) 3.104
Carvalho v Hull, Blyth (Angola) Ltd [1979] 1 WLR 1228 . . . . . .5.50, 5.71,
5.90, 5.93

(The) Caspian Basin Specialised Emergency Salvage Operation v
  Vouygues [1997] 2 Lloyd's Rep 507 . . . . .2.56
Castanho v Brown & Root (UK) Ltd [1981] AC 557 . . . .2.17, 3.147, 3.162,
  4.90, 4.93, 4.108, 4.109, 4.110, 4.111, 4.112, 4.113, 4.120,
  4.153, 4.181, 4.185, 4.190, 4.203
Chaney v Murphy (1948) 64 TLR 489 . . . . .3.75, 3.145
Channel Tunnel Group Ltd v Balfour Beatty Construction Ltd
  [1993] AC 334 . . . . .1.07, 4.88, 4.124, 4.146
(The) Chaparral [1968] 2 Lloyd's Rep 158; 407 US 1 (1972); [1972] 2
  Lloyd's Rep 315 . . . . .2.55, 4.121, 4.165, 5.03, 5.06, 5.08, 5.13,
  5.32, 5.33, 5.34, 5.41, 5.43, 5.55, 5.79, 5.80, 5.83, 5.86, 5.88, 5.90
Charm Maritime Inc v Kyriakou [1987] 1 Lloyd's Rep 433 . . . . .3.129,
  4.208, 4.211
Charman v WOC offshore BV [1993] 1 Lloyd's Rep 378 . . . . .4.260, 4.269,
  4.275, 4.287
Chartered Mercantile Bank of India v Netherlands India Steam
  Navigation Co Ltd (1883) 10 QBD 521 . . . . .2.39
Chase v Ram Technical Services Ltd [2000] 2 Lloyd's Rep 418 . . . . .3.118,
  4.198, 4.276
Chellaram v Chellaram [1985] 1 Ch 409 . . . . .4.56
China Trade and Development Corp v MV Choong Yong 837 F 2d
  33 (2d Cir, 1987) 4.120, 4.129, 4.130, 4.196, 4.209, 4.224, 4.273
Chowdhury v Mitsui OSK Lines Ltd [1970] 2 Lloyd's Rep 272 . . . . . .5.38
(The) Christianborg (1885) 10 PD 141 .3.112, 3.113
(The) Christos [1977] 1 Lloyd's Rep 109 . . . . .5.51
Citi-March v Neptune Orient Lines [1997] 1 Lloyd's Rep 72 . . .5.81, 5.96
Clarke v Lo Bianco (1991) 84 DLR (4th) 244 . . . . .4.299, 4.300
Clay, Re [1919] 1 Ch 66 . . . . .4.198, 4.263, 4.265, 4.269, 4.289
Cleveland Museum of Art v Capricorn Art International SA [1990] 2
  Lloyd's Rep 166 . . . . .3.105, 3.120
Club Méditerranée NZ v Wendell [1989] 1 NZLR 216 . . . . .4.39, 4.46
Coast Lines Ltd v Hudig & Veder Chartering NV [1972] 2 QB 34 . . .2.49,
  5.40
Cohen v Rothfield [1919] 1 KB 410 . . . . . . .3.98, 3.103, 4.205, 4.206, 4.207
Cole v Cunningham 133 US 107 (1890) 4.85
Commercial Bank of the Near East plc v A, B, C and D [1989] 2 Lloyd's
  Rep 319 . . . . .3.104, 4.273
Commonwealth Bank of Australia v White; ex parte The Society of
  Lloyd's [1992] 2 VR 681 . . . . .5.36, 5.38, 5.45
Compagnie des Bauxites de Guinea v Insurance Corp of North America
  651 F 2d 877 (3rd Cir, 1981) 3.27
Compagnie des Messageries Maritimes v Wilson (1954) 94
  CLR 577 . . . . .5.38

Compagnie Européenne de Cereals SA v Tradax Export SA [1986] 2
    Lloyd's Rep 301 . . . . .4.109, 4.213
Compagnie Tunisienne de Navigation SA v Compagnie d'Armement
    Maritime SA [1971] AC 572 . . . . .5.18
Computer Associations International Inc v Altai, Inc 126 F 3d 365 (2nd
    Cir, 1997) 4.120
Connelly v RTZ Corporation plc [1998] AC 854 . . . . .4.48, 4.52, 4.55
Connolly Brothers Ltd, In re [1911] 1 Ch 731 . . . . . .3.77, 4.95, 4.179, 4.194
Continental Bank NA v Aeakos Compania Naviera SA [1994] Lloyd's
    Rep 505; [1994] 1 WLR 588 . . . . .3.28, 4.151, 4.168, 4.173, 4.174,
                      4.176, 4.177, 4.178, 4.246, 5.59, 5.65
Cool Carriers AB v HSBC Bank (USA) [2001] 2 Lloyd's Rep 22 . . . . .4.03
Copin v Adamson (1875) 1 Ex D 17 . . . . .5.10, 5.101
Copperweld Steel Co v Demag-Mannesman-Boehler 578 F 2d 953 (3rd
    Cir, 1978) 5.88
(The) Coral Isis [1986] 1 Lloyd's Rep 413; [1986] 1 QB 413 . . . .3.99, 3.162,
                                    4.24
Coreck Maritime GmbH v Handels-reem BV [2000] ECR I-9337 . . . .5.70,
                             5.75, 5.76, 5.77, 5.78
Cover Europe, Re, 26 February 2002 . . . . .3.39
Crédit Suisse Financial Products v Société Générale d'Entreprises [1997]
    CLC 168 . . . . .5.26
Crédit Suisse First Boston (Europe) Ltd v MLC (Bermuda) Ltd [1999] 1
    Lloyd's Rep 767 . . . . .3.121
Crosley Corp v Hazeltine Corp 122 F 2d 925 (3d Cir 1941), cert denied
    315 US 813 (1942) 3.27
CSR v Cigna Insurance Australia (1997) 189 CLR 345 . . . . . . .3.63, 3.103,
        3.109, 3.111, 3.125, 4.38, 4.83, 4.95, 4.104, 4.105, 4.117, 4.183,
                       4.197, 4.222, 4.224, 4.230
CSR Ltd v New Zealand Insurance Co Ltd (1994) 36 NSWLR
    138 . . . . .1.39, 4.134, 4.227, 4.244
Curnow Shipping Ltd v National Bank of New Zealand Ltd (1990) 2
    PRNZ 67 . . . . .3.123

DA Technology Australia v Discreet Logic Inc (Federal Court of
    Australia, 10 March 1994) 3.140
(The) Daeyang Honey (1991) 109 ALR 120; (1994) 120 ALR 109 . . . . .4.70,
                                  4.246, 4.273
(The) Dai Yun Shan [1992] 2 SLR 508 . . . . .5.82
de Dampierre v de Dampierre [1988] AC 92 . . . . .1.38, 2.38, 3.87,
                                 3.104, 3.125
De la Vega v Vianna (1830) 1 B & Ad 284 . . . . .3.71
Deaville v Aeroflot [1997] 2 Lloyd's Rep 67 .4.238

Definitely Maybe (Touring) Ltd v Marek Lieberberg Konzert Agentur
    GmbH [2001] 1 WLR 1745 ....4.36
(The) Delfini [1988] 2 Lloyd's Rep 599 ....3.167
(The) Delos [2001] 1 Lloyd's Rep 703 ....5.25
(The) Delta (1876) 1 PD 393 ....3.112, 4.258
Deluxe Ice Cream Co v RCH Tool Corp 726 F 2d 1209 (7th Cir,
    1984) 4.30
Denby v The Hellenic Mediterranean Lines Co Ltd [1994] 1 Lloyd's
    Rep 320 ....4.171, 5.11
Denilauer v SNC Couchet Frères, Case 125/79 [1980] ECR
    1552 ....3.45, 4.35
Diethelm & Co v Bradley (1995) ATPR 41-388 ....1.06
Djoni Widjaja v Bank of America National Trust and Savings
    Association [1993] 3 SLR 678 ....4.93
Doherty v Allman (1873) 3 App Cas 709 ....4.153
Domansa v Derin Shipping & Trading Co Inc [2001] 1 Lloyd's Rep
    362 ....1.13, 5.38, 5.68
Donohue v Armco Inc [2000] 1 Lloyd's Rep 579; [2002] 1 Lloyd's Rep
    425 ....3.89, 3.118, 3.136, 4.05, 4.88, 4.93, 4.104, 4.113, 4.149,
                4.163, 4.164, 4.189, 4.216, 4.231, 5.10, 5.13, 5.27, 5.45, 5.50,
                                  5.65, 5.67, 5.79, 5.95, 5.100
Donovan v City of Dallas 377 US 408 (1964) 3.27
Dow Chemical Co v Castro Alfaro 786 SW2d 674 (Tex, 1990) 1.39,
                                  3.62, 3.64, 4.38, 4.76, 4.77
DR Insurance v Central National Insurance [1996] 1 Lloyd's
    Rep 74 ....2.43, 3.107
Dresser UK Ltd v Falcongate Freight Management Ltd [1992
    QB 502 ....3.29
Drouot Assurances v Consolidated Metallurgical Industries [1998] ECR
    I-3075 ....3.39
Du Pont de Nemours & Co v Agnew [1987] 2 Lloyd's Rep 585 .....2.56,
                                  3.10, 3.108, 3.120, 4.113, 5.95
Du Pont de Nemours & Co v Agnew (No 2) [1988] 2 Lloyd's Rep
    240 ....4.255, 4.269, 4.273
Dumez France v Hessische Landesbank, Case C-220/88 [1990]
    ECR I-49 ....2.36, 3.19, 3.20, 3.61
Dyson v Attorney-General [1911] 1 KB 410 ....4.262, 4.265

Earl of Mansfield v Stewart (1846) 5 Bell 139 ....4.268
Earl of Oxford's Case (1615) 1 Ch Rep 1 (21 ER 485) 4.85
(The) Eastern Trader [1996] 2 Lloyd's Rep 585 ....4.246
Effer SpA v Kantner, Case 38/81 [1982] ECR 825 ....3.13
Egon Olendorff v Libera Corporation [1996] 1 Lloyd's Rep 388 .....5.07

(The) El Amria [1981] 2 Lloyd's Rep 28 . . . . . . .2.31, 5.10, 5.22, 5.23, 5.80, 5.81, 5.94, 5.96, 5.97

(The) El Minia [1981] 2 Lloyd's Rep 539; [1982] 2 Lloyd's Rep 28 . . .2.31, 5.22, 5.23

Elefanten Schuh GmbH v Jacqmain [1981] ECR 1671 . . . . .5.28

(The) Eleftheria [1970] P 94 . . . . .5.10, 5.53, 5.79, 5.80, 5.83, 5.84, 5.85, 5.86, 5.89, 5.90, 5.91, 5.92, 5.93, 5.94, 5.96

Eli Lilly and Company v Novo Nordisk A/S [2000] ILPr 73 . . . . .4.63

Ellerman Lines Ltd v Read [1928] 2 KB 144 . . . . .4.124, 4.147, 4.250

Ellinger v Guinness, Mahon & Co [1939] 4 All ER 16 . . . . .5.93

(The) Emre II [1989] 2 Lloyd's Rep 182 .1.17, 5.22

Enforcement of an English Anti-Suit Injunction, Re the [1997] ILPr 320 . . . . .4.233

(The) Epar [1985] 2 MLJ 3 . . . . .5.38

Erie Railroad v Tompkins 304 US 64 (1938) 4.74

European Asian Bank AG v Punjab and Sind Bank [1981] 2 Lloyd's Rep 651 . . . . .3.161, 4.24, 4.25

Evans Marshall & Co Ltd v Bertola SA [1973] 1 WLR 349 . . . . .5.29, 5.58, 5.80, 5.81, 5.90

Evers v Firth (1986) 10 NSWLR 22 . . . . .2.12

Excess Insurance Co Limited v Allendale Mutual Insurance Co, Court of Appeal, 8 March 1995 . . . . .3.102

Fabrelle Wallcoverings & Textiles Ltd v North American Decorative Products Inc [1993] ILPr 381 . . . . .4.299, 4.300

FAI General Insurance Co Ltd v Ocean Marine Mutual Protection and Indemnity Association (1997) 41 NSWLR 559 . . . . .5.36, 5.58, 5.59

(The) Falstria [1988] 1 Lloyd's Rep 495 . . . . .2.52

Federal Deposit v Vanstone (1992) 88 DLR (4th) 448 . . . . .4.299, 4.300

(The) Fehmarn [1958] 1 WLR 159 . . . . .5.13, 5.32, 5.53, 5.80, 5.81, 5.83

Ferris v Plaister (1994) 34 NSWLR 474 . . . . .5.36

Feyerick v Hubbard (1902) 71 LJ KB 509 . . . . .5.10

Finnish Insurance Corporation v Protective Insurance Corporation 1990] 1 QB 1078 . . . . .4.260

First National Bank of Boston v Union Bank of Switzerland [1990] 1 Lloyd's Rep 32 . . . . .3.120, 4.04, 4.198, 4.251, 4.258, 4.269, 4.270, 4.286, 5.95

(The) Forum Craftsman [1985] 1 Lloyd's Rep 291 . . . . .5.62, 5.65

Francis Travel Marketing Pty Ltd v Virgin Atlantic Airways Ltd (1996) 39 NSWLR 160 . . . . .5.48, 5.67

(The) Frank Pais [1986] 1 Lloyd's Rep 529 . . . . .5.81, 5.89

Friends For All Children, Inc v Lockheed Aircraft Corp 717 F 2d 602 . . . . .3.93

(The) Frinton [1990]2 HKLR 700 . . . . .5.82, 5.97, 5.98
Frymer v Brettschneider (1994) 115 DLR (4th) 744 . . . . .4.39

G & E Auto Brokers Ltd v Toyota Canada Inc (1980) 117 DLR (3d)
    707 . . . . .5.79
Gadd v Gadd [1984] 1 WLR 1435 . . . . .2.38
GAF Corporation v Amchem Products Inc [1975] 1 Lloyd's
    Rep 601 . . . . .4.20, 4.23
Garpeg, Limited v United States 583 F Supp 789 (SDNY 1984) 4.121
Gascoine v Pyrah [1994] ILPr 82 . . . . .3.21, 3.22, 3.115
Gau Shan Co Ltd v Bankers Trust Co 956 F 2d 1349 (6th Cir, 1992)
    3.142, 4.120, 4.123, 4.225
General Electric Company v Deutz AG 270 F 3d 144 (2001) 4.120
(The) Giacinto Motta [1977] 2 Lloyd's Rep 221 . . . . .2.52
Gilmore, In the marriage of (1993) 16 Fam LR 285 . . . . . . .2.38, 2.59, 4.70
Glencore International AG v Exter Shipping Ltd [2002] 2 All ER
    (Comm) 1 . . . . .3.140, 4.134, 4.196, 4.197, 4.216
Glencore International Ltd v Metro Training International [2001] 1
    Lloyd's Rep 284 . . . . .2.47
(The) Goldean Mariner [1989] 2 Lloyd's rep 390 . . . . . . .1.38, 3.123, 3.124,
                                                                          3.126, 3.165, 4.38
(The) Golden Anne [1984] 2 Lloyd's Rep 489 . . . . .4.147, 4.153, 4.232
Goliath Portland Cement Co Ltd v Bengtell (1994) 33 NSWLR
    414 . . . . .1.41
Green v Australian Industrial Investment Ltd (1989) 25 FCR 532;
    (1989) 90 ALR 500 . . . . .4.70, 5.45
(The) Griesheim (Hong Kong Court of Appeal, No 70 of 1983) 5.23
Guaranty Trust Co of New York v Hannay & Co [1915]
    2 KB 536 . . . . .4.198, 4.250, 4.252, 4.260, 4.261, 4.262, 4.265, 4.269, 4.282
Gubisch Maschinenfabrik KG v Palumbo, Case 144/86 [1987] ECR
    4861 . . . . .3.34, 3.35, 3.39, 3.40, 4.65, 4.273, 4.290, 4.292
Guessefeldt v McGrath 342 US 308 (1952) 4.28
Gulf Bank KSC v Mitsubishi Heavy Industries Ltd [1994] 1 Lloyd's Rep
    323 . . . . .4.259, 5.55
Gulf Oil Corp v Gilbert 330 US 501 (1947) 1.24, 1.33, 3.90, 3.164, 4.74

(The) Hagen [1908] P 189 . . . . .3.145, 4.20, 4.23, 4.205
Haji-Ioannou v Frangos [1999] 2 Lloyd's Rep 337 . . . . . . .4.65, 4.66, 4.171
Hambros Bank Ltd v Thune (18 January 1991) No 6095/90 . . .4.90, 4.106,
                                                                          4.115, 4.147, 4.179
(The) Hamburg Star [1994] 1 Lloyd's Rep 399 . . . . .2.52, 3.120, 3.126, 4.60
(The) Handgate [1987] 1 Lloyd's Rep 142 . . . . .4.25
Hantarex SpA v SA Digital Research [1993] ILPr 501 . . . . .3.23

(The) Happy Pioneer [1983] HKLR 43 . . . . .5.63

Harbour Assurance Co (UK) Ltd v Kansa General International
  Insurance Co Ltd [1993] 1 Lloyd's Rep 455; [1993]
  QB 701 . . . . .5.36, 5.65

Harman v Home Office [1983] 1 AC 280 . . . . .2.25

Harris Corp v National Iranian Radio & Television 691 F 2d 1344 (11th
  Cir, 1982) 5.93

Harrods (Buenos Aires) Ltd, Re [1992] Ch 72 . . . . . . .3.58, 4.62, 4.63, 4.64,
                                                  4.65, 4.66, 4.288, 5.78

Hartford Fire Insurance Co v California 113 S Ct 2891 (1993) 1.23

Harvey Aluminium, Inc v American Cynamid Co, 203 F 2d 105
  (1953) 4.120

(The) Havhelt [1993] 1 Lloyd's Rep 523 . . . . .5.90

Haynsworth v Corporation of Lloyd's 121 F 3d 956 (1997) 5.45, 5.79

Helicopteros Nacionales de Colombia SA v Hall 466 US 408
  (1984) 1.14, 4.30

Hemain v Hemain [1988] 2 FLR 388 . . . . .4.113, 4.205

Henderson v Henderson (1843) 3 Hare 100 . . . . .5.102

Henry Geoprosco International Ltd [1976] QB 726 . . . . .4.43, 4.247, 5.103

Henry v Henry (1996) 185 CLR 571; (1997) 188 CLR 418 . . . . .1.08,
                                      2.59, 3.103, 3.104, 3.120, 4.205

(The) Herceg Novi [1998] 2 Lloyd's Rep 454 . . . . .2.56, 4.58

Hi-Fert Pty Ltd v Kiukang Maritime Carriers Inc (No 5) (1998)
  90 FCR 1 . . . . .5.15, 5.48, 5.67

Hi-Fert Pty Ltd v United Shipping Adriatic Inc (1998) 89 FCR
  166 . . . . .5.38

HIB v Guardian Insurance [1997] 1 Lloyd's Rep 414 . . . . .1.42, 4.283

(The) Hida Maru [1981] 2 Lloyd's Rep 206 . . . . .5.10, 5.51

Hilton v Guyot 159 US 113 (1895) 4.224

Hing Fat Plastic Manufacturing Co Ltd v Advanced Technology
  Products (HK) Ltd [1992] 2 HKLR 350 .4.209

HM Attorney-General v Arthur Andersen Co (United Kingdom)
  [1989] ECC 224 . . . . .3.113, 3.140, 4.216

Hoerter v Hanover Telegraph Works (1893) 10 TLR 103 . . . . .4.176, 5.56,
                                                            5.57, 5.60

(The) Hollandia [1983] AC 565 . . . . .5.37, 5.40

Holmes v Bangladesh Biman [1989] AC 1112 . . . . .2.48

Hope v Carnegie (1866) LR Vol 1 320 . . . . .4.143

Hopkins v Difrex Société Anonyme [1966] 1 NSWR 797 . . . . .5.82

Horn v York Paper Co Ltd (1990) 9 ACLC 60 . . . . .4.70

Hough v P & O Containers Ltd [1999] QB 834 . . . . .3.22

Houston v Sligo (1885) 29 ChD 448 . . . . .4.258

Huddart Parker Ltd v The Ship Mill Hill (1950) 81 CLR 502 . . . . .5.82

Hunt v BP Exploration Co (Libya) Ltd 492 F Supp 885 (ND Tex, 1980) 4.254
(EF) Hutton & Co (London) Ltd v Mofarrij [1989] 1 WLR 488 . . . . .3.120
Hyman v Helm (1883) 24 ChD 531 . . . . .3.103, 4.180, 4.200, 4.205
Hyslop v Society of Lloyd's (1992) 6 PRNZ 204 . . . . .3.109

Ilderton v Ilderton [1793] 2 HBl 145; ER 476 . . . . .1.01
Import of Italian Sports Cars, Re the [192] ILPr 188 . . . . . .5.28, 5.39, 5.69
(The) Indian Fortune [1985] 1 Lloyd's Rep 34 . . . . .5.90
(The) Indian Grace [1993] AC 410 . . . . .4.256
Industrie Tessili Italiana Como v Dunlop AG [1976] ECR 1473 . . . . . .3.58
Ingersoll Milling Machine Co v Granger 833 F 2d 680 (7th Cir, 1987) 3.141
Insurance Corporation of Hanover Inc v Latino Americana de Reassuregos SA 868 F Supp 520 . . . . .5.86
Insurance Corporation of Ireland Ltd v Compagnie des Bauxites 456 US 694 . . . . .4.78
Insurance Corporation of Ireland v Strombus [1985] 2 Lloyd's Rep 138 . . . . .3.131, 3.135, 4.283
International Credit and Investment Company (Overseas) Ltd v Badham [1998] BCC 134 . . . . .2.32
International General Electric Co of New York Ltd v Commissioner of Customs and Excise [1962] 1 Ch 784 . . . . .4.252
International Risk Management Group Ltd v Elwood Insurance Ltd (29 September 1993, Supreme Court of Bermuda, Nos 103 & 245/93) 4.43, 4.148, 4.162
International Shoe Co v Washington 326 (US) 310 (1945) 1.14, 1.24, 3.10, 4.28, 4.34
Ionian Bank Ltd v Couvreur [1969] 1 WLR 781 . . . . .3.74, 3.98
IP Metal Ltd v Ruote OZ SpA [1993] 2 Lloyd's Rep 60 . . . . . . .2.42, 4.273
(The) Iran Bohonar [1983] 2 Lloyd's Rep 621 . . . . .4.53
(The) Iran Vojdan [1984] 2 Lloyd's Rep 380 . . . .5.30, 5.32, 5.56, 5.58, 5.89
(The) Iran Zagubanski [2002] 1 Lloyd's Rep 106 . . . . .4.147
Irish Shipping Ltd v Commercial Union Assurance Co plc [1991] 2 QB 206 . . . . .2.02, 2.42, 4.60
Islamic Arab Insurance Co v Saudi Egyptian American Reinsurance Co [1987] 1 Lloyd's Rep 315 . . . . .3.126
Israel Discount Bank of New York v Hadjipateras [1984] 1 WLR 137 . . . . .5.102

Jackson v Spittall (1870) LR 5 CP 542 . . . . .3.71
(The) Jalakrishna [1983] 2 Lloyd's Rep 628 . . . . .2.31, 4.56
James, Ex parte (1874) LR 9 Ch App 609 . . . . .4.221

James Buchanan & Co Ltd v Babco Forwarding and Shipping (UK) Ltd
[1978] AC 141 ....2.45, 3.54
James Hardie v Grigor (1998) 45 NSWLR 20 ....3.90, 4.70
James Miller & Partners v Whitworth Street Estates Ltd [1970] AC
583 ....2.43
James Stoddard v Accupress Manufacturing Ltd [1944] 1 WWR
677 ....4.299, 4.301, 4.302
(The) Janera [1928] P 55 ....3.99
(The) Jemrix [1981] 2 Lloyd's Rep 544 ....5.98
Jeyaretnam v Mahmood, *The Times* 21 May 1992 ....2.03, 4.53
Jogia, Re [1988] 2 All ER 328 ....5.22
John Pfeiffer Pty v Rogerson (2000) 203 CLR 503 ....2.13, 3.152, 4.10
John Russell & Co Ltd v Cayzer, Irvine & Co Ltd [1916] 2 AC
298 ....4.22
Johnson v Coventry Churchill International Ltd [1992] 3 All
ER 14 ....2.39

Kaepa, Inc v Achilles Corporation 76 F 3d 624 (5th Cir, 1996) 4.122,
4.209, 4.244
Kalfelis v Bankhaus Schröder, Case 189/87 [1988] ECR 5565 ....3.18
(The) Kapetan Georgis [1988] 1 Lloyd's Rep 352 ....3.120
(The) Kapitan Shvetsov [1998] 1 Lloyd's Rep 199 ...2.52, 3.99, 3.100, 4.58
Kawasaki v 'Daeyang Honey' (1991) ALR 109 ....4.246
Keeton v Hustler Magazines Inc 465 US 770 (1984) 2.12
Kidd v van Heeren [1998] 1 NZLR 324 ....5.74
Kim Meller Imports Pty Ltd v Eurolevant SpA (1986) 7 NSWLR
269 ....5.38
King v Bristow Helicopters Ltd [2001] 1 Lloyd's Rep 95 ....2.02
Kinnear v Falconfilms NV (27 January 1994) 4.273
Kinoshita & Co, Re 287 F 2d 951 (1961) 5.64
Kirchner v Gruban [1909] 1 Ch 413 ....5.86, 5.90
(The) Kislovodsk [1980] 1 Lloyd's Rep 183 ....5.90, 5.96
Kitechnology BV v Unicor GmbH Plastmaschinen [1995] FSR 765 ...5.65
Klaxon v Stentor Electric Manufacturing 313 US 487 (1941) 4.74
Kloekner & Co AG v Gatoil Overseas Inc [1990] 1 Lloyd's Rep
177 ....3.28, 4.171, 4.273, 5.11
Knauf UK GmbH v British Gypsum Ltd [2002] 1 WLR
907 ....3.23, 3.30, 3.32
Koh Kay Yew v Inn Pacific Holdings Ltd [1997] 2 SLR 121 ....4.116
Kongress Agentur GmbH v Zeehaghe BV, Case C-365/88 [1990]
ECR I-1845 ....3.40, 4.289, 5.76
(The) Kribi [2001] 1 Lloyd's Rep 76 ....2.40, 4.151, 4.159
Kurz v Stella Musical Veranstaltungs GmbH [1992] Ch 196 ....3.23

Kuwait Airways Corporation v Iraq Airways Co [1994] 1 Lloyd's Rep
 276 . . . . .4.43, 4.247
Kuwait Airways Corporation v Iraq Airways Co (Nos 4 and 5)
 [2001] 1 Lloyd's Rep 161; [2002] 2 WLR 1353 . . . . .1.01, 1.23,
 4.59, 4.100
Kuwait Asia Bank EC v National Mutual Life Nominees Ltd [1991]
 AC 187 (PC) 4.14, 4.22

Labak v Graznar 6 NE 2d 790 (1935) 4.200, 4.213, 4.214
Ladenimar v Intercomfinanz, Case 314/92 . . . . .3.58
Laker Airways v Sabena, Belgian World Airways 731 F 2d 909 (DC Cir,
 1984) 3.27, 3.31, 3.142, 4.119, 4.120, 4.123,
 4.125, 4.129, 4.135, 4.213, 4.223, 4.237
Laminex (Australia) Pty Ltd v Coe Manufacturing (1998) 20 ATPR
 41-610, 40-669 . . . . .3.118
(The) Lanka Muditha [1991] 1 HKLR 741 . . . . .3.121
Lauritzen v Larsen 345 US 571 (1973) 2.01
Law v Garett (1878) 8 Ch D 26 . . . . .5.90
Leigh-Mardon Pty Ltd v PRC Inc (1993) 44 FCR 88 . . . . . .3.111, 5.38, 5.45
Lemmex v Bernard (2001) 204 DLR (4th) 192 . . . . .1.06, 1.22, 3.134
Lep International Pty Ltd v Atlantictrafic Express Service Inc (1987)
 10 NSWLR 614 . . . . .5.82
Lett v Lett [1906] 1 IR 618 . . . . .4.85, 4.147, 4.156
Lewis Construction Co Pty v M Tichauer Société Anonyme [1966]
 VR 341 Liddell's Settlement Trusts, Re [1936] Ch 365 . . . . .4.93
Lief Investments Pty Ltd v Conagra International Fertilizer Company
 [1998] NSWSC 481 . . . . .5.25
(The) Linda [1988] 1 Lloyd's Rep 175 . . . . .3.43
(The) Lisboa [1980] 2 Lloyd's Rep 546 . . . . .4.147, 4.149, 4.155, 4.160
(The) Lloydiana [1983] 2 Lloyd's Rep 313 . . . . .5.50
Logan v Bank of Scotland (No 2) [1906] 1 KB 141 . . . . . .3.75, 4.194, 4.200
(The) London [1931] P 14 . . . . .3.99
Longbeach Holdings Ltd v Bhanabhai & Co Ltd [1994]
 2 NZLR 28 . . . . .4.39
Lord Dillon v Alvares (1798) 4 Ves 357 (34 ER 867) 4.206
Lord Portarlington v Soulby (1834) 3 My & K 104 (40 ER 40) 4.85
Louvet v Louvet [1990] 1 HKLR 670 . . . . .2.38, 3.87, 4.48, 4.60
Love v Baker (1665) 2 Freem 125; 1 Ch Ca 67 (22 ER 698) 4.85
Lubbe v Cape [2000] Lloyd's Rep 139; [2000] 1 WLR 1545 . . . . .2.03, 2.05,
 3.90, 3.117, 4.52, 4.66
(The) Lucile Bloomfield [1964] 1 Lloyd's Rep 324 . . . . .3.75, 3.99

Machado v Fontes [1897] 2 QB 231 . . . . .2.39

(The) Maciej Rataj [1991] 2 Lloyd's Rep 458; [1992] 2 Lloyd's Rep
   552 . . . . .2.52, 4.269, 4.273, 4.282, 4.292
Mackay Refined Sugars (NZ) v NZ Sugar Co [1997] 3 NZLR
   476 . . . . .3.104, 3.140, 4.39
Mackender v Feldia AG [1967] 2 QB 590 . . . . .5.17, 5.27, 5.29, 5.36
Macquarie Bank v Bell and Berg (1999) 87 IR (NS) 126; 93 IR (NSW)
   191 . . . . .1.07
MacShannon v Rockware Glass Ltd [1978] AC 795 . . . . .1.29, 2.18,
      3.02, 3.62, 3.82, 3.83, 3.91, 3.93, 3.158, 3.159, 3.163, 4.49, 4.108
(The) Madrid [1937] P 40 . . . . .3.99
(The) Magnum [1989] 1 Lloyd's Rep 47 . . . . .2.55
Maharanee of Baroda v Wildenstein [1972] 2 QB 283 . . . . .1.16, 1.38, 2.30,
      3.75, 3.79
Maharani Woollen Mills Co v Anchor Line (1927) 29 Ll LR 169 . . . .5.37
(The) Mahkutai [1996] AC 650 . . . . .5.24, 5.25
Mainschiffahrts-Genossenschaft e G v Les Gravières Rhénanes SarL
   [1997] ECR I-911 . . . . .5.11
(The) Makefjell [1976] 2 Lloyd's Rep 29 . . . . .5.59, 5.63, 5.85, 5.96
(The) Maldive Importer [1986] 1 MLJ 12 . . . . .5.82
(The) Mali Ivo (1869) LR 2 A & E 356 .3.74, 3.112
Man (Sugar) Ltd v Haryanto (No2) [1991] 1 Lloyd's Rep 429 . . . . . .4.93,
      4.115, 4.146, 4.214, 5.52
Mantovani v Carapelli SpA [1978] 2 Lloyd's Rep 63; [1980]
   1 Lloyd's Rep 375 . . . . .4.147, 4.149
Marazura Navegaçion SA v Oceanus Mutual Underwriting Association
   [1997] 1 Lloyd's Rep 283 . . . . .4.147
Marc Rich & Co AG v Società Italiana Impianti PA, Case C-190/89
   [1991] ECR I-3855 . . . . .4.147, 4.161, 4.166, 4.252, 4.273
(The) Maria Gorthon [1976] 2 Lloyd's Rep 720 . . . . . . .4.147, 4.160, 4.228
Maritime Insurance Co Ltd v Geelong Harbour Trust Commissioners
   (1908) 6 CLR 194 . . . . .3.71, 3.151
Maritime Telegraph and Telephone Company v Pre Print Inc (1996)
   131 DLR (4th) 471 . . . . .5.79
Maxwell Communications Corporation plc (No 2), Re [1992]
   BCC 757 . . . . .4.93, 4.98, 4.113, 4.115, 4.144, 4.220, 4.235, 4.238
May v Reford (1969) 6 DLR (3d) 288 . . . . .5.82
(The) MC Pearl [1977] 1 Lloyd's Rep 566 . . . . .5.81, 5.96, 5.99
McConnell Dowell Constructors Ltd v Lloyd's Syndicate 396 [1988]
   2 NZLR 257 . . . . .3.126, 4.39, 4.252, 4.269, 5.95
McDonnell Douglas Corp v Islamic Republic of Iran 758 F 2d 341
   (8th Cir, 1985) 5.93
McHenry v Lewis (1882) 22 ChD 397 . . . . . . .3.72, 3.76, 3.98, 3.103, 3.112,
      4.179, 4.180, 4.194, 4.206, 4.207

McKain v RW Miller & Co (SA) Pty Ltd (1991) 174 CLR 1 . . . . .2.09, 2.12

McMickle v van Staaten (1992) 93 DLR (4th) 4.299, 4.300

Meadows Indemnity Co Ltd v The Insurance Corporation of Ireland
  plc [1989] 1 Lloyd's Rep 181; [1989] 2 Lloyd's Rep 298 . . .3.120, 3.138,
  4.269, 5.95

(The) Media (1931) 41 L Lr 80 . . . . .5.86

Mediterranean Enterprises Inc v Ssangyong Corporation 708 F 2d
  1458 (1983) 5.64

Medtronic, Inc v Catalyst Research Corp 518 F Supp 946 (1981),
  aff'd 664 F 2d 660 (8th Cir, 1981), 956 . . . . .4.100, 4.147, 4.214

Melan v Duke de Fitzjames (1797) 1 B & P 138 . . . . .3.71

(The) Merchant Prince [1892] P 179 . . . . .2.30

Mercury Communications Ltd v Communication Telesystems Interna-
  tional [1999] 2 All ER 33 . . . . .5.91

Meridian BIAO v Bank of New York [1997] 1 Lloyd's Rep
  437 . . . . .1.42, 3.104

Merrill Lynch v Raffa [2001] ILPr 437 . . . . .4.53

Merzario v Internationale Spedition Leitner [2001] 1 Lloyd's Rep
  490 . . . . .3.29

Messier-Dowty Ltd v Sabena SA [2000] 1 Lloyd's Rep 428; [2000]
  1 WLR 2040 . . . . .3.32, 3.106, 4.198, 4.269, 4.271, 4.274, 4.293

(The) Messiniaki Tolmi [1983] 1 Lloyd's Rep 666 . . . . .3.133

Metall & Rohstoff AG v Donaldson Lufkin & Jenrette [1990] 1 QB
  391 . . . . .4.14, 4.15, 4.190

Metall und Rohstoff AG v ACLI Metals (London) Ltd [1984] 1 Lloyd's
  Rep 598 . . . . .1.33, 4.113, 4.238

Metrocall Inc v Electronic Tracking Systems Pty Ltd (2000) 52
  NSWLR 1 . . . . .5.48, 5.67

Midland Bank plc v Laker Airways Ltd [1986] 1 QB 689 . . . . .2.15,
  2.26, 4.95, 4.97, 4.100, 4.137, 4.187, 4.195, 4.217,
  4.218, 4.220, 4.250, 4.269

Miller v United Technologies Corp 515 A 2d 390 (Conn, 1986) 4.77

Milor SRL v British Airways plc [1996] QB 702 . . . . .3.09, 3.169

Milwaukee County v ME White Co 296 US 268 . . . . .3.10

Minkler & Kirschbaum v Sheppard (1991) 60 BCLR (2d)
  360 . . . . .4.299, 4.300

Minories Finance v Afribank Nigeria [1995] 1 Lloyd's Rep 134 . . . . .2.32

Missing Share Certificates, Re [1991] I L Pr 298 . . . . .5.69

Mithras Management Ltd, Re (1992) 90 DLR (4th) 726 . . . . .5.82

Mitsubishi Motors Corp v Soler Chrysler-Plymouth Inc 473 US 614
  (1985) 5.45, 5.47

Mizokami Brothers of Arizona, Inc v Baychem Corp 556 F 2d 975 (8th
  Cir, 1977), cert denied 434 US 1035 . . . . .3.59

Modern Building Wales Pty Limited v Limmer & Trinidad Co Limited
 [1975] 1 WLR 1281 . . . . .5.25
Mogul Steamship Co v McGregor, Gow & Co [1892] AC 25 . . . . .4.99
Mohammed v Bank of Kuwait [1996] 1 WLR 1483 . . . . .4.53
Molins v GD SpA [2000] 1 WLR 1741 . . . . .3.29
(The) Monte Urbasa [1953] 1 Lloyd's Rep 587 . . . . .3.99
Moore v Moore (1896) 12 TLR 221 . . . . .4.200
(JP) Morgan Securities Asia Private Ltd v Malaysia Newsprint
 Industries Sdn Bhd [2001] 2 Lloyd's Rep 41 . . . . .5.91
Morguard Investments Ltd v de Savoye [1990] 3 SCR 1077 . . .1.04, 3.148,
            4.224, 4.296, 4.297, 4.298, 4.299, 4.301, 4.302, 4.303
Moses v Shore Boat Builders [1992] 5 WWR 282; (1993) DLR (4th)
 654 . . . . .4.298, 4.299
Muduroglu Ltd v TC Ziraat Bankasi [1986] QB 1225 . . . . .4.53, 4.191,
                               4.192, 4.193, 5.93
Multinational Gas and Petrochemical Co v Multinational Gas and
Petrochemical Services Ltd [1983] Ch 258 . . . . .4.19
(Joseph) Murphy Structural Engineers v Manitowoc (UK) Ltd, 30 July
 1985 . . . . .4.113

National Australia Bank Ltd v Idopost Pty Ltd [2002] NSWSC
 623 . . . . .4.142
National Mutual Holdings Pty Ltd v Sentry Corporation (1989) 87
 ALR 539 . . . . .4.105, 4.134, 4.135
National Westminster Bank Ltd v Utrecht-America Finance Co [2001]
 1 All ER (Comm) 7 . . . . .4.147, 4.232
Neptune Bulk Terminals Ltd v Intertec Internationale Technische
 Assistenz (1981) 127 DLR (3d) 736 . . . . .5.82
(The) Nerano [1996] 1 Lloyd's Rep 1 . . . . .5.24
(The) Netty [1981] 2 Lloyd's Rep 57 . . . . .3.162
Neuchatel Swiss General Insurance Co v Lufthansa Airlines 925 F 2d
 1193 (9th Cir, 1991) 3.141
New Hampshire Insurance v Aerospace Finance [1998] 2 Lloyd's Rep
 539 . . . . .2.22, 3.104
New Hampshire Insurance Co v Strabag Bau AG [1992] 1 Lloyd's Rep
 361 . . . . .3.120, 3.134, 3.135, 4.269, 5.95
(The) Nile Rhapsody [1992] 2 Lloyd's Rep 399 . . . . . .3.63, 4.56, 5.78, 5.80
Nolan, Re; ex parte Young (1991) 172 CLR 460 . . . . .4.191
North Eastern Marine Engineering Co v Leeds Forge Co [1906]
 1 Ch 324 . . . . .4.266
Northern Sales Co Ltd v Government Trading Corp of Iran (1991) 81
 DLR (4th) 316 . . . . .5.09
Norton's Settlement, In re [1908] 1 Ch 471 . . . . .4.194, 4.200

Nova (Jersey) Knit Ltd v Kammgarn Spinnerei GmbH [1977]
    1 WLR 713 . . . . .5.56

Ocarina Marine Ltd v Macard Stein & Co [1994] 2 Lloyd's Rep
    524 . . . . .5.61
Ocean Mutual Marine v FAI General Insurance, Commercial Court,
    16 June 1998 . . . . .4.99
Oceanic Sun Line Special Shipping Co Inc v Fay (1988) 165
    CLR 197 . . . . .1.04,
            1.06, 1.22, 3.31, 3.60, 3.78, 3.110, 3.149, 3.150, 3.151, 3.154, 3.156,
                4.26, 4.68, 4.70, 5.17, 5.19, 5.20, 5.21, 5.42
Oceano Grupo v Quintero [2000], Case C-240/98 . . . . .5.35
Oil Spill by the Amoco Cadiz off the Coast of France, In re, 1984 AMC
    2123 (ND Ill, 1984) 2.52
(The) Oinussin Pride [1991] 1 Lloyd's Rep 126 . . . . .3.135, 4.55
OK Petroleum AB v Vitol Energy SA [1995] 2 Lloyd's Rep 160 . . . . . .5.26
Olympic Corp v Société Générale 462 F 2d 376 (2nd Cir, 1972) 3.59
Omega Group Holdings Ltd v Kozeny (6 September 2001) [1996]
    CLC 252 . . . . .4.131
Oppenheimer v Cattermole [1976] AC 249 . . . . .5.93
Orr-Lewis v Orr-Lewis [1949] P 347 . . . . .4.205
OT Africa Line v Hijazy [2001] 1 Lloyd's Rep 76 . . . . .3.33, 4.174
Oulton Agencies Inc v Knolloffice Inc (1988) 48 DLR (4th)
    545 . . . . .5.79, 5.82
Overseas Union Insurance Ltd v Incorporated General Insurance Ltd
    [1992] 1 Lloyd's Rep 439 . . . . .3.126
Overseas Union Insurance Ltd v New Hampshire Insurance Company,
    Case C-351/89 [1991] ECR I-3317 . . . . .3.28, 3.36, 3.38, 3.47,
                4.65, 4.170, 4.283, 5.11
Owens Bank Ltd v Bracco [1992] 2 AC 443; Case C-129/92 [1994]
    ECR I-117 . . . . .3.37, 3.38, 5.102
Owens-Corning Fibreglass Corp v Baker 838 SW 2d 838 (Tex App,
    Texark, 1992) 4.138
Owens-Illinois Inc v Webb 809 SW 2d 899 (Tex App, Texrk,
    1991) 4.138
Owusu v Jackson [2002] ECWA Civ 877 . . . . .3.58, 4.66, 5.78

Pacific Resources Corporation v Credit Lyonnais Rouse (CA, 7 October
    1994) 5.65
(The) Pacific Senator [2001] 2 Lloyd's Rep 674 . . . . .5.58, 5.59, 5.86
Pain v United Technologies Corp 637 F 2d 775, 790 (DC Cir,
    1980) 3.141
Pan American World Airways Inc v Andrews [1992] SLT 268 . . . . . .4.238

Pan Lloyd Shipping Ltd v Cho Hung Bank [1992] 1 HKLR 356 . . . . .5.23
(The) Panseptos [1981] 1 Lloyd's Rep 152 . . . . .5.81, 5.96
Paper Products Pty Ltd v Tomlinsons (Rochdale) Ltd (1993) 43 FCR
 439 . . . . .5.67
Paramasivam v Flynn (1998) 90 FCR 489 . . . . .2.38
Pena Copper Mines Ltd v Rio Tinto Co Ltd [1911-1913]
 All ER 209 . . . . .4.147, 4.156, 4.223
Pendy Plastic Products v Pluspunkt [1982] ECR 2723 . . . . .4.35
Pennoyer v Neff 95 US 714 (1878) 1.20
Perfetto v Parlapiano [1993] ILPr 190 . . . . .5.69
Perkins v Benguet Consolidated Mining Co 342 US 437
 (1952) 1.14, 4.30
Peruvian Guano Co v Bockwoldt (1883) 23 ChD 225 . . . . .3.71, 3.72,
 3.73, 3.75, 3.76, 3.103, 3.112, 4.180, 4.205
Peters v ZNAV, Case 34/82 [1983] ECR 987 . . . . .3.20
(The) Petr Schmidt [1995] 1 Lloyd's Rep 202 . . . . .5.65
Philip Alexander Securities and Futures Ltd v Bamberger [1997]
 ILPr 73 . . . . .4.233
Phillips v Eyre (1870) LR 6 QB 1 .2.39, 4.99, 3.152
(The) Pia Vesta [1984] 1 Lloyd's Rep 169 . . . . .5.50, 5.81, 5.89
Picketts v International Playtex, Inc, 576 A 2d 518 (Conn, 1990) 4.77,
 4.245
(The) Pioneer Container [1994] 2 AC 324 . . . . .5.24, 5.66
Piper Aircraft Co v Reyno 454 US 235 (1981) 2.15, 2.44, 3.60, 3.62,
 3.90, 3.141, 3.164, 4.09, 4.41, 4.57, 4.58, 4.74, 5.33
Pirelli v United Thai Shipping Corporation [2000] 1 Lloyd's Rep
 663 . . . . .5.37
Pirrana Small Car v Rumm [1981] 5 WWR 79 . . . . .5.82, 5.89
Pittsburgh-Corning Corp v Askewe 823 SW 2d 759 (Tex App, Texark
 1992) 4.138, 4.243
(The) Playa Larga [1983] 2 Lloyd's Rep 171 . . . . .5.65
(The) Po [1990] 1 Lloyd's Rep 418 . . . . .3.162
Polito v GENSG [1960] Ex CR 233 . . . . .5.82
Polly Peck International plc v Citibank NA [1994] ILPr 71 . . . .3.28, 4.273
Powell Duffryn plc v Petereit, Case C-214/89 [1992]
 ECR I-1745 . . . . .5.28
Power Curber International Ltd v National Bank of Kuwait SAK
 [1981] 1 WLR 1233 . . . . .2.41
Prima Paint Corporation v Flood & Conklin Manufacturing Co 388 US
 395 (1967) 5.36
Purcell v Khayat, *The Times* 23 November 1987 . . . . .4.53

(The) Quo Vadis [1951] 1 Lloyd's Rep 425 . . . . .3.99

Radhakrishna Hospitality Service Private Ltd v EIH Ltd [1999]
  2 Lloyd's Rep 249 . . . . .4.50
Raguz v Sullivan (2000) 50 NSWLR 236 . . . . .5.01
Raiffeisen Zentralbank Österreich AG v Five Star Trading LLC [2001]
  1 QB 825 . . . . .1.15
Rasoulzadeh v Associated Press 574 F Supp 854 (SDNY) 1983, aff'd 767
  F 2d 908 (2d Cir, 1985) 5.93
Recyclers of Australia Pty Ltd v Hettinga Equipment Inc (2000)
  100 FCR 420 . . . . .5.52, 5.62
Reese Brothers Plastics Ltd v Hamon-Sobelco Australia Pty Ltd [1989]
  ACLD 35098 . . . . .4.70
(The) Reinbeck (1889) 6 Asp MLC 366 . . . . .3.85
Renault v Zhang (2002) 187 ALR 1 . . . . . . .1.06, 1.22, 1.41, 2.03, 2.13, 2.24,
                    2.39, 2.47, 3.60, 3.94, 3.103, 3.150, 3.152, 4.18, 4.26,
                                     4.70, 4.72, 4.73, 4.98
Réunion Européenne SA v Spliethoff's Bevrechtings-Kantoor [1998]
  ECR I-6511; [2000] QB 690 . . . . .3.18, 3.22, 3.24
(The) Rewia [1991] 1 Lloyd's Rep 69; [1991] 2 Lloyd's Rep 325 . . . . . .5.70
Richards v Lloyd's of London 135 F 3d 1289 (1998) 5.45, 5.79
Riley v Kingsley Underwriting Agencies Ltd 969 F 2d
  953 (1992) 5.45, 5.79
Roberts v Hampton & Sons [1989] 2 HKLR 89 . . . . .3.95
Roby v Corporation of Lloyd's 996 F 2d 1353 (1993) 5.45, 5.79, 5.86
Roneleigh Ltd v MII Exports Inc [1989] 1 WLR 618 . . . . .4.25, 4.55
Rösler v Rottwinkel, Case 241/83 [1985] ECR 99 . . . . .3.09, 4.62
Rothmans of Pall Mall (Overseas) Ltd v Saudi Arabian Airlines Corp
  [1981] 1 QB 368 . . . . .3.04, 3.05
(The) Rothnie [1996] 2 Lloyd's Rep 206 . . . . .5.10, 5.86
Rowan Companies, Inc v DiPersio (1990) 69 DLR (4th) 224 . . . . . . .4.144
(The) Ruben Martinez Villena [1998] 1 Lloyd's Rep 435 . . . . . . .5.53, 5.89
Russian Volunteer Fleet v United States 282 US 481 (1931) 4.28

S Megga Telecommunications Ltd v Etowaru Co Ltd [1995] 2 HKC
  761 . . . . .4.246
SA Mineracao da Trindade-Samitri v Utah International Inc 745
  F 2d 190 (1984) 5.66
Sanicentral GmbH v Collin, Case 25/79 [1979] ECR
  3423 . . . . .5.28, 5.39
Sarabia v 'Oceanic Mindaro' [1997] 2 WWR 116 . . . . .5.66, 5.79
Sarrio v Kuwait Investment Authority [1999] 1 AC 32 . . . . .3.42
Scherk v Alberto-Culver Company 417 US 506 (1974) 5.12
Schiffahrtsgesellschaft Detlev von Appen v Voest Alpine Intertrading
  GmbH [1997] 1 Lloyd's Rep 179 . . . . .4.147, 4.151, 4.228, 4.246

Sea Containers Ltd v Stena AB 890 F 2d 1205
(DC Cir, 1989) 4.120, 4.135
Seaconsar Far East Ltd v Bank Markazi Jomhouri Islami Iran [1994]
1 AC 438 . . . . .3.120, 3.145, 4.14, 4.17, 4.19, 4.21, 4.22, 4.25
Sealey (orse Callan) v Callan [1953] P 135 . . . . .2.38
(The) Seapearl v Seven Seas Corp [1983] 2 FC 161 . . . . .5.82
Seattle Totems Hockey Club v National Hockey League 652 F 2d 852
(9th Cir, 1981), cert denied 457 US 1105 (1982) 3.31, 4.121, 4.125
Seereederei Baco Liner GmbH v 'Al Aliyu' [2000] FCA 650 . . . . .4.54
(The) Sennar (No 2) [1958] 1 WLR 490 . . . . . . .1.17, 4.173, 5.10, 5.13, 5.61,
5.62, 5.63, 5.102
Sentry Corporation v Peat Marwick Mitchell & Co (1990) 95
ALR 11 . . . . .1.32, 4.127, 4.128
Settlement Corporation v Hochschild [1966] 1 Ch 10 . . . . . . .4.147, 4.155
Shaffer v Heitner 433 US 186 (1977) 1.20
Shearson Lehman Hutton Inc v TVB GmbH, Case C-89/91 [1993]
ECR I-139 . . . . .3.61
Shell v RW Sturge Ltd SS F 3d 1227 (1995) 5.45, 5.79
Shell International Petroleum Co Ltd v Coral Oil Co Ltd [1999]
2 Lloyd's Rep 606 . . . . .4.95
Showlag v Mansour [1995] 1 AC 431 . . . . .4.256
Sim v Robinow (1892) 19 R 665 . . . . .3.88, 3.90, 3.163
Simon Engineering plc v Butte Mining plc (No 2) [1996] 1 Lloyd's
Rep 91 . . . . .4.189
(The) Sindh [1975] 1 Lloyd's Rep 372 . . . . .5.62
Singh v Howden Petroleum Ltd (1979) 100 DLR (3rd) 121 . . . . .4.14
Sinochem International Oil (London) Co Ltd v Mobil Sales & Supply
Corporation [2000] 1 Lloyd's Rep 670 .5.81, 5.96
Siromath Pty Ltd (No 3), Re (1991) 25 NSWLR 25 . . . . .4.81, 4.134
(The) Siskina [1979] AC 210 . . . . .4.12, 4.19, 4.20, 4.109
Smith Kline French Laboratories Ltd v Bloch [1983] 2 All ER 72 . . . .1.38,
2.15, 2.17, 2.21, 4.95, 4.137, 4.190, 4.194, 4.250, 4.260
Société Azienda Stampaggio Acciaio v SA Phocéenne de Métalurgie
[1993] ILPr 253 . . . . .4.36
Société Commerciale de Reassurance v Eras International [1992] 1
Lloyd's Rep 570 . . . . .5.95
Société du Gaz de Paris v Société Anonyme de Navigation 'Les Arma-
teurs Français' 1926 SC (HL) 13 . . . . .2.05, 3.82, 3.88, 3.90
Société Générale de Paris v Dreyfus Brothers (1885)
29 ChD 239 . . . . .3.145, 4.16
Société Nationale Industrielle Aerospatiale v Lee Kui Jak [1987]
1 AC 871 . . . . .3.129, 3.142, 3.147, 4.05, 4.93, 4.102, 4.104, 4.105,
4.106, 4.108, 4.112, 4.113, 4.115, 4.116, 4.117, 4.124, 4.125,

4.179, 4.181, 4.182, 4.183, 4.185, 4.190, 4.200, 4.201, 4.203,
4.210, 4.214, 4.216, 4.238, 4.240, 4.273, 4.282, 5.98
Society of Lloyd's v Hyslop [1993] 3 NZLR 135 . . . . .4.39, 5.45, 5.79
Sohio Supply Co v Gatoil (USA) Inc [1989] 1 Lloyd's Rep 588 . . . . .3.121,
4.147, 4.155, 4.199, 4.215, 4.269, 4.273, 5.59
Sokana Industries Inc v Freyre & Co Inc [1994] 1 Lloyd's Rep 56 . . .4.163
Solorio v United States 483 US 435 (1987) 4.191
Somafer SA v Saar-Ferngas AG [1978] ECR 2183 . . . . .3.18
Sonantrach Petroleum Corp v Ferrell Int Ltd [2001] 1 All ER Comm
627 . . . . .5.36, 5.56
South Carolina Insurance Co v Assurantie NV [1987] AC 24 . . . . . . .2.23,
2.25, 4.105, 4.111, 4.112, 4.113, 4.115, 4.120, 4.125, 4.130,
4.132, 4.133, 4.146, 4.179, 4.190
South India Shipping Corp Ltd v Export-Import Bank of Korea [1985]
1 WLR 585 . . . . .1.14
(The) Soya Margareta [1961] 1 WLR 709 . . . . .4.209
Spiliada Maritime Corporation v Cansulex Ltd [1987] 1 AC 460 . . . .1.33,
1.38, 1.49, 2.01, 3.82, 3.83, 3.84, 3.86, 3.88, 3.89, 3.90, 3.91, 3.92,
3.93, 3.94, 3.95, 3.114, 3.120, 3.126, 3.134, 3.146, 3.156, 3.157,
3.158, 3.159, 3.161, 3.162, 3.163, 3.164, 3.165, 3.166, 4.12, 4.23,
4.24, 4.25, 4.26, 4.39, 4.40, 4.41, 4.46, 4.47, 4.51, 4.54, 4.55, 4.56,
4.57, 4.67, 4.68, 4.69, 4.73, 4.107, 4.108, 4.245, 5.10, 5.13, 5.54,
5.80, 5.85, 5.90, 5.91
SS Pharmaceuticals v Qantas Airways [1991] 1 Lloyd's Rep 288 . . . .2.45
St Pierre v South America Stores (Gath and Chaves) Ltd [1936] 1 KB
382 . . . . .3.72, 3.75, 3.80, 3.81, 3.159
Standard Steamship Owners' Protection and Indemnity Association
(Bermuda) Ltd v Gann [1992] 2 Lloyd's Rep
528 . . . . .3.107, 4.269, 4.273, 4.275
(The) Star of Luxor [1981] 1 Lloyd's Rep 139 .5.90
Sterling Pharmaceuticals Pty Ltd v The Boots Company (Australia) Pty
Ltd (1992) 34 FCR 287 . . . . .3.97, 3.104, 3.120, 3.140
Sternberg v O'Neil SSO A 2d 1105 (Del, 1988) 4.30
Stevens v Head (1993) 176 CLR 433 . . . . .2.09, 2.11, 2.12
(The) Stolt Marmaro [1985] 2 Lloyd's Rep 428 . . . . .3.120, 3.133,
4.273, 5.95
Street Sound Around Alecs Inc v M/V Royal Container 30 F Supp 2d
661 (SDNY) 5.58
Strombus v Insurance Corporation of Ireland [1985] 2 Lloyd's Rep
138 . . . . .3.139
(The) Stylt [1993] LMCLQ 433 . . . . .2.52
Svendborg v Wansa [1977] 2 Lloyd's Rep 183 . . . . .4.193
Sydbank v Bannerton Holdings Pty Ltd (1996) 68 FCR 539 . . . . .4.26

Takach, In the marriage of (1980) 47 FLR 441 . . . . .4.205
Tanning Research Laboratories Inc v O'Brien (1990) 169 CLR
    332 . . . . .3.137, 5.47
(The) Tatry [1994] ECR I-5439 . . . . . . .3.39, 3.42, 4.171, 4.282, 4.291, 4.292,
    4.293
Taunton-Collins v Cromie [1964] 1 WLR 633 . . . . .3.130
Terra International Inc v Mississippi Chemical Corporation 119 F 3d
    6988 (1997) 5.64
Tesam Distribution Ltd v Schuh Mode Team GmbH [1990]
    ILPr 150 . . . . .2.07
(TW) Thomas & Co Ltd v Portsea Steamship Co Ltd [1912]
    AC 1 . . . . .5.25
(WC) Thomas & Sons Pty Ltd v Bunge (Australia) Pty Ltd [1975] VR
    801 . . . . .3.135, 5.82
(The) Tillie Lykes [1977] 1 Lloyd's Rep 124 . . . . . . .3.32, 3.98, 3.100, 3.101
Toepfer International GmbH v Molino Boschi SRL [1996] 1 Lloyd's Rep
    510 . . . . .4.228
Toepfer International GmbH v Société Cargill France [1988] 1 Lloyd's
    Rep 379 . . . . .4.147, 4.233
Total Oil Great Britain Ltd v Marbonanza Compania Naviera SA
    (CA, 27 June 1975) 4.19
Tracer Research v National Environmental Services Co 42 F 3d 1292
    (1994) 5.64
Tracomin SA v Sudan Oil Seeds Co Ltd (Nos 1 & 2) [1983] 1 WLR
    1026 . . . . .4.147, 4.151, 4.212, 5.10
(The) Traugutt [1985] 1 Lloyd's Rep 76 . . . . .5.50
Trendtex Trading Corp v Crédit Suisse [1980] 3 All ER 721 . . . .2.23, 5.61,
    5.80, 5.92
(The) Tropaioforos (No 2) [1962] 1 Lloyd's Rep 410 . . . . .4.147, 4.157
Turner v Grovit [2000] QB 345; [2002] 1 WLR 107 . . . . . .1.07, 3.118, 4.83,
    4.94, 4.95, 4.96, 4.104, 4.105, 4.109, 4.113, 4.115, 4.134, 4.178, 4.195
Tyburn Productions Ltd v Conan Doyle [1991] Ch 75 . .4.100, 4.257, 4.269

Union Carbide Corp, In re 634 F Supp 842 (SDNY, 1986) 1.36, 3.64
Union Discount Company Ltd v Zoller [2002] 1 WLR 1517 . . . . .4.150
Union Insurance Society of Canton v SS Elikon 642 F 2d 721 (4th Cir,
    1981) 5.38
United Cigarette Machine Co v Wright 156 F 244 (1907), aff'd 193 F
    1023 (4th Cir, 1912) 3.27
United States v Aluminium Company of America 148 F 2d 416 (2nd Cir,
    1945) 1.23, 3.52
United States v International Brotherhood of Teamsters 728 F Supp
    1032 (SDNY 1990) 4.147

United States v Reliable Transfer Co Inc, 421 US 397 (1975); [1975] 2
    Lloyd's Rep 286 sub nom *The Mary A Whalen* 2.52
United States of America v Ivey (1996) 139 DLR (4th) 570 . . . . .4.299
United Technologies International, Inc v Malev Hungarian Airlines
    946 F 2d 97 (2nd Cir, 1992) 2.27
Unterweser Reederi GmbH, In re, 428 F 2d 888 (5th Cir, 1970) 4.121,
                                                            4.179, 5.41, 5.43

Van Dyck v Van Dyck [1990] 3 NZLR 624 . . . . .3.104
Van Uden Maritime BV v Kommanditgesellschaft In Firma Deco-Line
    [1988] ECR I-7091; [1999] QB 1225 . . . . .4.166
Vardopulo v Vardopulo (1909) 25 TLR 518 .4.205
(The) Varna [1994] 2 Lloyd's Rep 41 . . . . .3.104
(The) Vestris (1932) 43 Ll LR 86 . . . . .5.51
(The) Vishva Abha [1990] 2 Lloyd's Rep 313 . . . . .2.52, 3.139, 3.160
(The) Vishva Ajay [1989] 2 Lloyd's Rep 558 . . . . .4.55, 4.56
(The) Vishva Apurva [1991] 2 MLJ 440; [1992] 2 SLR 175 . . . . . .5.53, 5.80,
                                                            5.82, 5.90, 5.92
(The) Vishva Prabha [1979] 2 Lloyd's Rep 286 . . . . .5.81, 5.89, 5.90
Vitkovice Horni a Hutni Tezirstvo v Korner [1951] AC 869 . . . . .4.20
Vocalion (Foreign) Ltd, Re [1932] 2 Ch 196 . . . . .4.86, 4.144
Volkswagen Canada Inc v Auto Haus Frohlich Ltd [1986] 1 WWR
    380 . . . . .5.02
(The) Volvox Hollandia [1988] 2 Lloyd's Rep 361 . . . . .4.270, 4.276, 4.277,
                                                            4.282, 4.287
Voth v Manildra Flour Mills Pty Ltd (1991) 171 CLR 538 and 15
    NSWLR 513 . . . . .1.04, 1.11, 3.60, 3.83, 3.149, 3.150, 3.151, 3.162, 3.163,
                    4.05, 4.14, 4.18, 4.26, 4.40, 4.57, 4.67, 4.68, 4.69, 4.70,
                            4.71, 4.72, 4.78, 4.240, 4.245

Waterhouse v Reid [1938] 1 KB 743 . . . . .4.19
Watson v First Choice Holidays and Flights [2001] 2 Lloyd's Rep
    339 . . . . .3.22
(The) Waylink [1988] 1 Lloyd's Rep 475 . . . . .4.50
Westinghouse Electric Corporation [1978] AC 547, In re 4.218
WFM Motors Pty Ltd v Maydwell [1993] ACL Rep 85 NSW 2 . . . . . .4.70
Williams v The Society of Lloyd's [1994] 2 VR 274 . . . . .5.45
Williamson v North-Eastern Railway Co (1884) 11 R 596 (XI SC 4th
    Series) 2.12
(The) Wladyslaw Lokietek [1978] 2 Lloyd's Rep 520 . . . . .2.31
World-Wide Volkswagen Corp v Woodson 444 US (1980) 4.31
Worms v De Valdor (1880) 49 LJ Ch 261 . . . . .3.71

XAG v A Bank [1983] 2 All ER 464 . . . . .4.133, 4.148
XL Insurance Ltd v Owens Corning [2000] 2 Lloyd's Rep
   500 . . . . .2.48, 4.147

Youell v Kara Mara Shipping Co Ltd [2002] 2 Lloyd's Rep
   102 . . . . .4.91, 4.274
YTC Universal Ltd v Trans Europa SA [1973] 1 Lloyd's Rep 480 . . . .5.60

Zhang v Renault (2002) 187 ALR 1 . . . . .3.163
ZP v PS (1994) 181 CLR 639 . . . . .1.10
Zwartfeld, Re, Case 2/88 Imm [1990] ECR I-3365 . . . . .4.161

Table of Legislation

All references are to paragraph numbers.

Australia
Contracts Review Act 1980
(NSW) 5.42
Foreign Judgments Act
1991 (C'th) 5.10
s 7(4) 4.43
Foreign Proceedings (Excess of
Jurisdiction) Act 1984
(C'th) 3.52
Insurance Contracts Act
1984 (C'th) 4.100, 4.233, 5.46
ss 52, 54 . . . . .2.50, 2.51
International Arbitration Act
1974 (C'th) 5.48
s 7(2) 5.03
Jurisdiction of Courts (Cross-
Vesting) Act 1987 (C'th) . . .4.10
Motor Accidents Act 1988
(NSW) 2.11
Service and Execution of Process
Act 1992 (C'th) 3.27
Trade Practices Act 1974
(C'th) 4.99

Belgium
Code Judiciaire
Art 638 . . . . .1.20

Bermuda
Protection of Trading Interests Act
1981 . . . . .3.52

Canada
Foreign Extraterritorial Measures
Act 1984 . . . . .3.52

Denmark
Law on Civil Procedure
Art 248(2) 1.16, 1.20

European Union Directives
Directive 93/13/EC 5.35
Product Liability Directive . . .2.36
Art 7(e) 2.34
Art 16 . . . . .2.29

Regulations
Council Regulation 44/
2001 . . . . .1.13, 1.46, 1.48,
1.50, 2.29, 2.32, 2.35,
3.06, 3.10, 3.12, 3.48, 3.49, 3.50,
3.54, 3.56, 3.58, 3.65, 3.68, 3.114,
3.170, 3.171, 4.07, 4.08, 4.09, 4.12,
4.14, 4.27, 4.34, 4.62, 4.89, 4.166,
4.172, 4.252, 4.284, 4.285, 4.286,
5.10, 5.16, 5.35, 5.73, 5.76
Recital 15 . . . . .3.09
Chapter II 3.13, 3.14,
3.20, 3.23, 3.25, 3.38, 3.46, 5.39
Chapter III 3.38, 3.45
Art 2 . . . . . . .3.17, 3.20, 4.63, 5.75
Art 3 . . . . .4.295
Art 4 . . . . . . .3.36, 3.69, 4.63, 5.75
Art 5 . . . . .2.07
(3) 4.90
Art 6 . . . . .3.40, 3.1163.24
Art 13 . . . . .3.16
Art 16 . . . . .2.36
Art 17 . . . . .3.16
Art 19 . . . . .3.28
Art 20 . . . . .3.28
Art 21 . . . . .3.16
Art 22 . . . . .3.14, 3.16, 3.17,3.18,
3.28, 3.36, 3.69, 4.63, 5.77
Art 23 . . . .3.15, 3.17, 3.36, 3.69,
4.169, 4.178, 5.07, 5.11, 5.28,
5.37, 5.39, 5.50, 5.69, 5.74, 5.75

(1) 3.23
Art 24 . . . . . . .4.36, 4.63, 4.175,
5.37, 5.50, 5.74
Art 25 . . . . .3.14, 5.74, 5.77
Art 26 . . . . .4.35
Art 27 . . . . .3.26, 3.27, 3.28,
3.31, 3.32, 3.34, 3.36, 3.37, 3.38,
3.39, 3.40, 3.43, 3.53, 3.100, 4.62,
4.65, 4.169, 4.204, 4.290, 4.292,
4.293, 5.50
Art 28 . . . . .3.31, 3.40, 3.41,
3.43, 3.44, 3.116, 4.204
Art 29 . . . . .3.28
Art 30 . . . . .3.30
Art 33 . . . . .4.253
Art 34 . . . . .4.36, 4.253
(2) 4.37
(3) 3.25, 3.35
(4) 4.256
Art 35 . . . . . . .4.36, 4.253, 4.295
(2) 3.46
Art 36 . . . . .3.47
Art 41 . . . . .3.47, 4.36
Art 72 . . . . .3.46, 3.65, 4.295

France
Civil Code
Art 14 . . . .1.20, 1.21, 1.23, 4.295

Germany
Code of Civil Procedure (ZPO)
s 23 . . . . .1.20, 1.23

Greece
Civil Code
Art 919 . . . . .4.168, 4.176
Art 635(5) 1.20

Luxembourg
Civil Code
Art 14 . . . . .1.20

Netherlands
Code of Civil Procedure
Art 126(3) 1.20

United Kingdom
Administration of Justice Act
1920 . . . . .3.07, 4.207
Arbitration Act 1996
s 7 . . . . .5.36
s 9(4) 5.03
Carriage by Air Acts (Application
of Provisions) Order 1967 . .2.48
Carriage of Goods by Sea Act
1971 . . . . .5.37
Civil Jurisdiction and Judgments
Act 1982 . . . . .4.207, 5.76
s 3(1) 3.54
s 26 . . . . .1.17
s 32(1) 4.167, 5.10
(4) 4.167
s 33 . . . . .4.43, 5.103
s 41(6) 4.13
s 49 . . . . .4.288
Civil Procedure Rules 1998 . .1.23,
3.30, 3.146, 4.13, 4.14, 4.20, 4.22,
4.23, 4.24, 4.91, 5.10
Part 11 . . . . .1.28
r 6.20 . . . . .4.19
r 6.21 . . . . .4.21, 4.23
r 62.8 . . . . .1.28
Common Law Procedure Act
1852 . . . . .1.10
Consular Relations Act
1968 . . . . .1.18
Consumer Credit Act 1974
s 141(1) 5.38
Diplomatic Privileges Act
1964 . . . . .1.18
Fatal Accidents Act 1976 . . . . .5.38,
5.68
Foreign Judgments (Reciprocal
Enforcement) Act 1933 . . . .3.07,
4.207
Foreign Limitation Periods Act
1984 . . . . .5.90
Human Rights Act 1998 . . . . . .4.52
s 3 . . . . .4.159

Insolvency Act 1986
  s 13 . . . . .4.144
  s 239 . . . . .4.144
Judgments Extension Act
  1868 . . . . .4.206
Law Reform (Personal Injuries)
  Act 1948
  s 1(3) 5.38
Private International Law
  (Miscellaneous Provisions)
  Act 1995 . . . . .2.13, 4.99
Protection of Trading Interests Act
  1980 . . . . .3.52, 4.148, 4.218
Protection of Interests (US
  Antitrust Measures) Order
  1983 . . . . .4.219
Rules of the Supreme Court
  Order 11 . . . . .3.135, 3.146
  r 4(2) 4.21
  Order 15, r 16 . . . . .4.261
  Order 39, r 2 . . . . .4.131
State Immunity Act 1978
  s 2(3) 4.43

Supreme Court Act 1981
  s 37 . . . . .4.159
Trade Practices Act 5.38, 5.45
Unfair Terms in Consumer
  Contracts Regulations 1999
  Arts 13, 17, 21 . . . . .5.35

United States
Anti-Injunction Act 28 USC
  § 2283 . . . . .3.27
Bankruptcy Code
  § 547 . . . . .4.144
Federal Arbitration Act 2.48
Racketeer Influenced and Corrupt
  Organizations Act 1970
  (RICO Act) 4.128, 4.189,
                      5.45, 5.100
Securities Exchange Act
  1934 . . . . .4.189
  s 27 . . . . .4.28
Sherman Act 4.99
United States Constitution
  Art IV, § 1 . . . . .3.10

Table of Conventions

All references are to paragraph numbers.

Brussels Collision Liability
 Convention 2.52
Brussels Convention on Jurisdiction and Judgments in Civil
 and Commercial Matters . .1.46,
  1.48, 1.50, 2.07, 2.29, 2.32, 2.35,
  3.06, 3.07, 3.09, 3.10, 3.12, 3.13,
  3.19, 3.30, 3.48, 3.49, 3.51, 3.53,
  3.54, 3.55, 3.65, 3.66, 3.68, 3.114,
  3.170, 3.171, 3.172, 4.07, 4.09,
  4.62, 4.166, 4.289, 5.10, 5.75
 Title II 3.29
 Art 6 . . . . .5.76
  (1) 3.18, 3.21, 3.22, 3.24
  (2) 3.22
 Art 11 . . . . .5.35
 Art 16 . . . . .4.63
  (1) 5.77
 Art 17 . . . . . . .3.23, 4.169, 4.171,
  4.172, 4.178, 5.07, 5.11, 5.39,
  5.69, 5.74, 5.77
 Art 18 . . .4.63, 4.161, 4.175, 5.74
 Art 19 . . . . .5.74
 Art 21 . . . . .3.34, 3.35, 3.36,
  3.37, 3.38, 3.100, 4.65, 4.169,
  4.170, 4.171, 4.172, 4.173,
  4.277, 4.290, 4.292, 4.293, 5.11
 Art 22 . . . . .4.171, 4.172
 Art 26 . . . . .4.173
 Art 27 . . . . .3.35
 Art 59 . . . . .3.65
Brussels Convention on the
 Limitation of Liability of
 Owners of Seagoing
 Ships 4.277
Community Patent
 Convention 2.29

Convention on Limitation of
 Liability for Maritime Claims
 1976 . . . . .2.52
European Patent
 Convention 2.34
GATT agreement 1.04
Geneva Convention on the
 Contract for the International
 Carriage of Goods by
 Road 3.03, 3.05, 3.06
Hague Convention on the
 Recognition and Enforcement
 of Foreign Judgments in Civil
 and Commercial Matters and
 Additional Protocol 3.07,
  3.56, 3.57
Hague Service Convention . . .3.30
International Convention on
 Certain Rules in Matters of
 Collision 1952
 Art 1(3) 4.204
International Convention on Civil
 Liability for Oil Pollution
 Damage 2.52
International Convention relating
 to the Limitation of Liability of
 Owners of Sea-going Ships
 1957 . . . . .2.52
Limitation Convention
 1976 . . . . .2.56
Lugano Convention on Jurisdic-
 tion and Judgments 2.07,
  2.32, 2.35, 3.06,
  3.09, 3.48, 3.54, 3.57, 3.69, 4.07,
  4.08, 4.09, 4.12, 4.27, 4.62, 4.89,
  4.91, 4.166, 4.175, 4.204, 4.284,
  4.285, 4.286, 5.10, 5.73, 5.75, 5.77

Art 3 . . . . .4.295

Art 59 . . . . .4.295

Art 62(1)(b) 3.06

New York Convention on the
Recognition and Enforcement
of Foreign Arbitral
Awards 5.03, 5.07, 5.15, 5.52

Rome Convention on the Law
Applicable to Contractual
Obligations 2.02, 2.40, 3.68

Art 1(2)(d) 5.16, 5.57

Art 10(1) 5.57

San Sebastian Convention . . .2.35, 5.77

Scandinavian Convention for the
Recognition and Enforcement
of Judgments 3.56

Treaty of Rome 1957
Art 293 . . . . .3.06, 3.55

Warsaw Convention on Carriage
by Air 1929 . . . . .2.02, 2.45,
3.03, 3.04, 3.05, 3.06, 3.09

Table of Abbreviations

AC	Appeal Cases
ACLC	Australian Company Law Cases
ALJ	Australian Law Journal
All ER	All England Reports
ALR	Australian Law Reports
AMC	American Maritime Cases
ANZ Ins Cas	Australian and New Zealand Insurance Cases
ATPR	Australian Trade Practices Reports
BCC	British Company Cases
BCLC	Butterworths Company Law Cases
BCLR	British Columbia Law Reports
BYIL	British Yearbook of International Law
Ch	Chancery
CLC	Commercial Law Cases
CLJ	Cambridge Law Journal
CLP	Current Legal Problems
CLR	Commonwealth Law Reports (Australia)
Colum L Rev	Columbia Law Review
Com Cas	Commercial Cases
C'wth	Commonwealth
CPR	Civil Procedure Rules
DLR	Dominion Law Reports (Canada)
ECC	European Commercial Cases
ECR	European Court Reports
ER	English Reports
Exch	Exchequer Reports
Ex D	Law Reports, Exchequer Division
F	Federal Reports (US)
FCA	Federal Court of Australia
FCR	Federal Court Reports (Australia)
F Supp	Federal Supplement (US)
HKLR	Hong Kong Law Reports
ICLQ	International and Comparative Law Quarterly
I L Pr	International Litigation Procedure
I R (NSW)	Industrial Reports (NSW)
IR	Irish Reports
KB	King's Bench
LJQB	Law Journal, Queen's Bench
Lloyd's Rep	Lloyd's Reports

LMCLQ	Lloyd's Maritime & Commercial Law Quarterly
LQR	Law Quarterly Review
LRCP	Law Reports, Common Pleas
LT	Law Times
MLJ	Malaysian Law Journal
MLR	Modern Law Review
MULR	Melbourne University Law Review
NE	North Eastern
NILQ	Northern Ireland Law Quarterly
NILR	Northern Ireland Law Reports
NLJ	New Law Journal
NSWLR	New South Wales Law Reports
NSWR	New South Wales Reports
NZLR	New Zealand Law Reports
NZULR	New Zealand Universities Law Review
OJ	Official Journal
OJLS	Oxford Journal of Legal Studies
P	Probate Reports
QAC	Quebec Appeal Cases
QB	Queen's Bench
QSC	Queensland Supreme Court
RPC	Reports of Patent Cases
SC	Sessions Cases
SCR	Supreme Court Reports (Canada)
S Ct	Supreme Court Reports (United States)
SLR	Singapore Law Reports
SLT	Scottish Law Times
SW	South Western Reports
Syd L Rev	Sydney Law Review
TLR	Times Law Reports
UBCLR	University of British Columbia Law Review
US	United States Reports
VR	Victorian Reports
VSC	Victorian Supreme Court
WLR	Weekly Law Reports
WWR	Western Weekly Reports (Canada)
YEL	Yearbook of European Law

1

Introduction

I.	Transnational Litigation and the Global Economy	1.01
II.	Transnational Litigation and Concurrent Jurisdiction	1.10
	1. 'Modern' Defendants: Ubiquitous and Vulnerable	1.13
	2. 'Exorbitant' Jurisdiction	1.19
	3. The Problems of Concurrent Jurisdiction	1.26
III.	The Importance of Venue	1.31
IV.	Venue in Transnational Litigation: Outline	1.44

I. TRANSNATIONAL LITIGATION AND THE GLOBAL ECONOMY

Transnational litigation is to the domestic breed as three-dimensional chess is to the garden variety, or as the triphibious warfare of MacArthur is to a land battle of World War I.[1]

Litigation with a transnational dimension has the potential to raise a host **1.01** of interesting and difficult issues. These include questions of choice of law, the role of domestic public policy and the operation of mandatory laws of the forum, the scope of protective and provisional measures available to maintain the status quo or to satisfy future judgment debts, methods of obtaining evidence from the courts of foreign states, recognition and enforcement of judgments, and foreign state immunity.[2] Perhaps the most interesting issue of all, however, relates to the rules by which a venue is selected and settled upon for the resolution of any given transnational dispute. As Eyre LCJ once said, albeit in a slightly different context, 'our books are full of cases on the subject of venues and the doctrine is very nice and curious'.[3]

In his preface to *Essays in International Litigation and the Conflict of Laws*,[4] **1.02** the general editor of *Dicey and Morris on the Conflict of Laws* draws attention to the fact that traditional texts on private international law have

---

[1] The Hon Judge MR Wilkey, 'Transnational Adjudication: A View From the Bench' (1984) 18 International Lawyer 541, 543.

[2] For example, *Banca Carige v Banco Nacionale de Cuba* [2001] 2 Lloyd's Rep 147; *Kuwait Airways Corporation v Iraq Airways Co (Nos 4 and 5)* [2002] 2 WLR 1353.

[3] *Ilderton v Ilderton* (1793) 2 HBl 145, 161; 126 ER 476, 484.

[4] Collins, LA, *Essays in International Litigation and the Conflict of Laws* (1994).

tended to give a less than complete treatment to topics which he describes as being of 'great practical importance' in transnational litigation. These include the role of forum selection agreements, the doctrine of *forum non conveniens*, and the scope for, and propriety of, the use of the action for negative declaratory relief in transnational litigation.[5] To this list might be added the subject of injunctions to restrain foreign proceedings, so-called 'anti-suit' injunctions. The same lacuna has been observed in relation to United States jurisprudence in this area where it has been said that 'despite the vital importance of international civil litigation to US courts, lawyers and litigants, little systematic attention has been devoted to the subject by law schools or publishers of law books'.[6] More often than not, these topics receive relatively cursory treatment in chapters the main focus of which is typically on the rules prescribing the subject matter and personal jurisdiction of the courts. More recently, however, they have commanded heightened academic interest commensurate with their practical significance, so much so in fact that one commentator has heralded 'the coming of age of a subject which might aptly be called "international civil litigation" '.[7] That assessment is certainly consistent with the appearance of several specialist works in this field[8] in addition to the emergence of a plethora of what may be described as 'survey' works which detail aspects of practice and procedure from countries around the world, thereby highlighting the advantages and limitations of proceeding in different jurisdictions.[9]

1.03 Those incidents of the subject 'international civil litigation' or 'transnational litigation' which relate to the identification of the venue in which a

---

[5] Collins, LA, *Essays in International Litigation and the Conflict of Laws* (1994), vii.

[6] Born, GB and Westin, D, *International Civil Litigation in United States Courts* (2nd edn, 1992) 2. Born and Westin's work, now in its third edition (1996) under the sole authorship of Mr Born has done much to rectify this position in the United States as has Dr Ong's significant work *Cross Border Litigation within ASEAN* (1997) in relation to this subject in that region.

[7] Fentiman, RG, (Book Review) (1992) 41 ICLQ 229, 230.

[8] O'Malley, S and Layton, A, *European Civil Practice* (1989); Briggs, A and Rees, P, *Civil Jurisdiction and Judgments* (3rd edn, 2002). An important and influential American work is Born, GB and Westin, D (n 6 above).

[9] See, for example, Cromie, S, *International Commercial Litigation* (2nd edn, 1997); McIntosh, D and Holmes, M, *Civil Procedure in E.C. Countries* (1991); McIntosh, D and Holmes, M, *Personal Injury Awards in E.C. Countries* (1991); Hodges, CJS, *Product Liability: European Laws and Practice* (1993); Miller, DLC and Beaumont, PR, *The Option of Litigating in Europe* (1993); and the series of books issued under the auspices of the International Litigation Committee of the International Bar Association edited by Platto, C: *Obtaining Evidence in Another Jurisdiction in Business Disputes* (1988); *Enforcement of Foreign Judgments Worldwide* (1989); *Pre-Trial and Pre-Hearing Procedures Worldwide* (1990); *Trial and Court Procedures Worldwide* (1991); *Civil Appeal Procedures Worldwide* (1992); Campbell, D and Campbell, C (eds), *International Civil Procedures* (1995); Fawcett, JJ (ed), *Declining Jurisdiction in Private International Law* (1995); Nygh, P and McLachlan, C (eds), *Transnational Tort Litigation* (1996).

transnational dispute is to be resolved form the broad subject matter of this book. 'Transnational' is preferred to 'international' litigation throughout this book for two reasons: first, it avoids any confusion with litigation in the field of public international law (although public international law issues may arise in transnational litigation); secondly, it is thought that 'transnational' better conveys the fact that two or more jurisdictions may be concerned in the resolution of the parties' dispute.

The advent of the 'subject' of 'transnational litigation' has been coincident **1.04** both with the emergence of a truly global economy and the achievement in recent decades of great technological advances, particularly in the fields of transportation and telecommunications and, more generally, through the internet's facilitation of international commerce including the electronic transfer of funds and the ability to transact business in 'cyberspace'. These developments have been remarked upon by both courts[10] and commentators[11] alike. Part of the explanation for this economic trend lies in the fact that rapid and inexpensive transportation has led to greater international trade and an increase in labour mobility. The *relative* freedom of international trade, and efforts under the auspices of the GATT agreement to secure this goal to an even greater extent, mean that primary and secondary products are regularly penetrating new markets, especially since the end of the Cold War. The same may also be said in relation to various service industries.

One feature of economic globalization has been the great diversification **1.05** of corporate holdings, both in terms of commodity portfolios and geographical spheres of operation, and a company's plant, equipment, and other assets will frequently be located in a strategic range of countries. Such diversification characterizes the corporate behaviour of vast multinational corporations which are able to co-ordinate their businesses by virtue of sophisticated communications networks. More generally, the flow of international commerce has been facilitated by the development of systems of 'electronic funds transfer' and, more recently, 'e-commerce'. Furthermore, co-operative joint ventures often see corporations from different countries combining to invest in a third. As these developments have occurred, the world economy has not been a paragon of stability and

---

[10] See, for example, *Oceanic Sun Line Special Shipping Co Inc v Fay* (1988) 165 CLR 197, 212; *Voth v Manildra Flour Mills Pty Ltd* (1991) 171 CLR 538, 586 and (1989) 15 NSWLR 513, 533; *Morguard Investments Ltd v de Savoye* [1990] 3 SCR 1077, 1098; *Amchem Products Inc v Workers Compensation Board* [1993] 1 SCR 897, 911.

[11] For example, Collins, LA (ed), *Dicey and Morris on the Conflict of Laws* (13th edn, 2000) 388; Neale, AD and Stephens, ML, *International Business and National Jurisdiction* (1988) 4; Pryles, MC, 'Judicial Darkness on the Oceanic Sun' (1988) 62 ALJ 774, 775; Sir Michael Kerr, 'Commercial Dispute Resolution: The Changing Scene' in Bos, M and Brownlie, I, *Liber Amicorum for Lord Wilberforce* (1987) 115–119.

the effect of various international crises has produced great fluctuations in world currency, share, and commodity markets.[12]

1.06 Cheaper and improved transportation means not only more business travel but also more international travel for private purposes. Two of the leading Australian cases on discretionary stays involve plaintiffs sustaining injuries while on holiday, one in Greece and one in New Caledonia.[13] Similarly, the United States Supreme Court's decision in *Carnival Cruise Lines v Shute*,[14] relating to the enforcement of the jurisdiction clauses in consumer contracts, arose out of proceedings relating to an injury sustained on an ocean-going cruise. A further example is provided by the Ontario Court of Appeal's decision in *Lemmex v Bernard*,[15] where the court declined to stay proceedings brought in Ontario by an Ontario resident who had been injured while on vacation in Grenada.

1.07 The emergence of an ever more integrated global economy has obvious ramifications for transnational litigation. One commentator has observed that 'in a world where daily transactions routinely involve multiple countries, litigants are increasingly likely to find themselves embroiled in simultaneous contests in several theatres'.[16] Quite simply, more international trade means more transnational disputes, contractual, quasi-contractual, and arising from the negligent provision of goods and services. One consequence of a global economy—the posting of employees abroad—may also give rise to disputes as to the application of the employment law protections of the state from which the employee has been posted.[17] And another consequence is the diversification of assets against which judgments may be enforced. As Sir Michael Kerr observed extrajudicially, '*quot contractus, tot contentiones, tot lites*'.[18] This has had the consequence that 'the business of litigation, like commerce itself, has become increasingly international'.[19] It is no coincidence that the last twenty years have seen the burgeoning of 'international law firms', offering not only the personnel and facilities to co-ordinate complex trans-

---

[12] 'Exchange controls, devaluations, constant currency fluctuations, and universal inflation have played havoc with long term contracts and future obligations generally': per Sir Michael Kerr, ibid 116.

[13] *Oceanic Sun Line Special Shipping Co Inc v Fay* (1988) 165 CLR 197; *Renault v Zhang* (2002) 187 ALR 1. See also *Diethelm & Co v Bradley* (1995) ATPR 41–388.

[14] 499 US 585 (1991).   [15] (2001) 204 DLR (4th) 192.

[16] Teitz, LE, 'Taking Multiple Bites of the Apple: A Proposal to Resolve Conflicts of Jurisdiction and Multiple Proceedings' (1992) 26 The International Lawyer 21, 22.

[17] See, for example, *Turner v Grovit* [2002] 1 WLR 107; *Macquarie Bank v Bell and Berg* (1999) 87 IR (NSW) 126; 93 IR (NSW) 191.

[18] (n 11 above) 115.

[19] *Amchem Products Inc v Workers Compensation Board* [1993] 1 SCR 897, 911 per Sopinka J. See also *Channel Tunnel Group Ltd v Balfour Beatty Construction Ltd* [1993] AC 334, 341 where Lord Browne-Wilkinson referred to 'the international character of much contemporary litigation'.

national litigation but also knowledge of and familiarity with the procedural and other advantages to be secured through litigating in particular forums.[20]

This collective burgeoning of transnational activity is seen most clearly in, **1.08** but is by no means confined to, international commerce. Complexities of transnational litigation are also presented as a consequence of the growth of international tourism and greater mobility generally, meaning that one also encounters 'fights about where to fight' across the legal firmament, including, often sadly, in the context of family law both in the area of divorce[21] and in relation to the custody of children whose separated parents wish to live in different countries.[22]

The next section of this chapter introduces the fundamental prerequisite **1.09** for the phenomenon of transnational forum shopping, namely the factor of concurrent jurisdiction.

II. TRANSNATIONAL LITIGATION AND CONCURRENT JURISDICTION

It is a trite proposition that disputes as to the venue in which to resolve a **1.10** piece of transnational litigation only arise because there will invariably be a number of potential forums whose jurisdictional rules would, prima facie at least, permit the dispute to be entertained. As Lord Goff said in *Airbus Industrie GIE v Patel*,[23] there is 'a jungle of separate, broadly based jurisdictions all over the world'. The existence of concurrent jurisdiction is the *sine qua non* for the type of jurisdictional clashes with which this book is concerned. In common law countries, what has frequently been termed 'exorbitant' in the sense of not purely territorial jurisdiction is not a new phenomenon, dating back in the United Kingdom to the Common Law Procedure Act of 1852, and, together with civil law jurisdictional rules not premised upon a purely territorial theory of jurisdiction, has always guaranteed the possibility, in any given case, of a number of potential forums.[24]

The globalization of the world economy described in the previous section **1.11**

[20] See Wetter, JG, 'The Case for International Law Schools and an International Legal Profession' (1980) 29 ICLQ 206, 212–213 and 216; see also Pearson, N, 'The Case for Cross Border Co-operation' (1991) 5 The Lawyer 40/11.

[21] *Henry v Henry* (1996) 185 CLR 571.

[22] *ZP v PS* (1994) 181 CLR 639.

[23] [1999] 1 AC 199, 132.

[24] McLachlan, C, 'Transnational Tort Litigation: An Overview' in Nygh, P and McLachlan, C (eds), Transnational Tort Litigation (1996) 10–11.

is also not without significance in the context of a discussion of concurrent jurisdiction. This point was well made by Sopinka J in *Amchem Products Inc v Workers Compensation Board*.[25] After referring to the increase of free trade and the rapid growth of multinational corporations, he observed that:

> The defendant may not be identified with only one jurisdiction. Moreover, there are frequently multiple defendants carrying on business in a number of jurisdictions and distributing their products or services world wide. As well, the plaintiffs may be a large class residing in different jurisdictions. It is often difficult to pinpoint the place where the transaction giving rise to the action took place.[26]

1.12 This section proceeds to explore some of the ramifications of an increasingly globalized economy for concurrent jurisdiction.

1. 'MODERN' DEFENDANTS: UBIQUITOUS AND VULNERABLE

1.13 Corporations likely to be involved in transnational litigation frequently have a presence in more than one forum. They may be physically present in several jurisdictions by virtue of the existence either of a branch office or an agency arrangement or else a subsidiary which cannot be said to be wholly independent.[27] Whereas the English common law generally respects the separate legal status of subsidiaries for jurisdictional purposes,[28] other jurisdictions, even within the common law family,[29] may be more prepared to 'pierce the corporate veil' and conclude that a parent is present in a particular jurisdiction by virtue of the actual presence of a subsidiary. The American 'alter ego' doctrine provides one example.[30] Of that jurisdiction it has been said that 'any significant degree

---

[25] [1993] 1 SCR 897.

[26] ibid 911–912. See also *Voth v Manildra Flour Mills Pty Ltd* (1990) 171 CLR 538, 586 per Toohey J: 'particularly in the modern commercial world, there may be more than one forum available to a plaintiff'.

[27] See generally *Adams v Cape Industries plc* [1990] Ch 433, especially 530–531, and Articles 9 and 15 of European Council Regulation 44/2001.

[28] But see Fawcett, JJ, 'A New Approach to Jurisdiction over Companies in Private International Law' (1988) 37 ICLQ 645 for an argument that English courts should assert jurisdiction on the basis of the 'economic presence' of the company in the jurisdiction, irrespective of whether it is formally represented by a subsidiary.

[29] For examples from the Australian case law, see Nygh, P, in Nygh, P and McLachlan, C (eds), *Transnational Tort Litigation* (1996) 28.

[30] *Cannon Manufacturing Co v Cudahy Packing Co* 267 US 33 (1925) and see Born, GB and Westin, D (n 6 above) 137–144, who note that the relatively strict test set out in this case to establish 'alter ego' status has been somewhat diluted in more recent decisions. See also Sarno, GR, 'Haling Foreign Subsidiary Corporations into Court under the 1934 Act: Jurisdictional Bases and Forum Non Conveniens' (1992) 55 Law and Contemporary Problems 379; and also Westbrook, JL, 'Theories of Parent Company Liability and the Prospects for an International Settlement' (1985) 20 Texas International Law Journal 321 for a discussion of how multinational parent corporations may be held liable for the acts of subsidiaries, even *without* piercing the veil.

of *de facto* control or supervision of a subsidiary company in the United States is likely to be regarded as bringing the foreign parent company legitimately within the personal jurisdiction of an American court'.[31] Courts will also be astute in cases where jurisdiction is being resisted on the basis of an alleged lack of corporate presence to test this assertion and to ascertain the substance rather than the form of the matter.[32] It may be surmised that this sceptical view will frequently be brought to bear in cases where the defendant is a one-ship company.

Corporations which are 'physically' present within a jurisdiction are **1.14** vulnerable under common law principles to being sued 'as of right', even if the cause of action sued upon relates to an 'overseas' action or transaction of the corporation and has no connection with the corporation's 'presence' within the jurisdiction.[33] In the United States, courts may only be able to exercise 'general jurisdiction' under the due process standard enunciated in *International Shoe Co v Washington*[34] where the defendant has 'continuous and systematic' contacts with the forum.[35] In the absence of such contacts and in the event that the corporation is not registered to do business in the forum state, jurisdiction may only be asserted if the litigation arises out of a specific contact between the defendant corporation and the forum state.[36]

There is also the consideration, recently articulated by Mance LJ, that: **1.15**

Obligations are commonly enforced today not against the person, but against assets. Debtors often trade or hold some or even all of their assets overseas. Proceedings are as a result often begun and enforced against debtors in countries other than that of their residence (as in this case). A move towards single legal markets, like those involving countries party to the Brussels and Lugano Conventions, makes judgments readily exportable between countries.[37]

Individuals present within the jurisdiction are also vulnerable to being **1.16** sued 'as of right', at least within the common law tradition,[38] and this rule has been reasserted by the United States Supreme Court.[39] Individuals

---

[31] Neale, AD and Stephens, ML (n 11 above) 130; and see generally at 128–133.

[32] See, for example, *Domansa v Derin Shipping & Trading Co Inc* [2001] 1 Lloyd's Rep 362.

[33] *South India Shipping Corp Ltd v Export–Import Bank of Korea* [1985] 1 WLR 585.

[34] 326 US 310 (1945).

[35] *Perkins v Benguet Consolidated Mining Co* 342 US 437 (1952); *Helicopteros Nacionales de Colombia SA v Hall* 466 US 408 (1984).

[36] See further paras 4.27 ff below.

[37] *Raiffeisen Zentralbank Österreich AG v Five Star Trading LLC* [2001] 1 QB 825, 843.

[38] See also Article 248(2) of the Danish Law on Civil Procedure.

[39] *Burnham v Superior Court of California* 110 S Ct 2105 (1990) and see discussion by Collins, LA, 'Temporary Presence, Exorbitant Jurisdiction and the U.S. Supreme Court' (1991) 107 LQR 10, especially 13–14; and by Juenger, F, 'An Addendum on the United States Approach' in Nygh, P and McLachlan, C, *Transnational Tort Litigation* (1996) 39–40.

travelling from jurisdiction to jurisdiction are thus liable to be served with process in more than one forum[40] and, as the celebrated case of *Maharanee of Baroda v Wildenstein*[41] illustrates, this is notwithstanding the fact that an individual's presence in a particular jurisdiction might be quite fortuitous or, if not fortuitous, totally unrelated to that party's commercial interests or activity, as in that case where Daniel Wildenstein, a French art dealer, was in England for the Ascot races. This is an excellent illustration of the fact that even the purist view that jurisdiction should be strictly territorial may be based on tenuous links to the forum. So-called 'tag' jurisdiction has a potentially heightened vitality in an era of cheap and rapid international travel.

1.17 Ships have always been vulnerable to the exercise of such jurisdiction for the necessarily peripatetic nature of their business takes them from forum to forum, making maritime claims 'particularly vulnerable to forum shopping'[42] and rendering every port 'an admiralty emporium'.[43] In *The Atlantic Star*, Lord Simon offered the following justification for this broad jurisdiction:

> Ships are elusive. The power to arrest in any port and found thereon an action *in rem* is increasingly required with the custom of ships being owned singly and sailing under flags of convenience. A large tanker may by negligent navigation cause extensive damage . . . she will take very good care to keep out of the ports of the 'convenient' forum.[44]

1.18 Jurisdiction *in rem* against a ship is not limited in terms of the subject matter of the claim a court may be asked to examine. With very few exceptions,[45] this is also the case with respect to *in personam* jurisdiction.

---

[40] 'Despite the ease of international communications—by telephone, facsimile, and otherwise—business transactions inevitably involve face-to-face meetings and negotiations. For this and other reasons, "tag service" can often be accomplished as a practical matter': Born, GB and Westin, D (n 6 above, 2nd edn) 50.

[41] [1972] 2 QB 283.

[42] *The Sennar (No 2)* [1985] 1 WLR 490, 493 per Lord Diplock.

[43] *The Atlantic Star* [1974] AC 436, 475 per Lord Simon. See also Lord Denning MR in the Court of Appeal: [1973] 1 QB 364, 382: 'The owners of ships who engage in international trade are especially vulnerable. Any of their vessels is liable to arrest in any of the ports to which they go.'

[44] ibid 474. Section 26 of the Civil Jurisdiction and Judgments Act 1982, permitting the retention and application of any security obtained in England to the decision of a foreign court in favour of whose jurisdiction proceedings in England have been stayed, renders this justification less compelling: see *The Emre II* [1989] 2 Lloyd's Rep 182. See also *The Abidin Daver* [1984] AC 398, 410 per Lord Diplock.

[45] See Collins, LA (ed) (n 11 above), Rule 20 in relation to persons entitled to immunity under the Diplomatic Privileges Act 1964 or the Consular Relations Act 1968, and Rule 21 in relation to international organizations or their officials specially protected by or under statute.

2. 'Exorbitant' Jurisdiction

Corporations and individuals, even if not physically present in a particu-   **1.19**
lar forum in the sense described above, may still be subject to 'assumed',
'exorbitant', or 'long arm' jurisdiction in that forum if, for example, they
have been party to activities within the forum such as entry into a contract
or in circumstances where their activities have resulted in consequences
within the forum, such as the sustaining of damage. Rules prescribing
such jurisdiction are a common feature of many countries' legal systems
and it will suffice for the purposes of this book, which is not directly
concerned with the *content* of different countries' jurisdictional rules, to
mention but a few examples.

Article 14 of the French Civil Code provides that any French national may   **1.20**
sue a foreign defendant in the French courts without any further connection to France and a similar jurisdictional rule obtains in Luxembourg.[46]
In Belgium and The Netherlands, a similar rule applies with regard to
plaintiffs domiciled or resident in those countries.[47] In Germany, section
23 of the ZPO (Code of Civil Procedure) provides that jurisdiction may be
asserted in any action involving pecuniary claims over a defendant who
is not domiciled in Germany but who possesses assets in that jurisdiction.
Traditionally, this provision has been interpreted both literally and very
widely, with jurisdiction not being limited to the value of the asset nor any
factual connection between it and the claim being required. Accordingly,
the most trivial and modest asset could found jurisdiction in a case
involving a multimillion dollar claim. Although this particular example of
exorbitant jurisdiction has recently been somewhat emasculated in a
significant and, within Germany, much criticized[48] decision of the
Bundesgerichtshof which superimposed a requirement of 'sufficient
connection' with Germany on section 23 of the ZPO,[49] similar exorbitant
jurisdictional bases exist in Scotland and other continental jurisdictions
including Denmark, Greece, and Belgium.[50] A similar jurisdiction existed
in the United States up until 1977.[51]

---

[46] This is also Article 14 of the Luxembourg Civil Code.

[47] Article 638, *Code Judiciaire*; Article 126(3), Dutch Code of Civil Procedure.

[48] See the articles referred to by Walter, G and Dalsgaard, R, 'The Civil Law Approach' in Nygh, P and McLachlan, C, *Transnational Tort Litigation* (1996) 44, n 17.

[49] See Dannemann, G 'Jurisdiction Based on the Presence of Assets in Germany: A Case Note' (1992) 41 ICLQ 632, 633.

[50] Article 248(2), Danish Law on Civil Procedure; Article 40, Greek Code of Civil Procedure; Article 635(5), Belgian Judicial Code. See also in relation to Austria and The Netherlands: De Winter, LI, 'Excessive Jurisdiction in Private International Law' (1968) 17 ICLQ 706, 707–708; Sweden: Smit, H, 'Common and Civil Law Rules of In Personam Adjudicatory Authority' (1972) 21 ICLQ 335, 335 and 338.

[51] *Shaffer v Heitner* 433 US 186 (1977) overruled that aspect of *Pennoyer v Neff* 95 US 714

1.21 While Article 14 of the French Civil Code is often held up as perhaps the paradigm example of an exorbitant head of jurisdiction, with all the pejorative implications that that epithet connotes, it is not so very different from those common law jurisdictions which authorize the service of proceedings on foreign defendants in circumstances where the plaintiff brings a claim in tort and has suffered damage in the jurisdiction. In New South Wales, for example, that head of jurisdiction has been interpreted as permitting a plaintiff injured abroad but who continues to suffer damage on his or her return to New South Wales to bring proceedings against a foreign defendant.[52]

1.22 The position appears to be precisely the same in Canada. In *Lemmex v Bernard*,[53] an Ontarian injured while on holiday in Grenada brought his injury back with him to Ontario (in the sense that his damages endured) and jurisdiction was upheld over the stinging dissent of O'Leary J who said:

> To give jurisdiction to Ontario in such circumstances could not be in accordance with fairness and order and would not in my opinion be acceptable to the international community. A Toronto taxi driver should not have to defend himself in Australia or Japan or Grenada because his tourist passenger alleges he was injured through the taxi driver's negligence. And if the taxi driver were sued in one of those courts, the courts of Ontario ought not, in my opinion, to recognize that such foreign court had jurisdiction to entertain the suit.[54]

Under the current law in Australia and Canada, at least, that harsh consequence is a reality, mitigated only by the possibility of an application for a stay of proceedings which, as *Lemmex, Oceanic Sun*, and *Renault* all illustrate, tend to be unsuccessful at least where the plaintiff has suffered serious and ongoing injuries.

1.23 As may be gleaned from the examples given above, exorbitant or long arm jurisdiction may be specified in terms of particular heads of subject matter, as in the Civil Procedure Rules 1998 and their analogues in other common law countries, or expressed more generally, as in Article 14 of the French Civil Code or section 23 of the German ZPO. One particular type of jurisdiction perhaps warranting special mention in this context is that which in the United States is said to arise under the 'effects' doctrine enunciated in *United States v Aluminium Company of America*.[55] In this case, Judge Learned Hand stated that 'it is settled law . . . that any State may

---

(1878) which permitted the assertion of *quasi in rem* jurisdiction to litigate claims unrelated to the property attached: see 212.

[52] See, for example, *Oceanic Sun Line Special Shipping v Fay* (1988) 165 CLR 197; *Renault v Zhang* (2002) 187 ALR 1.
[53] (2001) 204 DLR (4th) 192.   [54] ibid 215.
[55] 148 F 2d 416 (2nd Cir, 1945).

impose liabilities, even upon persons not within its allegiance, for conduct outside its borders which has consequences within its borders which the State reprehends; and these liabilities other States will ordinarily recognize'.[56] This jurisdiction has been reinvested with a new potency in *Hartford Fire Insurance Co v California*.[57] Contrary to what is perhaps commonly supposed, the United States is not the only country that asserts such extraterritorial jurisdiction.[58] Whatever its status as a matter of public international law, such jurisdiction quite clearly contributes to the likelihood that courts of more than one state may assert jurisdiction in relation to the same claim, for physical acts in one jurisdiction will frequently produce economic effects in another, and courts in the respective states may both assert jurisdiction.

Although the precise content of rules prescribing exorbitant jurisdiction **1.24** will obviously vary between countries, a good general justification for such jurisdiction was provided by Justice Jackson of the United States Supreme Court who stated that it 'usually give[s] a plaintiff a choice of courts, so that he may be quite sure of some place to pursue his remedy'.[59] In the United States, the assertion of long arm jurisdiction is not inconsistent with the constitutional guarantee of 'due process' which requires only certain 'minimum contacts' with the forum.[60]

While the existence of exorbitant jurisdiction in different legal systems is **1.25** by no means a recent development and the pejorative 'exorbitant' is no longer always considered apposite,[61] the fact that potential corporate and individual defendants, while not actually present in a particular country, may yet have assets in the jurisdiction (as part of a programme of diversified holdings, for example) may encourage plaintiffs to have greater resort to 'exorbitant' bases of jurisdiction, confident in the knowledge that local assets can feed any judgment, making secondary attempts at enforcement unnecessary.

3. THE PROBLEMS OF CONCURRENT JURISDICTION

The ubiquitous 'presence' of multinational corporations and the ease of **1.26** international travel for individuals, the concomitant increase in

---

[56] ibid 444.

[57] 509 US 764 (1993), noted by Roth, P, 'Jurisdiction, British public policy and the U.S. Supreme Court' (1994) 110 LQR 194.

[58] See Whish, R and Sufrin, B, *Competition Law* (3rd edn, 1993) 373–374. For an extreme case, see the Iraqi Government's resolution 369 discussed in *Kuwait Airways Corporation v Iraq Airways Co (Nos 4 and 5)* [2001] 1 Lloyd's Rep 161, 223; and see, now, [2002] 2 WLR 1353.

[59] *Gulf Oil Corp v Gilbert* 330 US 501, 507 (1947).

[60] *International Shoe Co v Washington* 326 US 310 (1945).

[61] *Agar v Hyde* (2000) 201 CLR 552, 570–571.

transnational business activity, and the widespread existence of broad bases of exorbitant jurisdiction all have a common consequence. They contribute directly to the possibility that a number of courts in different countries may assert jurisdiction in respect of one and the same claim or related claims arising out of the same factual substratum of events. This 'possibility' is guaranteed in the case of defamation where the one libellous statement is treated, at least as a matter of domestic law, as an individual publication giving rise to the separate causes of action in as many jurisdictions as the statement is made.[62]

1.27 The problems of concurrent jurisdiction are not, of course, novel although the conditions of the modern global economy have no doubt underlined them. Moreover, and in part perhaps on account of this circumstance, jurists have demonstrated heightened sensitivity to notions of international judicial comity in recent decades. In this context, the type of cases considered in this book and the litigation patterns disclosed by it have provoked increased contemplation of the difficulties that can be produced by courts of different countries asserting jurisdiction over the same dispute. These difficulties extend beyond the immediate expense and inconvenience which fighting two or more sets of proceedings necessarily entails for the parties. They also involve the unattractive possibility of courts of two (or more) countries reaching different and inconsistent decisions on identical or related matters, a situation which hardly encourages respect for the rule of law and the role of courts in a civilized society. Further, where there is concurrent litigation, parties may seek to expedite proceedings in a particular forum with the intent of rendering proceedings in the other jurisdiction nugatory by virtue of a plea of *res judicata*, the so-called 'race to judgment'. Such a race necessarily embroils sovereign courts in the type of tactical battles and strategic warfare that, as shall be seen, are recurring features of modern transnational commercial litigation. In *The Abidin Daver*,[63] Lord Diplock expressed considerable disquiet at the prospect of multiple or concurrent proceedings, stating that '[c]omity demands that such a situation should not be permitted to occur as between courts of two friendly and civilized states. It is a recipe for confusion and injustice.'[64] An additional consideration in this context relates to court resources and concern in respect of court delays.

---

[62] See *Berezovsky v Michaels* [2000] 1 WLR 1004.   [63] [1985] AC 398.

[64] ibid 412. cf *Bayer AG v Winter* The Times, 24 March 1986, where Hoffmann J observed that 'while a multiplicity of suits was not desirable, a distinction should be drawn between proceedings to preserve assets and litigation of the substantive merits of the dispute. The plaintiff had no wish to litigate the merits in Austria and Switzerland and was willing to undertake, once protective measures were in place, to apply for a stay of proceedings in the Swiss and Austrian courts, pending the decision of the English court on liability.'

The problems of concurrent jurisdiction will be no more than theoretical in **1.28**
circumstances where all parties agree to the venue for resolution of any
disputes arising between them, whether by means of litigation or arbitration, although it should be appreciated that the often multidimensional and
multi-party nature of modern transnational litigation may make consensus
as to venue more difficult. Where there is accord between the parties, it may
be expressed formally in terms of a written 'jurisdiction agreement' or
'forum clause' in a contract, or, in the case of arbitration, an agreement to
submit disputes to arbitration. Such agreements need not be entered into
prior to the dispute between the parties arising. Alternatively, agreement as
to the venue for any litigation may be informal or, in the case of arbitration,
ad hoc. In these circumstances, the defendant will not oppose the forum
chosen by the plaintiff (or the mode of dispute resolution, in the case of
arbitration) whether directly by means of a jurisdictional challenge[65] or
indirectly through the institution of proceedings in another forum either for
substantive relief or for a declaration of non-liability.

Litigation or arbitration in a 'neutral' venue such as London, known for **1.29**
its particular expertise in certain branches of the law such as insurance
and shipping, may prove to be acceptable to all parties to a transnational
commercial dispute.[66] Indeed, many parties make express provision for
litigation or arbitration in London in their contractual arrangements. In
MacShannon v Rockware Glass Ltd,[67] Lord Salmon observed that
'[h]undreds if not thousands of commercial contracts, having nothing to
do with the United Kingdom, are made all over the world every year
between foreigners, containing a clause that . . . any difference or dispute
between the parties shall be arbitrated in London'.[68] Estimates that in
about 80 per cent of cases in the Commercial Court at least one of the
parties is not resident in the United Kingdom, and that in about 50 per
cent of cases all parties are foreign,[69] also confirm the supposition that, in

---

[65] By which is meant, in the context of proceedings in England, an application under Part
11 of the Civil Procedure Rules or CPR 62.8 in the case of an arbitration.

[66] Slater, AG, 'Forum Non Conveniens: A View from the Shop Floor' (1988) 104 LQR 554,
561: 'The reasons which lead foreigners to start proceedings in England are very complex.
They may include some particular substantive or procedural advantage. *More often, they are
based on general considerations of cost, convenience and confidence in the system*, (emphasis
added).

[67] [1978] AC 795 , 820.

[68] See also *The Abidin Daver* [1984] AC 398, 407 per Lord Diplock, and *Akai Pty Ltd v
People's Insurance Company* (1996) 185 CLR 571 in which there was evidence that the
Singaporean and Australian parties to a contract of insurance desired the neutrality of
London as the forum for resolution of any disputes.

[69] See Sir Michael Kerr in Bos, M and Brownlie, I (n 11 above) 113. McLachlan, C,
'Dispatching the Opposition: A Legal Guide to Transnational Litigation' (August 1992) IFL
Rev Special Supplement 38 places the figures slightly lower but the point is nevertheless
clear.

many cases, parties to a transnational dispute are perfectly content to litigate in England (or other large commercial centres such as New York or Sydney).

1.30 This book is not, however, concerned with those cases where there is no dispute as to the forum for litigation or as to the mode of dispute resolution, in the case of arbitration. Rather it is concerned with the opposite case, where several courts have concurrent jurisdiction and there *is* a serious dispute between the parties as to which should hear the case or as to whether it should be arbitrated or litigated.

III. THE IMPORTANCE OF VENUE

1.31 Although not a totally modern phenomenon, battles over the venue for transnational litigation and the law regulating the problems of concurrent jurisdiction in such circumstances have become increasingly prominent in the law reports and it is perhaps no coincidence that most of the case law to be considered in this book has arisen in the last twenty years.[70] Indeed, it has been said that '[t]here can be few subjects, outside the field of substantive law, which have received such extensive consideration by the courts over such a short period'.[71] If that comment were true in 1988 when it was expressed, it is, if anything, more apposite almost fifteen years later. Such has been the focus of the courts on this particular area that several academic writers have pointed to what they regard as an unmistakeable trend in the conflict of laws away from its traditional and arcane domain of choice of law towards problems of jurisdiction,[72] a trend consistent with the birth of the subject of 'transnational litigation'.

1.32 What lies behind clashes over jurisdiction in transnational disputes is a centrally important proposition which is the fundamental premise of this book, namely that *venue matters*. In the field of tort law, for example, it has

---

[70] In addition to English and European law, the case law that is considered in this book includes that of the United States, Canada, Australia, New Zealand, Hong Kong, Singapore, Malaysia, Scotland, and the Republic of Ireland.

[71] Slater, AG (n 66 above) 559.

[72] Briggs, A, 'Private International Law' in Birks, P (ed), *English Private Law* (2001) para 17.02; Briggs, A, 'Conflict of Laws: Postponing the Future?' (1989) 9 OJLS 251, 252–253; Fawcett, JJ, (Book Review) [1990] LMCLQ 296 and 'The Interrelationships of Jurisdiction and Choice of Law in Private International Law' [1991] CLP 39; Fentiman, RG, 'Foreign Law in English Courts' (1992) 108 LQR 142 , 155. As a matter of practice, Inglis has suggested that the apparent primacy of choice of law was always misleading: 'Jurisdiction, the Doctrine of Forum Conveniens, and Choice of Law in Conflict of Laws' (1965) 81 LQR 380, 380: 'Custom and usage conspire to place "choice of law" in the forefront of most academic discussions of conflict of laws. No emphasis could be more misleading in practice.'

been observed that '[t]he battle over where the litigation occurs is typically the hardest fought and most important issue in a transnational case'[73] and the battle may be just as fierce with regard to commercial disputes, although different motivations may be at play, as further explained in Chapter 2. The extent to which venue matters can be measured not only by the number but also by the intensity of many of the jurisdictional clashes to be considered in what follows. These clashes, as shall be seen, frequently reach appellate level and occasionally inspire metaphors of litigational warfare. Characteristic of the battle over venue is one Australian judge's reference to 'yet another round in a long battle between the parties which is being fought on two fronts, one in this country and the other in the United States of America'.[74]

The motivation for such clashes will inevitably vary and may be affected **1.33** by considerations not always apparent to the judge or which are not relevant to any determination he or she might have to make.[75] It may simply be that the parties are 'determined to litigate the other into the ground regardless of the cost or effort involved'.[76] It has also been observed that 'a plaintiff sometimes is under temptation to resort to a strategy of forcing the trial at a most inconvenient place for an adversary, even at some inconvenience to himself'.[77]

It is assumed in this book, however, that, for the most part, a rational **1.34** motivation informs a plaintiff's original choice of forum and subsequent clashes over jurisdiction in transnational disputes. It follows as a corollary of the premise that venue can be of vital importance in transnational litigation that 'forum shopping' will be at a premium. The principal reason why venue may be of critical significance and the pre-eminent explanation for the phenomenon of forum shopping lies in the law's lack of uniformity. Procedural differences between jurisdictions will make some forums far more attractive than others from a plaintiff's perspective; further, the relative lack of uniformity both in states' internal laws and choice of law rules dictates differences in the substantive principles which will be applied in a given case depending on the forum selected.

The importance of venue in transnational litigation is reinforced when it is **1.35** appreciated that much of the litigation in this area appears to be preliminary

---

[73] Robertson, DW and Speck, PK, 'Access to State Courts in Transnational Personal Injury Cases: Forum Non Conveniens and Antisuit Injunctions' (1990) 68 Texas Law Review 937, 938.

[74] *Sentry Corporation v Peat Marwick Mitchell & Co* (1990) 95 ALR 11, 24 .

[75] *Spiliada Maritime Corporation v Cansulex Ltd* [1987] 1 AC 460, 465 per Lord Templeman.

[76] *Metall und Rohstoff AG v ACLI Metals (London) Ltd* [1984] 1 Lloyd's Rep 598, 607 per Purchas LJ, citing Staughton J at first instance.

[77] *Gulf Oil Corp v Gilbert* 330 US 501 (1947), 507 per Jackson J.

not to substantive litigation but rather to the settlement or compromise of the plaintiff's claim. It may at first glance seem counter-intuitive that a case which is destined to settle or compromise would be the subject of litigation, at least litigation pursued to the stage of a formal judgment, albeit on an interlocutory matter. But that is to overlook the fact that the parties' formula for settlement will be in terms of an assessment of a range of contingencies. An American commentator has observed that 'even in cases where settlement is likely, the question of the appropriate forum is often litigated because it can define the parameters of the settlement'.[78] Similar observations have been made with respect to litigation over venue in England.[79]

1.36 This point is best demonstrated by way of an illustration. Where the two potential forums for the resolution of a dispute are the United States and India, for example,[80] the likely difference in quantum which a successful plaintiff would be awarded may be such that one of, if not *the* most important of, the contingencies for the parties to consider in settlement negotiations will be the plaintiff's ability to maintain suit in the United States. In this context, some commentators speak of a 'mid-Atlantic settlement formula' in which the different amounts which may be recovered in the potential forums represent polar figures.[81] Whether prospective courts will permit the case to proceed in their jurisdiction may, however, be uncertain and not be able to be ascertained without resorting to litigation. Paradoxically, therefore, in the absence of consensus as to what is the appropriate venue for resolution of the dispute, parties may be constrained to resort to litigation in order to settle the terms of a compromise. The stakes will frequently be such that any litigation as to venue will be keenly contested.

1.37 The necessarily impressionistic observations in the previous paragraph find support in recent case law. In *The Al Battani*, a case involving a jurisdictional contest between the courts of England and Egypt, Sheen J observed that:

---

[78] Silberman, LJ, 'Developments in Jurisdiction and Forum Non Conveniens in International Litigation' (1993) 28 Texas International Law Journal 501, 502.

[79] Briggs, A and Rees, P (n 8 above) para 4.17.

[80] As was the case with respect to the claims arising out of the Bhopal disaster: see *In re Union Carbide Corp* 634 F Supp 842 (SDNY, 1986).

[81] See, for example, Pannone, R, 'Forum Shopping—Trans-National Claims' (1987) 55 Medico-Legal Journal 224 , 232; Baade, HW, 'Foreign Oil Disaster Litigation Prospects in the United States and the "Mid-Atlantic Settlement Formula" ' (1989) 7 Journal of Energy and Natural Resources Law 125; Joseph, D, 'Disaster Litigation—the USA Way' (1989) 139 New Law Journal 1419; Silva, EJ, 'Practical Views on Stemming the Tide of Foreign Plaintiffs and Concluding Mid-Atlantic Settlements' (1993) 28 Texas International Law Journal 479, especially 496–497.

Cases of this class seldom come to trial. I cannot help thinking that the reality of the matter is that my decision as to the venue for trial will put one party or the other into a stronger position when negotiating any possible settlement of this claim.[82]

Staughton J had made strikingly similar observations at first instance in **1.38** *Spiliada Maritime Corporation v Cansulex Ltd*,[83] stating that 'I suspect that what I am in fact deciding is not where the *Spiliada* action will ultimately be tried, but whether a settlement will be reached against the background of litigation pending in England or of litigation pending in Canada'.[84] So also in *The Goldean Mariner*,[85] a case in which certain American marine underwriters sought to set aside or, in the alternative, to stay proceedings on the ground of *forum non conveniens*, Phillips J expressed the 'strong suspicion that the motive behind these applications . . . has been a desire to improve negotiating position rather than any real desire for trial in another forum'.[86]

The same pattern of settlement following litigation as to jurisdiction also **1.39** appears to apply in the United States and Australia.[87] In *Dow Chemical Co v Castro Alfaro*,[88] the vast majority of the Costa Rican workers who sought damages in this case accepted a settlement offer soon after the resolution of the jurisdictional question in their favour.[89] In Australia, commercially significant litigation between CSR Limited and New Zealand Insurance Co Limited and between Allstate Life Insurance Co and a range of defendants settled while appeals in relation to decisions to grant anti-suit injunctions were pending.[90]

---

[82] [1993] 2 Lloyd's Rep 219, 221. [83] [1987] AC 460.

[84] Cited in Lord Goff's speech, ibid 468–469.

[85] [1989] 2 Lloyd's Rep 390.

[86] ibid 403. See also *Maharanee of Baroda v Wildenstein* [1972] 2 QB 283, 298 per Stephenson LJ; *Smith Kline & French Laboratories Ltd v Bloch* [1983] 2 All ER 72, 77 per Lord Denning MR; *The Abidin Daver* [1984] AC 398, 412 per Lord Diplock; and *de Dampierre v de Dampierre* [1988] AC 92, 103 per Lord Templeman; *Baghlaf Al Zafer v PNSC* [1998] 2 Lloyd's Rep 229, 235 per Phillips LJ.

[87] See the articles by Baade, HW and Silva, EJ cited in n 81 above and Craft, RR, 'Factors Influencing Settlement of Personal Injury and Death Claims in Aircraft Accident Litigation' (1981) 46 Journal of Air Law and Commerce 895, 908–910.

[88] 786 SW2d 674 (Tex, 1990).

[89] Albright, AW, 'In Personam Jurisdiction: A Confused and Inappropriate Substitute for Forum Non Conveniens' (1992) 71 Texas Law Review 351, 352 n 4. See also Robertson, DW, '*Forum Non Conveniens* in America and England: A Rather Fantastic Fiction' (1987) 103 LQR 398, 419. His survey of the outcome of 55 personal injury cases and 30 commercial cases in which the question of venue had been resolved against trial in a US federal court indicates that, in the first category, 20 of the cases settled out of 55 and only 10 cases went to trial in an alternative forum and, of the 30 commercial cases, 16 settled and only 6 went to trial in an alternative forum.

[90] See *CSR Ltd v New Zealand Insurance Co Ltd* (1994) 36 NSWLR 138; *AllState Life Insurance Co Ltd v Australian and New Zealand Banking Group Ltd* (1996) 64 FCR 1 and 44.

1.40 In a well-known passage in *The Atlantic Star*, Lord Simon stated that:

> 'Forum-shopping' is a dirty word; but it is only a pejorative way of saying that, if you offer a plaintiff a choice of jurisdiction, he will naturally choose the one in which he thinks his case can most favourably be presented: this should be a matter neither for surprise nor for indignation.[91]

1.41 While the first limb of Lord Simon's conclusion may be readily accepted,[92] the second is considerably more controversial. Justice Michael Kirby, when President of the New South Wales Court of Appeal, located the opprobrium attaching to the pejorative phrase 'forum shopping' in the fabric of the rule of law. In his Honour's words:

> There can be no rule of law without certainty as to the rights and obligations of persons under the law. If different consequences could flow from the uncontrolled privilege of a party to bring proceedings in different jurisdictions of Australia, this would inject a high measure of uncertainty into the law. It would erode the principle of finality which limitation statutes defend. It would diminish the predictability of the application of the law to particular facts. It would interfere in the capacity of parties and their insurers to organise their affairs in a rational manner, including in accident cases. It would effectively destroy 'decisional harmony' and put a premium on legal inventiveness in invoking jurisdictions having no other connection or relevance save for a beneficial limitation or other procedural regime.[93]

1.42 In spite of Lord Simon's observation that the phenomenon of forum shopping should not be a matter for indignation, recent cases have made it clear that, where a contract's proper law, according to English rules of private international law, is English, English courts regard litigation in a forum that will not apply English law as a blatant and unacceptable form of forum shopping[94] even, it would appear, in a case where the litigation was initiated in a forum whose statutes either overrode or gave relief from the (English) proper law, notwithstanding that those statutes did not have extraterritorial effect.[95]

1.43 What is most important to note for present purposes is that forum shopping only becomes a possibility and, depending on one's viewpoint, a problem, where several forums have jurisdiction to entertain a particular claim. It is this factor that makes the differences between the procedural

---

[91] [1974] AC 436, 471.

[92] Gleeson CJ has described the term as 'dyslogistic and unhelpful': *Goliath Portland Cement Co Ltd v Bengtell* (1994) 33 NSWLR 414, 419.

[93] *Goliath Portland Cement Co Ltd v Bengtell* (1994) 33 NSWLR 414, 435; see also his Honour's remarks in *Renault v Zhang* (2002) 187 ALR 1.

[94] *HIB v Guardian Insurance* [1997] 1 Lloyd's Rep 414, 417; *Meridien BIAO v Bank of New York* [1997] 1 Lloyd's Rep 437, 442 and 466.

[95] *Akai v People's Insurance Company* [1998] 1 Lloyd's Rep 90.

and substantive (including conflicts) laws of different jurisdictions of significance for litigants and creates the necessary precondition for battles over venue in transnational disputes.

IV. VENUE IN TRANSNATIONAL LITIGATION: OUTLINE

This introductory chapter has sought to set the context in which the topic **1.44** of 'Forum Shopping and Venue in Transnational Litigation' can be considered. The setting is provided by the operation and realities of the modern global economy which ensure that the type of clashes over jurisdiction considered in this book are likely to increase in number. The prerequisite for such clashes has been seen to be the factor of concurrent jurisdiction which provides the environment for forum shopping. The motivations for this phenomenon are explained by differences in both procedural and substantive laws between jurisdictions. Plaintiffs' attempts to take advantage of such differences in turn often result in fierce battles being joined by *defendants* over the question of what forum should ultimately determine the transnational dispute. And, as has been seen, such battles will often be fought even if, or indeed because, a dispute is destined to be settled out of court. The factor of concurrent jurisdiction also creates the unseemly prospect of multiple proceedings and the possibility of inconsistent results in different courts. Such clashes of jurisdiction may redound to the cost of considerations of international judicial comity.

The main corpus of this book addresses, at both a conceptual and practi- **1.45** cal level, the problems raised by the existence of concurrent jurisdiction and the cognate phenomenon of forum shopping. Chapter 2 makes a detailed examination of the incentives for forum shopping. These are seen to be rooted not only in differences in procedure as between jurisdictions relating, for example, to the level of damages obtainable or the extent of pre-trial discovery available but also in lack of uniformity in both substantive principles of law and choice of law rules. As noted above, a plaintiff's attempt to take advantage of the various benefits offered by one forum over another typically signals the beginning of the battle for venue in transnational litigation.

Chapter 3 then examines two different conceptual responses to the prob- **1.46** lems of concurrent jurisdiction and the perceived 'evil' of forum shopping. The first is that exemplified by the Brussels Convention on Jurisdiction and Judgments (now, for all practical purposes, translated into European Council Regulation 44/2001) which, although it does not totally eliminate the scope for forum shopping, places a premium on certainty as far as matters of jurisdiction are concerned and seeks to ensure that litigation proceeds only in an appropriate forum. One of its aims is to eliminate what are perceived to be expensive and essentially unmeritorious clashes over venue for the resolution of a transnational dispute. Both the Convention and the Regulation are especially sensitive to the possibility of inconsistent decisions by courts of contracting and, under the Regulation, member states and, through a crude but largely effective mechanism, there is virtually no scope for concurrent jurisdiction actually being exercised.

1.47 The second conceptual response is that developed by the common law to mediate clashes over venue in transnational litigation. It centres around the notion that, for any given transnational dispute, there is a 'natural forum' in which it should be resolved. The concept of the natural forum lies at the core of many of the common law's responses to forum shopping and it will be seen that it, too, can be employed to a certain extent to forestall the undesirable consequences entailed in the existence and assertion of concurrent jurisdiction.

1.48 Chapter 4 moves from an examination of the theoretical merits and demerits of the two conceptual responses outlined above to a detailed consideration of the practical strategies available to a *defendant* in the battle over venue in transnational litigation. These strategies, which include challenging jurisdiction *in limine*, applications for a stay of proceedings on the basis of the doctrine of *forum non conveniens*, requests for the grant of an anti-suit injunction restraining foreign proceedings, and the action for negative declaratory relief pre-empting them, have been collectively described as 'reverse forum shopping'.[96] It will be evident from the brief reference made above to the scheme of the Brussels Convention and Council Regulation 44/2001 that there will be less scope for a defendant to challenge jurisdiction allocated by these instruments than under the common law, for, as was noted, one of the Convention's and Regulation's *raisons d'être* is to minimize jurisdictional clashes. That is not to say that a defendant may not attempt to deploy certain of the strategies mentioned above in order to secure the forum of its choice within the scheme of the Brussels Convention and the Regulation but, as will also be seen, some of these strategies are rather problematic in this arena.

1.49 The main focus in Chapter 4 is necessarily on common law issues. It contains a detailed examination of 'reverse forum shopping' strategies with a view to establishing their tactical value to a defendant in the battle

---

[96] Boyce, D, 'Foreign Plaintiffs and Forum Non Conveniens: Going Beyond *Reyno*' (1985) 64 Texas Law Review 193, 216 n 149.

for venue in transnational litigation. The first section examines, in a necessarily general way, the course of challenging a court's jurisdiction. Recent
common law developments in both England and Australia have important ramifications in this respect with both making a plaintiff's task in
establishing and upholding jurisdiction considerably easier. It will also be
seen that, in certain contexts, challenging a court's jurisdiction may introduce constitutional issues of considerable complexity. The second section
of the chapter considers the extent to which the *Spiliada* doctrine,[97] which
embraces the notion of the 'natural forum', has been successfully
employed by the courts which have adopted it to redirect litigation to the
natural forum. It also notes that, in those jurisdictions with either a
diluted version of this doctrine, a different doctrine of *forum non conveniens*, or no such doctrine at all, the prospects for a defendant of securing
a stay will be correspondingly diminished. The third section focuses upon
the increasingly important topic of anti-suit injunctions and the extent to
which "defendants" will meet with success when requesting a court to
restrain foreign proceedings. Such relief may be sought in a rich variety of
circumstances and an attempt at classification is made. Such contextual
differentiation also has important ramifications for the role of comity in
this area. That topic is fully considered. The fourth section concerns
attempts not to restrain but rather to pre-empt foreign proceedings and
issue is taken with the orthodoxy of the common law's distaste for negative declarations. A final section considers perhaps the simplest strategy
of all which a defendant may employ in the context of transnational litigation, namely ignoring the institution of foreign proceedings and resisting any attempt at enforcement in its country of domicile or residence. It
will be seen that this strategy is not always as secure as may have been
formerly supposed.

Chapter 5 then addresses a topic of immense practical importance in **1.50**
transnational litigation, namely the use of jurisdiction and arbitration
agreements to resolve questions of venue. Such agreements are recognized by most legal systems as being an essential part of international
commerce and, on their face, they offer a relatively straightforward means
of avoiding costly and acrimonious disputes over jurisdiction. But, even
in this area, such is the potential importance of venue in transnational litigation and dispute resolution that there is a surprisingly large amount of
case law involving attempts by parties to extricate themselves from such
agreements. The arguments deployed by parties endeavouring to secure
this result range from simple appeals to the discretion of the court to
complex questions relating to choice of law and the formation of

---

[97] *Spiliada Maritime Corp v Cansulex Ltd* [1987] AC 460.

contracts. In tending on the whole to uphold and give effect to such agreements, the approach of both the common law, on the one hand, and the Brussels Convention and Council Regulation 44/2001, on the other, exhibit much similarity.

1.51 A final chapter then briefly seeks to gather together various themes that can be detected in a study of venue in transnational litigation and the practice of forum shopping. It will be seen that the central premise of the book, namely that *venue matters*, is confirmed by the sheer number of cases in recent years that have involved this fundamentally important issue. It is an issue which is worthy of detailed academic appraisal and this book responds to observations that insufficient attention has hitherto been paid to the principles of law which govern the question of venue in transnational litigation. Every attempt has been made to lend a practitioner's perspective to the discussion.

2

Venue and the Plaintiff—The Incentives for Forum Shopping

I.	Three Dimensions of Uniformity	2.01
II.	The Significance of Procedure	2.09
	1. The United States—A Forum Shopper's Delight	2.14
	2. Beyond America: Further Procedural Inducements	2.28
III.	Lack of Uniformity in Domestic Law	2.33
IV.	Divergence in Choice of Law Rules and Practice	2.37
V.	Conclusion	2.58

I. THREE DIMENSIONS OF UNIFORMITY

'Since Savigny, it has been customary to regard the attainment of uniform **2.01** solutions as the chief purpose of private international law.'[1] The intuitively attractive corollary of this succinct statement of the guiding aspiration of the modern conflict of laws is that the venue in which a piece of litigation is tried should not affect the outcome or result of that litigation. As Justice Jackson said in a leading choice of law case, 'the purpose of a conflict-of-laws doctrine is to assure that a case will be treated in the same way under the appropriate law regardless of the fortuitous circumstances which often determine the forum'.[2] Consequently, there should be no occasion for parties to a dispute 'to litigate in order to determine where they shall litigate'.[3]

In an ideal world, such a contest would be devoid of practical significance **2.02** for the 'same substantive rules [would obtain], irrespective of the court where they are pleaded'.[4] In such a world, it would seem, the much maligned practice of forum shopping would not flourish. But this ideal world does not of course exist, and the goal of harmonization and unification *either* of internal laws *or* choice of law rules, though occasionally

---

[1] Rabel, E, *The Conflict of Laws: A Comparative Study* (2nd edn, 1958, prepared by Ulrich Drobnig) Vol 1, 94. See also *The Amazonia* [1990] 1 Lloyd's Rep 236, 246.

[2] *Lauritzen v Larsen* 345 US 571, 591 (1953).

[3] *Spiliada Maritime Corporation v Cansulex Ltd* [1987] AC 460, 464.

[4] Rabel, E (n 1 above) 94. See also *Irish Shipping Ltd v Commercial Union* [1991] 2 QB 206, 229.

realized in limited cases[5] and partially achieved in certain regional areas (and then only in certain fields),[6] remains utopian.[7]

2.03   *Even if* extensive harmonization of substantive law were achieved or a set of uniform choice of law rules did exist, however, it would still not be the case that uniform results would obtain and that forum shopping would correspondingly dissipate. 'The true causes of forum shopping', it has been said, 'are to be found elsewhere than in the divergences of the rules of private international law. The plaintiff usually shops in the forum with which he is most familiar or in which he gains the greatest procedural advantage or puts the defendant to the greatest procedural disadvantage.'[8] In the most extreme cases, a choice of forum will be dictated by a genuinely held view that an alternate, obvious forum will not yield a fair trial[9] or where the sheer expense of litigation in that forum will be prohibitive.[10]

2.04   It is plain that the conditions for litigation will not be the same in every forum. Legal costs, the speed and mode of litigation, and the quality and ability of the judiciary and the legal profession are factors which serve to differentiate the legal systems of different countries, making them more or less attractive to litigants, depending on their motivations. Other procedural matters will be enshrined in actual rules or laws of the forum, relating for example to the nature and scope of discovery or disclosure, recovery of costs, and the availability of certain remedies including interlocutory remedies such as freezing and search orders, known in the common law world as Mareva injunctions and Anton Piller orders, security for costs, and, in some jurisdictions requiring, for example, the filing by defendants of a bond, security for a claim. It has been observed that 'these factors should not be discounted. Every practising litigator knows that they are often the decisive determinants in a case overriding considerations of fact and substantive law.'[11]

---

[5] For example, the Warsaw Convention on Carriage by Air 1929. But even here, see *King v Bristow Helicopters Ltd* [2001] 1 Lloyd's Rep 95.

[6] For example, the Rome Convention on the Law Applicable to Contractual Obligations.

[7] Rabel, for example, has described it as 'an ideal remote from reality' (n 1 above) 94, Juenger as 'illusory': 'Forum Shopping, Domestic and International' (1989) 63 Tulane Law Review 553, 574.

[8] Collins, LA, 'Contractual Obligations—The EEC Preliminary Draft Convention on Private International Law' (1976) 25 ICLQ 35, 36. See also Juenger, FK, *Choice of Law and Multistate Justice* (1993) 4.

[9] See *Jeyeretnam v Mahmood* The Times, 21 May 1992, discussed in Bottomley, S and Kinley, D, *Commercial Law and Human Rights* (2002) 121–122.

[10] *Lubbe v Cape* [2000] 1 WLR 1545; *Renault v Zhang* (2002) 187 ALR 1.

[11] Pearl, S, 'Forum Shopping in the EEC' (1987) 15 International Business Lawyer 391, 393.

Although, as a practice, 'forum shopping' has pejorative connotations— **2.05**
Dr Morris recording that it was considered a 'deadly sin' at The Hague[12]—
in seeking to maximize a client's chances of success in litigation, it is not
only unremarkable but also entirely understandable.[13] It has even been
described, in the context of the adversary system, as an aspect of a solicitor's professional obligation to his or her client[14] and as an inevitability.[15]
Nor, it should be appreciated, is forum shopping (or the judicial desire to
curtail it) necessarily a recent phenomenon. In *Société du Gaz de Paris v
Société Anonyme de Navigation 'Les Armateurs Français'*,[16] Lord Sumner
observed that he was:

perfectly certain that the London underwriters . . . would never have thought of
entering the forum . . . unless they had thought, and had been advised, that by so
doing they gained for themselves some substantial advantage in the contest,
either some direct inconvenience to their opponent, or, at any rate, something
which would involve his disadvantage and increase their chances of winning.[17]

The mindset of plaintiffs and their advisers has evidently not altered from **2.06**
Lord Sumner's day.

The *raison d'être* for forum shopping lies in lack of uniformity throughout **2.07**
the world's legal systems, in terms both of internal laws and choice of law
rules and the procedural rules developed by different countries to facilitate the enforcement of those laws. To overlook or understate the significance of these differences to litigants 'is to fly in the face of reality'[18] for
lack of uniformity in any one of these three areas produces the consequence that the legal result in any given fact situation may vary according to the forum in which litigation takes place. Even apparently uniform
rules remain susceptible to differing judicial interpretation. A good example of this is Article 5 of European Council Regulation 44/2001 and the

---

[12] *The Conflict of Laws* (1st edn, 1971) 149–150. See also *Boys v Chaplin* [1971] AC 356, 378,
383, and 406; *The Atlantic Star* [1974] AC 436, 454. Dr Ong relates that it is 'abhorred in the
Philippines as well as in the other three common law ASEAN countries' (Malaysia,
Singapore and Brunei): *Cross-border Litigation within ASEAN* (1997) 484; see also 539–545.
[13] *The Atlantic Star* [1974] AC 436, 471. Whether it is acceptable is considered at paras 3.85
ff below.
[14] Pannone, R, 'Forum Shopping—Trans-National Claims' (1987) 55 Medico-Legal
Journal 224, 236; Joseph, D, 'Disaster Litigation—the USA Way' (1989) 139 New Law Journal
1419; Juenger, FK (n 8 above) 572; 'Forum Shopping Reconsidered' (1989–90) 103 Harvard
Law Review 1677, 1690–1691. See also *Bank of America v Bank of New York* (1995) 17 ATPR
41–390, 40, 337; Weintrub, R, 'International Litigation and Forum Non Conveniens' (1994) 29
Texas International Law Journal 321, 322.
[15] *Lubbe v Cape plc* [2000] 1 Lloyd's Rep 139, 154.
[16] 1926 SC (HL) 13.
[17] ibid 22.
[18] Slater, AG, 'Forum Non Conveniens: A View from the Shop Floor' (1988) 104 LQR 554,
563.

Brussels and Lugano Conventions[19] which, in England, requires, at the threshold jurisdictional level, a party asserting jurisdiction to show a good arguable case as to the existence of a contract or a tort[20] whereas, in continental states, it is apparently sufficient for jurisdictional purposes for the plaintiff simply to assert the relevant fact to establish jurisdiction.[21]

2.08 While, as was seen in Chapter 1, the existence of concurrent jurisdiction in two or more courts provides the necessary precondition for a plaintiff to seek to exploit these differences, it is lack of uniformity which is critical in igniting strategic battles over venue. It is a valuable exercise, therefore, to explore in some more detail precisely how differences in procedural, substantive, and choice of law rules between jurisdictions may affect the outcome of a particular piece of litigation. This inquiry serves to highlight the often large prizes which accompany victory in the battle for venue in transnational litigation and therefore helps to explain the incentives for forum shopping.

II. THE SIGNIFICANCE OF PROCEDURE

2.09 The precept that matters of substance are governed by the *lex causae* and matters of procedure by the *lex fori* has been described as 'perhaps the most inveterate doctrine of the conflict of laws'.[22] It has obvious ramifications for forum shopping for it operates irrespective of the fact that the *lex causae* may treat a given procedural question differently from the *lex fori*, even where this has the consequence that the outcome of the case will differ from that which would have obtained had the litigation taken place in the forum whose law was applicable to the substantive dispute. It has been rightly pointed out that the broader the interpretation which courts place upon what matters are to be classified as procedural, the greater will be the scope for forum shopping[23] for the reality is, in the words of Mason CJ, that 'all rules typically classified as procedural have the potential to affect substantive rights'.[24]

---

[19] For a full discussion of the relationship between, and spheres of operation of, the Regulation and the Conventions, see Briggs, A and Rees, P, *Civil Jurisdiction and Judgments* (3rd edn, 2002).

[20] *Tesam Distribution Ltd v Schuh Mode Team GmbH* [1990] I L Pr 150.

[21] See Walter, G and Dalsgaard, R, 'The Civil Law Approach' in Nygh, P and McLachlan, C, *Transnational Tort Litigation*, 55.

[22] Ailes, EH, 'Substance and Procedure in the Conflict of Laws' (1941) 39 Michigan Law Review 392, 392.

[23] *McKain v RW Miller & Co (SA) Pty Ltd* (1991) 174 CLR 1, 23 and 25; *Stevens v Head* (1993) 176 CLR 433, 452 and 462. See also *Breavington v Godleman* (1988) 169 CLR 41, 113 and 161.

[24] *McKain v RW Miller & Co (SA) Pty Ltd* (1991) 174 CLR 1, 25.

This section considers various aspects of procedure such as the mode of **2.10**
litigation (including the role of juries in the assessment of damages), the
scope of discovery and rules relating to fees and cost recovery, all of
which may affect the outcome of any given piece of litigation.[25]
Procedural advantages offered by the courts of the United States make
them a particularly attractive destination for plaintiffs and a subsection is
specifically devoted to them. Before embarking upon a more detailed
inquiry, it is first useful to illustrate just how a court's classification of a
matter as substantive or procedural may be critical.

In *Stevens v Head*,[26] the plaintiff, a New Zealander in Australia to visit the **2.11**
'Expo' exhibition in Brisbane, Queensland, was injured in the New South
Wales city of Tweed Heads. Tweed Heads is situated on the border
between New South Wales and Queensland and the only reason for the
plaintiff's presence in New South Wales was that she had been unable to
secure accommodation in Queensland, presumably due to Expo's popularity. The plaintiff commenced proceedings in Queensland rather than
New South Wales where legislation placed certain statutory caps on the
amount of damages recoverable in a case such as the plaintiff's. While the
decision to commence proceedings in Queensland rather than New South
Wales may not be deprecated as a blatant case of forum shopping, it is
plain that the majority's decision in this case to classify the statutory caps
on damages for economic loss imposed under New South Wales law as
the *lex loci delicti*[27] as procedural rather than substantive constituted a
standing invitation to forum shopping.[28]

That decision is to be contrasted with *Williamson v North-Eastern Railway* **2.12**
Co,[29] one of the early Scottish decisions embracing the doctrine of *forum
non conveniens*. It provides an excellent illustration of a plaintiff's attempt
to take advantage of the rule that matters of procedure are for the *lex fori*
in order to improve her chances of success. By seeking to invoke this rule,
the plaintiff hoped to escape the consequences of English law relating
both to title to sue and the limitation period for an action under Lord
Campbell's Act. But the Court of Session was firm and resolute in disal-
lowing such forum shopping even though, 'in consequence of our decision a poor widow, living in Leith, whose husband has been killed in

---

[25] For a useful comparative survey work, see Campbell, D and Campbell, C, (eds),
International Civil Procedures (1995).
[26] (1993) 176 CLR 433.
[27] Motor Accidents Act 1988 (NSW).
[28] (1993) 176 CLR 433, 452 and see Opeskin, BR, 'Statutory Caps on Damages in
Australian Conflict of Laws' (1993) 109 LQR 533.
[29] (1884) 11 R 596 (XI SC 4th Series).

England, may be practically deprived of all remedy'.[30] A 'hard case' was not allowed to make bad law whereas in both *Stevens v Head* and *McKain v RW Miller & Co (SA) Pty Ltd*,[31] an earlier case concerning the classification of statutes of limitation, one is left with the impression that the majorities (identical in both cases) were prepared to tolerate a broad interpretation of procedure, notwithstanding any consequent frustration or circumvention of applicable choice of law rules,[32] in order to permit the plaintiff to recover, in *Stevens*, a greater amount and in *McKain*, at all. The consequences in terms of the increased scope for forum shopping were trenchantly pointed out in the minority judgments.

2.13 The minority views in both *McKain* and *Stevens* were subsequently vindicated by the High Court of Australia's decision in *John Pfeiffer v Rogerson*[33] which made it plain that, within Australia, questions both of limitations and quantification of damages were to be treated as substantive and not procedural. However, in the transnational field, with which this book is concerned, that Court has expressly reserved its position on those two questions.[34] In the United Kingdom, apart from questions of limitations, nothing in the Private International Law (Miscellaneous Provisions) Act 1995 puts an end to the issue of whether quantification of damages is substantive or procedural and the prevailing case law continues to support the latter characterization with the consequence that a negligence claim litigated in England may be governed by Russian law, for example, but the assessment of damages may fall to be determined by reference to English law. Where there is a discrepancy between the amount of damages recoverable under the *lex loci delicti* and England as the law of the forum, the incentive for forum shopping is apparent.

1. The United States—A Forum Shopper's Delight

2.14 If it is the case that procedural advantages offered by particular forums provide, above all else, the incentive for forum shopping, then there can be little doubt that the United States is the most attractive destination for the forum shopping plaintiff, especially one with an action in tort.[35]

---

[30] ibid 600. cf *Evers v Firth* (1986) 10 NSWLR 22, 25: 'A litigant can hardly be accused of forum shopping when all the other shops are shut', referring to the fact that the limitation period had run in Queensland, the natural forum. New South Wales proceedings were not stayed. See also *Keeton v Hustler Magazines Inc* 465 US 770 (1984).

[31] (1991) 174 CLR 1.

[32] Collins, LA (ed), *Dicey and Morris on the Conflict of Laws* (13th edn, 2000) 157.

[33] (2000) 203 CLR 503.

[34] *Renault v Zhang* (2002) 187 ALR 1, 21.

[35] See, generally, Born, G, *International Civil Litigation in United States Courts* (3rd edn, 1996), 3–5.

In the United States, as Justice Thurgood Marshall expressly acknow- **2.15** ledged in *Piper Aircraft Co v Reyno*,[36] procedural factors such as expansive rules of pre-trial discovery, jury trials, large damages awards, and the non-recovery of costs rule conspire to produce the result, so graphically described by Lord Denning, that 'as a moth is drawn to the light, so is a litigant drawn to the United States'.[37] Other procedural inducements offered by litigation in the United States include low filing fees, the possibility of class actions, and liberal joinder rules[38] as well as relatively loose (from an Anglo-Commonwealth perspective) rules of pleading, thereby reducing the prospect of summary dismissal of speculative or vaguely cast claims. The contingency fee system greatly facilitates a plaintiff's ability to enjoy many of these procedural advantages and may, in itself, be a reason for bringing suit in the United States (or other jurisdictions) where lawyers are permitted to (and do) act 'on spec'. [39] Weintrub put it succinctly: 'The United States is a magnet for the afflicted of the world. The costs of litigating here are lower and the recovery is higher.'[40]

Most of these advantages represent corresponding disadvantages for a **2.16** defendant, a fact which will often also be attractive in itself to a plaintiff because it will enhance the prospects of settlement. On the other hand, at least in commercial cases, some of the procedural advantages of litigating in the United States may be double-edged:

At the same time, aspects of US litigation can make it distinctly unattractive to some foreign (and domestic) plaintiffs. Few litigants welcome the prospect of participating in any proceeding, far from home, in an unfamiliar forum that may be inconvenient, parochial, and worse. In the United States, legal proceedings can be uniquely expensive and, compared to at least some foreign alternatives, relatively slow. The availability of broad discovery can be a threat, as well as an inducement, for potential plaintiffs, as can the extensive public, press, and governmental access to US judicial proceedings and discovery materials. And the possibility of large damages awards, by potentially unpredictable local lay juries, can be a disincentive where counterclaims are likely.[41]

---

[36] 454 US 235 (1981) 252.

[37] *Smith Kline & French Laboratories Ltd v Bloch* [1983] 2 All ER 72, 74.

[38] Boyce, D, 'Foreign Plaintiffs and Forum Non Conveniens: Going Beyond *Reyno*' (1985) 64 Texas Law Review 193, 196.

[39] See *Midland Bank plc v Laker Airways Ltd* [1986] 1 QB 689, 704 and *Bank of Tokyo Ltd v Karoon* (Note) [1987] AC 45, 55. cf *Smith Kline & French Laboratories Ltd v Bloch* [1983] 2 All ER 72, 74. See also Silva, EJ, 'Practical Views on Stemming the Tide of Foreign Plaintiffs and Concluding Mid-Atlantic Settlements' (1993) 28 Texas International Law Journal 479, 480 n 4.

[40] 'International Litigation and Forum Non Conveniens' (1994) 21 Texas International Law Journal 321, 352.

[41] Born, G, *International Civil Litigation in United States Courts* (3rd edn, 1996) 5.

Jury Trials and Higher Damages

2.17 Of the factors referred to in the previous paragraphs (and accepting that it will partly be a function of the type of case at bar), it is the 'notorious generosity'[42] of the American jury that stands out as the greatest carrot for foreign plaintiffs.[43] An excellent illustration of the potency of this factor is provided by the litigational history of a Portuguese seaman's claim against a Panamanian company for damages for personal injury.[44] Castanho sustained injury on board the defendant's ship while at dock in Great Yarmouth harbour in Norfolk, England. Having initially commenced an action in England, he then sought, at the prompting of American attorneys, to discontinue this action and instead instituted fresh proceedings in Texas, the only connection with this forum being the ultimate beneficial ownership of shares of the defendant by Brown & Root, a Texas-based company. The simple explanation for Castanho's decision to change forum is supplied by the procedural differences between the two jurisdictions for there was:

> no ostensible difference between Texas law and English law as to the defendant's liability for negligence or even as to the measure of damages as a matter of law. But on the same facts and guided (or ostensibly and in any event, unreversably guided) by the same legal standards, an English judge would probably have awarded not much more than £300,000 and an East Texas jury might have come in with more than the $3 million for which the case was settled.[45]

2.18 In the Court of Appeal, Lord Denning MR and Brandon LJ, disagreed sharply on the propriety of this form of forum shopping, the latter seeing it as 'entirely legitimate'.[46] Together with Shaw LJ, who saw the case as 'about money, not morality',[47] it was this latter view which prevailed in the House of Lords.[48] There was no attempt to elevate a concern to discourage forum shopping into a basis for the grant of anti-suit injunctive relief, the remedy sought by the defendants in the English proceedings. That the defendants were prepared to fight all the way up to the

---

[42] Fleming, JG, *The American Tort Process* (1988) 125.

[43] *Smith Kline & French Laboratories Ltd v Bloch* [1983] 2 All ER 72, 74. See also Fleming, JG (n 42 above) 125 n 101.

[44] The background of this case is found in *Castanho v Brown & Root (UK) Ltd* [1981] AC 557. A more colourful account is provided by Lord Denning at [1980] 3 All ER 72, 76–78.

[45] Baade, HW, 'Foreign Oil Disaster Litigation Prospects in the United States and the "Mid-Atlantic Settlement Formula" ' (1989) 7 Journal of Energy and Natural Resources Law 125, 126.

[46] [1980] 3 All ER 72, 92, cf Lord Denning at 76–78 and 82–83. cf the House of Lords' decision two years earlier in *MacShannon v Rockware Glass Ltd* [1978] AC 795, discussed in Schuz, R, 'Controlling Forum Shopping: The Impact of *MacShannon v Rockware Glass Ltd*' (1986) 35 ICLQ 374.

[47] ibid 90.   [48] [1981] AC 557.

House of Lords to have the Texas proceedings restrained underlines the great significance which parties attach to the issue of the venue in which a transnational dispute is to be resolved.

Fleming has described the civil jury in American tort litigation as 'the **2.19** darling of plaintiffs and the scourge of defendants'.[49] Three particular facets of the civil jury system should be noted. First, although characterized as procedural, it is indubitable that the civil jury system has had a profound (and expansive) impact on substantive legal principles, particularly in the shift in the United States from fault-based to strict liability.[50] This is largely because the open-ended formulae of negligence law have permitted the infiltration of community values and prejudices through the jury system.[51] In addition, as Baade has observed, the 'aggressive plaintiffs' bar is constantly seeking to expand legal notions of tort liability, and the absence of counsel fee awards to prevailing defendants encourages the testing of new tort theories'.[52] This is the climate in which American juries consider their verdicts.

Secondly, in their assessment of damages, juries are inclined to stray from **2.20** the orthodoxy of compensation and rather relate quantum to the defendant's financial resources and degree of fault.[53] In doing so, it would appear that there is little scope for judicial control or supervision, especially where state as opposed to federal juries are concerned.[54] Fleming states that 'while the judge's instructions [as to jury's discretion in damages] are mired in vacuous generalities, the jury is presented with extravagant demands by the plaintiff's attorney. ... The proclivity of juries to empty deep pockets has been repeatedly noted. But judicial efforts to blindfold the jury have been largely thwarted.'[55]

Thirdly, it should be appreciated that the central importance of the jury is **2.21** not unrelated to several of the other procedural advantages which have been referred to above. Thus, one of the reasons commonly offered for American juries' inflated damages awards is that they make allowance for contingency fees, sometimes amounting to up to 40 per cent and which will be deducted from any award.[56] Moreover, it has also been said that juries compensate for the absence in American law of the common law practice of allowing a successful litigant to recover its costs from the losing side.[57] Damages awards may also therefore include an element of

---

[49] (n 42 above) 103. [50] ibid 115–116 and 120.
[51] ibid 118. [52] (n 45 above) 127.
[53] Fleming, JG (n 42 above) 123–125. [54] ibid 125–127. [55] ibid 135.
[56] ibid 125 and 226. See also *Smith Kline & French Laboratories Ltd v Bloch* [1983] 2 All ER 72, 74 per Lord Denning MR who noted this practice.
[57] Fleming, JG (n 42 above) 226.

surreptitious fee-shifting. The three considerations enumerated above are pertinent even in circumstances where foreign law is held to govern not only the claim but also the issue of quantum of damages.[58]

2.22 Supplementing the significance of the civil jury in United States proceedings is the fact that 'many US state and federal statutes provide for mandatory awards of multiple damages while state common law often permits jury awards of punitive damages based on vague, discretionary standards'.[59] *New Hampshire Insurance v Aerospace Finance*[60] was a case, for example, where the US proceedings in question sought recovery of punitive damages under Pennsylvania's Bad Faith Act.

The Scope and Importance of Discovery

2.23 In other cases, procedural advantages apart from or additional to generous damages awards will provide the incentive for forum shopping; the more striking the differences of procedure, the greater the occasion for this practice. One area which especially stands out is that of pre-trial discovery or disclosure and, again, the United States is a conspicuously attractive destination for plaintiffs. Civil law and common law systems proceed upon diametrically opposed views as to how best to ascertain the truth[61] and this is reflected in respective attitudes towards discovery. Within the common law tradition, there are also controversial differences. Thus, in allowing oral pre-trial discovery, the United States is more generous than other common law jurisdictions[62] but these, in turn, are more generous than civil law countries such as Switzerland,[63] Germany, and Japan.[64]

2.24 The advantage of broad discovery rules may be particularly significant in product liability and intellectual property suits where access to a defendant's internal documents may be vital in establishing its knowledge of a product's technical defects or appreciation of possible improvements or

---

[58] See Silva, EJ (n 39 above) 493. cf *Smith Kline & French Laboratories Ltd v Bloch* [1983] 2 All ER 72, 83.

[59] Born, G, *International Civil Litigation in United States Courts* (3rd edn, 1996) 5.

[60] [1998] 2 Lloyd's Rep 539, 541.

[61] Zweigert, K and Kötz, H, *An Introduction to Comparative Law* (2nd rev'd edn, 1992, trans Weir, A) 280–283.

[62] McLachlan, C, 'Dispatching the Opposition: A Legal Guide to Transnational Litigation' (August 1992) IFL Rev Special Supplement 43. Also see generally Levine, J, *Discovery: A Comparison Between English and American Civil Discovery Law* (1982) especially 8–11. The differences between UK and US pre-trial procedures are discussed in *South Carolina Insurance Co v Assurantie NV* [1987] AC 24, 35–37.

[63] *Trendtex Trading Corp v Crédit Suisse* [1980] 3 All ER 721, 736.

[64] Park, WD and Cromie, S, *International Commercial Litigation* (1990) 180 and 196–198.

available safety precautions not implemented.[65] In a civil law country such as Germany, by contrast, a plaintiff 'cannot expect the defendant to help him build his case by supplying damaging evidence from his own files'.[66] Indeed, in the product liability field, Germany has been described as a haven for defendants.[67] Significant differences in the procedural rules relating to discovery in France, on the one hand, and New South Wales, on the other hand, were prayed in aid by the plaintiff in *Renault v Zhang*,[68] a negligent manufacture/design case, as a reason for resisting Renault's application to have the New South Wales proceedings stayed.

Differences such as these, apart from encouraging outright forum shop- **2.25** ping, also promote parallel litigation whereby a party suing in one forum seeks to take advantage of another forum's wider discovery rules for the purposes of the original and substantive litigation. As one commentator has observed, 'evidence produced in parallel litigation will cross procedural defenses. No discovery serves local purposes only.'[69] This observation no doubt reflects the reality of the matter, the principle in *Harman v Home Office*[70]—insisting on an implied undertaking only to use discovered documents in the proceedings in which they were discovered—notwithstanding.

As has been seen in the case of the jury trial and the related availability of **2.26** higher damages, the United States' generous discovery laws take on an added appeal when combined with other aspects of that country's procedure. Referring to United States pre-trial discovery as 'long drawn out' and 'very expensive', Dillon LJ has observed that:

any defendant, even if ultimately dismissed from the suit or successful when the suit comes on for trial, has in practice virtually no chance of recovering its costs. Conversely, the plaintiff, if it can find a United States lawyer prepared to undertake the suit on a contingency fee basis, has no worry over costs and, even if insolvent, will not have to give security for costs.[71]

---

[65] Boyce, D (n 38 above) 200; Freedman, W, *Foreign Plaintiffs in Products Liability Actions* (1988) 28; Fawcett, J and Torremans, P, *Intellectual Property and Private International Law* (1998) 198–199.

[66] Park, WD and Cromie, S (n 64 above) 180. This observation must be qualified in part, for a defendant will be ordered to produce specific documents if they are known to be in its possession: O'Malley, S and Layton, A, *European Civil Practice* (1989) 1305. See also Fawcett, J and Torremans, P (n 65 above) 199.

[67] Schlosser, P, 'Product Liability' in Nygh, P and McLachlan, C, *Transnational Tort Litigation* 76.

[68] (2002) 187 ALR 1, 42.

[69] Baade, HW, 'An Overview of Transnational Parallel Litigation: Recommended Strategies' (1981) 1 The Review of Litigation 191, 206. See also the discussion of *South Carolina Insurance Co v Assurantie NV* [1987] AC 24 in paras 4.130 ff below.

[70] [1983] 1 AC 280.

[71] *Midland Bank plc v Laker Airways Ltd* [1986] 1 QB 689, 703–704.

2.27 The attractions of this procedure to a plaintiff, not least its potential to force an early settlement, cannot be gainsaid. These have, if anything, been enhanced by a recent decision of the United States Court of Appeals for the Second Circuit which holds that, not only may a party to *foreign* litigation seek discovery in the United States where the other party is subject to that country's personal jurisdiction,[72] but that there is no need for the discovery first to be sought in the substantive foreign proceedings.[73] On the other hand, the width and generosity of United States discovery laws will not always be unattractive to a defendant for a 'litigant may contrive to dump truckloads of unassorted files on the party demanding discovery, hoping, often not in vain, that the searcher will be so exhausted that the damaging items will be overlooked or never reached'.[74]

2. BEYOND AMERICA: FURTHER PROCEDURAL INDUCEMENTS

2.28 It should not of course be thought that the United States is the only destination of the dedicated forum shopper—various aspects of its procedure are replicated elsewhere[75]—nor should it be thought that plaintiffs have an unlimited ability to shop in that country's many forums. Rules of jurisdiction, though often widely drawn, do impose some limits as to choice of forum in any given case and, moreover, are subject to constitutional scrutiny.[76] Given a choice of forum, however, a plaintiff is likely to choose that in which its chances of success are most propitious. This section considers the ways in which forums other than those to be found in the United States may prove attractive to plaintiffs.

2.29 To the extent that the jurisdictional scheme encapsulated in the Brussels Convention on Jurisdiction and Judgments and now European Council Regulation 44/2001 permits forum shopping,[77] different levels of damages available in the different member and contracting states will be of relevance to a plaintiff's determination of where to sue.[78] This is

---

[72] As to which, see paras 4.27 ff below.

[73] *United Technologies International, Inc v Malev Hungarian Airlines* 946 F 2d 97 (2nd Cir, 1992), discussed by Mundiya, T, 'U.S. Court Invites Foreign Litigants To Use U.S. Discovery Laws' (1993) 42 ICLQ 356.

[74] Frankel, ME, *Partisan Justice* (1978) 18.

[75] Japan, for example, permits the use of contingency fees and follows the non-recovery of legal costs rule: Schlesinger, R, Baade, H, Damaska, M, Herzog, P, *Comparative Law: Cases-Text-Materials* (5th edn, 1988) 353 n 29 and 366 n 52c; and France has extremely liberal joinder rules: see ibid 385 n 72q. The United Kingdom, Canada, New Zealand, and Australia all permit lawyers to appear for plaintiffs on a 'no-win no-pay' basis.

[76] See paras 4.27 ff below.   [77] See paras 3.23 ff below.

[78] On this issue, see McIntosh, D and Holmes, M, *Personal Injury Awards in E.C. Countries* (1991) and Holding, FJ and Kaye, P, *Damages for Personal Injuries: A European Perspective* (1993).

perhaps especially the case in the field of product liability where, despite harmonization of substantive principles, 'the awards which may be made in different countries in respect of identical injuries can vary considerably, even dramatically'.[79] Further, several states have opted to limit a producer's total liability for damage pursuant to Article 16 of the Product Liability Directive.[80] Apart from matters affecting the level of damages which may be recovered, other procedural features of different countries' judicial systems, in particular the extent to which discovery of documents is permitted, may also have a very real impact upon a plaintiff's choice of forum in a product liability case.[81] Procedural differences as between the member states of the European Union are also likely to be of increasing importance under the Community Patent Convention.[82]

Other procedural considerations not already mentioned may also attract **2.30** plaintiffs in certain types of case. In *The Atlantic Star*,[83] for example, the Dutch plaintiff commenced proceedings in England, wishing to take advantage of the common law's oral tradition and thereby undermine the impact of a report of the Antwerp Court Surveyor which it judged would not support its claim but which would have been heavily relied on in Belgian proceedings, certainly more so than in any English proceedings.[84] The plaintiff was also evidently attracted to England in this case on account of the Court of Admiralty's rule that colliding with another ship at anchor constitutes primary evidence of negligence.[85]

In Israel, the traditional procedural facility of preventing a defendant **2.31** from leaving the country may provide a powerful incentive for forum shopping.[86] Less drastically, the ability to obtain full security for a claim provides another example of a procedural consideration which will render a forum attractive to a plaintiff[87] as will the prospect of a relatively more expeditious trial[88] and the existence of a more generous limitation period, at least in jurisdictions where matters of limitation are construed

---

[79] Hodges, CJS, *Product Liability: European Laws and Practice* (1993) 164.

[80] ibid 171.

[81] ibid 160–188 and paras 2.23 ff above.

[82] See Young, D and Birss, C, 'Forum Shopping under the Community Patent Convention' [1992] EIPR 361, especially 364.

[83] [1974] AC 436.

[84] This emerges most clearly from Brandon J's decision at first instance: [1972] 1 Lloyd's Rep 534, 537. See also *Maharanee of Baroda v Wildenstein* [1972] 2 QB 283, 293.

[85] *The Merchant Prince* [1892] P 179. See *The Atlantic Star* [1973] 1 QB 364, 384 per Lord Denning MR. The forum's rules of evidence are treated as matters of procedure in the conflict of laws: North, PM and Fawcett, JJ, *Cheshire and North's Private International Law* (13th edn, 1999) 74–78.

[86] Fawcett, J (ed), *Declining Jurisdiction in Private International Law* (1995) 269–270.

[87] *The Atlantic Star* [1974] AC 436, 470; *The Wladyslaw Lokietek* [1978] 2 Lloyd's Rep 520, 540; *The El Amria and El Minia* [1981] 2 Lloyd's Rep 539, 542.

[88] *The Jalakrishna* [1983] 2 Lloyd's Rep 628, 631.

as procedural and not substantive.[89] Considerations pertaining to the financing of legal services may also, in a given case, greatly influence the choice of forum.[90] Related to this, the existence and extent of any system of legal aid in a particular forum may provide an inducement to forum shopping and, in extreme cases, a reason in itself justifying forum selection.[91]

2.32 A reason to forum shop in the courts of European Union or EFTA countries is that, by reason of Council Regulation 44/2001 and the Brussels and Lugano Conventions on Jurisdiction and Judgments, a judgment from a court in any one of the signatory states may almost always be enforced in any other.[92] That is to say that recognition and enforcement will not be subject to the traditional common law approach that the court giving judgment may have its judgment examined *ex post* to see that it did have jurisdiction in the international sense. These rules, moreover, extend to judgments based on the assertion of exorbitant jurisdiction over non-European Union or EFTA domiciliaries.[93] A vivid illustration of this advantage is provided by the case of *Minories Finance v Afribank Nigeria*,[94] where one of the reasons why England as opposed to Nigeria was treated as the more convenient forum was the ready enforceability of any English judgment against assets of the defendant in Ireland, a party to the Lugano Convention. That facility of enforcement was to be contrasted with perceived practical difficulties in enforcing any Nigerian judgment, in particular, having currency under various bills of exchange allocated by the Nigerian Central Bank. To similar effect is the decision of the Court of Appeal in *International Credit and Investment Company (Overseas) Ltd v Badham*.[95]

[89] Compare the situation that formerly existed at common law in Australia in federal cases (*McKain v RW Miller & Co (SA) Pty Ltd* (1991) 174 CLR 1 but now see *John Pfeiffer Pty Ltd v Rogerson* (2000) 203 CLR 503) and which may continue to obtain in transnational cases (see *Renault v Zhang* (2002) 187 ALR 1) with that in the United Kingdom where the Foreign Limitation Periods Act 1984 provides that limitation periods should be treated as substantive and not procedural and therefore be governed by the applicable foreign law.

[90] See Chapter 11 of Miller, DLC and Beaumont, PR, *The Option of Litigating in Europe* (1993), entitled 'Financing Legal Services: A Comparative Perspective', 149–173.

[91] *Lubbe v Cape plc* [2000] 1 WLR 1545.

[92] Article 38 of European Council Regulation 44/2001 and Article 31 of the Brussels and Lugano Conventions.

[93] Article 4. See paras 3.45 ff below.

[94] [1995] 1 Lloyd's Rep 134.

[95] [1998] BCC 134.

III. LACK OF UNIFORMITY IN DOMESTIC LAW

Apart from procedural advantages, other considerations, perhaps more **2.33** obvious, also contribute to the possibility of variance of outcome or result as between jurisdictions and thereby also provide important incentives for forum shopping. Most basically, the fact that attempts to unify the internal laws of different countries have met with only limited success, the endeavours of bodies such as UNIDROIT and UNCITRAL notwithstanding, ensures the fundamental and substantive basis for forum shopping.[96]

Even in areas where there has been some success in securing unification, **2.34** such as the law relating to product liability and intellectual property within the European Union,[97] derogation from certain aspects of any general agreement can seriously undermine the efficacy of any unification as far as preventing forum shopping is concerned. Thus, in relation to the Product Liability Directive, the fact that some states opted not to include the 'development risks defence' provided for in Article 7(e) of the Directive in their national legislation[98] may act as an inducement to plaintiffs to sue in a particular forum in a given case, so far as this is permitted by the relevant jurisdictional rules.[99] In the realm of patent law, under the European Patent Convention, the fact that there is reserved to Contracting States the basis upon which to decide what constitutes an infringement highlights the scope for differences in outcome, especially in borderline cases.[100]

Jurisdictional questions relating to product liability and intellectual prop- **2.35** erty infringements within Europe are governed by European Council Regulation 44/2001 and in certain residual cases[101] the Brussels, Lugano, and San Sebastian Conventions. The jurisdictional scheme of these instruments is considered at greater length at paragraphs 3.13 ff below but it should be noted here that, while they are as a general proposition concerned to limit cases of concurrent jurisdiction and the scope for forum shopping, there are likely to be several potential forums in both product liability and intellectual property cases.

---

[96] For those areas in which attempts at unification have met with some success, see North, PM and Fawcett, JJ (n 85 above) 10.

[97] Pursuant to Directive 85/374.

[98] For those countries not including such a defence, see Hodges, CJS (n 79 above) 171.

[99] See Pearl, S (n 11 above) 393–394 and Pannone, R (n 14 above) 235.

[100] Fawcett, J and Torremans, P (n 65 above) 199–200; see also 597.

[101] See generally Briggs, A and Rees, P, *Civil Jurisdiction and Judgments* (3rd edn, 2002).

2.36 In product liability cases, this is because of the broad interpretation given to the phrase 'place where the harmful event occurred' in Article 5(3) of the instruments,[102] the provisions of the instruments relating to consumer contracts[103] allowing a plaintiff to sue, exceptionally, in the courts of its own domicile, and by virtue of the fact that Article 6(1) permits a defendant to be sued in the place of domicile of any other defendant. It will be unusual for a manufacturer to be the sole defendant in a product liability case and a supplier or importer will also be jointly and severally liable under the Directive.[104] It is therefore clear that a plaintiff in a product liability case is likely to have a wide choice of forums, thereby being able to exploit differences in each jurisdiction's substantive (and procedural)[105] laws. In intellectual property cases, the fact that there will frequently be a number of defendants in cases of infringement gives rise to an immediate choice of forum as does the fact that Articles 2 and 5(3) will invariably be available to found jurisdiction.[106]

IV. DIVERGENCE IN CHOICE OF LAW RULES AND PRACTICE

2.37 It might be supposed that differences in substantive laws as between jurisdictions can be overcome by the operation of choice of law rules. While this is certainly their purpose, as shall be seen, their ability to ameliorate the problems of differing internal laws (and forum shopping pursuant to such differences) is limited. This is both by reason of a lack of uniformity at this level and also as a result of derogation by courts from the appropriate choice of law rule in certain circumstances. The inability of choice of law rules to secure uniformity of result irrespective of venue can be seen in at least seven ways, all of which may provide an inducement to a plaintiff to initiate litigation in a particular forum.

2.38 First, a choice of law rule in a particular area may be in favour of the *lex fori*, such as the common law rule for divorce and maintenance. In *de Dampierre v de Dampierre*,[107] for example, this 'choice of law' rule had the consequence that the venue for divorce proceedings would significantly affect the amount of maintenance to which the wife was entitled, hence

---

[102] Case 21/76, *Bier BV v Mines de Potasse D'Alsace SA* [1976] ECR 1735 but cf Case C–220/88, *Dumez France v Hessische Landesbank* [1990] ECR I–49.

[103] Article 16 of Council Regulation 44/2001 and Article 14 of the Conventions.

[104] See generally Geddes, A, 'Forum Shopping in the EEC' (1988) 138 NLJ 542.

[105] See nn 65 and 79 above.

[106] Fawcett, J and Torremans, P (n 65 above) 196–197 and 330–331.

[107] [1988] AC 92.

the wife's eagerness to proceed in England rather than France.[108] In at least some areas where equitable relief is sought, there is a respectable view (although the matter awaits full academic consideration)[109] that the law of the forum should provide the governing law.[110] If this view be correct, and it is proper to regard, for example, claims for a constructive trust as institutional rather than remedial, this identifies another broad area where forum shopping may be at a premium.

A choice of law rule which entails at least a partial application of the *lex* **2.39** *fori*, such as the common law choice of law rule for tort enunciated by Willes J in *Phillips v Eyre*,[111] may also encourage forum shopping, especially where it is interpreted as giving a predominant role to the *lex fori*, as in *Machado v Fontes*.[112] In *Boys v Chaplin*,[113] Lord Pearson adverted to the possibilities for forum shopping encouraged by such a choice of law rule.[114] On the other hand, it might be argued that the choice of law rule in *Phillips v Eyre*, far from encouraging forum shopping, in fact operated to *disadvantage* a plaintiff by requiring actionability to be established in two jurisdictions. This objection is not valid, however, on those interpretations of that rule that afford a predominant role to the *lex fori* and only require that the act was not justifiable by the law of the place where it was done. Finally, where a maritime accident occurs on the high seas, other than one wholly on or within the vessel, there is no *lex loci delicti*, and common law courts will apply the *lex fori*.[115]

Secondly, different jurisdictions apply different choice of law rules[116] and **2.40** here also, notwithstanding the efforts in this case of the Hague Conference on Private International Law, only limited success has been

---

[108] ibid 100. See also *Sealey (orse Callan) v Callan* [1953] P 135, 144; *Gadd v Gadd* [1984] 1 WLR 1435; *Louvet v Louvet* [1990] 1 HKLR 670, 677; *In the marriage of Gilmore* (1993) 16 Fam LR 285.

[109] Barnard, L, 'Choice of Law in Equitable Wrongs: A Comparative Analysis' [1992] CLJ 474.

[110] *Paramasivam v Flynn* (1998) 90 FCR 489.

[111] (1870) LR 6 QB 1. This rule has some continuing vitality in the United Kingdom (see Collins, LA (ed), *Dicey and Morris on the Conflict of Laws* (13th edn, 2000) Chapter 35) notwithstanding the passage of the Private International Law (Miscellaneous Provisions) Act 1995 (UK) and in those common law jurisdictions where it has not been overruled, cf Australia: *Renault v Zhang* (2002) 187 ALR 1.

[112] [1897] 2 QB 231.

[113] [1971] AC 356.

[114] ibid 406. cf *Johnson v Coventry Churchill International Ltd* [1992] 3 All ER 14, 25–26.

[115] *Chartered Mercantile Bank of India v Netherlands India Steam Navigation Co Ltd* (1883) 10 QBD 521, 537 and see Collins, LA (ed), (n 111 above) 1539.

[116] *The Kribi* [2001] 1 Lloyd's Rep 76, 91 provides a recent example where, had the litigation been permitted to proceed in Belgium, Belgian substantive law would have applied whereas the express contractual choice of English law would apply in England.

achieved in securing agreement to uniform choice of law rules.[117] A notable exception in the case of the European Union is the Rome Convention on the Law Applicable to Contractual Obligations and it is interesting to note that one of the motivations behind the work on the Convention was to forestall forum shopping.[118] But even here, the absence of any ultimate court to interpret the Convention has generated different views as to the operation and application of the provisions among signatory states.[119]

2.41 Lack of uniformity in choice of law rules is seen most prominently (but by no means solely) in cases where personal law either provides or forms part of a choice of law rule. The schism between the common law's adoption of domicile and the civil law's support for nationality is responsible for laying 'to rest the hope that multilateralism could achieve its goal of decisional harmony'.[120] The most important ramification of different choice of law rules is, of course, that a plaintiff's choice of forum can be critical, as *Power Curber International Ltd v National Bank of Kuwait SAK*[121] illustrates. In this case, the bank's liability to pay on a letter of credit depended upon its proper law. If it was Kuwaiti, then the bank may have had an arguable defence. If, as it was held to be, it was the law of North Carolina, then no such defence existed. Kuwaiti law would have governed, however, had the case been heard in that forum.

2.42 In *IP Metal Ltd v Ruote OZ SpA*,[122] venue was also all-important in terms of the substantive outcome. If proceedings took place in Italy, it was likely that Italian law would be held to govern the contract, affording Ruote a possible defence. On the other hand, if the actions were heard in England, where the relevant choice of law rule pointed to English law, Ruote would have no defence to IP Metal's claims.[123] Even where different forums have the same choice of law rules, different approaches to characterization may yield different substantive results.[124]

2.43 Thirdly, what is prima facie the same choice of law rule may be uncertain in its operation or susceptible of different interpretations in different jurisdictions. The common law choice of law rule for contract in the absence

---

[117] See generally Lipstein, K, 'One Hundred Years of Hague Conferences on Private International Law' (1993) 42 ICLQ 553.
[118] Collins, LA (n 111 above) 1199.
[119] *Raiffeisen Zentralbank Österreich AG v Five Star Trading LLC* [2001] 1 QB 825, 838–849.
[120] Juenger, FK (n 8 above) 42.
[121] [1981] 1 WLR 1233.
[122] [1993] 2 Lloyd's Rep 60.
[123] ibid 62. See also *Irish Shipping Ltd v Commercial Union* [1991] 2 QB 206, 229 where, as a result of the respective choice of law regimes, English law would have been applied in England, and Belgian law in Belgium, with different substantive consequences.
[124] Juenger, FK (n 8 above) 51 and 74.

of an express choice provides one such example, it not being clear whether reference should be made to the *system of law* or the *country* with which the transaction has the closest connection.[125] In *DR Insurance v Central National Insurance*,[126] it was recognized that a New York court would probably come to a different view from an English court as to the proper law of the insurance contracts there under consideration.

Referring to a *lex loci delicti* choice of law rule for tort and the frequent **2.44** difficulties in identifying the locus of a tort, Juenger has observed that '[a]pplied in practice, a rule that at first blush looks simple and even-handed soon reveals its complexities and capriciousness'.[127] 'Proper law' choice of law rules, as especially favoured in the US Second Restatement, lend themselves to diverse applications on account of the raft of factors and considerations which may be taken into account.[128] In *Piper Aircraft Co v Reyno*,[129] Justice Marshall stated that:

the tort plaintiff may choose, at least potentially, from among 50 jurisdictions if he decides to file suit in the United States. Each of these jurisdictions applies its own set of *malleable* choice of law rules.[130]

In this context, it has been observed that modern American choice of law theories present a plaintiff with a 'cornucopia of opportunities for forum-shopping'.[131]

Fourthly, the universal 'homing trend' in private international law **2.45** conduces towards forum shopping[132] for where a court has a choice of applying its own or a foreign law, the former will generally be applied.[133] As one American scholar has put it: 'Even if the forum's choice-of-law rules direct that foreign law will apply, the choice of an American forum can still have a significant effect because the foreign law is applied with local sensibilities.'[134] The same may be said for a forum's substantive law

---

[125] *James Miller & Partners v Whitworth Street Estates Ltd* [1970] AC 583 illustrates that this distinction is capable of yielding different answers.

[126] [1996] 1 Lloyd's Rep 74, 82.

[127] Juenger, FK (n 8 above) 51.

[128] Boyce, D (n 38 above) provides a good illustration at 222 n 178.

[129] 454 US 235 (1981).

[130] ibid 252 n 18 (emphasis added). See also Juenger, FK (n 8 above) 129–130.

[131] Brown, GD, 'The Ideologies of Forum Shopping—Why Doesn't a Conservative Court Protect Defendants?' (1993) 71 North Carolina Law Review 649, 674.

[132] Juenger, FK (n 8 above) 3–4.

[133] Silberman, LJ, 'Developments in Jurisdiction and Forum Non Conveniens in International Litigation: Thoughts on Reform and a Proposal for a Uniform Standard' (1993) 28 Texas International Law Journal 501, 503 n 7.

[134] Albright, AW, 'In Personam Jurisdiction: A Confused and Inappropriate Substitute for Forum Non Conveniens' (1992) 71 Texas Law Review 351, 352 n 14. See also Maier, HG and McCoy, TR, 'A Unifying Theory for Judicial Jurisdiction and Choice of Law' (1991) 39 American Journal of Comparative Law 249, 253–255.

where it represents the domestic implementation of an international treaty or convention notwithstanding the importance of an 'internationalist' interpretation of international instruments, such as the Warsaw Convention on Carriage by Air 1929, in order to avoid an unequal application and the consequent encouragement of forum shopping.[135]

2.46 Fifthly, proof of the applicable foreign law may introduce factual uncertainty which would or may not have been encountered had the litigation proceeded in the forum supplying the applicable law. It has been observed that 'there are several cases in which the judge has had to pick his way through subtly conflicting bodies of evidence of foreign law, with the result that one may applaud the effort yet still lack confidence in the outcome'.[136] This circumstance may appeal to a plaintiff who wishes either to obtain a more favourable interpretation of the *lex causae* or to avoid its application altogether and have the forum law applied in default.[137]

2.47 An example of the profound complexity that may be involved in the proof of foreign law is supplied by the decision of Moore-Bick J in *Glencore International Ltd v Metro Training International*,[138] involving competing claims to the title of substantial quantities of oil commingled in one of the United Arab Emirates. Foreign law 'proved' in common law courts as a question of fact, especially foreign law not expressed in the English language and necessarily lifted out of the procedural parameters in which it is invariably applied, may suffer in the literal and metaphorical translation to the benefit of one side. Important nuances may be lost. In this regard, the High Court of Australia in *Renault v Zhang*[139] arguably showed no sensitivity to what a comparativist might consider a basic reality in assessing the significance of the fact that the cause of action in that case was governed by French law.

2.48 Sixthly, a mandatory law of a particular forum may override any foreign applicable law, whether that law was identified by uniform choice of law principles or not.[140] This may or may not make a particular forum attractive to a plaintiff. In *Holmes v Bangladesh Biman*,[141] the issue was whether

---

[135] *SS Pharmaceuticals v Qantas Airways* [1991] 1 Lloyd's Rep 288, 294. See also *James Buchanan & Co Ltd v Babco Forwarding and Shipping (UK) Ltd* [1978] AC 141, 152; [1977] QB 208, 221.

[136] Briggs, A, *The Conflict of Laws* (2002) 6.

[137] See generally Fentiman, RG, 'Foreign Law in English Courts' (1992) 108 LQR 142; Fentiman, RG, *Foreign Law in English Courts* (1999).

[138] [2001] 1 Lloyd's Rep 284.   [139] (2002) 187 ALR 1, 18–21.

[140] For a detailed discussion of the identification and operation of mandatory laws and, in particular, the way in which they may override contractual choice of law, see Nygh, P, *Autonomy in International Contracts* (1999) 199–234.

[141] [1989] AC 1112.

the plaintiff's claim was governed by schedule 1 to the Carriage by Air Acts (Application of Provisions) Order 1967 (UK) as a mandatory law of the forum or by Bangladeshi law as the proper law of the contract.[142] If, as was held at first instance and in the Court of Appeal, the English provisions applied, the plaintiff's claim could only be capped at £83,763 whereas if, as had been contended and was ultimately accepted by the House of Lords, the English provisions were inapplicable on the facts of the case, the maximum the plaintiff could have recovered was £913, the limit set under Bangladeshi law. What is significant for present purposes is that the plaintiff's choice of forum created, for her, the possibility of a far more attractive result. Although ultimately unsuccessful in this case, in another case a party less inclined to fight all the way up to the House of Lords may well have been prepared to reach a settlement. Importantly, this would have been negotiated in the context of the higher amount apparently recoverable in England than in Bangladesh. *Holmes v Bangladesh Biman* was thus a case where the availability of what was clearly a plausible argument in favour of the mandatory operation of the law of the forum provided a significant inducement to the plaintiff to commence suit in that jurisdiction.[143] In *XL Insurance Ltd v Owens Corning*,[144] an anti-suit injunction was granted restraining Owens Corning from suing in the United States where, the evidence disclosed, the Federal Arbitration Act would override the proper law of the contract. It was said to be manifestly unjust to XL to expose it to this situation.

An example of a case where it was very much in the plaintiff's interests to **2.49** avoid the mandatory operation of a particular forum's laws is provided by *Coast Lines Ltd v Hudig & Veder Chartering NV*.[145] A different result would have obtained had proceedings been commenced in The Netherlands rather than England because a mandatory provision of the Dutch Commercial Code would have overridden the English choice of law.

---

[142] [1988] 2 Lloyd's Rep 120, 122. The corresponding (although in one crucial respect, different) Bangladeshi provisions had also been expressly incorporated in the contract between the passenger (the plaintiff's deceased husband) and the airline.

[143] It is perhaps surprising that a stay was not sought in this case on the basis that Bangladesh was the natural forum. Not only did its law govern the contract of carriage but the plaintiff's husband had died on an internal flight in Bangladesh and had purchased his ticket there. cf *The Adhiguna Meranti* [1988] 1 Lloyd's Rep 384 where, although Indonesia was the natural forum, the Hong Kong Court of Appeal refused to stay proceedings on account of the fact that, in Indonesia, the defendant shipowners could establish a derisory liability fund.

[144] [2000] 2 Lloyd's Rep 500.

[145] [1972] 2 QB 34.

2.50 Another example, and interesting case study, is supplied by the transnational litigation that occurred between Akai Pty Ltd, an Australian company, and the People's Insurance Company of Singapore.[146] The People's Insurance Company was party to a policy of credit insurance with Akai, insuring Akai against the failure of persons to whom it supplied goods on credit to make payment for goods. Akai made a claim on the policy when a company to which it distributed electrical goods went into liquidation. The policy of insurance was governed by English law and contained a clause referring any dispute arising from the policy to the English courts. Notwithstanding these provisions, Akai commenced litigation in the Supreme Court of New South Wales, seeking a declaration that the People's Insurance Company was liable to indemnify it under the policy. Apart from wishing to sue in its home forum, which was probably also the natural forum in the context of the issues in dispute, what made New South Wales a particularly attractive forum for Akai was the existence of the Insurance Contracts Act 1984, a Commonwealth Act, section 54 of which excused certain breaches of conditions contained in the policy relating, for example, to the time for making a claim, and section 52 of which proscribed any 'contracting out' of the Act.

2.51 The People's Insurance Company sought a stay of the proceedings in favour of litigation in England on the basis that that is what the parties had agreed. The High Court of Australia, reversing a decision granting that relief,[147] held by majority that the Insurance Contracts Act was a mandatory law of the forum, the contracting out from which was not permissible. Accordingly, notwithstanding the existence of the jurisdiction and choice of law clause and the majority's acknowledgement that, ordinarily, parties should be held to their bargains, the mandatory operation of the Insurance Contracts Act and an express statutory proscription on contracting out of the benefits of that Act meant that the choice of law and jurisdiction clause would not be given effect and no stay would be granted.[148]

2.52 A particular forum may be attractive to a plaintiff because of the absence of a mandatory law commonly found in other jurisdictions. In both *The*

---

[146] *Akai Pty Ltd v People's Insurance Company* (1996) 185 CLR 571.

[147] (1995) 8 ANZ Ins Cas 61–254.

[148] This case had an intriguing twist for, shortly after the decision of the High Court of Australia dissolving the stay, the People's Insurance Company secured anti-suit injunctions in both Singapore and England restraining Akai from continuing its claim in the Supreme Court of New South Wales: *Akai Pty Ltd v People's Insurance Co Ltd* [1998] 1 Lloyd's Rep 90. This case, and what it has to say about comity, in particular, are considered further in Chapter 4.

Giacinto Motta[149] and *In re Oil Spill by the Amoco Cadiz off the Coast of France*,[150] the United States proved attractive to the plaintiffs because that country was *not* a signatory to either the Brussels Collision Liability Convention or the International Convention on Civil Liability for Oil Pollution Damage respectively. In *United States v Reliable Transfer Co Inc*,[151] referring to the former Convention, Justice Potter Stewart stated that 'the United States is now virtually alone among the world's major maritime nations in not adhering to the Convention with its rule of proportional fault—a fact that encourages transoceanic forum shopping'.[152] In a similar context, where shipowners seek to establish a limitation fund, their choice of forum may be dictated according to whether or not a particular jurisdiction is a party to the Convention on Limitation of Liability for Maritime Claims of 1976 or only the International Convention relating to the Limitation of Liability of Owners of Sea-going Ships of 1957 which mandates a substantially lower limit of liability.[153]

The operation and potential significance of mandatory laws may vary **2.53** depending upon the subject matter of the rights in question. Thus, for example, by reason of their territorial foundations and the clear capacity to impact upon competition law considerations, it has been observed that intellectual property rights are particularly susceptible to the operation of a forum's mandatory law.[154] The situation is rendered more complicated by the inherently difficult task of characterizing a particular forum statute as having a sufficient quality so that it overrides the foreign law otherwise selected by the forum's statutory or common law choice of law rules.

One form of forum law likely to be held to be mandatory in operation are **2.54** the provisions of a particular country's Constitution and/or Bill of Rights. In *Dow Jones v Gutnick*, it may fairly be surmised that one of the strongly motivating factors underpinning Dow Jones's application to

---

[149] [1977] 2 Lloyd's Rep 221, 224.

[150] 1984 AMC 2123 (ND Ill, 1984).

[151] 421 US 397 (1975); [1975] 2 Lloyd's Rep 286 sub nom *The Mary A Whalen*.

[152] ibid 403–404 (289 of Lloyd's). See also Nixon, EB, 'Limitation of Shipowners' Liability under U.S. Law—Does Any Other Law Apply?' in Sharpe, DJ and Spicer, WW, *New Directions in Maritime Law 1984* (1985) 117–118.

[153] See *The Vishva Abha* [1990] 2 Lloyd's Rep 313; *The Falstria* [1988] 1 Lloyd's Rep 495; *The Maciej Rataj* [1992] 2 Lloyd's Rep 552, 555; *The Hamburg Star* [1994] 1 Lloyd's Rep 399, 409; *Caltex Singapore Pte Ltd v BP Shipping Ltd* [1996] 1 Lloyd's Rep 286; *The Kapitan Shvetsov* [1998] 1 Lloyd's Rep 199. See also in this context the decision of the Hoge Raad in *The Stylt*, noted and criticized by Berlingieri, F, in [1993] LMCLQ 433, holding that limitation of liability should be governed by the same law as that governing *the* (which is problematic because there may be many) substantive claim. Accordingly, if the state whose law governs the claim in respect of which limitation is invoked is not party to one of the two Limitation Conventions, then the defendant will not be able to claim limitation under the law of the forum party to one of these Conventions.

[154] Fawcett, J and Torremans, P (n 65 above) 577–587.

have defamation proceedings commenced in the Supreme Court of Victoria[155] stayed in favour of litigation in the United States was the public figure defence derived from the First Amendment.[156] In a related context, the First Amendment has been successfully invoked to resist the enforcement of an English defamation verdict against a defendant's assets in the United States.[157]

2.55 Finally, and related to the previous consideration, aspects of a forum's public policy may also attract plaintiffs. It was the possible application of Spanish public policy that lay behind the defendant's (unsuccessful) attempt to stay English proceedings in favour of Spain in *The Magnum*.[158] The *Bisso*[159] doctrine in the United States, according to which no effect is given to exclusion of liability clauses in contracts as a matter of that forum's public policy, was the strategic consideration which led to the institution of proceedings in Florida in breach of an exclusive jurisdiction clause for England in the celebrated case of *Bremen v Zapata Offshore Co* ('*The Chaparral*').[160] In this case, Douglas J stated that 'Judges in this country have traditionally been hostile to attempts to circumvent the public policy against exculpatory agreements. For example, clauses specifying that the law of a foreign place (which favours such releases) should control have regularly been ignored.'[161]

2.56 A third example is provided by the case of *Du Pont de Nemours & Co v Agnew*,[162] where insurers sought to take advantage of Illinois public policy which apparently precluded indemnification of an assured against an award of punitive damages based on personal liability.[163] A still further example is provided by a trilogy of cases relating to the 1976 Limitation Convention which has been characterized as representing not just a manifestation of English public policy but also as 'an internationally sanctioned and objective view of where substantive justice is now seen as lying'.[164] That view, however, was later repudiated by the Court of Appeal.[165]

---

[155] *Gutnick v Dow Jones* [2001] VSC 305. This case was appealed to the High Court of Australia, with argument being heard in May 2002. See also 'Before the High Court: The Message, Not the Medium' (2002) 24 Sydney Law Review 263.

[156] *New York Times v Sullivan* 376 US 254 (1964).

[157] *Bachchan v India Abroad Publications Inc* 585 NYS 2d 661 (1992).

[158] [1989] 1 Lloyd's Rep 47, 51.

[159] *Bisso v Inland Waterways Corp* 349 US 85 (1955).

[160] 407 US 1 (1972); [1972] 2 Lloyd's Rep 315.

[161] ibid 24 (324 of Lloyd's).

[162] [1987] 2 Lloyd's Rep 585.   [163] ibid 587.

[164] *The Caspian Basin Specialised Emergency Salvage Operation v Vouygues* [1997] 2 Lloyd's Rep 507, 530; *Caltex Singapore Pte Ltd v BP Shipping Ltd* [1996] 1 Lloyd's Rep 286; *The Herceg Novi* [1998] 1 Lloyd's Rep 167.

[165] *The Herceg Novi* [1998] 2 Lloyd's Rep 454, 460.

Public policy is of course an infamously 'unruly horse' and the nature and **2.57**
scope of its application in private international law is difficult to describe
and even more difficult to predict. Juenger has articulated this circumstance well: 'When conceptual constraints collide with the natural judicial
reluctance to apply inferior foreign law, doctrinal purity and common
sense vie for the upper hand. But it requires soothsayers, rather than
jurists, to foretell which of the two will prevail in a particular situation.'[166]
What is clear is that the potential application of a forum's public policy to
the dispute in question may provide an important incentive for a party to
seek to institute litigation in that forum.

V. CONCLUSION

From the conspectus in the preceding section of the application (or non- **2.58**
application) of choice of law rules in private international law, it is clear
that the venue chosen for a piece of litigation may be of critical importance for the outcome of a particular case for it may directly affect the
substantive law to be applied. It was earlier seen that a forum's procedural rules may also provide a powerful incentive for forum shopping. In
some cases a plaintiff will consciously seek out a forum with a view to
taking advantage of its procedural advantages or in the knowledge that
that forum will or will not apply a particular substantive law. In other
cases, the very uncertainty of what substantive law is to be applied will
be attractive to a plaintiff and victory in a successful jurisdictional battle
may convert an unpromising case into an eminently winnable one[167] or at
least one wherein the certainty of an opponent's victory (or indeed the
speed in which it may be able to be achieved) is considerably diminished,
paving the way for a settlement where one was either not feasible prior to
the jurisdictional battle or on far better terms for the jurisdictional
victor.[168]

As a generalization, it is probably the case that forum shopping with a **2.59**
view to securing an advantage in terms of the *substantive* law to be
applied tends to be a characteristic of transnational commercial
disputes[169] while forum shopping designed to secure any or all of the

---

[166] (n 8 above) 81.

[167] See *Britannia Steamship Insurance Association v Ausonia Assicurazioni SpA* [1984] 2
Lloyd's Rep 98 and *Banco Atlantico SA v The British Bank of the Middle East* [1990] 2 Lloyd's
Rep 504, discussed further at paras 4.57 ff below.

[168] Fentiman, RG (n 137 above) 153: 'many litigants seek to exploit the possibility of delay
and uncertainty, if only to force the other party's capitulation or to engineer a settlement'.

[169] In such cases, disputes over venue will often not arise as they will have been anticipated by the parties in contractual negotiations and a forum will have been agreed upon.

procedural advantages detailed earlier in this chapter is primarily the province of product liability claims and personal injury litigants. A related consequence of this is that the forum shopper's destination in the latter category of case will frequently be the United States. It should not be overlooked that forum shopping may well occur outside either of these two contexts. It may be particularly discernible in the realm of family law as the following observation of Fogarty J of the Full Court of the Family Court of Australia reveals:

> Since the laws relating to the redistribution of the property of married persons upon their separation appear to vary almost infinitely and in subtle ways from country to country and since parties may have property, both real and personal, in different jurisdictions, the choice of forum to determine those issues will be important not only as a matter of personal convenience and cost but also because it may have a significant impact on the ultimate result.[170]

2.60 This passage admirably captures the importance of those considerations which it has been the task of this chapter to convey.

Even in such cases, however, jurisdictional battles may be fought as one party seeks to circumvent the agreed choice of forum. This is explored more fully in Chapter 5.

[170] *In the marriage of Gilmore* (1993) 16 Fam LR 285, 293. See also the subsequent case of *Henry v Henry* (1996) 185 CLR 571 in which the High Court of Australia reversed a decision of the Full Court of the Family Court of Australia refusing to stay Australian divorce proceedings in circumstances where related property proceedings concerning matrimonial property had been commenced at an earlier point in time in Monaco.

3

Conceptual Responses to Forum Shopping and Concurrent Jurisdiction

I.	Introduction	3.01
II.	Jurisdiction Allocated by Convention	3.03
	1. The Jurisdictional Scheme of the Brussels Convention/Council Regulation 44/2001	3.13
	2. Multiple Proceedings and Council Regulation 44/2001	3.25
	3. Recognition and Enforcement of Judgments under Council Regulation 44/2001	3.45
	4. The Brussels Convention and Regulation 44/2001—A Model for Others?	3.49
III.	Common Law Regulation of Jurisdiction	3.68
	1. The Traditional Common Law Approach	3.71
	2. The 'Natural Forum'—Emergence of a Concept	3.78
	3. The Natural Forum—The Concept Considered	3.84
	4. The Natural Forum—The Concept Criticized	3.149
IV.	Conclusion	3.170

I. INTRODUCTION

3.01 The previous chapter sought to demonstrate that differences in the procedural, internal and conflicts laws of different countries may produce significant incentives for forum shopping. It was seen in Chapter 1 that the *sine qua non* for such activity was the existence of jurisdiction in more than one forum, whether by reason of the fact that a defendant is present in several forums (either simultaneously, in the case of corporations, or sequentially, in the case of individuals or ships) or because of so-called exorbitant or assumed jurisdiction. The combination of concurrent jurisdiction and the various advantages offered by one 'competent' forum over another in any given case creates the environment for vigorous battles over the issue of venue in transnational litigation. Further, the availability of multiple venues obviously entails the possibility of multiple suits and in turn the prospect of inconsistent judicial decisions.

3.02 Bearing in mind that 'destinations that are very close to one another may be reached by different routes',[1] this chapter explores two *conceptual*

---

[1] *MacShannon v Rockware Glass Ltd* [1978] AC 795, 811 per Lord Diplock.

responses to the problems posed by concurrent jurisdiction. The first involves both a stricter conception and the co-operative allocation of jurisdiction by international treaty or convention. The second, a creation of the common law (and therefore of perhaps limited efficacy and appeal in this area because of its necessarily limited scope), centres around the notion that there is a 'natural forum' for any given piece of transnational litigation and that it is to this venue that jurisdictional rules should direct litigants. By allocating jurisdiction according to a strict set of rules contained in a written convention and specifically addressing the problem of concurrent jurisdiction, the first response reduces but by no means eliminates the scope for litigation about where to litigate and forum shopping. The second response, on the other hand, arguably increases the scope for interlocutory litigation about the question of venue in transnational disputes because of the abstract nature of the notion of the natural forum. Nevertheless, this response presents a core and, at least in theoretical terms, highly attractive concept for resolving such clashes. In practical terms, and perhaps paradoxically, it may hasten resolution of the dispute.[2]

II. JURISDICTION ALLOCATED BY CONVENTION

3.03 In particular subject matter areas, the jurisdiction of the court of a given country is prescribed by international conventions to which that country is a signatory.[3] Other signatory states will have a similar regime of jurisdictional rules in relation to the subject matter covered by the convention. Such conventions generally form part of an overall programme designed to secure uniformity in the *internal* laws of the subscribing states in relation to the convention's particular subject matter. The Warsaw Convention on Carriage by Air and the Geneva Convention on the Contract for the International Carriage of Goods by Road provide two examples of conventions which demarcate jurisdiction in this way for those countries party to them.

3.04 Where such conventions apply, there may, depending upon the proper construction of the convention in question, be no scope for application of the common law rules relating to the assumption of jurisdiction.[4]

---

[2] Briggs, A and Rees, P, *Civil Jurisdiction and Judgments* (3rd edn, 2002) at 4.12, especially at text accompanying n 60.

[3] In respect of the United Kingdom, see generally Chapter 15 of Collins, LA (ed), *Dicey and Morris on the Conflict of Laws* (13th edn, 2000).

[4] For example, the ordinary presence of the defendant in the forum: see *Rothmans of Pall Mall (Overseas) Ltd v Saudi Arabian Airlines Corp* [1981] 1 QB 368.

Examples can be found of cases where a defendant, over whom jurisdiction is asserted by reason of a convention, has succeeded in obtaining a stay of those proceedings on grounds of *forum non conveniens*. This was, in essence, the situation in *The Atlantic Star*[5] where jurisdiction was conferred under the 1952 Brussels Collision Convention. In *Rothmans of Pall Mall (Overseas) Ltd v Saudi Arabian Airlines Corp*,[6] Ormrod LJ contemplated that a defendant may seek a stay of proceedings on the grounds of *forum non conveniens* in cases where jurisdiction is established under the Warsaw Convention on Carriage by Air[7]—a view that has expressly been held to be the case in the United States[8]—however, subsequent English authority denies this possibility in the context of that Convention.[9]

Although both the Warsaw Convention and the Geneva Convention on **3.05** Carriage by Road give the plaintiff *some* choice of forum, within those jurisdictions party to them (or other applicable conventions) there will be reduced scope for a plaintiff to forum shop as far as seeking to benefit from differences in the substantive law is concerned for, as noted above, the very purpose of such conventions is to effect a measure of uniformity in substantive principle. The negation of forum shopping possibilities under the Warsaw Convention was remarked upon by Mustill J in *Rothmans of Pall Mall (Overseas) Ltd v Saudi Arabian Airlines Corp*.[10] Referring to Articles 28 and 32 of that Convention, he observed that their policy was 'to prevent forum shopping by the plaintiff, and at the same time to prevent the defendant from imposing, through the medium of his standard conditions of carriage, a choice of jurisdiction likely to be favourable to his interests'.[11] Such conventions, however, do not entirely eliminate forum shopping or interlocutory disputes in relation to venue. A good example in relation to the Carriage by Road Convention is supplied by *Andrea Merzario v Internationale Spedition Leitner*,[12] which involved litigation about whether first-commenced but second-served Austrian proceedings were 'pending' at the time of the second-commenced but first-served English proceedings.

The most significant conventions affecting jurisdiction to which the **3.06** United Kingdom is a party are the Brussels and Lugano Conventions on Jurisdiction and Judgments.[13] While the Brussels and Lugano

---

[5] [1974] AC 436.   [6] [1981] 1 QB 368.   [7] ibid 388.
[8] *Trivelloni-Lorenzi v Pan American World Airways* 821 F 2d 1147 (5th Cir,1987); *Feng Zhen Lu v Air China International Corporation* (1992) 24 Avi 17, 369.
[9] *Milor SRL v British Airways plc* [1996] QB 702.
[10] [1981] 1 QB 368.   [11] ibid 377.
[12] [2001] 1 Lloyd's Rep 490.
[13] For reasons of convenience, these Conventions will in general be referred to compendiously as the 'Brussels Convention'.

Conventions remain in force, for the most part the work done by those conventions is now done by European Council Regulation 44/2001.[14] Unlike the Warsaw or Geneva Conventions referred to above, the jurisdictional rules set out in the Brussels and Lugano Conventions as well as in Council Regulation 44/2001 are not part of a larger package designed to effect uniformity in terms of principles of *substantive* law in particular subject matter areas. Their scope, extending as to 'civil and commercial matters', is simply too broad for that goal even to be contemplated. Rather, the principal rationale of the Brussels Convention, as for the Regulation, was to further the ideals of a common market by allowing the free movement, as it were, of judgments within the member states[15] or, as stated in the Convention's Preamble, 'to secure the simplification of formalities governing the reciprocal recognition and enforcement of judgments of courts or tribunals'. This language reflects the terms of what is now Article 293 (formerly Article 220) of the Treaty of Rome which provided the impetus for and indeed imposed an obligation upon the original six member states of the European Economic Community, as it then was, to enter into negotiations for a convention providing for the recognition and enforcement of judgments between member states.[16]

3.07 The Committee of Experts entrusted with responsibility for the drafting of the Brussels Convention recognized that the goal of facilitating the reciprocal recognition and enforcement of judgments could be achieved by two different techniques, entry into either a *convention simple* or a *convention double*.[17] A *convention simple* is based on rules of 'indirect jurisdiction', that is to say, it provides for recognition and enforcement of judgments which have been founded upon jurisdiction of the kind specified in the relevant

---

[14] Denmark chose not to participate in the adoption of the Regulation and thus the Brussels Convention continues to apply as between Denmark and member states. The texts (which are not identical) of the Regulation, the Brussels, and Lugano Conventions are conveniently reproduced in Briggs, A and Rees, P, *Civil Jurisdiction and Judgments* (3rd edn, 2002), Appendices I, II, and III. For convenience, except where context otherwise requires, reference to the scheme of jurisdictional allocation first enshrined in the Brussels Convention will be made by referring to the relevant articles of Regulation 44/2001 in order to reflect the reality that, from March 2002, it is the Regulation that will, generally, allocate jurisdiction between member states in litigation concerning persons domiciled in member states.

[15] Jenard Report [1979] OJ C59/1, 52.

[16] The Lugano Convention, extending the terms of the Brussels Convention, with some minor variations, to EFTA countries is necessarily not based on a desire to effectuate the wishes of Article 293 (formerly 220) of the Treaty of Rome. Moreover, Article 62(1)(b) of this Convention provides for accession by non-European Union and non-EFTA states by invitation: see Jenard/Möller Report [1990] OJ C189/57, 84–85.

[17] Jenard Report [1979] OJ C59/1, 7. This distinction is elaborated below; for further consideration, see von Mehren, AT, 'Recognition and Enforcement of Sister-State Judgments: Reflections on General Theory and Current Practice in the European Economic Community and the United States' (1981) 81 Columbia Law Review 1044, 1058 and Lipstein, K, 'One Hundred Years of Hague Conferences on Private International Law' (1993) 42 ICLQ 553, 642.

convention. Judgments whose jurisdiction is not so founded are correspondingly not entitled to recognition or enforcement but it is important to note that the original court's jurisdiction is not otherwise restricted; its judgment will clearly be enforceable against any of the defendant's assets within the jurisdiction, and may even be enforceable in a state party to the convention under common law (or equivalent) rules of recognition or enforcement in that state in circumstances where the convention is not intended to be an exclusive code. Innumerable bilateral conventions to which the United Kingdom is a party, for example, follow this model and both the Administration of Justice Act 1920 and the Foreign Judgments (Reciprocal Enforcement) Act 1933 specify the types of jurisdiction upon which any foreign judgments must be founded to be entitled to recognition or enforcement under these Acts. The Hague Convention on the Recognition and Enforcement of Judgments in Civil and Commercial Matters of 1 February 1971 also provides an example of a *convention simple*.[18]

A *convention double*, on the other hand, is based on rules of direct jurisdic- **3.08** tion. Common jurisdictional standards are set and, in cases covered by the scope of such a convention, courts of signatory states may not assert jurisdiction beyond these standards. With very limited exceptions, a court of a signatory state in which recognition and/or enforcement of any judgment is sought will neither be required nor indeed permitted to examine the jurisdictional basis of the foreign judgment. Recognition and enforcement is virtually automatic and much simplified under this model, although consensus between participating states as to appropriate heads of jurisdiction may be difficult to achieve.

The Committee of Experts responsible for the drafting of the Brussels **3.09** Convention settled on the model of a *convention double*, recognizing certain ancillary benefits which such a model provides. These included increased harmonization of laws relating to jurisdiction among contracting states,[19] the abandonment of national rules of exorbitant jurisdiction (at least as they applied to parties domiciled in contracting states),[20] and greater certainty for litigants, both as to where to sue and where they may be sued.[21] This last concern seems to have been of particular importance

---

[18] This Convention is referred to further at para 3.56 below.

[19] Jenard Report [1979] OJ C59/1, 7. Given its more integrationist aspirations, this concern was arguably of greater importance for member states of the European Union than for those of the EFTA countries subscribing to the later Lugano Convention.

[20] ibid. In this regard it should be noted that the Preamble to the Brussels Convention lays stress on the need 'to strengthen in the Community the legal protection of persons therein established'.

[21] ibid 15. In Case 241/83, *Rösler v Rottwinkel* [1985] ECR 99, 127, the European Court of Justice referred to the 'purpose of the Convention, which is to assign jurisdiction in a certain and predictable way'.

and is well reflected in the observation by Schlosser that 'a plaintiff must be sure which court has jurisdiction. He should not have to waste his time and money risking that the court concerned may consider itself less competent than another.'[22] Further, as has been alluded to above, the *consequences* of suit in a particular forum will also be more certain in so far as there will be virtual automatic recognition and enforcement of any judgment in contracting states. A further benefit of a *convention double* is that it permits the regulation through jurisdictional rules of the problem of concurrent suits or *lis pendens*,[23] a feature specifically drawn attention to in Recital 15 of Regulation 44/2001 and of particular relevance to the concerns of this book.

3.10 The similarity between both the aims and the benefits of this model in the context of the Brussels Convention and now Regulation 44/2001, on the one hand, and the United States Constitution, on the other, is striking and several useful comparisons have been made.[24] The due process clause of the United States Constitution, as interpreted in *International Shoe Co v Washington*[25] to require 'minimum contacts' between a case and the forum in which it is being heard, and the application of the Constitution's full faith and credit clause[26] to sister-state judgments may together be seen to create a scheme analogous to a *convention double*. In this context, it is instructive to note that the purpose of the full faith and credit clause was:

> to alter the status of the several states as independent foreign sovereignties, each free to ignore obligations created under the laws or by the judicial proceedings of the others, and to make them integral parts of a single nation throughout which a remedy upon a just obligation might be demanded as of right irrespective of the state of its origin.[27]

3.11 Also and equally significantly, the full faith and credit clause precluded parties from 'contesting matters that they have had a full and fair oppor-

---

[22] Schlosser Report [1979] OJ C59/71, 97. Phillips LJ, speaking in the context of the Warsaw Convention, has observed that 'there is something to be said for a regime which restricts the choice of forum in a manner which excludes those that are likely to be inappropriate, but which does not otherwise permit the plaintiff's choice to be challenged': *Milor SRL v British Airways plc* [1996] QB 702, 710.

[23] Jenard Report [1979] OJ C59/1, 7.

[24] See, for example, von Mehren, AT (n 17 above), especially at 1058, and Juenger, FK, 'Judicial Jurisdiction in the United States and the European Communities; A Comparison' (1984) 82 Michigan Law Review 1195 *passim*. Contrast Borchers, PJ, 'Comparing Personal Jurisdiction in the United States and the European Community: Lessons for American Reform' (1992) 40 American Journal of Comparative Law 121, who emphasizes the differences and in particular what he considers to be the deficiencies of the far less specific American model for the assumption and allocation of jurisdiction.

[25] 326 US 310 (1945).

[26] Article IV, §1.

[27] *Milwaukee County v ME White Co* 296 US 268, 277 (1935).

tunity to litigate', thus protecting 'their adversaries from the expense and vexation attending multiple lawsuits, conserv[ing] judicial resources, and foster[ing] reliance on judicial action by minimizing the possibility of inconsistent decisions'.[28]

Attention is now turned to the jurisdictional scheme of the Brussels **3.12** Convention and Council Regulation 44/2001 with particular focus being placed upon the ways in which those regimes seek to minimize forum shopping and address the problem of concurrent or overlapping proceedings.

1. The Jurisdictional Scheme of the Brussels Convention/Council Regulation 44/2001

According to the Jenard Report, the official and authoritative[29] report of **3.13** the Committee of Experts responsible for drafting the Brussels Convention, 'the rules of jurisdiction codified in Title II [now Chapter II of Regulation 44/2001] determine which State's courts are *most appropriate* to assume jurisdiction, taking into account all relevant matters'.[30] In codifying specific rules of jurisdiction, the Committee diverged from the approach in the United States where the Supreme Court prescribes only the outer limits of permissible state and federal court jurisdiction.[31] As will be seen below, like Regulation 44/2001, the 'modern' common law rules of jurisdiction are also concerned to identify the 'most appropriate' court or 'natural forum' for transnational litigation. Unlike the common law, however, and in accord with its desire to afford litigants certainty with respect to matters of jurisdictional competence, both the Brussels Convention and Regulation 44/2001 identify which member state's courts are most appropriate to assume jurisdiction in particular civil and commercial matters. In *Effer SpA v Kantner*,[32] it was observed that 'the Convention [Regulation] provides a collection of rules ... which, in the interests of legal certainty and for the benefit of the parties, confer jurisdiction upon the national court territorially best qualified to determine a dispute'.[33]

---

[28] *Montana v United States* 440 US 147, 153–154 (1979).

[29] Section 3(3) of the Civil Jurisdiction and Judgments Act 1982 states that the Jenard and Schlosser Reports ([1979] OJ C59/1 and C59/71 respectively) 'may be considered in ascertaining the meaning and effect of any provision of the Conventions and shall be given such weight as is appropriate in the circumstances'.

[30] Jenard Report [1979] OJ C59/1, 15 (emphasis added).

[31] Juenger, FK (n 24 above) 1206.

[32] Case 38/81 [1982] ECR 825.

[33] ibid 834.

3.14 A small number of cases, including matters relating to land, the constitutional existence and status of corporations, the validity of entries on public registries, and the registration and validity of certain intellectual property rights, is considered to be territorially so closely linked to particular forums that courts of those member states are afforded 'exclusive' jurisdiction under Article 22 of Regulation 44/2001 and a court of another member state seised of a claim falling within Article 22's scope is required to declare of its own motion that it has no jurisdiction.[34] Moreover, a judgment founded upon jurisdiction assumed contrary to Article 22 will not be subject to recognition.[35] To the extent that this is also the case with respect to judgments founded on jurisdiction assumed contrary to the provisions of Sections 3 and 4 of Chapter II of the Regulation, relating to insurance and consumer contracts, those sections may also be said to provide an exclusive code of jurisdiction.

3.15 In Article 23, Regulation 44/2001 also permits parties to enter into agreements giving a court or the courts of a member state exclusive or other jurisdiction to settle disputes arising in connection with a particular legal relationship. The Committee of Experts responsible for the drafting of the Brussels Convention recognized the particular importance of such agreements in the commercial world.[36] Article 23 is discussed much more fully in Chapter 5 of this book but it is significant to observe that, as a general proposition, the Regulation respects parties' decisions to resolve questions of venue consensually. Where there is such consensus, there is simply no point in imposing further or alternative jurisdictional requirements. This entirely commonsensical position is also reflected in Article 24 which provides that a court will have jurisdiction where a defendant enters an appearance other than one solely to contest the court's jurisdiction.

3.16 There are four exceptional situations where the Regulation will not permit jurisdiction to rest upon an agreement between the parties: those cases specified in Article 22;[37] and special provisions relating to insurance, consumer, and employment contracts. Articles 13, 17, and 21 of the Regulation respectively limit the circumstances in which jurisdiction agreements may be entered into in these areas. This special treatment is justified by reference to the perceived weaker economic position (and therefore unequal bargaining power) of consumers, assureds, and employees but, even in this context, jurisdiction agreements entered into *after* the dispute has arisen will be effective to provide a further basis of jurisdiction.[38]

---

[34] Article 25.   [35] Article 35.   [36] Jenard Report [1979] OJ C59/1, 37.
[37] ibid 34.   [38] See Articles 13(1) and 17(1).

While Articles 22 and 23 are of undoubted importance in the overall **3.17** framework of Regulation 44/2001, it is Article 2 which forms the cornerstone of the Regulation's jurisdictional scheme, providing that 'subject to this Regulation, persons domiciled in a member state shall, whatever their nationality, be sued in the courts of that member state'. This principle is predicated on the maxim *actor sequitur forum rei*[39] and it follows from the language of the Jenard Report[40] that the courts of the defendant's country of domicile will almost always be appropriate.[41] It has been said that 'the domicile of the defendant provides for a just and reasonable criterion of jurisdiction because of its relative simplicity and foreseeability'.[42]

So central is the principle that the most appropriate forum for a defendant **3.18** to be sued in is that of its domicile that the European Court of Justice has interpreted the derogations from it restrictively (including those cases specified in Article 22)[43] and in a way which encourages a plaintiff who has a choice of jurisdictions in which to bring its case nevertheless to sue the defendant in the courts of the defendant's domicile. In *Kalfelis v Bankhaus Schröder*,[44] the Court held that:

a court which has jurisdiction under Article 5(3) over an action in so far as it is based on tort or delict does not have jurisdiction over that action in so far as it is not so based. Whilst it is true that disadvantages arise from different aspects of the same dispute being adjudicated upon by different courts, . . . a plaintiff is always entitled to bring his action in its entirety before the courts for the domicile of the defendant.[45]

Earlier, in *Somafer SA v Saar-Ferngas AG*,[46] it opined that:

multiplication of the bases of jurisdiction in one and the same case is not likely to encourage legal certainty and the effectiveness of legal protection throughout the territory of the Community and therefore it is in accord with the objective of the [Regulation] to avoid a wide and multifarious interpretation of the exceptions to the general rule of jurisdiction contained in Article 2.

---

[39] Jenard Report [1979] OJ C59/1, 18–19. [40] See para 3.13 above.

[41] The exceptions are the cases presented by Articles 22 and 23 discussed in the previous two paragraphs but even here, as a general proposition, the courts of the defendant's domicile will supplant a forum nominated in an Article 23 jurisdiction agreement entered into prior to the dispute arising in certain types of cases involving insurance and consumer contracts: see Articles 12 and 16 of the Regulation.

[42] Walter, G and Dalsgaard, R, 'The Civil Law Approach' in Nygh, P and McLachlan, C, *Transnational Tort Litigation*, 43.

[43] See, for example, Case 73/77, *Sanders v van der Putte* [1977] ECR 2383; Case 241/83, *Rösler v Rottwinkel* [1985] ECR 99; Case C–115/88, *Reichert v Dresdner Bank (No 1)* [1990] ECR I–27.

[44] Case 189/87 [1988] ECR 5565.

[45] ibid 5585–5586. cf Case 34/82, *Peters v ZNAV* [1983] ECR 987, 1003. See also Walter, G and Dalsgaard, R, 'The Civil Law Approach' in Nygh, P and McLachlan, C, *Transnational Tort Litigation*, 43. [46] [1978] ECR 2183, 2191.

A more recent example of the pre-eminence of the precept that defendants ought be sued in the courts of their domicile is the restrictive interpretation afforded by the Court of Justice to Article 6(1) of the Brussels Convention in *Réunion Européene SA v Spliethoff's BV*.[47]

3.19 In its drafting of the Brussels Convention, the Committee of Experts was, and, in its interpretation, the Court of Justice continues to be, conscious of the fact that any multiplication of courts of competent jurisdiction serves to heighten the risk of irreconcilable decisions.[48]

3.20 The main body of exceptions to the Regulation's central rule of jurisdiction encapsulated in Article 2 is found in Section 2 of Chapter II, entitled 'Special Jurisdiction'. The articles in this section provide *additional* bases of jurisdiction and do not supplant the application of Article 2 to the particular situations to which they are directed. The heads of 'special jurisdiction' are justified on the basis of 'a close connecting factor between the dispute and the court with jurisdiction to resolve it'[49] or by reference to 'the interests of the proper administration of justice', including the desire to minimize the scope for irreconcilable judgments.[50]

3.21 There may seem to be an element of paradox in the fact that increasing the heads of potential jurisdiction for a plaintiff to choose from in deciding where to bring its case could minimize the scope for irreconcilable decisions but the contexts to which this last observation relates concern complex litigation involving either multiple (and differently domiciled) defendants or third parties. For example, in *Gascoine v Pyrah*, Hirst LJ, referring to the court's assumption of jurisdiction under Article 6(1) of the Brussels Convention, stated that 'the result of this appeal will, far from leading to a multiplication of proceedings, avoid a duplication of proceedings both here and in Germany'.[51] Article 6 permits a party domiciled in one member state also to be sued, where it is one of a number of defendants, in the courts for the place where any one of them is domiciled or, in third party proceedings, in the court seised of the original proceedings.[52]

3.22 While Article 6 may be thought to be a powerful tool to facilitate the resolution of all aspects of dispute between all parties in one jurisdiction (and

---

[47] [1998] ECR I–6511; [2000] QB 690. See para 3.22 below.

[48] Jenard Report [1979] OJ C59/1, 23; Case C–220/88, *Dumez France SA v Hessische Landesbank* [1990] ECR I–49, 80.

[49] Jenard Report [1979] OJ C59/1, 22; Case 33/78, *Somafer SA v Saar-Ferngas AG* [1978] ECR 2183, 2191; Case 34/82, *Peters v ZNAV* [1983] ECR 987, 1002; Case C–220/88, *Dumez France SA v Hessische Landesbank* [1990] ECR I–49, 79–80.

[50] Jenard Report [1979] OJ C59/1, 27 and 32.   [51] [1994] I L Pr 82, 95.

[52] Article 6 also permits a party to be sued on a counterclaim in the court in which the original claim is pending. See also Article 10, paragraph 3.

the decision of the Court of Appeal in *Gascoine v Pyrah*[53] supports its use in this way), the European Court of Justice's decision in *Réunion Européenne SA v Spliethoff's Bevrechtingskantoor*[54] to the effect that 'two claims in one action for compensation directed against different defendants and based in one instance on contractual liability and in the other on liability in tort or delict cannot be regarded as connected' strongly undermines this goal. This issue was the subject of a reference to the Court of Justice in *Watson v First Choice Holidays and Flights*.[55] Other provisions of the Convention and Regulation may also work to undermine the ability of Article 6 to group litigation and result in fragmentation. In *Hough v P & O Containers Ltd*,[56] the existence of a German jurisdiction clause meant that jurisdiction could not be exercised in England in third party proceedings pursuant to Article 6(2) notwithstanding the Court's regret as to the consequential multiplicity of proceedings.

The existence of 'special jurisdiction' in Section 2 of Chapter II has the **3.23** consequence that, in certain situations, two or more courts within the Regulation's reach will have jurisdiction to hear the same dispute between the same parties. This was the case where parties had entered into a non-exclusive jurisdiction agreement, at least according to the interpretation afforded Article 17 of the Brussels Convention by Hoffmann J in *Kurz v Stella Musical Veranstaltungs GmbH*,[57] and is also the case under Article 23(1) of the Regulation which provides, in effect, that a non-exclusive jurisdiction clause will have effect according to its terms, namely it will confer non-exclusive jurisdiction on the nominated court.[58] This means that there will still be some scope for forum shopping within the jurisdictional parameters imposed by the Regulation.[59] It must be doubted, however, whether it is appropriate to invoke the ordinarily pejorative connotations

---

[53] [1994] I L Pr 82. [54] [1998] ECR I–6511 at para [50].

[55] [2001] 2 Lloyd's Rep 339. The question referred was 'whether the statement in paragraph 50 of the judgment in *Réunion Européenne* is a rule applying to article 6(1) or whether the fact that one claim relates to contract and the other to tort, delict or quasi-delict is no more than one of the factors to be taken into account by the national court in deciding whether a sufficient connection exists between the respective claims to justify adding as a party to proceedings brought in one Contracting State against a party domiciled in that State, another party domiciled in a different Contracting State'.

[56] [1999] QB 834, 845.

[57] [1992] Ch 196, discussed at paras 5.54 ff below (and see *Hantarex SpA v SA Digital Research* [1993] I L Pr 501).

[58] Previously, as a result of unhappy draftsmanship, some courts had interpreted Article 17 of the Brussels Convention as requiring non-exclusive jurisdiction clauses to be treated as exclusive.

[59] See Pearl, S, 'Forum Shopping in the EEC' (1987) 15 International Business Lawyer 391; Bogaert, PWL, 'Ius Vigilantibus: Tactics of Forum Shopping under the EEC Judgments Convention' [1988] ECLR 1; Geddes, A, 'Forum Shopping in the EEC' (1988) 138 NLJ 542; Joseph, D, 'Disaster Litigation—the USA Way' (1989) 139 New Law Journal 1419. See also *Knauf UK GmbH v British Gypsum Ltd* [2002] 1 WLR 907, discussed in para 3.30 below.

of this phrase to describe any choice of jurisdiction open to a plaintiff under the Regulation. All permitted forums are necessarily appropriate and Schlosser's observation that 'where the courts of several states have jurisdiction, the plaintiff has *deliberately* been given a right of choice',[60] strongly implies that that choice is not to be deprecated.

3.24 It should be noted that the Committee of Experts was sensitive to any efforts by plaintiffs to abuse the Brussels Convention's jurisdictional scheme for improper motives relating to choice of forum. Thus, commenting on Article 6(1) which permits the joinder of a non-domiciled defendant in another defendant's domicile, Jenard observed that 'there must be a connection between the claims made against each of the defendants, as for example in the case of joint debtors. It follows that an action cannot be brought solely with the object of ousting the jurisdiction of the courts of the State in which the defendant is domiciled.'[61] The requirement for a close connection is now expressly stated in Article 6(1) of the Regulation.[62]

2. MULTIPLE PROCEEDINGS AND COUNCIL REGULATION 44/2001

3.25 Apart from the possibility of 'forum shopping', concurrent jurisdiction also presents the prospect of parallel or concurrent proceedings, whether brought by the same plaintiff against the same defendant in two or more jurisdictions, or as a result of one set of proceedings being commenced by the 'plaintiff' and the other by the 'defendant' in the form of a counterclaim or application for a negative declaration. As was seen in paragraphs 1.26 ff above, concurrent proceedings present the unattractive prospect of irreconcilable decisions being given on the same set of facts. An important feature of the Brussels Convention was the desire to minimize the scope for such decisions and this concern remains prominent in Regulation 44/2001. Although recognizing in Article 34(3) that it will not always be possible to escape this outcome, the provisions of Section 9 of Chapter II of the Regulation entitled 'Lis Pendens' directly address the potential for irreconcilable decisions created by the existence in certain circumstances of concurrent jurisdiction.[63]

---

[60] Schlosser Report [1979] OJ C59/71, 97 (emphasis added).

[61] [1979] OJ C59/1, 26. The requirement for such a connection appears expressly in Article 6(1) of Council Regulation 44/2001.

[62] See, also, *Réunion Européenne SA v Spliethoff's Bevrechtingskantoor* [1998] ECR I–6511; [2000] QB 690.

[63] Jenard anticipated that the provisions of this section would 'greatly reduce the number of irreconcilable judgments': [1979] OJ C59/1, 45.

II. Jurisdiction Allocated by Convention

Article 27 of the Regulation is of particular importance, providing that: **3.26**

Where proceedings involving the same cause of action and between the same parties are brought in the Courts of different member states, any court other than the court first seised shall of its own motion stay its proceedings until such time as the jurisdiction of the court first seised is established. Where the jurisdiction of the court first seised is established, any court other than the court first seised shall decline jurisdiction in favour of that court.

In its emphasis on the chronological sequence of proceedings, Article 27 **3.27** establishes something akin to the American domestic 'first filed rule'.[64] This rule, which has only ever been considered to apply to parallel proceedings commenced *within* the United States and has no application to transnational cases,[65] provides that, when similar cases have been filed in different federal district courts, the court which first obtained jurisdiction should enjoin the prosecution of subsequent proceedings in the court second seised. The rule has been extended to apply to parallel proceedings commenced in both a federal and state court[66] and in two or more state courts (although state courts' power to enjoin federal proceedings is limited by the doctrine of federal pre-emption).[67] There is no equivalent rule in Australia. Indeed, anti-suit injunctive relief within the Australian federation is proscribed by section 21 of the Service and Execution of Process Act 1992 (C'th).

Returning to the scheme of the Regulation, under Article 27, unlike the **3.28** American 'first filed' rule, the first seised court is not expressly empowered to enjoin proceedings in courts subsequently seised although English courts evidently consider themselves free to do so. In *Continental Bank NA v Aeakos Compania Naviera SA*,[68] the first of an important series of decisions discussed more extensively in Chapter 4, the Court of Appeal confirmed Gatehouse J's decision to restrain proceedings which had been commenced in the Court of Athens which, in this case, was in fact the first seised court. On this authority, an English court's ability to restrain proceedings in a court seised *second* would be *a fortiori*.[69] The absence of power or at least of specific provision in the Regulation for the making of

---

[64] This rule was established in *Crosley Corp v Hazeltine Corp* 122 F 2d 925 (3d Cir 1941), cert denied 315 US 813 (1942).

[65] *Compagnie des Bauxites de Guinea v Insurance Corp of North America* 651 F 2d 877, 877 (3rd Cir, 1981); *Laker Airways v Sabena, Belgian World Airways* 731 F 2d 909, 927 n 49 (1984) but cf *United Cigarette Machine Co v Wright* 156 F 244 (1907), aff'd 193 F 1023 (4th Cir, 1912).

[66] cf The Anti-Injunction Act 28 USC §2283.

[67] *Donovan v City of Dallas* 377 US 408 (1964).

[68] [1994] 1 WLR 588.

[69] The jurisdictional ability to restrain proceedings in another member state and the propriety of this course if jurisdiction exists are discussed in some detail at paras 4.166 ff below.

orders restraining proceedings in another member state is, however, by no means fatal to the effective operation of Article 27. Consistent with the Regulation's intended self-executing operation,[70] under Article 27, the second seised court is *required* to decline jurisdiction and may not, subject to a possible exception,[71] examine the jurisdiction of the first seised court.[72] *Polly Peck International plc v Citibank NA*[73] provides an example of an assiduous application of this principle. Where both courts are vested with exclusive jurisdiction, Article 29 requires that jurisdiction should be declined by all courts other than that first seised.

3.29 Under the Brussels Convention, the time at which a court became seised was a matter for national procedural law. An important difference between the common law position as to when a court was seised (service on the defendant) and the continental position (issue of the initiating process) emerged in the case law. There was, however, ultimately some convergence on the part of English courts in this area towards a prevalent continental position that, at least for the purposes of Section 8 of Title II of the Brussels Convention, a court was 'seised' when service of the writ was effected.[74] Even this convergence did not eliminate hard-fought litigation in relation to the sequence of commencement. In *Molins v GD SpA*,[75] the Court of Appeal was called upon to decide which party was served first with mirror image process. What may have been thought to be a straightforward, indeed mechanical, chronological inquiry, was complicated by the fact that the Italian process had been (first) served on the English defendant by facsimile in a manner consistent with Italian procedural law but not authorized by English law regarding service where the defendant's prior consent had not been obtained. The English process was held to have been served first.

3.30 Under Regulation 44/2001, the question of 'when seised' has been removed from national procedural law by Article 30 although it may be

---

[70] Jenard Report [1979] OJ C59/1, 8 and see Articles 19 and 20. *The Sargasso* [1993] 1 Lloyd's Rep 424 provides an example of the operation of the 'simple test of chronological priority' (at 429).

[71] Namely, where the second seised court considers, first, that it has exclusive jurisdiction, at least under the provisions of Article 22 of the Regulation, and secondly, that the first seised court lacks such jurisdiction: Case C–351/89 *Overseas Union Insurance Ltd v New Hampshire Insurance Company* [1991] ECR I–3317, 3351; cf *Kloekner & Co AG v Gatoil Overseas Inc* [1990] 1 Lloyd's Rep 177.

[72] Case C–351/89, *Overseas Union Insurance Ltd v New Hampshire Insurance Company* [1990] ECR I–3317, 3350.

[73] [1994] I L Pr 71.

[74] *Dresser UK Ltd v Falcongate Freight Management Ltd* [1992] QB 502; and see Briggs, A, 'Get Your Writs Out' [1992] LMCLQ 150. See also *Merzario v Internationale Spedition Leitner* [2001] 1 Lloyd's Rep 490, 496–497.

[75] [2000] 1 WLR 1741.

confidently expected that the uniform rule, which necessarily incorporates a measure of national procedural law relating to service of process, will throw up fact situations giving rise to litigation about where to litigate in circumstances where the potential consequences of venue justify such a contest. An example of such a contest is supplied by *Knauf UK GmbH v British Gypsum Ltd*,[76] where, in order to win the 'race to seise', the claimant in England sought to circumvent the service provisions contained in the Hague Service Convention by seeking, *ex parte*, an order under the Civil Procedure Rules to serve the German defendant by post. The attempt was unsuccessful, the Court of Appeal emphasizing that this course not only circumvented the Service Convention but, also, the Brussels Convention because 'precedence was [sought to be] achieved only by taking an a priori view of where it was convenient for the litigation to be conducted'.[77]

A mechanistic first filed rule such as that embodied in Article 27 of the **3.31** Regulation has the merit of simplicity and is designed to avoid the twin evils of inconsistent decisions and a race to judgment in those courts exercising jurisdiction.[78] The motivation for such a race is the possibility of being able to plead in the ongoing foreign proceedings that the first judgment renders those proceedings *res judicata* or establishes an issue or cause of action estoppel.[79] Apart from averting such a race, the requirement in Article 27 that the second seised court decline jurisdiction (and the discretion afforded to such a court under Article 28 to do the same in the case of related proceedings)[80] has the additional and salutary result that judicial resources are not wasted through duplicated proceedings, a concern that necessarily looms large in jurisdictions which, in what is perceived to be in the interests of comity, tolerate the existence and exercise of concurrent jurisdiction.[81] Moreover, under Article 27, courts with concurrent jurisdiction are not required nor indeed permitted, whether implicitly or explicitly, to make assessments of or comparisons with the courts of the other jurisdiction or their procedural facilities. The danger that reflections on the appropriateness of courts of different countries to

---

[76] [2002] 1 WLR 907.

[77] ibid 924.

[78] See paras 1.26 ff above.

[79] As to which, see generally Barnett, P, *Res Judicata, Estoppel and Foreign Judgments* (2001).

[80] See discussion at paras 3.40–3.41 below.

[81] As shall be seen at paras 4.223 ff below, this is the predominant approach taken by American courts: see *Laker Airways v Sabena, Belgian World Airlines* 731 F 2d 909 (1984). For cases which have expressed concern about the cost and waste of duplicated proceedings, see *Seattle Totems Hockey Club v National Hockey League* 652 F 2d 852 (9th Cir, 1981), cert denied 457 US 1105 (1982); *American Home Assurance Co v Insurance Corp of Ireland* 603 F Supp 636 (1984); *Cargill v Hartford Accident & Insurance Co* 531 F Supp 710 (D Minn, 1982).

exercise jurisdiction may necessarily involve invidious comparisons, inimical to notions of judicial comity, is thus avoided.[82]

3.32 A blunt rule such as Article 27 is not without its faults. One such fault is the potential for the rule, in cases of multiple defendants, to bifurcate litigation which, ideally, should be heard in a single forum.[83] Those faults may, however, be a necessary price to pay for the virtues enumerated in the previous paragraph. As Lord Goff has said: 'This system achieves its purpose, but at a price. The price is rigidity and rigidity can be productive of injustice.'[84] The most obvious weakness of the rule embodied in Article 27 is that the 'race to judgment' is simply replaced by the 'race to seise'. More significantly, the premium placed on commencing proceedings first may well serve to increase and promote litigation as opposed to other, arguably more desirable and less costly, forms of dispute resolution. In *Messier-Dowty Ltd v Sabena SA*,[85] Lord Woolf MR drew attention to the tension between a blunt rule such as Article 27 of the Regulation with the incentive for parties to rush into proceedings and 'the culture which our Civil Procedure Rules are seeking to promote'. Once a party has set the 'litigation ball rolling', so to speak, it may be more difficult to arrive at a negotiated settlement. Further, the simple chronological criterion for resolving jurisdictional clashes may operate quite fortuitously in the circumstances of any given case. As Brandon J once observed, 'the date on which a party begins an action may be a matter of luck without great significance'.[86]

3.33 Matters are not completely out of the hands of a party that has been gazumped in its choice of preferred forum, however. In *OT Africa Lion v Hijazy*,[87] Aikens J granted an anti-suit injunction restraining defendants in English proceedings from pursuing a claim in the first seised Antwerp court in circumstances where the Antwerp proceedings had been commenced in breach of an exclusive jurisdiction clause nominating English law and English courts. Such cases (which remain controversial) apart, however, the rule embodied in Article 27 has important ramifications for practice. Briggs has noted that:

---

[82] See generally *Voth v Manildra Flour Mills Pty Ltd* (1990) 171 CLR 538, 558–559 and *Oceanic Sun Line Special Shipping Co Inc v Fay* (1988) 165 CLR 197, 240 per Brennan J.

[83] This was the apparent motivation for the claimant's conduct in *Knauf UK GmbH v British Gypsum Ltd* [2002] 1 WLR 907, discussed in para 3.30 above. Had the English court been first seised, the claimant's positive claim against both defendants could have been heard in the one forum whereas this may not have been the case had the German defendant's own anticipated claim in Germany against the claimant in the English proceedings been served first.

[84] *Airbus Industrie GIE v Patel* [1999] 1 AC 119, 132.

[85] [2000] 1 Lloyd's Rep 428, 432.

[86] *The Tillie Lykes* [1977] 1 Lloyd's Rep 124 , 128.

[87] [2001] 1 Lloyd's Rep 76.

the courteous solicitor's habit of writing a letter before action is, from the client's point of view, disastrous. In effect, it invites the opponent to snatch the jurisdictional advantage by launching proceedings in the court of *his* choosing. . . . in a case in which pressure may be exerted, or some strategic or other advantage may be obtained by choosing the forum for the battle, there is no justification for surrendering one's best point before one has begun.[88]

The force of these observations is, in part, a reflection of the very broad **3.34** interpretation accorded to the phrase 'cause of action' in Article 21 of the Brussels Convention (now Article 27 of the Regulation) by the European Court of Justice in *Gubisch Maschinenfabrik KG v Palumbo*.[89] In this case the Court held that, in circumstances where one party brought an action in Germany to enforce an international sales contract and the other party subsequently brought proceedings in Italy seeking rescission of the same contract, both sets of proceedings involved the same cause of action and the same subject matter.[90] The Italian court was accordingly required to decline jurisdiction. A very strong purposive interpretation underpinned this decision, certainly one which went further than that recommended by Advocate-General Mancini who favoured a more literal construction of Article 21 of the Brussels Convention (Article 27 of the Regulation),[91] and the Court reflected the Brussels Convention's concern to avoid irreconcilable decisions, stating that Article 21 of the Convention was 'designed to preclude [this prospect], *in so far as is possible and from the outset*'.[92]

Gubisch extended Article 21's operation beyond that envisaged in the **3.35** Jenard Report where, in relation to Article 27(3) of the Brussels Convention (now Article 34(3)),[93] it was stated that 'a French court in which recognition of a Belgian judgment awarding damages for failure to perform a contract is sought will be able to refuse recognition if a French court has already given judgment in a dispute between the same parties declaring that the contract was invalid'.[94] In light of *Gubisch*, it is difficult

---

[88] 'Anti-European Teeth for Choice of Court Clauses' [1994] LMCLQ 158, 158–159 (emphasis added). See also Bogaert, PWL, *'Ius Vigilantibus*: Tactics of Forum Shopping under the EEC Judgments Convention' [1988] ECLR 1, 6: 'When a dispute in contract arises, it may thus be useful to seise the court of one's choice so as to be certain that only that court will have jurisdiction.'

[89] Case 144/86 [1987] ECR 4861.

[90] The textual requirement that the proceedings involve the 'same subject matter' did not appear in the English or German language versions of Article 21 of the Brussels Convention but it is clear from *Gubisch* that those versions are to be interpreted as though they did contain that phrase: ibid 4875.

[91] ibid 4868–4870.

[92] ibid 4874 (emphasis added).

[93] This provides that a judgment shall not be recognized if it is 'irreconcilable with a judgment given in dispute between the same parties in the State in which recognition is sought'.

[94] [1979] OJ C59/1, 45.

to see how this situation could ever properly arise as between courts of Contracting States. Thus it is plain that Article 27, which in itself represented, when introduced by the Brussels Convention, an 'innovative' mechanism among Contracting States for resolving clashes of jurisdiction,[95] has emerged as an extremely powerful jurisdictional tool and a central element in the Regulation's overall scheme, designed to further the efficient administration of justice by minimizing the scope for irreconcilable judgments.

3.36 The Court of Justice laid further stress on the important jurisdictional task which (then) Article 21 (now Article 27) is expected to perform in its decision in *Overseas Union Insurance Ltd v New Hampshire Insurance Company*.[96] In this case it was held, *inter alia*, that the Article's operation was not confined to circumstances where the jurisdiction of the two courts in question derived directly from the Brussels Convention pursuant to Articles 2 or 3 (that is to say, it is not confined to proceedings in which the defendant is domiciled in a Contracting State) but rather extended to *all* cases of concurrent jurisdiction in member states meeting the description in Article 21 of the Convention (Article 27 of the Regulation), whether or not one or both sets of proceedings were based upon (residual) national rules of jurisdiction.[97] Thus, in *Overseas Union*, the Court of Justice confirmed that the High Court should decline its Article 4 jurisdiction in proceedings which had been brought against a New Hampshire domiciled defendant in circumstances where that defendant had itself earlier commenced proceedings against the plaintiff in the English proceedings in France.[98]

3.37 This decision is to be contrasted to *Owens Bank Ltd v Bracco*,[99] where the Court of Justice held that Article 21 of the Brussels Convention (Article 27 of the Regulation) had no application to apparently similar sets of proceedings in Italy and England relating to the recognition and enforcement of a judgment of a court of a non-Contracting State, St Vincent. This conclusion was expressed on the basis that such proceedings fell outside the scope of the Brussels Convention and, while the decision is defensible, it is perhaps somewhat surprising in light of *Overseas Union*.

---

[95] Case 144/86, *Gubisch* [1987] ECR 4861, 4869 per Advocate-General Mancini. For an account of the prior positions under the domestic laws of various Contracting States, see Szászy, I, *International Civil Procedure* (1967) 541–544.

[96] Case C–351/89 [1991] ECR I–3317.

[97] Article 4 of Regulation 44/2001 provides that, subject to the exclusive jurisdiction provisions of Articles 22 and 23, jurisdiction over non-member state domiciled defendants is to be determined according to national law.

[98] Case C–351/89 [1991] ECR I–3317, 3348.

[99] Case C–129/92 [1994] ECR I–117.

Although Chapter II of the Regulation does not prescribe rules of juris- **3.38**
diction relating to the recognition and enforcement of judgments of non-
member states and Chapter III does not provide for the recognition or
enforcement of such judgments, the possibility of pleading the result of
one state's recognition and enforcement proceedings (which in this case
raised the issue of fraud) in the courts of the other state in order to establish an issue or cause of action estoppel presents *exactly* the kind of jurisdictional clash which Article 27 and *Overseas Union* seemed concerned to
avoid. On the other hand, and in favour of the decision, it may have been
that, as a decision of the Italian court on the question of whether the St
Vincent judgment was tainted by fraud and was therefore unenforceable
in Italy was unlikely to have been recognized in England[100] (and was
certainly not bound to be recognized),[101] and as any English decision was
unlikely to have been recognized in Italy,[102] there would be no point in
holding that Article 21 of the Brussels Convention (Article 27 of the
Regulation) operated. This reasoning is present though rather less explicit
in the Court of Justice's decision in *Owens Bank Ltd v Bracco*.[103]

Article 27 of the Regulation, although having much work to do in the fore- **3.39**
stalling of irreconcilable decisions, especially in the light of *Gubisch*, only
has application to proceedings between 'the same parties'. The European
Court of Justice's decision in *The Tatry*[104] established that proceedings
would be between the 'same parties' within the meaning of now Article
27 notwithstanding that, in one or other (or both) sets of proceedings,
there are also other and different parties. Article 27 of the Regulation only
operates, however, between the same parties. The Court of Justice's later
decision in *Drouot Assurances v Consolidated Metallurgical Industries*[105]
established that 'a party' for the purposes of Article 27 need not be the
same juristic entity in both jurisdictions so long as its interests have identical and indissociable interests (for example, a liquidator and the
company in liquidation[106] or, in at least some cases, an insurer and its
assured).

---

[100] Because the common law rule is that fraud may be raised anew in any recognition or
enforcement proceedings and the court is bound to examine it for itself: *Owens Bank Ltd v
Bracco* [1992] 2 AC 443.

[101] Article 27(5) of the Brussels Convention provided that 'A judgment shall not be recognised if the judgment is irreconcilable with an earlier judgment given in a non-Contracting
State involving the same cause of action and between the same parties, provided that this
latter judgment fulfils the conditions necessary for its recognition in the State addressed.' See
now Article 34(4) of the Regulation.

[102] See the Jenard Report [1979] OJ C59/1, 45.

[103] [1994] ECR I–117.

[104] [1994] ECR I–5439.

[105] [1998] ECR I–3075.

[106] *Re Cover Europe*, 26 February 2002.

3.40 The prospect of irreconcilable decisions will still remain as a possibility in cases where there are multiple defendants whom a plaintiff may, for whatever reason,[107] choose to sue in the courts of their respective domiciles, Article 6 notwithstanding. It may also be that a plaintiff is constrained to sue multiple defendants in different jurisdictions because local rules of procedure do not permit such joinder.[108] Similarly, there will be cases between the same parties but in which the 'causes of action' are not held to be the 'same' within the meaning of *Gubisch*. They may nevertheless be so closely connected, for example because of a common factual substratum, that they are quite capable of producing inconsistent results. Article 28 is the Regulation's mechanism for minimizing the possibility of inconsistent or irreconcilable decisions in these contexts and indeed it has been said that it is 'of more practical importance' than Article 27.[109] Although this may be somewhat less so after *Gubisch*, it is by no means the case that that decision has emasculated the role of Article 28 of the Regulation, as the factual examples given above which illustrate the 'non-reach' of Article 27 seek to show.

3.41 Article 28 of Regulation 44/2001 permits a second seised court to stay its proceedings in circumstances where 'related actions' are pending in the courts of another member state. It also permits a second seised court to decline jurisdiction over actions 'related' to those pending in an earlier seised court, if the first seised court has jurisdiction over the actions in question and its law permits the consolidation of proceedings. The consequence of this, of course, is to allow the first seised court to assume jurisdiction over *both* sets of proceedings through the consolidation of the related actions and so avoid the possibility of irreconcilable decisions. Indeed this purpose is manifest in the very definition given to 'related actions' by the third paragraph of Article 28: 'actions are deemed to be related where they are so closely connected that it is expedient to hear and determine them together to avoid the risk of irreconcilable judgments resulting from separate proceedings'.

3.42 The ambit of this definition and the word 'irreconcilable' in particular was the subject of the important decision in *The Tatry*,[110] where it was held that proceedings would be related if there was involved the 'risk' of conflict-

---

[107] Schlosser observed that a plaintiff's choice of forum may be dictated, for example, by a desire to enforce any decision obtained in that same forum: [1979] OJ C59/71, 97. This illustration may seem a little contrived given the Regulation's very *raison d'être* of facilitating recognition and enforcement.

[108] See Case C–365/88, *Kongress Agentur Hagen GmbH v Zeehaghe BV* [1990] ECR I–1845. Alternately, joinder may be a matter of discretion for the national court.

[109] Collins, LA, *The Civil Jurisdiction and Judgments Act 1982* (1983) 97.

[110] [1994] ECR I–5439.

ing decisions although not necessarily decisions bearing mutually exclusive legal consequences. This decision left undecided an important question of degree in relation to the extent of the risk—a risk may range from remote to high. In England, at least, following the decision in *Sarrio v Kuwait Investment Authority*,[111] Lord Saville tended away from the standard of a high degree of risk,[112] thus encouraging the discretionary staying of second seised proceedings. The nature of the concept 'related action' and the questions of degree necessarily raised and difficult to elucidate means that any formula ultimately arrived at will leave a considerable discretion with the court asked to stay the second set of proceedings, thus providing a further avenue for hard-fought battles concerning venue.

The exact basis upon which this discretion is to be exercised is nowhere **3.43** made explicit in the Regulation although Jenard stated that 'where actions are related, the first *duty* of the court is to stay its proceedings'.[113] The Schlosser Report, although generally of the view that the doctrine of *forum non conveniens* has no role to play in the Convention's jurisdictional scheme, arguably does not totally exclude it.[114] In *The Linda*,[115] Sheen J was adamant that 'the doctrine of forum non conveniens can have no relevance in cases to which Article 21 [now Article 27] or Article 22 [now Article 28] applies'.[116] Earlier, he had stated that:

The question 'Which court would be the more convenient or the more appropriate?' does not arise. . . . If Article 22 is applicable, then any court other than the court first seised may stay its proceedings. As the Netherlands court has no power under Article 22 to stay its proceedings, it would be absurd to decline to stay these proceedings because to do otherwise would be to run the risk of irreconcilable judgments resulting from separate proceedings.[117]

This view would appear to admit of no discretion to retain or decline **3.44** jurisdiction. In reality, however, questions of discretion will inevitably be bound up or subsumed in deciding whether the proceedings are 'related' for the purposes of Article 28 of the Regulation. It certainly appears from Sheen J's decision that, once a conclusion is reached that the proceedings satisfy the description of being related, the imperative of minimizing the prospect of irreconcilable decisions compels the second seised court to

---

[111] [1999] 1 AC 32.

[112] See Briggs, A and Rees, P, *Civil Jurisdiction and Judgments* (3rd edn, 2002) section 2.200.

[113] [1979] OJ C59/1, 41 (emphasis added).

[114] [1979] OJ C59/71, 97–98: 'The practical reasons in favour of the doctrine of forum conveniens will lose considerably in significance, as soon as the 1968 Convention becomes applicable in the United Kingdom and Ireland . . . To correct rules of jurisdiction in a particular case by means of the concept of forum conveniens will then be largely unnecessary.'

[115] [1988] 1 Lloyd's Rep 175.   [116] ibid 180.

[117] ibid 179.

decline jurisdiction or stay the proceedings.[118] According to two English decisions, this will not be the case, however, in circumstances where the related proceedings in the second seised court are governed by a jurisdiction agreement in favour of that court.[119]

3. RECOGNITION AND ENFORCEMENT OF JUDGMENTS UNDER COUNCIL REGULATION 44/2001

3.45 The final point of significance arising from Regulation 44/2001 to be noted for present purposes regards the provisions concerned with recognition and enforcement of judgments. It will be recalled from the discussion at the beginning of this chapter that one of the advantages of following the model of a *convention double* is that recognition and enforcement is greatly facilitated because all contracting states subscribe to common rules of jurisdiction and are required to examine their jurisdiction in each case at the outset.[120] In *Denilauer v SNC Couchet Frères*,[121] the Court of Justice observed that 'it is because of the guarantees given to the defendant in the original proceedings that the Convention [Regulation], in Title III, is very liberal in regard to recognition and enforcement'.[122] It follows that, unlike the case of a *convention simple* (or, indeed, common law rules) in relation to the recognition and enforcement of foreign judgments, there will be little scope either for impugning the jurisdiction of the original court at the enforcement stage or for resisting recognition and enforcement on other grounds. This is reflected in some of the key provisions of Chapter III of Regulation 44/2001.

3.46 After stating that 'a judgment shall not be recognised if it conflicts with the provisions of Sections 3, 4 or 6 of Chapter II,[123] or in a case provided for in Article 72',[124] Article 35(2) of the Regulation continues:

> In its examination of the grounds of jurisdiction referred to in the foregoing paragraph, the court or authority applied to shall be bound by the findings of fact on which the court of the member state of origin based its jurisdiction. Subject to paragraph 1, the jurisdiction of the member state of origin may not be reviewed. The test of public policy referred to in point 1 of Article 34 may not be applied to the rules relating to jurisdiction.

---

[118] This is consistent with the Jenard Report.

[119] *Kloekner & Co AG v Gatoil Overseas Inc* [1990] 1 Lloyd's Rep 177, 206; *IP Metal Ltd v Ruote OZ SpA* [1993] 2 Lloyd's Rep 60, 67.

[120] Articles 25 and 26 of the Regulation and see the Jenard Report [1979] OJ C59/1, 8.

[121] Case 125/79 [1980] ECR 1552.   [122] ibid 1569.

[123] These are the sections which confer 'exclusive' jurisdiction on courts in specific situations. It is important to note that 'exclusive' jurisdiction conferred under an Article 23 'prorogation' agreement falls within Section 6 and so is not subject to Article 35's exception.

[124] Article 72 is described in n 176 below.

Article 36 of the Regulation further provides that 'under no circumstances **3.47** may a foreign judgment be reviewed as to its substance.' This is reiterated in Article 41 of the Regulation. The very narrow scope permitted a court to review a judgment given under jurisdiction allocated by the Brussels Convention and, now, Regulation 44/2001 was also emphasized by the Court of Justice in *Overseas Union*.[125] The extremely circumscribed possibilities of review of a foreign judgment at the recognition and enforcement stage also extend to judgments given by courts of member states under national rules of jurisdiction in cases where the defendant is not domiciled in a member state. This feature of the Convention and Regulation 44/2001 is discussed further below and also in paragraph 4.295 below.

The previous three sections have sought to provide an overview of the **3.48** scheme and structure of the Brussels Convention and, now, Regulation 44/2001. That sphere of operation is, of course, extended through the Lugano Convention to member states of the European Free Trade Association. Consideration now turns to the question of its value as a paradigm in an even broader context.

4. The Brussels Convention and Regulation 44/2001—A Model for Others?

There is much that is desirable in a legislative scheme such as is enshrined **3.49** in the Brussels Convention and Regulation 44/2001 which, in addition to (and as a critical element in) facilitating the recognition and enforcement of judgments, provides both for the clear allocation of jurisdiction (including prevention of the commencement of litigation in a jurisdictionally inappropriate forum) and anticipates and in the vast majority of cases prevents the possibility of irreconcilable decisions. As will be seen in paragraphs 3.68 ff below, it must be doubted whether the common law has been nearly as successful in developing *clear* rules for the allocation and retention of jurisdiction in a transnational case. It is similarly to be doubted whether the common law has evolved a wholly satisfactory approach to situations where concurrent proceedings are on foot. This necessarily leads one to consider the question whether a *convention double* in the tradition of the Brussels Convention on Jurisdiction and Judgments, as now manifested in Regulation 44/2001, could have a wider operation in the realm of transnational litigation, to avert or minimize the phenomenon of forum shopping and the problems of concurrent jurisdiction.

---

[125] Case C–351/89 [1991] ECR I–3317, 3350.

3.50 In theoretical terms, the answer would seem reasonably clear. Such a convention would be eminently desirable for the same reasons as has been argued make Regulation 44/2001 and its antecedents valuable jurisdictional instruments. Clashes of jurisdiction are positively discouraged and irreconcilable decisions are invariably avoided by preventing the exercise of concurrent jurisdiction from the outset. Moreover, the 'evils' of forum shopping are greatly ameliorated. Prior to litigation arising, a potential defendant will be able to ascertain from the jurisdictional scheme of the convention the forum or forums in which it may be sued. Such a defendant will thereby also be able to ascertain the content of its rights and liabilities by reference to the substantive law of that jurisdiction. Further, parties *entering into* contracts will be able to identify the potential forums for litigation (and therefore the content of future rights and liabilities) from the outset. Indeed, this may even affect the actual contract terms.[126]

3.51 The real obstacle to entry into a *convention double* to govern questions of jurisdiction in transnational litigation and the recognition and enforcement of foreign judgments is a *practical* one, that of securing sufficiently widespread agreement to a convention, its structure, core concepts, and sphere of operation. In this context, it must not be forgotten or underestimated just how radical was the change to jurisdictional rules originally effected by the Brussels Convention, not only in the United Kingdom but also throughout Europe. The impact of this change in the original states party to the Convention has been summarized in the following way:

> Jurisdiction rules in cases with a foreign element, and rules on the recognition of foreign judgments, which took centuries to develop, no longer had any validity. Jurisdictional privileges and other expressions of national interest had to be foregone.[127] Labyrinths of dogmas which had assumed awe-inspiring proportions in continental jurisprudence in connection with international procedural law were overturned.[128]

3.52 Considerable external pressures compelled the sacrifices which Kohler refers to in this passage. In the absence of such pressures and as more recent experience under the auspices of the Hague Conference, discussed further below, demonstrates, widespread mutual agreement as to accept-

---

[126] This point is made more fully at paras 5.01 ff below in relation to jurisdiction and arbitration agreements.

[127] What was in fact yielded by the original six was considerably less than this and the previous sentence claim; with the exception of suits against domiciliaries of Contracting States, exorbitant heads of jurisdiction were retained and indeed invested with greater potency in terms of the enforceability of judgments given under them.

[128] Kohler, C, 'Practical Experience of the Brussels Jurisdiction and Judgments Convention in the Six Original Contracting States' (1985) 34 ICLQ 563, 563.

able bases of jurisdiction would seem a remote possibility. Apart from fundamental points of distinction between the civil and common law traditions,[129] there may be considerable disagreement as to appropriate jurisdictional bases *within* a particular tradition. In this context, the apparently intractable hostility between some common law jurisdictions and the United States with respect to the legitimacy of asserting extraterritorial jurisdiction pursuant to the 'effects' doctrine provides a ready example.[130] Any meaningful *convention double* would need to address and accommodate the competing tensions rooted in this disagreement as well as in areas on the recognition and enforcement side such as disquiet at the level of damages awarded by American juries. A *convention simple* in relation to the recognition and enforcement of judgments between the United Kingdom and the United States has fallen on such hurdles.[131]

The argument has been made that a convention which is designed not **3.53** only to facilitate the recognition and enforcement of judgments but also to harmonize rules of jurisdictional competence is only possible and workable within an international 'law system' that is reasonably homogeneous.[132] This observation may be particularly apposite if a provision similar to the centrally important Article 27 of Regulation 44/2001 is to have any role to play in such a convention. In the absence of relative homogeneity of substantive and procedural laws, the 'race to seise' will be even more dramatic and keenly contested. In considering the need for homogeneity, it is pertinent to recall that the Brussels Convention was only drafted by the original six member states of the European Economic Community, all of which shared a common civil law heritage, and, although there have been some amendments at the time of other states'

---

[129] These are explored at greater length at paras 3.58–3.65 below.

[130] Contrast the American approach as first and most famously enunciated by Learned Hand J in *United States v Aluminium Company of America* 148 F 2d 416 (2nd Cir, 1945) with Commonwealth statutory responses: Protection of Trading Interests Act 1980 (UK); Protection of Trading Interests Act 1981 (Bermuda); Foreign Proceedings (Excess of Jurisdiction) Act 1984 (Aust); Foreign Extraterritorial Measures Act 1984 (Can).

[131] See North, PM, *Essays in Private International Law* (1993) 201–223. At 202, North quotes the Lord Chancellor's statement to the House of Lords that 'a substantial proportion of the bodies which commented on the Consultative Paper [on the draft Convention] felt that a Convention might be harmful in view of the very high damages awarded by American juries, especially in personal injury and product liability cases; and that it would not be possible to devise any means of mitigating the enforcement of such judgments which would not be excessively difficult to operate in practice'. See also Baade, HW, 'An Overview of Transnational Parallel Litigation: Recommended Strategies' (1981) 1 The Review of Litigation 191, 194.

[132] von Mehren, AT (n 17 above) 1046–1050 stresses that similarity in the institutional characteristics of the administration of justice of participating states is a vital element for the achievement of a *convention double*. See also Baer, T, 'Injunctions Against Prosecution of Litigation Abroad: Towards a Transnational Approach' (1984–5) 37 Stanford Law Review 155, 158 n 8.

accession, these have done little to alter the essential scheme of the Convention or its core concepts.[133] It is certainly a matter open to conjecture whether agreement as to the form and basic structure of the Brussels Convention would have been as readily attainable had all of the ultimate Contracting States been party to the original drafting process. This is particularly so with regard to the United Kingdom and the Republic of Ireland, the nature and philosophy of whose national jurisdictional rules differ markedly from those of Contracting States in the civil law tradition.[134] One member of the British delegation responsible for negotiating the terms of the United Kingdom's accession to the Convention has stated that 'the issues raised by acceptance of the Brussels Convention proved to be many, far-reaching, and in some cases intractable'.[135] Accession to the Convention was not optional for the United Kingdom.[136] States not so compelled by such extraneous considerations as a desire to join the European Union may be far less likely to accede to a convention in the face of such obstacles and felt incompatibility.

3.54 The practical feasibility of securing agreement to a *convention double* may be compounded by the fact that, although it would obviously be hoped that all contracting states would afford the terms of any convention an internationalist interpretation,[137] it must be ultimately desirable that there be a court or tribunal whose decisions as to the convention's scope and meaning are authoritative and binding. The European Court of Justice obviously represents such a body in the context of Regulation 44/2001 and the Brussels (but not the Lugano) Convention.[138] However, in the context of the wider convention envisaged, the creation of such a supranational court or the investiture of an existing body such as the International Court of Justice with jurisdiction to provide authoritative guidance on questions arising under such a convention must be regarded as an extremely remote possibility.

3.55 In considering questions of the practical feasibility of securing widespread agreement to a *convention double* governing civil jurisdiction and judgments, it must be borne in mind that the impetus for entry into the

---

[133] A very useful summary of the amendments to the Convention over time is provided by Newman, KL, 'The 1968 Brussels Convention and Subsequent Developments' in Miller, DLC and Beaumont, PR, *The Option of Litigating in Europe* (1993) 6–12.

[134] See the Schlosser Report [1979] OJ C59/71, 97–98 but cf Kennett, W, '*Forum Non Conveniens* in Europe' (1995) 54 CLJ 552. This perception also emerges strongly and tellingly in Newman's account of negotiations prior to the United Kingdom's accession and subsequent accessions: see Newman, KL in Miller, DLC and Beaumont, PR, ibid.

[135] ibid 2.

[136] See para 3.55 below.

[137] *James Buchanan & Co Ltd v Babco Forwarding and Shipping (UK) Ltd* [1978] AC 141, 152 per Lord Wilberforce; [1977] QB 208, 221 per Roskill LJ.

[138] See s 3(1) of the Civil Jurisdiction and Judgments Act 1982.

Brussels Convention was not simply what has been suggested to be the theoretical desirability of such an arrangement but rather the far more compelling pressures of European unification. As has been seen, entry into the Convention was in fact mandated by Article 293 (formerly 220) of the Treaty of Rome of 1957. For states other than the original six of the European Economic Community, a similar compulsion was supplied by making accession to the Brussels Convention a precondition to membership of the European Union.[139] While there was no similar legal compulsion for members of the EFTA states to enter into the parallel Lugano Convention, economic and political pressures due to EFTA's geographical propinquity to the European Union undoubtedly influenced the decision to enter into the parallel convention.[140] The decision was doubtless also facilitated by the essentially common legal heritage of both the EFTA states and the majority of the member states of the European Union.

The practical difficulties in securing a convention along the lines of **3.56** Regulation 44/2001 are confirmed by historical precedent and recent experience. Previous and far less ambitious conventions than the one envisaged have been unable to achieve support resulting in ratification. Thus the Hague Convention of 1 February 1971 on the Recognition and Enforcement of Foreign Judgments in Civil and Commercial Matters and Additional Protocol, a *convention simple*, has to date only been ratified by The Netherlands, Cyprus, and Portugal.[141] Lipstein has observed that this Convention's structure 'leaves a wide choice of solutions to contracting States, and the addition of a Protocol which is of a persuasive character, only show[s] up the wide differences among the original parties to the Convention.'[142] In this context, the Hague Convention may be contrasted to the Scandinavian Convention for the Recognition and Enforcement of Judgments, the success of which has been largely attributed to the homogeneous nature of the laws and legal traditions of the member states.[143] That so little agreement was possible in relation to a *convention simple* such as the Hague Convention of 1 February 1971 presented a strong basis for scepticism about the likely future prospects of agreement to a *convention double* where, as has been seen, in terms of principles of national jurisdiction, much more is required to be yielded.

---

[139] Article 63 of the Convention provides that 'any State which becomes a member of the European Economic Community [as it then was] shall be required to accept this Convention'.

[140] See the Jenard/Möller Report [1990] OJ C189/57.

[141] Lipstein, K (n 17 above) 644 and 650–651.

[142] ibid 644.

[143] Philip, A, 'The Scandinavian Conventions on Private International Law' [1959] I Recueil des Cours 245, especially 325–341.

3.57 Notwithstanding the considerable practical obstacles in the way of securing agreement to an effective and wide-ranging convention governing the allocation of jurisdiction in transnational civil and commercial disputes and providing for recognition and enforcement of judgments based upon such jurisdiction, at the Centenary Session of the Hague Conference of May 1993 it was agreed to convene a Special Commission in mid-1994 to discuss a United States initiative for a new Hague Convention on the Recognition and Enforcement of Foreign Judgments. While the American delegation at this Session envisaged that this would be a *convention simple* and identified certain bases of jurisdiction which would and would not warrant the recognition and enforcement of any foreign judgment founded upon them, a proposal was subsequently presented to the Special Commission in 1994 in the form of a draft *convention double*, adopting the Lugano Convention as its model.[144] Between then and 2001, significant progress appeared to be being made in the negotiation of a global *convention double* prescribing heads of jurisdiction and providing for ready enforcement of judgments by member states.[145] By 2002, however, the hopes of that initiative appeared to have been dashed when agreement was ultimately unable to be achieved as to mutually acceptable bases of jurisdiction. Particularly controversial appeared to be the 'doing business' jurisdictional basis propounded by the United States delegation. A change of United States administration also appears to have played a role in terms of dampening the project's ambition with reference to the breadth of its coverage, namely a *convention double* for civil and commercial matters.

3.58 Even if there were a common will and desire to enter into a genuinely international convention regulating jurisdiction and the enforcement of foreign judgments, it must further be doubted whether Regulation 44/2001, as the most obvious precedent, would provide the most suitable and acceptable model. Not only in its conception, but also in its interpretation and development,[146] is it a profoundly European instrument, tailored to specific European concerns[147] and reflecting continental legal traditions such as the clear dividing line between civil and commercial

---

[144] These developments were briefly noted at (1993) 28 Texas International Law Journal 531, 537.

[145] An account of these developments and a copy of the text of the proposed Convention as at 30 October 1999 is contained in Chapter 8 of Barnett, PR (n 79 above).

[146] See, for example, Case 12/76, *Industrie Tessili Italiana Como v Dunlop AG* [1976] ECR 1473, 1484 where the European Court of Justice stressed that not only was the Convention to be interpreted by reference to its principles and objectives but also with regard to its relationship with the EEC Treaty.

[147] See Kohler, C (n 128 above) 565 who refers to a common description of the Convention as a 'European Law of Procedure'.

law, on the one hand, and public law, on the other.[148] It adopts as a central element a notion of domicile that is foreign to common law countries.[149] But perhaps the clearest point of distinction between the common law and civil law traditions enshrined in Regulation 44/2001 lies in the absence of any discretion in the assumption and exercise of jurisdiction under the Regulation,[150] a precept that may even operate to confine an English court's discretion in cases apparently beyond the Regulation's territorial sphere of competence[151] and which, if held so to do,[152] would further underline the sacrifices of jurisdictional principle and tradition originally entailed in accession to the Brussels Convention. It is difficult to imagine that other common law jurisdictions which place great store in the discretion to accept, maintain, or reject jurisdiction would readily cede such control over the exercise of jurisdiction in a transnational case. Moreover, some jurisdictions, of which the United States stands out as the most prominent and important example, would appear in their case law at least not wholeheartedly to accept the Convention's *grundnorm*, namely the principle that the prima facie appropriate forum in which a defendant may be sued is that of its domicile. There is a positive and a negative reason for this position, both of which tend to confirm the view advanced by one Canadian commentator that questions of judicial jurisdiction are 'deeply political.'[153]

[148] See the Schlosser Report [1979] OJ C59/71, 83–84. Its European flavour is highlighted by Dr Ong's magnum opus, *Cross Border Litigation within ASEAN* (1997), which considers in exhaustive detail areas where the Brussels Convention would require adaptation were it to be adopted as a core or base model for ASEAN.

[149] Schlosser Report [1979] OJ C59/71, 95–97. For a discussion of the differences between the common law and Convention understandings of the concept of domicile, see Collins, LA (ed) (n 3 above) 285–290.

[150] With the exception of Article 28. See, on this point, Newman, KL in Miller, DLC and Beaumont, PR (n 133 above) 3. Kohler (n 128 above) 582 has observed that 'rigidity is in fact a characteristic of the system. It accords with the continental notion of legal certainty in questions of jurisdiction, which in some cases takes precedence over a more "equitable" solution.' For a different perspective, to the effect that commonly assumed differences between the civil law and common law in relation to the discretionary assumption of jurisdiction may be overstated, see Kennett, W (n 134 above).

[151] Compare Collins, LA, 'Forum Non Conveniens and the Brussels Convention' (1990) 106 LQR 535 with Briggs, A, 'Forum Non Conveniens and the Brussels Convention Again' (1991) 107 LQR 180 and see further discussion of this issue at paras 4.62 pp below.

[152] In *Re Harrods (Buenos Aries) Ltd* [1992] Ch 72, the question of the extent to which English courts retain a discretion to decline jurisdiction was referred to the European Court of Justice: Case 314/92, *Ladenimor v Intercomfinanz*. This case subsequently settled and the reference was withdrawn so that the Court of Appeal's decision in *Re Harrods* to the effect that an element of discretion survives where an English domiciliary is sued in England and the natural forum is a non-member state represents the state of the law at present: see paras 4.62–4.66 below. The question has been referred again to the European Court of Justice in *Owusu v Jackson* [2002] ECWA Civ 877.

[153] Black, V, 'The Other Side of *Morguard*: New Limits on Judicial Jurisdiction' (1993) 22 Canadian Business Law Journal 4, 14–17.

3.59 The positive reason arises out of the notion that a state's courts exist primarily for the benefit and protection of its citizens who, apart from anything else, support them with their taxes.[154] Accordingly, their right of access should not be lightly denied, an argument which is made powerfully and not surprisingly by the American trial lawyers' lobby.[155] While few would advocate this as an absolute policy,[156] it is significant that, in the leading decision of the United States Supreme Court in this area, it was stated that 'when the [plaintiff's] home forum has been chosen it is reasonable to assume this choice is convenient'.[157] This bias comports with an earlier assessment of state practice by Professor, now Justice, Ginsburg:

> Although important efforts to acquaint jurists with foreign procedural systems and to improve judicial assistance among nations have been made in recent years, legislatures as well as courts are understandably reluctant to force domiciliaries to litigate abroad by withholding a forum at home.[158]

3.60 The philosophy reflected in this observation and the Supreme Court's decision in *Piper Aircraft Co v Reyno* has also manifested itself in a number of decisions of the High Court of Australia which draw attention to a court's 'obligation to exercise jurisdiction'.[159] In *Oceanic Sun Line Special Shipping Co Inc v Fay*,[160] a case which provides an extremely clear example of a national court's desire and willingness to make its courts available for a national plaintiff, Brennan J observed that:

> Generally speaking, it is of the nature of a legal right that the person in whom it is vested is entitled to invoke the State's power to enforce it. For that purpose the courts are at the service of litigants, and the rule of law rests on the courts' duty to exercise their jurisdiction when litigants invoke it.[161]

---

[154] This argument is explored by Wolinsky, MO, 'Forum Non Conveniens and American Plaintiffs in the Federal Courts' (1980) 47 University of Chicago Law Review 373, 388–393.

[155] See, for example, Kennelly, JJ, 'Choice of Forums in Tort Cases (and Some Controversial Suggestions)' (1992) 36 Trial Lawyers' Guide 172, especially 181–199. See also *The Atlantic Star* [1974] AC 436, 475 per Lord Simon, who spoke of 'unrestricted access to the seat of judgment'.

[156] For academic criticism see, for example, Freedman, W, *Foreign Plaintiffs in Products Liability Actions* (1988) 26.

[157] *Piper Aircraft Co v Reyno* 454 US 235, 125–126 (1981). See also *Olympic Corp v Société Générale* 462 F 2d 376, 378 (2nd Cir, 1972). cf *Mizokami Brothers of Arizona, Inc v Baychem Corp* 556 F 2d 975, 978 (8th Cir, 1977), cert denied 434 US 1035.

[158] Ginsburg, RB, 'The Competent Court in Private International Law: Some Observations on Current Views in the United States' (1965) 20 Rutgers Law Review 89, 99.

[159] *Voth v Manildra Flour Mills Pty Ltd* (1990) 171 CLR 538, 560.

[160] (1988) 165 CLR 197.

[161] ibid 239; see also 252 per Deane J: 'It is a basic tenet of our jurisprudence that, where jurisdiction exists, access to the courts is a right.'

More recently, in *Renault v Zhang*,[162] the High Court of Australia refused to stay proceedings commenced by a permanent resident in circumstances where the only connection with the forum of New South Wales (or any other Australian State for that matter) was the fact that the plaintiff resided in New South Wales and returned there for further treatment after sustaining injuries in New Caledonia.

The approach manifested in these cases is to be contrasted to that of the **3.61** Brussels Convention and Regulation 44/2001. In *Dumez France SA v Hessische Landesbank*,[163] the European Court of Justice referred to the 'hostility of the Convention towards the attribution of jurisdiction to the courts of the plaintiff's domicile'.[164]

The negative reason which stands against the central philosophy under- **3.62** pinning Article 2 of the Brussels Convention and Regulation 44/2001, namely the prima facie appropriateness of suing a defendant in its place of domicile, is that there is simply no acceptance in common law jurisdictions of the blanket proposition that it is always appropriate to sue a defendant in the courts of its country of domicile. The contrast in this regard to civilian notions is such that the decision of the House of Lords in *MacShannon v Rockware Glass Ltd*[165] and that of the United States Supreme Court in *Piper Aircraft Co v Reyno*[166] have been described as 'astonishing to continental eyes'.[167] Continental lawyers may have found even more astonishing the view of the dissentients in *Dow Chemical Co v Castro Alfaro*.[168] Their view, which argued for the application of the doctrine of *forum non conveniens* and which, it is thought, would now prevail,[169] was characterized by Justice Doggett in colourful but not factually inaccurate terms as being to the effect that it was:

inconvenient and *unfair* for [Costa Rican] farmworkers allegedly suffering permanent physical and mental injuries ... to seek redress by suing a multinational corporation in a court three blocks away from its world headquarters and another corporation, which operates in Texas this country's largest chemical plant.[170]

---

[162] (2002) 187 ALR 1.   [163] Case C–220/88 [1990] ECR I–49.

[164] ibid 79; see also Case C–89/91, *Shearson Lehman Hutton Inc v TVB Gmbh* [1993] ECR I–139, 187.

[165] [1978] AC 795.

[166] (1981) 454 US 235.

[167] Verheul, JP, 'The Forum (Non) Conveniens in English and Dutch Law and Under Some International Conventions' (1986) 35 ICLQ 413, 415.

[168] 786 SW2d 674 (Tex, 1986).

[169] This is because the majority's decision to the effect that the doctrine of *forum non conveniens* did not exist in Texas was based on an interpretation of the Texas Civil Practice and Remedies Code which has now been amended expressly to confirm the existence of the doctrine in that State: see further paras 4.74 ff below.

[170] 786 SW (2d) 674, 680 per Justice Doggett.

3.63 In this context, there might also be noted the High Court of Australia's decision in *CSR v Cigna Insurance Australia*,[171] where CSR, a company incorporated in New South Wales and having its head office in Sydney, succeeded in having proceedings commenced in the Supreme Court of New South Wales by a syndicate of insurers, the lead of which in fact also had its head office in the same street at CSR's Sydney office, stayed in favour of proceedings which CSR had commenced shortly beforehand in New Jersey. *The Nile Rhapsody*[172] provides another English example of acceptance of a *forum non conveniens* motion resulting in a stay of English proceedings in circumstances where 'the defendant's place of business is in England, and they have a firm and solid connection with this country'.[173]

3.64 The unsuccessful attempt to sue Union Carbide in America in the wake of the Bhopal chemical disaster[174] provides another example of the common law's refusal to be fettered by the maxim *actor sequitur forum rei*, so central to the civil law's jurisdictional traditions and, as has been seen, of pre-eminent importance in the context of the Brussels Convention and Regulation 44/2001. Cases such as *Dow Chemical* and *Union Carbide* have certainly provoked extensive academic debate about the propriety of United States multinationals invoking the doctrine of *forum non conveniens* with a view to minimizing their liability[175] and there is an undoubted element of paradox, not to say blatant strategic manoeuvring (on the part of both parties), in cases where a foreign plaintiff desires to litigate in the United States and an American defendant seeks a stay in favour of proceedings in another forum. While the academic debate cuts in both directions, the result in *Union Carbide* and the minority position in *Dow Chemical* are hardly maverick decisions and there has been no indication from the courts that applications for the staying of a suit made by United States domiciled defendants in an appropriate case are illegitimate. In the case of corporate defendants, reluctance by common law courts fully to embrace the maxim *actor sequitur forum rei* may also be explained by reference to the fact that corporate domicile is frequently highly artificial or contrived, influenced for example by consideration of the taxation conditions in a particular jurisdiction.

---

[171] (1997) 189 CLR 345.   [172] [1992] 2 Lloyd's Rep 399, 413.

[173] Hirst J, whose decision was upheld on appeal ([1994] 1 Lloyd's Rep 382), stated that 'the place of business of the respective parties is an entirely neutral consideration'. cf *Banco Atlantico SA v The British Bank of the Middle East* [1990] 2 Lloyd's Rep 504, 510 per Bingham LJ.

[174] *In re Union Carbide Corp* 634 F Supp 842 (SDNY, 1986).

[175] Compare, for example, Kennelly, JJ (n 155 above) with Mitnick, LA, 'Multinationals Fight Back with the Doctrine of Forum Non Conveniens' (1989) Defense Counsel Journal 391; Prince, P, 'Bhopal, Bougainville and OK Tedi: Why Australia's Forum Non Conveniens Approach is Better' (1998) 47 ICLQ 573.

A further reason why Regulation 44/2001 or a variant thereon would be **3.65** unlikely to secure the support of countries such as the United States is that it permits national rules of exorbitant jurisdiction to be exercised against non-contracting state domiciled defendants. Moreover, it invests such jurisdiction with great potency by making judgments given in the exercise of such exorbitant jurisdiction enforceable in all other member states. Unless there was widespread accession to a convention containing this feature, which would largely nullify its discriminatory effect, to subscribe to such a convention could legitimately be seen to be tantamount to a diplomatic affront to other friendly but non-signatory states.[176] The hostile reaction of many American commentators to this aspect of the Brussels Convention casts doubt upon its acceptability as a wider paradigm.[177] The diplomatic price of acceding to a convention with such a blatantly discriminatory feature might reasonably be considered to be not worth paying.

The conclusion that one is drawn to is that, notwithstanding the obvious **3.66** theoretical attractions of a convention which allocates jurisdiction in transnational disputes, anticipates and addresses the peculiar problem of concurrent proceedings, and greatly facilitates the recognition and enforcement of foreign judgments, the practical obstacles in the path of the achievement of such a convention are all but insuperable. The success in establishing such an arrangement in the form of the Brussels Convention is to be largely explained by the larger political context in which it had its genesis. Subsequent accession to it by states joining the European Community is also to be explained by reference to these larger political concerns. Further, it has been seen that original consensus as to the Brussels Convention's core concepts was largely due to the common legal heritage of the original parties to it. The influence of that heritage on the ultimate form of the Brussels Convention, moreover, makes it unlikely that it could serve as a model for any broader convention for it differs in certain fundamental respects from the established approach to jurisdiction in common law jurisdictions in particular. Historical experience in turn highlights the very great difficulty in securing meaningful agreement to a global *convention double.*

---

[176] It is true that Article 59 of the Convention (Article 72 of the Regulation) mitigates against the harshness of this rule and the possible damage to diplomatic relations to a certain extent by permitting bilateral treaties to be entered into providing for the non-recognition in the member state of an exorbitantly grounded judgment of another member state against a domiciliary of the third state.

[177] See, for example, von Mehren, AT (n 17 above) 1059, who described the fact that judgments based on exorbitant jurisdiction are automatically enforceable around member states as 'the single most regressive step that has occurred in international recognition and enforcement practice this century'. See also Nadelmann, KH, 'Common Market Assimilation of Laws and the Outer World' (1964) 58 American Journal of International Law 724.

3.67 The pessimistic analysis offered above concerning the likelihood of a meaningful international convention to govern questions of venue in transnational litigation makes it necessary to consider common law responses to the problems of concurrent jurisdiction, multiple proceedings, and forum shopping in transnational litigation. The remainder of this chapter essays that task.

III. COMMON LAW REGULATION OF JURISDICTION

3.68 The Brussels Convention did not come into force in the United Kingdom until 1 January 1987. Up until that time, the rules in relation to the assumption of jurisdiction in transnational disputes were governed exclusively by rules of court and a body of common law principles that had built up around those rules. Those rules continue to play an important role, however, for unlike the Rome Convention on the Law Applicable to Contractual Obligations, for example, which supplants the common law rules for choice of law in contract, the advent of the Brussels Convention and, now, Regulation 44/2001 has effected a multiplication of the English rules of jurisdiction.[178]

3.69 Article 4 of the Regulation provides that 'if the defendant is not domiciled in a member state, the jurisdiction of the courts of each member state shall, subject to Articles 22 and 23, be determined by the law of that member state'.[179] Thus the common law rules continue to apply, albeit by virtue of the Regulation's diktat, to situations where the defendant is not domiciled in a member state.[180] They are of particular importance in the context of this book for, as has already been seen, a favourite destination for the concerted forum shopper is the United States of America. They are obviously also of importance for those common law countries including Canada, New Zealand, Australia, India, Singapore, Malaysia, and Brunei that are not party to the Lugano Convention on Jurisdiction and Judgments.

3.70 The first part of this section of the chapter notes the common law's traditional response to arguments by defendants seeking to have proceedings stayed in favour of another forum. It will be seen that English and common law courts following their lead were notoriously unsympathetic to arguments to the effect that trial in England (or the relevant

---

[178] See, generally, Briggs, A and Rees, P (n 2 above).
[179] Articles 22 and 23 relate to certain limited situations in which relevant courts of member states are to have exclusive jurisdiction regardless of the defendant's domicile.
[180] Unless domiciled in Denmark (or otherwise involving a connection with Denmark), in which case the Brussels Convention continues to apply.

Commonwealth jurisdiction) would be inconvenient and inappropriate in light of the factual circumstances of the case, even if proceedings in another jurisdiction between the same parties were also pending. This attitude has undergone a major revision in the course of the last thirty years, culminating (with the conspicuous exception of Australia), in conceptual terms, in the emergence of the notion of the 'natural forum' and acceptance of the doctrine of *forum non conveniens*. That development is traced and an examination is made of the policies underpinning it. A final section examines and seeks to answer various conceptual criticisms made of the natural forum and the doctrine of *forum non conveniens*.

1. The Traditional Common Law Approach

'We have no sort of right, moral or legal, to take away from a plaintiff any **3.71** real chance he may have of advantage', stated Bowen LJ in *Peruvian Guano Co v Bockwoldt*.[181] Some ninety years later, Lord Denning MR observed that 'if a plaintiff considers that the procedure of our courts, or the substantive law of England, may hold advantages for him superior to that of any other country, he is entitled to bring his action here'.[182] These two dicta reflect what was the consistent and generous disposition which English courts (and Commonwealth courts following their lead)[183] displayed towards plaintiffs who had 'regularly' commenced proceedings in England, that is to say, plaintiffs who had commenced proceedings by serving the defendant with process within the territorial confines of the given forum. And this was the case 'though every fact arose abroad, and the dispute was between foreigners'.[184] All that was required was the defendant's presence (or that of any ship) within the jurisdiction, however accidental or fortuitous this presence might be.

In *The Atlantic Star*,[185] Lord Denning stated that 'it may be that the plaintiff **3.72** is able to catch the defendant here when he is on a short visit . . . or to arrest his ship when it puts into an English port for a few hours. But so long as he can catch him here, he is entitled as of right to bring his action here.' There was little chance for a defendant so served with process to object successfully to an English court's assumption and exercise of jurisdiction.

---

[181] (1883) 23 ChD 225, 234; see also 230 per Jessel MR.

[182] *The Atlantic Star* [1973] 1 QB 364, 382.

[183] See, for example, *Maritime Insurance Co Ltd v Geelong Harbour Trust Commissioners* (1908) 6 CLR 194.

[184] *Jackson v Spittall* (1870) LR 5 CP 542, 549; see also *The Atlantic Star* [1973] 1 QB 364, 382 per Lord Denning MR: 'This right to come here is not confined to Englishmen. It extends to any friendly foreigner.' For early cases permitting 'aliens' to commence proceedings in England, see *Melan v Duke de Fitzjames* (1797) 1 B & P 138; *De la Vega v Vianna* (1830) 1 B & Ad 284; *Worms v De Valdor* (1880) 49 LJ Ch 261.

[185] [1973] 1 QB 364, 382.

However tenuously connected the case with England and however inappropriate it would be for the plaintiff's claim to be adjudicated upon in English courts, the traditional approach of the common law was only to grant a stay of proceedings if the defendant could demonstrate that their continuance would be 'vexatious or oppressive' and that a stay would not work an injustice to the plaintiff. This qualification, often associated with the judgment of Scott LJ in *St Pierre v South American Stores (Gath and Chaves) Ltd*[186] but in truth dating back more than fifty years earlier,[187] was construed by the courts in an extremely narrow manner, making 'any application for a stay ... purely academic'.[188]

3.73 The 'vexatious and oppressive' formula, alternatively referred to *passim* as the '*St Pierre* test', was defined negatively in the sense that, if the plaintiff could point to even the most slender advantage in favour of continuing in England, it was inferred that the proceedings were not vexatious or oppressive. In *Hyman v Helm*,[189] Brett MR stated that 'if it is of some advantage to him [plaintiff], it is not right for the other party to say that the bringing it is vexatious and oppressive as against him'.[190] Such advantages could be either procedural or substantive, in terms of the remedy available. In *McHenry v Lewis*,[191] Jessel MR gave the illustration of a plaintiff who 'might have a personal remedy in one country and a remedy only against the goods in another'.[192] In *Hyman v Helm*,[193] Bowen LJ considered that if a forum offered superior facility both of procedure before judgment and execution of judgment once obtained, then institution of proceedings in that forum would not be vexatious or oppressive, *even if proceedings in another jurisdiction were also on foot.*

3.74 The existence of a single advantage to a plaintiff effectively immunized an action from the taint of vexation or oppression.[194] Indeed, it was sufficient to negative vexation or oppression if the plaintiff merely *thought* that proceedings in England offered some advantage—'an unsubstantiated but bona fide belief by the plaintiff or his legal advisers in an advantage to be obtained for him by suing in the English courts might be a sufficient

---

[186] [1936] 1 KB 382, 398.

[187] *McHenry v Lewis* (1882) 22 ChD 397; *Peruvian Guano Co v Bockwoldt* (1883) 23 ChD 225.

[188] *The Atlantic Star* [1973] 1 QB 364, 385 per Phillimore LJ.

[189] (1883) 24 ChD 531.

[190] ibid 538. This case in fact involved the question whether foreign proceedings were 'vexatious and oppressive' but the analysis of this concept is pertinent.

[191] (1882) 22 ChD 397, 401.

[192] This example approaches the factual circumstances of *Peruvian Guano Co v Bockwoldt* (1883) 23 ChD 225.

[193] (1883) 24 ChD 531, 543–544.

[194] cf *The Mali Ivo* (1869) LR 2 A & E 356, referred to at para 3.112 below.

answer to the defendant's application for a stay'[195]—and there was a virtual presumption that this was the case. In *Ionian Bank Ltd v Couvreur*,[196] Davies J observed that 'these plaintiffs obviously think that it will be advantageous for them to go on with their English action; for otherwise they would not be pressing on with it'.[197] Application of the traditional rules made it unsurprising that a stay was refused in this case. It is plain that forum shopping for either procedural or substantive advantages was thus not only sanctioned but positively encouraged by English courts, for a plaintiff could resist an application for a stay of proceedings by demonstrating the efficacy of its forum shopping expedition.[198]

The assessment of vexation and oppression by reference to the question **3.75** whether trial in a given forum offered any advantage or indeed hope of advantage to the plaintiff also meant that considerations of inconvenience to a defendant as a result of proceeding in that forum were not thought germane to the enquiry into vexation or oppression. In *St Pierre*,[199] after noting that there were 'several strong reasons for contending that the Chilean Court is a more convenient forum', Scott LJ observed that 'these grounds go only to convenience; they do not come near to establishing the allegations of the summons',[200] namely that the proceedings in England were vexatious and oppressive. Inconvenience, even of a considerable nature, was not regarded as coextensive with vexation or oppression. The Court of Appeal in *Chaney v Murphy*[201] reaffirmed this viewpoint, stating that 'inconvenience to the defendants cannot of itself afford any ground for staying an action properly and *bona fide* brought according to the rules'.[202]

The respect which was afforded a plaintiff's choice of forum was such that **3.76** the plaintiff's concomitant freedom in that regard was often couched in

---

[195] *MacShannon v Rockware Glass Ltd* [1978] AC 795, 812 per Lord Diplock, describing the traditional approach of the English courts. See also *The Atlantic Star* [1974] AC 436, 453 per Lord Reid.

[196] [1969] 1 WLR 781.

[197] ibid 787. See also *Peruvian Guano Co v Bockwoldt* (1883) 23 ChD 225, 232 per Lindley LJ.

[198] Fawcett, JJ, 'Forum Shopping—Some Questions Answered' (1984) 35 NILQ 141, 148: 'The greater the advantage (that is, the more adept the plaintiff is at forum shopping) the less likely there is to be a stay.'

[199] [1936] 1 KB 382.

[200] ibid 397.

[201] (1948) 64 TLR 489.

[202] ibid 492; see also *Peruvian Guano Co v Bockwoldt* (1883) 23 ChD 225, 230 per Jessel MR; *Maharanee of Baroda v Wildenstein* [1972] 2 QB 283, 297–298 per Stephenson LJ; *The Atlantic Star* [1973] 1 QB 364, 381 per Lord Denning MR. cf *Logan v Bank of Scotland (No 2)* [1906] 1 KB 141, 152 per Sir Gorrel Barnes P; *The Lucile Bloomfield* [1964] 1 Lloyd's Rep 324, 329 per Hewson J.

terms of a *right*, even a right to commence parallel proceedings in different jurisdictions. In *Peruvian Guano Co v Bockwoldt*,[203] Jessel MR stated that a plaintiff 'has the *right* to bring an action, and if there are substantial reasons to induce him to bring the two actions, why should we deprive him of that *right*?'[204] Similarly, in *McHenry v Lewis*,[205] another case where concurrent proceedings were on foot, Cotton LJ declared that the courts should be cautious in restraining a plaintiff from proceeding 'when he has a *right* of action as against the defendant'.[206] Where a plaintiff had only commenced one set of proceedings, in England, however tenuous their connection to that jurisdiction, the plaintiff's 'right' was even more absolute. Thus Dicey stated:

When the defendant is in England, the jurisdiction of the Court is not discretionary; the plaintiff has a right to demand that if it exist it shall be exercised.[207]

3.77 Any interference with a plaintiff's ability to exercise or enjoy this 'right' was considered to be a 'very serious thing'.[208] Correlative to a plaintiff's *right* was the court's *duty* 'to award him the redress to which he is entitled'.[209]

2. THE 'NATURAL FORUM'—EMERGENCE OF A CONCEPT

3.78 It has been seen above that the traditional approach of the English courts towards staying proceedings constituted something of an inducement towards forum shopping, or at least provided no effective bar, even in blatant cases.[210] For, so long as a plaintiff was able to serve the defendant while present in the jurisdiction, however fleeting or fortuitous that presence might be, there was little chance of a stay being secured. In *The Atlantic Star*,[211] in a passage the candour of which is only matched by the notoriety it subsequently attained, Lord Denning MR averred:

You may call this 'forum-shopping' if you please, but if the forum is England, it is a good place to shop in, both for the quality of the goods and the speed of service.[212]

3.79 That Lord Denning attached no moral disapprobation to this practice clearly proceeded from a particular view both of substantive principles of English law (including private international law) and the procedural

---

[203] (1883) 23 ChD 225.

[204] ibid 230 (emphasis added).

[205] (1882) 22 ChD 397.

[206] ibid 406 (emphasis added).

[207] Dicey AV, *The Conflict of Laws* (1st edn, 1896) 239.

[208] *In re Connolly Brothers Ltd* [1911] 1 Ch 731, 746 per Fletcher Moulton LJ.

[209] *The Atlantic Star* [1973] 1 QB 364, 381 per Lord Denning MR.

[210] *Oceanic Sun Line Special Shipping Co Inc v Fay* (1988) 165 CLR 197, 212 per Wilson and Toohey JJ.

[211] [1973] QB 364.

[212] ibid 382.

amenities and reputation of the English courts.[213] In the House of Lords, Lord Reid censored that view as unduly chauvinistic and emphasized the need for judicial comity.[214] The unusual circumstances of, and the decision in, *Maharanee of Baroda v Wildenstein*,[215] where the defendant was served during a brief visit from France to the Ascot races, together with the candour of Lord Denning's judgment in *The Atlantic Star*, combined to cast the traditional English rules in relation to the assumption and retention of jurisdiction in transnational cases in stark relief. Although open to conjecture, it is perhaps no coincidence that the revision of these rules commenced in the wake of these two decisions. The importance of this revision is reflected in the fact that the first of the House of Lords' decisions in this area, *The Atlantic Star*,[216] has been described by Lord Diplock as 'a landmark in the development of English law'.[217]

The reappraisal of the English rules regarding the staying of proceedings **3.80** regularly commenced within the jurisdiction was underpinned by a concern relating to the propriety of the practice of forum shopping. Some five years prior to *The Atlantic Star*, in the context of examining the appropriate choice of law rule for tort in *Boys v Chaplin*,[218] several of their Lordships had occasion to comment adversely on this practice, both Lords Hodson and Pearson expressing the view that it was in the interests of public policy to discourage it.[219] But if this was the case, then a fundamental incompatibility existed between the traditional 'St Pierre' rule relating to the staying of actions which, as has been seen, acted as an inducement towards, or at least provided no effective bar to, forum shopping and the policy of and interest in discouraging that practice. Robert Goff QC, counsel for the applicant in *The Atlantic Star*, was astute to this incongruity as one of his submissions records:

> As to the contention that the court will not grant a stay in order to deprive a plaintiff of an advantage, if, as is the case, it is the policy of English law to discourage forum shopping, then ipso facto that principle to be given effect to must deprive a plaintiff of an advantage because a plaintiff goes forum shopping for the very purpose of endeavouring to obtain an advantage.[220]

The House of Lords' response to this conundrum was to make the circum- **3.81** stances in which a defendant might obtain a stay easier to satisfy than on the *St Pierre* test, although initially the terms of this test were formally retained.[221] An advantage to the plaintiff in proceeding in England was

---

[213] See also *The Abidin Daver* [1983] 1 WLR 884, 889. [214] [1974] AC 436 , 453.
[215] [1972] 2 QB 283. [216] [1974] AC 436.
[217] *The Abidin Daver* [1984] AC 398, 407. [218] [1971] AC 356.
[219] ibid 378, and 401 and 406. [220] [1974] AC 436, 444.
[221] ibid 454 per Lord Reid, 468 per Lord Wilberforce, 477 per Lord Kilbrandon.

no longer decisive[222] and the defendant was put 'in the scales'.[223] A stay
was granted in this case in favour of the Commercial Court of Antwerp,
this revealingly being the first Admiralty action *in rem* ever to meet this
jurisdictional fate.[224] Significantly, also, Lord Reid's speech was informed
by a desire to curtail the practice of forum shopping, his Lordship observing that 'there have been many recent criticisms of "forum shopping" and
I regard it as undesirable'.[225]

3.82 The House of Lords' decision in *The Atlantic Star* set in train a quintes-
sentially common law process of judicial law-making.[226] The decisions in
MacShannon v Rockware Glass Ltd[227] and *The Abidin Daver*[228] were significant steps in the evolutionary process which culminated some twelve
years later with the decision of the House in *Spiliada Maritime Corporation
v Cansulex Ltd*.[229] This decision embraced as part of English law the
Scottish doctrine of *forum non conveniens* and elevated to centre stage the
concept of the 'natural forum'—described by one commentator as 'the
holy grail'.[230] It established that a stay would be granted if the defendant
could point to a forum other than England in which the case could most
suitably be tried for the interests of all the parties and the ends of
justice.[231] This jurisdiction was the 'natural forum' and would be identified by its nexus with the dispute. In short, *Spiliada* established that the
natural forum was that with which the action had 'the most real and
substantial connection'[232] and the adoption of the doctrine of *forum non
conveniens* was a form of 'self-denying ordinance under which the Court
will stay (or dismiss) proceedings in favour of another clearly more
appropriate forum'.[233]

3.83 The phrase 'the natural forum' is first found in one of the Scottish decisions followed in *Spiliada, Société du Gaz de Paris v Société Anonyme de*

---

[222] ibid 468–469 per Lord Wilberforce.
[223] ibid 454 per Lord Reid.
[224] See *The Atlantic Star* [1973] 1 QB 364, 385 per Phillimore LJ.
[225] [1974] AC 436, 454.
[226] *The Abidin Daver* [1984] AC 398, 408 per Lord Diplock.
[227] [1978] AC 795.
[228] [1984] AC 398.
[229] [1987] AC 460. It is not proposed to trace the path of that evolutionary development in
detail. That territory has been exhaustively covered: see, for example, Briggs, A, 'Forum Non
Conveniens—Now We Are Ten?' (1983) Legal Studies 74; Briggs, A, 'The Staying of Actions
on the ground of "Forum Non Conveniens" in England Today' [1984] 2 LMCLQ 227; Briggs,
A, 'Forum non Conveniens—An Update' [1985] 3 LMCLQ 360; Barma, A and Elvin, D,
'Forum Non Conveniens: Where To From Here?' (1985) 101 LQR 48; Schuz, R, 'Controlling
Forum Shopping: The Impact of MacShannon v Rockware Glass Ltd' (1986) 35 ICLQ 374.
[230] Nygh, P, in Nygh, P and McLachlan, C, *Transnational Tort Litigation* (1996) 92.
[231] [1987] AC 460, 480.
[232] ibid 477–478.
[233] *Airbus Industrie GIE v Patel* [1999] 1 AC 119, 132.

Navigation 'Les Armateurs Français'.[234] In this case, Lord Shaw stated that if 'there is a real unfairness to one of the suitors in permitting the choice of a *forum* which is not *the natural or proper forum* . . . then the doctrine of *forum non conveniens* is properly applied'.[235] The concept of 'the natural forum' was employed in all four of the House of Lords' decisions referred to in the previous paragraph and has entered into the vocabulary of the courts in this area of the law.[236] It is also significant to note that it was employed by Lord Pearson in *Boys v Chaplin*[237] in the context of describing forum shopping. He characterized that practice as involving:

a plaintiff by-passing his *natural forum* and bringing his action in some alien forum which would give him relief or benefits which would not be available to him in his *natural forum*.[238]

Although Lord Pearson referred to the *plaintiff's* natural forum, the concept which emerged from the line of decisions commencing with *The Atlantic Star* emphasized the objectivity of the exercise and thus focused on the natural forum, taking *all parties'* interests into account. Thus, the development of a jurisdictional test that permits the staying of proceedings when, in broad terms, they are not commenced in the natural forum has the salutary effect of also acting to prevent forum shopping.[239] The advantages of this development are explored below.

3. THE NATURAL FORUM—THE CONCEPT CONSIDERED

In a 1972 article on jurisdiction in transnational disputes, Pryles **3.84** concluded with the observation that a 'new general or all-embracing conception of jurisdiction is required'.[240] The conception which has emerged is that of the 'natural forum'. This section considers the concept of the natural forum in some detail and examines how the courts have employed and refined it since its ultimate recognition in *Spiliada*.

---

[234] 1926 SC (HL) 13.
[235] ibid 20 (emphasis added).
[236] *The Atlantic Star* [1974] AC 436, 453 per Lord Reid; *MacShannon* [1978] AC 795, 809, 811–812, and 815–816 per Lord Diplock, 818 and 820 per Lord Salmon, 826, 828–829, and 831 per Lord Keith; *The Abidin Daver* [1984] AC 398, 410–411 per Lord Diplock, 415 per Lord Keith; and *Spiliada* [1987] AC 460, 477–478 per Lord Goff.
[237] [1971] AC 356.
[238] ibid 401 (emphasis added); see also 406.
[239] *Voth v Manildra Flour Mills Pty Ltd* (1989) 15 NSWLR 513, 526 per Gleeson CJ.
[240] 'The Basis of Adjudicatory Competence in Private International Law' (1972) 21 ICLQ 61, 80. See also Granger, C, 'The Conflict of Laws and Forum Shopping: Some Recent Decisions on Jurisdiction and Free Enterprise in Litigation' (1974) 6 Ottawa Law Review 416, 417. Remarking on the problems of forum shopping and the difficulty of unifying domestic and conflicts rules, Granger concluded that 're-examination and perhaps reformation of our own rules relating to jurisdiction may be worthwhile'.

The Natural Forum, Fairness, and Forum Shopping

3.85 An examination of what is wrong with forum shopping serves at the same time to highlight what is attractive about the concept of the natural forum and the tool of *forum non conveniens* as a means of directing litigation into that forum. It was seen in Chapter 2 that, as a result of lack of uniformity at the levels of procedural law, substantive principle, and choice of law rules throughout the international legal system, very different results may obtain in the resolution of any given legal dispute according to the forum in which that dispute is tried. It is not surprising in this circumstance, therefore, that a plaintiff will seek to litigate in that forum which offers the best chances of success.[241] But if that in itself is not a matter for surprise, whether it should be a matter for concern or indignation[242] is another question.[243]

3.86 Lord Morris, who, together with Lord Simon, dissented in *The Atlantic Star*, clearly thought not, taking the view that it was not the province of the courts to make assessments of the propriety of a plaintiff's choice of forum—'[The plaintiff] believes that in the advancement or for the protection of his legitimate financial interests his prospects of success are better in this country than in Belgium. It is not our province to decide whether he is right or wrong.'[244] But if, as a result of a combination of the law's lack of uniformity and the existence of concurrent jurisdiction, the option of 'shopping' for a forum is a real and potentially significant one, why, it may legitimately be asked, should a plaintiff be able unilaterally to enhance its prospects of success by the choice of forum? Put another way, 'as a matter of abstract justice',[245] it seems intuitively offensive to notions of procedural fairness that 'the action goes for trial in the country thus selected by the plaintiff . . . [who] chooses the country which suits him best'.[246]

---

[241] See *The Reinbeck* (1889) 6 Asp MLC 366, 388 per Lord Esher MR: 'You may expect men of business to act as such, in a good stand up fight', cited by Lord Wilberforce in *The Atlantic Star* [1974] AC 436, 471.

[242] cf *The Atlantic Star* [1974] AC 436, 471 per Lord Simon who demurred on this matter. See also Juenger, FK, 'Environmental Damage' in Nygh, P and McLachlan, C, *Transnational Tort Litigation*, 213 who argues that, in environmental cases, a wide choice of forum avails a plaintiff of the socially useful opportunity of protecting the environment.

[243] See generally the exchange between Juenger, FK, 'What's Wrong with Forum Shopping?'; Opeskin, BR, 'The Price of Forum Shopping: A Reply to Professor Juenger'; and Juenger, FK, 'Forum Shopping: A Rejoinder' in (1994) 16 Sydney Law Review 5, 14, and 28 respectively. See also Brown, GD, 'The Ideologies of Forum Shopping—Why Doesn't a Conservative Court Protect Defendants?' (1993) 71 North Carolina Law Review 649, especially 666–675.

[244] [1974] AC 436, 459. See also 461.

[245] *Spiliada* [1985] 2 Lloyd's Rep 116, 135 per Oliver LJ.

[246] *The Atlantic Star* [1973] 1 QB 364, 382 per Lord Denning MR.

A large measure of the attraction in the doctrine of *forum non conveniens* is **3.87**
that it seeks to identify the 'tribunal, having competent jurisdiction, in
which the case may be tried more suitably for the interests of *all the parties*
and for the ends of justice',[247] not just that party which has the advantage
of instituting the litigation. The objectivity[248] of the quest for the natural
forum has the happy consequence expressed, somewhat ironically, by
Lord Denning that the plaintiff 'no longer wins the toss on every throw'[249]
as far as matters of choice of forum are concerned. Considerations of fairness and equity enter the picture.[250] This was made explicit by Lord Goff
in *de Dampierre v de Dampierre*.[251] In concluding that paragraph 9 of
Schedule 1 of the Matrimonial Proceedings Act 1973 represented a statutory equivalent of *forum non conveniens*, Lord Goff acknowledged that the
phrase 'balance of fairness' found in the statute identified the 'underlying
purpose' of the common law doctrine.[252] This sentiment is also reflected
in *Louvet v Louvet*, where Hunter JA stated that the court must 'try to
determine in each case which is the *fairer* jurisdiction to the parties collectively or, perhaps putting it more brutally, which overall produces the
least unjust result'.[253]

These analyses of the reason for the search for the natural forum, based **3.88**
upon notions of fairness, are consistent with the Scottish decisions upon
which *Spiliada* is so firmly based. As in Lord Shaw's judgment in *Société
du Gaz*,[254] Lord Sumner also emphasized the importance of an even-
handed approach as between the parties in relation to the choice of
forum.[255] In this, he echoed the sentiments of Lord Low in *Sim v
Robinow*[256] who stated that the plea of *forum non conveniens* applies 'whenever it can be shown that the case cannot, *consistently with fairness and
justice*, be tried in this country'.[257] The focus on fairness as between the
parties as to the choice of venue is mediated through the concept of the
natural forum. This analysis of the burden of *Spiliada* is supported by

---

[247] *Sim v Robinow* (1892) 19 R 665, 668 per Lord Kinnear (emphasis added).

[248] 'Simply to give the plaintiff his advantage at the expense of the defendant is not consistent with the objective approach inherent in Lord Kinnear's statement of principle in *Sim v
Robinow*': *Spiliada* [1987] AC 460, 482 per Lord Goff.

[249] *Smith Kline & French Laboratories Ltd v Bloch* [1983] 2 All ER 72, 78.

[250] Robertson, DW, 'Forum Non Conveniens in America and England: A Rather Fantastic
Fiction' (1987) 103 LQR 398, 425: 'the new forum non conveniens doctrine can be seen as
bringing a "fairness" dimension . . . to the issue of personal jurisdiction in England'. See also
Pryles, MC, 'Judicial Darkness on the Oceanic Sun' (1988) 62 ALJ 774 , 785 and 790.

[251] [1988] AC 92.　　　　　　　　　　　　　　　　　　　　　[252] ibid 108.

[253] [1990] 1 HKLR 670, 677 (emphasis added).　　　　　　[254] 1926 SC (HL) 13, 20.

[255] ibid 21.　　　　　　　　　　　　　　　　　　　　　　　　[256] (1892) 19 R 665.

[257] ibid 666 (emphasis added). For an even earlier reference to the need for fairness in the
choice of forum, see *Longworth v Hope* (1865) 3 M 1049, 1057 per Lord Deas.

Lord Goff's insistence that 'the question is not one of convenience, but of the suitability or appropriateness of the relevant jurisdiction'.[258]

3.89 It is important to appreciate that, for the most part, English courts and other common law courts that have adopted and applied *Spiliada* are not so concerned with the quest to identify the 'natural forum' that they will stay proceedings *of their own accord* if of the view that another forum merits the epithet 'natural'.[259] Nor will English courts generally override a contractual choice of forum in favour of the natural forum, even though the chosen forum would not otherwise constitute the natural forum.[260] It is plain that this concept only comes into play where the defendant objects to the assumption of jurisdiction. But it is suggested that this serves only to underline what animates the quest for the natural forum. That concept is designed to provide a neutral and objective solution to clashes between parties relating to the venue for the resolution of a transnational dispute— something of a tie-breaker in cases of contested jurisdiction and at the same time a corrective to the phenomenon of forum shopping. On this analysis, if the natural forum is conceived of as that which provides the fairest venue for the resolution of a transnational dispute, the forum nominated in an exclusive jurisdiction clause will become the natural forum, at least in a simple two party case.

Convenience and the Natural Forum

3.90 In the United States, application of the doctrine of *forum non conveniens* is designed primarily to point to the most 'convenient' forum for litigation.[261] Convenience in this context encompasses not only that of the parties but also that of the courts. This is most clearly borne out by the fact that one of the matters which an American court faced with a stay application may consider is the state of 'docket congestion' in that particular court.[262] In England and other common law jurisdictions that have adopted *Spiliada*, on the other hand, the 'convenience' of the parties, the

---

[258] [1987] AC 460, 475.

[259] 'If both parties are content to proceed here there is no need to object': *The Atlantic Star* [1974] AC 436, 453 per Lord Reid.

[260] An important qualification to this is in cases involving multiple parties, not all of whom are party to the jurisdiction agreement. See, for example, *Donohue v Armco Inc* [2002] 1 Lloyd's Rep 425 and *Bouygues Offshore SA v Caspian Shipping Co (Nos 1, 3, 4 and 5)* [1998] 2 Lloyd's Rep 461 and the discussion in paragraphs 4.146 ff and Chapter 5 below.

[261] 'The central purpose of any forum non conveniens inquiry is to ensure that 'the trial is convenient': *Piper Aircraft Co v Reyno* 454 US 235, 256 (1981).

[262] *Gulf Oil Corp v Gilbert* 330 US 501, 508–509 (1947). In *Lubbe v Cape plc* at first instance, Buckley J did not consider that *Spiliada* excluded the taking into account of these considerations: [2000] 1 Lloyd's Rep 139, 155 but this was denied by the House of Lords [2000] 1 WLR 1545; cf *James Hardie v Grigor* (1998) 45 NSWLR 20, 40–41.

court, or both is neither the reason behind adoption of the doctrine of *forum non conveniens* nor the cornerstone of the concept of the natural forum although it is plain that proceedings in a forum other than the natural forum may well be inconvenient to the defendant and even the plaintiff.[263] Considerations of convenience are certainly not central to the Scottish jurisprudence in this area.[264]

In *Spiliada*, adopting the definition offered by Lord Keith in both   **3.91** *MacShannon*[265] and *The Abidin Daver*,[266] Lord Goff identified the natural or most appropriate forum as that forum with which the action has 'the most real and substantial connection'.[267] In favouring this definition, his Lordship must be taken to have rejected Lord Diplock's equation in *MacShannon* of the natural forum with that forum in which 'justice can be done at substantially less inconvenience and expense' than England.[268] Consistent with the analysis advanced below, this difference is more than purely semantic.

In *Spiliada*, Lord Goff stated that, in its identification of the natural forum,   **3.92** the court must look to 'connecting factors' including the location and availability of witnesses, the place where the parties respectively reside or carry on business, and the law governing the relevant transaction.[269] Courts will place varying weight upon the significance of these factors. At least in commercial disputes, an element of scepticism may be justified when pro forma affidavits or witness statements are filed relating to inconvenience of witnesses having to travel and the need to move documents given that business travel is an everyday feature of international commerce.[270] The significance of the location of witnesses has more force with regard to third party witnesses who may include persons formerly employed but no longer under the control of the party who wishes to call that witness. The significance of the 'location' of witnesses may also be reduced by reason of advances in videoconferencing technology but experience teaches that, at least at its current stage of development, that is not a wholly satisfactory substitute for cross-examination of witnesses, at least where issues of credit are involved or the cross-examination is of any

---

[263] ibid 507.
[264] *Sim v Robinow* (1892) 19 R 665, 668 per Lord Kinnear; *Société du Gaz* 1926 SC (HL) 13, 22 per Lord Sumner.
[265] [1978] AC 795, 829.
[266] [1984] AC 398, 415.
[267] [1987] AC 460, 477–478. This is also the definition favoured by academic commentators: Briggs, A, 'Forum Non Conveniens—Now We Are Ten?' (1983) Legal Studies 74, 88; Schuz, R (n 229 above) 382; Barma, A and Elvin, D (n 229 above) 62.
[268] [1978] AC 795, 812. See also *The Abidin Daver* [1984] AC 398, 409.
[269] [1987] AC 460, 478.
[270] *Agar v Hyde* (2000) 201 CLR 552, 571.

great length of time. Differences in time zones may also generate a measure of unfairness if important evidence is required to be given in the very early hours of the morning.

3.93 Identification of the natural forum is not restricted in terms of a physical or geographical nexus and the situs of the natural forum may in some circumstances change over time. This emerges from *Spiliada* itself where Lord Goff concluded that what was critical in establishing England as the natural forum was the so-called 'Cambridgeshire' factor.[271] The 'Cambridgeshire' factor related to the fact that another set of proceedings had raised very similar issues to those likely to be in contention in *Spiliada* and, given their complexity and the detailed knowledge necessary to be acquired for such litigation combined with the fact that the same solicitors instructed by the same insurers were retained in both cases, the 'efficiency, expedition and economy' yielded by such expertise meant that litigation in England was in 'the objective interests of justice'.[272] The 'Cambridgeshire' factor necessarily did not arise or become of significance until well after the events giving rise to the dispute between the two parties involved.

3.94 Although Lord Goff eschewed the language of 'convenience' in *Spiliada*— 'it is most important not to allow it [the Latin *forum non conveniens*] to mislead us into thinking that the question at issue is one of "mere practical convenience" '[273]—it is evident that the indicia of the 'natural forum' which he identified will point to a venue which is convenient both for the parties and the court. But it is thought that the point of Lord Goff's disavowal of the language and notion of convenience was to underline why the courts are concerned to identify the natural forum. That is *not* to locate the most efficient and inexpensive venue for the disposition of litigation. Rather, as has been argued above, in circumstances where the parties have not themselves agreed to a forum, the principal rationale of the search for the natural forum is to achieve a measure of fairness by identifying it according to objective connecting factors. For example, it is the forum (in tort and property cases at least) that is likely to supply the governing law and it is not simply convenient, but, significantly, most fair for both parties, to have their dispute determined by a court whose

---

[271] [1987] AC 460, 484–486.

[272] ibid 486. It is interesting to note that no significance whatsoever was placed in a very similar circumstance in *MacShannon* where some 44 similar cases had been commenced in England involving many of the same solicitors on the plaintiffs' side: see [1978] AC 795, 813. For an American equivalent of the 'Cambridgeshire' factor, recommending retention of proceedings, see *Friends For All Children, Inc v Lockheed Aircraft Corp* 717 F 2d 602, 608–609 (DC Cir, 1983).

[273] [1987] AC 460, 475.

system of law supplies the governing law, in the procedural and institutional setting in which that law is designed to apply.[274]

The natural forum is *primarily* a neutral venue and secondarily a convenient one. It must be viewed not as the end in itself of English jurisdictional rules but rather as the means to a different end. In this light, in England and countries that have adopted *Spiliada*, the undoubted administrative efficiency and judicial convenience that follow from the process of identifying the natural forum are consequential benefits rather than the reason for the search for such a forum.[275] **3.95**

Comity, the Natural Forum, and Concurrent Litigation

It will be recalled that, in *The Atlantic Star*,[276] Lord Reid referred to the need to replace judicial chauvinism with judicial comity. In the context of the type of case under consideration (ie one with a transnational dimension), there will, *ex hypothesi*, be the prospect of multiple proceedings if, indeed, proceedings have not already been commenced in another jurisdiction at the time of the institution of the English action, a case of *lis alibi pendens*. Moreover, there will frequently be more than two parties involved in transnational litigation, as many shipping and insurance cases in particular demonstrate. This circumstance is apt to give rise to a complex array of claims, cross-claims, indemnity, and other third party proceedings, not all of which will necessarily be heard in the same forum. In some cases, there will not even be the possibility of hearing all aspects of the dispute in one forum. **3.96**

As was seen in paragraphs 1.26 ff above, multiple proceedings, treating the same or substantially the same subject matter, entail not only inefficiency and the waste of judicial resources through duplication[277] but also raise the highly unappealing prospect of inconsistent decisions, either on the facts or in relation to the legal consequences attaching to those facts, or both.[278] Indeed, according to Lord Kilbrandon, the simple articulation **3.97**

---

[274] cf *Renault v Zhang* (2002) 187 ALR 1, where the High Court of Australia, consistent with its own jurisprudence in relation to the granting of a stay of proceedings, plainly saw the significance of the applicability of foreign law in terms of convenience rather than objective fairness as between the parties.

[275] *Roberts v Hampton & Sons* [1989] 2 HKLR 89 provides a good example of considerations of convenience being subordinated to concerns of fairness as between the parties as to choice of forum and thus illustrates the true role of the doctrine of *forum non conveniens*.

[276] [1974] AC 436, 453.

[277] For a good example and description of the type of waste involved, see *Sterling Pharmaceuticals Pty Ltd v The Boots Company (Australia) Pty Ltd* (1992) 34 FCR 287, 292.

[278] Multiple proceedings may have been perfectly justifiable 'at a time when a judgment obtained in one country was of little use in any other': *The Atlantic Star* [1974] AC 436, 454 per Lord Reid.

of this predicament 'should be enough to invite the contemplation of some remedy for it'.[279] The importance of comity is that it requires an English court to take account of the possible impact of its assumption and retention of jurisdiction on proceedings or prospective proceedings in courts of other friendly states. They may affect the question of the location of the natural forum.

3.98 In calling for the replacement of judicial chauvinism with judicial comity, Lord Reid was referring *inter alia* to the scant regard which English jurisdictional rules had traditionally paid to the existence of concurrent litigation. It has already been seen that considerable latitude was afforded to a plaintiff's choice of forum, even where it chose to commence parallel proceedings in two jurisdictions.[280] If there was some advantage to be had in pursuing parallel proceedings (and this could be simply illustrated by virtue of the lack of 'identity of proceedings, remedies and benefits' in either jurisdiction),[281] then English courts would neither stay domestic proceedings nor restrain foreign proceedings on the grounds of vexation or oppression. In *The Tillie Lykes*,[282] Brandon J reflected the traditional approach of English courts to multiple proceedings, whether parallel or concurrent, in the sense that the plaintiff in one forum was defendant in the other:

> What this case involves . . . is the inherent disadvantage of having two sets of proceedings in two different countries in respect of the same subject-matter. The disadvantages involved in that situation, by themselves, have never hitherto been considered sufficient to justify a stay.[283]

3.99 Later he observed that 'it would no doubt be possible to have a doctrine of law under which the Court would regard the avoidance of a multiplicity of proceedings as something to be secured at all costs' but that 'such a doctrine is no part of the law of England'.[284] This attitude may in part be explained by reference to a sanguine expectation that the commercial pressures of settlement mean that multiple proceedings rarely eventuate

---

[279] ibid 474.
[280] Note, however, that the situation may have been different where both sets of proceedings were commenced in the Queen's Courts: *McHenry v Lewis* (1882) 22 ChD 397, 400–401 per Jessel MR; *Cohen v Rothfield* [1919] 1 KB 410, 414 per Scrutton LJ.
[281] *Cohen v Rothfield* [1919] 1 KB 410, 414 per Scrutton LJ.
[282] [1977] 1 Lloyd's Rep 124.
[283] ibid 126. This decision was endorsed by the Court of Appeal in *The Abidin Daver* [1983] 1 WLR 884. See also *Ionian Bank Ltd v Couvreur* [1969] 1 WLR 781, 787 per Davies J and *The Atlantic Star* [1974] AC 436, 469 per Lord Wilberforce.
[284] [1977] 1 Lloyd's Rep 124, 128. For cases illustrating this proposition, see *The Janera* [1928] P 55; *The London* [1931] P 14; *The Madrid* [1937] P 40; *The Quo Vadis* [1951] 1 Lloyd's Rep 425; *The Monte Urbasa* [1953] 1 Lloyd's Rep 587; *The Lucile Bloomfield* [1964] 1 Lloyd's Rep 324; *The Kapitan Shvetsov* [1998] 1 Lloyd's Rep 199.

in any substantive sense. In *The Coral Isis*,[285] Sheen J opined that 'the reality is that there will not be two trials; there may not even be one trial. The hypothetical difficulty that two different Courts will reach different apportionments of blame for the collision is most unlikely to arise.' [286]

It falls, then, to consider just how the actuality of concurrent proceedings **3.100** affects the question of venue and the calculus of the natural forum in light of heightened modern sensitivity to the need for international judicial comity. The first point to note is that, unlike Article 21 of the Brussels Convention or Article 27 of Regulation 44/2001, the chronological sequence of proceedings has never been determinative in the common law[287] and, as shall be seen below, this position has not altered with the emergence of the concept of 'the natural forum'. Accordingly, no automatic jurisdictional prize hangs on victory in the 'race to seise'. The decision of the Hong Kong Court of Appeal in *The Kapitan Shvetsov*[288] provides an illustration of this point. As Lord Templeman observed in *The Abidin Daver*,[289] 'an ugly rush to get one action decided ahead of the other is not to be replaced by an ugly rush to issue proceedings in one country before the issue of proceedings in another'.[290] That is not to say, however, that the existence of concurrent proceedings continues to be overlooked by English and common law courts and that only lip-service is paid to observing the demands of comity.

The decision in *The Abidin Daver*[291] illustrates this proposition. After a **3.101** maritime collision in Turkish territorial waters between a Turkish-owned and a Cuban-owned ship, the Turkish shipowners promptly commenced proceedings in the District Court of Sariyer, Turkey against the Cuban shipowners, claiming damages for negligence in the navigation and management of their ship. Approximately three months later, the defendants counterclaimed, not in Turkey but through the commencement of proceedings in England. The Turkish shipowners, defendants in these proceedings, successfully applied for a stay. This decision, though reversed in the Court of Appeal,[292] was confirmed by the House of Lords in which Lord Brandon effectively denuded his earlier judgment in *The Tillie Lykes*[293] of any authoritative status. He stated that the instant case was not one 'of mere disadvantage of multiplicity of suits, it was a case which was liable to cause, if both actions continued, much difficulty and

---

[285] [1986] 1 QB 413, 417.
[286] See also *The Abidin Daver* [1984] AC 398, 412 per Lord Diplock.
[287] *The Tillie Lykes* [1977] 1 Lloyd's Rep 124, 128 per Brandon J. See also *Du Pont de Nemours & Co v Agnew* [1987] 2 Lloyd's Rep 585, 593 per Bingham LJ.
[288] [1998] 1 Lloyd's Rep 199, 215.   [289] [1984] AC 398.
[290] ibid 426.   [291] [1984] AC 398.
[292] [1983] 1 WLR 884.   [293] [1977] 1 Lloyd's Rep 124.

trouble'.[294] This of course will invariably be the case where concurrent jurisdiction is being exercised.

3.102 In *Excess Insurance Co Limited v Allendale Mutual Insurance Co*,[295] in a passage cited with approval by Rix LJ in *Ace Insurance SA-NV v Zurich Insurance Co*,[296] and which is an illustration of the law of comity in operation in the context of concurrent proceedings, Hobhouse LJ said:

> The question of liability will have to be determined in Rhode Island. It is not proper or appropriate that the Courts of this country should at the same time try to determine on an order 11 basis, the matters which, within the jurisdiction of the Rhode Island Court, are being determined by that Court. There, on that hypothesis, this is not a suitable case to give leave to serve out of the jurisdiction.

3.103 In Australia, there may be discerned a difference of approach between applications to stay proceedings where no other proceedings are on foot[297] as compared to the situation where more than one proceeding has been commenced.[298] Whereas, in the former situation, Australia really stands alone among common law jurisdictions in having eschewed the role of the natural forum, in cases of *lis alibi pendens* or, at the very least, overlapping jurisdiction, the approach of the High Court of Australia appears to adopt a more orthodox approach. Thus, in *Henry v Henry*,[299] the Court said that 'there are more compelling considerations in favour of a stay of the local proceedings if, as can happen, there are proceedings in another country which has jurisdiction to entertain those proceedings and the proceedings are between the same parties and with respect to the same issue or controversy'.[300] Having drawn attention to decisions such as *McHenry v Lewis, Peruvian Guano v Bockwoldt, Hyman v Helm,* and *Cohen v Rothfield* as cases where it was held that it was not prima facie vexatious in the strict sense of that word to bring two sets of proceedings in different countries, the Court went on to state that:

> The problems which arise if the identical issue or the same controversy is to be litigated in different countries which have jurisdiction with respect to the matter are such, in our view, that, prima facie, the continuation of one or the other should be seen as vexatious or oppressive.[301]

---

[294] *The Abidin Daver* [1984] AC 398, 424; see also 411–412.
[295] Court of Appeal, 8 March 1995.
[296] [2001] 1 Lloyd's Rep 658, 629–630.
[297] As to which, see most recently *Renault v Zhang* (2002) 187 ALR 1.
[298] See Nygh, P & Davies, M, *Conflict of Laws in Australia* (7th edn, 2002) xvii–xviii and 130–132.
[299] (1996) 185 CLR 571.
[300] ibid 590. See also *CSR v Cigna Insurance Australia* (1997) 189 CLR 345.
[301] ibid 591.

Where concurrent proceedings are on foot, a significant difference in **3.104**
terms of the stage to which the respective proceedings have advanced
may be of importance in any decision whether or not to grant a stay.[302] In
de Dampierre v de Dampierre,[303] Lord Goff drew a distinction between
'genuine' proceedings, on the one hand, and proceedings which have
been commenced simply for the purpose of demonstrating the existence
of another competent forum—what one judge has termed a 'makeshift
claim'[304] and what another has described as 'forum shopping of the worst
kind'[305]—or proceedings which have not advanced beyond the stage of
initiating process, on the other. He observed that if 'genuine' proceedings:

have not merely been started but have developed to the stage where they have
had some impact upon the dispute between the parties, especially if such impact
is likely to have a continuing effect, then this may be a relevant factor to take into
account when considering whether the foreign jurisdiction provides the appropriate forum for the resolution of the dispute between the parties.[306]

Not only is this observation sound as a matter of principle and common **3.105**
sense but it is also consistent with the courts' concern to ensure fairness
as between the parties as to the choice of forum. If a defendant in the
foreign proceedings has a cross-claim which it wishes to bring against the
plaintiff in another jurisdiction or wishes otherwise to object to litigation
in the foreign forum, it is reasonable to expect that party either to make its
claim abroad and/or object to the foreign court's jurisdiction at an early
stage of the foreign proceedings. It is not unfair that failure to take this
course should effectively preclude a party from arguing that its preferred
forum is in fact the natural forum for the disposition of its claim. A party's
delay in these circumstances may therefore be taken to constitute its
acquiescence in the foreign jurisdiction's claim or entitlement to be called
the natural forum. *Cleveland Museum of Art v Capricorn Art International
SA*[307] was a case where a stay of English proceedings was granted in
circumstances where proceedings in Ohio had been under way for over

---

[302] *The Varna* [1994] 2 Lloyd's Rep 41; *Henry v Henry* (1996) 185 CLR 571.

[303] [1988] AC 92.

[304] *Carter Holt Harvey Timber Ltd v Pacifico Timber Importers Pty Ltd* (High Court of New
Zealand, 7 December 1992), noted by Paterson, RJ, 'Conflict of Laws' (1992) New Zealand
Recent Law Review 368, 376. See also Saville J's characterization of the counterclaim in
Greek proceedings in *Commercial Bank of the Near East plc v A, B, C and D* [1989] 2 Lloyd's Rep
319, 322.

[305] *Meridian BIAO v Bank of New York* [1997] 1 Lloyd's Rep 437, 446. See also *New Hampshire
Insurance v Aerospace Finance* [1998] 2 Lloyd's Rep 539, 542.

[306] [1988] AC 92, 108. See also *Sterling Pharmaceuticals Pty Ltd v The Boots Company
(Australia) Pty Ltd* (1992) 34 FCR 287, 291 and 293, where Lockhart J considered it pertinent
in such a case to consider the stage to which proceedings had advanced in each court; and
Van Dyck v Van Dyck [1990] 3 NZLR 624 , 627 per Barker J; *Mackay Refined Sugars (NZ) v NZ
Sugar Co* [1997] 3 NZLR 476.

[307] [1990] 2 Lloyd's Rep 166.

two years and substantial pre-trial expenses had been incurred in relation to preparation not readily transferable to proceedings in England.[308]

3.106 English courts have in the past tended to place one important qualification upon which foreign proceedings are taken into account for the purposes of the inquiry as to whether England is the natural forum. Where the foreign proceedings were for negative declaratory relief, it has been held that the existence of such proceedings should not affect an English court's view as to whether it or another court is the natural forum.[309] This view has been echoed in Australia.[310] This view was predicated on the basis that, as a general proposition, English law traditionally viewed with hostility this form of action and permitting such actions to be taken into account in any assessment of the natural forum would be to encourage them.[311] The traditional hostility evinced by English courts to the action for negative declaratory relief is examined in paragraphs 4.250 ff below and, as shall be seen, there has been a significant change of attitude to actions for negative declaratory relief in light of Lord Woolf's leading judgment in *Messier Dowty Ltd v Sabena*,[312] although a degree of residual suspicion about the motives of parties seeking this form of relief is likely to endure.

3.107 There is no justification for ignoring the existence of *foreign* proceedings for negative declaratory relief in considering whether a particular jurisdiction provides the natural forum for the resolution of a given transnational dispute. Whatever the traditional common law view of such proceedings, they are accepted as legitimate in Europe and the United States and, significantly for present purposes, are equally capable of producing inconsistent decisions. This is a circumstance which it has been seen courts should be astute to avoid in the interests of comity. It is therefore not legitimate for English and other common law courts to discount the existence of foreign proceedings for negative declaratory relief in assessing their own jurisdictional claims. Hirst J's decision in *The Standard Steamship Owners' Protection and Indemnity Association (Bermuda) Ltd v Gann*,[313] although refusing to set aside service in the circumstances of the

---

[308] [1990] 2 Lloyd's Rep 166, especially 173.

[309] Collins, LA, 'The Marc Rich Case and Actions for Negative Declarations' in *Essays in International Litigation and the Conflict of Laws* (1994) 282. See, for example, *Arkwright Mutual Insurance Co v Bryanston Insurance Co Ltd* [1990] 2 QB 649, 665 and, more generally, *Du Pont de Nemours & Co v Agnew* [1987] 2 Lloyd's Rep 585; *The Stolt Marmaro* [1985] 2 Lloyd's Rep 428.

[310] *The Daeyang Honey* (1994) 120 ALR 109, 117; and *CSR v Cigna Insurance Australia* (1997) 189 CLR 345.

[311] See *Sohio Supply Co v Gatoil (USA) Inc* [1989] 1 Lloyd's Rep 588, 593 per Staughton LJ.

[312] [2000] 1 Lloyd's Rep 428, 435.

[313] [1992] 2 Lloyd's Rep 528.

case, demonstrates this more enlightened approach. In assessing England's claims to be the natural forum, he took into account negative declaratory proceedings that had been commenced in San Diego, noting that their sole purpose was not to demonstrate the existence of a competing jurisdiction.[314] Similarly, in *DR Insurance v Central National Insurance*,[315] leave to serve negative declaratory proceedings out of the jurisdiction was refused in circumstances where there were concurrent proceedings already on foot in New York.

It should also be noted in the context of examining the relevance of **3.108** foreign proceedings to a jurisdiction's claim to be the natural forum that where, because of its subject matter, a dispute is only capable of being resolved in one particular forum, then the existence of any *related* foreign proceedings will not recommend or be of relevance to an application to stay the domestic proceedings. In *Apple Computer Inc v Apple Corps SA*,[316] a case in which relief was sought under the New Zealand Trade Marks Act 1953, Henry J observed that, as such relief could not be effectively granted in England, the existence of proceedings in that jurisdiction was of no relevance to the question of whether a stay should be granted in New Zealand.[317] Similarly, the ultimate lack of significance attributed by the Court of Appeal to American proceedings in a stay application in *Du Pont de Nemours & Co v Agnew*[318] was because of the view that a question of English public policy could only properly be decided by English courts.[319] In declining to grant a stay of proceedings in *Akai Pty Limited v People's Insurance Company*,[320] the High Court of Australia was concerned that, were the proceedings stayed in favour of proceedings in England, where a protective writ had been filed, an English court may not have entertained Akai's claim to be relieved from 'technical' breaches of contract under the Insurance Contracts Act 1984 (C'th), a piece of reformist consumer-protection legislation.

Conversely, where a court is of the view that an aspect of the dispute **3.109** before it is only capable of being resolved in the foreign forum, then this will recommend a stay of all related proceedings in the domestic forum. The fact that a claim was made under section 52 of the Australian Trade Practices Act 1974 in *Australian Commercial Research and Development Ltd v ANZ McCaughan Merchant Bank Ltd*[321] was critical in Browne-Wilkinson VC's decision to stay related English proceedings for he considered that

---

[314] ibid 537.   [315] [1996] 1 Lloyd's Rep 74, 84.   [316] [1990] 2 NZLR 598.
[317] ibid 602; see also *Apple Corps Ltd v Apple Computer Inc* [1992] RPC 70 in which reference is made to the equivalent litigation between the parties with regard to the defendant's German patent.
[318] [1987] 2 Lloyd's Rep 585.   [319] ibid 594 per Bingham LJ.
[320] (1997) 188 CLR 418.   [321] [1989] 3 All ER 65.

that claim could only be resolved by an Australian court.[322] In *Hyslop v Society of Lloyd's*,[323] the New Zealand court granted a partial stay of New Zealand proceedings but declined to stay proceedings to the extent that they raised claims under the Securities Act 1978 (NZ) and the Fair Trading Act 1986 (NZ). In *CSR v Cigna Insurance Australia*,[324] the High Court of Australia placed particular emphasis upon its view that proceedings which CSR had commenced in New Jersey under the Sherman Act could only be entertained in a United States court and that the attempt to restrain CSR from pursuing those proceedings, including, as they did, a Sherman Act claim, albeit related to conduct which appeared to have occurred in Australia, should not be permitted. Proceedings in New South Wales commenced by Cigna Insurance Australia were stayed.

3.110 The technique of either seeking a stay in one court on the basis that a statutory claim lies in another jurisdiction also seised of the matter or of resisting a stay of domestic proceedings on the basis that a foreign court will not be capable of providing the relief sought under a domestic statute[325] is subject to abuse, especially perhaps in the former case where the foreign court will be unlikely to be familiar with another jurisdiction's legislation. Referring to *Apple Computer Inc v Apple Corps SA*,[326] which also involved questions arising under the New Zealand Commerce Act 1986, Paterson has observed that the 'obvious inference is that a plaintiff in New Zealand proceedings, who wishes to avoid a stay sought on the basis that New Zealand is *forum non conveniens* because of litigation pending in a foreign court, should claim relief under a New Zealand statute'.[327]

3.111 It is significant to note that the Trade Practices Act claim in *Australian Commercial Research and Development Ltd v ANZ McCaughan Merchant Bank Ltd*[328] was added to the English pleadings just prior to the hearing of the stay application.[329] Where statutory claims are made and are relied on either to support or resist an application for a stay in favour of litigation in the natural forum, courts should be astute to examine whether the statute in question essentially codifies or reflects the common law, as was arguably the case in *Australian Commercial Research and Development Ltd v ANZ McCaughan Merchant Bank Ltd*, or whether the foreign statute is suffi-

---

[322] ibid 72, but see para 3.111 below. Browne-Wilkinson VC's views may no longer be valid since the passage of the Private International Law (Miscellaneous Provisions) Act 1995. If a statutory claim under the Australian Trade Practices Act is characterized by English law as a tort, the 1995 Act may allow it to be litigated in the United Kingdom.

[323] (1992) 6 PRNZ 204, referred to in [1997] 3 NZLR 476, 484.

[324] (1997) 189 CLR 345.

[325] As happened, for example, in *Oceanic Sun Line Special Shipping Co Inc v Fay* (1988) 165 CLR 197 in relation to the application of the Contracts Review Act 1980 (NSW).

[326] [1990] 2 NZLR 598.   [327] (n 304 above) 376.

[328] [1989] 3 All ER 65.   [329] ibid 72.

ciently similar to legislation in the natural forum so that equivalent and effective relief will be available to the party in that jurisdiction.[330] Attention should also be paid to whether the local forum's choice of law rules will permit the foreign statutory claim to be litigated in that court. Too often, it would appear a negative answer to this question is assumed (as was arguably the case in *CSR v Cigna Insurance Australia*[331] with respect to the ability to litigate the Sherman Act claim in New South Wales).

Where proceedings have been commenced by the same plaintiff in differ- **3.112** ent jurisdictions, the traditional remedy for a defendant was to require the plaintiff to make an election as to which set of proceedings to continue with. In *The Mali Ivo*,[332] actions had been instituted both in the High Court of Admiralty and the Austrian consular court of Constantinople. Sir Robert Phillimore stated that if he were satisfied 'that there was a lis alibi pendens before a tribunal which could afford the plaintiff a complete remedy, whether the proceedings were technically instituted *in rem* or *in personam*', then he would be under a 'duty either to suspend proceedings in this Court, or to put the parties to their election as to which court they would have recourse to'.[333]

Although putting a party to its election still accommodates the plaintiff's **3.113** traditional control over the venue of litigation by permitting *it* to choose in which forum to continue, if the defendant's only objection is as to the fact that it is being constrained to defend identical proceedings in two different jurisdictions, putting a plaintiff to its election effects a fair result as between the parties, especially where the plaintiff may be ordered to pay the defendant's costs in the discontinued proceedings.[334] Where, however, the defendant objects not simply to the fact that two sets of proceedings are on foot but that one set of proceedings is not taking place in the natural forum, then the court will be required to consider whether it is the natural forum, bearing in mind, as has been seen above, the stage of proceedings in the other forum. If the court does not consider itself to be the natural forum, then a stay should be granted. If, on the other hand, the court considers that it, rather than the other jurisdiction, is the natural forum and that the plaintiff's institution and continuance of two sets of

---

[330] See, for example, *Leigh-Mardon Pty Ltd v PRC Inc* (1993) 44 FCR 88, 104–105.
[331] (1997) 189 CLR 345.
[332] (1869) LR 2 A & E 356.
[333] ibid 359. See also *The Delta* (1876) 1 PD 393, 404; *McHenry v Lewis* (1882) 22 ChD 397, 400 per Jessel MR; *Peruvian Guano Co v Bockwoldt* (1883) 23 ChD 225; and *The Christianborg* (1885) 10 PD 141, 153 per Baggallay LJ.
[334] *Australian Commercial Research and Development Ltd v ANZ McCaughan Merchant Bank Ltd* [1989] 3 All ER 65, 73 per Browne-Wilkinson VC.

proceedings is vexatious and oppressive, then the plaintiff *may* be restrained from continuing with its proceedings in the other forum.[335]

Complex Litigation and the Natural Forum

3.114 It follows from the preceding discussion that the conception of the natural forum need not be a static one, that is that it will not necessarily be fixed in time, once and for all. This is also clear from the potential significance of the *'Cambridgeshire'* factor.[336] It may be affected by the existence, stage, and, in the case of actions for negative declaratory relief, nature of proceedings pending elsewhere. While this fact necessarily adds some complexity to the inquiry into the situs of the natural forum, the inquiry nevertheless remains faithful to what have been suggested to be the key policy considerations underpinning it. The significance of concurrent proceedings will in part depend on the respective parties' conduct and the part they have played in permitting the concurrent litigation not only to arise but to continue. Fairness as between the parties is respected[337] and an endeavour is made to reduce the scope for concurrent proceedings, a factor which must also be in all parties' interests. The common law can in this way be seen to be striving for at least one of the same goals as the Brussels Convention and Regulation 44/2001.

3.115 The same phenomenon can be seen in a related area, also involving a comparison of the 'modern' common law and the Regulation. It has already been observed that any given transnational dispute will frequently involve several parties and may spawn a complex array of claims and cross-claims *inter se*, not all of which will necessarily be heard in the same forum.[338] In this context, it is important to appreciate that inconsistency of results may arise not only in proceedings in one forum which are simply the converse of those in another[339] but also in related proceedings, not necessarily between the same parties, involving a common substratum of facts.[340]

---

[335] *The Christianborg* (1885) 10 PD 141, 152–153 per Baggallay LJ. In *Australian Commercial Research and Development Ltd v ANZ McCaughan Merchant Bank Ltd* [1989] 3 All ER 65, Browne-Wilkinson VC considered that Queensland rather than England was the natural forum and therefore gave leave to discontinue the English proceedings and granted a stay of the defendant's cross-claim. See also *HM Attorney General v Arthur Andersen & Co (United Kingdom)* [1989] ECC 224.

[336] See at para 3.93 above.

[337] In *Spiliada*, Lord Goff emphasized that the *'Cambridgeshire'* factor did not constitute any disadvantage to Cansulex: [1987] AC 460, 486.

[338] See, generally, Fawcett, J, 'Multiparty litigation in Private International Law' (1995) 44 ICLQ 744.

[339] A common example of this is a 'collision case' where comparative fault is at issue between the two parties; see, for example, *The Abidin Daver* [1984] AC 398.

[340] See, for example, *Gascoine v Pyrah* [1994] I L Pr 82, 94 per Hirst LJ, who observed that

It has been seen that the Regulation attempts to deal with such problems **3.116** through Article 28, permitting a second seised court to decline jurisdiction in favour of a first seised court if it has jurisdiction over the second action and the ability to consolidate proceedings, and Article 6, permitting a co-defendant to be sued in the courts of another defendant's domicile and third party proceedings to take place in the court originally seised rather than the courts of the third party's domicile. In this way and in 'the interests of the proper administration of justice', the scope for inconsistent decisions is reduced *from the outset* through jurisdictional rules permitting the grouping of all litigation arising out of one set of events in a single forum.

It will not always be possible to secure resolution of all issues in one **3.117** forum, especially in multi-party cases. This gives rise to the scope for a certain degree of manipulation by parties in the manoeuvring to secure what is perceived to be the best forum for a particular party's purposes. One example of such manoeuvring is by defendants offering to submit to (their) preferred forum where they are not otherwise present, for the purposes of being able to point to that forum as the one forum in which all parties or all issues may be able to be resolved. This technique was employed by Cape plc in proceedings commenced against it in England by a number of South African claimants who had been employed by South African subsidiaries of Cape.[341] In earlier proceedings, Evans LJ described this as 'almost a case of forum shopping in reverse'[342] and one to be deprecated or at least to be regarded with a measure of scepticism. A differently constituted Court of Appeal in the same proceedings, however, plainly did not regard it as a significant obstacle to granting a stay in favour of what it considered to be the natural forum, albeit one to which Cape plc had 'made' itself amenable.[343]

On the plaintiff's side, 'local' subsidiaries are also often sued together **3.118** with the foreign parent and/or related corporations which are the true target of a suit in order to lend a nexus to the plaintiff's desired forum.[344]

different findings of fact 'are virtually impossible to reconcile if different judges in different jurisdictions . . . hearing and seeing different witnesses reach different conclusions which have hinged on an assessment of the reliability of individual witnesses; and of course the problem may be compounded in cases where there are different procedures in different national courts in the way in which they hear the evidence and assess it. Moreover, different findings of fact also frequently lead to different conclusions of law.'

[341] See *Lubbe v Cape plc* [2000] 1 Lloyd's Rep 139, 144–145 and 156–157. When this matter reached the House of Lords [2000] 1 WLR 1545, the significance of this point disappeared because of the decision to lift the stay and to permit the proceedings to continue in England.

[342] Cited in *Lubbe v Cape plc* [2000] 1 Lloyd's Rep 139, 156.

[343] *Lubbe v Cape plc* [2000] 1 Lloyd's Rep 139.

[344] See, for example, *Laminex (Australia) Pty Ltd v Coe Manufacturing* (1998) 20 ATPR 41–610, 40–669.

Courts must be astute to guard against such colourable joinders in juris-dictional fights. In *Chase v Ram Technical Services Ltd*,[345] there were paral-lel proceedings in England and Canada. The English proceedings were stayed, it being held that the claim against the third defendant, an English company, was contrived or colourable. All of the other defendants were Canadian. In *Turner v Grovit*,[346] in the Court of Appeal, Laws LJ described the nomination of a Spanish subsidiary of Mr Grovit's group of compa-nies as claimant in Spanish proceedings as 'nothing but a device to confer putative jurisdiction on the Spanish Court', saying that it was a 'sham and pretence'.[347] The position will not always be clear, however, especially at an early stage of any litigation. The House of Lords, for example, differed markedly from what the Court of Appeal in *Donohue v Armco Inc*[348] thought of the legitimacy of the claims of various 'friends and relations' who had joined the litigation in New York and were not party to the exclusive jurisdiction clause (unsuccessfully) sought to be enforced in the English proceedings.

3.119 While common law jurisdictions typically permit the consolidation of proceedings, on the face of it, the jurisprudence of the natural forum would seem ill-equipped to prevent the fracturing of various aspects of litigation in a complex transnational dispute for, given the fact that the indicia of the natural forum include the domicile or residence of the parties, it is clear that, as regards *particular* claims between various parties to the transnational dispute, the *situs* of the natural forum may well differ. As argued below, however, the flexibility of the concept of the natural forum is such that it can be adapted to the circumstances of a complex transnational dispute involving several parties. Such flexibility has not escaped criticism.[349]

3.120 Coincident with the emergence of the concept of the natural forum, common law judges have displayed a markedly heightened sensitivity in recent years to the need to resolve and the desirability of resolving all liti-gation arising out of the same set of events in the same court. The cases in which this observation has been made are now legion. Thus, in *Du Pont de Nemours & Co v Agnew*,[350] Bingham LJ stated that 'the policy of the law must nonetheless be to favour the litigation of issues only once, in the most appropriate forum',[351] and in *First National Bank of Boston v Union Bank of Switzerland*,[352] Russell LJ stated that 'as a general rule concurrent

---

[345] [2000] 2 Lloyd's Rep 418.   [346] [2000] QB 345.
[347] ibid 362.
[348] Compare [2002] 1 Lloyd's Rep 425 with [2000] 1 Lloyd's Rep 579, 590–591.
[349] See para 3.156 below.   [350] [1987] 2 Lloyd's Rep 585.
[351] ibid 589.   [352] [1990] 1 Lloyd's Rep 32.

proceedings in different jurisdictions are not to be encouraged; they can lead to inconsistent judgments and they can undermine comity'.[353]

Litigation which gives rise to the possibility of inconsistent results and which may result in 'an ugly rush to judgment' is rightly viewed as inherently undesirable.[354] If courts are concerned with the need to avoid inconsistent or incompatible decisions, the natural forum needs to be identified in the context of the *entire dispute between all of the parties* rather than a discrete aspect of it between only two parties. Thus in *The Lanka Muditha*,[355] for example, Kempster JA of the Hong Kong Court of Appeal considered that: **3.121**

. . . other factors being equal, New York would be the forum in which the litigation could be tried more suitably than in Hong Kong in the interests of all parties presently *and potentially involved* and for the ends of justice.[356]

The potential complexity of particular litigation involving a multiplicity of parties and claims may be such that it will not always be possible for all aspects of a dispute to be resolved in one forum.[357]

A series of insurance cases, however, illustrate the proposition that, in complex transnational litigation, courts required to identify the natural forum for whatever jurisdictional purpose[358] should have reference to the dispute in its entirety (including potential third party claims and cross-claims) if there is a prospect of inconsistent decisions. **3.122**

In *The Goldean Mariner*,[359] the first plaintiff, Golden Ocean Assurance Ltd, a Bermudan insurance company, had arranged through its agents CE Heath & Co, to syndicate 100 per cent of its risk. The syndicate included **3.123**

---

[353] ibid 39. See also *Camilla Cotton Oil Co v Granadex SA* [1976] 2 Lloyd's Rep 10, 14; *The Stolt Mamaro* [1985] 2 Lloyd's Rep 428, 436; *Spiliada* [1987] AC 460, 485; *The Kapetan Georgis* [1988] 1 Lloyd's Rep 352, 361–362; *Meadows Indemnity Co Ltd v The Insurance Corporation of Ireland plc* [1989] 1 Lloyd's Rep 181, 190, [1989] 2 Lloyd's Rep 298, 305; *EF Hutton & Co (London) Ltd v Mofarrij* [1989] 1 WLR 488, 496; *Australian Commercial Research and Development Ltd v ANZ McCaughan Merchant Bank Ltd* [1989] 3 All ER 65, 70–71; *Cleveland Museum of Art v Capricorn Art International SA* [1990] 2 Lloyd's Rep 166, 174; *New Hampshire Insurance Co v Strabag Bau AG* [1992] 1 Lloyd's Rep 361, 371; *Sterling Pharmaceuticals Pty Ltd v The Boots Company (Australia) Pty Ltd* (1992) 34 FCR 287, 291; *Seaconsar Far East Ltd v Bank Markazi Jomhouri Islami Iran* [1994] 1 AC 438; *The Hamburg Star* [1994] 1 Lloyd's Rep 399, 408; *Henry v Henry* (1997) 188 CLR 418.
[354] See *The Abidin Daver* [1984] AC 398, 423; *Sohio Supply Co v Gatoil (USA) Inc* [1989] 1 Lloyd's Rep 588, 593.
[355] [1991] 1 HKLR 741.
[356] ibid 748 (emphasis added).
[357] See, for example, *Crédit Suisse First Boston (Europe) Ltd v MLC (Bermuda) Ltd* [1999] 1 Lloyd's Rep 767, 781.
[358] There may be several—service out, stay applications, anti-suit relief and, in Canada, recognition and enforcement of judgments (as to which, see paras 4.296 ff below).
[359] [1989] 2 Lloyd's Rep 390.

English, American, French, and Swiss underwriters. The plaintiffs commenced proceedings in England to recover under their policies certain sums awarded to marine salvors in relation to repairs undertaken to the 'Goldean Mariner'. The American defendants sought either to set aside, or a stay of, these proceedings on the basis that New York rather than England was the *forum conveniens*. Phillips J stated that:

> Where, as is often the case, a vessel is insured on the world market with individual insurers around the globe each covering a comparatively small proportion of the risk it is vital in the interests of all concerned that if the validity of a claim has to be determined by litigation, this should occur in a single hearing binding on all concerned.[360]

3.124 The defendants in *The Goldean Mariner* argued that it was unfair that they be compelled to litigate in England, a forum which they were unaware had any connection to the insurance, in circumstances where they had accepted the risk, which had been placed by New York brokers, in New York. Phillips J, apart from doubting the state of the defendants' ignorance, stated that 'at all events it seems to me that the American defendants, when writing this insurance, could reasonably have contemplated the possibility that proceedings might be initiated in England'.[361] Phillips J thus may be seen to have sought to accommodate the 'fairness' concerns which it has been argued provide the leading rationale for the search for the natural forum with another important policy consideration, namely the desire to minimize the likelihood of inconsistent decisions on account of multiple proceedings. By invoking the concept of what the defendants could or ought reasonably to have contemplated, echoes can be detected of the doctrines of 'legitimate expectation' and 'procedural fairness'.

3.125 It might be observed in this context that courts are more wary of applications by insurers and reinsurers to stay proceedings against them in a forum in which the vast majority of claims can be resolved because of a perception that concurrent litigation in an alleged natural forum is often initiated for strategic purposes and, as such, does not constitute 'genuine' proceedings.[362] Unless courts are prepared to draw bold inferences, however, it may be difficult as a matter of practice to ascertain whether proceedings have been brought solely for strategic purposes. An inference of this kind was drawn by the High Court of Australia in *CSR Ltd v Cigna Insurance Australia Ltd*.[363]

---

[360] ibid 400. For another case where refusal to grant a stay permitted all proceedings to be resolved in one jurisdiction, see *Curnow Shipping Ltd v National Bank of New Zealand Ltd* (1990) 2 PRNZ 67, 70, noted by Paterson, RJ (n 304 above) 377.

[361] ibid 401.

[362] See Lord Goff's reference to 'genuine' proceedings in *de Dampierre v de Dampierre* [1988] AC 92, 108.

[363] (1997) 189 CLR 345.

It might legitimately be thought that, given the size and global signifi- **3.126** cance of the London insurance market, an analysis of the kind found in *The Goldean Mariner* is apt to produce a jurisdictional 'homeward trend' in reinsurance and insurance litigation where English courts are concerned. As Potter J observed in *Arkwright Mutual Insurance Co v Bryanston Insurance Co Ltd*,[364] a dispute 'involving the meaning and effect of a reinsurance contract made in the London market . . . is, on first impression at least, peculiarly appropriate to trial in this court'.[365] This may also be the case in many standard insurance cases if the insurer and not the assured is regarded as *dominus litis*, as was suggested should be the case by Lord Goff in *Spiliada*.[366] *McConnell Dowell Constructors Ltd v Lloyd's Syndicate 396*,[367] however, apart from providing an excellent example of the need to take an expansive view of the natural forum in complex transnational cases involving several parties in different countries, also illustrates a competing viewpoint.

McConnell Dowell was a New Zealand-based construction company **3.127** principally operating in New Zealand. Together with subsidiary and other related companies, it held a group insurance policy against liability to third parties for negligence. This insurance existed on two layers, the first being largely subscribed by English underwriters. These policies were issued in London but were silent as to the governing law. Arranged contemporaneously with this insurance was 'second layer' insurance subscribed by a New Zealand insurer, Cigna Insurance New Zealand Ltd, and which was made expressly subject to New Zealand law. Cigna had a 14.5 per cent involvement in the first layer insurance and its total insurance commitment amounted to some two-thirds of the overall cover. Upon a claim being made under both layers of insurance, the underwriters of the first layer commenced proceedings in England 'on behalf of all other insurers concerned', seeking declarations that the first layer insurance did not cover the claims made or, in the alternative, that they were entitled to avoid the contracts on the grounds of non-disclosure. Some ten days later, McConnell Dowell commenced proceedings in New Zealand under both layers of insurance, having obtained an order to serve the English underwriters outside the forum. The English underwriters sought

---

[364] [1990] 2 QB 649.

[365] ibid 665–666. England was considered to be the natural forum for the purposes of service out of the jurisdiction in reinsurance disputes in *Britannia Steamship Association v Ausonia Assicurazioni SpA* [1984] 2 Lloyd's Rep 98; *Islamic Arab Insurance Co v Saudi Egyptian American Reinsurance Co* [1987] 1 Lloyd's Rep 315; and *Overseas Union Insurance Ltd v Incorporated General Insurance Ltd* [1992] 1 Lloyd's Rep 439.

[366] [1987] AC 460, 486; see also *The Abidin Daver* [1984] AC 398, 426 per Lord Templeman and *The Hamburg Star* [1994] 1 Lloyd's Rep 399, 410.

[367] [1988] 2 NZLR 257.

to have service set aside or, in the alternative, to have the action stayed. Cigna sought a stay pending the outcome of the English proceedings.

3.128 At first instance in the New Zealand proceedings, Sinclair J held that the first layer policies were governed by English law and that the commencement of proceedings against Cigna in New Zealand was a stratagem designed to bring in the overseas underwriters. He dismissed the action against the English underwriters for want of jurisdiction and stayed the action brought against Cigna. Some four and a half months later, Evans J of the Queen's Bench Division refused an application by McConnell Dowell to stay the English proceedings for declaratory relief but made this ruling on the condition that the decision of Sinclair J stood.[368] On appeal, however, Sinclair J's decision was overturned.

3.129 The argument presented to both Sinclair J and Evans J was that if, in the English action, the plaintiffs succeeded, then the factual and legal issues in the New Zealand proceedings would disappear (including the question of liability on the second layer because it was in identical terms to the first layer and the principles of New Zealand and English insurance law were the same). At the very least it was put that the English proceedings could be treated as discrete and preliminary. The New Zealand Court of Appeal, on the other hand, put considerable emphasis on the fact that New Zealand was the only forum in which *all issues* could be resolved, including questions of quantum and reinstatement which would arise in the event that the insurers were held to be liable on the policies and could not avoid them for non-disclosure.[369] Of particular interest is Cooke P's observation that:

> Although recognising that it was concerned with the different subject of injunctions restraining foreign proceedings, I think that the recent judgment of the Privy Council in *SNI Aerospatiale*[370] . . . is not without relevance for present purposes. Great importance was attached there to the ability to join Bristow Malaysia as a third party in Brunei. The analogy, certainly imperfect but nonetheless plain enough, is with the comprehensiveness of the New Zealand action as a vehicle for disposing of the present dispute.[371]

---

[368] He stated that 'I have not sought to deal with the situation which will arise if the higher Courts in New Zealand come to conclusions which mean that the prospect of a dual and conflicting jurisdiction becomes a reality.' (Cited in Bisson J's judgment in the New Zealand Court of Appeal, ibid 281.)

[369] ibid 274–275 per Cooke P; 277 per Somers J; 277 per Bisson J.

[370] *Société Nationale Industrielle Aerospatiale v Lee Kui Jak* [1987] AC 871. This case is discussed fully in paras 4.79 ff below.

[371] [1988] 2 NZLR 257, 276. See also in this context *Charm Maritime Inc v Kyriakou* [1987] 1 Lloyd's Rep 433, where one of the reasons for refusing a stay in favour of Greece was that it was only in England that both the defendants were able to be sued and as, on the facts, one or the other had to be liable, suit in England was necessary to ensure in the interests of justice

Sinclair J had been conscious of the desirability of having the whole **3.130** dispute resolved in one forum and in fact had expressed the hope that 'the insured would immediately commence independent proceedings in England allowing, if it becomes necessary, the two actions to become consolidated'.[372] The fact that he saw England as the only forum in which there was a possibility of having the whole dispute resolved was driven by his conclusion, reversed on appeal, that the New Zealand courts lacked jurisdiction over all of the first layer underwriters save Cigna. However, the Court of Appeal considered, *inter alia*, that their degree of involvement in the total package of insurance made them proper parties to the New Zealand proceedings and that jurisdiction therefore existed. It then examined the dispute *in globo*, as it were, holding that New Zealand was clearly the natural forum. This global perspective was perhaps most clearly painted by Bisson J, who observed that 'the insurances are all part of a package arranged in respect of the same period of indemnity for a New Zealand company and its associated companies in respect of operations predominantly in New Zealand or directed from New Zealand with Cigna, a New Zealand company carrying overall the greater part of the risk'.[373]

Two other insurance cases demonstrate that the policy of 'grouping' liti- **3.131** gation and identifying the natural forum as that in which the overall dispute may be resolved with the least prospect of inconsistent decisions does not always result in the retention of jurisdiction by the English courts or a decision to permit service out of the jurisdiction. In *Insurance Corporation of Ireland v Strombus*,[374] reinsurers sought a declaration in England against certain insurers that the reinsurance contracts in question were null and void on the ground of non-disclosure. This action was commenced after the assured had made a claim against his insurer which had been duly passed on to the reinsurers. No proceedings on the insurance policy had at that stage been commenced. These were, however, commenced in California on the day after the defendant insurance company (Strombus) were served with a writ in the English proceedings. In those proceedings, the insurance company cross-claimed against the reinsurers. Delivering the judgment of the Court, Mustill LJ stated that:

The Californian proceedings will continue [attempts by the reinsurers to stay the Californian proceedings had been unsuccessful[375]]. The issue is whether the

---

that the plaintiff was not denied any recourse because of a fracturing of the proceedings. See also the discussion of *Taunton-Collins v Cromie* [1964] 1 WLR 633 by Kerr J in *Bulk Oil Zug AG v Trans-Asiatic Oil Ltd SA* [1973] 1 Lloyd's Rep 129, 136–137.

[372] Referred to in Cooke P's judgment, ibid 274.   [373] ibid 282.

[374] [1985] 2 Lloyd's Rep 138.

[375] ibid 142.

English proceedings should also continue. In our judgment they should not, notwithstanding that they were commenced a short time before the foreign action . . . The substance of the dispute is being litigated in California. . . . We see no sufficient reason why the reinsurers should be allowed to proceed in England with a dispute which is no more than a shadow of the action already afoot overseas.[376]

3.132 Mustill LJ was here demonstrating what in another case he described as 'the good management of the concurrent sets of proceedings'.[377] Although the claim by the reinsurers against the insurers related to a contract which had been broked in England and which was governed by English law,[378] the Court did not look narrowly at the relationship between the reinsurers and insurers alone. Rather, it looked to the 'substance of the dispute' and was alive to the undesirability of what it described as 'an unacceptable degree of duplication'.[379] In ascertaining the 'most appropriate forum', the broadest view of the dispute was taken in order to minimize the possibility of inconsistent results.

3.133 In *The Stolt Marmaro*[380] at first instance, Mustill J would have declined to exercise his discretion to allow service out of the jurisdiction had he found that the case fell within one of the heads of Order 11, rule 1 partly on the basis that the plaintiffs could equally have exercised their option to have all the proceedings in New York.[381] On the other hand, in *The Messiniaki Tolmi*,[382] in refusing to grant a stay, Mustill J held that 'it is to my mind very far from clear that the Court of Taiwan is the appropriate tribunal for trying separately, or by way of duplication, a part of what is really one multi-faceted dispute'.

3.134 In *New Hampshire Insurance Co v Strabag Bau AG*,[383] a case where the indicia of the natural forum set out in *Spiliada* pointed to England as the natural forum, Lloyd LJ, taking a view of the larger dispute between all interested parties, identified Germany as the natural forum. Two of the three defendants were required to be sued there[384] and, in light of this circumstance, Lloyd LJ stated that 'it seems almost self-evident that the proceedings against the third defendant should also be heard in Germany'.[385] *Lemmex v Bernard*[386] provides an illustration of the same approach in Canada, O'Leary J stating that the real and substantial

---

[376] ibid 146.
[377] *HM Attorney-General v Arthur Andersen & Co* [1989] ECC 224, 229.
[378] [1985] 2 Lloyd's Rep 138, 143.   [379] ibid 144.
[380] [1985] 2 Lloyd's Rep 428.   [381] See Goff LJ's judgment at 436.
[382] [1983] 1 Lloyd's Rep 666, 673.   [383] [1992] 1 Lloyd's Rep 361.
[384] This was by virtue of the fact that they were domiciled in Germany and Article 11 of the Brussels Convention, providing that 'an insurer may bring proceedings only in the courts of the Contracting State in which the defendant is domiciled', applied.
[385] [1992] 1 Lloyd's Rep 361, 371. The third defendant was domiciled in Austria.
[386] (2001) 202 DLR (4th) 192.

connection test 'requires the court to take a broad perspective of the subject matter of the action, one that is not limited to a consideration of the event of the accident alone'.[387]

The policy considerations underpinning the approaches adopted in both **3.135** *Insurance Corporation of Ireland v Strombus*[388] and *New Hampshire Insurance Co v Strabag Bau AG*[389] are also illustrated in a number of shipping cases. In *The Oinoussin Pride*,[390] Pride Shipping Corporation ('Pride'), a Liberian registered but Greek controlled shipowner, had obtained leave under Order 11 of the Rules of the Supreme Court to serve Taiwanese receivers of cargo out of the jurisdiction. These defendants had themselves commenced proceedings in Alabama against both Pride and stevedores responsible for the loading of the cargo in Mobile, Alabama. Pride had itself claimed in these proceedings against the stevedores and the charterers but not the receivers. In granting the defendant receivers' application to set aside the Order 11 service, Webster J emphasized the desirability of resolving as much of the dispute as was possible in one forum (there were separate arbitration proceedings between Pride and the charterers in London).[391] After noting that the receivers had agreed to submit to the jurisdiction in Alabama, Webster J stated that 'it is unlikely that the claim by the plaintiffs against the stevedores could be heard in England and, as the claim against the stevedores is so closely connected to the issues arising between the plaintiffs and the defendants, it is appropriate for them to be heard by the [Alabama] Court so as to avoid the possibility of inconsistent decisions'.[392]

In *Bouygues Offshore SA v Caspian Shipping Co (Nos 1, 3, 4 and 5)*,[393] not only **3.136** was a similar policy given effect to in a complex shipping dispute involving multiple parties where the global centre of gravity of the dispute was South Africa but, further, this policy was permitted to prevail over an exclusive jurisdiction clause for England contained in a towage contract and trumped the otherwise strong disposition of English courts to give effect to such clauses. Only one of a number of interested parties to the dispute had the benefit of this clause. A strikingly similar approach to that adopted in *Bouygues Offshore SA* was taken by the House of Lords in *Donohue v Armco Inc*.[394]

---

[387] ibid 201.
[389] [1992] 1 Lloyd's Rep 361.
[391] ibid 134.
[392] ibid. See also, for an example of a case where the granting of a stay of proceedings prevented the possibility of inconsistent findings and the avoidance of hardship and expense for the applicant, *Thomas & Sons Pty Ltd v Bunge (Australia) Pty Ltd* [1975] VR 801, 806–807.
[393] [1998] 2 Lloyd's Rep 461.
[394] [2002] 1 Lloyd's Rep 425. See further paras 5.94 ff.

[388] [1985] 2 Lloyd's Rep 138.
[390] [1991] 1 Lloyd's Rep 126.

3.137 It may be observed that, had the jurisdiction clauses in either of these cases been a London arbitration rather than an English exclusive jurisdiction clause, the mandatory requirement for a stay of proceedings in favour of arbitration under the New York Convention would have had the result of fracturing the litigation unless one were to read that Convention's requirement that 'the matter be capable of settlement by arbitration' as referring only to discrete elements of the dispute between the parties to the arbitration agreement with the consequence that where the dispute between the parties to the arbitration agreement is so closely bound up with the claims and counterclaims of other parties to the global dispute so as not to be able to be severed, the 'matter' cannot be regarded as capable of settlement by arbitration.[395]

3.138 The policy of favouring litigation in the forum most capable of disposing of all aspects of a dispute was also in evidence at first instance in *Meadows Indemnity Co Ltd v The Insurance Corporation of Ireland plc*,[396] but was ignored in changed circumstances in the Court of Appeal.[397] This case stands as a notable exception to the line of cases discussed above which have emphasized the need, so far as is possible, to resolve all aspects of transnational disputes in one forum. In *Meadows*, proceedings had been commenced in the Irish courts by International Commercial Bank plc ('ICB') against Insurance Corporation of Ireland ('ICI'). ICB had provided ICI with financial guarantee insurance on an outstanding loan which it had made to a Swiss company. Meadows had reinsured ICI. Before Meadows had been made a party to these proceedings, it commenced proceedings in England seeking various negative declarations against ICI. Meadows further sought, as against ICB, declarations that ICI was entitled to avoid the insurance and that ICI was not bound to indemnify ICB in respect of losses on the loan agreement. ICB sought, *inter alia*, to have these proceedings stayed in favour of the Irish courts. In weighing the elements for and against a stay, Hirst J concluded that:

> Lastly there is the consideration to which I attach considerable importance that England is the only forum in which all three parties, i.e. Meadows, ICI and ICB, are at present all before the Court in one single action. It is obviously convenient that all three parties should be involved together in one action, if only to avoid the risk of inconsistent findings.[398]

3.139 By the time an appeal was heard from Hirst J's decision, not only had Meadows been served with a third party notice in the Irish proceedings

---

[395] In *Tanning Research Laboratories Inc v O'Brien* (1990) 169 CLR 332, 351, reference was made to the need for the relevant 'matter' to be a 'discrete' controversy.
[396] [1989] 1 Lloyd's Rep 180.
[397] [1989] 2 Lloyd's Rep 298.
[398] [1989] 1 Lloyd's Rep 180, 190.

but Costello J. had confirmed the Court's jurisdiction to give leave to serve a third party notice outside the jurisdiction (which had been challenged by Meadows) and had refused to decline jurisdiction to hear the third party claim. All parties were now before the Irish Court which was thus in a position to hear all aspects of the dispute and all claims in one action. The English Court of Appeal did not advert to this change in circumstances (which must be considered significant in the light of the observation of Hirst J cited above) in refusing to interfere with the exercise of the trial judge's discretion in not granting a stay of the English proceedings.[399] That refusal had the consequence, which Neill LJ for one was alive to,[400] that there would be proceedings on both sides of the Irish Sea with the possibility of inconsistent results and the duplication of expense and judicial resources. This case is somewhat curious for the absence of any reference to the concerns of judicial comity which may have recommended staying the English proceedings in favour of the Irish court if it provided the natural forum and that was where, to borrow the language of the Court of Appeal in *Strombus v Insurance Corporation of Ireland*,[401] the 'substance of the dispute was being litigated'.[402] The result is also surprising in light of the fact that the English proceedings involved claims for negative declaratory relief.[403]

Earlier in this chapter, reference was made to what Mustill LJ once **3.140** described as the 'good management of concurrent sets of proceedings'.[404] He was referring in the context of the case before him to the granting of a temporary stay of one set of proceedings pending the resolution of a related set of proceedings. That is a technique which has been employed in some intellectual property litigation.[405] A temporary stay was granted in *Mackay Refined Sugars (NZ) v NZ Sugar Co*[406] in circumstances where proceedings between the same parties in Australia were at an advanced stage of preparation.[407] On one view, although never explicitly justified on case management grounds, anti-suit injunctions granted in *Glencore*

---

[399] [1989] 2 Lloyd's Rep 298.   [400] ibid 305.

[401] [1985] 2 Lloyd's Rep 138, 144.

[402] See also *The Vishva Abha* [1990] 2 Lloyd's Rep 312, where Sheen J accorded little significance to related proceedings in South Africa in which the defendants in the English proceedings were involved and which could have produced inconsistent findings on the central issue of liability for the maritime collision.

[403] See paras 4.250 ff below.

[404] *HM Attorney-General v Arthur Andersen & Co* [1989] ECC 224, 229.

[405] See, for example, *Sterling Pharmaceuticals v The Boots Company (Australia)* (1992) 34 FCR 287.

[406] [1997] 3 NZLR 476.

[407] See also *DA Technology Australia v Discreet Logic Inc* (Federal Court of Australia, 10 March 1994), where Gummow J granted a temporary stay pending the outcome of proceedings in Canada but, significantly, on the condition that the party seeking the stay would not assert issue estoppel arising out of the Canadian litigation.

International AG v Exter Shipping Ltd[408] and *Allstate Life Insurance Co v Australia and New Zealand Banking Group Ltd*[409] may be viewed as a variation on the theme to which Mustill LJ alluded.[410]

3.141   It is interesting and not surprising to note that there is evidence of a similar sensitivity to the dangers of the exercise of concurrent jurisdiction in American jurisprudence in this area and it has been stated that 'dismissal [on *forum non conveniens* grounds] is more likely if there are related actions pending in the foreign forum'.[411] Familiar themes emerge. Thus, the desirability of resolving 'all claims in one trial'[412] was an important factor in the dismissal of proceedings in *Piper Aircraft Co v Reyno*[413] and *Pain v United Technologies Corp*,[414] for example. Cognate with this concern is a consciousness of the waste of judicial resources where proceedings are duplicated. In *Banco Nominees Ltd v Iroquois Brands Ltd*,[415] for example, it was stated that:

> It is a waste of judicial resources to require two courts to attend to this matter when there is the chance that the cases could be consolidated in England. This factor weighs in favour of dismissing the case so that it may be pursued in England.[416]

3.142   The concern to minimize the scope for concurrent litigation and to consolidate proceedings wherever possible may, of course, conversely, recommend the retention of jurisdiction in the United States because of the ability to implead third parties,[417] although it should be noted that, where a third party defendant is foreign, constitutional obstacles may stand in this course.[418] As shall be seen in the next chapter, two lines of authority have emerged in United States Circuit courts concerning the propriety of issuing anti-suit injunctions. One line of authority, championed by Posner CJ, favours the relatively free use of anti-suit injunctions

---

[408] [2002] 2 All ER (Comm) 1.

[409] (1996) 64 FCR 1 and 44.

[410] See further the discussion in paras 4.204 ff below.

[411] Reynolds, WL, 'The Proper Forum for a Suit: Transnational Forum Non Conveniens and Counter-Suit Injunctions in the Federal Courts' (1992) 70 Texas Law Review 1663, 1683 and see Born, GB and Westin, D, *International Civil Litigation in United States Courts* (2nd edn, 1992) 292. The following cases provide examples: *Brinco Mining Ltd v Federal Insurance Co* 552 F Supp 1233 (DDC,1982); *Ingersoll Milling Machine Co v Granger* 833 F 2d 680 (7th Cir, 1987); cf *Neuchatel Swiss General Insurance Co v Lufthansa Airlines* 925 F 2d 1193 (9th Cir, 1991).

[412] *Piper Aircraft Co v Reyno* 454 US 235, 259 (1981).

[413] ibid.

[414] 637 F 2d 775, 790 (DC Cir, 1980).

[415] 748 F Supp 1070 (D Del, 1990).

[416] ibid 1078.

[417] See *American Home Assurance Co v Insurance Corporation of Ireland* 603 F Supp 636, 643 (1984) and Freedman, W (n 156 above) 83.

[418] See paras 4.27 ff below and see Kennelly, JJ (n 155 above) 181–199.

to avoid the standard problems of concurrent proceedings.[419] On the other hand, and in sharp contradistinction to this approach, is another line of authority that, by reason of a perception of the requirements of comity, all but mandates parallel litigation in the absence of a stay of proceedings being granted.[420]

The preceding pages have endeavoured to focus in considerable detail **3.143** upon the particular problems of identifying the natural forum in typically complex cases of transnational litigation involving several parties. This examination has revealed an especially strong concern on the part of the courts to 'group' related litigation in so far as is possible, with a view to minimizing the likelihood of inconsistent results and avoiding the waste of resources which multiple proceedings necessarily entail. In this context, the natural forum has been seen to be that with which the *entire dispute* has the closest and most real connection, as opposed to that forum (not necessarily the same) having the closest and most real connection to a dispute which is but an aspect of the larger contest. It may be objected that this clear policy goal is in tension with what has been argued to be the primary reason for the emergence of the concept of the natural forum, namely the desire to effect some measure of fairness as between the parties as to choice of forum. A court's desire to resolve all aspects of a dispute in one set of proceedings may mean that, from a particular defendant's perspective, resolution of that aspect of the dispute in which it is involved may not take place in the natural forum.

There are several responses to this apparent tension. First, in a two party **3.144** case, the problem is unlikely to arise; secondly, the forum in which proceedings can be grouped will often be the natural forum according to the ordinary process of identification; thirdly, in certain types of case, a defendant should have a reasonable expectation that litigation will be fought out 'in the round' so that the decision to proceed in one forum or not to proceed in favour of another forum will not be unfair to the party affected; finally, in those cases where the policies do clash, one must simply be viewed as taking priority over the other.

The Unifying Conception of the Natural Forum

The final observation of a conceptual nature to be made with regard to the **3.145** natural forum is that its evolution in the context of the staying of proceedings

---

[419] *Allendale Insurance Corp v Bull Data Systems Inc* 10 F 3d 425 (7th Cir, 1993). The decision of Lindgren J in the Federal Court of Australia in *Allstate Life Insurance Co v Australia and New Zealand Banking Group Ltd [No 4]* (1996) 64 FCR 1 and 44 as well as the actual result in *Société Nationale Industrielle Aerospatiale v Lee Kui Jak* [1987] AC 871 are to similar effect.

[420] *Laker Airways v Sabena* 731 F 2d 909 (DC Cir, 1984); *Gau Shan* 956 F 2d 1349 (6th Cir, 1992).

permitted some assimilation with the common law's approach to granting leave to a plaintiff to serve a defendant with process while outside the jurisdiction. Apart from the need to satisfy the court that it is authorized to entertain proceedings against a party not served within the jurisdiction by reference to applicable rules of court, and that there is a serious question to be tried,[421] in England a plaintiff is also required to establish to the court that England is a *forum conveniens* for the resolution of the dispute.[422] Failure to demonstrate this has the consequence that no leave will be granted.[423] The older cases put the need for the satisfaction of this requirement on the basis that to bring a defendant, *ex hypothesi* not resident in the forum, to England to contest a claim constituted a serious imposition in terms of inconvenience and disruption.[424] Such an imposition could only be justified if the claim was so closely related to England that it could be described as *forum conveniens*. In this limited circumstance, therefore, it would be neither unreasonable nor unfair to subject a defendant to the exercise of exorbitant jurisdiction.

3.146 The term 'natural forum' does not appear to have been employed in the context of establishing *forum conveniens* for the purposes of service out of the jurisdiction, but, even if what was traditionally required to be shown to satisfy that description was something less than that England was 'clearly and distinctly the more appropriate forum', the House of Lords' decision in *Spiliada*, in point of fact an Order 11 case,[425] completed the process of assimilation.[426] Lord Goff was clear that both cases in essence involved the same inquiry, namely what was the natural forum for the resolution of the dispute.[427] If England was the natural forum in a service out case (and the other requirements imposed by the Civil Procedure Rules were satisfied, for example, that the case concerned a contract breached in England), leave would be granted to serve the defendant out of the jurisdiction; if England was not the natural forum in a case in which

---

[421] To express the test in its most recent formulation, see *Seaconsar Far East Ltd v Bank Markazi Jomhouri Islami Iran* [1994] 1 AC 438 and see further discussion in paras 4.13 ff below.

[422] See Collins, LA, 'Some Aspects of Service Out of the Jurisdiction in English Law' (1972) 21 ICLQ 656, 657–663.

[423] See, for example, *Chaney v Murphy* (1948) 64 TLR 489, 493; *Amin Rasheed Corp v Kuwait Insurance* [1984] AC 50, 65 per Lord Diplock, 72 per Lord Wilberforce.

[424] *Société Générale de Paris v Dreyfus Brothers* (1885) 29 ChD 239, 242–243 per Pearson J; approved at (1887) 37 ChD 215. See also *The Hagen* [1908] P 189, 201; *The Brabo* [1949] AC 326, 350.

[425] See now the Civil Procedure Rules.

[426] cf *Amin Rasheed Shipping Corp v Kuwait Insurance Co* [1984] AC 50, 72, where Lord Wilberforce had expressed some doubt about the help to be derived in Order 11 cases from those concerned with the staying of proceedings.

[427] [1987] AC 460, 480–481.

a stay was sought, and the natural forum could be identified elsewhere, then a stay would be granted in favour of that jurisdiction.

In addition to stay and service out cases, the 'natural forum' has emerged **3.147** as something of a *core* concept in related areas of the law concerned with jurisdiction in transnational litigation. In *Castanho v Brown & Root (UK) Ltd* ('*Castanho*'),[428] a case in which an injunction was sought to restrain the institution of proceedings in Texas, Lord Scarman stated that 'the principle is the same whether the remedy sought is the stay of English proceedings or a restraint upon foreign proceedings'.[429] On this view, an injunction should lie wherever, in the converse situation, a stay would be granted, that is, where litigation is not proceeding in the natural forum.[430] Concluding that 'Texas is as natural and proper a forum for suing a group of Texan-based companies as England',[431] Lord Scarman declined to grant the anti-suit injunctive relief in this case. Although the approach adopted in *Castanho* was subsequently revised by the Privy Council in *Société Nationale Industrielle Aerospatiale v Lee Kui Jak*,[432] the natural forum still has an important role to play in any decision to grant anti-suit injunctive relief, as the later decision in *Airbus Industrie v Patel*[433] made plain. With the exception of the so-called 'single forum' class of cases,[434] it is a general prerequisite to the grant of such relief that the court issuing anti-suit injunctive relief itself be the natural forum for the resolution of the substantive litigation.[435]

The Supreme Court of Canada has put the concept to even further use in **3.148** this context by holding that such relief should not be granted if the court in which the foreign proceedings have been commenced could itself reasonably be described as the natural forum.[436] Furthermore, in another important common law development in Canada, the Supreme Court appears to have identified an important role for the natural forum to play in the recognition and enforcement of foreign country judgments, holding that a foreign default judgment may be enforced in circumstances where it was handed down in what the enforcing court considers to be the

---

[428] [1981] AC 557. [429] ibid 574–575.

[430] This was the approach adopted by the Brunei Court of Appeal in *Société Nationale Industrielle Aerospatiale v Lee Kui Jak*: see [1987] AC 871, 887–891.

[431] [1981] AC 557, 576.

[432] [1987] AC 871, 896.

[433] [1999] 1 AC 119. See, also, *Turner v Grovit* [2002] 1 WLR 107, 118–119.

[434] See *British Airways Board v Laker Airways Ltd* [1985] AC 58, discussed below at paras 4.109 ff.

[435] *Société Nationale Industrielle Aerospatiale v Lee Kui Jak* [1987] AC 871, 896.

[436] *Amchem Products Inc v Workers Compensation Board* [1993] 1 SCR 897, 932 and see discussion of this case by Edinger, ER at (1993) 72 Canadian Bar Review 366.

natural forum.[437] It has also been suggested that the 'natural forum' may play a role in the *non*-recognition of foreign country judgments where jurisdiction has been assumed solely on the basis of the defendant's temporary presence within the jurisdiction.[438]

4. THE NATURAL FORUM—THE CONCEPT CRITICIZED

3.149 On an abstract and conceptual level, the 'natural forum' is an extremely attractive notion, a claim which even its strongest critics accept.[439] At least in circumstances where there is contention between the parties as to where to litigate, it has been seen that it appears to offer an effective, efficient, and even-handed solution. In both stay and 'service out' cases, it operates to allocate litigation to that forum with which the dispute has 'the most real and substantial connection'. And in injunction cases, although larger questions of sovereignty and comity are at play because the grant of anti-suit injunctive relief may be perceived to constitute an interference with the process of another court, it has been seen that reference to the natural forum is an important aspect of the inquiry for, if injunctive relief is granted, it will constrain the parties to proceed in the natural forum. As for its incipient role in the realm of recognition and enforcement of judgments, so far only taking root in Canada, it acts as a discipline to plaintiffs to proceed in the natural forum, at least in so far as a particular plaintiff may wish to enforce its judgment in a third forum.

3.150 Although widely welcomed in academic circles[440] and extensively followed in other common law jurisdictions with one notable exception,[441] the concept of the natural forum has not been without its critics. These criticisms relate to both matters of fundamental principle and practical shortcomings involved in the search for the natural forum. These criticisms warrant close and careful scrutiny for, as has been seen, the 'natural forum' is the core concept which has been developed by common law courts to deal not only with the particular problem of forum shopping

---

[437] *Morguard Investments Ltd v de Savoye* [1990] 3 SCR 1077 and see Briggs, A, 'Foreign Judgments: More Surprises' (1992) 109 LQR 449. For further discussion of this development, see paras 4.296 ff below.

[438] Briggs, A, 'Which Foreign Judgments Should We Recognise Today?' (1987) 36 ICLQ 240; and 'Foreign Judgments: More Surprises' (1992) 109 LQR 449.

[439] *Voth v Manildra Flour Mills Pty Ltd* (1990) 171 CLR 538, 557 per Mason CJ, Deane, Dawson, and Gaudron JJ. See also *Oceanic Sun Line Special Shipping Co Inc v Fay* (1988) 165 CLR 197, 234 per Brennan J.

[440] See, for example, Briggs, A, 'Forum Non Conveniens—The Last Word?' [1987] LMCLQ 1; Pryles, MC, 'Liberalising the Rule on Staying of Actions—Towards the Doctrine of Forum Non Conveniens' (1978) 52 ALJ 678.

[441] Australia: see *Oceanic Sun Line Special Shipping Co Inc v Fay* (1988) 165 CLR 197; *Voth v Manildra Flour Mills Pty Ltd* (1990) 171 CLR 538; *Renault v Zhang* (2002) 187 ALR 1.

but also with the more general problem of several forums having concurrent jurisdiction over an ever increasing number of transnational disputes.

The Natural Forum and the Rule of Law

In *Oceanic Sun Line Special Shipping Co Inc v Fay*,[442] Brennan J suggested **3.151** that the broad discretion reposed in the courts by the doctrine of *forum non conveniens* was inconsistent with the rule of law which imposed upon courts a 'duty to exercise their jurisdiction when litigants invoke it',[443] a view similar to that adopted by McHugh JA in the New South Wales Court of Appeal.[444] Invocation of the rule of law in order to attack the concept of the natural forum is, however, ill-conceived. Indeed one commentator has argued that, on the contrary, traditional jurisdictional rules of the type advocated by Brennan J[445] and which lend themselves to forum shopping are themselves contrary to the rule of law:

So long as the legal consequences of a defendant's actions depend on the discretion of the plaintiff in choosing a forum for litigation, it is not possible for the defendant to know his or her rights and obligations with sufficient certainty in advance of acting.[446]

A similar view was powerfully expressed in practical terms by Callinan J **3.152** of the High Court of Australia in dissent in *Renault v Zhang*:[447]

'Forum shopping' has a capacity to affect all nations, including Australia, with established and fair judicial systems. If persons injured or damaged elsewhere are free to pursue their claims in this country because they think that they will enjoy greater prospects of success here than in the jurisdiction in which the damage was inflicted, then it is only to be expected that other nations, whose curial proceedings provide more generous results for plaintiffs, whether by way of huge awards of exemplary damages or otherwise, will be receptive to forum shopping in those nations' courts by their nationals and others who have been damaged or injured in this country. The consequences in these circumstances for people and corpora-

---

[442] (1988) 165 CLR 197.   [443] ibid 239.   [444] (1987) 8 NSWLR 242, 267–268.

[445] In *Oceanic*, Brennan J advocated retention of a test which had been adopted by the High Court in *Maritime Insurance Co Ltd v Geelong Harbour Trust Commissioners* (1908) 6 CLR 194 and which was similar in content to the St Pierre test. It is to be noted that in *Voth v Manildra Flour Mills Pty Ltd*, though arriving at a different conclusion on the facts, his Honour subscribed to what had emerged as a majority approach in *Oceanic* in the interests of *stare decisis*: see (1990) 171 CLR 538, 572.

[446] Opeskin, BR (n 243 above) 17. On arguments concerning the rule of law, see especially 15–17, where Opeskin draws on Joseph Raz, *The Authority of Law* (1979). See also 'Forum Shopping Reconsidered' (1990) 103 Harvard Law Review 1677, 1687 where the author observes that acceptance of forum shopping 'threatens not only the concept of the rule of law, but also the image of apolitical neutrality that the legal system tries to create'.

[447] (2002) 187 ALR 1, para 196.

tions in this country who have complied with all relevant laws and standards, have paid their taxes and insured against risks on the basis of the law applying where they live or operate in this country, could be grave and unpredictable and, ultimately devastating.

There is no little irony in the fact that one of the justifications for the adoption by the majority of the High Court of Australia in *Renault v Zhang*[448] of the *lex loci delicti* as the choice of law rule for tort with no flexible exception was, as it had been in the Court's earlier federal choice of law decision in *John Pfeiffer v Rogerson*,[449] that the traditional rule in *Phillips v Eyre* lent itself, at least on one view, to forum shopping.

3.153 Cavers has also expressed the view that widely drawn rules of jurisdiction untempered by a doctrine of *forum non conveniens* rather than the operation of that doctrine itself are inimical to the rule of law.[450]

3.154 Justice Brennan's concern for the infraction of the rule of law proceeded from his view that it was illegitimate for the courts, through the exercise of a discretion 'guided by no more specific a touchstone than the ends of justice',[451] to alter parties' rights. The concern of the courts, in his view, was 'the enforcement of *existing* rights and liabilities', not 'the creation, modification or abolition of rights and liabilities'.[452] It is certainly the case, as was made clear in Chapter 2, that decisions concerning jurisdiction in private international law *do* have the potential to affect rights and liabilities. But the very point about parties' rights and liabilities in the type of case under consideration in this book is that they are not necessarily fixed and immutable. The greater the number of potential forums, the greater the potential disparity in content of the parties' respective rights and liabilities, hence the need for a doctrine which minimizes the plaintiff's ability to determine the content of those rights and liabilities in its own interest through a unilateral choice of forum.[453]

3.155 The perceived danger to the rule of law represented by the doctrine of *forum non conveniens* is, at best, overstated. While, as shall be seen, the 'natural forum' will not always be easy to identify, it offers greater prospects to defendants of identifying the content of their rights or liabilities than jurisdictional rules by which their content may be determined by nothing more than a chance presence in the forum. Another way of expressing this may be to say, borrowing perhaps not coincidentally from the realm of administrative law and notions of procedural fairness, that a party's legitimate

---

[448] (2002) 187 ALR 1.
[449] (2000) 203 CLR 503.   [450] Cavers, DF, *The Choice of Law Process* (1965) 23.
[451] *Oceanic* (1988) 165 CLR 197, 239.   [452] ibid (emphasis added).
[453] Pryles, MC, 'Judicial Darkness on the Oceanic Sun' (1988) 62 ALJ 774, 782–783 makes a similar criticism of this aspect of Brennan J's analysis.

expectations as to its rights and liabilities are best assessed by reference to prevailing standards in the natural forum. It is significant to note that, in *Amchem Products Inc v Workers Compensation Board*,[454] Sopinka J spoke in this language when discussing the natural forum.[455]

Uncertainty and the Natural Forum

As noted above, Brennan J stated that the court's discretion in a *forum non conveniens* case is 'guided by no more specific a touchstone than the ends of justice'.[456] While one of the most frequent criticisms of the doctrine concerns its uncertain operation, in making this observation, Brennan J seems, with respect, to have greatly oversimplified the approach enunciated by Lord Goff in *Spiliada*. There his Lordship made it clear that the primary search is for the natural forum, understood in the sense of that forum with which the dispute has 'the most real and substantial connection', with the sensible proviso that justice is available in that jurisdiction.[457] Brennan J's criticism nonetheless touches upon what is seen to be the doctrine of *forum non conveniens's* greatest practical weakness, namely its uncertain operation in an area where certainty should be at a premium. **3.156**

In *Spiliada*, Lord Templeman who, it should be noted, embraced the concept of the natural forum, stated that the factors which a court may take into account in the process of its ascertainment are 'legion' and that 'the authorities do not, perhaps cannot, give any clear guidance as to how these factors are to be weighed in any particular case'.[458] This is an observation which has been seized upon by critics of the 'natural forum' approach who argue that it is necessarily uncertain and, indeed, unworkable because it requires the comparison of 'incomparables'.[459] One commentator has observed that 'the risk in having a flexible discretionary **3.157**

---

[454] [1993] 1 SCR 897.

[455] At 920 ibid, he stated that 'a party whose case has a real and substantial connection with a forum has a legitimate claim to the advantages that that forum provides. The legitimacy of this claim is based on a reasonable expectation that in the event of litigation arising out of the transaction in question, those advantages will be available', and at 933 he expressed the same view in negative terms: 'A party can have no reasonable expectations of advantages available in a jurisdiction with which the party and the subject matter of the litigation has little or no connection' (emphasis added).

[456] *Oceanic* (1988) 165 CLR 197, 239.

[457] [1987] AC 460, 476–478.

[458] [1987] AC 460, 465. See also *The Atlantic Star* [1974] AC 436, 468 per Lord Wilberforce, who stated that drawing the 'critical equation' will frequently be difficult and be done 'by an instinctive process'.

[459] 'The exercise of this discretion involves the balancing of diverse and unquantifiable objective factors of "appropriateness" ': Carter, PB, 'Decisions of British Courts During 1972–1973: Private International Law' (1972–1973) 46 BYIL 428, 430; Slater, AG, 'Forum Non Conveniens: A View from the Shop Floor' (1988) 104 LQR 554, 572.

test which is based upon a "legion" of connecting factors is that it will not yield consistent and predictable results'.[460] But it may be questioned whether the factors to be taken into account are, in fact, 'legion' and whether the process of assessment is quite as difficult as Lord Templeman's observation has been taken to imply.

3.158 Much of the difficulty and confusion which is said to arise in the identification of the natural forum may be attributed to the pre-*Spiliada* dictum of Lord Diplock in *MacShannon*:

> In order to justify a stay two conditions must be satisfied, one positive and one negative: (a) the defendant must satisfy the court that there is another forum to whose jurisdiction he is amenable in which justice can be done between the parties at substantially less inconvenience or expense, and (b) the stay must not deprive the plaintiff of a legitimate personal or juridical advantage which would be available to him if he invoked the jurisdiction of the English court.[461]

3.159 In the tradition of the common law's evolutionary modus operandi, this statement was a self-conscious reformulation of Scott LJ's leading statement in *St Pierre*.[462] Notwithstanding the opinion voiced by Lord Goff that Lord Diplock would only have regarded the passage cited above 'as a tentative statement [of the law] at an early stage of a period of development',[463] this passage has been particularly influential, even after *Spiliada*, and lower courts have from time to time continued to employ the language of a plaintiff's 'legitimate personal or juridical advantage'. It is no doubt true that the 'weighing' of advantages and disadvantages to the parties of litigation in a particular forum is a difficult and at times impossible exercise.[464] Such a process, however, forms no part of the inquiry into the natural forum; rather it represents something of a hangover of the common law's traditional focus on the advantages to the parties, especially the plaintiff, of suing in a particular forum. Writing between the decisions in *MacShannon* and *Spiliada*, Barma and Elvin were right to point out that:

> [a]t present, the court is required to consider the nature and possible effect of largely speculative questions of advantage and disadvantage. The weighing-up in the proposed 'natural forum' principle ['most real and substantial connection'] is a consideration of *much more certain and objectively demonstrable factors*.[465]

---

[460] Hayes, EL, 'Forum Non Conveniens in England, Australia and Japan: The Allocation of Jurisdiction in Transnational Litigation' (1992) 26 UBCLR 41, 64.

[461] [1978] AC 795, 812.   [462] See para 3.72 above.

[463] *Spiliada* [1987] AC 460, 475.

[464] 'The balancing of advantage and disadvantage is uncertain in that it puts a misplaced trust in the weighing of what are in reality imponderables, for it is often impossible to state accurately the value, if any, of the alleged advantages claimed before a matter actually is tried and disposed of (and sometimes the effect of the alleged advantage remains unclear even then)': Barma and Elvin (n 229 above) 55.

[465] (n 229 above) 62 (emphasis added).

The subsequent experience of the courts suggests that identification of the **3.160** natural forum is not usually a hopelessly imponderable task. As Bingham LJ observed in *Banco Atlantico SA v The British Bank of the Middle East*,[466] 'the question itself is defined by authority and there is clear authoritative guidance on the matters which may and may not be considered in answering it'.[467] Similarly Sheen J, who, as the Admiralty judge, probably had more occasion to identify the natural forum than most judges, has observed 'that there are cases in which the facts speak for themselves in showing in which country there is an appropriate forum'.[468] Statements such as these in large measure answer claims that the task of identifying the natural forum is one ridden with uncertainty.

Notwithstanding such affirmations that *Spiliada* is workable in practice, it **3.161** must be conceded that in some transnational disputes the identification of the natural forum may be an extremely difficult task because various factors can point to different forums; the preponderance of evidence, the location and availability of witnesses, and the law to be applied as a result of the choice of law process will often not be geographically coincident. So much was in fact conceded by Lord Goff in *Spiliada*:

there are cases where no particular forum can be described as the natural forum for the trial of the action. Such cases are particularly likely to occur in commercial disputes, where there can be pointers to a number of different jurisdictions, or in Admiralty, in the case of collisions on the high seas.[469]

In many cases, the indicia of the natural forum will be in such tension that **3.162** it will be scarcely sensible to speak of the dispute in question as having a 'natural forum', let alone a forum that is clearly the most appropriate forum.[470] Alternatively, it could be that several forums attract this description.[471] The difficulty of identifying the natural forum in some cases provides no reason, however, for renouncing it or the doctrine of *forum non conveniens* as a general proposition. In cases where more than one natural or appropriate forum can be identified, the most egregious instances of forum shopping will still be thwarted. Further, in many of the types of disputes referred to by Lord Goff in the passage from *Spiliada*

---

[466] [1990] 2 Lloyd's Rep 504. [467] ibid 506.
[468] *The Vishva Abha* [1990] 2 Lloyd's Rep 312, 313.
[469] [1987] AC 460, 477. See also *European Asian Bank AG v Punjab and Sind Bank* [1981] 2 Lloyd's Rep 651, 658.
[470] See, for example, *The Coral Isis* [1986] 1 Lloyd's Rep 413, 416 and *The Po* [1990] 1 Lloyd's Rep 418, 423.
[471] *Castanho* [1981] AC 557, 576 per Lord Scarman; *The Netty* [1981] 2 Lloyd's Rep 57, 60 per Sheen J; *Amchem Products Inc v Workers Compensation Board* [1993] 1 SCR 897, 912 per Sopinka J. See also *Voth v Manildra Flour Mills Pty Ltd* (1990) 171 CLR 538, 558; cf 586 per Toohey J: 'There can, in theory, be only one such forum, however difficult it may be, in practice, to identify it.'

cited above, the parties will previously have made an agreement as to which forum should provide the venue for the resolution of any subsequent disputes so that the need to identify the natural forum as an independent exercise will not arise.[472]

3.163 The most telling attack based on the uncertainty and unpredictability of the task of identifying the natural forum relates to the fact that this process will occur at a necessarily early stage of proceedings so that it will often be difficult to assess matters of convenience and likely expense at that time. Indeed, so much was recognized by Lord Diplock in *MacShannon*.[473] Slater has trenchantly observed that 'to debate these questions at length at an early stage is frequently a speculative and futile exercise'.[474] In some cases at least this observation must be correct,[475] although it might be pointed out that one of the virtues of the 'most real and substantial connection' version of the test for identifying the natural forum is that it de-emphasizes the significance of matters of 'convenience' and 'expense'. Further, as to the duration of battles over venue in transnational litigation, parties will be conscious of the firm suggestion of Lord Templeman in *Spiliada* that jurisdictional challenges or applications for stays of proceedings should be 'measured in hours and not days'.[476] The High Court of Australia would prefer 'minutes not hours'[477] but this aspiration has not been borne out in practice and, bearing in mind that Court's view that, where, on such an application, if anything is to be made of the substantive content of an arguably applicable foreign law, the differences between that law and the local law must be identified in a full and admissible way,[478] it is quite unrealistic if any attention is to be paid to the significance of the fact that a foreign law will govern the dispute.

3.164 It is important to note that criticisms as to the uncertain and unpredictable operation of the doctrine of *forum non conveniens* in the United States—'trying to predict what courts will rule regarding ... forum non conveniens is like trying to tattoo soap bubbles'[479]—should be treated with considerable reserve and not automatically translated in order to criticize the use of that doctrine in other common law jurisdictions. Apart from the fact that much of the confusion in America arises because the individual

---

[472] Jurisdiction agreements form the subject matter of Chapter 5 of this book.
[473] [1978] AC 795, 813. See also *Sim v Robinow* (1892) 19 R 665, 668 per Lord Kinnear.
[474] (n 459 above) 568.
[475] See also *Voth v Manildra Flour Mills Pty Ltd* (1990) 171 CLR 538, 558.
[476] [1987] AC 460, 465.
[477] *Voth v Manildra Flour Mills* (1991) 171 CLR 538, 565.
[478] *Zhang v Renault* (2002) 187 ALR 1.
[479] Kennelly, JJ (n 155 above) 177; and see Robertson, DW (n 250 above) 426; Hay, P, 'Transient Jurisdiction After Burnham' (1990) Uni of Illinois L Rev 593, 603 n 76; and also see *Gulf Oil Corp v Gilbert* 330 US 501 (1947), 516 per Black J (dissenting).

States are not bound to follow federal precedent in this area,[480] the two leading Supreme Court decisions proceed from a different policy concern to that which it has been argued underpins the line of cases culminating in *Spiliada*.[481] The concerns of fairness which lie at the heart of the common law's use of the doctrine of *forum non conveniens* are, to a certain extent, accommodated in the United States by the requirements imposed by the due process clause of the Constitution.[482] This has the consequence that the role of *forum non conveniens* is not expected to cover the same territory as its common law counterpart. A further element of this difference is that, in addition to the weighing of the private interests of the parties, questions of public interest such as the state of docket congestion and the forum's occasional interest in regulating the activities of resident corporations are taken into account. As was also seen above, under *Piper Aircraft Co v Reyno*,[483] special consideration is given to a plaintiff's American nationality in *forum non conveniens* dismissal applications.

The Natural Forum and Abuse of Process

A final criticism of the doctrine of *forum non conveniens* and the elevation **3.165** to centre stage of the concept of the natural forum is that interlocutory litigation over the question of venue is likely to be encouraged and the process of the courts abused. One such perceived abuse is the use of stay applications to delay or 'buy time'.[484] Writing extrajudicially at the time of the decision in *Spiliada*, Sir Michael Kerr had cause to comment that:

> with the rise in interest rates, the value of cash in hand has become greater in all aspects of commerce than the cost of fighting losing cases, particularly since judgments and awards—if their payment could not be avoided altogether—have normally carried interest at far lower rates than the cost of borrowing in the interim. Dragging out disputed legal processes as long as possible has become a commercial objective in itself.[485]

It is no doubt tempting for critics of the natural forum to link the **3.166** doctrine's operation with the use and clogging of the courts for illegitimate tactical purposes.[486] There are several responses to such charges. First, there is the direction of Lord Templeman in *Spiliada* itself that stay

---

[480] See further at paras 4.74 ff below.
[481] Namely, a primary focus on convenience, including that of the court, rather than fairness as between the parties.
[482] See further at paras 4.27 ff below.
[483] 454 US 235, 125–126 (1981).
[484] See, for example, *The Goldean Mariner* [1989] 2 Lloyd's Rep 390, 403.
[485] 'Commercial Dispute Resolution: The Changing Scene' in Bos, M and Brownlie, I, *Liber Amicorum for Lord Wilberforce* (1987) 116.
[486] See, for example, Hayes, E (n 460 above) 64.

applications should be dealt with expeditiously.[487] There is also the strongest indication given in that case that the prospects of success on appeal are extremely limited.[488] Secondly, if the principal incentive for delay is the low rates of official interest awarded on any ultimate money judgment, then the appropriate course is to amend the relevant rules of court so as to link awards with prevailing rates of inflation and commercial interest rates. Finally, if the court's process really is being abused, it is always open to it to prevent such abuse in the exercise of its inherent jurisdiction.

3.167 More generally, the advent of the natural forum and the cognate doctrine of *forum non conveniens* have elicited judicial murmurings and what is perhaps a certain naïve apprehension that the court processes are becoming embroiled in the undoubted strategic warfare that transnational litigation often entails. In *The Delfini*,[489] for example, Phillips J observed that:

> The doctrine of forum conveniens has become a firmly established part of English law. Defendants have not been slow to take advantage of this . . . For better or worse this has led defendants and their advisers to focus attention on the question of jurisdiction . . . at the outset of legal proceedings.[490]

3.168 The unwritten assumption is that the doctrine of *forum non conveniens* lends itself peculiarly to such interlocutory skirmishes. Obviously the doctrine is less certain than the traditional jurisdictional rules considered in paragraphs 3.71 ff above but the law frequently has to trade off the value of certainty against the requirements of fairness to litigants.[491] If, as it is strongly considered to be the case, the plaintiff is not to have the freedom unilaterally to decide what may be the highly significant issue of venue for the resolution of a transnational dispute, then an increase in litigation in relation to this question is the necessary price to pay. It is preferable that such litigation should occur by reference to rules developed by the courts to effect a fair outcome than that one party should be able to secure a favourable result at the defendant's expense simply by virtue of the fact that a state's broadly drawn jurisdictional rules permit a plaintiff to enhance its prospects of success. As Weintrub has observed, 'forum non conveniens furthers efficient and fair use of our judicial resources'.[492]

---

[487] [1987] AC 460, 465.
[488] ibid.
[489] [1988] 2 Lloyd's Rep 599.
[490] ibid 612.
[491] See, for example, Gleeson, AM, 'Clarity or Fairness: Which is More Important?' (1990) 12 Sydney Law Review 305.
[492] 'International Litigation and Forum Non Conveniens' (1994) 23 Texas International Law Journal 321, 352.

Moreover if it is the case that interlocutory proceedings play 'a very **3.169** significant part' in securing the settlement of many commercial cases[493] and the policy of the law is to encourage such settlement, then it is no valid criticism that litigation occurs in relation to an interlocutory matter rather than the substantive dispute. Where the interlocutory litigation concerns the question of the venue for the resolution of a transnational dispute, it has been seen in paragraphs 1.31 ff above that the determination of this matter will frequently be a prelude to settlement of the substantive dispute.[494]

IV. CONCLUSION

This chapter has explored two different conceptual responses to forum **3.170** shopping and the more general problems of venue in modern transnational litigation. Its examination of the scheme of the Brussels Convention and Council Regulation 44/2001 and the relatively recent emergence in the common law of the core notion of the 'natural forum' has revealed strikingly similar concerns: first, an interest to prevent plaintiffs from commencing litigation in an inappropriate forum; and secondly, to guard against, so far as is possible, the consequences of litigation concerning the same or related matters in more than one forum. While both approaches have certain virtues, neither is without its flaws.

There is much that is theoretically attractive in the scheme enshrined in **3.171** the Brussels Convention and now Regulation 44/2001 and, more generally, in the model of a *convention double*. The appeal of that model is essentially twofold. First, it specifies *certain* rules of jurisdiction which are designed to benefit litigants and minimize the scope for what are perceived to be essentially unmeritorious and, in terms of resources, wasteful clashes over the issue of jurisdiction. Secondly, it introduces a mechanism for reducing the likelihood of concurrent and related litigation, thereby anticipating and avoiding not only the prospect of inconsistent decisions but also the unseemly spectacle of a 'race to judgment'. On the other hand, it provides no panacea to the reality that the venue of any given transnational litigation is often itself worth litigating about or at least perceived to be worth litigating about. It has been said that:

---

[493] Sir John Donaldson, Foreword to the first edition of Goldrein, IS and Wilkinson, KHP, *Commercial Litigation: Pre-Emptive Remedies* reprinted in the 2nd edition (1991) vii.

[494] So much was explicitly recognized by Phillips LJ in *Milor SRL v British Airways plc* [1996] QB 702, 710.

The Brussels Convention system, despite its many advantages in securing a common basis for jurisdiction and, with that, an extensive basis for the enforcement of foreign judgments, has not eliminated forum shopping, nor has it prevented jurisdictional issues from becoming major pieces of interlocutory litigation leading, in particular where reference to the European Court is required, to considerable delay to the litigation process. [495]

3.172 It has been doubted, moreover, whether, as a practical matter, the Brussels Convention provides a paradigm for a wider jurisdiction and judgments convention. It is perhaps no coincidence that, with the exception of the United Kingdom and the Republic of Ireland, whose accession to the Brussels Convention is to be explained by extraneous political and economic exigencies, those states least likely to accept the bases and scheme of jurisdiction encapsulated in the Convention share a common law heritage. Fundamental differences of approach to the issue of jurisdiction between the civil and common law traditions also suggest that the unanimity of attitude necessary to secure agreement to a wider jurisdiction and judgments convention is unlikely to be achieved. The seeming collapse of the Hague Conference project for a global *convention double* testifies to this difficulty.

3.173 It is perhaps not surprising that, in these circumstances as well as in response to the need to develop sensitive and appropriate rules for the assumption and retention of jurisdiction at a time when transnational litigation is on the increase, the 'jurisdictional' rules of the common law have undergone a radical revision in the last twenty years. The discretionary aspect of the common law's attitude to questions of jurisdiction, which has always been one of its defining features, has, if anything, been increased. That discretion has been seen principally to operate by reference to the concept of the natural forum. Both in its origin and implementation, this concept is designed to thwart forum shopping which has generally been viewed by the courts with disdain. Moreover, it has been argued that, within certain limits, the natural forum is a sufficiently sophisticated and sensitive concept that it is able to accommodate the complexities of the question of what is an appropriate and fair venue for the resolution of typical modern transnational disputes, frequently involving multiple parties from different jurisdictions.

3.174 The advent of the doctrine of the natural forum has attracted criticism, the most powerful of which relates to what is perceived to be its uncertain compass. While such criticism is not to be lightly dismissed, a measure of uncertainty bred by the existence of a discretion is of the essence of the difference between the common law and civil law approaches in this area.

---

[495] Nygh, P and McLachlan, C, *Transnational Tort Litigation* (1996) 19

Discretion concerning the exercise of jurisdiction, moreover, is jealously guarded by common law courts. Provided that the discretion is exercised by reference to reasonably predictable criteria and the policy considerations which underpin its existence are sound, then the concept of the natural forum constitutes an appropriate and, in the majority of cases in which it is called into operation, effective cornerstone of the common law's response to the complex problems of venue in modern transnational litigation.

4

Venue and the Defendant—Reverse Forum Shopping

I.	Options for the Defendant	4.01
II.	Challenging Jurisdiction	4.12
	1. Challenging the Jurisdiction of Common Law Courts	4.13
	2. Constitutional Dimensions to Jurisdictional Challenges	4.27
III.	Staying Proceedings—*Forum Non Conveniens*	4.38
	1. *Spiliada* Applied	4.44
	2. Australian Abstention	4.67
	3. *Forum Non Conveniens* in the United States	4.74
IV.	Anti-Suit Injunctions	4.79
	1. Jurisdiction to Restrain Foreign Proceedings	4.84
	2. 'Protective' Anti-Suit Injunctions	4.125
	3. Anti-Suit Injunctions Upholding Legal Rights	4.146
	4. Restraint of Vexatious and Oppressive Foreign Proceedings	4.179
	5. Anti-Suit Injunctions and the Claims of Comity	4.223
V.	Negative Declaratory Proceedings	4.250
	1. The Mechanics of Negative Declaratory Relief	4.251
	2. Negative Declarations in the Common Law	4.261
	3. Negative Declarations and Council Regulation 44/2001	4.284
VI.	Ignoring Foreign Proceedings	4.294
	1. Threats to the Strategy—I	4.295
	2. Threats to the Strategy—II	4.296
VII.	Conclusion	4.304

I. OPTIONS FOR THE DEFENDANT

Chapter 1 of this book drew attention to the fact that, in relation to any **4.01** given transnational dispute, there are likely to be several forums willing prima facie to exercise jurisdiction. The phenomenon of concurrent jurisdiction highlighted the extent of choice open to a plaintiff as to the venue in which a transnational dispute may be resolved. In Chapter 2, various incentives for forum shopping were identified. These have the consequence that the plaintiff's 'right' to choose the forum can be an extremely valuable and important one. In the previous chapter, two conceptual responses were explored which are designed to ensure that this right is not abused and that jurisdiction is allocated between courts according to a rational set of principles or a unifying theme. Apart from regulating the relationship between plaintiff and defendant, it was seen that these conceptual responses also exhibited a common concern for the larger problems of concurrent jurisdiction, namely the possibility of inconsistent decisions and the wasteful duplication of judicial resources. This chapter seeks to move from the conceptual to the practical and explores the various strategies that are open to *defendants* in the battle for venue in transnational litigation.

4.02 In this context it has been said that 'the economics of modern commercial litigation, more than ever before, dictate that there is for defendants an enormous advantage in winning by way of an interlocutory proceeding, even if that involves appeals to the High Court, the House of Lords or the Privy Council'.[1] Even if ultimately unsuccessful, engaging in such a battle may yield ancillary benefits, not the least of which may be the deferment of any final payment to the plaintiff, a consideration of special importance at a time of high inflation.[2]

4.03 If the premise of the book is well founded and it is the case that venue will often be of crucial significance in transnational litigation, then it follows that a defendant will have as much interest as a plaintiff in securing a forum in which it is most likely to meet with success (or further its particular strategic motivation, which may be fragmentation, delay, or an impact on the sequence of complex proceedings—all with a view to enhancing the environment for commercial settlement). In *Cool Carriers AB v HSBC Bank (USA)*,[3] Tomlinson J sanguinely observed that, had the claimants' interpleader proceedings been able to be brought within a head of jurisdiction under the Civil Procedure Rules, not only would their own position have been safeguarded but there could have been a rapid resolution of all matters in dispute between all parties without prejudice to anyone 'assuming that all parties desire a swift and economic disposal of their disputes'.[4] Tomlinson J concluded 'of course, they do not'. On the morning of judgment, the Court was informed that the ship-owning parties, resisting a one-stop resolution, had filed for Chapter 11 protection in the United States of America.

---

[1] O'Brien, B, 'Stays of Proceedings and Transnational Injunctions' (1989) 12 Adelaide Law Review 201, 201.

[2] See Baade, HW, 'An Overview of Transnational Parallel Litigation: Recommended Strategies' (1981) 1 The Review of Litigation 191, 195 and Sir Michael Kerr, 'Commercial Dispute Resolution: The Changing Scene' in Bos, M and Brownlie, I, *Liber Amicorum for Lord Wilberforce* (1987) 116, cited in para 3.162 above.

[3] [2001] 2 Lloyd's Rep 22.

[4] ibid 30.

Forum shopping must not only be regarded as a positive phenomenon in **4.04** the sense that it consists solely of *plaintiffs* seeking out the most propitious forum in which to conduct litigation.[5] It is also negative. A *defendant* may seek to force the litigation into another forum by challenging a particular court's jurisdiction, applying for a stay of proceedings, or having those proceedings restrained by means of an anti-suit injunction. Another means by which a defendant may engage in forum shopping is through the commencement of proceedings in its own preferred forum in anticipation of substantive litigation in another jurisdiction chosen by the plaintiff and less congenial to the defendant. Such proceedings may themselves be for substantive relief or otherwise for a declaration of non-liability. If a defendant is able to obtain the latter type of relief, this may be sufficient to rob the plaintiff's proceedings in another jurisdiction of any potency, especially if the defendant's assets are in the forum. All of the above strategies, which may collectively be described as 'reverse forum shopping',[6] operate to negative any procedural or substantive disadvantages to the defendant in the plaintiff's preferred forum. Indeed it has been said that 'defensive interests are currently as aggressive as plaintiffs in pursuing a favourable forum'.[7]

A defendant's strategy will often be accompanied by the offer of various **4.05** undertakings in relation to proceedings in the alternate forum 'such as submitting to the jurisdiction of the foreign tribunal, waiving any statute of limitations . . . making witnesses and documents available and guaranteeing the satisfaction of the foreign judgment'.[8] Frequently courts will require certain undertakings to be given by the party seeking interlocutory relief in relation to venue[9] or, indeed, resisting such relief. An example of the latter is supplied by *Donohue v Armco Inc*,[10] where, as part of the price for not restraining the pursuit of proceedings in New York in breach of an English exclusive jurisdiction clause, the plaintiffs in those proceedings were required to undertake not to enforce against the party with the benefit of that clause any multiple or punitive damages awarded pursuant to RICO.

---

[5] *The Atlantic Star* [1974] AC 436, 471; *First National Bank of Boston v Union Bank of Switzerland* [1990] 1 Lloyd's Rep 32, 38.

[6] Boyce, D, 'Foreign Plaintiffs and Forum Non Conveniens: Going Beyond *Reyno*' (1985) 64 Texas Law Review 193, 216 n 149.

[7] Robertson, DW, 'Conflict of Laws and Forum Non Conveniens Determinations in Maritime Personal Injury and Death Cases in United States Courts' in Sharpe, D and Spicer, W, *New Directions in Maritime Law 1984* (1985) 52.

[8] Robertson, DW, ibid 71 and see, for example, *Société Nationale Industrielle Aerospatiale v Lee Kui Jak* [1987] AC 871, 903–904.

[9] See, for example, the conditions imposed as the price for the grant of a stay of proceedings in *Voth v Manildra Flour Mills Pty Ltd* (1990) 171 CLR 538.

[10] [2002] 1 Lloyd's Rep 425, 437.

4.06 Another strategy, albeit passive, which a defendant may employ is simply to allow foreign proceedings to continue and then resist any attempt at enforcement by reference to this non-submission or arguments founded in the public policy of the forum in which enforcement is being sought. As shall be seen, this approach is of limited efficacy and is not without legal risk and potentially adverse commercial ramifications.

4.07 Not all of the strategies outlined above will be available in circumstances where the plaintiff commences proceedings in a court whose jurisdiction derives from the Brussels or Lugano Conventions or Council Regulation 44/2001. It will not be possible, for example, to obtain a stay of proceedings, at least in circumstances where another contracting or member state provides an alternative forum and the defendant is not domiciled in that state.[11] By way of contrast, the English Court of Appeal has consistently (albeit somewhat problematically) held that anti-suit injunctive relief *is* available to restrain proceedings in the courts of another contracting or member state, at least in circumstances where those proceedings appear to have been commenced in violation of an exclusive jurisdiction clause for the English courts.[12] On the other hand, there is nothing problematic about the availability of negative declaratory relief in the context of the Brussels and Lugano Conventions and Council Regulation 44/2001. Indeed, in those jurisdictional settings, its efficacy is enhanced because of the emasculation of English courts' ability to withhold (and traditional custom of withholding) it on discretionary grounds.[13]

4.08 The range of potential strategies available to a defendant both at common law and, to a more limited extent and where applicable, in the context of Council Regulation 44/2001 and under the Lugano Convention certainly bears out the truth of the observation that 'with much of the law in this area, it is not simply a question of looking at both sides of the coin, but at all sides of a polygon'.[14]

4.09 Just as what may be described as the federalizing of jurisdiction in Europe initially through the Brussels and Lugano Conventions and now by way of the Regulation has made the position more complex, within federations such as the United States and Australia there is added scope for both forum shopping and reverse forum shopping. In the United States, a case may be removed from a state to a federal court[15] or transferred from one federal court to another,[16] so-called 'vertical' and 'horizontal' forum

---

[11] See paras 4.62 ff below.   [12] See paras 4.166 ff below.
[13] See paras 4.284 ff below.
[14] Briggs, A and Rees, P, *Civil Jurisdiction and Judgments* (1st edn, 1993) vi, reproduced in the 3rd edn, 2002.
[15] 28 USC § 1441 (1988).   [16] 28 USC § 1410(a) (1988).

shopping. The defendants in *Piper Aircraft Co v Reyno*[17] in fact resorted to both courses, first removing the case from the state to the federal court in California, and then transferring it to the federal court in Pennsylvania.[18] This manoeuvring allowed the defendants to avoid California's then doctrine of *forum non conveniens* which, on the facts, was unlikely to yield the stay ultimately granted by the Supreme Court under federal principles of *forum non conveniens*. By way of contrast, it has been observed that:

'Plaintiffs' lawyers have become expert at bringing . . . cases *in state courts* and in environments *where there can be no removal to a federal court* and *where the doctrine of forum non conveniens does not apply as a matter of state law*. They have also, by and large, avoided causes of action sounding in maritime law which is federal even if applied by state courts, for arguably, *forum non conveniens* is then applicable in such courts by virtue of federal supremacy'.[19]

In Australia, by way of contrast, although the possibility of vertical and **4.10** horizontal transfers of proceedings was introduced by the Jurisdiction of Courts (Cross-Vesting) Act 1987 (C'th) and corresponding state legislation,[20] the incentives for forum shopping as between the States and between state and federal courts are considerably fewer than in the United States.[21] Indeed, the introduction of the cross-vesting scheme has arguably hastened moves towards increased uniformity of both procedural and choice of law rules within Australia.[22] That is certainly now the case in tort cases.[23]

The five main 'reverse forum shopping' strategies open to a defendant in **4.11** the battle for venue in transnational litigation which have been outlined above are now considered in greater detail.

II. CHALLENGING JURISDICTION

It is not the remit of this book to consider the *specific* rules of jurisdiction **4.12** of various forums and the respective methods by which they may be challenged. Accordingly, a certain level of generality necessarily attends the following discussion. That is not, however, to underestimate the potential

---

[17] (1981) 454 US 235.   [18] ibid 240–241.

[19] Baade, HW, 'Foreign Oil Disaster Litigation Prospects in the United States and the "Mid-Atlantic Settlement Formula" ' (1989) 7 Journal of Energy and Natural Resources Law 125, 139 (emphasis added).

[20] See, generally, Mason, K and Crawford, J, 'The Cross-Vesting Scheme' (1988) 62 ALJ 328.

[21] Opeskin provides an excellent account of the reasons for this in 'The Price of Forum Shopping: A Reply to Professor Juenger' (1994) 16 Sydney Law Review 14, 18–21.

[22] See Mason, K and Crawford, J (n 20 above) 345–346 and Opeskin, BR ibid.

[23] *John Pfeiffer Pty Limited v Rogerson* (2000) 203 CLR 503.

importance of what is perhaps the most basic step a defendant can take in seeking to prevent the continuance of litigation in a particular forum. This section proceeds by first examining some typical objections which a defendant may make to the exercise of jurisdiction by common law courts over parties outside the forum, sometimes referred to as exorbitant jurisdiction.[24] Special considerations which may affect, in relation to the United States, the *nature* and, in relation to states subject to Council Regulation 44/2001 or party to the Lugano Convention, the *method* of any jurisdictional challenge are then explored. In the former case, these considerations are constitutional and this term may also be used aptly to describe the process by which courts assuming jurisdiction under Council Regulation 44/2001 and the Lugano Convention ensure that standards of fairness to a defendant are met.

1. CHALLENGING THE JURISDICTION OF COMMON LAW COURTS

4.13 In cases where a defendant is not physically present in the jurisdiction, a forum's rules permitting the exercise of jurisdiction may be quite technical and in turn invite technical objections. In some circumstances, these may be made more simply than an application for a stay of proceedings, for example, which could require considerable evidence to be adduced and expense to be incurred.[25] To draw an illustration from the Civil Procedure Rules, if a claimant or plaintiff has served a defendant outside the jurisdiction on the basis that the defendant was domiciled in England, relying solely on the defendant's residence in England for the last three months or more,[26] the defendant may make a clean and simple objection to jurisdiction by demonstrating absence of the requisite residence for the period in question.

4.14 Similarly, as under English law a plaintiff seeking permission to serve a defendant out of the jurisdiction must demonstrate at least a good arguable case that its claim falls within a case authorized by the Civil Procedure Rules.[27] Where there has been service on the basis, for exam-

---

[24] See *The Siskina* [1979] AC 210, 254 and *Amin Rasheed Shipping Corp v Kuwait Insurance Co Ltd* [1984] AC 50, 65 but compare *Spiliada* [1987] AC 460, 48; *Agar v Hyde* (2000) 201 CLR 552, 570–571; and Collins, LA (ed), *Dicey and Morris on the Conflict of Laws* (13th edn, 2000) 307 n 18.

[25] See generally paras 4.38 ff below. Often an application for a stay of proceedings will be made in the alternative to a challenge to jurisdiction if that challenge fails.

[26] Section 41(6) of the Civil Jurisdiction and Judgments Act 1982.

[27] The test of 'a good arguable case' was endorsed by Lord Goff in *Seaconsar Far East Ltd v Bank Markazi Jomhouri Islami Iran* [1994] 1 AC 438, 454–455. Two earlier Court of Appeal decisions had advocated a more strenuous test on the basis that the issue of jurisdiction is unlikely to be revisited at the trial: *Attock Cement Ltd v Romanian Bank of Foreign Trade* [1989] 1 WLR 1147, 1153–1156; *Metall & Rohstoff AG v Donaldson Lufkin & Jenrette* [1990] 1 QB 391,

ple, that a contract was breached in England by reason of non-payment of the claimant, a defendant who is able to demonstrate by reference to simple propositions of law that payment was not due in England and, hence, that no breach occurred there would be well advised to challenge jurisdiction on this elementary ground. The possibility of such challenges is not impaired in those jurisdictions where there is no requirement for the prior leave of the court before serving a defendant outside the forum.[28]

In this context, the facts of a particular case may disclose a lacuna in a **4.15** particular forum's long arm jurisdiction. In *Metall und Rohstoff AG v Donaldson Lufkin & Jenrette Inc*,[29] a transnational fraud case, for example, the Court of Appeal held that no claim could be brought against a United States parent company in aid of relief sought by way of constructive trust as there was no independent head of jurisdiction under what was then Order 11 of the Rules of the Supreme Court. The claim against the United States parent was only maintainable in so far as it sought damages for the tort of inducing breach of contract that, on the facts, may have been more difficult to sustain than the constructive trust remedy.

Common law courts have traditionally exhibited great caution when exer- **4.16** cising jurisdiction over foreign defendants under rules of court conferring long arm jurisdiction, Pearson J's dictum in *Société Générale de Paris v Dreyfus Brothers*[30] perhaps constituting the leading statement in this regard:

It becomes a very serious question, and ought always to be considered a very serious question, whether . . . this Court ought to put a foreigner, who owes no allegiance here, to the inconvenience and annoyance of being brought to contest his rights in this country, and I for one say, most distinctly that I think this Court ought to be exceedingly careful before it allows a writ to be served out of the jurisdiction.[31]

Initially, this cautious approach was self-interested, being based on a **4.17** desire not to encourage the similar treatment of English defendants by foreign courts, but it came ultimately to rest on broad considerations of international comity,[32] premised on the view that such jurisdiction was

---

434–435. This test affords more scope to a defendant seeking to challenge jurisdiction but its status is unclear in light of *Seaconsar* which did not consider the point directly.

[28] There is no such requirement in England, for example, where jurisdiction is assumed under Council Regulation 44/2001. In relation to the various Australian jurisdictions, the position was surveyed in *Voth v Manildra Flour Mills Pty Ltd* (1990) 171 CLR 538, 564. See also *Kuwait Asia Bank EC v National Mutual Life Nominees Ltd* [1991] AC 187 (PC) in relation to New Zealand; *Singh v Howden Petroleum Ltd* (1979) 100 DLR (3rd) 121 in relation to Ontario; *Canadian Commercial Bank v Carpenter* (1990) 62 DLR (4th) 734 in relation to British Columbia.

[29] [1990] 1 QB 391. This particular lacuna has now been rectified by CPR 6.20.
[30] (1885) 29 ChD 239.   [31] ibid 242–243, approved at (1887) 37 ChD 215.
[32] Collins, LA, 'Some Aspects of Service Out of the Jurisdiction in English Law' (1972) 21 ICLQ 656, 657–659.

exceptional and amounted to a derogation from a theory of jurisdiction aligned with notions of territorial sovereignty. In *Seaconsar Far East Ltd v Bank Markazi Jomhouri Islami Iran*,[33] Lord Goff observed that 'it is, of course, true to say that any inconvenience involved has been much reduced by modern methods of communication; but the point of principle remains'. He went on to observe, however, that this consideration is very largely met by *forum conveniens* analysis.

4.18 The High Court of Australia, while also noting that 'contemporary developments in communications and transport make the degree of "inconvenience and annoyance" to which a foreign defendant would be put, if brought into the courts of this jurisdiction, of a qualitatively different order to that which existed in 1885', has also expressed the view that 'the considerations of comity and restraint, to which reference has so often been made in cases concerning service out of the jurisdiction, will often be of greatest relevance in considering questions of forum non conveniens'.[34] There is much to be said for this view, as a matter of principle. In the context of Australian jurisprudence in this field, however, this observation is difficult to reconcile with the same Court's rejection of the doctrine of *forum non conveniens* in *Voth v Manildra Flour Mills Pty Ltd*,[35] especially given the way that the 'not clearly inappropriate forum test' enunciated in that case has been subsequently applied.[36]

4.19 Considerations of comity have traditionally informed various canons of construction and principles of practice which a defendant wishing to challenge the court's jurisdiction may seek to take advantage of. *Seaconsar* indicates that they remain of some relevance in England; in light of *Agar v Hyde*,[37] this may not be so in Australia. Examples of the infusion of considerations of comity include the fact that pendent jurisdiction may not be asserted in relation to a claim not founded on a particular sub-rule of rule 6.20 of the Civil Procedure Rules but having the same factual basis as a properly founded claim[38] and courts will be vigilant against the abuse of the Civil Procedure Rules to serve 'necessary' or 'proper' parties. In this context it has been said that 'if in substance those within the jurisdiction are made parties, without a plausible cause of action, merely that their presence may be used to support an application to issue a writ against persons without the jurisdiction, leave will not be granted'.[39]

---

[33] [1994] 1 AC 438, 455.
[34] *Agar v Hyde* (2000) 201 CLR 552, 571.
[35] (1990) 171 CLR 538.
[36] See, for example, *Renault v Zhang* (2002) 187 ALR 1.
[37] (2000) 201 CLR 552.
[38] *Waterhouse v Reid* [1938] 1 KB 743 and *Total Oil Great Britain Ltd v Marbonanza Compania Naviera SA* (CA, 27 June 1975), cited by Lord Diplock in *The Siskina* [1979] AC 210, 255.
[39] *The Brabo* [1949] AC 326, 339. See also *Multinational Gas and Petrochemical Co v Multinational Gas and Petrochemical Services Ltd* [1983] Ch 258, noted by Fawcett, JJ, 'Jurisdiction Over Foreign Companies' (1984) 100 LQR 17.

Moreover, if there is any doubt or uncertainty in the construction of **4.20** particular sections of the Civil Procedure Rules, Farwell LJ's judgment in *The Hagen*[40] is authority for the proposition that such doubt or uncertainty ought to be resolved in favour of the foreign defendant. This approach has been taken further, for both Lord Tucker in *Vitkovice Horni a Hutni Tezirstvo v Korner*[41] and Megarry J in *GAF Corporation v Amchem Products Inc*[42] have suggested that a foreign defendant should be given the benefit of the doubt not solely in relation to matters of construction but also 'quite generally'.[43] Nothing in the relatively new English Civil Procedure Rules indicates any revision to this approach.

Under the Civil Procedure Rules, a party seeking permission to serve out **4.21** of the jurisdiction must provide written evidence that it believes that the claim has a reasonable prospect of success[44] and the court is directed not to give permission unless satisfied that England and Wales is the proper place in which to bring the claim.[45] The concept of a 'proper place' is narrower than the concept of a 'proper case' which was the language of Order 11, rule 4(2) of the Rules of the Supreme Court in England and Wales. The concept had been interpreted as containing two elements, the first relating to the strength of the plaintiff's claim on the merits; the second to the appropriateness of the jurisdiction as a forum for the hearing of the dispute. In *Seaconsar Far East Ltd v Bank Markazi Jomhouri Islami Iran*,[46] the concept of a 'proper case' was essentially denuded of its first element, Lord Goff stating that he could 'see no good reason why any particular degree of cogency should be required in relation to the merits of the plaintiff's case'.[47] It was held to be sufficient if it were simply established that there was a 'serious question to be tried' rather than there needing to be demonstrated a 'good arguable case' on the merits,[48] the position now established under the Civil Procedure Rules.

Both *Seaconsar* and the amendments effected by the Civil Procedure Rules **4.22** made life more difficult for a foreign defendant in England seeking to challenge the exercise of jurisdiction over it,[49] in many cases effectively robbing a defendant of a potential argument in the battle over venue. In essence, a foreign defendant is now in no different position to any defendant wishing to strike out or move for summary dismissal of a claim. It

---

[40] [1908] P 189, 201, approved in *The Siskina* [1979] AC 210, 255.
[41] [1951] AC 869, 889.   [42] [1975] 1 Lloyd's Rep 601, 605.
[43] ibid. See also Collins, LA (n 32 above) 672. cf Megaw LJ in *Buttes Gas & Oil Co v Hammer* [1971] 3 All ER 1025, 1028.
[44] Civil Procedure Rules, rule 6.21(1)(b).
[45] Civil Procedure Rules, rule 6.21 (2A).   [46] [1994] 1 AC 438.
[47] ibid 767.   [48] ibid.
[49] See Briggs, A, 'Service Out of the Jurisdiction Gets Easier: Defendant, Beware!' [1994] LMCLQ 1, 2–4.

remains open to a foreign defendant to seek to set aside service on the basis of the manifest weakness of the case pleaded against it;[50] the relevant point being that the fact that the defendant is a foreign party no longer makes this task simpler, as it once did. [51]

4.23 As noted above, the Civil Procedure Rules now speak of the 'proper place' in which to bring the claim.[52] Translated into the language of the established case law, it will be incumbent upon a claimant seeking to serve a defendant out of the jurisdiction to satisfy the court that England is the natural forum. It is important to recall that *Spiliada*[53] was a service out of the jurisdiction case and that the considerations germane to the identification of the natural forum, including the existence of proceedings in another jurisdiction,[54] are equivalent for stay and service out purposes with the important difference that the burden is on the plaintiff to demonstrate that England is clearly more appropriate.[55]

4.24 Where there is no natural forum, a possibility that may well arise in some commercial and admiralty cases,[56] the logic of *Spiliada* may appear to dictate that a defendant may always successfully resist a claimant's attempt to serve it out of the forum.[57] That may be disputed, however. Although Lord Goff spoke of the need to show England as being *the* appropriate forum and the Civil Procedure Rules speak of *the proper place*, a claimant need show only that England is clearly and distinctly more appropriate than any other court in which suit could be brought. Where no natural forum can be shown and where there is no obvious alternative venue, an English court may simply consider itself to be *forum conveniens* by default.

4.25 In *The Handgate*,[58] Lloyd LJ stated that it was only when there was an alternative forum 'that the question arises whether England is more or

---

[50] *Kuwait Asia Bank EC v National Mutual Life Nominees Ltd* [1991] AC 187, where the Privy Council described the plaintiff's claims against the first appellant as 'so clearly untenable that they cannot possibly succeed' (224), and *Agar v Hyde* (2000) 201 CLR 552 provide examples.

[51] *The Brabo* [1949] AC 326, 351. See also *John Russell & Co Ltd v Cayzer, Irvine & Co Ltd* [1916] 2 AC 298 , 304: 'the words "properly brought" enure to the protection of the person out of the jurisdiction whom it is proposed to serve with process'.

[52] Civil Procedure Rules, rule 6.21 (2A).

[53] [1987] AC 460.

[54] See *The Hagen* [1908] P 189, 202; *GAF Corporation v Amchem Products Inc* [1975] 1 Lloyd's Rep 601, 605 and 608.

[55] *Spiliada* [1987] AC 460, 480–481.

[56] See *European Asian Bank AG v Punjab and Sind Bank* [1981] 2 Lloyd's Rep 651, 658; *The Coral Isis* [1986] 1 Lloyd's Rep 413, 416; *Spiliada* [1987] AC 460, 477.

[57] Slater, AG, 'Forum Non Conveniens: A View from the Shop Floor' (1988) 104 LQR 554, 574.

[58] [1987] 1 Lloyd's Rep 142.

less suitable than the alternative forum'.[59] On the other hand, it might be argued that the forum in which the defendant may be sued as of right, that is its place of residence or domicile, always provides an alternative forum and, if England is no more appropriate than this jurisdiction, the claimant ought to sue the defendant there. In line with this, Lord Goff stated in *Seaconsar* that, in a service out case, a strong argument that England is *forum conveniens* is required.[60] Even if a plaintiff is unable to demonstrate that England is the natural forum and another forum in fact exists which either merits that epithet or else is where the defendant resides and is no less appropriate than England, a claimant or plaintiff may still obtain an order for service out of the jurisdiction if it can show that 'substantial justice' is not likely to be done in the foreign and natural forum.[61]

For completeness it should be noted that one consequence of the High **4.26** Court of Australia's decision not to adopt *Spiliada*[62] is that, in that jurisdiction,[63] it is considerably easier for a plaintiff (and correspondingly more difficult for a defendant seeking to challenge jurisdiction) to obtain leave to serve a defendant out of the jurisdiction (or to confirm service out of the jurisdiction in circumstances where prior leave is not required), it only being necessary to establish that Australia is not a 'clearly inappropriate forum' for the hearing of the case.[64] In *Oceanic Sun Line Special Shipping Co Inc v Fay*,[65] the High Court appeared to favour the plaintiff to an even greater extent by placing the burden of showing that Australia was 'clearly inappropriate' on the defendant.[66] The subsequent decision in *Voth v Manildra Flour Mills Pty Ltd*[67] appeared to restore orthodoxy to a certain extent by making it clear that the burden in this respect lies on the plaintiff seeking leave,[68] although the position is less clear in those jurisdictions

---

[59] ibid 145. See also *European Asian Bank AG v Punjab and Sind Bank* [1981] 2 Lloyd's Rep 651, 656.

[60] [1993] 3 WLR 756, 767.

[61] See, for example, *Roneleigh Ltd v MII Exports Inc* [1989] 1 WLR 618 and *Britannia Steamship Insurance Association Ltd v Ausonia Assicurazioni SpA* [1984] 2 Lloyd's Rep 98. For reasons of convenience, the 'substantial justice' exception to *Spiliada* is discussed (and, in its application in recent service *ex juris* and stay cases, criticized) in paras 4.47 ff below.

[62] Discussed in greater detail at paras 4.67 ff below.

[63] Unlike the United States, decisions of the High Court are binding on state courts in matters of state as well as federal law although it is always open to state legislatures to alter the common law rules for service out of the jurisdiction.

[64] See *Oceanic Sun Line Special Shipping Co Inc v Fay* (1988) 165 CLR 197; *Voth v Manildra Flour Mills Pty Ltd* (1990) 171 CLR 538.

[65] (1988) 165 CLR 197.

[66] It appears that New Zealand courts, while following *Spiliada*, also take the view that the burden of persuading the court that the forum is not appropriate in a service *ex juris* context lies on the defendant: see Paterson, RJ, 'Forum Non Conveniens in New Zealand' (1989) 13 NZULR 337, 364–369.

[67] (1990) 171 CLR 538.   [68] ibid 564.

within Australia where prior leave is not required.[69] Notwithstanding this principled and entirely appropriate retreat with regard to onus, as Collins has observed, the 'not clearly inappropriate forum' formulation of the test for service out of the jurisdiction is novel and the 'effect is to shift the balance in favour of plaintiffs suing defendants outside the jurisdiction further than in any other Commonwealth country'.[70] The High Court's effective resurrection of the language of 'vexation and oppression' in *Renault v Zhang*,[71] which, while not formally abandoned in *Voth*, was assumed by many to have been effectively denuded of its content in favour of the language of 'clearly inappropriate forum', only serves to shift the balance even further in favour of plaintiffs.

2. Constitutional Dimensions to Jurisdictional Challenges

4.27 It was seen in paragraphs 3.84 ff above that considerations of fairness in relation to the choice of forum underpinned the common law's decision to embrace the doctrine of *forum non conveniens*. In other legal systems, this concern is built into jurisdictional rules themselves as opposed to being treated as a matter of discretion (although there may be less of a distinction than this difference perhaps implies).[72] Further still, in some states, a measure of fairness in relation to the exercise of jurisdiction is constitutionally mandated. This section considers two such constitutional guarantees, first in relation to the United States and second in the context of jurisdiction assumed under Council Regulation 44/2001 and the Lugano Convention on Jurisdiction and Judgments.

4.28 In the United States, challenging a court's jurisdiction has a constitutional dimension arising from the due process clause of the United States Constitution. A constitutional challenge will be coextensive with a regular jurisdictional challenge in circumstances where a state or federal long arm statute extends personal jurisdiction to the limits of due process.[73]

---

[69] In *Sydbank v Bannerton Holdings Pty Ltd* (1996) 68 FCR 539, the Full Court of the Federal Court placed the burden of this issue on the foreign defendant resisting service. See also the decision of the Supreme Court of Queensland in *Borek v Answer Products Inc* [2000] QSC 379.

[70] Collins, LA, 'The High Court of Australia and Forum Conveniens: The Last Word?' (1991) 107 LQR 182, 187.

[71] (2002) 187 ALR 1, 21–22.

[72] See, for example, in relation to Japan, Hayes, EL, '*Forum Non Conveniens* in England, Australia and Japan: The Allocation of Jurisdiction in Transnational Litigation' (1992) 26 UBCLR 41, 54–63; in relation to The Netherlands, Verheul, JP, 'The *Forum (Non) Conveniens* in English and Dutch Law and Under Some International Conventions' (1986) 35 ICLQ 413, 416–419; and, to a lesser extent, in relation to Germany, Dannemann, G, 'Jurisdiction Based on the Presence of Assets in Germany: A Case Note' (1992) 41 ICLQ 632. See also the Schlosser Report [1979] OJ C59/71, 97.

[73] Section 27 of the Securities Exchange Act 1934 provides an example, discussed by

Significantly for present purposes, the protection afforded by this clause is *not* confined solely to American defendants.[74] The value of this protection will be especially great for those foreign defendants which or who are sued in a state court which does not adhere to the doctrine of *forum non conveniens*. In *International Shoe Co v Washington*,[75] the Supreme Court held that the due process clause required that a state court's exercise of jurisdiction over a party located outside the State must not offend 'traditional notions of fair play and substantial justice'.[76] To this end, certain 'minimum contacts' between the defendant and the forum were required. An extraordinarily complex body of case law has been built upon this simple concept and ascertaining its content in any given case is no straightforward task.[77] All of this provides a fecund environment for interlocutory jurisdictional skirmishes.

In broad terms, the constitutional requirement of due process has **4.29** spawned a bifurcation between 'general' and 'specific' jurisdiction. These concepts are explored below in relation to a foreign defendant's[78] ability to invoke due process protection and thus resist litigation in the United States.

If general jurisdiction can be established over a particular defendant, then **4.30** it will be liable to suit irrespective of the relationship between the forum and the particular claim made.[79] The fact that a corporation is registered to do business in a particular State will not necessarily mean that it is subject to that State's general jurisdiction[80] and improper inducements to register[81] may result in general jurisdiction asserted on the basis of such registration being impugned.[82] Absent registration, general jurisdiction may still be asserted over a corporation if it has carried out 'continuous and systematic' activities within the forum.[83] This concept equates to

Sarno, GR, 'Haling Foreign Subsidiary Corporations into Court under the 1934 Act: Jurisdictional Bases and Forum Non Conveniens' (1992) 55 Law and Contemporary Problems 379, 383–384.

[74] *Guessefeldt v McGrath* 342 US 308, 318 (1952); *Russian Volunteer Fleet v United States* 282 US 481, 492 (1931); and see Born, GB, *International Civil Litigation in United States Courts* (3rd edn, 1996) 92, 137–138.

[75] 326 US 310 (1945).   [76] ibid 316.   [77] Born, GB (n 74 above) 74.

[78] This term does not encompass non-US nationals resident in the United States.

[79] This is of course subject to any *forum non conveniens* arguments which a defendant may make: see paras 4.74 ff below.

[80] Born, GB (n 74 above) 101.

[81] Such as the denial of certain defences in the event that the corporation is sued in that State, jurisdiction being otherwise established.

[82] *Bendix Autolite Corp v Midwesco Enterprises, Inc* 108 S Ct 2218 (1988); cf *Sternberg v O'Neil* 550 A 2d 1105 (Del, 1988).

[83] *Perkins v Benguet Consolidated Mining Co* 342 US 437 (1952); *Helicopteros Nacionales de Colombia SA v Hall* 466 US 408 (1984).

what is sometimes referred to as the 'doing business' standard.[84] It is perhaps not a matter of inordinate surprise that judges have expressed different views as to what constitute sufficiently 'continuous' or 'systematic' activities to satisfy the standard for general jurisdiction, a proposition illustrated by the division of opinion among the members of the Supreme Court in *Helicopteros Nacionales de Colombia SA v Hall*.[85]

4.31 In the absence of a defendant's 'continuous and systematic' presence in the forum, a plaintiff may still seek to convince a court to assume 'specific jurisdiction' under which a single or occasional 'contact' with the forum may suffice to ground jurisdiction if the dispute 'arises out of' that contact. Once again, considerable difficulty attends the task of isolating the precise circumstances in which a court will be justified in asserting specific jurisdiction.[86] A court must determine whether the defendant has 'purposefully availed' itself of the protections and benefits of the forum's law and make an assessment of whether the exercise of jurisdiction over the defendant would be 'reasonable' in the circumstances.[87] As to the first requirement, there is division of opinion, for example, as to whether the mere placing of a product in the 'stream of commerce' in the knowledge that it could end up in the United States constitutes 'purposeful availment'.[88] Similarly, there is debate as to whether a court will have specific jurisdiction over a defendant in relation to a tort occurring outside the forum by reason of the fact that the defendant solicited business in that forum.[89] So also there is considerable difference of opinion as to the width of the concept 'arising out of'. The scope for imprecision afforded by the term 'reasonable', moreover, is notorious. It is important to note in this context, however, that the Supreme Court has observed that 'the unique burdens placed upon one who must defend oneself in a foreign legal system should have significant weight in assessing the reasonableness of stretching the long arm of personal jurisdiction over national borders'.[90]

4.32 The obvious uncertainties evident in the various formulations of what is required for 'due process' suggest that it may be well worth a foreign

---

[84] See, for example, *Deluxe Ice Cream Co v RCH Tool Corp* 726 F 2d 1209 (7th Cir, 1984).

[85] 466 US 408 (1984). Born, GB (n 74 above) 103–104, 111–116 provides examples of what have and have not been held to be sufficient continuous and systematic activities.

[86] 'Defining the scope of special jurisdiction and when such jurisdiction may be exercised has proved at least as difficult as resolving questions of general jurisdiction': ibid 69.

[87] *World-Wide Volkswagen Corp v Woodson* 444 US 286 (1980).

[88] See, for example, the different opinions expressed in *Asahi Metal Industry Co v Superior Court of California, Solano County* 480 US 102 (1987).

[89] See Richman, WM, '*Carnival Cruise Lines*: Forum Selection Clauses in Adhesion Contracts' (1992) 40 American Journal of Comparative Law 977, 980 n 16.

[90] *Asahi Metal Industry Co v Superior Court of California, Solano County* 480 US 102, 114 (1987).

defendant's while to mount a challenge to American proceedings at the threshold constitutional stage. This will especially be the case where a plaintiff can only make a plausible due process defence under either the specific or general jurisdiction bases but not both although it must be noted that, while due process protection extends to a foreign defendant, a suit brought by an American national against a foreign defendant will be relatively more impregnable on due process grounds.

There may be some ancillary benefits for a defendant challenging juris- **4.33** diction. Born and Westin have observed that 'raising a credible jurisdictional defense will, as a practical matter, often provide the defendant with more time in which to develop its defence of the merits. This is particularly true if the trial court can be persuaded to stay discovery on the merits while the jurisdictional challenge is resolved.'[91] On the other hand, it has rightly been said that 'even the limited issue of personal jurisdiction will force the parties to expend an enormous amount of time and effort gathering materials, interviewing witnesses and preparing pleadings'.[92] Such considerations may well induce a settlement offer, especially in light of the inability in the United States to recover costs. Selecting a prima facie competent forum with a view to engineering such a result is in the nature of modern transnational litigation.

Where a plaintiff seeks to sue a defendant which is domiciled in a member **4.34** state of the European Union in the courts of one of those states, certain safeguards are provided under Council Regulation 44/2001[93] in order to ensure fairness to the defendant in the assumption and exercise of jurisdiction. This, it will be recalled, is the same broad concern that underpinned the United States Supreme Court's decision in *International Shoe Co v Washington*.[94] In stark contrast to the United States, however, where a defendant wishing to oppose jurisdiction might be put to considerable expense and inconvenience in mounting a jurisdictional challenge, a defendant domiciled in a member state will be in a superior position.

Apart from the general fact that the bases upon which jurisdiction may be **4.35** exercised under the Regulation are far more specific than those standards examined in the previous paragraphs,[95] Article 26 of the Regulation requires a court seised to undertake an examination of its jurisdiction *of its*

---

[91] Born, GB and Westin, D, *International Civil Litigation in United States Courts* (2nd edn, 1996) 151.

[92] See Silva, EJ, 'Practical Views on Stemming the Tide of Foreign Plaintiffs and Concluding Mid-Atlantic Settlements' (1993) 28 Texas International Law Journal 479, 484.

[93] As well as under the Brussels and Lugano Conventions.

[94] 326 US 310 (1945).

[95] See Juenger, FK, 'Judicial Jurisdiction in the United States and the European Communities; A Comparison' (1984) 82 Michigan Law Review 1195, 1207.

own motion if the defendant who is domiciled in another member state does not make an appearance and the court must decline jurisdiction where it is not founded under an article of the Regulation. The Jenard Report stated in relation to the cognate provision in the Brussels Convention that 'the courts must apply the rules of the Convention whether or not they are pleaded by the parties'.[96] This represented part of the Convention's general concern, continued in the Regulation, that 'proceedings leading to the delivery of judicial decisions take place in such a way that the rights of the defence are observed'.[97]

4.36 On the other hand, in so far as the underlying facts of the dispute may affect the issue of whether jurisdiction exists,[98] a defendant opposed to a plaintiff's choice of forum would be well advised to appear to make its case as, with limited exceptions,[99] this course will not be open to the defendant at the recognition and enforcement stage.[100] An initial jurisdictional challenge will not constitute submission under Article 24 of Regulation 44/2001. The French Cour de Cassation has correctly held that, in cases where a defendant appears, the procedure for establishing a lack of jurisdiction is for the *lex fori*.[101] Accordingly in the case in question, because under French law a jurisdictional challenge must be lodged prior to a defence on the merits, no objection to jurisdiction was permitted to be made for the first time on appeal.

4.37 The imperative of challenging jurisdiction at the outset is *a fortiori* in circumstances where the defendant is not a domiciliary of a member state. For such a defendant, there are few procedural safeguards[102] or meaningful exceptions permitting the challenge of the original court's jurisdiction at the recognition and enforcement stage.[103] As one commentator has observed, 'defendants, regardless of whether they are Community domiciliaries, are under great pressure to participate in the original proceedings'.[104]

---

[96] [1979] OJ 59/1, 8.

[97] Case 125/79, *Denilauer v SNC Couchet Frères* [1980] ECR 1552, 1569. See also Case 228/81, *Pendy Plastic Products v Pluspunkt* [1982] ECR 2723, 2736.

[98] See, for example, *Definitely Maybe (Touring) Ltd v Marek Lieberberg Konzert Agentur GmbH* [2001] 1 WLR 1745.

[99] Articles 34 and 35 of Regulation 44/2001.

[100] Article 41.

[101] *Société Azienda Stampaggio Acciaio v SA Phocéenne de Métalurgie* [1993] I L Pr 253.

[102] cf Article 34(2).

[103] See further in para 4.295 below.

[104] von Mehren, AT, 'Recognition and Enforcement of Sister-State Judgments: Reflections on General Theory and Current Practice in the European Economic Community and the United States' (1981) 81 Columbia Law Review 1044, 1055.

III. STAYING PROCEEDINGS—*FORUM NON CONVENIENS*

The commitment of defendants to joining the battle for venue in transna-   **4.38**
tional litigation is perhaps most frequently evidenced by applications for
a stay of proceedings on the basis of the doctrine of *forum non conveniens*
or by reference to jurisdiction or arbitration agreements. Indeed it has
been said in the context of jurisdictional clashes in the United States that
'defendants are now using forum non conveniens as a weapon rather than
as a legitimate defense'.[105] Consistent with that observation is the somewhat paradoxical truth that, in America, 'parties often are arguing *against*
their own convenience—the foreign plaintiff wishing to litigate in
America, and the domestic defendant moving to have the case heard
abroad'.[106] With the possible exception of Australia, because of a materi-
ally differently formulated test for the granting of a stay, the defensive
and strategic use of *forum non conveniens* motions would appear to be
equally prevalent in other common law jurisdictions.[107] This section
proceeds with that consideration in mind.

An examination is undertaken in paragraphs 4.47 ff below of the way in   **4.39**
which *Spiliada* has been applied, not simply in England but also in the
courts of those common law jurisdictions which have embraced it.[108]
Particular attention is focused upon those cases where applications for
stays have been unsuccessful. The question of the extent to which a stay
based on *forum non conveniens* grounds is available where an English or
other member state domiciliary is sued in England in circumstances
where no other member state of the European Union or no other
Contracting State to the Lugano Convention, as appropriate, appears to
have an interest in proceedings is then considered in paragraphs 4.62 ff
below.

---

[105] (Note) (1992) 105 Harv LR 1813, 1817.
[106] Reynolds, WL, 'The Proper Forum for a Suit: Transnational Forum Non Conveniens
and Counter-Suit Injunctions in the Federal Courts' (1992) 70 Texas Law Review 1663, 1672.
See also Boyce, D (n 6 above) 215 and, for an example, see *Dow Chemical Co v Castro Alfaro*
786 SW 2d 674 (Tex, 1990), cert denied 111 S Ct 671 (1991). In an Australian context, see *CSR
Ltd v Cigna Insurance Australia* (1997) 189 CLR 345.
[107] See, for example, *The Goldean Mariner* [1989] 2 Lloyd's Rep 390, 403, cited in para 1.38
above.
[108] For example, New Zealand: *Club Mediterranée NZ v Wendell* [1989] 1 NZLR 216;
McConnell Dowell Constructors Ltd v Lloyd's Syndicate 396 [1988] 2 NZLR 257; *Society of Lloyd's
v Hyslop* [1993] 3 NZLR 135; *Longbeach Holdings Ltd v Bhanabhai & Co Ltd* [1994] 2 NZLR 28;
Mackay Refined Sugars NZ v NZ Sugar Co [1997] 3 NZLR 476; Canada: *Amchem Products Inc v
Workers Compensation Board* [1993] 1 SCR 897; *Frymer v Brettschneider* (1994) 115 DLR (4th)
744; Hong Kong: *The Adhiguna Meranti* [1988] 1 Lloyd's Rep 384, [1987] HKLR 904.

4.40 Paragraphs 4.67 ff below turn to Australia. It has been noted at various stages of this book that the High Court of Australia has declined to embrace the concept of the natural forum as embodied in the doctrine of *forum non conveniens*. In *Voth v Manildra Flour Mills Pty Ltd*,[109] however, it essayed the view that there was little practical difference between the *Spiliada* and the Australian 'not clearly inappropriate' test.[110] That view, never in truth sustained by subsequent decisions, must now be regarded as open to serious doubt.

4.41 Finally, paragraphs 4.74 ff below make a brief assessment of the role of *forum non conveniens* in the United States. At a federal level, that doctrine is reasonably coherent and largely recognizable although it differs in certain important respects from *Spiliada's* conception of it. At a state level, however, it will be seen that there is a wide spectrum of opinion, ranging from the wholesale non-recognition of the doctrine in certain jurisdictions to a faithful adherence to it at the other end of the scale so that a defendant's prospects of securing a stay may depend first on whether or not it is sued in the federal or a state jurisdiction[111] and, if the latter, in which particular jurisdiction. Even if it is one subscribing to the doctrine of *forum non conveniens*, it may yet be difficult to predict the prospects of a motion for a stay being granted.

4.42 Before considering these three areas, two more general points should be borne in mind. First, as was seen in paragraphs 3.78 ff above, the doctrine of *forum non conveniens* is a creature of the common law with the consequence that the strategy outlined in this section will generally not be available to defendants sued in civil law systems.[112] This has the obvious and not unimportant consequence that:

> Experienced international practitioners are increasingly aware of the fact that by a combination of exorbitant jurisdiction and the absence of forum non conveniens some civil-law countries have become litigation havens.[113] Clever plaintiffs' lawyers are quick to make use of such havens when they look for a forum that is both surprising and inconvenient for the defendant.[114]

---

[109] (1990) 171 CLR 538.

[110] ibid 558.

[111] This encompasses the issue of whether state proceedings may be removed to a federal court: see the discussion of the course of the *Piper Aircraft* litigation at para 4.09 above.

[112] But see n 72 above for the view that similar questions to those which arise in a *forum non conveniens* application may be canvassed upon a challenge to jurisdiction in some civil law countries.

[113] Footnote 95c to quoted text: 'German practitioners have exhibited no signs of regret in observing that this adds to the volume of their litigation business.'

[114] Schlesinger, R, Baade, H, Damaska, M, Herzog, P, *Comparative Law: Cases-Text-Materials* (5th edn, 1988) 403.

In this context, it is significant to note that the civil law tradition of the State of Louisiana has dictated that there is no inherent jurisdiction to stay proceedings on the basis of *forum non conveniens* in that forum.[115] This is of heightened significance when it is appreciated that the full faith and credit clause of the United States Constitution renders any Louisiana judgment enforceable throughout that country. The province of Quebec has also traditionally not subscribed to the doctrine of *forum non conveniens*[116] although the consequences of this for interprovincial enforcement throughout Canada are not plain.[117] The situation has been clarified by the passage of the Civil Code of Quebec, § 3135 of which introduces a statutory version of *forum non conveniens*. This section provides that 'even though a Quebec authority has jurisdiction to hear a dispute, it may exceptionally and on an application by a party, decline jurisdiction if it considers that the authorities of another country are in a better position to decide'.[118]

In those forums where a stay of proceedings on the grounds of *forum non* **4.43** *conveniens* is available, one danger which may lie in store for a defendant seeking such relief is that, in jurisdictions which do not permit conditional appearances, a stay application may be held to constitute submission to the foreign court. In *Kuwait Airways Corporation v Iraq Airways Co,*[119] Nourse LJ opined that 'a defendant who seeks a stay on the ground of forum non conveniens will usually take a step in the proceedings'.[120] Even if a defendant takes no further part in proceedings after an unsuccessful stay application, under the common law doctrine as enunciated by the English Court of Appeal in *Henry v Geoprosco International Ltd,*[121] the foreign court's judgment would probably be enforceable in the defendant's home forum. While this doctrine may be readily criticized[122] and indeed has been reversed by statute in both England[123] and Australia,[124]

---

[115] See *Fox v Board of Supervisors of LSU* 576 So 2d 978 (La, 1991); *American Dredging Co v Miller* 114 S Ct 981 (1994); *Lejano v Bandak* 705 So 2d 158 (La, 1997). Article 123 of the Louisiana Civil Code permits a limited statutory right of transfer or dismissal in cases where the plaintiff is not domiciled in Louisiana.

[116] *Dominion of Canada General Insurance Co v Johns-Manville Corp* (1991) 40 QAC 124.

[117] Edinger, ER, 'Morguard v De Savoye: Subsequent Developments' (1993) 22 Canadian Business Law Journal 29, 37.

[118] This provision is discussed in Woods, JA, 'Recognition and Enforcement of Judgments Between Provinces: The Constitutional Dimensions of *Morguard Investments Ltd*' (1993) 22 Canadian Business Law Journal 104, 112 ff.

[119] [1994] 1 Lloyd's Rep 276.

[120] ibid 283. In this case, the significance of 'a step in the proceedings' related to s 2(3) of the State Immunity Act 1978 which provides that 'a State is deemed to have submitted . . . if it has intervened or taken any step in proceedings'.

[121] [1976] QB 726.

[122] See, for example, Collins, LA, 'Harris v Taylor Revived' (1976) 92 LQR 268.

[123] Section 33 of the Civil Jurisdiction and Judgments Act 1982.

[124] Section 7(4) of the Foreign Judgments Act 1991 (C'th).

for example, in those jurisdictions where it still represents good law, seeking a stay of foreign proceedings in order to defeat a forum shopping plaintiff may not be a risk-free enterprise. The same caveat applies to jurisdictional challenges. In Texas, for example, while a conditional appearance to contest jurisdiction is permitted, an unsuccessful challenge is deemed to constitute submission with possible ramifications for subsequent enforcement proceedings.[125]

1. *SPILIADA* APPLIED

4.44 The discussion of the emergence of the natural forum and consideration of that concept in paragraphs 3.78 ff and 3.84 ff above was largely in the context of applications for a stay of proceedings based upon the doctrine of *forum non conveniens* and much of that discussion is of relevance here. Certain key points can be briefly recapitulated.

4.45 Most fundamentally, where a defendant can show that another forum is 'clearly more appropriate' in the sense that it has a more real and substantial connection to the case than the forum seised, then in most cases a stay should be granted. Critical factors which may establish such a nexus include the governing law, the residence of the parties, and the location of witnesses and relevant evidence. Moreover, the assessment of the natural forum may be affected by the existence of concurrent or related proceedings in another forum whose claims to be the natural forum may be enhanced if such proceedings are bona fide, more advanced than in the forum seised and/or capable of resolving all aspects of a multidimensional transnational dispute. These, then, are some of the key factors that a defendant will need to point to in seeking to secure a stay.

4.46 In *Club Méditerranée NZ v Wendell*,[126] Cooke P emphasized the fact that burden of convincing the court to stay proceedings in favour of a more appropriate forum rested upon the defendant and that 'cogent material' was required to be produced to discharge this onus.[127] The task of the defendant wishing to seek a stay of proceedings in those jurisdictions subscribing to *Spiliada* would thus appear to be reasonably clear. The following subsection considers an important qualification to this proposition.

---

[125] *International Risk Management Group Ltd v Elwood Insurance Ltd* (29 September 1993, Supreme Court of Bermuda, Nos 103 & 245/93.)
[126] [1989] 1 NZLR 216.
[127] ibid 220.

Spiliada and the 'Justice' Exception

In *Spiliada*, Lord Goff made one important qualification to the general **4.47** availability of a stay in the circumstances described above. He stated that, upon a defendant's establishing that the natural forum lies other than in England, the court would:

ordinarily grant a stay unless there are circumstances by reason of which justice requires that a stay should nevertheless not be granted. In this inquiry, the court will consider all the circumstances of the case, including circumstances which go beyond those taken into account when considering connecting factors with other jurisdictions. One such factor can be the fact, if established objectively by cogent evidence, that the plaintiff will not obtain justice in the foreign jurisdiction.[128]

Lord Goff expressed the view that the unavailability in the natural forum **4.48** of certain advantages which a plaintiff might derive from suing in England should not lead a court to refuse a stay on the basis that 'justice' would not be available in that forum.[129] He elaborated upon this theme in *Connelly v RTZ Corporation plc*,[130] where he observed that:

a general principle may be derived, which is that, if a clearly more appropriate forum overseas has been identified, generally speaking the plaintiff will have to take that forum as he finds it, even if it is in certain respects less advantageous to him than the English forum. He may, for example, have to accept lower damages, or do without the more generous English system of discovery. The same must apply to the system of court procedure, including the rules of evidence, applicable in the foreign forum. This may display many features which distinguish it from ours, and which English lawyers might think render it less advantageous to the plaintiff. Such a result may in particular be true of those jurisdictions, of which there are many in the world, which are smaller than our own, and are in consequence lacking in financial resources compared with our own. But that is not of itself enough to refuse a stay. Only if the plaintiff can establish that substantial justice cannot be done in the appropriate forum, will the court refuse to grant a stay.

'Justice' in this context is clearly not simply 'English justice' as Hunter JA realized in *Louvet v Louvet*[131] when he stated that 'it is quite plain that you cannot judge by the standards of the individual jurisdictions because you reach a headlong conflict'.[132]

---

[128] [1987] AC 460, 478, citing *The Abidin Daver* [1984] AC 398, 411.
[129] ibid 482.
[130] [1998] AC 854, 872–3
[131] [1990] 1 HKLR 670.
[132] ibid 677. See also Schuz, R, 'The Further Implications of *Spiliada* in light of Recent Case Law: Stays in Matrimonial Proceedings' (1989) 38 ICLQ 946, 951: 'It is clear that injustice cannot be looked at in a vacuum but only in the context of the background and expectation of the parties.'

4.49 The examples of procedural advantages given by Lord Goff in the above passage as not relevant to the 'justice' inquiry are factors which, under the approach enunciated by Lord Diplock in *MacShannon v Rockware Glass Ltd*,[133] may well have counted as 'legitimate personal or juridical advantages',[134] the existence of which might have operated to defeat a stay application. Several cases illustrate the significance of this difference in approach.

4.50 In *Brinkerhoff Maritime Drilling Corp v PT Airfast Services Indonesia*,[135] an argument that justice would not be available in the natural forum because the limitation period had run was rejected and proceedings in Singapore were stayed in favour of Indonesia. On the other hand, in *Baghlaf al Zafer Factory v Pakistan Shipping Co [No 2]*,[136] in circumstances where the court considered it had not been unreasonable for the plaintiff to have commenced in England and not to have filed a protective writ in Pakistan, justice was ultimately said to require continuation of proceedings in England in relation to a very small claim where litigation in Pakistan involved a difficult limitation question on which, had it been resolved adversely to the plaintiff, would inevitably have involved an application to lift the stay. In *The Waylink*,[137] proceedings in Gibraltar were stayed notwithstanding the fact that the far more limited discovery available in Germany would make it more difficult for the plaintiffs to establish their case. A further example of an unsuccessful attempt to rely on less generous discovery, evidentiary, and cost recovery rules as creating the requisite injustice to justify suit in other than the natural forum was *The Polessk*[138] where English proceedings were stayed in favour of proceedings in St Petersburg.[139]

4.51 Notwithstanding the clarity of Lord Goff's counsel that the 'justice' exception to *Spiliada* was not intended to be triggered by reason of mere differences in procedures available in alternate forums, there will come a point on the spectrum when particular procedural differences are so pronounced that the borderline between invidious comparison and the individual justice of the case may be crossed. The difficulty in this lies in the lack of any useful or meaningful guidelines in relation to the crossing of that boundary.

4.52 This point has been best exposed in the context of asbestos litigation brought in England by a large number of South African and Namibian plaintiffs who resisted arguments that South Africa was the natural forum

---

[133] [1978] AC 795. [134] ibid 812. [135] [1992] 2 SLR 776.
[136] [2000] 1 Lloyd's Rep 1. [137] [1988] 1 Lloyd's Rep 475.
[138] [1996] 2 Lloyd's Rep 40.
[139] See also *Radhakrisha Hospitality Service Private Ltd v EIH Ltd* [1999] 2 Lloyd's Rep 249.

for the resolution of their particular disputes by reference to the availability of legal aid and lawyers prepared to act on spec in England together with the availability of a class action procedure in that jurisdiction. Illustrating that this is an area where judicial minds may radically differ, in *Lubbe v Cape plc*[140] in the Court of Appeal, Pill LJ said:

Justice does not in my judgment require the refusal of a stay. As explained in *Connelly*, the exception identified in *Spiliada* is a narrow one. The general rule is that the Court will not refuse to grant a stay simply because the plaintiff has shown that no financial assistance will be available to him in the appropriate forum. It may exceptionally be a relevant factor but the plaintiff has far from established that substantial justice cannot and will not be done in South Africa. I have already referred to the high repute in which the South African Courts are held. There is also in South Africa a legal profession with high standards and a tradition of public service, though I do not suggest that lawyers in South Africa, any more than those anywhere else, can be expected to act on a large scale without prospects of remuneration. While I would not be prepared to apply the second stage of the *Spiliada* test, so as to permit English litigation, even in the absence of evidence that legal representation will be available, I am unable to conclude that in the circumstances it would not become available for claims in South African Courts. Moreover, given the accessibility to the wealth of scientific, technical and medical evidence available in this context, I am confident that it could be made available in a South African Court to the extent required to achieve a proper consideration of the plaintiffs' cases. The action would by no means be novel or speculative.

On appeal to the House of Lords, Lord Bingham reached a different view on what he regarded as the special facts of the case where the lack of means of several thousand claimants to prosecute their claims to a conclusion meant that justice required that the stay be lifted, permitting proceedings to continue in England which was not the natural forum.[141] This reflected his Lordship's earlier views in the Court of Appeal in *Connelly v RTZ Corporation plc*[142] where he invoked the requirement of Article 6(1) of the European Convention on Human Rights that 'in the determination of his civil rights and obligations . . . everyone is entitled to a fair and public hearing within a reasonable time by an independent and impartial tribunal established by law'[143] to support his view that proceedings should not be stayed in favour of the natural forum if that would have the practical effect of preventing a plaintiff from pursuing his or her rights anywhere.[144]

---

[140] [2000] 1 Lloyd's Rep 139, 164.   [141] [2000] 1 WLR 1545, 1559.
[142] [1997] 4 All ER 335. For the decision of the House of Lords in this case, see [1998] AC 854.
[143] This Article now has direct effect in the United Kingdom as a result of the passage of the Human Rights Act 1998.
[144] Briggs, A and Rees, P, *Civil Jurisdiction and Judgments* (3rd edn, 2002) 1.17–1.18 discuss

4.53 In considering exactly what will count as 'injustice' to warrant derogation from the natural forum, Lord Goff's citation of Lord Diplock's speech in *The Abidin Daver* noted above is significant in two respects. First, it makes it plain that the burden of establishing injustice in the natural forum switches to the plaintiff in the main proceedings. Secondly and more importantly, it suggests, *eiusdem generis*, the type of 'injustice' which will need to be shown to override the reversion of litigation to the natural forum. This is nothing less than the denial of 'even-handed' justice in the sense of explicit bias from the bench or some other factor such as political or ideological persecution that dictates that a fair trial will not be available.[145] This appraisal is confirmed by observations of Sir John Donaldson MR and Mustill LJ in *Muduroglu Ltd v TC Ziraat Bankasi*.[146] In *Purcell v Khayat*,[147] the Court of Appeal considered that the fact that the plaintiff in England had been convicted in his absence in Lebanon, the natural forum, in proceedings instituted by the defendant to the English proceedings, and faced three years' imprisonment was a sufficient reason to invoke the 'justice' exception.[148]

4.54 Bias or unfairness, moreover, has to be asserted candidly and established with 'positive and cogent evidence'.[149] This may place a plaintiff in something of an invidious and delicate position. As has been observed, 'the plaintiff has a distinctly unenviable choice. If he makes such allegations, but fails to win, . . . he will have to return to the court about which he has been so disparaging to pursue his claim. His position may not be a happy one.'[150] From the defendant's perspective, however, the apparent narrowness of the 'justice' exception incorporated in the *Spiliada* test evidences a strong fidelity to the conceptual desideratum that litigation should take place in the natural forum.

4.55 A defendant more anxious about the practical feasibility of this goal than its abstract appeal would have cause to be disappointed by certain deci-

---

the impact of the Human Rights Act on matters pertaining to civil jurisdiction and judgments. This is an area in which an expansion of the case law may be readily anticipated.

[145] See also *The Iran Bohonar* [1983] 2 Lloyd's Rep 621.

[146] [1986] QB 1225.

[147] *The Times*, 23 November 1987.

[148] See also *Mohammed v Bank of Kuwait* [1996] 1 WLR 1483, 1497; *Askin v Absa Bank* [1999] I L Pr 471; *Merrill Lynch v Raffa* [2001] I L Pr 437 but compare *Jeyaretnam v Mahmood* The Times, 21 May 1992, discussed in Bottomley, S and Kinley, D (eds), *Commercial Law and Human Rights* (2001) 121–123.

[149] *Seereederei Baco Liner GmbH v 'Al Aliyu'* [2000] FCA 656 provides an example of a case where it was unsuccessfully contended that the plaintiff in *in rem* proceedings in Australia (a forum with no connection to the dispute other than the defendant ship occasionally plied its trade in Australian waters) would not receive a fair or impartial trial in the Guinea courts.

[150] Briggs, A and Rees, P, *Civil Jurisdiction and Judgments* (1st edn, 1993) 166; see also 3rd edn, 2002, 150.

sions of English and Commonwealth courts applying the 'justice' exception to the *Spiliada* principle. If they represent any sort of trend, it is one that could result in the emasculation of the *Spiliada* doctrine and greatly undermine its fundamental goal of levelling the playing field in the battle over venue in transnational litigation. In *The Vishva Ajay*,[151] a standard collision case which occurred in the port of Okha in India, Sheen J came to the clear conclusion that India was the natural forum, stating in fact that this was 'self-evident'.[152] Nevertheless, he declined to grant a stay of proceedings on the basis of the 'justice' exception. Two factors influenced this decision. First, he noted that it appeared that 'a successful litigant in India will not be awarded costs upon a realistic basis and will have to bear a substantial part of the litigation costs himself'[153] and concluded that 'a successful plaintiff should not be deprived of part of the fruits of victory by paying a large sum in costs'.[154] It is to be noted parenthetically that such a rule is a feature of several legal systems, including those of Japan[155] and the United States,[156] and it would appear that Sheen J's reasoning, if valid, would apply to every case in which the natural forum does not award costs to a successful litigant. Sheen J sought to justify his decision on the basis that the 'costs' rule in England would favour both parties, the plaintiff, for the reasons already cited, and the defendant, by nullifying any 'pressure to settle the action for fear of paying a large sum in costs even when he has been successful'.[157] The obvious point to be made here is that if the defendant had wished to avoid such a situation, it would clearly not have sought a stay in favour of a forum which would present it. It seems odd, to say the least, that a defendant should be deprived of the opportunity to litigate in the natural forum by reference to a 'benefit' which it clearly does not value or seek to enjoy. Moreover, taking into account a factor which is a general aspect of a state's legal system rather than merely being specific to the case and concluding that its operation will result in the denial of 'substantial justice' to the plaintiff

---

[151] [1989] 2 Lloyd's Rep 558.   [152] ibid 559.   [153] ibid 560.

[154] ibid. Sheen J did not point out that, if the plaintiff lost in India, it would not have to pay the defendant's costs: *The Oinoussin Pride* [1991] 1 Lloyd's Rep 126, 135.

[155] Schlesinger, R, Baade, H, Damaska, M, Herzog, P (n 114 above) 353 n 29.

[156] The non-recovery of costs rule in the United States was central to the decision to go even further and to grant leave to serve the defendant out of the jurisdiction in *Roneleigh Ltd v MII Exports Inc* [1989] 1 WLR 618 on the basis that it meant that 'substantial justice' could not be obtained in that forum, at least in the context of the amount ($250,000) involved in the case. cf *Agrafax Public Relations Ltd v United Scottish Society Inc* [1995] CLC 862. See also *Berisford plc v New Hampshire Insurance Co* [1990] 2 QB 631, 647–648 and *Arkwright Mutual Insurance Co v Bryanston Insurance Co Ltd* [1990] 2 QB 649, 669.

[157] [1989] 2 Lloyd's Rep 558, 560. In *The Al Battani* [1993] 2 Lloyd's Rep 219, 224, Sheen J relied upon an identical argument in relation to the Egyptian costs rule to justify his decision not to stay English proceedings in favour of Egypt which he had identified as the natural forum.

exhibits 'a natural prejudice in favour of a procedure with which English lawyers are familiar'.[158] Such an approach was clearly proscribed and deprecated by both Lord Wilberforce and Lord Diplock in *Amin Rasheed Shipping Corp v Kuwait Insurance Co*[159] and, later, by Lord Goff in *Spiliada* and *Connelly*, and seriously undermines the deference to foreign legal systems and their procedural rules implicit in the concept of comity which *Spiliada* so clearly embraces.

4.56 Sheen J's decision in *The Vishva Ajay* was not solely based upon the Indian 'non-recovery of costs' rule although that consideration was clearly important, as indeed it was in his later decision in *The Al Battani*.[160] The second factor relied upon was the fact that evidence was led that the case would not reach the trial stage for at least six years if heard in India. This was arguably more defensible than reference to the local costs rule.[161] Sheen J concluded that a 'delay of this magnitude seems to me to be a denial of justice'.[162] A similar argument was made to Hirst J in *The Nile Rhapsody*[163] in relation to alleged delay in the Egyptian courts. Notwithstanding this a stay was granted. The period in question was shorter than in *The Vishva Ajay* (three to four years) but, on a more general level, it is important to note that Hirst J's decision to give 'minimal weight to the delay factor' was largely based on his sensitivity to warnings 'on more than one occasion by appellate courts not to make invidious comparisons with foreign Courts'.[164] In contrast to Hirst J's decision, upheld on appeal,[165] in *The Al Battani*,[166] a case where Egypt was also the natural forum, Sheen J once again took possible delay into account in his decision not to stay English proceedings. He was also influenced by the fact that delay would be compounded by the need to translate certain documents from English into Arabic, the fact that interest in Egypt is only awarded as from the date of the judgment, and, as noted above, the effects of the non-recoverability of costs rule. The effect of these considerations on the availability of 'substantial justice' in the natural forum seems far removed from the situation of a biased and hostile foreign court postu-

---

[158] *Amin Rasheed Shipping Corp v Kuwait Insurance Co* [1984] AC 50, 67.

[159] 'It is not appropriate in my opinion to embark upon a comparison of the procedures, or methods, or reputation or standing of the courts of one country as compared with those of another' per Lord Wilberforce, ibid 72; 67 per Lord Diplock. See also *The Abidin Daver* [1984] AC 395, 410.

[160] [1993] 2 Lloyd's Rep 219, 224. cf *The Nile Rhapsody* [1992] 2 Lloyd's Rep 399, 413.

[161] In *The Abidin Daver* [1984] AC 398, 411, Lord Diplock envisaged that a stay might be refused if there would be 'excessive delay' in the courts of the natural forum.

[162] [1989] 2 Lloyd's Rep 558, 560. See also *Chellaram v Chellaram* [1985] 1 Ch 409, 435–436 where a stay was refused on the basis of likely delay in the Indian courts.

[163] [1992] 2 Lloyd's Rep 399, 413–414.

[164] ibid 414.

[165] [1994] 1 Lloyd's Rep 382.

[166] [1993] 2 Lloyd's Rep 219, 223–224.

lated as the paradigm case for the invocation of the 'justice' exception contained in *Spiliada*.[167]

Another example of an appeal to the 'justice' exception contained in **4.57** *Spiliada* being successfully invoked is provided by *Banco Atlantico SA v The British Bank of the Middle East*.[168] At first instance, the United Arab Emirates were accepted as being, if not the natural forum, certainly 'clearly more appropriate' than England for the resolution of the dispute, all that is strictly necessary to be established on the *Spiliada* test, and a stay was granted. This decision was reversed on appeal. It is not entirely clear whether the Court of Appeal disagreed with the assessment of the natural forum. More likely, it considered that justice could not be done in the Sharjah court because it had no established conflict of laws doctrine and thus would apply local law rather than Spanish law which the Court of Appeal identified as being the proper law of the bills of exchange in question. It was plain that this would have ramifications for the result in the case and a stay was refused. This decision is to be contrasted to one of the central aspects of *Piper Aircraft Co v Reyno*[169] where the United States Supreme Court held that the fact that the plaintiff would secure a less favourable result in the alternate forum was not a relevant consideration on a *forum non conveniens* inquiry.[170] The only exception to this was where the remedy offered in the alternative forum was 'so clearly inadequate or unsatisfactory that it is no remedy at all'.[171]

Banco Atlantico was arguably a case where the remedy in the natural forum **4.58** met the description offered in *Piper Aircraft Co v Reyno*. Bingham LJ stated that he did not regard it as conducive to justice to require the plaintiff which had an arguable claim under what the Court considered to be the proper law 'to litigate, if at all, in a jurisdiction where it would be bound on the evidence to face summary rejection of its claims'.[172] The decision may also arguably be justified by reference to the fact that the English choice of law rule applied in this case was that contained in an international instrument, namely the Geneva Convention on Bills of Exchange of 1932, and was described as 'the accepted rule in the world of international commerce'.[173] In this sense the decision bears a close similarity to that of

---

[167] It can be said in Sheen J's defence that he is consistent: see *The Jalakrishna* [1983] 2 Lloyd's Rep 628.

[168] [1990] 2 Lloyd's Rep 504.

[169] 454 US 235 (1981).

[170] ibid 250. In a sense similar to this is the observation in *Voth v Manildra Flour Mills Pty Ltd* (1990) 171 CLR 538, 560 that 'in deciding whether to grant or refuse a stay, the court does not, indeed cannot, evaluate the justice or relative merits of the substantive laws of the available forums'.

[171] 454 US 235, 254 (1981).

[172] [1990] 2 Lloyd's Rep 504, 509.

[173] ibid 508.

the Hong Kong Court of Appeal in *The Adhiguna Meranti*,[174] where a stay in favour of Indonesia, the natural forum, was refused in circumstances where the limitation on the shipowner's liability in Indonesia would produce a derisory sum, based, as it appeared to be, on an amount specified in Article 474 of the original 1848 version of the Indonesian Civil Code.[175] In justifying its decision, the Court stated that the Hong Kong limit, based upon the 1957 Brussels Convention, reflected 'international public policy'.[176] A similar approach, appealing to a 'generally accepted rule of international law', is evident in *Britannia Steamship Insurance Association Ltd v Ausonia Assicurazioni SpA*,[177] a service *ex juris* case.[178]

4.59 While an appeal to 'international practice' or to an 'accepted rule of international commerce' may distinguish these cases from those in which courts have indulged parochial perceptions of what constitutes 'justice', characterizing a rule as one of 'international public policy' may be somewhat problematic in itself. If the concept is meaningful, courts should be astute to avoid the temptation of assuming too readily that local practice reflects international rules and custom. The decision of the House of Lords in *Kuwait Airways Corporation v Iraqi Airways Company*[179] provides a good example of the manner in which international public policy may be deployed in a clear case in private international law.

4.60 Where decisions to retain or assume jurisdiction are based on the perceived unavailability of 'justice' in the natural forum, courts should be vigilant in not assuming that, if a different substantive law is to be applied in the foreign forum which may produce a different result to that available in the local forum, whether as a result of the application of the foreign forum's domestic or conflicts laws, justice will not therefore be available. In *Irish Shipping Ltd v Commercial Union Assurance Co plc*,[180] Staughton LJ accepted the first part of this proposition, stating that 'so far as concerns domestic law, it would be wrong for us to suppose that our system is better than any other', but, for reasons which are unexplained, continued that 'in the case of conflict rules, which ought to be but are not the same internationally, there is a case for saying that we should regard our rules

---

[174] [1988] 1 Lloyd's Rep 384, [1987] HKLR 904.
[175] ibid 391; see also *The Andhika Samyra* [1989] 1 HKLR 198 and *The Kapitan Shvetsov* [1998] 1 Lloyd's Rep 199 in which the Hong Kong Court of Appeal declined to grant a stay of Hong Kong proceedings brought by Russian shipowners in favour of litigation in Singapore in circumstances where Thailand in fact provided the natural forum.
[176] ibid 396.
[177] [1984] 2 Lloyd's Rep 98, 102.
[178] cf *The Herceg Novi* [1998] 2 Lloyd's Rep 454 which questions the existence of a single international public policy in this context.
[179] [2002] 2 WLR 1353.
[180] [1991] 2 QB 206.

as the most appropriate'.[181] Far preferable, it is thought, is the view of Hunter JA of the Hong Kong Court of Appeal who, in *Louvet v Louvet*,[182] observed that there should be a recognition of the fact that:

there is going to be one loser and one winner in the result. The court has accordingly to resort to wider considerations, to perhaps a supra-national standpoint, and try to determine in each case which is *the fairer jurisdiction to the parties collectively*.[183]

This view certainly calls into question the decisions in *Banco Atlantico SA v The British Bank of the Middle East*[184] and *Britannia Steamship Insurance Association Ltd v Ausonia Assicurazioni SpA*.[185] Except in a case where its applicable law is so out of step with international practice, assuming that that concept is a meaningful one, or where it will lead to disregard of a contractual choice of law and so, constructively, amount to a breach, and in the absence of bias or manifest prejudice in the courts of the natural forum, the jurisdiction which Hunter JA described in the last sentence of the passage cited above will always be the natural forum. In line with the argument advanced in paragraphs 3.85 ff above, it is perfectly legitimate that defendants be entitled to insist that disputes in which they are involved are resolved in this forum by reference to its laws, both domestic and conflicts.   **4.61**

Spiliada and Council Regulation 44/2001

It remains to address the question of the extent to which a defendant to proceedings commenced in England can request a stay of proceedings in favour of the natural forum in light of the operation of Council Regulation 44/2001.[186] At first sight, the answer might appear obvious. As was seen in paragraphs 3.49 ff above, one of the features of the Regulation and the Brussels and Lugano Conventions is that there is no occasion for the exercise of discretion in the assumption or retention of jurisdiction. This is based on the policy consideration that a plaintiff 'should not have to waste his time and money risking that the court concerned may consider itself less competent than another'.[187] Schlosser's reference to 'another'   **4.62**

---

[181] ibid 229–230; see also 246–247.   [182] [1990] 1 HKLR 670.

[183] ibid 677 (emphasis added). See also *The Hamburg Star* [1994] 1 Lloyd's Rep 399, 410 per Clarke J, who stated that, on a stay motion, it will rarely if ever be appropriate 'to weigh in the balance the prospects of success of any of the parties at the trial'.

[184] [1990] 2 Lloyd's Rep 504.

[185] [1984] 2 Lloyd's Rep 98.

[186] A comprehensive discussion of this issue is contained in Briggs, A and Rees, P (n 144 above) 2.211–2.217.

[187] Schlosser Report [1979] OJ C59/71, 97. See also Case 241/83, *Rösler v Rottwinkel* [1985] ECR 99, 127.

allows one to conclude, as Dillon LJ did in *Re Harrods (Buenos Aires) Ltd*,[188] that where another member or contracting state may take jurisdiction over the case under the provisions of the Regulation or applicable Convention, a first seised court should not stay its proceedings. A stay of proceedings in favour of a court of another member or contracting state would, moreover, not be an effective strategy for, as the English court would remain seised of proceedings, Article 27 of the Regulation (Article 21 of the Conventions) would prevent the other court from exercising jurisdiction.

4.63 On the view expressed in *Re Harrods (Buenos Aires) Ltd*, it may have been assumed that, in all cases where the defendant in English proceedings was a domiciliary of a member or contracting state other than England, proceedings should not be stayed for, with the exception of Article 22 (Article 16 of the Conventions) cases relating to land (where a stay would be highly unlikely in any event), Article 2 dictates that the courts of the defendant's domicile will have jurisdiction so that there will always be 'another' state which may assume jurisdiction.[189] But *Re Harrods* has been interpreted as extending beyond cases where no other contracting or member state could have assumed jurisdiction. Thus, stays of English proceedings were granted at the behest of Danish and Swiss domiciled defendants in favour of proceedings in the United States notwithstanding that Denmark and Switzerland would have had jurisdiction under the Brussels and Lugano Conventions respectively.[190]

4.64 In *Arkwright Mutual Insurance Co v Bryanston Insurance Co Ltd*[191] and *Berisford plc v New Hampshire Insurance Co*,[192] Potter J and Hobhouse J respectively considered that, even in a situation where a stay was sought in favour of a non-Contracting State to the Brussels Convention and where no other Contracting State could assume jurisdiction over the dispute, there was no scope for the exercise of discretion and they were bound to retain jurisdiction. The Court of Appeal in *Re Harrods (Buenos Aires) Ltd*[193] took a different view, considering that the Convention was only concerned to regulate questions of jurisdiction between Contracting States *inter se* and was not intended to touch upon a clash of jurisdiction

---

[188] [1992] Ch 72, 96.

[189] A submission to the court of a member or contracting state by a non-member or contracting state domiciliary will not give that court jurisdiction under Article 24 of the Regulation (Article 18 of the Conventions). This is because Article 4 dictates that jurisdiction over such parties is to be asserted in accordance with the national law of the state in which proceedings have been commenced.

[190] *Eli Lilly and Company v Novo Nordisk A/S* [2000] I L Pr 73; *Ace Insurance SA-NV v Zurich Insurance Co* [2001] 1 Lloyd's Rep 618.

[191] [1990] 2 QB 649.   [192] [1990] 2 QB 631.

[193] [1992] Ch 72.

between a Contracting and a non-Contracting State.[194] The issues arising from *Re Harrods* were referred to the European Court of Justice in that case but the matter settled in the interim.[195]

While some commentators have welcomed the decision in *Re Harrods*, **4.65** others have raised serious objections to it which go beyond those articulated at first instance in both *Arkwright Mutual Insurance Co v Bryanston Insurance Co Ltd*[196] and *Berisford plc v New Hampshire Insurance Co.*[197] It has been pointed out with considerable force, for example, that the Conventions (and now the Council Regulation) are not mono-dimensional, concerned solely with the allocation of jurisdiction between member states, the principal basis upon which the decision in *Re Harrods* rested.[198] The operation of Article 27 of the Regulation (Article 21 of the Conventions), for example, has the consequence that a court which stays its proceedings prevents courts in other member states from assuming jurisdiction with respect to the 'same cause of action', a concept which, as has been seen, is very broad.[199] This is the case, moreover, whether or not jurisdiction is assumed under the direct rules of the Regulation or under national law pursuant to Article 4.[200] Furthermore, it is not correct that a decision to stay proceedings in favour of a non-member state in the circumstances postulated will not touch upon the concerns of other member states for it will have the consequence that any subsequent foreign judgment in the case will not be automatically enforceable in member states. Especially in cases where the plaintiff is a domiciliary of a member state other than the United Kingdom, it is difficult to conclude that other member states will not have an interest in an English court's decision to stay proceedings in favour of the courts of a non-member state.

---

[194] This was a view which had been put by Collins, LA in '*Forum Non Conveniens* and the Brussels Convention' (1990) 106 LQR 535, and which was cited by Bingham LJ in the Court of Appeal.

[195] This was also the fate of proceedings due to be heard in the House of Lords on appeal from the Court of Appeal's decision in *Ace Insurance SA-NV v Zurich Insurance Co* [2001] 1 All ER (Comm) 802 in respect of Article 21 of the Lugano Convention.

[196] [1990] 2 QB 649.

[197] [1990] 2 QB 631.

[198] Briggs, A and Rees, P (n 144 above) 2.212. See also Briggs, A, '*Forum Non Conveniens* and the Brussels Convention Again' (1991) 107 LQR 180.

[199] See Case 144/86, *Gubisch Maschinenfabrik KG v Palumbo* [1987] ECR 4861 and the discussion in paras 3.25 ff above but see also *Haji-Ioannou v Frangos* [1999] 2 Lloyd's Rep 337, 351 for a case in which Article 21 was held not to apply by reason of the fact that the 'object' of the two sets of proceedings was not the same.

[200] Case C-351/89, *Overseas Union Insurance Ltd v New Hampshire Insurance Company* [1991] ECR I-3317.

4.66 In *Haji-Ioannou v Frangos*,[201] Lord Bingham said of the decision in *Re Harrods*:

> The decision has excited considerable controversy and may no doubt be overruled or varied hereafter. But it is at present authority binding upon us for whatever the case decided. The case must be taken to have decided that, where the choice is between the exercise of jurisdiction properly conferred on the English Court and the exercise of jurisdiction by a foreign Court in a non-Contracting State, the power to stay on grounds of forum non conveniens is not excluded by the Convention.

> In *Lubbe v Cape*,[202] although the point was argued, it was unnecessary for the House of Lords to resolve it by reason of the fact that the English proceedings were not stayed. The question has been referred again to the European Court of Justice by the Court of Appeal in *Owusu v Jackson*.[203]

2. AUSTRALIAN ABSTENTION

4.67 In *Voth v Manildra Flour Mills Pty Ltd*,[204] the High Court of Australia adopted what may loosely be described as a variant of *Spiliada* as the appropriate test for the stay of proceedings.[205] Rather than focusing on the identification of the natural or clearly more appropriate forum for the resolution of a given transnational dispute, the Court considered it more desirable to ask the question whether or not Australia or a particular constituent State was a 'clearly inappropriate' forum.[206] If not, there would be no occasion for the staying of Australian proceedings (and, in the context of service out of the jurisdiction, there would be a valid basis for the exercise of the court's discretion).

4.68 It is not intended to appraise the merits of this approach as opposed to that espoused in *Spiliada* in any detail here.[207] On one view, the decision simply represents a compromise of the divergent approaches which had emerged in the earlier decision of *Oceanic Sun Line Special Shipping Co Inc v Fay*[208] and it was presumably thought important to speak with one voice

---

[201] [1999] 2 Lloyd's Rep 337, 346.   [202] [2000] 1 WLR 1545.

[203] [2002] ECWA Civ 877.   [204] (1990) 171 CLR 538.

[205] The majority make it plain that its decision represents something of a compromise of competing viewpoints: ibid 552 and see Brennan J at 572.

[206] ibid 552–561.

[207] The High Court set out its reasons for preferring the 'not clearly inappropriate' test in *Voth*, ibid 557–561. For criticism, see Pryles, MC, 'Judicial Darkness on the Oceanic Sun' (1988) 62 ALJ 774 and 'Forum Non Conveniens—The Next Chapter' (1991) 65 ALJ 442; Reynolds, FMB, 'Forum Non Conveniens in Australia' (1989) 105 LQR 40; Briggs, A, 'Forum Non Conveniens in Australia' (1989) 105 LQR 200; Collins LA, 'The High Court of Australia and *Forum Non Conveniens*: A Further Comment' (1989) 105 LQR 364.

[208] (1988) 165 CLR 197.

on such an important practical matter. Suffice it to say that in eschewing any utilization of the concept of the natural forum, a concept whose significance goes beyond simply that of applications for the stay of proceedings, the High Court of Australia has departed from the mainstream of Commonwealth jurisprudence in this area and, it is suggested, undervalued the importance of the role of the natural forum in effecting an even-handed mechanism for the resolution of jurisdictional clashes in transnational litigation. This is especially the case in circumstances where the Australian Constitution contains no equivalent to the American 'due process' clause which, as *Asahi Metal Industry v Superior Court*[209] illustrates, does much of the same work as the doctrine of forum non conveniens.[210] Kirby J, when President of the New South Wales Court of Appeal, accurately observed, the 'bias of the Australian test is plainly towards upholding the Australian jurisdiction, lawfully invoked' whereas 'the bias of the *Spiliada* test . . . is towards a *modern* search for that jurisdiction with which a multinational transaction has the most natural connection'.[211]

When *Voth* was handed down, there were grounds for believing that **4.69** Australia's deviation from the mainstream in this area would not be of great significance in practice, especially in light of the High Court's endorsement of Lord Goff's identification in *Spiliada* of the relevant 'connecting factors' germane to a stay application.[212] It was stated in the majority joint judgment in *Voth* that:

The 'clearly inappropriate forum' test is similar to and, for that reason, likely to yield the same result as the more appropriate forum test in the majority of cases. The difference between the two tests will be of critical significance only in those cases—probably rare—in which it is held that an available foreign tribunal is the natural or more appropriate forum but in which it cannot be said that the local tribunal is a clearly inappropriate one.[213]

Experience in the application of *Voth* has not borne out this prediction and **4.70** few have been the cases in which a stay of Australian proceedings has been granted.[214] In a number of the cases refusing a stay, it was made

---

[209] 480 US 102 (1987).
[210] See Weintrub, R, 'International litigation and forum non conveniens' (1994) Texas International Law Journal 321, 333.
[211] *Voth* (1989) 15 NSWLR 513, 534 (emphasis added).
[212] *Voth* (1990) 171 CLR 538, 564–565.
[213] ibid 558.
[214] An excellent survey of the cases up until 1999 is contained in Garnett, R, 'Stay of Proceedings in Australia: a *"clearly inappropriate"* test' (1999) 23 MULR 30. For examples of cases refusing a stay, see *Anglo-Australian Foods Ltd v Von Planta* (1988) FCR 34, *Green v Australian Industrial Investment Ltd* (1989) 25 FCR 532, and *Reese Brothers Plastics Ltd v Hamon-Sobelco Australia Pty Ltd* [1989] ACLD 35098, applying the clearly inappropriate standard

explicit that the competing jurisdiction was the natural or more appropriate forum.[215] Most recently, in *Renault v Zhang*,[216] a stay of New South Wales proceedings was declined in a case where the only connection with New South Wales was that that was where the plaintiff lived and the place to which he returned having been injured while driving a hired Renault motor vehicle in New Caledonia. The suit was for damages for negligent manufacture and design, both of which acts occurred in France, and it was French law that supplied the *lex causae*.

4.71 If there is such a thing as the 'homeward trend' in the application of jurisdictional rules, then it is surely illustrated by the application of the test enunciated in *Voth*. In commercial causes in Australian courts, the broad reach of the Trade Practices Act, which proscribes misleading or deceptive conduct in trade or commerce including 'innocent conduct', is regularly pleaded and the presence of a plea under this statute is regularly deployed to 'anchor' litigation whose centre of gravity may lie elsewhere. By and large, Australian courts have resisted the possibility that that Act may be picked up in a foreign court by that forum's choice of law rules and have regarded the absence of identical legislation in the alternate forum as a juridical disadvantage militating against the grant of a stay.[217]

4.72 Notwithstanding Kirby P's observation that 'sensitivity to what is "clearly inappropriate" will necessarily differ from one judge to another',[218] Australian judges have exhibited remarkable unanimity in finding that Australia is not a clearly inappropriate forum. The implication for defendants regularly served within the federal Territories or States of the Australian Commonwealth is plain, namely that it will be extremely difficult to obtain a stay of proceedings on the footing that a particular state or territory is clearly inappropriate for the resolution of the dispute, and there would appear to be no practical leavening of this position when the foreign defendant is served outside the jurisdiction.[219]

---

derived from Deane J's judgment in *Oceanic Sun Line Special Shipping Co Inc v Fay* (1988) 165 CLR 197; *Horn v York Paper Co Ltd* (1990) 9 ACLC 60; *Al Ru Farm Pty Ltd v Hedleys Humpers Ltd* [1991] ACL Rep 85 SA 1; *Banque Paribas v Jarret* [1991] ACL Rep 325 VIC 94; *In the marriage of Gilmore* (1993) 16 Fam LR 285; *WFM Motors Pty Ltd v Maydwell* [1993] ACL Rep 85 NSW 2; *The Daeyang Honey* (1994) 120 ALR 109.

[215] In *WFM Motors Pty Ltd v Maydwell* [1993] ACL Rep 85 NSW 2, Bryson J refused to stay proceedings 'although the courts of Hong Kong would be a highly suitable forum for the disposition of the disputes between these parties, and there are respects in which the connection between the disputes and the territory of New South Wales is tenuous'. See also *In the marriage of Gilmore* (1993) 16 Fam LR 285, 310; *James Hardie v Grigor* (1998) 45 NSWLR 20.

[216] (2002) 187 ALR 1.

[217] Garnett, R (n 214 above) 46–48.

[218] *Voth* (1989) 15 NSWLR 513, 535.

[219] *Renault v Zhang* (2002) 187 ALR 1.

The now radical difference between the approach of Australian courts, **4.73** post *Renault*, with that represented by *Spiliada* is best illustrated by contrasting the actual decision in *Renault* with what *Spiliada's* architect, Goff LJ, as he then was, said in *The Albaforth*,[220] namely that 'if the substance of the alleged tort is committed within a certain jurisdiction, it is not easy to imagine what other facts could displace the conclusion that the courts of that jurisdiction are the natural forum'.

3. *Forum Non Conveniens* in the United States

It is vital to appreciate that in the United States, which, as has been **4.74** observed, is a particularly attractive destination for forum shopping litigants, there is no single and overarching body of conflict of laws doctrine (apart from the extent to which the subject has a constitutional dimension). Thus, although the Supreme Court has endorsed the doctrine of *forum non conveniens* in two significant decisions[221] and it is this law which is followed by federal courts applying federal law and *semble* when exercising federal diversity jurisdiction,[222] it is by no means the case that every State subscribes to this doctrine and that those that do do so in every respect or in the same sense.[223] But before turning to consider the wide spectrum of state law on *forum non conveniens*, several aspects of the doctrine as it operates at a federal level should be noted. The first emerges from *Gulf Oil Corp v Gilbert*,[224] a domestic case but of seminal importance in a transnational context as well. In this case it was stated that 'unless the balance is strongly in favor of the defendant, the plaintiff's choice of forum should rarely be disturbed'.[225] This dictum must be read in light of *Piper Aircraft Co v Reyno*,[226] which established that, where proceedings have been commenced by an American citizen or resident, a stay will be even more difficult to obtain.[227] The discrimination apparent in this holding appears to go even further than might at first appear for Scoles and

---

[220] [1984] 2 Lloyd's Rep 91, 96.

[221] *Gulf Oil Corp v Gilbert* 330 US 501 (1947); *Piper Aircraft Co v Reyno* 454 US 235 (1981). It also discussed the doctrine in *American Dredging Co v Miller* 114 S Ct 981 (1994).

[222] This is notwithstanding *Erie Railroad v Tompkins* 304 US 64 (1938) and *Klaxon v Stentor Electric Manufacturing* 313 US 487 (1941): see Baade (n 19 above) 138–139; Weintrub, R, 'International Litigation and forum non conveniens' (1994) 29 Texas International Law Journal 321, 340–341; cf Miller, LE, 'Forum Non Conveniens and State Control of Foreign Plaintiff Access to U.S. Courts in International Tort Actions' (1991) 58 University of Chicago Law Review 1369, 1387ff.

[223] See Robertson, DW and Speck, PK, 'Access to State Courts in Transnational Personal Injury Cases: Forum Non Conveniens and Antisuit Injunctions' (1990) 68 Texas Law Review 937, 950–953; and Born, GB (n 74 above) 298.

[224] 330 US 501.   [225] ibid 508.

[226] 454 US 235 (1981).   [227] ibid 252 and 255.

Hay observe that 'dismissals for *forum non conveniens* in cases brought by *foreign* plaintiffs have been substantial in number in the wake of *Piper*'.[228]

4.75   It is impossible in a work of this nature to attempt a summary of the extent to which various States observe the doctrine of *forum non conveniens*. Indeed, it may be questioned to what extent such a survey could be carried out accurately if the observations of critics of the doctrine of *forum non conveniens* are to be believed, for its application in the United States has been described as 'instinctive' and 'haphazard'.[229] Robertson and Speck nevertheless carried out such a survey in 1990, reporting, with an appropriate lack of dogmatism, that:

> Thirty-two states and the District of Columbia seem to have adopted either the federal doctrine or something very closely resembling it. Four other states have given more equivocal indications of following the federal doctrine. Still four other states have adopted more limited versions of forum non conveniens that might nevertheless be broad enough to lead to dismissal in many transnational personal injury and wrongful death actions. In five states the existence of a forum non conveniens doctrine is a completely open question. Courts in Montana and West Virginia have rejected forum non conveniens in FELA cases, otherwise leaving the doctrine's existence an open question. Louisiana law precludes forum non conveniens dismissal except in a narrow range of situations . . . and at this writing the decisions in Georgia and Texas seem to reject the doctrine altogether.[230]

4.76   The reference to Texas's rejection of the doctrine is now out of date as the decision in *Dow Chemical Co v Castro Alfaro*[231] has been, in large measure, reversed by statute.[232] The Supreme Court's decision in *American Dredging Co v Miller*,[233] however, makes it abundantly clear that States are free to reject the doctrine or variants of it and that, contrary to suggestions sometimes made, the federal doctrine does not bind the States when non-United States litigants are involved by virtue of the foreign relations power.[234]

4.77   The dissentients in *Dow Chemical* were not reticent in predicting the consequences of the absence of a doctrine of *forum non conveniens* for Texas.

---

[228] Scoles, EF and Hay, P, *Conflict of Laws* (2nd edn, 1992) 377 (emphasis added).

[229] Baade, HW (n 19 above) 140.

[230] Robertson, DW and Speck, PK (n 223 above) 950–951 (footnotes omitted).

[231] 786 SW 2d 674 (Tex, 1990), cert denied 111 S Ct 671 (1991).

[232] See Subchapter D of Chapter 71 of the Texas Civil Practice and Remedies Code. The amended legislation is set out in Silberman, LJ, 'Developments in Jurisdiction and Forum Non Conveniens in International Litigation: Thoughts on Reform and a Proposal for a Uniform Standard' (1993) 28 Texas International Law Journal 501, 519–521. The doctrine will not apply when a claimant's injury is due to a violation of the laws of Texas or the United States.

[233] 114 S Ct 981 (1994).

[234] cf *American Dredging Co v Miller* 114 S Ct 981, 995 per Kennedy J dissenting.

Thus Justice Gonzalez considered that Texas would become 'an irresistible forum for all mass disaster lawsuits'[235] and Justice Hecht characterized it as 'the courthouse for the world'.[236] While these predictions must now be checked in relation to Texas, the consequences for forum shopping articulated by the dissentients are equally applicable to those other States, such as Florida and Louisiana, which do not subscribe to any doctrine of *forum non conveniens*. They are also of relevance to those States whose version of the doctrine is more pro-plaintiff oriented than the federal standard. One commentator has observed that 'states that reject the *Piper* approach will likely become litigation magnets for product liability lawsuits'.[237] The variations in state courts' understanding of the doctrine are also illustrated by a recent decision of the Supreme Court of Connecticut which, although purporting to apply *forum non conveniens*, demonstrates a very strong pro-plaintiff disposition. In *Picketts v International Playtex, Inc*,[238] the Court emphasized the plaintiffs' presumptive right to their chosen forum and that the defendant's burden was to show that Connecticut was a *seriously inconvenient* forum for the purposes of the case's evidentiary requirements. It expressly acknowledged that this inquiry was very different from 'a more evenhanded inquiry into which alternative jurisdiction would furnish the more appropriate forum'.[239]

As with the Australian version of *forum non conveniens* developed in *Voth*, **4.78** the consequence for a defendant sued in certain state courts in the United States is that application for a stay of proceedings on grounds of *forum non conveniens* is unlikely to prove a profitable litigational strategy, especially where the plaintiff is American. The Supreme Court itself has observed that 'one can rarely count on the fact that jurisdiction will be declined'.[240] Furthermore, as a general proposition, it should be pointed out that even a successful *forum non conveniens* motion will not free a defendant from the necessity of complying with a plaintiff's requests for discovery in the United States for these will often be for the very purpose of *establishing* jurisdiction and hence will *precede* any stay application. Moreover, the Supreme Court has held that non-compliance with such requests may be sanctioned by striking out the defendant's objection to jurisdiction.[241] The doctrine of *forum non conveniens* is therefore perhaps not the panacea which it might at first blush appear to be for the 'victims' of forum shopping.

---

[235] 786 SW 2d 674, 690 (1986).   [236] ibid 707.

[237] Silberman (n 232 above) 523.   [238] 576 A 2d 518 (Conn, 1990).

[239] ibid 525. See also *Miller v United Technologies Corp* 515 A 2d 390 (Conn, 1986).

[240] *American Dredging Co v Miller* 114 S Ct 981, 989 (1994).

[241] *Insurance Corporation of Ireland Ltd v Compagnie des Bauxites* 456 US 694, especially 707–709 (1982).

IV. ANTI-SUIT INJUNCTIONS

4.79 For a defendant either unhappy with the plaintiff's choice of forum or desirous, for tactical reasons, that litigation proceed in a different jurisdiction, or both, challenging a court's jurisdiction or seeking a stay of proceedings in a particular forum are obviously the two most direct strategies which may be employed in the battle over venue in transnational litigation. But a foreign court seised of proceedings may have extremely widely drawn jurisdictional rules or else lack a doctrine of *forum non conveniens* so that these expedients will be of limited value to the defendant.

4.80 Alternatively, even if the foreign court's jurisdiction may be challenged on either technical or discretionary grounds, a defendant may be reluctant to do so for several reasons. Such a course may count as submission to the proceedings in that jurisdiction with the consequence that any judgment ultimately given may be enforceable in another jurisdiction. The risk of this approach will be especially great where any substantive defence and/or cross-claim is required to be made at the time of a jurisdictional challenge. Secondly, notwithstanding the existence of a doctrine of *forum non conveniens* (or a variation thereon), a party may be sceptical as to its prospects of obtaining such relief, especially where the plaintiff in the foreign proceedings is a citizen or resident of that forum, especially perhaps one that has sustained physical injuries. Thirdly, a defendant may be reluctant to incur the expense and inconvenience of challenging foreign proceedings if a cheaper method of doing so is available, including one which offers the prospect of the recovery of costs in contested proceedings. Fourthly, issues of timing may in certain circumstances dictate moving swiftly and a response may be able to be made more swiftly by commencing suit in a forum with which the foreign defendant is most familiar or comfortable.

4.81 The expedient, where a defendant lacks assets in the foreign jurisdiction, of not submitting to the proceedings so that any subsequent default judgment is without immediate practical effect may also not be attractive to a defendant, for the existence of an outstanding judgment may represent a professional or personal embarrassment to individuals[242] or be prejudicial to a corporation's credit rating or appeal as a potential takeover target, not to mention an impairment to possible future business activity, including obtaining insurance or other services in the foreign forum.[243]

---

[242] *Re Siromath Pty Ltd (No 3)* (1991) 25 NSWLR 25, 30.
[243] It may also be a less viable option for reasons explored in paras 4.295 and 4.296 ff below.

In any or all of these contexts, one potential strategy open to a defendant **4.82** is to apply to a domestic court for an injunction restraining either the institution or the continuance of foreign proceedings (an 'anti-suit' injunction). Unlike the strategy of seeking a stay discussed in the preceding section, the question of the availability of anti-suit injunctive relief is one which has attracted scant academic attention despite what will be seen to be its fecund heritage and a veritable flood of recent case law both within the Commonwealth and in the United States.

The terminology 'anti-suit injunction' is now controversial as a result of **4.83** observations by Lord Hobhouse in *Turner v Grovit*,[244] in which he described this term as misleading 'since it fosters the impression that the order is addressed to and intended to bind another court' and 'suggests that the jurisdiction of the foreign court is in question and that the injunction is an order that the foreign court desist from exercising the jurisdiction given to it by its own domestic law'. While it is undoubtedly correct that an anti-suit injunction is not an order directed to the foreign court and also correct that anti-suit injunctions have been, on occasion, so regarded by foreign courts,[245] it may be doubted whether such misconceptions are as a result of the use of the term 'anti-suit injunction' as opposed to perceptions of the effect of such relief. It may also be doubted whether Lord Hobhouse's preferred terminology—'restraining order'— accommodates the considerations that actuated his concern. While it is important that the *in personam* nature of the remedy be always appreciated, lest there be concern that its modus operandi be misunderstood, that apprehension should be accommodated in clear reasons for judgment. The term 'anti-suit injunction' is a convenient and useful label which, as the High Court of Australia has observed, is 'now in common use'.[246] It also allows its various siblings—the anti-anti-suit injunction, the anti-anti-anti-suit injunction, and the anti-deposition injunction, all forms of restraining order—to be differentiated and better understood.

1. JURISDICTION TO RESTRAIN FOREIGN PROCEEDINGS

The first part of this section considers the jurisdiction to grant anti-suit **4.84** injunctive relief. Jurisdiction is here used in its broad sense to encompass both the technical competence of the courts to grant such relief and the discretionary principles which govern its exercise. It is first useful, however, to say a little about the historical origins of this jurisdiction.

---

[244] [2002] 1 WLR 107, 117.
[245] See *Re the Enforcement of an English Anti-Suit Injunction* [1997] I L Pr 320.
[246] *CSR Ltd v Cigna Insurance Australia Ltd* (1997) 189 CLR 345.

4.85 The existence of an equitable jurisdiction in the courts of common law countries and the United States of America to restrain parties from either commencing or continuing litigation in foreign jurisdictions is of ancient pedigree. The first report of an application for such relief was the case of *Love v Baker*[247] and, although Lord Clarendon LC doubted the basis of the jurisdiction in this case, it was confirmed by Lord Brougham LC in *Lord Portarlington v Soulby*[248] and by Lord Cranworth LC in *Carron Iron Co v Maclaren*.[249] It has its historical root in the pre-Judicature Act creature, the 'common injunction', which courts of Chancery could issue to restrain a party from commencing or continuing a suit in the courts of common law where to do so would be contrary to conscience.[250] Such injunctions were not directed to the courts of common law, as was the prerogative writ of prohibition, for example, but rather were in the form of an order, operating *in personam* on the conscience of the party proceeding or proposing to proceed at common law, directing it to desist therefrom.[251] It was the *in personam* nature of the jurisdiction that allowed a variant of the common injunction to be employed to restrain parties or prospective parties to *foreign proceedings* from continuing or commencing litigation abroad.[252] It was axiomatic, therefore, that this jurisdiction was founded:

> not on any arrogant assumption of power in our courts over foreign tribunals, but upon an undoubted control over the subjects of the realm, as a personal right to restrain them from committing injustice by prosecuting inequitable claims.[253]

4.86 The comfortable fiction resting on the *in personam* operation of the jurisdiction and the view that the grant of such relief constituted no interference with foreign proceedings meant that considerations of what is now termed 'comity' were not seen to arise. In *Bent v Young*,[254] Shadwell VC considered 'that in the contemplation of the Court of Chancery, every

---

[247] (1665) 2 Freem 125; 1 Ch Ca 67 (22 ER 698).

[248] (1834) 3 My & K 104, 107 (40 ER 40, 41).

[249] (1855) 5 HL Cas 416, 437. That the same equitable jurisdiction existed in the United States, see *Cole v Cunningham* 133 US 107, 117–119 (1890). For a valuable discussion of the early exercise of this equitable jurisdiction, see McLean, JD, 'Jurisdiction and Judicial Discretion' (1969) 18 ICLQ 931, especially 935–943.

[250] cf *Earl of Oxford's Case* (1615) 1 Ch Rep 1 (21 ER 485); see, generally, Holdsworth, WS, *A History of English Law* (5th edn, 1931) Vol 1, 459–465.

[251] In the *Earl of Oxford's Case* ibid, Lord Ellesmere LC stated that equity intervenes not 'from any error or defect in the judgment, but for the hard conscience of the party' at 10 (487 of ER).

[252] Paterson, JM, *Kerr on Injunctions* (6th edn, 1927) 596–605; *White & Tudor's Leading Cases in Equity* (9th edn, 1928) Vol 1, 631–636; Joyce, W, *The Law and Practice of Injunctions in Equity* (1872) Vol II, 1053–1071; Story, J, *Commentaries on Equity Jurisprudence* (14th edn, 1918) ss 1224–1225.

[253] *Lett v Lett* [1906] 1 IR 618, 629. See also *Carron Iron Co v Maclaren* (1855) 5 HL Cas 416, 437.

[254] (1838) 9 Sim 180.

foreign court is an inferior court'.[255] The sanction for a party disobeying an order to desist from foreign proceedings was to deem it to be in contempt of court and any foreign judgment obtained in defiance of such an order would not be enforceable.[256] The efficacy of such injunctive relief thus turned on the amenability of the plaintiff in the foreign proceedings to the foreign court's jurisdiction or the location of its assets in the forum granting the injunction. In *Re Vocalion (Foreign) Ltd*,[257] Maugham J stated that 'the Court ought to be satisfied before making the order that it will not hesitate if the order is disobeyed to commit or sequestrate the property of the person or company in default'.[258]

Before a court is in a position to assess whether in its discretion equitable **4.87** relief should be granted, actual jurisdiction over the defendant has to be established. This is the logical starting point of the inquiry.

Personal Jurisdiction over the Defendant

It is an elementary point, but one the significance of which has perhaps **4.88** been underestimated in this area, that a court must have personal jurisdiction over a defendant, whether by service of the defendant or authorization by the applicable rules of court, before it may grant an injunction directing the defendant to desist from commencing or pursuing foreign proceedings.[259]

Traditionally, in common law countries, a defendant within the jurisdic- **4.89** tion could be served as of right. That is now no longer the case in the United Kingdom and Ireland where the defendant is a domiciliary of a member state of the European Union or of Denmark or of a Contracting State to the Lugano Convention. Actual presence in England is irrelevant for the purposes of an English court's jurisdiction over such a defendant unless one of the articles of Council Regulation 44/2001 or the Convention prescribes jurisdiction in the circumstances of the case. This point can be demonstrated by reference to two cases in which anti-suit injunctions were sought prior to the Regulation and Convention coming into force.

In *Hambros Bank Ltd v Thune*,[260] an injunction was sought against two **4.90** Norwegian trustees of a Norwegian bankrupt estate. Leave had been

---

[255] ibid 191.
[256] *Bushby v Munday* (1821) 5 Madd 297, 307 (56 ER 908, 913).
[257] [1932] 2 Ch 196.
[258] ibid 205; Joyce (n 252 above) 1054.
[259] *Donohue v Armco Inc* [2002] 1 Lloyd's Rep 425, 432; *Channel Tunnel Group Ltd v Balfour Beatty Construction Ltd* [1993] AC 334, 342.
[260] (18 January 1991) No 6095/90.

obtained to serve them outside the jurisdiction under what was then Order 11 of the Rules of the Supreme Court. Were similar relief sought today, on the facts of that case, an English court would lack the requisite jurisdiction to grant the anti-suit relief. *Castanho v Brown & Root (UK) Ltd*[261] provides another example of a case in which the jurisdiction of the English court to grant the anti-suit injunctive relief sought would today be governed by Council Regulation 44/2001, Castanho being a Portuguese domiciliary. Unlike the *Hambros* case, as Castanho was in fact injured in England, jurisdiction would exist by virtue of Article 5(3) of the Regulation. Had the accident occurred elsewhere, however, it might also be argued that an English court would have had jurisdiction under Article 24 of the Regulation on the basis that Castanho had submitted to the jurisdiction of the English courts by himself initially instituting proceedings in England. Such a conclusion may be somewhat problematic, however, given that Castanho was given leave to discontinue the English proceedings.

4.91 Where a defendant is not domiciled in a member state of the European Union, Denmark or a Contracting State to the Lugano Convention, the need to first establish personal jurisdiction may still provide an obstacle to the grant of anti-suit relief in circumstances where the defendant is not present or able to be served in the forum. In these circumstances, it will be necessary to obtain an order for leave to serve the defendant outside the jurisdiction, in those jurisdictions where prior leave is required, and, in any event, to bring the claim within one of the authorized heads of jurisdiction, where leave is not required, to forestall a challenge to the court's jurisdiction. *Youell v Kara Mara Shipping Co Ltd*[262] provides an example of an unsuccessful challenge to the court's jurisdiction to issue proceedings seeking anti-suit injunctive relief. In this case, Aikens J accepted that a claim which solely sought such relief was permissible and legitimate.[263] In so far as the claim had as its basis a contractual right for suit exclusively to take place in England, the judge was satisfied on a good arguable case basis that this claim fell within that clause of the Civil Procedure Rules that authorized service out of the jurisdiction in a case where there was a claim 'which affects a contract'. By way of contrast, in *Amoco (UK) Exploration Co Ltd v British American Offshore Ltd*,[264] Langley J held that 'where the claim itself is not based on a contract or some other cause of

---

[261] [1981] AC 557. The facts of this case are set out in para 2.17 above.
[262] [2000] 2 Lloyd's Rep 102.
[263] In *Associated Newspapers Group plc v Insert Media Ltd* [1988] 1 WLR 509, 514, Hoffmann J observed that anti-suit injunctions are 'most commonly sought by defendants who are not seeking to assert any independent cause of action but simply a right not to be sued in the foreign court'.
[264] [1999] 2 Lloyd's Rep 772, 781.

action or recognized legal or equitable concept, in my judgment it cannot qualify for leave [for service out]'.

One particular difficulty, at least in cases where an anti-suit injunction is **4.92** sought on the basis of the defendant's vexatious, oppressive, or unconscionable conduct and that defendant is not present or able to be served in the forum, lies in the fact that many of the sub-heads of 'exorbitant' or long arm jurisdiction traditionally authorized by rules of court in common law jurisdictions are tied back to conduct or effects *within* the jurisdiction and what is being sought in an anti-suit injunction is precisely the opposite, namely the restraint of unconscionable conduct *outside* the jurisdiction.

The necessity that the defendant to an application for anti-suit relief be **4.93** 'amenable', to use Lord Goff's word in *Société Nationale Industrielle Aerospatiale v Lee Kui Jak*,[265] to English personal jurisdiction also reflects the fact that courts are sensitive to making an order which will be an empty threat.[266] In *Donohue v Armco*,[267] Sedley LJ said that:

an orderly use of available national forums depends upon a combination of mutual respect and self-denial on the part of their respective Courts. The risk inherent in an anti-suit injunction, if it is unwisely granted, is that it will not succeed in stopping a party whose assets are located outside the jurisdiction from litigating abroad nor dissuade the Courts of other countries from entertaining the litigation.

On the other hand, it has been said that an English court 'does not contemplate the possibility that it will not be obeyed'.[268]

An important question, which may be thought to go to subject matter **4.94** jurisdiction rather than personal jurisdiction or discretion, has been raised by dicta of Lord Hobhouse in *Turner v Grovit*,[269] where his Lordship said, by reference to his understanding of what he described as 'the point decided in *Airbus Industrie GIE v Patel*',[270] that:

The Applicant for a restraining order must have a legitimate interest in making his application and the protection of that interest must make it necessary to make the

---

[265] [1987] AC 871.

[266] See, for example, *Re Maxwell Communications Corporation plc (No 2)* [1992] BCC 757, 767, and 778.

[267] [2000] 1 Lloyd's Rep 579, 600.

[268] *In re Liddell's Settlement Trusts* [1936] Ch 365, 374. See also *The Tropaioforos (No 2)* [1962] 1 Lloyd's Rep 410, 420; *Castanho v Brown & Root (UK) Ltd* [1981] AC 557, 574; *Man (Sugar) Ltd v Haryanto (No 2)* [1991] 1 Lloyd's Rep 429, 439; *Djoni Widjaja v Bank of America National Trust and Savings Association* [1993] 3 SLR 678, 684.

[269] [2002] 1 WLR 107, 119. Dicta because the actual decision in this case was simply to refer a question to the European Court of Justice.

[270] [1999] 1 AC 119.

order. Where the Applicant is relying upon a contractual right not to be sued in the foreign country (say because of an exclusive jurisdiction clause or an arbitration clause), then, absent some special circumstance, he has by reason of his contract a legitimate interest in enforcing that right against the other party to the contract. But *where he is relying upon conduct of the other person which is unconscionable for some non-contractual reason, English law requires that the legitimate interest must be the existence of proceedings in this country which need to be protected by the grant of a restraining order* [emphasis added].

4.95 It is not immediately apparent why the unconscionable conduct necessary to enliven equity's jurisdiction, in an appropriate case, to grant anti-suit relief should be confined, as the passage from Lord Hobhouse's judgment would appear to do, to unconscionable conduct relative, or in some way tied, to existing local proceedings or, indeed, to proceedings at all. His observations are inconsistent with the anti-suit injunctions granted by the Court of Appeal in *Midland Bank plc v Laker Airways*[271] and in *Smith Kline & French Laboratories Ltd v Bloch*[272] as well as with the fact that 'vexation may assume innumerable shapes',[273] a recent example of which is supplied by *Shell International Petroleum Co Ltd v Coral Oil Co Ltd*,[274] where an anti-suit injunction was issued to restrain proceedings that had been commenced in Lebanon in circumstances where there were no English proceedings on foot and where the applicant for anti-suit relief could point to no applicable contractual or other legal entitlement to it. No decision prior to *Turner v Grovit* had suggested a limitation to equity's jurisdiction to grant anti-suit relief of the kind identified by Lord Hobhouse. The better view, it is suggested, is that the limits of the jurisdiction should be determined by the 'dictates of equity and good conscience'.[275]

4.96 Before turning to identify with more precision the various discretionary bases upon which anti-suit relief may be granted, a little more needs to be said about what have been described as 'single forum' cases, that is to say, cases in which it is sought to restrain proceedings in a forum which is the *only* forum in which particular relief is available. It should be noted that this line of cases cannot sit with the observations of Lord Hobhouse in *Turner v Grovit* cited above and are not reconcilable with those observations.

---

[271] [1986] QB 689.
[272] [1983] 2 All ER 72.
[273] *In re Connolly Brothers Ltd* [1911] 1 Ch 731, 746 .
[274] [1999] 2 Lloyd's Rep 606.
[275] *CSR Ltd v Cigna Insurance Australia Ltd* (1997) 189 CLR 345, 394.

'Single Forum' Cases

The distinction said to exist between 'single forum' and *'forum conveniens'* **4.97** or alternative forum cases was described by Lord Diplock as 'crucial'[276] and is one which, if valid, will necessarily bear on the analysis which follows. In *British Airways*, Lord Diplock identified as a 'novel' circumstance the fact that there was 'a single forum only that is of competent jurisdiction to determine the merits of the claim'[277] and considered that the grant of anti-suit injunctive relief in such a case should be approached differently from one where there were two or more alternative forums. This was because, in a case where the merits could only be tried in one forum, restraint of proceedings in that forum was ultimately dispositive, one of the reasons, no doubt, why the decision of the Court of Appeal in *Midland Bank plc v Laker Airways Ltd* attracted such a hostile reaction in the United States.[278]

In *Re Maxwell Communications (No 2)*,[279] Glidewell LJ described 'single **4.98** forum' cases as those where 'there is no equivalent legislation in England' and seemed to suggest that, as a consequence of this, there was 'no right of action in this country'.[280] Care must be taken not to conclude too readily, however, that the mere fact that a party seeks to agitate a cause of action which derives from a statute of a particular forum has the consequence that that claim is therefore only able to be litigated in that forum. The conflict of laws would hasten to a quick death if that were the case. Moreover, every claim in a civilian system necessarily derives from statute and, yet, there has never been any suggestion that a claim for delict arising under the Code Civile, for example, may not be litigated outside France.[281] As a general proposition, there is no reason in principle why a cause of action derived from a statute of a particular country is any less able to be litigated in a foreign forum than is a 'common law' claim in tort or contract arising in that country or governed by its laws.

On this analysis, the status of *British Airways* as a 'single forum' case may **4.99** be somewhat problematic for it is difficult to see how the factual circumstances in that case did not give rise to a justiciable controversy in England (as well as the United States) involving potential claims in conspiracy. It was said that such a claim in England would be 'ruled out' because of the decision in *Mogul Steamship Co v McGregor, Gow & Co*,[282] but that was not a case where the controversy was said to be non-justiciable, merely the

---

[276] *British Airways* [1985] AC 58, 85.   [277] ibid 80.
[278] [1986] 1 QB 689.   [279] [1992] BCC 757.   [280] ibid 771.
[281] This was the very point of the identification of the governing law in *Renault v Zhang* (2002) 187 ALR 1.
[282] [1892] AC 25: see *British Airways* [1985] AC 58, 79–80.

claim was not able to be made out on the facts.[283] Why, as a matter of principle and to the extent that choice of law rules permit, should a claim arising under the Australian Trade Practices Act, for example, not be able to be litigated in England[284] or a claim under the Sherman Act not be able to be litigated in Canada, at least to the extent that such an action is not held to constitute the enforcement of a foreign public law? The short point is that not every case where there is a statutory claim in the foreign forum will be a single forum case.

4.100 It may be that the term 'single forum' case will be appropriate in circumstances where it is sought to restrain a party pursuing a claim in a foreign forum under a statute of that forum in circumstances where, had that claim been brought in the forum in which the injunction is sought, that forum's choice of law rules would not have permitted the foreign statutory claim to be entertained. An example of such a case was *Akai Pty Ltd v People's Insurance Company*,[285] where the effect of the English anti-suit injunction, restraining proceedings in Australia, was that Akai was denied the benefit of the Australian Insurance Contracts Act in negative declaratory proceedings commenced in England by the insurance company by reason of its prior agreement to English law. Another example of a true single forum case may be one where any attempt to bring the foreign statutory claim in the forum granting the injunctive relief would fail, not by reason of the fact that that forum's choice of law rules did not 'pick up' the foreign statute but by reason of the fact that that forum's public policy declined to give effect to that statute, whether by reason of its offensive extraterritorial operation[286] or, for example, the fact that it may be repugnant to international law or universal human rights.[287] Another example, and perhaps the paradigm 'single forum' case is a case which is only justiciable in one forum, such as cases involving questions of title to land and certain intellectual property rights whose existence is geographically delimited.[288]

---

[283] [1892] AC 25, 50 and 59.

[284] For a case suggesting that it could be, subject to any application for a stay of proceedings, see *Ocean Mutual Marine v FAI General Insurance* (Commercial Court, 16 June 1998, Tuckey, J) but cf *Australian Commercial Research and Development Ltd v ANZ McCaughan Merchant Bank Ltd* [1989] 3 All ER 65. Assuming that a claim under this statute were characterized for choice of law purposes as a tort, the Private International Law (Miscellaneous Provisions) Act 1995 (UK) arguably makes it simpler to 'pick up' a foreign statutory claim than it was under *Phillips v Eyre*.

[285] [1998] 1 Lloyd's Rep 90.

[286] *Midland Bank v Laker Airways* [1986] QB 689.

[287] *Kuwait Airways Corporation v Iraqi Airways Company* [2002] 2 WLR 1353.

[288] See *Apple Computer Inc v Apple Corps SA* [1990] 2 NZLR 598; *Tyburn Productions Ltd v Conan Doyle* [1991] Ch 75; *Canadian Filters (Harwich) Ltd v Lear-Siegler, Inc* 412 F 2d 577 (1st Cir, 1969); and *Medtronic, Inc v Catalyst* 518 F Supp 946, aff'd 664 F 2d 660 (8th Cir, 1981).

Apple Corps Ltd v Apple Computer Inc[289] provides an example of a true **4.101** single forum case in which injunctive relief was granted. In this case, the parties had entered into, *inter alia*, a 'no challenge' agreement with regard to certain patents. One party brought a challenge in Germany to the validity of the other's German patent—a question which Hoffmann J expressly acknowledged could not be litigated in England.[290] The patentee sought injunctive relief in England on the basis of the 'no challenge' clause. In reply, it was argued that relief should not be granted because the 'no challenge' clause could be pleaded in defence in the German objection proceedings, a course which would necessarily entail the German court interpreting the parties' agreement. An injunction was granted although Hoffmann J was at pains to point out that it was only interlocutory and that if, at the final hearing, the 'no challenge' clause was not upheld, the German objection proceedings could proceed. Nonetheless, the relief granted in this case had the effect of ensuring that the decisive question, namely the construction of the 'no challenge' agreement, would be determined by an English court and that, depending on the outcome, the German court would be denied the opportunity of ruling on the validity of a German patent.

The significance of drawing a distinction between single forum and alter- **4.102** native forum cases is that, where a genuine single forum case is isolated, a court asked to restrain proceedings in that forum should have regard to the fact that the consequences of anti-suit injunctive relief will be more far-reaching than in an ordinary case which is justiciable in more than one forum for, in a single forum case, an anti-suit injunction will effectively determine the suit.[291] Lord Goff's preliminary requirement in *Aerospatiale*[292] that England be the natural forum before an English court may grant anti-suit injunctive relief cannot be reconciled with the 'single forum' cases, a fact which he recognized in a more acute fashion in *Airbus Industrie GIE v Patel*,[293] where it was said that, as a general rule, this requirement was necessary in the interests of comity. Lord Goff was careful, however, to avoid rigidity and observed that 'there may be extreme cases, for example where the conduct of the foreign state exercising jurisdiction is such as to deprive it of the respect normally required by comity, where no such limit is required to the exercise of the jurisdiction to grant an anti-suit injunction'.[294]

Consideration now turns to the various bases and jurisprudential roots **4.103** that have been identified in the case law as justifying the grant of anti-suit injunctive relief.

---

[289] [1992] RPC 70. [290] ibid 77. [291] *British Airways* [1985] AC 58, 80.
[292] [1987] AC 871, 896. [293] [1999] 1 AC 119. [294] ibid 140.

Discretionary Bases of Jurisdiction

4.104 In *Société Nationale Industrielle Aerospatiale v Lee Kui Jak*,[295] a decision of the Privy Council on appeal from Brunei, Lord Goff identified 'certain basic principles' from the long history of the equitable jurisdiction to restrain foreign proceedings. In short form these basic principles are that, in addition to establishing jurisdiction over the defendant, the court's jurisdiction is to be exercised when the interests of justice so demand; that the order granting injunctive relief is directed to the plaintiff in the foreign proceedings and not to the foreign tribunal; but that, notwithstanding the *in personam* operation of this jurisdiction, caution is required in its exercise by reason of its implicit interference with the foreign tribunal.[296] These principles, which have been endorsed by the House of Lords on three subsequent occasions,[297] are commonly accepted as non-controversial in both the Commonwealth[298] and in the United States.[299]

4.105 While the equitable jurisdiction to restrain foreign proceedings is not in doubt and certain basal principles can be succinctly stated, the *precise basis* upon which the discretion to grant such injunctions should be exercised has been a source of no little confusion in the courts of common law countries. Justice Gummow, then of the Federal Court of Australia, observed that 'the judicial root of this well-established jurisdiction has not been appreciated as well as it might have been in the recent British decisions'[300] and returned to this theme in *Australian Broadcasting Corporation v Lenah Game Meats Pty Ltd*.[301] As shall be seen, there was for a time at least a degree of doctrinal confusion in the English cases as the relationship between the basis for granting anti-suit injunctions and the then incipient doctrine of *forum non conveniens* came to be worked out.[302] There was and remains a distinctly uneven application of whatever test is in currency. For example, since 1985, three of the four House of Lords' decisions in this area,[303] the Privy Council's advice in *Aerospatiale*, and the High Court of Australia's decision in *CSR Ltd v Cigna Insurance Australia Ltd*[304] all

---

[295] [1987] AC 871.

[296] ibid 893.

[297] *Airbus Industrie GIE v Patel* [1999] 1 AC 119; *Turner v Grovit* [2002] 1 WLR 107; *Donohue v Armco* [2002] 1 Lloyd's Rep 425.

[298] See, for example, *CSR Ltd v Cigna Insurance Australia Ltd* (1997) 189 CLR 345; *Amchem Products Inc v Workers Compensation Board* [1993] 1 SCR 897.

[299] *Bank of Tokyo Ltd v Karoon* (Note) [1987] AC 45, 59–60.

[300] *National Mutual Holdings Pty Ltd v Sentry Corporation* (1989) 87 ALR 539, 563.

[301] (2001) 185 ALR 1, 26–27.

[302] See Briggs, A, 'Restraint of Foreign Proceedings' [1987] LMCLQ 391, 394.

[303] Excluding *Turner v Grovit* [2002] 1 WLR 107, which was an order staying proceedings pending a reference to the European Court of Justice.

[304] (1997) 189 CLR 345.

reversed the decisions reached at the intermediate appellate level. The fourth of the House of Lords' decisions, *South Carolina Insurance Co v Assurantie NV*,[305] upheld a majority Court of Appeal decision that had discharged an injunction granted at first instance.

Even the apparent doctrinal clarification in *Aerospatiale*[306] has not left the **4.106** position wholly clear and the very breadth of the formula articulated in that case identifying the circumstances when anti-suit relief is warranted—at its narrowest, 'vexatious, oppressive or unconscionable conduct' and, at its broadest, 'what justice requires'—has had the inevitable consequence that considerable uncertainty remains as to the *content* of the test proposed by Lord Goff in that case[307] and its relationship with other stated bases for injunctive relief.[308] In *Hambros Bank Ltd v Thune*,[309] Browne-Wilkinson VC candidly conceded that he had 'not found it easy to comprehend what the current law is covering the grant of injunctions, restraining a party from pursuing foreign proceedings'.[310] This section aims to redress that situation in order to ascertain the scope for parties to transnational disputes resorting to anti-suit injunctive relief in the battle for venue. The first task is to examine the leading case law from both Commonwealth jurisdictions and the United States with a view to identifying the *bases* upon which anti-suit injunctive relief in relation to foreign proceedings is granted.

The current status of the law in common law countries in relation to the **4.107** grant of injunctions to restrain foreign proceedings can only be properly understood by reference to the earlier and cognate development of the law relating to stays of actions regularly commenced in England and the setting aside of service in proceedings outside the jurisdiction. That development has been treated in considerable detail in paragraphs 3.78 ff above and, as was seen there, is most clearly marked by the emergence of the concept of the natural forum. The line of decisions culminating in *Spiliada*[311] did not, however, refer to cases where the plaintiff had chosen to commence proceedings in a jurisdiction other than England and where the defendant to those proceedings sought injunctive relief in England in relation to the foreign proceedings. Indeed Lord Goff expressly doubted

---

[305] [1987] AC 24.
[306] See paras 4.112–4.113 below.
[307] Hartley, TC, 'Comity and the Use of Antisuit Injunctions in International Litigation' (1987) 35 American Journal of Comparative Law 487, 493.
[308] See Briggs A, (n 302 above) 397.
[309] (18 January 1991) No 6095/90.
[310] ibid 37 of transcript. See also *Amchem Products Inc v Workers Compensation Board* (1990) 75 DLR (4th) 1, 3 where McEachern CJBC spoke of the 'serious deficiencies and uncertainties' in this area of the law.
[311] [1987] AC 460.

whether the line of cases, mainly from the late nineteenth century, where such relief had been granted was at all useful for the purposes of his reconsideration of the grounds upon which a stay of proceedings regularly instituted in England or an order for service out of the jurisdiction might be granted.[312]

4.108 In *Castanho v Brown & Root (UK) Ltd*,[313] a decision which pre-dated *Spiliada* but post-dated *MacShannon v Rockware Glass Ltd*,[314] Lord Scarman had expressed the view that 'the principle is the same whether the remedy sought is the stay of English proceedings or a restraint upon foreign proceedings'.[315] Accordingly, he suggested that an injunction should lie wherever, in the converse situation, a stay would be granted; that is, in circumstances where England was a forum in which justice could be obtained at substantially less inconvenience or expense and where the plaintiff would not be denied any legitimate personal or juridical advantages which might be available to him in the foreign forum. The combination of this reasoning and the decision in *Spiliada* would have meant that, by the time of that decision, it *appeared* that the basis upon which an injunction could be issued to restrain foreign proceedings was that England and not the foreign country was the natural forum for the conduct of the trial and that justice did not otherwise require that the trial nevertheless proceed in the foreign forum.[316] This view had the consequence that the broad right traditionally afforded a plaintiff to commence litigation wheresoever he or she wished was similarly curtailed whether a plaintiff chose to institute proceedings in England or abroad. The operative principle limiting such a choice was that litigation take place in the 'natural forum'.

4.109 In addition to *Castanho*, the House of Lords had two other opportunities in the 1980s to consider the proper basis for the grant of injunctive relief in relation to proceedings commenced outside England. In *British Airways Board v Laker Airways Ltd*,[317] Lord Diplock, who had agreed with Lord Scarman in *Castanho*, stated that a plaintiff may seek to restrain a defendant, by means of injunction, from bringing suit against him in a foreign court 'upon the ground that the plaintiff is entitled under English law to a legal or equitable right *not* to be sued in that foreign court by that person upon the cause of action that is the subject of such proceedings'. A contractual agreement that any dispute arising out of the contract be exclusively resolved by litigation in England was cited as an example of a

---

[312] ibid 480.   [313] [1981] AC 557.
[314] [1978] AC 795.   15 [1981] AC 557, 574–575.
[316] This in fact was the approach of the Brunei Court of Appeal in *Aerospatiale*: see [1987] AC 871, 887–891.
[317] [1985] AC 58, 81.

legal right not to be sued in a particular foreign forum. The use of an injunction in this context bears the familiar mark of equity intervening to restrain the breach of a negative stipulation or covenant. Lord Diplock then suggested that an *equitable right* not to be so sued would exist where a party had an equitable defence under English law such as estoppel, election, waiver, laches, or 'blowing hot and cold'—all of which, he suggested, could result in what could be generically described as 'unconscionable conduct'.[318] Such defences could 'be given anticipatory effect as a *right* not to be sued that is enforceable by injunction in an action for a declaration of non-liability'.[319] The translation of such equitable defences into 'rights' perhaps represented an attempt to reconcile the basis for the grant of anti-suit injunctions with Lord Diplock's own leading statement in respect of the basis for the grant of injunctions generally in *The Siskina*.[320] It is immediately of note that what Lord Diplock said in relation to 'equitable rights' not to be sued did not contain any hint of the gloss apparently sought to be placed upon the jurisdiction to grant anti-suit injunctions otherwise than in aid of a legal right by Lord Hobhouse in *Turner v Grovit*[321] which was identified and criticized above.

With the exception of a brief reference[322] to a general observation of Lord **4.110** Scarman in *Castanho*, Lord Diplock did not in *British Airways* draw any support from that decision, distinguishing it on the basis, as he saw it, of the novel circumstance that the claim against British Airways was only justiciable in the United States.[323]

In *South Carolina Insurance Co v Assurantie NV*,[324] Lord Brandon expressed **4.111** the opinion that there were two general circumstances where injunctive relief would be available: first, where there was an actual or threatened invasion of a legal or equitable *right*; and, secondly, in order to restrain unconscionable conduct.[325] Unlike Lord Diplock in *British Airways*, Lord Brandon apparently did not consider that a plaintiff's ability to apply to the courts for injunctive relief against unconscionable conduct vested in that plaintiff any sort of 'equitable right'. Lord Brandon offered no definition of

---

[318] *British Airways* [1985] AC 58, 81. Lord Scarman also adopted the language of 'equitable rights' (at 95). See also *Compagnie Européene de Cereals SA v Tradax Export SA* [1986] 2 Lloyd's Rep 301, 304.

[319] *British Airways*, ibid (emphasis added).

[320] [1979] AC 210, 256: 'A right to obtain an . . . injunction is not a cause of action. . . . It is dependent on there being a pre-existing cause of action against the defendant arising out of an invasion, actual or threatened by him, of a legal or actual right of the plaintiff for the enforcement of which the defendant is amenable to the jurisdiction of the court.' See also Collins, LA, *Essays in International Litigation and the Conflict of Laws* (1994), 4.

[321] [2002] 1 WLR 107, 119 and see paras 4.94–4.95 above.

[322] *British Airways* [1985] AC 58, 81.

[323] ibid 80. The validity of this point of distinction is considered at paras 4.99–4.101 above.

[324] [1987] AC 24.   [325] ibid 40.

'unconscionable conduct' although he did state that it included conduct that was 'oppressive or vexatious or which interferes with the due process of the court'.[326] He had observed earlier in his speech that 'unconscionable conduct' was *not* a necessary prerequisite for the grant of an injunction restraining foreign proceedings.[327] As such, injunctions of this kind were said to be exceptional: they could be granted absent any legal or equitable right of the applicant or any unconscionable conduct on the part of the respondent (although, presumably, these considerations could also justify such relief). In this way, Lord Brandon affirmed, in line with *Castanho*, that the court had 'power to restrain [a party] from continuing his foreign proceedings on the ground that there is another forum in which it is more appropriate, in the interests of justice, that the dispute between the parties should be tried'.[328]

4.112 In *South Carolina*,[329] Lord Goff reiterated an explanation he had offered in *Bank of Tokyo Ltd v Karoon*[330] that the general basis for the grant of such injunctions was the 'protection of English jurisdiction'.[331] In *Aerospatiale*,[332] he considered that even this broad view was too narrow and eschewed all attempts at categorization. In that case, delivering the advice of the Privy Council, Lord Goff was concerned with a similar situation to that which had arisen in *Castanho*, namely a claim in negligence where damages were available and were being sought in more than one forum. In *Aerospatiale*, an application had been made to the courts of Brunei to restrain proceedings in the District Court of Texas. Lord Goff stated:

> In a case such as the present where a remedy for a particular wrong is available both in the English (or, as here, the Brunei) court and in a foreign court, the English or Brunei court will, generally speaking, only restrain the plaintiff from pursuing proceedings in the foreign court if such pursuit would be *vexatious or oppressive*.[333]

He went on to add that 'this presupposes that, as a general rule, the English or Brunei court must conclude that it provides the natural forum for the trial of the action'.[334]

4.113 *Aerospatiale*, although a Privy Council decision, was taken by lower courts as having supplanted the earlier decisions of the House of Lords and, in particular, *Castanho*, to the extent that it identified a different jurisprudential basis for the grant of anti-suit relief.[335] As noted above, the later

---

[326] [1987] AC 24 41.   [327] ibid 40.   [328] ibid.
[329] [1987] AC 24.   [330] (Note) [1987] AC 45, 60.
[331] [1987] AC 24, 45.   [332] [1987] AC 871, 893.
[333] ibid 896 (emphasis added).   [334] ibid.
[335] *Du Pont de Nemours & Co v Agnew (No 2)* [1988] 2 Lloyd's Rep 240, 243–244 and 249; *Hemain v Hemain* [1988] 2 FLR 388, 390–392; and *Re Maxwell Communications Corporation plc (No 2)* [1992] BCC 757, 771.

House of Lords decisions in *Airbus Industrie, Turner v Grovit*,[336] and *Donohue v Armco* all endorse its central reasoning. Lord Goff's key concern in *Aerospatiale* was to sever the doctrinal connection—described by Carter as having 'an obvious but meretricious attraction'[337]—between stay and injunction cases.[338] As has been seen, this connection was central to Lord Scarman's judgment in *Castanho*, had carried the continued support of the House of Lords in *British Airways*,[339] and was affirmed by Lord Brandon in *South Carolina*.[340] In stating that, as a general rule, an English court could not grant injunctive relief unless it concluded that it provided the natural forum for the trial of the action, Lord Goff in effect transformed what the logical extension of *Castanho* (post-*Spiliada*) suggested should be the test for the grant of anti-suit injunctions into a precondition. That England was the natural forum became a necessary although not sufficient condition for the grant of anti-suit injunctive relief; the existence of vexatious, oppressive, or otherwise unconscionable conduct was also required.

The later decision of the House of Lords in *Airbus Industrie GIE v Patel*[341] made explicit the requirement that, for this form of relief to be granted, England (or the forum in which it is sought) must, other than in what have been described as single forum cases,[342] be the natural forum, as a general rule. Lord Goff saw this requirement as in large measure discharging an English court's obligation to 'do comity' to the foreign state in which the proceedings sought to be restrained had been commenced.[343] **4.114**

Notwithstanding its status as the leading authority, *Aerospatiale* leaves several issues unclear. For example, Lord Goff made no reference to the attempted formulations by both Lord Diplock in *British Airways* and Lord Brandon in *South Carolina* of the more general bases upon which such injunctions might be granted.[344] Similarly, and apart from uncertainty as **4.115**

---

[336] Save for the gloss of Lord Hobhouse criticized in para 4.96 above.

[337] (Note) (1988) BYIL 342.

[338] For the explicit statement of this conclusion, see *Aerospatiale* [1987] AC 871, 895–896.

[339] [1985] AC 58, 95.

[340] See also, in the Court of Appeal, *Metall und Rohstoff AG v ACLI Metals (London) Ltd* [1984] 1 Lloyd's Rep 598. The doctrinal connection drawn in *Castanho* was accepted by the Irish Supreme Court in *Murphy (Joseph) Structural Engineers v Manitowoc (UK) Ltd* (30 July 1985), noted in Binchy, W. *Irish Conflicts of Law* (1988) 167 and 170–171.

[341] [1999] 1 AC 119.

[342] See paras 4.97–4.101 above.

[343] Briggs has suggested that a choice of law analysis may provide the proper lens for what others, including the House of Lords in *Airbus*, regard as considerations of comity: 'The unrestrained reach of an anti-suit injunction: a pause for thought' [1997] LMCLQ 90.

[344] Browne-Wilkinson VC drew attention to this fact in *Hambros Bank Ltd v Thune* (18 January 1991) No 6095/90.

to its own content, the question of whether vexatious and oppressive behaviour is synonymous with unconscionable conduct is not plain.[345] Nor is it clear what kind of interference with the 'due process of the court'[346] is required before an English court will be justified in intervening by means of injunction to protect its jurisdiction and the integrity of its own processes.[347] Finally, there is the difficult question of what comity requires in any given case, or, indeed, whether it has any role to play at all in this field of discourse. In this context, the question whether an English court may restrain a party from commencing or continuing proceedings in another member state of the European Union on the basis of vexatious, oppressive, or unconscionable conduct has been referred to the European Court of Justice.[348]

4.116 *Aerospatiale* was approved by the Supreme Court of Canada as the 'foundation' for the test for the grant of anti-suit relief in *Amchem Products Inc v Workers Compensation Board*.[349] The Canadian approach to this field of discourse, however, is profoundly affected by perceptions of the demands of comity, considered more fully below. This has implications for the way in which the core principles identified in *Aerospatiale* are played out in Canada. Thus, whereas *Aerospatiale* comes more or less directly to a consideration of the quality of the defendant or respondent's conduct and whether or not it is of such a character as to warrant injunctive relief, the approach favoured by the Supreme Court in *Amchem* places an initial focus on the jurisdictional rules of the forum in which the proceedings sought to be restrained are pending or threatened. In short, if those rules broadly coincide with what Canadian courts evidently regard as the civilized doctrine of *forum non conveniens* and the organizing concept of the natural forum, comity and confidence in the ability and willingness of the foreign court fairly and responsibly to apply that doctrine will dictate judicial restraint. It is only if the foreign forum's jurisdictional rules do not exhibit those characteristics that a Canadian court will then move on to consider whether or not the conduct of the moving party in that foreign court warrants restraint.[350]

---

[345] Notwithstanding Lord Brandon's equation of the two in *South Carolina* [1987] AC 25, 41, they were treated as distinct by Steyn J in *Man (Sugar) Ltd v Haryanto (No 2)* [1991] 1 Lloyd's Rep 161, 167.   [346] *South Carolina* [1987] AC 25, 41.

[347] This question was not raised, let alone addressed, either by Hoffmann J or the Court of Appeal in *Re Maxwell Communications (No 2)* [1992] BCC 757, even though the American proceedings sought to be restrained would in effect undermine the avoidance of preference policy of the British insolvency legislation. See discussion of this case at para 4.144 below.

[348] *Turner v Grovit* [2002] 1 WLR 107.

[349] [1993] 1 SCR 897, 930. It has also been followed by the Singapore Court of Appeal: *Koh Kay Yew v Inn Pacific Holdings Ltd* [1997] 3 SLR 121.

[350] See Briggs, A, 'Anti-Suit Injunctions in a Complex World' in Rose, F (ed), *Lex Mercatoria* (2000), 222–223.

Aerospatiale was also referred to with approval by the High Court of **4.117**
Australia in *CSR Ltd v Cigna Insurance Australia Ltd.*[351] In that case, the
High Court undertook a review of the varying jurisdictional bases for the
grant of anti-suit relief. The jurisdiction was described, in part at least, as
a 'counterpart of a court's power to *prevent* its processes being abused' by
reason of the 'power to *protect* the integrity of those processes once set in
motion' through the grant of anti-suit relief.[352] The Court went on to
observe that:

Quite apart from the inherent power of a court to protect its own processes, a court
may, in the exercise of the power deriving from the Chancery Court, make orders
in restraint of unconscionable conduct or the unconscientious exercise of legal
rights. If the bringing of legal proceedings involves unconscionable conduct or the
unconscientious exercise of a legal right, an injunction may be granted by a court
in the exercise of its equitable jurisdiction in restraint of those proceedings no
matter where they are brought. In some cases, the equitable jurisdiction to restrain
unconscionable conduct may be exercised in aid of legal rights.[353]

Although referring to *Aerospatiale* with approval, there is room for debate
in relation to whether certain dicta in the High Court's judgment operate
to limit or constrain the circumstances in which anti-suit relief is available
in Australia.[354]

There is no decision of the United States Supreme Court dealing with anti- **4.118**
suit injunctions in a transnational context. The United States federal case
law divides into two overlapping yet distinct lines regarding the bases for
the grant of anti-suit injunctive relief.[355]

The decision of the District of Columbia Court of Appeals in *Laker Airways* **4.119**
Ltd v Sabena, Belgian World Airways [356] contains perhaps the most compre-
hensive judicial analysis of anti-suit injunctions in the American case law.
In his leading judgment, Judge Wilkey observed that:

There are no precise rules governing the appropriateness of anti-suit injunctions.
The equitable circumstances surrounding each request for an injunction must be
carefully examined . . . Injunctions are most often necessary to protect the jurisdiction of the enjoining court or to prevent the litigant's evasion of the important
public policies of the forum.[357]

---

[351] (1997) 189 CLR 345 and see Briggs, A, 'Self-Restraint in the High Court of Australia'
(1998) 114 LQR 27.
[352] ibid 391 (emphasis added).
[353] ibid 392.
[354] Briggs, A, and Rees, P (n 144 above) 5.46, and see paras 4.179 ff below.
[355] See, generally, Born, GB (n 74 above) 475 ff.
[356] 731 F 2d 909 (DC Cir, 1984).
[357] ibid 927.

4.120 The cautious language of this passage reveals a familiar reluctance to confine the equitable jurisdiction and the courts' discretion to certain limited categories.[358] *Laker*, however, has been interpreted in subsequent decisions in certain circuits as doing just that. Thus, in *Gau Shan Co Ltd v Bankers Trust Co*,[359] the Court of Appeals for the 6th Circuit, heavily influenced by what it perceived to be the demands of international judicial comity in transnational litigation, noted that: 'the Second and D.C. Circuits hold that the *only* proper grounds to grant a foreign anti-suit injunction are: 1) to protect the forum's jurisdiction, or 2) to prevent evasion of the forum's important public policies'.[360] This test was adopted by the 6th Circuit in this case[361] and the narrow view of the jurisdiction with a premium of comity has most recently been endorsed by the 3rd Circuit Court of Appeals.[362] Under this line of authority, an anti-suit injunction will not lie simply to restrain vexatious, oppressive, or otherwise unconscionable conduct. Parallel proceedings are accepted as an unfortunate fact of transnational life but, unless able to be avoided by the grant of a stay of proceedings in one or other forum, an anti-suit injunction will not lie to restrain one set of proceedings, even if that set of proceedings could be seen, even clearly seen, to be the engine of oppression or vexation to the applicant for anti-suit relief.

4.121 This line of authority is to be contrasted with that which may be traced to the decision of the 5th Circuit in *In re Unterweser Reederi GmbH*.[363] Unlike *Laker* which held that 'duplication of parties and issues alone is not sufficient to justify issuance of an anti-suit injunction',[364] in this case it was held that an anti-suit injunction may issue to restrain the 'simultaneous prosecution of the same action in a foreign forum thousands of miles away'.[365] *Unterweser* has been cited with approval by the Court of

---

[358] In *Castanho* [1981] AC 557, Lord Scarman cautioned that 'the width and flexibility of equity are not to be undermined by categorisation' (573). See also *South Carolina* [1987] AC 25, 44–45.

[359] 956 F 2d 1349 (6th Cir, 1992).

[360] ibid 1354 (emphasis added).

[361] See also *China Trade and Development Corp v MV Choong Yong* 837 F 2d 33 (2nd Cir, 1987), superseding older 2nd Circuit authority which had granted injunctive relief on the grounds of vexatiousness: *Harvey Aluminium, Inc v American Cynamid Co*, 203 F 2d 105 (1953); *Sea Containers Ltd v Stena AB* 890 F 2d 1205 (DC Cir, 1989); *Computer Associations International Inc v Altai, Inc* 126 F 3d 365 (2nd Cir, 1997). The *Laker* decision has been followed on numerous occasions at first instance.

[362] *General Electric Company v Deutz AG* 270 F 3d 144 (2001).

[363] 428 F 2d 888 (5th Cir, 1970), affirmed on rehearing *en banc*, 446 F 2d 907 (1971), reversed on other grounds sub nom *Bremen v Zapata Offshore Co* 407 US 1 (1972); [1972] 2 Lloyd's Rep 315.

[364] 731 F 2d 909, 927 (1984).

[365] 428 F 2d 888, 896 (1984). In *American Home Assurance Co v Insurance Corp of Ireland* 603 F Supp 636 (1984), it was stated (643) that 'adjudication of the same issue in separate actions

Appeals for the 9th Circuit in *Seattle Totems Hockey Club v National Hockey League*[366] and been followed in several first instance decisions.[367] A similar approach has been adopted by the 7th Circuit. In *Allendale Mutual Insurance Company v Bull Data Systems, Inc,*[368] Posner CJ characterized the two lines of authority as imposing, respectively, 'strict' and 'laxer' standards. He then sought to explain the difference in this way:

When we say we lean toward the laxer standard we do not mean that international comity should have no weight in the balance: we do not interpret the 'lax' cases as assigning it no weight. The difference between the two lines of case has to do with the inferences to be drawn in the absence of information. The strict cases presume a threat to international comity whenever an injunction is sought against litigating in a foreign court. The lax cases want to see some empirical flesh on the theoretical skeleton. . . . When every practical consideration supports the injunction, it is reasonable to ask the opponent for some indication that the issuance of an injunction really would throw a monkey wrench, however small, into the foreign relations of the United States. . . . The injunction merely prevents a French company from seeking to revive a dormant proceeding before an arbitral tribunal in France. The only concern with international comity is a purely theoretical one that ought not trump a concrete and persuasive demonstration of harm to the applicant for the injunction, if it is denied, not offset by any harm to the opponent if it is granted.[369]

Posner CJ's theme was, in turn, developed by the 5th Circuit in *Kaepa, Inc v Achilles Corp,*[370] where it was said that: **4.122**

We decline, however, to require a district court to genuflect before a vague and omnipotent notion of comity every time that it must decide whether to enjoin a foreign action. In the instant case, for example, it simply cannot be said that the grant of the antisuit injunction actually threatens relations between the United States and Japan. First, no public international issue is implicated by the case: Achilles is a private party engaged in a contractual dispute with another private party. Second, the dispute has been long and firmly ensconced within the confines of the United States judicial system: Achilles consented to jurisdiction in Texas; stipulated that Texas law and the English language would govern any dispute; appeared in an action brought in Texas; removed that action to a federal court in Texas; engaged in extensive discovery pursuant to the directives of the federal court; and only then, with the federal action moving steadily toward trial, brought identical claims in Japan. Under these circumstances, we cannot conclude that the district court's grant of an antisuit injunction in any way trampled on notions of comity.

---

would result in delay, inconvenience, expense, inconsistency or a race to judgment' and would 'engender considerable vexation and oppression'.

[366] 652 F 2d 852 (9th Cir, 1981), cert denied 457 US 1105 (1982).
[367] *Cargill Inc v Hartford Accident & Indemnity Co* 531 F Supp 710 (D Minn, 1982); *Garpeg, Limited v United States* 583 F Supp 789, 798 (SDNY 1984); and *American Home Assurance Co v Insurance Corp of Ireland* 603 F Supp 636 (1984). [368] 10 F 3d 425 (7th Cir, 1993).
[369] ibid 431–433. [370] 76 F 3d 624 (5th Cir, 1996).

4.123 From this conspectus of the leading English, Commonwealth, and United States cases, and noting the narrower approach exemplified by *Laker* and *Gau Shan*, three main bases for relief can be identified: first, the protection of courts' jurisdiction, including prevention of the evasion of important public policies of the forum; second, the effectuation of legal or equitable rights; and third, the forestalling of vexatious, oppressive, or unconscionable conduct.

4.124 In the following subsections, with the caveat that the various bases identified are not to be regarded as confining the courts' discretion[371] and noting that there is a degree of conceptual overlap between bases, an exploration is made of what is entailed in the notion of acting to protect the jurisdiction of the court; the circumstances where an injunction will be granted to enforce certain legal rights not to be sued, whether at all or abroad, are considered; and an attempt is made to give content to the concept of vexatious and oppressive conduct. There is then a consideration of the concept and claims of comity in this area of the law. Related to that assessment, possible limitations on the availability of anti-suit relief will also be considered.

2. 'Protective' Anti-Suit Injunctions

4.125 In *Bank of Tokyo Ltd v Karoon*,[372] Robert Goff LJ stated that 'the golden thread running through the rare cases where an injunction has been granted appears to have been the protection of the jurisdiction; an injunction has been granted where it was considered proper for the protection of the jurisdiction of the English court'.[373] Although he was subsequently to disavow this description in so far as it purported to summarize the limits of this head of equitable jurisdiction,[374] the protection of the court's jurisdiction remains one basis upon which a court may grant injunctive relief in relation to foreign proceedings. In *South Carolina*, Lord Brandon stated that unconscionable conduct included that 'which interferes with the due processes of the court'.[375] Protection of jurisdiction may be considered in three contexts: first, in the sense in which Lord Brandon referred to the term in *South Carolina*, namely the protection of the integrity of a court's own processes; secondly, and related to the first, the protection of a court's very ability to hear a case; and thirdly, protection of jurisdiction in the broader sense of preventing the evasion of a forum's important public policies.[376]

---

[371] *Aerospatiale* [1987] AC 871, 892; and *Channel Tunnel Group Ltd v Balfour Beatty Construction Ltd* [1993] AC 334, 340–341, 341–343, and 362–363.
[372] (Note) [1987] AC 45.   [373] ibid 60.
[374] See *Aerospatiale* [1987] AC 871, 893.   [375] [1987] AC 24, 41.
[376] *Laker* 731 F 2d 909, 927 (DC Cir, 1984).

Integrity of Process

Armstrong v Armstrong[377] provides an early illustration of a court enjoin- **4.126** ing foreign proceedings in order to preserve the integrity of its own processes. In that case, divorce proceedings had been instituted in England. The husband, whose order for a commission to examine witnesses in Vienna had been suspended, applied to the Viennese courts under provisions of the Austrian Code to summon witnesses before it and examine them on oath. It was conceded that any evidence taken pursuant to the provisions of the Austrian Code would be inadmissible in the English proceedings so that the Viennese proceedings yielded no advantage to the husband. Whatever other advantage he stood to gain was considered to be illegitimate not on the basis that it was vexatious and oppressive to the defendant but because it would represent an 'interference with the proper course of the administration of justice in this Court'.[378]

In *Sentry Corporation v Peat Marwick Mitchell & Co*,[379] the Full Court of the **4.127** Federal Court of Australia upheld a decision to grant an injunction to restrain an apprehended contempt of proceedings in the Federal Court. The apprehended contempt lay in the taking of oral depositions in Sydney pursuant to the order of the Wisconsin Circuit Court in related proceedings involving parent companies or companies associated with the parties to the Australian proceedings. Critically, the persons sought to be examined on oath were involved in the preparation of the case in the Federal Court and the complaint brought in the Wisconsin proceedings depended on the outcome of the Australian proceedings.[380]

The commencement of proceedings under the Racketeer Influenced and **4.128** Corrupt Organizations Act 1970 (RICO Act) in California against a party whose written evidence was to be relied upon by a party in fraud proceedings in England was held not to be intimidatory or an interference with the jurisdiction or process of the court by Hoffmann J in *Arab Monetary Fund v Hashim*.[381] Unlike the decision in *Sentry Corporation v Peat Marwick Mitchell & Co*, Hoffmann J did not consider the fact that the Californian proceedings may have constituted a contempt of the English

---

[377] [1892] P 98.
[378] ibid 101. See also *Omnium Lyonnais D'Etanchei et Revetement Asphalte v Dow Chemical Co* 441 F Supp 1385 (CD Cal, 1977) which was a case in which the use, in French proceedings, of documents discovered in the United States without the permission, as required, of the Special Master was restrained as abusive.
[379] (1990) 95 ALR 11.
[380] ibid 33 and 39–41.
[381] Financial Times, 23 July 1992.

proceedings to be determinative.[382] Hoffmann J considered that the motive behind the commencement of the Californian proceedings was 'the opportunity to examine Mr al Hafidh on discovery or at trial in Los Angeles'.[383] He concluded that, while 'this may or may not be an abuse of the process in California', it 'does not in my judgment constitute an interference with the proceedings in England'.[384] Questions of degree are clearly involved and it is suggested that, had Mr al Hafidh been a central witness, Hoffmann J's decision may have been different.

4.129 It is self-evident that a central element of protecting the integrity of a court's process is the maintenance of control of proceedings before it. In *Laker*, one of the few situations which Wilkey J would countenance as outweighing considerations of comity and therefore appropriate for anti-suit injunctive relief was where foreign proceedings concerned a matter which had already been litigated in the forum in which injunctive relief was sought.[385] Such relief was justified by reference to the need to 'protect the integrity of [the court's] judgments'.[386] Given the effort courts invest in familiarizing themselves with the details of particular sets of proceedings and the time set aside for their resolution, it is reasonable to suppose that the need to maintain control over litigation is more pressing (and indeed justified) the further litigation has advanced,[387] *ex hypothesi* the case where judgment has in fact been entered.

4.130 *South Carolina*[388] was a case in which the issue of control over the course of English proceedings arose at an early stage. Re-reinsurers sought an order for pre-trial discovery in the United States against companies not party to the English proceedings. No substantive proceedings were on foot in the United States. Both Hobhouse J at first instance and the Court of Appeal came to conclusions radically different from those of the House of Lords on the question of whether the United States proceedings constituted an interference with the jurisdiction of the English courts and therefore warranted restraining by the grant of an injunction. Griffiths LJ presented an amalgam of reasons for upholding the injunction granted by Hobhouse J. In particular, and in line with the decision at first instance, he considered that 'once the parties have chosen or accepted the court in which their dispute is to be tried they must abide by the procedure of that country and that court must be master of its own procedure'.[389] The

---

[382] He stated that 'it is open to the court to entertain proceedings for contempt without enjoining the foreign action'.

[383] ibid 7.   [384] ibid.

[385] 731 F 2d 909, 928 n 52 (1984).   [386] ibid.

[387] See *China Trade and Development v MV Choong Yong* 837 F 2d 33, 40 (2nd Cir, 1987).

[388] [1987] AC 24.

[389] [1986] 1 QB 348, 358.

reason for this rested squarely on grounds of public policy. Griffiths LJ continued:

Severe dislocation to the timetable of the English litigation is a readily foreseeable consequence of unrestrained access to foreign procedural remedies. This is likely to cause hardship or inconvenience not only to the other party to that litigation but will also affect other litigants whose cases are listed upon forecasts dependent on litigation being conducted in accordance with our own rules of procedure. As the judge said, the court will lose control of its own proceedings.[390]

The re-reinsurers could have, but did not, make a request to the High **4.131** Court under RSC, Order 39, rule 2 (as it then was) for letters of request to issue to the courts of the United States with a view to obtaining evidence. In addition to letters rogatory issued by foreign courts, any 'interested person' may make an application directly to a United States district court for testimony to be given or documents to be produced.[391] The re-rein-surers made such a direct request. Hobhouse J and the Court of Appeal felt that any request should come through the English court which would no doubt exercise its discretion in deciding whether to issue letters roga-tory. In this way, RSC, Order 39, rule 2 was interpreted as a mandatory procedure for the gathering of evidence from foreign sources where such evidence was not volunteered. The House of Lords took a different view and answered the public policy arguments that had been invoked by Griffiths LJ with the assertion that the court could control excessive delay by fixing dates for trial and that any inconvenience produced by resort to the foreign procedure was a necessary cost of justice.[392] The point can be made that proceeding via the mechanism prescribed by the Rules of the Supreme Court allows the court in control of the substantive case to decide, in the exercise of its discretion, the bounds of necessity. It is a process which ensures that the court remains master of its own house.[393]

The actual decision in *South Carolina* can be contrasted to that of the Court **4.132** of Appeal in *Bank of Tokyo Ltd v Karoon*,[394] where New York proceedings were in part restrained. These proceedings were for breach of confidence

---

[390] ibid. The greater the amount of time a court has invested in a case, the more dislocat-ing the effect of foreign litigation and the stronger the basis for injunctive relief to protect the jurisdiction: see *China Trade and Development v MV Choong Yong* 837 F 2d 33, 40 (2nd Cir, 1987).

[391] 28 USC § 1782.

[392] [1987] AC 24, 43.

[393] Compare *Allstate Life Insurance Co v Australia and New Zealand Banking Group Ltd* (1996) 64 FCR 61, where an injunction was granted restraining the taking of an oral deposition in the United States of a particular witness in the period shortly prior to the commencement of a major and complex piece of commercial litigation in Australia. See also *Omega Group Holdings Ltd v Kozeny* (6 September 2001); *Bankers' Trust International v PT Dharmala Sakti Sejahtera* [1996] CLC 252.

[394] (Note) [1987] AC 45.

and privacy violations which were said to have resulted from the provision to the Bank of Tokyo, for use in English proceedings, of information relating to Mr Karoon's account by its New York subsidiary. The New York proceedings against the Bank of Tokyo were considered to impeach rights which the Bank of Tokyo had acquired in England by its successful resistance of an application by Mr Karoon to strike out interpleader proceedings which it had commenced in London. The allegedly confidential information was employed in the opposition to the strike out application. The New York proceedings against the Bank of Tokyo, in so far as they might have resulted in a finding that the English decision relied on information obtained in breach of confidence, were restrained in order, in effect, to ensure that the English decision and the processes employed in reaching that decision were not impeached.

4.133 The reaction to New York proceedings of this kind is difficult to reconcile with Leggatt J's decision in *XAG v A Bank*,[395] where an injunction was granted restraining an English bank from providing documents in response to a subpoena issued by a New York bank in foreign proceedings as the provision of such information would involve a breach of banker/customer confidentiality. In *Bank of Tokyo Ltd v Karoon*, had the Bank of Tokyo sought letters rogatory from the English court in the strike out application, a New York court could have resolved the issues of United States confidentiality and privacy law in proceedings which were effectively an extension of English pre-trial procedure. There could have been no question of any interference with the integrity of the processes of the English court. Such an approach, consistent with that favoured by the lower courts in *South Carolina*, militates against the free and uncontrolled resort to foreign procedure for the purposes of English proceedings.[396]

4.134 Retention of control over local proceedings has underpinned at least four Australian decisions to issue anti-suit injunctive relief. In *National Mutual Holdings Pty Ltd v Sentry Corporation*,[397] a party to litigation before the Federal Court of Australia commenced proceedings in New York seeking to enjoin its former solicitors from acting for an opposing party in the Australian proceedings. In granting an injunction, Gummow J described the New York proceedings as 'a procedure apt to bring about a situation whereby that other party changes its solicitor, a step of primary and paramount concern to this court'.[398] In *Re Siromath Pty Ltd (No 3)*,[399] McLelland J of the Supreme Court of New South Wales restrained

---

[395] [1983] 2 All ER 464.
[396] See further discussion of resort to foreign procedure in transnational litigation at paras 4.185 ff below.
[397] (1989) 87 ALR 539.
[398] ibid 564.
[399] (1991) 25 NSWLR 25.

proceedings which had been commenced in Pennsylvania against the liquidator and the provisional liquidator of a New South Wales company which was in the process of being wound up. He spoke of the need to protect officers of the court in the discharge of their official duties and described the Pennsylvanian proceedings, brought by a trade creditor of the company, as 'intimidatory and oppressive'.[400] In both *CSR Ltd v NZ Insurance Co Ltd*[401] and *Allstate Life Insurance Co v Australia and New Zealand Banking Group Ltd*,[402] proceedings in the Supreme Court of New South Wales and the Federal Court of Australia, respectively, were at an advanced stage of preparation having been the subject of intensive case management and allocation of court time when foreign proceedings were commenced which threatened not only hearing dates but also to undermine careful case management by the courts of the proceedings to date. In this context, these two cases bear a very close affinity with the decisions of the English Court of Appeal to uphold a decision to restrain proceedings that had been commenced in the United States in *Glencore International AG v Exter Shipping Ltd*[403] and to restrain the Spanish proceedings in *Turner v Grovit*.[404]

The protection of a court's jurisdiction is not just a matter of judicial self-esteem. It is intimately bound up with the provision of justice to the parties in accordance with a forum's rules of procedure which are designed not just with the desideratum of efficiency in mind but also, and perhaps pre-eminently, are concerned with the affording of fairness to the parties before the court.[405] In some jurisdictions, the protection of the jurisdiction of the courts is constitutionally mandated. In the United States, for example, it has been said that 'courts need not stop to find all the usual prerequisites for equitable relief when they are acting to protect their jurisdiction from conduct which impairs their ability to carry out Article III functions'.[406] **4.135**

It should be pointed out that, in the cases which have been considered in this subsection, a narrow view, relating to the integrity of the court's processes, has been taken of the concept of 'jurisdiction'. Any broader view of the concept of protecting the court's jurisdiction could result in injunctions being granted simply in cases where another court has also **4.136**

---

[400] ibid 30.
[401] (1994) 36 NSWLR 138.
[402] (1996) 64 FCR 1 and 44.
[403] [2002] 2 All ER (Comm) 1.
[404] [2000] QB 345, but note that the House of Lords referred the issue to the European Court of Justice [2002] 1 WLR 107.
[405] See *Laker* 731 F 2d 901, 927 (DC Cir, 1984).
[406] See *Sea Containers Ltd v Stena AB* 890 F 2d 1205, 1214–1215 (DC Cir, 1989). See also *National Mutual Holdings Pty Ltd v Sentry Corp* (1989) 87 ALR 539, 563.

assumed jurisdiction over a possible dispute and there is the possibility of inconsistent decisions. While it may be the case that an injunction granted in this situation can be justified,[407] it is analytically desirable not to ground such injunctions on the basis of the protection of the court's jurisdiction; that concept should be tightly confined. The next subsection considers the use of anti-suit injunctions, or, more precisely, anti-anti-suit injunctions, not to prevent another court from hearing a case but rather to ensure the issuing court's ability *itself* to continue to exercise jurisdiction.

Anti-Anti-Suit Injunctions

4.137 The view has already been noted that caution should be exercised in the grant of anti-suit injunctions because of their ability to interfere as a practical if not theoretical matter with the process of and proceedings in a foreign court. Anti-suit injunctions are employed by American courts in particular to prevent what those courts perceive to be attacks on their jurisdiction, including by anti-suit injunctions granted by courts of foreign forums. Such attacks do not relate to the mere potential threat posed by 'competing' proceedings in a foreign jurisdiction; rather they are represented by cases where 'the foreign proceeding is not following a parallel track but attempts to carve out exclusive jurisdiction over concurrent actions'.[408] The hostile reaction of the American courts to the injunctions granted by the Court of Appeal in both *British Airways*[409] and *Midland Bank plc v Laker Airways Ltd*[410] arose directly in this context. Their 'sole purpose' was seen as being 'to *terminate* the American action'.[411] In such circumstances, Wilkey J stated that 'an injunction may be necessary to avoid the possibility of losing validly invoked jurisdiction. This would be particularly true if the foreign forum did not offer the remedy sought in the domestic forum.'[412] To this end, the mechanism of the so-called 'anti-anti-suit injunction' or 'defensive' anti-suit injunction has been developed. This is an injunction which orders a party not to seek injunctive relief in another forum in relation to proceedings in the issuing forum. Considerations of comity are cancelled out prospectively by anticipation that the foreign forum will grant anti-suit relief.[413]

---

[407] See the discussion at paras 4.204 ff below.

[408] 731 F 2d 909, 930 (1984).

[409] [1984] QB 142. The injunction was subsequently dissolved by the House of Lords: [1985] AC 58.

[410] [1986] QB 689.

[411] *Laker* 731 F 2d 909, 930 (1984).

[412] ibid.

[413] Such an injunction was granted by a Philadelphian court against the American parent in the *Smith Kline* litigation: see *Smith Kline & French Laboratories Ltd v Bloch* [1983] 2 All ER 72, 75.

In the *Amchem* litigation,[414] 'corporate citizens' of Texas, defendants to a **4.138** class action brought in Texas involving asbestos-related injuries, succeeded in obtaining simple anti-suit injunctive relief in the courts of British Columbia against the plaintiffs.[415] Not all of the plaintiffs, however, were amenable to that province's jurisdiction. Accordingly and in anticipation of similar anti-suit applications in other provinces, those plaintiffs not affected by the British Columbian injunction sought and secured anti-anti-suit relief in Texas against the corporate defendants.[416] Such injunctions were designed to ensure that what the Texas courts considered to be their legitimately conferred and assumed jurisdiction would be exercised (although, unlike *British Airways*, there was no prospect in the case of the *Amchem* litigation that the suit would not be able to be heard on the merits in Canada).

With, as shall be seen below, the increasing willingness of the English **4.139** courts in particular to enforce exclusive jurisdiction and arbitration clauses by an injunction restraining proceedings perceived to have been commenced in breach of such a clause, it is reasonable to expect well-advised litigants proposing to commence other than in a contractually stipulated forum to accompany the filing of their suit with an application, typically *ex parte*, for an anti-anti-suit injunction ordering the defendant to those proceedings not to seek to thwart them indirectly by seeking, in another forum, an anti-suit injunction. The efficacy of this strategy will depend, in part, on the defendant's amenability to the forum asked to issue the anti-anti-suit relief and in part on an expectation that the court order will be respected by a court in the foreign forum.

It was the failure of Akai Pty Ltd to obtain such an injunction, following **4.140** its successful resistance of a stay application fought all the way to the High Court of Australia,[417] that saw it effectively robbed of the fruits of its jurisdictional victory in that forum when the party that had failed to obtain a stay, having studiously not entered an appearance in the New South Wales proceedings, moved swiftly and *ex parte* in both Singapore and England to obtain anti-suit relief restraining the continuation of the proceedings in New South Wales.[418]

---

[414] The factual background to this classic example of tactical jockeying for venue in a transnational dispute is fully described in *Amchem Products Inc v Workers Compensation Board* [1993] 1 SCR 897.

[415] The anti-suit injunction was subsequently discharged, however, by the Supreme Court, ibid.

[416] (1990) 75 DLR (4th) 1. See *Owens-Illinois Inc v Webb* 809 SW 2d 899 (Tex App, Texark, 1991); *Pittsburgh-Corning Corp v Askewe* 823 SW 2d 759 (Tex App, Texark, 1992); and *Owens-Corning Fibreglass Corp v Baker* 838 SW 2d 838 (Tex App, Texark, 1992).

[417] *Akai Pty Ltd v People's Insurance Company* (1997) 188 CLR 418.

[418] See [1998] 1 Lloyd's Rep 90.

4.141 The expedient of seeking an anti-anti-suit injunction will be especially important where there is a difference in the substantive law to be applied in the competing forums, whether by reason of the operation of a mandatory law of one forum that overrides an expressly chosen law, as was the case in *Akai*, or simply by dint of different choice of law rules. To take the case of a mandatory law of the forum, because that law's operation will only be local, an exclusive jurisdiction clause in a contract with a foreign law clause may be rendered void or inoperative in that forum in which proceedings have been commenced with the consequence that the breach of the jurisdiction clause will, there, only be apparent whereas it will be real in the stipulated forum where the mandatory law does not operate. What the judge of one country would see as no breach of an exclusive jurisdiction clause by virtue of the beneficial operation of the mandatory law would be seen by a judge of another country as a flagrant breach of contract.

4.142 In this context, reference should also be made to that rare but not unheard of bird, the anti-anti-anti-suit injunction. This is an injunction which may be sought in circumstances where a party considers it has a good case for restraining foreign proceedings on the grounds of vexation or oppression but is also conscious of the possibility that, if the moving party in the foreign forum has notice of the proposed application to restrain its proceedings, it may itself seek to protect its (vexatious) strategy by seeking anti-anti-suit relief from its own forum.[419] It has already been seen that, even on the strict strand of United States authority, anti-anti-suit injunctions are not seen to infringe comity and that parallel proceedings are tolerated and indeed protected, irrespective of the vexation that they may occasion. In *Allstate Life Insurance Co v Australia and New Zealand Banking Group Ltd*,[420] Lindgren J of the Federal Court of Australia granted an anti-anti-anti-suit injunction to secure one party's 'right' to seek to have United States proceedings restrained on the ground that they were vexatious and oppressive, relief that was ultimately granted[421] but which may have been foreclosed or pre-empted had not the anti-anti-anti-suit injunction been obtained. On the application for the relief, Lindgren J was referred to the decision in *Bank of New York v Bank of America*[422] in which, at a time when there was before an Australian court an application for an anti-suit injunction, the New York judge made an order restraining any further proceedings on that application.

---

[419] See Briggs, A and Rees, P (n 144 above) 5.48.
[420] 21 September 1995. A similar injunction was granted in *National Australia Bank Ltd v Idopost Pty Ltd* [2002] NSWSC 623.
[421] (1996) 64 FCR 1 and 44.
[422] 861 F Supp 225 (1994).

Evasion of Public Policies

Under the rubric of the protection of the court's jurisdiction comes consid- **4.143** eration of the grant of anti-suit relief to guard against the evasion of important public policies of the forum. This provides perhaps one of the most uncontroversial and time-honoured occasions for the grant of this form of injunctive relief. Whereas, as shall be seen in the case of vexatious or oppressive conduct, proceedings are restrained because no legitimate or just advantage can be said to lie for a plaintiff in proceeding in a particular foreign forum, it is the very existence of an advantage outside the forum which may justify injunctive relief in cases where a plaintiff is considered to be evading the forum's important public policies.[423] The classic instance of such a case is where a creditor of a bankrupt estate or company in liquidation seeks to move against assets outside the jurisdiction and thus secure an advantage over other creditors whose claims will be met according to a legislatively prescribed order of priorities and in accordance with the principle of *pari passu* distribution.[424] In the context of corporate insolvency, such injunctive relief is specifically provided for, in the case of the United Kingdom, for example, in section 126 of the Insolvency Act 1986. Similar injunctive relief has been held to be appropriate in cases concerned with the administration of the assets of a deceased estate.[425]

In *Re Maxwell Communications Corporation plc (No 2)*,[426] Barclays Bank **4.144** unsuccessfully sought to restrain foreign proceedings commenced by administrators appointed under section 13 of the Insolvency Act 1986. This case is noteworthy for the reason that no attempt seems to have been made to argue that the administrators' action in seeking to avoid the payment to Barclays as a preference under § 547 of the American Bankruptcy Code was an evasion of the British avoidance provisions. This was arguably the case for the reason that it was accepted that there was little chance of recovering the payment under section 239 of the Insolvency Act 1986. True it is that anti-suit injunctions in such circumstances will typically be directed against a creditor seeking to move against an insolvent debtor's foreign assets. The public policy which protects unsecured creditors to the extent of treating them equally on their common debtor's insolvency is therefore upheld. If, however, a payment is not avoidable under English legislation, it is not readily apparent why

---

[423] *Bank of Tokyo Ltd v Karoon* [1987] AC 45, 60.

[424] On this topic, see Smart, PStJ, *Cross-Border Insolvency* (1991) 180–192 and the cases cited there; Fletcher, I, *Insolvency in Private International Law* (1999) 84–86.

[425] See, for example, *Hope v Carnegie* (1866) LR Vol 1 320.

[426] [1992] BCC 757. A valuable discussion of various aspects of international insolvency is contained in Fletcher, I (n 424 above).

an English creditor's recovery against an English debtor and its interest in the equitable distribution of available assets among all unsecured creditors should be imperilled by another creditor's actions in foreign proceedings, the more so when that creditor is an officer of the court. Neither Hoffmann J at first instance nor the Court of Appeal manifested any concern that the jurisdiction vested in the court to preside over the insolvency of an English company according to the policies embodied in the provisions of the Insolvency Act was in a sense being undermined by the United States proceedings.[427]

4.145 Discussion now turns to the second broad basis for the exercise of the discretion to issue anti-suit injunctive relief, namely anti-suit injunctions upholding legal rights.

3. ANTI-SUIT INJUNCTIONS UPHOLDING LEGAL RIGHTS

4.146 It will be recalled that, in *British Airways*,[428] Lord Diplock stated that a plaintiff may seek to restrain a defendant from bringing suit against him in a foreign court 'upon the ground that the plaintiff is entitled under English law to a legal or equitable right *not* to be sued in that foreign court by that person upon the cause of action that is the subject of such proceedings'. Equitable rights, he said, arose from conduct which could be generically described as 'unconscionable'. The terminology of 'equitable rights' has appeared to cause some difficulty in this area,[429] however such rights arise on account of the foreign plaintiff's vexatious, oppressive or otherwise unconscionable conduct.[430] The use of anti-suit injunctions in response to such conduct is considered in paragraphs 4.179 ff below. Accordingly, this section will concentrate on the protection and enforcement of *legal rights* not to be sued abroad or at all. It should be read in conjunction with Chapter 5 which considers, *inter alia*, arguments relating to the existence and efficacy of jurisdiction and arbitration agreements.

4.147 The cases disclose three categories of contractually conferred legal rights which parties have sought to protect by means of an injunction to prevent the breach of a stipulation not to commence foreign proceedings. These

---

[427] Some support for the criticism of this decision may be derived from *In re Vocalion* [1932] 2 Ch 196, especially 204–207. For an unsuccessful attempt to gain injunctive relief on the basis that the plaintiff was evading an important forum policy, see *Rowan Companies, Inc v DiPersio* (1990) 69 DLR (4th) 224.

[428] [1985] AC 58, 81.

[429] See, for example, *South Carolina* [1987] AC 24, 41; *Man (Sugar) Ltd v Haryanto (No 2)* [1991] 1 Lloyd's Rep 429, 437. The problem of the need to define this concept may be reduced in light of *Channel Tunnel Group Ltd v Balfour Beatty Construction Ltd* [1993] AC 334.

[430] In *South Carolina*, Lord Brandon stated that unconscionable conduct included that which was vexatious and oppressive—[1987] AC 24, 41.

are, first, rights created by exclusive jurisdiction or choice of court clauses,[431] secondly, agreements to submit any disputes arising under a contract to arbitration,[432] and, thirdly, agreements not to sue at all, whether these be in deeds of settlement and release in which parties give up any existing rights to litigate,[433] in agreements to be bound by the results of particular litigation,[434] or else in other commercial agreements.[435] As between the first two categories, there has been said to be no difference in principle.[436]

In addition, a contractual duty of confidence may warrant the grant of an **4.148** injunction restraining a party owing the duty from complying with a subpoena issued in foreign proceedings.[437] A further type of legal right which may form the basis for the grant of anti-suit injunctive relief is one conferred by statute. If, for example, it could be said that the Protection of Trading Interests Act 1980 confers a right on a party not to have a foreign judgment for multiple damages enforced against it in England, it may be that such a party could seek to rely on this right to secure anti-suit injunctive relief restraining foreign proceedings, especially in circumstances where the defendant's only assets were in England.[438] A further statutory

---

[431] *The Lisboa* [1980] 2 Lloyd's Rep 546; *Sohio Supply Co v Gatoil (USA) Inc* [1989] 1 Lloyd's Rep 588.

[432] *Pena Copper Mines Ltd v Rio Tinto Co Ltd* [1911–1913] All ER 209; *The Maria Gorthon* [1976] 2 Lloyd's Rep 720; *Marazura Navegaçion SA v Oceanus Mutual Underwriting Association* [1977] 1 Lloyd's Rep 283; *Mantovani v Carapelli SpA* [1980] 1 Lloyd's Rep 375; *Tracomin SA v Sudan Oil Seeds Co Ltd (Nos 1 & 2)* [1983] 1 WLR 1026; *The Golden Anne* [1984] 2 Lloyd's Rep 489; *Canadian Home Assurance Co v Cooper* (1985) 29 DLR (4th) 419; *Marc Rich & Co AG v Società Italiana Impianti PA* (11 November 1991) approved sub nom *The Atlantic Emperor (No 2)* [1992] 1 Lloyd's Rep 624; *The Angelic Grace* [1994] 1 Lloyd's Rep 168; [1995] 1 Lloyd's Rep 87; *Schiffahrtsgesellschaft Detlev von Appen v Voest Alpine Intertrading GmbH* [1997] 1 Lloyd's Rep 179; *Toepfer International GmbH v Société Cargill France* [1998] 1 Lloyd's Rep 379; *Bankers Trust Co v Pt Jakarta International Hotels & Development* [1999] 1 Lloyd's Rep 910; *XL Insurance Ltd v Owens Corning* [2000] 2 Lloyd's Rep 500; *The Iran Zagubanski* [2002] 1 Lloyd's Rep 106. See also Thomas, DR, 'Restraining Concurrent Legal Proceedings' [1983] LMCLQ 692.

[433] *Lett v Lett* [1906] 1 IR 618; *United States v International Brotherhood of Teamsters* 728 F Supp 1032 (SDNY 1990); *Hambros Bank Ltd v Thune* (18 January 1991) No 6095/90; *National Westminster Bank Ltd v Utrecht-America Finance Co* [2001] 1 All ER (Comm) 7.

[434] *The Tropaioforos (No 2)* [1962] 1 Lloyd's Rep 410.

[435] *Ellerman Lines Ltd v Read* [1928] 2 KB 144; *Settlement Corporation v Hochschild* [1966] 1 Ch 10; *Medtronic, Inc v Catalyst Research Corp* 518 F Supp 946 (1981), aff'd 664 F 2d 660 (8th Cir, 1981); *Apple Corps Ltd v Apple Computer Inc* [1992] RPC 70; *National Westminster Bank v Utrecht-America Finance Co* [2001] 2 All ER (Comm) 7. The injunction unsuccessfully sought in *Bank of Africa Ltd v Cohen* [1909] 2 Ch 129 may also be classified with this group of cases. The basis on which injunctive relief was sought appears to have been an implied promise not to commence proceedings for the return of the title documents.

[436] *The Angelic Grace* [1995] 1 Lloyd's Rep 87, 96; *Bankers Trust Co v PT Jakarta International Hotels and Development* [1999] 1 Lloyd's Rep 910.

[437] *XAG v A Bank* [1983] 2 All ER 464, discussed at para 4.133 above.

[438] cf *British Airways* [1984] QB 142, 161–163; *International Risk Management Group Ltd v Elwood Insurance Ltd* (29 September 1993, Supreme Court of Bermuda, Nos 103 and 245/93).

right which a defendant may seek to rely on in an application for anti-suit injunctive relief is one which it could be argued is conferred by a particular jurisdiction's statutory compensation scheme. If the plaintiff and defendant both reside in that jurisdiction, a plaintiff's endeavour to take advantage of more generous damages available under the common law, for example, in another jurisdiction might be legitimately restrained on the basis of the defendant's 'right' only to provide compensation in accordance with the forum's statutory scheme.[439]

4.149 Where one party commences litigation in a foreign forum, contrary to its contractual obligation, and the other party seeks an anti-suit injunction to restrain the foreign proceedings, the first and important point to note is that equitable relief will not generally be afforded in aid of a legal right where a remedy at law is available. In *Mantovani v Carapelli SpA*[440] and *The Lisboa*,[441] Donaldson J and Dunn LJ respectively contemplated a remedy in damages for breach of such contractual undertakings as a possible alternative to anti-suit injunctive relief.[442] In relation to the breach of an agreement to arbitrate, Mustill and Boyd also envisage an action for damages to recover any losses suffered, including damages tantamount to an indemnity if the plaintiff in England 'were able to persuade the English Court that if the matter had gone to arbitration he would have been bound to win (for example, if the foreign court took the wrong view on a question of English law)'.[443] In *Donohue v Armco*,[444] it was a concession as to the availability of a claim for damages for breach of contract that was in part responsible for the House of Lords' decision in that case not to enforce an exclusive jurisdiction clause for England by way of an anti-suit injunction.

4.150 In this context, the decision in *Union Discount Company Ltd v Zoller*[445] should be noted. There, the English Court of Appeal awarded damages in a sum reflecting the unrecoverable costs of a jurisdictional challenge to proceedings commenced in New York in breach of an exclusive jurisdiction clause. The Court of Appeal had little difficulty in holding that the general rule of public policy which precludes any attempt to recover irrecoverable costs from one set of proceedings in another set of proceedings did not apply to a 'person who starts totally unnecessary proceedings in a foreign jurisdiction in breach of an exclusive jurisdiction clause'. The significance of this decision should not, however, be overstated. The Court of Appeal was careful to confine its decision to the narrow facts of

---

[439] cf *Breavington v Godleman* (1988) 169 CLR 41.   [440] [1978] 2 Lloyd's Rep 63.

[441] [1980] 2 Lloyd's Rep 546.

[442] [1978] 2 Lloyd's Rep 63, 73; [1980] 2 Lloyd's Rep 546, 551.

[443] Mustill, MJ and Boyd, SC, *Commercial Arbitration* (2nd edn, 1989) 461, especially at n 14.

[444] [2002] 1 Lloyd's Rep 425, 437 and 439.   [445] [2002] 1 WLR 1517.

the instant case, namely a case where a party breaches an exclusive jurisdiction clause by litigating in a jurisdiction which does not award costs to
a party successfully moving to strike out or challenge those proceedings.

The award of damages for breach of an exclusive jurisdiction clause in **4.151**
circumstances where the party, who has lost the benefit of its contract by
the foreign suit, has also lost the substantive proceedings in the foreign
jurisdiction is far more problematic. In these circumstances, the theoretical availability of damages is not a particularly practicable or desirable
alternative. This is because their assessment would entail the effective
relitigation of a dispute already tried, with or without third parties who
may have participated in the original hearing, and an award of anything
more than nominal damages would carry the conclusion that the court in
which proceedings took place abroad erred in its determination. Such a
conclusion is not a basis for the non-recognition of or a refusal to enforce
a foreign judgment but an award of more than nominal damages would
be to that effect. The limited scope of an award of damages for breach of
such a contractual undertaking has been recognized in a number of
cases.[446] This leads one ineluctably to the conclusion that, prima facie, an
anti-suit injunction should lie to restrain a breach of a promise not to sue
other than in a particular jurisdiction, by a particular mode of procedure,
or at all. Such a conclusion is the obvious corollary of the High Court of
Australia's view that a party suing in breach of an arbitration clause 'may
by suing expose himself to an action for breach of his contract to refer but,
having regard to the measure of damages, that is a risk which he could
lightly encounter'.[447]

It is necessary, therefore, to consider what precisely must be shown for the **4.152**
grant of anti-suit injunctive relief in this context.

The Requirements for Relief

The principal question to be considered here is whether, in accordance **4.153**
with the doctrine of *Doherty v Allman*[448] and subject to matters of discretion and equitable defences such as laches, an anti-suit injunction will lie
in every case of a breach of an undertaking either not to sue at all or not
to sue in other than the specified forum or whether, as is sometimes
suggested, the breach must be shown to be vexatious or oppressive. In

---

[446] *Tracomin SA v Sudan Oil Seeds Co Ltd (Nos 1 & 2* [1983] WLR 1026, 1036–1037; *Continental Bank v Aeakos* [1994] 1 Lloyd's Rep 505, 512 and 598; *Schiffahrtsgesellschaft Detlev von Appen v Voest Alpine Intertrading GmbH* [1997] 1 Lloyd's Rep 179; *Bankers Trust v Jakarta International Hotels & Development* [1999] 1 Lloyd's Rep 910, 915; and *The Kribi* [2001] 1 Lloyd's Rep 76, 93.
[447] *Anderson v GH Michell & Sons Ltd* (1941) 65 CLR 543, 549.
[448] (1873) 3 App Cas 709, 720.

Castanho in the Court of Appeal, Shaw LJ appeared to take the former position, stating that:

an English court . . . must not seek to meddle officiously with the jurisdiction of foreign tribunals . . . The only apparent (but not real) exception is where the parties to litigation have contracted to sue only in the courts of this country. In such a case the courts might grant an injunction if proceedings were to be instituted abroad, but this would be no more than the enforcement of an English contract not to sue abroad.[449]

4.154 A different view would only countenance anti-suit injunctive relief in this context where the breach was vexatious and oppressive. The difference in these views disappears if the breach of a covenant not to sue other than in a particular forum or at all is considered to be vexatious and oppressive in itself.

4.155 In *Sohio Supply Co v Gatoil (USA) Inc*,[450] Staughton LJ stated that 'the continuance of foreign proceedings in breach of contract where the contract provides for exclusive English jurisdiction may well in itself be vexatious and oppressive in any given case'.[451] This observation was delivered in the context of reflection on the decision of the Court of Appeal in *The Lisboa*[452] which, following *Settlement Corporation v Hochschild*,[453] held that a mere breach of a contractual undertaking not to sue would not, *ipso facto*, justify injunctive relief and a further element of vexatious or oppressive conduct was required. *Settlement Corporation v Hochschild* itself followed the decision of the Court of Appeal in *Cohen v Rothfield*,[454] which summarized the leading nineteenth-century authorities on the staying of both domestic and foreign proceedings.[455] Significantly, none of these authorities concerned the grant of an injunction in aid of a *legal right* not to be sued abroad.

4.156 Vexation and oppression were not referred to as necessary requirements for the grant of interlocutory relief in either *Lett v Lett*[456] or *Pena Copper Mines Ltd v Rio Tinto Co Ltd*.[457] Mere breach was sufficient. In the latter case, Cozens-Hardy MR said:

There is a plain bargain between the parties . . . that any dispute should be determined in one way only—namely by reference to arbitration . . . I can scarcely imagine a case in which the discretion ought to be exercised more plainly than it is here.[458]

---

[449] [1980] 3 All ER 72, 89. cf *The Golden Anne* [1984] 2 Lloyd's Rep 489, 498.
[450] [1989] 1 Lloyd's Rep 588.   [451] ibid 592.
[452] [1980] 2 Lloyd's Rep 546.   [453] [1966] 1 Ch 10.
[454] [1919] 1 KB 410.   [455] See paras 3.13 ff above.
[456] [1906] 1 IR 618, 635.   [457] [1911–1913] All ER 209.
[458] ibid 212–213.

In *The Tropaioforos (No 2),*[459] vexatious and oppressive conduct was **4.157** suggested by counsel for the applicant for anti-suit injunctive relief as what was required to be demonstrated[460] and, given that vexatious and oppressive conduct was established in that case, the question of the appropriate test was not considered by the court. It should be noted, however, that, on the facts of that case, the only real conduct in question was the breaking of the contractual undertaking not to sue. This was also the case in *The Angelic Grace,*[461] where proceedings had been commenced in Italy in breach of a London arbitration clause. Rix J considered that the charterers' intention to litigate in Italy in circumstances where their claim fell within the scope of the arbitration agreement was 'vexatious'.[462]

When *The Angelic Grace* reached the Court of Appeal, a particularly robust **4.158** attitude towards the enforcement of jurisdiction and arbitration agreements by way of anti-suit relief manifested itself. This was the first of a series of decisions where anti-suit injunctions have been issued by the English courts to restrain breach of an exclusive jurisdiction or arbitration clause almost as of right. Thus, Millett LJ said:

In my judgment, the time has come to lay aside the ritual incantation that this is a jurisdiction which should only be exercised sparingly and with great caution. There have been many statements of great authority warning of the danger of giving an appearance of undue interference with the proceedings of a foreign Court. Such sensitivity to the feelings of a foreign Court has much to commend it where the injunction is sought on the ground of forum non conveniens or on the general ground that the foreign proceedings are vexatious or oppressive but where no breach of contract is involved. In the former case, great care may be needed to avoid casting doubt on the fairness or adequacy of the procedures of the foreign Court. In the latter case, the question whether proceedings are vexatious or oppressive is primarily a matter for the Court before which they are pending. But in my judgment there is no good reason for diffidence in granting an injunction to restrain foreign proceedings on the clear and simple ground that the defendant has promised not to bring them.[463]

Perhaps unsurprisingly, it has recently been argued that the passage of the **4.159** Human Rights Act 1998 (UK) operates to cut down the traditional equitable jurisdiction of the High Court of Justice in England to grant anti-suit relief in aid of a legal right contained in an exclusive jurisdiction clause. In *The Kribi,*[464] Aikens J considered and dismissed an argument that article 6 of the Human Rights Convention, providing a right of access to an 'independent and impartial tribunal established by law', dictated that relief the effect of which was to shut out a party from proceeding in a

[459] [1962] 1 Lloyd's Rep 410. [460] ibid 418.
[461] [1994] 1 Lloyd's Rep 168. [462] ibid 182.
[463] [1995] 1 Lloyd's Rep 87, 96. [464] [2001] 1 Lloyd's Rep 76, 86–87.

foreign court, violating this right. Aikens J rejected a similar argument that section 3 of the Human Rights Act required the power in section 37 of the Supreme Court Act 1981 to 'stay, sist, strike out or dismiss any proceedings' to be read down in accordance with the Convention right. Aikens J was right to take this view, at least in circumstances where the English Court granting the anti-suit relief provided a forum, accessible in a meaningful way to the foreign plaintiff, in which to agitate its claims. The Human Rights Act point may, however, have more legitimacy in so-called single forum cases where the effect of an anti-suit injunction is to prevent a plaintiff from suing in the foreign forum with no alternative forum available.

4.160 It should be noted that, even in the clearest case of breach of a contractual undertaking not to sue, an injunction will not automatically be granted because of the ultimately discretionary nature of equitable remedies. Examples of the discretionary nature of the remedy and the operation of equitable defences in this context include *The Lisboa*,[465] where equitable considerations clearly intruded to compel the refusal to grant injunctive relief,[466] and *The Maria Gorthon*,[467] where an injunction was not granted despite the breach of an arbitration clause essentially because the defences of laches and waiver were made out.

4.161 A classic instance of arguably inadvertent waiver is provided by *Marc Rich v Società Italiana Impianti PA*,[468] where the existence of a London arbitration clause was in dispute. While answers to various questions referred to the European Court of Justice by the Court of Appeal were being awaited in England, the Italian Corte di Cassazione held that the contract in question contained no London arbitration clause and that therefore the Italian courts had jurisdiction to try the contractual dispute. Hobhouse J (whose decision was approved by the Court of Appeal)[469] stated that he would have been prepared to grant an injunction restraining Italian proceedings pending the determination by the English courts of whether an arbitration clause existed were it not for the fact that Marc Rich had submitted to the Italian courts. Hobhouse J described this as amounting 'to a waiver of the right to specific performance of the alleged arbitration agreement'.[470] While it is not clear that he considered this submission to

---

[465] [1980] 2 Lloyd's Rep 546.
[466] Dunn LJ stated that 'there is a serious risk if the injunction were granted that the vessel would be sold, the proceeds of sale distributed, and the defendants would lose all security for their counterclaim, the plaintiffs having refused to give a bond or other alternative security', ibid 552.
[467] [1976] 2 Lloyd's Rep 720.
[468] 11 November 1991.
[469] sub nom *The 'Atlantic Emperor' (No 2)* [1992] 1 Lloyd's Rep 624, 633–634.
[470] Transcript, 21–22.

give the Italian court jurisdiction under Article 18 of the Brussels Convention or simply under Italian jurisdictional provisions, he was clear that, by its submission, Marc Rich had lost any basis on which it could challenge the recognition and enforcement of the Italian judgment in any English enforcement proceedings.[471]

This case teaches an important lesson as to why it may be in a party's **4.162** interest to seek anti-suit injunctive relief rather than challenging a foreign court's jurisdiction directly. In certain jurisdictions, challenges to jurisdiction may not be dealt with at an interlocutory stage. Accordingly, if parties wish to avoid a default judgment in the event that their jurisdictional challenge is unsuccessful, they must also make their substantive defence and enter any cross-claim at the same time as their jurisdictional challenge. In doing so, they run the risk of being held to have submitted to the foreign proceedings with important ramifications for enforcement in third jurisdictions. Seeking anti-suit injunctive relief may be a way to avoid treading this 'legal tightrope'.[472]

Apart from cases of equitable defences, the only other circumstance in **4.163** which English courts have shown a preparedness to depart from the strictures of *pacta sunt servanda* when asked to enforce an exclusive jurisdiction or arbitration agreement by anti-suit injunction are cases where the foreign proceedings involve third parties in addition to those parties to the jurisdiction or arbitration agreement and the interests of justice, overall, recommend litigation in the foreign forum. The interests of justice are likely to so recommend in circumstances where, looking at the dispute globally rather than simply as solely between the parties to the relevant contractual arrangement, the foreign forum could be described as the natural forum. *Donohue v Armco Inc*[473] was just such a case as was *Sokana Industries Inc v Freyre & Co Inc*,[474] in which Coleman J declined on discretionary grounds to restrain proceedings in Florida brought in breach of a London arbitration clause in circumstances where Florida appeared to be

---

[471] See at 22 of transcript. The factual context in which the battle for venue took place in this case raises the intriguing question as to whether the European Court of Justice could itself grant anti-suit injunctive relief. In Case C–2/88 Imm, *Re Zwartveld* [1990] ECR I–3365, the Court discovered an inherent jurisdiction, founded on the 'mutual duties of sincere cooperation' imposed upon member states and Community institutions, to order the Commission to furnish certain documents to a Dutch court. It is not inconceivable that this same source of power could be exercised to order a *court* of a member state (as opposed to an individual party) to stay proceedings before it where a court of another member state has made a reference under the 1971 Protocol.

[472] *The Angelic Grace* [1994] 1 Lloyd's Rep 168, 180. See also *International Risk Management Group Ltd v Elwood Insurance Ltd* (29 September 1993, Supreme Court of Bermuda, Nos 103 and 245/93) and discussion at para 4.43 above.

[473] [2002] 1 Lloyd's Rep 425.

[474] [1994] 1 Lloyd's Rep 56.

the natural forum and where the impleading of a third party in those proceedings meant that an injunction would generate a multiplicity of suits.

4.164 These cases suggest a means for parties seeking to extricate themselves from what may be real strategic burdens represented by jurisdiction or arbitration clauses, namely to join or implead other defendants not party to the suit and/or to raise claims falling outside the scope of the applicable clause. A measure of vigilance will be required on the part of courts faced with the need to resolve what may be a profound tension between a desire to uphold the benefit of a freely negotiated bargain, on the one hand, and the instinctive desire to avoid a multiplicity of suits with attendant costs burdens and the potentiality for inconsistent decisions, on the other. 'Policing' the bona fides of multi-party suits in this context is not easy given the appropriate reluctance and practical inability of courts to enter into the merits of a dispute at an early stage, the very time when interlocutory remedies such as anti-suit relief are likely to be sought. In *Donohue v Armco Inc*,[475] the House of Lords made an assessment of the exisiting claims, potential claims, and cross-claims in the New York litigation between parties other than those bound by an exclusive jurisdiction agreement for England, and sought to locate the respective centres of gravity of those claims, as part of the process of determining whether or not to enforce the jurisdiction clause by way of an anti-suit injunction.

4.165 Jurisdiction agreements have been described as 'an indispensable element in international trade, commerce and contracting'[476] and, as such, there are strong policy reasons for enforcing them.[477] Subject to equitable defences and cases of genuine multi-party complex litigation in a forum that in a global sense supplies the natural forum, common law courts will in general grant anti-suit injunctive relief restraining the institution or continuance of foreign proceedings.

Anti-Suit Injunctions, Jurisdiction Agreements, and Council Regulation 44/2001

4.166 The robust enthusiasm of English courts, in particular, for the granting of anti-suit injunctive relief where there has been a breach of a jurisdiction agreement has extended to cases where the relevant foreign proceedings have been commenced in the courts of a Contracting State to the Brussels and Lugano Conventions and, by parity of reasoning, in courts of coun-

---

[475] [2002] 1 Lloyd's Rep 425.
[476] *The Chaparral* 407 US 1, 13 (1972), [1972] 2 Lloyd's Rep 315, 320.
[477] See generally paras 5.01 ff below.

tries whose jurisdictional rules are in part at least governed by European Council Regulation 44/2001.[478]

As was seen in paragraphs 3.13 ff above the Conventions and now the **4.167** Regulation prescribe the circumstances in which courts in member states may assume jurisdiction. They make no reference to the possibility of courts in one state issuing orders which, while *in personam*, are nonetheless recognized as interfering with proceedings in another jurisdiction. This silence is by no means surprising given that anti-suit injunctive relief appears to be a creature of the common law, having its origins in the courts of Chancery.[479] The question therefore arises as to whether an English court could restrain proceedings in a court of a member or contracting state where jurisdiction was assumed in the face of what the English court considers to be an English exclusive jurisdiction clause. This question has heightened significance because of the absence in the Conventions or the Regulation of any defence to recognition or enforcement of a foreign judgment equivalent to section 32(1) of the Civil Jurisdiction and Judgments Act 1982.[480]

In *Continental Bank NA v Aeakos Compania Naviera SA*,[481] the Court of **4.168** Appeal upheld Gatehouse J's decision to restrain the defendants from continuing proceedings in Greece contrary to a jurisdiction agreement to submit to the English courts. The jurisdiction clause in question in *Continental Bank* was contained in a loan agreement between the parties and both Gatehouse J and the Court of Appeal construed it as conferring *exclusive* jurisdiction on the English courts, an arguably surprising result as jurisdiction clauses in loan agreements are typically non-exclusive, designed merely to give the lending bank enforcement rights in the nominated forum. The Greek proceedings, commenced by the borrower defendants in the Court of Athens, were brought under Article 919 of the Greek Civil Code which provides for damages for the violation of 'the commands of morality'. These proceedings were served on Continental Bank in America in March 1991. Proceedings for injunctive relief were commenced before Gatehouse J in April of the same year.

---

[478] It should be noted that, while arbitration agreements fall outside the scope of the Conventions and the Regulation—Article 1(4) and see Case C–190/89, *Marc Rich & Co AG v Società Italiana Impianti PA* [1991] ECR I–3855—the Court of Justice's later decision in *Van Uden Maritime BV v Kommanditgesellschaft In Firma Deco-Line* [1998] ECR I–7091; [1999] QB 1225 suggests that provisions of the Regulation may still be invoked to give effect to an arbitration agreement.

[479] See para 4.85 above.

[480] Section 32(1) disallows the recognition and enforcement of any foreign judgment or arbitration award given in breach of the terms of a jurisdiction or arbitration agreement but section 32(4) excludes this from the context of Convention or Regulation judgments.

[481] [1994] 1 WLR 588.

4.169 The first question for the court was whether it in fact had *jurisdiction* to grant the relief sought. As the defendants in the proceedings for anti-suit relief were domiciled in a Contracting State, the issue of jurisdiction fell to be determined under the Brussels Convention. Article 17 appeared to yield a simple answer to the question. It provided that 'if the parties, one or more of whom is domiciled in a Contracting State, have agreed that a court or the courts of a Contracting State are to have jurisdiction to settle any disputes which have arisen or which may arise in connection with a particular legal relationship, that court or those courts shall have exclusive jurisdiction'.[482] This apparently simple answer, however, was complicated by Article 21[483] which provided that:

> where proceedings involving the same cause of action and between the same parties are brought in the Courts of different Contracting States, any court other than the court first seised shall of its own motion stay its proceedings until such time as the jurisdiction of the court first seised is established. When the jurisdiction of the court first seised is established, any court other than the court first seised shall decline jurisdiction in favour of that court.

4.170 It was uncontroversial that the Court of Athens was the court first seised within the meaning of Article 21. Moreover, the fact that the Bank was not domiciled in a Contracting State did not take the case outside the scope of Article 21.[484] Accordingly, the defendants argued that the English court lacked any jurisdictional basis for the grant of the anti-suit injunction and should decline jurisdiction in favour of the Court of Athens or, at the very most, stay the English proceedings, pending any challenge to the Greek court's jurisdiction. The defendants placed reliance on the fact that it was implicit in Article 21 that the jurisdiction of a court of a Contracting State may only be contested *directly* in that court and not indirectly in the courts of other Contracting States.

4.171 At first instance, Gatehouse J rejected this argument on the basis that different causes of action were involved so that Article 21 simply did not enter the picture,[485] a view that may be supported by the European Court of Justice's later decision in *The Tatry*.[486] More significantly, he implied that, even if 'the same cause of action' were involved in the Greek and English proceedings, Article 17 would have overriding effect. The Court of Appeal was more explicit, stating that 'if Article 17 applies, its provi-

---

[482] See now Article 23 of Council Regulation 44/2001.
[483] See now Article 27 of Council Regulation 44/2001.
[484] Case C–351/89, *Overseas Union Insurance Ltd v New Hampshire Insurance Co* [1991] ECR I–3317.
[485] Additionally, Gatehouse J did not see any reason to stay proceedings under Article 22 of the Convention on the basis that the causes of action were related.
[486] [1995] 1 Lloyd's Rep 302. See also *Haji-Ioannou v Frangos* [1999] 2 Lloyd's Rep 337, 351.

sions take precedence over the provisions of Articles 21 and 22'. It held that the *lis pendens* provisions of the Convention did not provide a jurisdictional obstacle to the grant of injunctive relief in aid of the legal right contained in the Article 17 agreement. In insisting on the primacy of Article 17, the Court of Appeal drew support from *Kloeckner & Co AG v Gatoil Overseas Inc.*[487]

Whereas the Brussels Convention made explicit provision in Articles 21 **4.172** and 22 for the resolution of jurisdictional clashes, the Court of Appeal's view of the primacy of Article 17 did great violence to the coherence of the Convention (and, now, Council Regulation 44/2001). An international treaty such as the Brussels Convention is based on an assumption that signatories to it will be faithful to its terms and not seek to undermine its operation. It is predicated, moreover, on an assumption of mutual trust and co-operation between Contracting States. The position is *a fortiori* under Council Regulation 44/2001.

In *Continental Bank*, not only did the Court of Appeal refuse to decline **4.173** jurisdiction of its own motion, it also refused to stay the English proceedings until such time as the Greek court had examined its jurisdiction. The grant of the injunction effectively deprived the Greek court of this opportunity, an opportunity which Article 21 strongly suggests it should have had. This was an even more egregious interference with the structure and operation of the Convention than refusing to respect the decision of a court of another Contracting State as to its jurisdiction. Indeed, it is noteworthy that, had the Greek court already published a decision as to its jurisdiction, an English court would have been bound to recognize it under Article 26 of the Convention and the issue as to the Greek court's jurisdiction would have been *res judicata* as between the parties.[488]

Continental Bank was followed in *OT Africa Line Ltd v Hijazy*[489] in a context **4.174** where proceedings were first commenced in Antwerp in breach of what the English court considered an exclusive English jurisdiction clause notwithstanding (unlike the *Continental Bank* case) that the Antwerp court had scheduled a preliminary hearing on the jurisdiction point and this challenge was available without any requirement (as again there had been in the *Continental Bank* proceedings) for a defence on the merits to be filed as an element of the challenge.

---

[487] [1990] 1 Lloyd's Rep 177. This decision did not involve an application for anti-suit injunctive relief but rather a clash of jurisdiction between a court in which proceedings had first been commenced and a second seised court which considered itself to have exclusive jurisdiction. See also *Denby v The Hellenic Mediterranean Lines Co Ltd* [1994] 1 Lloyd's Rep 320.

[488] *The Sennar (No 2)* [1985] 1 WLR 490.

[489] [2001] 1 Lloyd's Rep 76.

4.175 A court of a member state of the European Union or a Contracting State to the Lugano Convention is required to declare of its own motion that it has no jurisdiction where a claim is made under a contract containing a jurisdiction clause for a court or the courts of another member or contracting state and where the defendant has not entered an appearance within the meaning of Article 24 of the Regulation and 18 of the Convention.[490] This will only be the case, however, where that court is satisfied that the exclusive jurisdiction agreement depriving it of jurisdiction exists and is valid or that the dispute the subject of proceedings falls within the agreement's scope.

4.176 One key question which arose in *Continental Bank* was whether the Greek Article 919 proceedings fell within the agreement's scope. Steyn LJ stressed the fact that the loan agreement containing the jurisdiction agreement was governed by English law and, in line with long-established authority,[491] held that English law as the proper law of the jurisdiction agreement should govern questions of construction arising out of the agreement. He favoured a broad construction of the agreement and that the Article 919 proceedings fell within its scope.[492] Although there is nothing to cavil at in this approach per se, it underplays the significance of the fact that it should have been the *Greek* and not the English court whose construction of the jurisdiction agreement's scope mattered. In its examination of its own jurisdiction and in particular the question whether the Article 919 proceedings fell outside the agreement's scope, thereby removing any jurisdictional impediment to them, it was not necessarily the case that the Greek court would have applied the same choice of law rule as the English court to this question of construction, the Rome Convention not applying to jurisdiction or arbitration agreements.[493] Although not the position under English law, the construction question could, for example, quite plausibly have been seen as a matter of procedure and therefore for Greek law as the *lex fori*. It was not at all inconceivable on this footing that the Greek court might *properly* have seen the dispute as falling *outside* the agreement's scope.

4.177 As shall be seen in Chapter 5, English courts applying English choice of law rules from time to time conclude that, for any number of reasons, litigation may proceed in England notwithstanding the existence of an exclusive jurisdiction agreement nominating the courts of another state. Such differences in construction are inevitable in the conflict of laws. In any

---

[490] Schlosser Report [1979] OJ C59/71, 81.

[491] *Hoerter v Hanover Telegraph Works* (1893) 10 TLR 103.

[492] For a more detailed consideration of approaches to the scope and nature of exclusive jurisdiction clauses, see Chapter 5 below.

[493] Article 1(2)(d).

event, in *Continental Bank*, it was equally possible that the Greek court may have come to the conclusion that the proceedings did in fact fall within the agreement's scope, in which case it would have been bound to decline jurisdiction pursuant to Article 17 of the Convention. The unhappy fact, however, is that the English court did not even give it a chance to do this.

Article 17 is the Convention's, and Article 23, the Regulation's, chosen **4.178** mechanism for enforcing exclusive jurisdiction agreements. It is difficult to accept that they admit of any scope for the granting of anti-suit injunctive relief on the basis of the breach of such clauses. Far from reinforcing the 'structure and logic' of the Convention, as Steyn LJ claimed, the Court of Appeal's decision to uphold the anti-suit injunctive relief in *Continental Bank* disrupted it. The spirit of cooperation implicit in the Brussels Convention and now Council Regulation 44/2001 is seriously subverted where courts of one member or contracting state are denied the opportunity of examining their own jurisdictional base by the courts of another member or contracting state. Whether or not the European Court of Justice will take the opportunity in *Turner v Grovit*[494] to express a view as to the propriety of the practice of English courts in issuing anti-suit injunctions restraining suit in other member states of the European Union commenced in breach of an exclusive English jurisdiction clause, given that the precise issue referred in that case related to anti-suit injunctions granted to restrain unconscionable conduct, it is inevitable that another vehicle will present itself permitting the propositions for which the *Continental Bank* case stands to be tested in that ultimate Court.

4. Restraint of Vexatious and Oppressive Foreign Proceedings

It is clear that, subject to differing perceptions as to the requirements of **4.179** comity, throughout the Commonwealth and at least according to one strand of authority in the United States, a court will be justified in restraining foreign proceedings if it considers their pursuit to be either vexatious or oppressive.[495] The meaning of the phrase 'vexatious and oppressive' has been considered at an earlier stage in this book[496] but courts have shied away from providing any precise definition of it.[497] In

---

[494] [2002] 1 WLR 107.
[495] *South Carolina* [1987] AC 25, 41; *Aerospatiale* [1987] AC 871, 896; *In re Unterweser* 428 F 2d 888, 890 (5th Cir, 1970).
[496] See paras 3.72 ff above.
[497] Although approving *Aerospatiale*, the Supreme Court of Canada has abjured the use of the phrase 'vexatious and oppressive', preferring to ask whether it is 'unjust to deprive the plaintiff in the foreign proceeding of some personal or juridical advantage that is available in that forum': *Amchem Products Inc v Workers Compensation Board* [1993] 1 SCR 897, 932–933.

McHenry v Lewis,[498] Bowen LJ advised that 'it would be most unwise . . . to lay down any definition of what is vexatious or oppressive'.[499] This reluctance may be partly ascribed to a desire not to fetter what is perceived to be a very wide and discretionary jurisdiction, partly to the fact that the phrase's meaning 'must vary with the circumstances of each case',[500] and that 'vexation may assume innumerable shapes',[501] and partly because 'the law on the subject is in a continuous state of development'.[502] In this section, while acknowledging that their exact content may differ, 'vexation', 'oppression', and 'unconscionability' will be treated together as they were in *South Carolina*[503] and in *Hambros Bank Ltd v Thune*.[504] An attempt is made to divine the meaning of the key phrase, 'vexatious and oppressive' from an examination of the cases in this area.

4.180 The first question is whether it is legitimate to consider those decisions, up to and including *The Atlantic Star*,[505] which considered the meaning of 'vexatious and oppressive' in the context of applications to stay local proceedings. Tradition would suggest an affirmative answer. The principles in *McHenry v Lewis*[506] and *Peruvian Guano Co v Bockwoldt*,[507] stay and election cases respectively, were applied in *Hyman v Helm*[508] where an injunction was sought to restrain proceedings commenced in San Francisco. Indeed, 'stay' and 'injunction' cases were grouped together and treated as one in the first nine editions of *Dicey and Morris*. On the other hand, increased sensitivity to considerations of comity and the heightened appreciation of the artifice implicit in the explanation that anti-suit injunctions operate *in personam* and do not interfere with foreign tribunals indicate that different policy factors are at play in the two forms of action.[509]

4.181 In *Castanho*,[510] Lord Scarman stated that 'it is unnecessary now to examine the earlier case law'.[511] This view, however, proceeded from the assumption that the policy concerns were in fact *the same* in stay and injunction cases and that, as the 'old cases' on stays had been superseded, so also they were no longer useful in the context of injunctions. This view, however, was subsequently discredited[512] and, as such, Lord Scarman's

---

[498] (1882) 22 ChD 397.   [499] ibid 407–408.
[500] ibid 408.   [501] *In re Connolly Brothers Ltd* [1911] 1 Ch 731, 746.
[502] *Aerospatiale* [1987] AC 871, 896. See also *The Atlantic Star* [1974] AC 436, 464, 468, and 477.
[503] [1987] AC 24, 41.   [504] 18 January 1991, No 6095/90.
[505] [1974] AC 436.   [506] (1882) 22 ChD 397.
[507] (1883) 23 ChD 225.   [508] (1883) 24 ChD 531.
[509] See Briggs, A, 'No Interference with a Foreign Court' [1982] 31 ICLQ 189, especially 191–195.
[510] [1981] AC 557.   [511] ibid 574.
[512] See paras 4.112–4.113 above.

assessment of the status of the old case law is not considered helpful. In *Aerospatiale*, Lord Goff stated that 'the long line of English cases concerned with injunctions restraining foreign proceedings still provides useful guidance on the circumstances in which such injunctions may be granted'.[513] Carter demurred, predicting that 'the concept of "oppression" may be ripe for refurbishment'.[514] More forcefully, the authors of *Cheshire and North* argue that:

Despite what was said in [*Aerospatiale*], older cases can be of little value in ascertaining [the meaning of vexation or oppression]. The problem faced by the courts nowadays is that of plaintiffs' forum shopping in countries, such as the United States, where a very wide jurisdiction is taken, a very different sort of problem from that faced by courts in the 19th century. The use of language from the 19th century only serves to obscure the basic considerations that should be taken into account in this area: the interests of the parties; the connections with the alternative fora; the dictates of comity and the need for caution before restraining foreign proceedings.[515]

It will be recalled from paragraphs 3.71 ff above that domestic proceed- **4.182** ings were not considered to be vexatious or oppressive so as to warrant a stay if the plaintiff could point to any remedial or procedural advantage in the forum. The same analysis applied *mutatis mutandis* to foreign proceedings. In *Aerospatiale*,[516] Lord Goff stated that 'the court will not grant an injunction if, by doing so, it will deprive the plaintiff of advantages in the foreign forum of which it would be unjust to deprive him'.[517] The significant difference between this formulation and that to be found in the older line of cases is that the exercise of the discretion to grant injunctive relief turns on an assessment of whether it would be *unjust* to deprive a plaintiff of whatever advantages were available as opposed to a more mechanical test based simply on the *existence* of such advantages.

The High Court of Australia in *CSR Ltd v Cigna Insurance Australia Ltd* [518] **4.183** appears to have committed itself to the more mechanical test by stating that 'foreign proceedings are to be viewed as vexatious or oppressive only if there is nothing which can be gained by them over and above what may be gained in local proceedings', a view which, applied literally, would never permit an Australian court to grant anti-suit injunctive relief in a 'single forum' case, no matter how oppressive or vexatious the commencement of proceedings in such a forum might be. Ironically, the Court derived the proposition quoted above from observations by Robert Goff LJ in *Bank of Tokyo v Karoon*,[519] which his Lordship appeared to move

---

[513] [1987] AC 871, 896.   [514] Carter, PB (n 337 above) 347.
[515] North, PM and Fawcett, JJ (13th edn, 1999) 365.   [516] [1987] AC 871.
[517] ibid 896.   [518] (1997) 189 CLR 345, 393.
[519] [1987] AC 45, 60.

away from in *Aerospatiale*. Whether or not the High Court of Australia's limitation on the jurisdiction to grant anti-suit relief applies in the case of *subsequently* commenced foreign proceedings which provide some advantage to the foreign plaintiff not available in the local forum may be doubted.[520]

4.184 Five broad areas have been identified where courts are most likely to intervene to restrain foreign proceedings on the basis that those particular proceedings are vexatious and oppressive. It is to these that attention is now turned.

Subjection to Oppressive Foreign Procedures

4.185 As was seen in paragraphs 2.09 ff above, a plaintiff may be attracted to a foreign forum on account of perceived procedural or other advantages in that forum, relating for example to pre-trial procedures, a contingency fee system, the possibility of a jury trial, or the level or types of damages recoverable. As was also seen, many of these advantages are associated with the United States and it is no coincidence that many of the cases in which anti-suit injunctions are sought concern proceedings commenced in the federal or under various state jurisdictions of that country. Were the *Castanho* test still in currency, focusing solely on the question of whether litigation was taking place in the natural forum, it might have been the case that evidence of concerted 'forum shopping', designed to enhance and maximize a plaintiff's chance of success, would have justified or at least played an important role in any grant of injunctive relief. Under the more stringent test laid down in *Aerospatiale*, however, the question for a court to determine is whether taking advantage of foreign procedures is vexatious and oppressive.

4.186 As a general proposition, common law courts have been reluctant to conclude that the mere taking advantage of the procedural facilities of the court system of another country is vexatious or oppressive and similar statements with respect to the need to accommodate and accept differences in the procedures of particular forums have already been noted in the context of stay applications.[521] As an injunction granted in such circumstances carries a judgment on the *inherent* nature of such procedures, their merits, and fairness, rather than operating as a response to any particular unconscionable conduct for which the plaintiff in the foreign forum is personally responsible, considerations of comity loom large.[522] On the other hand, it may be that what Hartley has described as

---

[520] (1997) 189 CLR 345, 394.   [521] See para 4.48 above.
[522] The significance of comity on the availability of anti-suit injunctive relief is considered more fully in paras 4.223 ff below.

the fundamentally different conceptions of the role of civil litigation in England and the United States will ensure that this is an area where the limits of comity are most likely to be tested[523] and where an applicant for anti-suit injunctive relief may successfully claim that resort to the foreign court's procedure is vexatious and oppressive in the circumstances. Several cases illustrate the ambivalence of English judges to such questions.

In *Midland Bank plc v Laker Airways Ltd*,[524] Neill LJ observed that: **4.187**

[I]t is right to treat with great caution the argument that pre-trial discovery is oppressive. The American courts have developed this form of discovery as part of their ordinary procedure and it cannot be right for this court, while paying lip-service to the principle of comity, to treat the possibility of exposure to pre-trial discovery as a source per se of injustice.[525]

On the other hand, Dillon LJ's judgment in the same case was exactly to **4.188** the opposite effect. He described the building up of an antitrust suit under United States pre-trial procedure as 'a farrago of suspicion upon innuendo upon suspicion'[526] and continued:

That the United States pre-trial procedure in an anti-trust suit is, by English thinking, oppressive has been said many times. The procedure is long drawn out and very expensive, and any defendant, even if ultimately dismissed from the suit or successful when the suit comes on for trial, has in practice virtually no chance of recovering its costs.[527]

In a similar vein to *Midland Bank* is the decision in *Simon Engineering plc v* **4.189** *Butte Mining plc (No 2)*,[528] where an injunction was granted to restrain a party from proceeding in the Courts of Montana with an action for alleged securities fraud contrary to the United States Securities Exchange Act 1934. The party was claiming treble damages under the Racketeering Influenced and Corrupt Organizations Act (1970) (RICO Act) and certain other relief.[529] In granting the injunction, it was held that the RICO Act provided a remedy rather than a cause of action and that, in this context, English law afforded alternative causes of action which were also alleged

---

[523] (n 307 above) 504–505. He draws attention to the fact that private litigation in England is almost exclusively concerned with private objectives while the possibility of punitive or treble damages, for example, in American proceedings serves public purposes such as promoting product safety and the preservation of competition in business in addition to remedying private disputes. See also Fleming, JG, *The American Tort Process* (1988) vii.

[524] [1986] 1 QB 689.

[525] ibid 714. See also *British Airways* [1984] QB 142, 185.

[526] [1986] 1 QB 689, 709–710.

[527] ibid 703–704.   [528] [1996] 1 Lloyd's Rep 91.

[529] That English courts will not regard RICO as per se offensive but will rather focus upon the circumstances in which it has been invoked, see *Donohue v Armco* [2002] 1 Lloyd's Rep 425.

in Montana. Further, it was held that, on the evidence, England was manifestly the natural forum for the action and none of the connecting factors with Montana relied upon by the defendants were of sufficient weight to displace that conclusion. In holding that the applicants for the anti-suit injunction had made out a sufficient case of oppression, it was held that the advantages of proceeding in Montana, namely the availability of contingency fee arrangements and the breadth of United States' pre-trial discovery, were not legitimate in circumstances where England was plainly the natural forum.

4.190 Whether or not it would be vexatious or oppressive to commence foreign proceedings simply to take advantage of that jurisdiction's pre-trial procedures for the purposes of English proceedings is an open question[530] although, as has been seen in relation to the *South Carolina* case, making use of American pre-trial discovery procedure will not, in and of itself, be held to constitute an interference with the English court's jurisdiction. One may also contrast the diametrically opposed attitudes taken by Brandon LJ in *Castanho*[531] and Lord Denning MR in *Smith Kline & French Laboratories Ltd v Bloch*[532] to damages awarded in litigation in the United States. An assessment of whether various procedural features of trial in the United States were vexatious or oppressive was avoided in *Aerospatiale* by reason of undertakings offered by the plaintiffs in the Texas proceedings not to invoke them.[533] The combination of *Aerospatiale's* reassertion of vexation and oppression as the wellspring for injunctive relief[534] and Lord Diplock's candid reference in *British Airways* to 'what an English court would be entitled to regard as the oppressive consequences that the American system of pre-trial discovery and non-recovery of costs by successful defendants will have on a defendant to an action which is bound to fail'[535] may suggest that considerations of comity will not always outweigh the particular facts of any given case and result in the denial of injunctive relief to a 'worthy' plaintiff.

4.191 If the grant of an injunction restraining proceedings designed merely to take advantage of foreign procedures is a delicate matter, restraint of foreign proceedings on the basis that the defendant in those proceedings will not be able to obtain a fair trial will be even more delicate. The broad basis of the jurisdiction—an injunction will be warranted 'when the interests of justice so demand'[536]—must contemplate the possibility of injunc-

---

[530] In *Metall und Rohstoff AG v ACLI Metals (London) Ltd* [1984] 1 Lloyd's Rep 598, 605, the prospect of the English action in effect being tried by a combination of both New York and English pre-trial procedures was counted as a 'substantial disadvantage' for the defendant.
[531] [1980] 3 All ER 72, 92.   [532] [1983] 2 All ER 72, 74–75.
[533] [1987] AC 871, 899.   [534] See paras 4.111–4.112 above.
[535] [1985] AC 58, 86.   [536] See para 4.104 above.

tive relief in such circumstances. The concept of the 'interests of justice' must have the same content whether or not a stay or an anti-suit injunction is in issue. As was seen in paragraphs 4.47 ff above, it has been said that an English court may decline to stay a proceeding in favour of what is clearly the natural forum in circumstances where the court was not convinced that a fair trial could be obtained in that jurisdiction.[537] In *Muduroglu Ltd v TC Ziraat Bankasi*,[538] Mustill LJ intimated that a fair trial may not be attainable where a Turkish military court was involved.[539] It should not be assumed, moreover, that matters before a 'military' court would not be justiciable in England (not that that in itself would preclude injunctive relief),[540] for the jurisdiction of such a court may be nowhere near as circumscribed as that exercised by military tribunals in common law countries.[541]

In *The Anita*,[542] Mocatta J held, for the purposes of an insurance claim, **4.192** that a 'Special Court' established in Vietnam was no more than an organ of government and that its acts were in reality those of the executive. Although overturned on appeal,[543] this decision and the judgments of the Court of Appeal in *Muduroglu* illustrate that English courts will not refrain from examining the nature and procedures of foreign courts, including questions relating to their independence and the integrity of their officers.

In *Muduroglu*, Sir John Donaldson MR was sensitive to the threat to **4.193** natural justice in countries where a career judiciary, not independent from the executive and subject to a bureaucratic system of promotion, presided over cases to which state-owned instrumentalities were party.[544] That will by no means be a rare event and, although involving issues of the most extraordinary delicacy, both Donaldson MR and Mustill LJ were adamant that English courts should be alive to the possibilities of abuse and react where it is established by the applicant to be appropriate.[545] One reaction may take the form of a grant of anti-suit injunctive relief. An example of such an injunction being granted is supplied by the facts of *Svendborg v Wansa*,[546] where there was evidence

---

[537] *Muduroglu Ltd v TC Ziraat Bankasi* [1986] QB 1225, 1248 and 1268.
[538] ibid.   [539] ibid 1248.
[540] See discussion of the 'single forum' cases at paras 4.97–4.101 above.
[541] For the narrow jurisdictional compass afforded to military tribunals in common law countries, see, for example, *Solorio v United States* 483 US 435 (1987); *Re Nolan; ex parte Young* (1991) 172 CLR 460.
[542] [1970] 2 Lloyd's Rep 265. The 'Special Court' was a 'military court', staffed by military officers (none of whom had any legal training), but whose jurisdiction purportedly extended to superintending the customs regulations.
[543] [1971] 1 Lloyd's Rep 487.   [544] [1986] QB 1225, 1268.
[545] ibid 1268 and 1248.   [546] [1997] 2 Lloyd's Rep 183.

that it would not be safe for the applicant's solicitor to return to Sierra Leone for a prolonged period of time and that both he and the shipping line's former senior representative in West Africa had received death threats.

Mala Fide Foreign Proceedings

4.194 English courts have traditionally restrained the mala fide prosecution of suits, including suits commenced abroad. In *McHenry v Lewis*, Scrutton LJ stated that vexation and oppression would exist where there was 'some motive other than a bona fide desire to determine disputes'.[547] In *Logan v Bank of Scotland (No 2)*,[548] the plaintiff sought to justify the commencement of English proceedings on the ground that one of the defendants resided in England. The fact that that defendant was an undischarged bankrupt who was unable to afford even to defend the action led Sir Gorrel Barnes P to conclude that his joinder to proceedings was not bona fide and that the commencement of the English proceedings was vexatious. Whereas *Logan v Bank of Scotland (No 2)* was a stay case, *In re Connolly Brothers Ltd*[549] was a case where an injunction was granted to restrain the appointment by the Lancaster Palatine Court of a receiver on the ground that the equitable chargee's application was made mala fide. *Smith Kline & French Laboratories Ltd v Bloch*[550] is an illustration of injunctive relief lying where mala fides can be demonstrated in the institution of foreign proceedings. This, at least, was the explanation of the *Smith Kline* case offered by Lord Diplock in *British Airways*. He stated that 'the decision was justifiable on the ground that the vexatious character of the proceedings against the American company was that its inclusion as defendants in the American proceedings was made mala fide for the sole purpose of laying an ostensible foundation for American jurisdiction for the claim against the English company'.[551]

4.195 In *Midland Bank plc v Laker Airways Ltd*,[552] Dillon LJ drew a subtle distinction between the *use* of foreign procedures and the *motivation* for having recourse to them.[553] A similar distinction was drawn by Ackner LJ in *Bank of Tokyo Ltd v Karoon* in relation to contingency fees.[554] Thus, if, for example, proceedings can be shown to have been brought 'mala fide to put blackmailing pressure on an English party because of the expense and harassment of the pre-trial procedure', it would be an 'abdication' of

---

[547] (1882) 22 ChD 397, 414; see also *In re Norton's Settlement* [1908] 1 Ch 471, 479.
[548] [1906] 1 KB 141.   [549] [1911] 1 Ch 731.
[550] [1983] 2 All ER 72.   [551] [1985] AC 58, 86.
[552] [1986] 1 QB 689.   [553] ibid 702.
[554] (Note) [1987] AC 45, 55.

responsibility for an English court not to intervene.[555] To similar effect, Hobhouse J has described proceedings 'directed not to the obtaining of a legal remedy but rather to misusing the legal process to bring improper pressure on the party sued' as 'vexatious in the narrower sense of the term'.[556] This is certainly how Laws LJ viewed the commencement of Spanish proceedings in *Turner v Grovit*.[557] He stated that it was 'plain beyond the possibility of argument' that these proceedings were 'launched in bad faith in order to vex the Plaintiff in his pursuit of the application before the Employment Tribunal here. . . . All the credible evidence points one way. The documents lead to the ineluctable conclusion that the Spanish proceedings were intended and intended only to oppress the Plaintiff and as such fall to be condemned as abusive as a matter of elementary principle.'[558] He also characterized the selection of another company within the group as the claimant in the Spanish proceedings as 'nothing but a device to confer putative jurisdiction on the Spanish Court' saying that it was a 'sham and pretence'.

Pressure is in the nature of litigation and although there is no doubt that, **4.196** in the world of commerce, litigation is often resorted to with no intention of bringing it to a final conclusion but rather with a view to raising the stakes to effect a beneficial settlement,[559] explicit evidence of illegitimate motivation is likely to be rare. This will have the consequence that the cases in which injunctions will be issued to restrain the mala fide prosecution of foreign suits will be correspondingly few, at least in the absence of judicial willingness to infer such lack of good faith. In this context, the forceful dissent of an American judge in *China Trade and Development v MV Choong Yong*[560] should be noted:

[I]n this day of exceedingly high costs of litigation . . . courts have an *affirmative duty* to prevent a litigant from hopping halfway around the world to a foreign court as a means of confusing, obfuscating and complicating litigation already pending for trial in a court in this country.[561]

This observation strikingly anticipated the facts of *Glencore International AG v Exter Shipping Ltd*,[562] in which the Court of Appeal dismissed an appeal from the decision of Moore-Bick J who granted an injunction

---

[555] *Midland Bank plc v Laker Airways Ltd* [1986] 1 QB 689, 702.
[556] *Cannon Screen Entertainment v Handmade Films* (11 July 1989).
[557] [2000] QB 345.
[558] ibid 362
[559] See discussion of this point in paras 1.31 ff above.
[560] 837 F 2d 33 (2nd Cir, 1987).
[561] ibid 40 (emphasis added). See also the discussion of injunctions issued to protect a court's jurisdiction in paras 4.125 ff above.
[562] [2002] EWCA Civ 524.

restraining certain shipowners from pursing proceedings in the United States in circumstances where they had, at the time of the commencement of those proceedings, participated in complex multi-party litigation in England which, by necessity, had been extensively case managed. Rix LJ made the observation[563] that:

> the inference to be drawn in such circumstances is that the ship owners' complaint in Georgia is simply a part of the deliberate strategy of harassment and vexation, designed to wear down Glencore by making it as difficult and expensive as possible for it to bear the burden of litigation on several fronts; and designed always to put off to another day, and another court and another forum the possibility of reaching a conclusion on the issues which divide the parties. The consequences of the Georgia complaint, if indeed it is not worthless, would be embarrassing not only for Glencore, but also for the other litigants in the Metro litigation and for the English Court: for all to face, in theory, the complexities and multiplicity of litigation in a situation where the Georgia Court was being invited to make finding as to MTI's rights over and in dealing with the oil which would fly in the face of findings in London.

4.197 One can only conclude that the institution of litigation for an illegitimate or improper purpose is a matter on which judicial impressions will vary but cases such as *Glencore* arguably betray an increasing willingness to draw inferences as to the propriety of decisions made in relation to the choice of forum.[564]

4.198 In this context, the propriety of a plaintiff seeking negative declaratory relief in a foreign jurisdiction must also be considered. As will be seen in paragraphs 4.251 ff below, although the jurisdiction of common law courts to grant negative declaratory relief has been long acknowledged,[565] at least up until the Court of Appeal's important decision in *Messier-Dowty Ltd v Sabena SA*,[566] the implication has never been far beneath the surface that, with the possible exception of insurance cases, a party seeking it may well lack a certain good faith. Thus, in *Re Clay*,[567] Duke LJ spoke of 'a great danger of needless and costly controversy fomented by parties who delight in litigation'.[568] Kerr LJ described an application for such relief as 'an *abuse of the process* of our Courts'[569] and cases since *Messier-Dowty* have, in the particular circumstances of those cases, continued to stigmatize this form of relief.[570]

---

[563] ibid at para [69] of judgment.
[564] See also in this context *CSR Ltd v Cigna Insurance Australia Ltd* (1997) 189 CLR 345, 401.
[565] *Guaranty Trust Co of New York v Hannay & Co* [1915] 2 KB 536.
[566] [2000] 1 WLR 2041.   [567] [1919] 1 Ch 66.   [568] ibid 78.
[569] *First National Bank of Boston v Union Bank of Switzerland* [1990] 1 Lloyd's Rep 32, 38 (emphasis added).
[570] See, for example, *Chase v Ram Technical Services Ltd* [2000] 2 Lloyd's Rep 418, where 'negative' proceedings against the local defendant were held to be colourable.

Although it is by no means self-evident that a similar form of action in a **4.199** foreign jurisdiction should be so characterized and that to do so may represent no more than 'an exercise in mechanical jurisprudence',[571] it is clear that the notion, that an application for negative declaratory relief in the United States constituted evidence of bad faith on the part of a foreign plaintiff, informed Staughton LJ's decision to confirm the grant of anti-suit injunctive relief in *Sohio Supply Co v Gatoil (USA) Inc*.[572] The very form of relief sought was treated as evidence of bad faith.

Inconvenient Foreign Proceedings

Although in *Aerospatiale* Lord Goff was at pains to point out that vexation **4.200** and oppression are far more stringent criteria than those considerations of convenience which may be reflected in a determination of the natural forum for litigation,[573] he did not refer to *Logan v Bank of Scotland (No 2)*[574] which illustrates that questions of degree must intrude on an assessment of convenience with the result that it *may* be oppressive for a plaintiff to commence proceedings in a highly inconvenient forum. In that case, Sir Gorrel Barnes P stated that:

> where the difficulty for the defendant of trying in the country in which the action is brought is such that it is impracticable to properly try the case by reason of the difficulty of procuring the attendance of busy men as witnesses, and keeping them during a long trial, and of having to deal with masses of books, documents and papers which are not in the country where the action is brought, and of dealing with law foreign to the tribunal, it appears to me that a case of vexation in some circumstances may be made out if the plaintiff chooses to sue in that country rather than in that where everybody is and where all the witnesses and material for the trial are.[575]

It is evident that extreme inconvenience may indicate bad faith. The close **4.201** relationship between these two factors was demonstrated in *Cannon Screen Entertainment v Handmade Films*,[576] a decision post-dating *Aerospatiale*. Hobhouse J restrained Californian proceedings on account of the highly inconvenient nature of the forum given the subject matter and nature of the dispute. There, the acts alleged took place in England, the

---

[571] Carter, PB, 'The Role of Public Policy in English Private International Law' (1993) 42 ICLQ 1, 2.
[572] [1989] 1 Lloyd's Rep 588, 593.
[573] He cited *Hyman v Helm* (1883) 24 ChD 531 for the proposition that 'proceedings are not to be regarded as vexatious merely because they are brought in an inconvenient place': [1987] AC 871, 894.
[574] [1906] 1 KB 141.
[575] ibid 152. See also *Moore v Moore* (1896) 12 TLR 221, 222; *In re Norton's Settlement* [1908] 1 Ch 471, 482–483; *Labak v Graznar* 6 NE 2d 790 (1935).
[576] 11 July 1989.

parties alleged to have suffered loss were English companies carrying on business in England, and the loss was alleged to have been suffered in the United Kingdom. The alleged 'theatre contract' was English as were the parties to it. Hobhouse J concluded that 'under these circumstances, to sue in California is not merely to sue in an inconvenient forum but to engage in a crude form of oppression'.[577]

4.202 In *Amchem Products Inc v Workers Compensation Board,*[578] the British Columbia Court of Appeal upheld the grant of an injunction restraining proceedings in Texas against predominantly American corporate defendants on the basis that British Columbia was '*the one and only* natural forum for this action'[579] as opposed to the *more appropriate* of two natural forums, in other words, litigation in the foreign jurisdiction would be plainly inconvenient. This essentially factual conclusion was reversed by the Supreme Court[580] which had the benefit of further evidence relating to the connection between the respondents and Texas.[581] The injunction was discharged.

4.203 Seen from the perspective of the Court of Appeal, however, the distance between the principles enunciated in *Castanho* and *Aerospatiale* is far less than might have at first appeared and the relative convenience of the alternative forums may retain some significance. This may especially be seen in circumstances where the litigation is complex and involves a number of parties. In this context, inconvenience rising to the level of vexation or oppression necessary to warrant anti-suit relief will not be confined to the geographical inconvenience of the foreign forum.

Multiple Foreign Proceedings/*Lis Alibi Pendens*

4.204 Where two or more sets of proceedings have been commenced in several forums, vexation and oppression may lie in the multiplicity of actions in all the circumstances of the case, including questions of timing, scope of proceedings, parties, and issues. 'Inconvenience' may shade into oppression, whether subjectively intended or because it is the objective consequence of the shape the litigation has assumed. Before turning to examples of anti-suit relief granted in such cases, it should be noted that other remedies will, of course, be available to a defendant in this situation apart from injunctive relief. As was seen in paragraphs 4.12 ff above, an application may be made to stay proceedings or an order may be sought

---

[577] See also *Canadian Home Assurance Co v Cooper* (1986) 29 DLR (4th) 419, 423; *Allied-Signal Inc v Dome Petroleum Ltd* [1989] 5 WWR 326.
[578] (1990) 75 DLR (4th) 1.   [579] ibid 18 (emphasis added).
[580] [1993] 1 SCR 897.   [581] ibid 908.

which puts the plaintiff to its election (assuming that both sets of proceedings have been commenced by the same plaintiff).[582] This latter course, as noted in paragraphs 3.96 ff above, is the one which was traditionally followed by the courts upon concluding that concurrent proceedings were vexatious and oppressive. It has also been seen that, in the context of Council Regulation 44/2001 and the Lugano Convention, a regime has been introduced to govern the position of multiple suits.[583] This leads one to consider in what circumstances the common law will 'impose' a choice on a plaintiff responsible for parallel proceedings by restraining the continuance of the foreign set of proceedings. It must also be considered whether the existence of multiple proceedings may be said to be vexatious and oppressive where they are commenced by different parties in different jurisdictions.

The earlier common law cases placed importance on whether both sets of **4.205** proceedings had been commenced by the same plaintiff or whether, in lieu of or in addition to counterclaiming, the defendant in the English proceedings commenced proceedings against the plaintiff in another forum.[584] In this second situation, common law courts have traditionally been reluctant to restrain the foreign proceedings as vexatious or oppressive. As Farwell LJ stated in *The Hagen*,[585] 'there is no question of him [the plaintiff abroad] commencing double litigation so as to harass, and therefore no personal equity against him'.[586] Such were the advantages perceived to be enjoyed by *plaintiffs* that to enjoin prosecution of the foreign action would deprive the plaintiff of his status as *dominus litis* and the advantage of *control* over the conduct of the litigation. In *Cohen v Rothfield*,[587] Scrutton LJ stated that 'where the plaintiff in the foreign action is not plaintiff, but defendant, in the English action, the case against interference is even stronger, for the person to be stayed has not himself initiated two actions. He has initiated one, and has been compelled to appear in another over which he has, as defendant, no *control*'.[588] Parallel proceedings were more likely to be held to be vexatious and oppressive[589]

---

[582] Article 1(3) of the International Convention on Certain Rules in Matters of Collision 1952 enshrines the principle of election, providing that a 'claimant shall not be allowed to bring a further action against the same defendant on the same facts in another jurisdiction, without discontinuing an action already instituted'.

[583] Articles 27 and 28 of the Regulation, discussed in paras 3.25 ff above.

[584] *Hyman v Helm* (1883) 24 ChD 536; *Vardopulo v Vardopulo* (1909) 25 TLR 518. Matrimonial proceedings perhaps provide the most common instance of the defendant in one set of proceedings being plaintiff in another action. See, for example, *Orr-Lewis v Orr-Lewis* [1949] P 347; *In the marriage of Takach* (1980) 47 FLR 441; *Hemain v Hemain* [1988] 2 Fam LR 388; *Henry v Henry* (1996) 185 CLR 571.

[585] [1908] P 189.   [586] ibid 202.

[587] [1919] 1 KB 410, 414.   [588] [1919] 1 KB 410, 414 (emphasis added).

[589] See Paterson, JM (n 252 above) 596–599.

although this was by no means invariable. 'If there is a fair possibility that [the plaintiff] may have an advantage by prosecuting a suit in two countries, why should this Court interfere and deprive him of it?'[590]

4.206 In *McHenry v Lewis*,[591] a distinction was drawn between two actions commenced by the same plaintiff in the Queen's Courts, on the one hand, and a situation where the same plaintiff commenced one action in the Queen's Court and another in a court of a foreign sovereign. The former situation only was considered prima facie vexatious and called for relief.[592] Extrapolating from the pre-Judicature Act Chancery practice of putting a plaintiff to his election if he was suing for the same cause of action both at law and in equity's auxiliary jurisdiction, Jessel MR stated that 'the same principle applies, it appears to me, wherever the judgment can be enforced, and for that reason I think that the case of *Lord Dillon v Alvares* can no longer be relied on'.[593] *Lord Dillon v Alvares*[594] was a case where proceedings in Ireland were not restrained notwithstanding parallel litigation in England. Significantly, however, this case was decided at a time when there was no mutual enforceability of judgments in England or Ireland.[595]

4.207 If, as appears both from Jessel MR's dictum in *McHenry v Lewis* and the result in that case,[596] the reason why parallel proceedings were not regarded as vexatious or oppressive where one of the two actions was commenced outside the realm was because of the lack of enforceability of the English decision in that forum, then it is at least arguable that the modern passage of direct enforcement legislation[597] dictates the result that parallel proceedings in which the same remedy is sought and which

[590] *Peruvian Guano Co v Bockwoldt* (1883) 23 ChD 225, 234.
[591] (1882) 22 ChD 397.
[592] ibid 400–401 and 408–409. See also *Cohen v Rothfield* [1919] 1 KB 410, 414.
[593] (1882) 22 ChD 397, 400.
[594] (1798) 4 Ves 357 (34 ER 867).
[595] The Judgments Extension Act 1868 (31 & 32 Vict c 54) provided for the direct and mutual enforceability of judgments of the superior courts of England, Scotland, and Ireland through a process of registration. Objections to recognition and enforcement, such as may be made at common law, could not be made in this system of 'extension of judgments': *Bailey v Welpley* 4 Ir RCL 243 (1869). See Read, HE, *Recognition and Enforcement of Foreign Judgments in the Common Law Units of the British Commonwealth* (1938) 296–298.
[596] The plaintiff's advantage in bringing concurrent proceedings and the reason why the American action was neither restrained nor the plaintiff put to his election lay in the fact that any English judgment would not be enforceable in America—'We have got these parties to the litigation who could not be made liable in *England*, and who could be made liable in *America*, and we have got this also, that the parties to the action in *America* who are resident in *England* can be made liable in *England* and cannot be made liable in America; for although you may get judgment against them in *America*, you cannot enforce that judgment in England, you must bring an action upon it.': (1882) 22 ChD 397, 402–403.
[597] See, for example, Administration of Justice Act 1920; Foreign Judgments (Reciprocal Enforcement) Act 1933; Civil Jurisdiction and Judgments Act 1982.

are commenced in jurisdictions which have mutual recognition and enforcement arrangements would be prima facie vexatious and oppressive. This argument depends on whether Jessel MR used the term 'enforced' only in the sense of *direct* enforcement (ie free from any objections to the judgment being able to be made) under the Judgments Extension Act or whether he would have included in his understanding a system of registration subject to a limited number of objections or defences (as in current enforcement legislation). If the latter (and assuming that the same remedy was being sought in both jurisdictions), the ability to enforce either the English judgment abroad or a foreign judgment in England would result in one set of proceedings being redundant for, *ex hypothesi*, the same remedy would be available in both jurisdictions. Such parallel proceedings would therefore be vexatious and oppressive. This analysis is consistent with the occasional use of the phrase 'vexatious and *useless*' as a statement of the basis upon which foreign proceedings would be restrained.[598]

While it has been said that 'it is not prima facie vexatious for the same **4.208** plaintiff to commence two actions relating to the same subject matter, one in England and one abroad',[599] a preferable view is found in *Australian Commercial Research & Development Ltd v ANZ McCaughan Merchant Bank Ltd*.[600] In that case, Browne-Wilkinson VC stated that:

where a plaintiff seeks to pursue the same defendant in two jurisdictions in relation to the same subject matter, the proceedings verge on the vexatious . . . the outcome is vexatious.[601]

This view is consistent with the argument advanced in the preceding **4.209** paragraphs. In the United States, as has been seen, one line of authority holds that the existence of parallel litigation occasions a justification for injunctive relief where a court comes to the conclusion that there is no basis for staying proceedings before it on grounds of *forum non conveniens*. Indeed, the maintenance of concurrent proceedings is considered vexatious and oppressive even where both sets of proceedings have not been commenced by the same plaintiff.[602] In *China Trade and Development v MV*

---

[598] See, for example, *Cohen v Rothfield* [1919] 1 KB 410, 414; *Armstrong v Armstrong* [1892] P 98, 100, where 'useless' foreign proceedings were restrained.

[599] *Bank of Tokyo Ltd v Karoon* (Note) [1987] AC 45, 59.

[600] [1989] 3 All ER 65.

[601] ibid 69. See also *The Cap Bon* [1967] 1 Lloyd's Rep 543, 548 and *Charm Maritime Inc v Kyriakou* [1987] 1 Lloyd's Rep 433, 450–451, where it is at least implicit in Dillon LJ's judgment that the maintenance of parallel proceedings would be oppressive.

[602] *American Home Assurance Co v Insurance Corp of Ireland* 603 F Supp 636 (1984). Note that the stricter line of authority, on the other hand, rejects such reasoning and holds that multiple or parallel proceedings must be tolerated on the footing that it is the price required by considerations of comity.

Choong Young,[603] Bright J (dissenting in the result) observed, in a passage referred to with approval by Kirby P in *Bank of America v Bank of New York*,[604] that 'in this day of exceedingly high costs of litigation . . . courts have an affirmative duty to prevent a litigant from hopping half way around the world to a foreign court as a means of confusing, obfuscating and complicating litigation already pending for trial in a court of this country'.[605] Where a plaintiff does make an election to discontinue the foreign set of proceedings, courts will occasionally reinforce this course in the defendant's interest by granting anti-suit injunctive relief.[606]

4.210 In *Aerospatiale*,[607] although parallel proceedings had been commenced in both Brunei and Texas by Lee, the widow of a victim of a helicopter crash, against the helicopter's manufacturer, Société Nationale Industrielle Aerospatiale ('SNIA'), and operator, Bristow Malaysia, an injunction was sought not on the basis that it was vexatious and oppressive to be sued concurrently but on the basis that the Texas proceedings were, in themselves, oppressive. The factual circumstances giving rise to the claim of oppression are of interest for they raise the more general issue of whether the existence of multiple proceedings, *whether commenced by the same plaintiff or not*, may be classified as vexatious and oppressive. To return to the facts of the case, the actions against Bristow Malaysia had been settled. After attempting unsuccessfully to have the Texas proceedings dismissed on grounds of *forum non conveniens*, SNIA sought an injunction from the Brunei courts to restrain the continuation of the Texan proceedings. When that injunction was eventually granted by the Privy Council, the circumstance that was deemed oppressive arose from a combination of the fact that SNIA wished to seek contribution from Bristow Malaysia and the strong doubt which existed as to whether Bristow Malaysia was subject to the Texas court's jurisdiction.[608] This gave rise to the possibility that, in the event of SNIA being held liable in Texas, an inconsistent conclusion as to liability might be reached in any contribution claim subsequently made in Brunei. The conceivable result of this, as envisaged by Lord Goff, was as follows:

[SNIA] might be held liable to the plaintiffs in Texas without any right over against Bristow Malaysia in that court, and might be held not liable to the plaintiffs in Brunei, in which event they would have no claim over against Bristow

---

[603] 837 F 2d 33 (2nd Cir, 1987).
[604] (1995) 17 ATPR 41-390 at 40-337.
[605] 837 F 2d 33, 40. See also *Kaepa Inc v Achilles Corporation* 76 F 3d 624, 627 (5th Cir, 1996).
[606] See *The Soya Margareta* [1961] 1 WLR 709, 717; *Hing Fat Plastic Manufacturing Co Ltd v Advanced Technology Products (HK) Ltd* [1992] 2 HKLR 350, 355.
[607] [1987] AC 871.
[608] That jurisdiction was being contested at the time of the Privy Council's decision: [1987] AC 871, 900.

Malaysia, even though negligence on the part of Bristow Malaysia may in fact have been a substantial cause of the accident.[609]

Distilled to its essence, the oppression lay in the possibility of ongoing liti- **4.211** gation which could spawn inconsistent decisions with resulting hardship to the applicant for injunctive relief. In this context, the decision is strikingly similar to *Charm Maritime Inc v Kyriakou*.[610] Here, the possibility of effectively being left without a remedy, in circumstances where it was uncontroversial that if the plaintiff did not succeed against the first defendant then he would succeed against the second, resulted in the denial of a stay of action in favour of what was otherwise the natural forum. In both cases, the entire controversy was capable of being resolved in the courts of one country[611] and, in the latter case, Dillon LJ observed that 'the ends of justice require that the issues between the plaintiffs and Mr Kyriakou and the issues between the plaintiffs and Mr Mathias . . . should be tried at the same time in the same jurisdiction'.[612] These decisions also accord entirely with a more general concern of common law courts to minimize the scope for multiple litigation and the prospect of inconsistent decisions, a theme which was seen to feature prominently in the discussion of the natural forum in the previous chapter.

Another case in which the prospect of ongoing litigation played a signifi- **4.212** cant role in the grant of anti-suit injunctive relief was *Tracomin SA v Sudan Oil Seeds Co Ltd (No 2)*.[613] Unlike *Aerospatiale*, however, an injunction was granted not because of any resultant hardship to any of the parties (it was thought that that could be accommodated by an award of damages for breach of a London arbitration clause)[614] but because of the undesirable consequences per se of inconsistent decisions. In stating that he could not 'believe that the Swiss courts will be unduly perturbed at the English courts intervening to avoid the rather unseemly spectacle . . . of trade arbitrators considering a Swiss judgment and deciding whether it is right or wrong',[615] Donaldson MR clearly saw comity as more threatened by the scenario he envisaged than infringed by the foreclosing to the Swiss courts of the opportunity of making a decision in a matter in which they had assumed jurisdiction.[616]

---

[609] ibid 901.   [610] [1987] 1 Lloyd's Rep 433.

[611] Bristow Malaysia had acknowledged their preparedness to accept service of third party proceedings in Brunei (see [1987] AC 871, 901). To similar effect, the second defendant in *Charm Maritime Inc v Kyriakou* was amenable to English but probably not to Greek jurisdiction because of the effect of a jurisdiction clause.

[612] [1987] 1 Lloyd's Rep 433, 451.   [613] [1983] 1 WLR 1026.

[614] ibid.   [615] ibid.

[616] See also *The Angelic Grace* [1994] 1 Lloyd's Rep 168, 182.

4.213 United States authority may be found for the proposition that the prospect of ongoing litigation constitutes vexation and oppression sufficient to warrant injunctive relief. In *Labak v Graznar*,[617] it was said that 'if Labak is allowed to proceed to final judgment in Czechoslovakia, he might next resort to and relitigate his claim in a court of any other sister state or foreign country which might entertain jurisdiction, and the defendants in error thus be dragged by a foreign court to the ends of the earth to defend only upon the rule of res judicata'.[618] In *Laker*, Judge Wilkey made it clear that one legitimate instance for the grant of an anti-suit injunction is where the issuing court has delivered judgment and a party to it seeks to relitigate the question out of the forum.[619] It should be noted, however, that Judge Wilkey would justify such relief not on the basis of preventing vexatious and oppressive conduct per se but in order to 'protect the integrity of [the court's] judgments by preventing their evasion through vexatious and oppressive relitigation'.[620]

4.214 A complex version of this situation arose in *Man (Sugar) Ltd v Haryanto (No 2)*.[621] In this case, the threat of ongoing litigation lay in the prospect of opposing attempts to enforce an Indonesian judgment in countries other than England where a judgment relating to the same disputed contract had already been obtained in Man's favour, a situation much like *Labak v Graznar*.[622] Man, however, was unsuccessful in his application for injunctive relief although Neill LJ did state that he found the case a 'very difficult' one[623] and only upheld Steyn J's decision 'with reluctance'.[624] What perhaps distinguished the prospect of ongoing litigation in *Man (Sugar) Ltd v Haryanto (No 2)* from a similar prospect in *Aerospatiale* was the fact that whereas, in the latter case, the Texas court had not yet heard the substantive claim let alone reached any decision on it,[625] the Indonesian court in the former case had not only reached a decision but had done so in an action initiated by the party now seeking injunctive

---

[617] 6 NE 2d 790 (1935).   [618] ibid 792.

[619] 731 F 2d 909, 928 n 52 (1984).

[620] ibid. cf *Compagnie Européene de Cereals SA v Tradax Export SA* [1986] 2 Lloyd's Rep 301, 304 where, in a slightly different though closely analogous context, Hobhouse J stated that '[i]f what Tradax are seeking to do is to litigate or arbitrate a second time before a different forum a matter already decided between the parties in this Court, CEC has an equitable right to have the further proceedings restrained. The aggrieved party has an equitable right not to be harassed by successive proceedings; it is unconscionable.'

[621] [1991] 1 Lloyd's Rep 161 and 429 (Court of Appeal).

[622] 6 NE 2d 790 (1935).

[623] *Man (Sugar) Ltd v Haryanto (No 2)* [1991] 1 Lloyd's Rep 429, 436.

[624] ibid 438.

[625] To similar effect is *Medtronic, Inc v Catalyst Research Corp* 518 F Supp 946, 956 (1981), aff'd 664 F 2d 660 (8th Cir, 1981), where one of the reasons favouring the restraining of foreign proceedings in two other countries was the fact that neither had yet entered a judgment.

relief in England. Mann LJ spoke of 'respect for the *decisions* of foreign Courts properly given within their jurisdictions'.[626] Had an injunction been sought prior to the Indonesian court either hearing the case or delivering judgment, the English court may been far more prepared to enjoin Mr Haryanto from continuing those proceedings. The injunction sought in *Man (Sugar) Ltd v Haryanto (No 2)* was intended to prevent the Indonesian judgment being enforced anywhere in the world.

One theme which emerges from those cases which have detected vexation **4.215** or oppression in the prospect of ongoing litigation is the desirability of consolidating litigation as far as possible and minimizing the scope for inconsistent judgments. In *Sohio Supply Co v Gatoil (USA) Inc*,[627] Staughton LJ remarked, in the context of granting injunctive relief, that it was 'inherently undesirable that there should be concurrent proceedings in different jurisdictions, about the same subject matter'.[628] Apart from the potentially oppressive consequences for a dual defendant and concern to avoid the risk of inconsistent judgments, this sentiment may also be fuelled by a distinctly contemporary concern regarding judicial resources and the need for economy in the courts. In *American Home Assurance Co v Insurance Corporation of Ireland*,[629] the importance of an 'efficient' use of judicial resources was explicitly recognized, it being observed that 'all parties in the consolidated litigation are before this court while neither [various parties are referred to] are parties to the United Kingdom action. Thus, in the further interest of conservation of judicial resources, this forum seems best situated to adjudicate the entire controversy.' The English actions were enjoined.[630] In this context, there is a plain overlap between courts granting anti-suit relief in order to protect the exercise of their jurisdiction and the prevention of vexation or oppression to parties embroiled in multiple suits.

In *HM Attorney-General v Arthur Andersen and Co*,[631] Mustill LJ resolved a **4.216** problem of multiple proceedings by considering what 'the good management of the concurrent sets of proceedings' required[632] and dicta in related areas of the law can be pointed to in support of the proposition

---

[626] [1991] 1 Lloyd's Rep 429, 440 (emphasis added). This case is to be contrasted to *Ellerman Lines Ltd v Read* [1928] 2 KB 144, where an injunction was granted to restrain the enforcement of a Turkish judgment obtained through fraudulent misrepresentations and in breach of a contractual agreement not to arrest the defendant's ship.

[627] [1989] 1 Lloyd's Rep 588

[628] ibid 593.

[629] 603 F Supp 636, 643 (1984).

[630] See also *Seattle Totems Hockey Club v National Hockey League* 652 F 2d 852 (9th Cir, 1981), cert denied 457 US 1105 (1982); *Cargill v Hartford Accident & Insurance Co* 531 F Supp 710 (D Minn, 1982).

[631] [1989] ECC 224.

[632] ibid 239.

that all litigation arising out of the same set of events should be resolved in one comprehensive set of proceedings.[633] This is an area where it is thought, especially perhaps in view of the decision in *Aerospatiale* and later cases such as *Glencore*[634] and *Allstate Life Insurance Co v Australia and New Zealand Banking Group Ltd*[635] involving multiple parties and myriad cross-claims, that there is in fact increased scope for anti-suit injunctive relief for, as has been observed throughout this book, much modern transnational commercial litigation involves more than two parties and may spawn a complex array of related claims. By the same token, the decisions of the Court of Appeal in *Bouygues Offshore SA v Caspian Shipping Co (Nos 1, 3, 4 and 5)*[636] and of the House of Lords in *Donohue v Armco*[637] illustrate that the very same considerations may recommend against an anti-suit injunction and in favour of a stay of proceedings.

Jurisdictionally 'Improper' Foreign Proceedings

4.217 The fifth category of vexatious and oppressive conduct warranting the grant of anti-suit injunctive relief that can be identified from the case law involves cases where proceedings in the foreign court are founded on an assertion of extraterritorial jurisdiction. Anti-suit injunctive relief was granted in *Midland Bank plc v Laker Airways Ltd*[638] on the basis that the commencement of antitrust proceedings against Midland Bank in New York was unconscionable. Unconscionability was considered to lie in the attempt to take advantage of the extraterritorial application of United States anti-trust law.[639]

4.218 In *British Airways*,[640] on the other hand, the airlines' participation in business in America meant that those laws were not being given extraterritorial effect and that the commencement of antitrust proceedings against them was not, for that reason, unconscionable.[641] In this light, the injunction granted in the *Midland Bank* litigation gave effect to a negative conception of British public policy—the view that the extraterritorial application of laws should not be countenanced.[642]

---

[633] See paras 2.33 ff above.

[634] [2002] 2 All ER (Comm) 1.

[635] (1996) 64 FCR 1 and 44.

[636] [1998] 2 Lloyd's Rep 461.

[637] [2002] 1 Lloyd's Rep 425.

[638] [1986] 1 QB 689.

[639] ibid 700, 710, 714–715. See the cogent criticism of this decision by Crawford JR (Note) [1986] BYIL 413.

[640] [1985] AC 58.

[641] ibid 84.

[642] See, for example, the Protection of Trading Interests Act 1980 UK and *In re Westinghouse Electric Corporation* [1978] AC 547. For an argument that American courts should mitigate the impact of the Protection of Trading Interests Act on American antitrust litigation by enjoining British defendants from pursuing their rights under the Act, see (Note) 79 Michigan Law Review 1574 (1981).

It is interesting to observe that, in *British Airways* in the Court of **4.219**
Appeal,[643] the decision to grant injunctive relief was ultimately made on
the basis that neither British Airways not British Caledonian would be
able to obtain justice in the United States.[644] Importantly, this was *not*
because of the Court of Appeal's perception of aspects of American procedure[645] nor because of any view as to the fairness of United States
antitrust law. Rather, the Court felt that British Airways and British
Caledonian would be denied justice by virtue of directions made under
the Protection of Trading Interests (US Antitrust Measures) Order 1983
preventing both of those parties from furnishing the plaintiff and the
United States District Court with certain information and documentation
which might be relevant to their defence.[646]

Re Maxwell Communications Corporation plc (No 2)[647] is authority for the **4.220**
view that not every action which seeks to take advantage of the extraterritorial operation of United States legislation will be unconscionable and
therefore liable to be restrained by anti-suit injunction. After all, international commerce may not be capable of being confined to purely intra-
territorial legislation. Hoffmann J opined that antitrust legislation may be
a special case.[648] *Re Maxwell Communications Corporation plc (No 2)*
involved an attempt to restrain an application to a United States bankruptcy court to set aside a payment received by Barclays in their Holborn
branch in respect of an overdraft facility which had been extended to
Maxwell Communications, a company incorporated in England. In refusing to enjoin this application, Hoffmann J considered, somewhat tenuously it is suggested, that, as the source of the repayment was the sale of
an asset located in the United States, a connection with that jurisdiction
was more apparent than any in the *Midland Bank* case so that the assertion
of jurisdiction by the United States court did not involve 'so egregious a
claim of extra-territoriality that justice requires that it should be
prevented by injunction'.[649] In what was presumably a reference to public
international law notions of jurisdiction, Hoffmann J suggested that an
injunction would be justified where the foreign court took jurisdiction in
'violation of the principles of customary international law'.[650]

This decision was approved by the Court of Appeal.[651] It might be **4.221**
observed that, had an injunction been granted in this case, it would have
carried the conclusion that an officer of the court was acting vexatiously
and oppressively. In other areas of the law, such officers have been held to

---

[643] [1984] QB 142.   [644] ibid 202.
[645] cf the attitude of Dillon LJ in *Midland Bank*, noted at para 4.195 above.
[646] [1984] QB 142, 202.   [647] [1992] BCC 757.
[648] ibid 764.   [649] ibid 766.
[650] ibid 762.   [651] ibid.

have a 'higher moral duty' than ordinary litigants.[652] The position in this case was complicated, however, by the fact that the administrators also wore another hat under United States law in that they also had an official capacity under Chapter 11 of the Bankruptcy Code.[653]

4.222 In *CSR Ltd v Cigna Insurance Australia Ltd*,[654] Brennan CJ alone of all the judges of the High Court of Australia characterized the commencement of antitrust proceedings in New Jersey by one Australian company against another Australian company, being the lead insurer of a syndicate of insurers, as conduct warranting equity's intervention through the grant of an anti-suit injunction. The Chief Justice took the view that the conduct underpinning the antitrust complaint had all relevantly occurred in Australia and that CSR's invocation of the Sherman Act with what, on the facts of the case, was its extraterritorial reach, was 'unjust and oppressive'.[655] The majority joint judgment did not see the case in the same way as the Chief Justice.

5. Anti-Suit Injunctions and the Claims of Comity

4.223 The preceding three sections have revealed a perhaps surprisingly wide variety of circumstances in which common law courts may and do grant anti-suit injunctive relief. The injunction, however, being an equitable remedy, is discretionary and, in the context of transnational litigation, one of the key elements affecting the exercise of that discretion is the consideration of comity.[656] While this has not always been so,[657] the somewhat bland invocation of comity is certainly a feature of all the modern cases in which anti-suit injunctive relief has been sought. Comity has been described as:

---

[652] See, for example, *Ex parte James* (1874) LR 9 Ch App 609; *Re Carnac; Ex Parte Simmonds* (1885) 16 QBD 308, 312.

[653] [1992] BCC 757, 760.   [654] (1997) 189 CLR 345.   [655] ibid 376–377.

[656] It is the role of comity that makes reference to and reliance upon anti-suit injunction cases within a federal judicial system problematic in a transnational context. In *Laker*, Judge Wilkey explained that 'the rules against antisuit injunctions are more relaxed when the injunction runs against concurrent litigation within a single forum. In this situation respect for a co-equal sovereign's jurisdiction is not implicated and is more easily outweighed by the economies achieved through avoidance of duplicative actions': 731 F 2d 909, 927, n 49 (1984). The enigmatic nature of comity is illustrated, however, by the fact that in Australia the very prospect of a court of one state restraining proceedings in another state has been described as 'unseemly' and 'offensive': *Beecham (Aust) Pty Ltd v Roque Pty Ltd* (1987) 11 NSWLR 1, 3 and 6. The power to grant such relief has also been constitutionally doubted: *Bond Brewing Holdings Ltd v Crawford* (1989) 92 ALR 154 and is now proscribed by s 21 of the Commonwealth Service and Execution of Process Act 1992.

[657] In *The Angelic Grace* [1994] 1 Lloyd's Rep 168, 181, Rix J, referring to *Pena Copper Mines Ltd v Rio Tinto Co Ltd* [1911–1913] All ER 209, states that 'there is no hint of the consideration of caution for the sake of judicial comity which more modern authorities have stressed'.

not an absolute value, but it is no more flexible or optional than others . . . the term denotes the deference we should give to foreign judicial proceedings, a deference which arises not because we think those proceedings correct but because they are the judicial proceedings of a friendly state.[658]

4.224 In *Morguard Investments Ltd v De Savoye*,[659] La Forest J observed that a nation's respect for the commands of comity in the sense described above had to be balanced with the regard due 'to the rights of its own citizens or of other persons who are under the protection of its laws'.[660] The concept of comity has not been without its critics, the Chief Justice of British Columbia describing it as a 'little understood concept upon which so much depends, and which is often more a matter of legal fiction than of reality or principle'[661] and an American federal appellate judge expressing the view that 'no comity principles between nations are at stake in resolving a piece of commercial litigation'.[662] For FA Mann, comity was 'so elusive and imprecise a term as to render its use unhelpful and confusing'[663] and Dicey described it as 'a singular specimen of confusion of thought produced by laxity of language'.[664]

4.225 Notwithstanding such criticism, there is no doubt that a court asked to grant anti-suit injunctive relief should be sensitive to the foreign court because of the possible perception of interference with that court's processes. Views differ, however, as to what is required by such sensitivity in a practical sense. At one end of the spectrum is the view, espoused by those Circuit Courts in the United States following the 'strict' standard of *Gau Shan*, that comity requires that anti-suit injunctions never, or virtually never, be granted. This approach necessarily increases the likelihood of parallel proceedings and the inevitable attendant race to judgment. In the middle of the spectrum is the view that considerations of comity are relevant but are no more than a matter to be weighed by the trial judge in the overall exercise of his or her discretion. At the other or sceptical end of the spectrum is the view that considerations of comity have little or no role to play in this area of international private litigation and should only be taken into account when there is some demonstration of likely damage to the international relations of the sovereign states whose courts are or

---

[658] Black, V, 'The Anti-Suit Injunction Comes To Canada' (1987–1988) 13 Queens Law Journal 102, 119. See also Collins, LA (n 24 above) 5–7.

[659] [1990] 3 SCR 1077.

[660] ibid 1096. See also *Hilton v Guyot* 159 US 113, 163–164 (1895) and *CSR Ltd v Cigna Insurance Australia Ltd* (1997) 189 CLR 345, 396.

[661] *Amchem Products Inc v Workers Compensation Board* (1990) 75 DLR (4th) 1, 4.

[662] *China Trade and Development v MV Choong Yong* 837 F 2d 33, 40 (2nd Cir, 1987) per Judge Bright (dissenting).

[663] *Foreign Affairs in English Courts* (1986) 136.

[664] 1st edn, 1896, 10, cited in Collins, LA (n 24 above) 5.

may be seised of the matter. In *Allendale Mutual Insurance Co v Bull Data Systems Inc*, Posner CJ reacted to the argument for restraint on the basis of comity advanced by the respondent by concluding that 'the only concern with international comity is a purely theoretical one that ought not trump a concrete and persuasive demonstration of harm to the applicant for the injunction not offset by harm to the opponent if it is granted'.[665] Posner CJ's decision places sharp focus upon the invariably untested assertion that the grant of anti-suit relief will be offensive to the foreign court.

4.226 As a general proposition, the significance of the claims of comity will vary according to the facts of each case and also by reference to the reason why injunctive relief is being sought. It may be doubted whether there has been a sufficient appreciation in recent cases of the need for contextual differentiation in this area. Too often, no real consideration is given to the questions of how, or indeed whether, the grant of anti-suit injunctive relief will constitute an infringement of comity or genuinely affront a foreign court nor, indeed, whether comity is relevant in all cases.[666]

4.227 The following general observations may be made about the role of comity in this field. First, 'if an anti-suit injunction is issued for cogent reasons appearing from the facts of the case, there can be no reasonable suggestion that the Court issuing the injunction had little confidence in the foreign Court'.[667] Secondly, a finding that the commencement or continuation of foreign proceedings would be vexatious, oppressive, or unconscionable focuses on the conduct of the plaintiff in the foreign proceedings and not that of the foreign *court*. Thirdly, the courts recognize the need for 'sensitivity' in this area; the jurisdiction is an 'exceptional' one and caution should be employed in its exercise. Fourthly, caution is also ensured (and thus comity accommodated) by the stringency of the test for anti-suit relief in the exclusive jurisdiction, a test which ensures that anti-suit relief is not simply granted where the local court disagrees with the foreign court's assessment of the natural forum but requires there to be vexatious, oppressive, or unconscionable conduct. Fifthly, in so far as comity encompasses the notion of mutual respect and reciprocity of treatment among nations, it is noteworthy that anti-suit injunctions are granted by courts of common law countries including the United States of America. Finally, where the foreign proceeding involves an attempt to invoke the extraterritorial operation of a foreign law (at least a law whose

---

[665] 10 F 3d 425, 432 (1993).

[666] In this context, it should perhaps be noted that an order requiring an election entails no infringement of comity as the decision as to venue in a real sense remains that of the plaintiff and not the court.

[667] *CSR Ltd v NZI Insurance Ltd* (1994) 36 NSWLR 138, 158–159.

reach travels beyond generally accepted limits), or to impose punitive penalties under that foreign law, the claim for comity is much weaker.

Circumstances where it is more likely that comity may be infringed by the **4.228** grant of an anti-suit injunction are where the foreign court has already invested a great deal of time in pre-trial directions or has even started hearing the matter, or where the applicant for the injunction has, up to that point, evinced a willingness to be sued in the foreign court. In this respect, however, comity is served by well-established principles of equity and, in particular, the discretionary nature of equitable relief. An injunction will not lie in circumstances where the applicant for injunctive relief has allowed foreign proceedings to continue for some time before seeking that relief,[668] or where the applicant has itself participated in the foreign proceedings to such an extent as to waive its legal or equitable rights to seek to restrain those proceedings. Equitable considerations such as laches and waiver thus may be seen in the particular context of anti-suit injunctions to promote comity. The corollary of this, which has already been stated, is that an anti-suit injunction issued in circumstances where the foreign court has invested little or no time in the hearing of a matter will be far less 'offensive', if indeed offensive at all, than one granted in circumstances where proceedings have been on foot for some considerable period and the foreign court has invested time in the management and conduct of those proceedings.[669]

Consideration now turns to an analysis of the claims of comity in the **4.229** context of each of the general bases for the discretionary jurisdiction to grant anti-suit injunctive relief identified earlier in this chapter.

Where the basis for the grant of anti-suit relief relates to the protection of **4.230** the jurisdiction of the court issuing the injunction, once a court has determined that the integrity of its process is being abused, that proper control over pending proceedings is threatened, or that the court's jurisdiction is in some way being improperly evaded or impeached, arguments for restraint based on considerations of comity are least strong[670] and it may even be that, in this situation, courts are or may be *bound* to grant anti-suit injunctive relief. Certainly it is in this area that the approaches of United States and Commonwealth jurisdictions are most in unison.

---

[668] For example, *The Maria Gorthon* [1976] 2 Lloyd's Rep 510, 516; *Toepfer International GmbH v Molino Boschi SRL* [1996] 1 Lloyd's Rep 510; but cf *Schiffahrtsgesellschaft Detlev von Appen v Voest Alpine Intertrading GmbH* [1997] 1 Lloyd's Rep 179, where there had been delay in seeking anti-suit relief. While an injunction was granted in this case, it was conditional upon the applicant for that relief paying the costs of the Brazilian proceedings that had been permitted to continue.
[669] *The Angelic Grace* [1995] 1 Lloyd's Rep 86, 96.
[670] See *CSR Ltd v Cigna Insurance Australia Ltd* (1997) 189 CLR 345, 398.

4.231 Where a foreign court has taken jurisdiction in what an English court may regard as the face of a choice of court clause, it has been doubted how compelling the claims of international judicial comity are. Lord Hoffmann has observed that an injunction restraining foreign proceedings in aid of a legal right 'involves no finding whatever about the suitability of the foreign forum but merely the universal principle that until some good contrary reason has been shown, men should be held to their bargains'.[671] In *Donohue v Armco*[672] in the Court of Appeal, Sedley LJ went so far as to say that:

> it is universally contrary to comity for Courts to stand by while a party who has contracted to litigate in one country reneges on the agreement. Comity creates an expectation that the Courts of other countries will collaborate in holding the parties to the terms of an exclusive jurisdiction clause.

4.232 Observations to similar effect were made by Millett LJ in *The Angelic Grace*.[673] At first instance in that case,[674] Rix J took the view that comity actually *called for* the grant of anti-suit injunctive relief. This proactive stance recommended itself to Rix J because the concurrent Italian proceedings were at an early stage and, were they permitted to continue, the clash of jurisdictions was likely to be exacerbated. He stated that he was:

> fully conscious of the need for caution and the desirability of the need for judicial comity in this area. Yet it seems to me that much greater damage is done to the interests which that caution and that comity are intended to serve, if this Court adjourns these proceedings to await the outcome of a challenge to the jurisdiction in Italy . . . and then proceeds to issue an injunction.[675]

His decision was upheld on appeal, Leggatt LJ describing a proposal that the Italian court first be asked to stay proceedings as 'not only invidious but the reverse of comity' and stating, graphically, that 'contrary to Mr Bumble's view, the law is not normally an ass and comity does not require it to behave like one'.[676]

---

[671] *Apple Corps Ltd v Apple Computer Inc* [1992] RPC 70, 79. See also Bermann, GA, 'The Use of Anti-Suit Injunctions in International Litigation' (1990) 28 Columbia Journal of Transnational Law 589, 623: 'Given their independent bases in prior commitments by the parties, such claims [for anti-suit relief] simply do not connote the intrusiveness and insult to foreign nations to which courts entertaining issuance of international anti-suit injunctions need to be alert.'

[672] [2000] 1 Lloyd's Rep 579, 600. Note that this decision was reversed—[2002] 1 Lloyd's Rep 425.

[673] [1995] 1 Lloyd's Rep 87, 96; see also *National Westminster Bank Ltd v Utrecht-America Finance Co* [2001] 1 All ER (Comm) 7.

[674] [1994] 1 Lloyd's Rep 168.

[675] ibid 182. cf *The Golden Anne* [1984] 2 Lloyd's Rep 498, 498.

[676] [1995] 1 Lloyd's Rep 87, 95.

Whether no message is impliedly conveyed to the foreign court as to the **4.233** propriety of it assuming jurisdiction in the face of such a clause may be debatable, especially in circumstances where the foreign court takes a different view with regard to the scope or enforceability of the clause in question or where the other proceedings are in a member state of the European Union.[677] In *Akai Pty Ltd v People's Insurance Co Ltd*,[678] Thomas J rejected the argument that the English court should, as a matter of comity, give effect to Australian law and public policy by staying the proceedings. His reasoning, in essence, was that comity did not require an English court to give effect to an Australian statute which, for reasons of public policy, expressly overrode a choice of law clause for, as it happened, England. Thomas J regarded it as no part of the English court's role to give effect to Australian public policy as expressed in the Insurance Contracts Act 1984 (C'th), notwithstanding the fact that the People's Insurance Company had chosen to do business in Australia with an Australian company, Akai Pty Limited, and notwithstanding the fact that the High Court of Australia had delivered judgment on the matter and declined, by majority, to enforce the exclusive jurisdiction clause. Thomas J concluded, with the minority of the High Court, that:

this Court should give effect to the bargain of the parties and their freely negotiated choice of law and jurisdiction. It should not, as a matter of comity, give effect to the decision of the High Court that overrode that bargain and that choice.[679]

This case perhaps provides an illustration of what Rix J was referring to in *The Angelic Grace* in the passage cited above. The perception that the decision of Thomas J in *Akai* infringes comity is surely more powerful in circumstances where the effect of his decision, enforcing the exclusive jurisdiction clause, was to render nugatory the result of a court at the apex of another judicial system closely bound to English law by history.

Where anti-suit injunctive relief lies to restrain foreign proceedings which **4.234** are considered to be vexatious or oppressive, various instances of vexation and oppression have been gleaned from the cases. Here, too, it is necessary to make some differentiation between the various instances, for comity will be implicated to differing degrees, but it is important to note, as was made plain in *Airbus Industrie v Patel*,[680] that the general requirement under English law that injunctive relief will not be granted to restrain vexatious and oppressive foreign proceedings unless the English

---

[677] See *Re the Enforcement of an English Anti-Suit injunction* [1997] I L Pr 320 and cf *Phillip Alexander Securities and Futures Ltd v Bamberger* [1997] I L Pr 73, 104 at 115–117 and *Toepfer International GmbH v Société Cargill France* [1998] 1 Lloyd's Rep 379.
[678] [1998] 1 Lloyd's Rep 90.
[679] ibid 100.
[680] [1999] 1 AC 119.

court considers itself to be the natural forum for the resolution of a particular set of proceedings in itself represents an important commitment to comity.

4.235 In *Re Maxwell Communications (No 2)*,[681] Hoffmann J, emphasizing the importance of comity, stated that 'although the injustice which can justify an anti-suit injunction must inevitably be judged according to English notions of justice, it will usually be assumed that a similar quality of justice is available in the foreign court'.[682] Where the vexation or oppression warranting the grant of anti-suit injunctive relief is due to the extremely inconvenient nature of the foreign forum, no adverse inference is being cast on the 'quality of justice' in that forum by the grant of an anti-suit injunction so that comity is not infringed in that respect. The inference to be drawn from the grant of an anti-suit injunction in this situation may be qualitatively different from the lack of respect implicit in one granted on the basis of the oppressive nature of foreign procedure which *does* reflect upon the quality of justice available in the foreign forum. Where what is considered to be vexatious or oppressive is the prospect of ongoing litigation, the significant 'public' concerns in relation to the unattractive prospect of inconsistent decisions and the appeal of efficient utilization of judicial resources which at the least reinforce a court's willingness to grant anti-suit injunctive relief in this situation may mean that any affront to comity will be relatively minor in this context on the footing that the courts of all countries have a mutual interest in securing such goals.

4.236 There is an echo of this concern in sentiments expressed by Lord Diplock in *The Abidin Daver*.[683] Referring to the prospect of concurrent proceedings, his Lordship stated that 'comity demands that such a situation should not be permitted to occur as between courts of two friendly and civilized states. It is a recipe for confusion and injustice.'[684] The grant of an anti-suit injunction may be one way of effectuating this goal.

4.237 It should be noted, however, that the position just expressed is one with which most American commentators[685] and the *Laker* line of cases in the United States would strongly disagree.[686] This viewpoint holds that

---

[681] [1992] BCC 757.
[682] ibid 762.
[683] [1984] AC 398.
[684] ibid 412.
[685] See Raushenbush, RW, 'Antisuit Injunctions and International Comity' (1985) 71 Virginia Law Review 1039; Baer, T, 'Injunctions Against Prosecution of Litigation Abroad: Towards a Transnational Approach' (1984–5) 37 Stanford Law Review 155; Schimek, DM, 'Anti-Suit and Anti-Anti-Suit Injunctions: A Proposed Texas Approach' (1993) 45 Baylor Law Review 499.
[686] cf Teitz, LE, 'Taking Multiple Bites of the Apple: A Proposal to Resolve Conflicts of Jurisdiction and Multiple Proceedings' (1992) 26 The International Lawyer 21, 29, who argues that tolerance of parallel proceedings 'merely defers battle to a later stage . . . [i]n

comity is infringed where the courts of one sovereign state seek to assert *exclusive* control over a particular issue.[687] On this view, the use of anti-suit injunctions to avert the particular problems of multiple or parallel proceedings cannot be tolerated. What Posner CJ in *Allendale* described as the 'laxer' (from the point of view of comity) standard of cases is certainly more in accordance with the traditional attitude United States courts have taken to the use of anti-suit injunctions to restrain foreign proceedings in circumstances of concurrent transnational litigation. In a Note entitled 'Injunctions To Restrain Foreign Proceedings' written in 1919, it is stated that 'practically all courts are agreed today that a multiplicity of suits, if vexatious—and such is true in most instances—presents a fair case for the exercise of the Chancellor's discretion ... the defendant's conduct is clearly inequitable in putting the complainant to the expense and annoyance of defending several suits, and restricting him to a signal action assures him sufficiently of the justice he seeks'.[688] By contrast, in *Laker*, Judge Wilkey stated that 'avoiding hardship to parties and promoting the economies of consolidated litigation are more properly considered in a motion for dismissal for *forum non conveniens*'.[689] The suggestion that seeking anti-suit injunctive relief is a very much inferior and less appropriate course than seeking to have foreign proceedings stayed by the court seised has provided what may be considered to be a significant obstacle to a defendant's ability to obtain anti-suit injunctive relief. The next section considers how this is so.

Consonant with Judge Wilkey's view of comity, it has been argued by **4.238** both commentators and judges that a court should decline to entertain an application for anti-suit injunctive relief until an application has first been made to the foreign court.[690] This is on the basis that it 'gives the foreign court the chance to regulate its own process rather than have it controlled from afar'.[691] Further, it has been suggested that, generally, any vexation

---

cases of inconsistent judgment, with no international consensus on recognition and enforcement, who to pay (and in what currency) under which judgment becomes the next focus of litigation'. She illustrates this proposition at 29–31 with an example of parallel proceedings in the courts of Texas and Abu Dhabi.

[687] Schimek, DM (n 685 above) 503.

[688] (1919–1920) 33 Harvard Law Review 92.

[689] 731 F 2d 909, 928 (1984).

[690] See Baer, T (n 685 above) 179–180; Hartley, TC (n 307 above) 507 and 509; Black V (n 658 above) 122; Bermann, GA (n 671 above) 614.

[691] Black, V, ibid. Purchas LJ favoured this approach in *Metall und Rohstoff AG v ACLI (Metals) London Ltd* [1984] 1 Lloyd's Rep 509, 609, as did Robert Goff LJ in *Bank of Tokyo Ltd v Karoon* (Note) [1987] AC 45, 63; Lord Kirkwood in *Pan American World Airways Inc v Andrews* [1992] SLT 268; Glidewell LJ in *Re Maxwell Communications (No 2)* [1992] BCC 757, 773; see also *Deaville v Aeroflot* [1997] 2 Lloyd's Rep 67. It has also won the approval of the Supreme Court of Canada: *Amchem Products Inc v Workers Compensation Board* [1993] 1 SCR 897, 931.

and oppression alleged to arise from the foreign proceedings, such as inconvenience, expense, and non-recovery of costs, will not begin to 'bite' unless and until an application to stay those proceedings has been refused.[692] In *Arab Monetary Fund v Hashim*,[693] Hoffmann J considered that:

> generally speaking, as a matter both of comity and common sense, the foreign judge is in the best position to decide whether it is just and equitable that proceedings in his or her own court should be stayed or allowed to proceed. . . . There must be some good reason why the decision has to be made here rather than there.[694]

4.239 More recently, in *Amoco (UK) Exploration v British American Offshore Ltd*,[695] Langley J said:

> The 'comity' argument has in my judgment particular force where the relief sought is only an anti-suit injunction, the parties sought to be injuncted are proceeding in their local jurisdiction, and the local courts have not been asked to rule on forum conveniens issues themselves although applications can be made to them to do so. Mr Pollock submitted that, absent an exclusive jurisdiction clause, in principle, a party should not pursue an anti-suit injunction before exhausting remedies in the local Court. In my judgment it would be wrong to endorse any absolute rule to that effect but I do think that such considerations are material to the exercise of the Court's discretion. . . . In terms of comity there is in my judgment much to be said for leaving such questions to the Texan Courts . . . The existence of such remedies [stay and refusal of jurisdiction] in the Texan Courts also serves to diminish any 'oppression' to the claimants arising from the Texan proceedings.

4.240 The cogency of this course will largely be dependent upon the criteria according to which the foreign court regulates its proceedings and, in particular, the extent to which the doctrine of *forum non conveniens* is observed. In this context, Lord Goff's reference in *Aerospatiale* to the 'now very widely recognised principle of forum non conveniens'[696] may represent judicial overstatement.[697] So much was recognized by Gleeson CJ in

---

[692] *Pan American World Airways Inc v Andrews* [1992] SLT 268, 271.

[693] Financial Times, 23 July 1992.

[694] It is important to note that the fact that the foreign court has ruled that it has jurisdiction to hear the dispute and will not decline to exercise it does not mean that an English court will *not* grant injunctive relief in appropriate circumstances. Thus, in *Aerospatiale* itself, an application to stay the Texas proceedings was not only refused but so were three attempts to appeal that decision ([1987] AC 871, 886) and an injunction was granted nevertheless. *Akai Pty Ltd v People's Insurance Company* [1998] 1 Lloyd's Rep 90 supplies another example of this.

[695] [1999] 2 Lloyd's Rep 772, 780.

[696] [1987] AC 871, 894.

[697] See paras 4.69, 4.70, and 4.74 above.

Voth v Manildra Flour Mills Pty Ltd[698] and Sopinka J in *Amchem Products Inc v Workers Compensation Board.*[699]

Where the foreign jurisdiction does observe the doctrine of *forum non* **4.241** *conveniens* and an application to stay proceedings on the basis of that doctrine has been refused, greater deference is likely to be paid to such a decision on the footing that the employment of that doctrine represents a commitment to comity that is correspondingly lacking in jurisdictions which do not allow actions to be stayed on *forum non conveniens* grounds. Such deference probably falls short of actual recognition of the foreign decision although the Supreme Court of Canada's decision in *Amchem Products Inc v Workers Compensation Board*[700] approaches this position:

> when a foreign court assumes jurisdiction on a basis that generally conforms to our rule of private international law relating to *forum non conveniens*, that decision will be *respected* and a Canadian court will not purport to make the decision for the foreign court.[701]

Recognizing that many jurisdictions do not employ a *forum non conveniens* **4.242** doctrine,[702] Sopinka J stated that what was important was whether the foreign court's assumption of jurisdiction was *consistent* with the doctrine of *forum non conveniens* as employed in the common law provinces of Canada.[703] Accordingly, if it *would* have been reasonably open to the foreign court to conclude that it was the natural forum, then no injunction should be granted. Sopinka J was keen to diminish the significance to be attached to the absence in the foreign forum of the doctrine of *forum non conveniens*, a factor which had been of great significance in the lower courts in that case.[704] He stated that comity 'does not require that the decision of the foreign court be based on the doctrine of *forum non conveniens'*.[705]

Any stipulation that a stay first be sought in the foreign court bears a strong **4.243** similarity to the doctrine of 'exhaustion of local remedies' in public international law.[706] The parallel is perhaps apt because both the grant of an anti-suit injunction and the taking of jurisdiction by an international tribunal constitute something of an infringement of sovereignty. The candour of the courts in admitting that the grant of anti-suit relief may constitute an interference with the foreign tribunal has already been noted.[707]

---

[698] (1989) 15 NSWLR 513, 525–526. [699] [1993] 1 SCR 897, 914 and 937.
[700] [1993] 1 SCR 897.
[701] ibid 934 (emphasis added). The language of recognition is used at 936.
[702] ibid 937. [703] ibid 934 and 937–938.
[704] (1989) 65 DLR (4th) 567, 592; (1990) 75 DLR (4th) 1, 18. [705] [1993] 1 SCR 897, 937.
[706] See, generally, Brownlie, I, *Principles of Public International Law* (4th edn, 1991) 494–504.
[707] In this context, a further resonance of public international law is found in *Pittsburgh-Corning Corp v Askewe* 823 SW 2d 759 (Tex App, Texark, 1992), where it was argued that the

4.244 A number of powerful criticisms may be advanced against the suggested 'preferable course' articulated in *Amchem* of first seeking a stay of foreign proceedings before making any application for anti-suit relief. That course is based upon a major and untested assumption, namely that the foreign court would be insulted if proceedings pending before it were restrained. This assumption has been and should be questioned, especially in circumstances where the court issuing the injunction makes plain the reasons for its decision, focusing as they must on the defendant's unconscionable conduct, and the basis for the grant of the relief entails no criticism of the foreign court.[708]

4.245 The approach advocated in *Amchem* also rests upon another important assumption, namely that a party will be able to apply for and, in an appropriate case, obtain a stay or dismissal of the foreign proceedings in a quick and convenient manner, with a minimum of inconvenience, cost, and disruption to itself as envisaged, for example, by Lord Templeman in *Spiliada Maritime Corporation v Cansulex Ltd*[709] and by the High Court in *Voth v Manildra Flour Mills Pty Ltd*,[710] and also without prejudice to itself. That assumption is simply unwarranted. In some countries, including many European countries in the civil law tradition, there is no equivalent of the doctrine of *forum non conveniens*.[711] Those countries include France, Germany, Greece, Italy, and Switzerland.[712] In other countries, the applicable doctrine is heavily biased towards a retention of jurisdiction, whether in terms,[713] or in its application. The United States Supreme Court has acknowledged that 'one can rarely count on the fact that jurisdiction will be declined'.[714]

---

court's asserted jurisdiction to restrain Canadian proceedings was in violation of the 'act of State' doctrine. Interestingly, the argument was rejected in this case by resort to the *in personam* fiction: 'the Texas district court did not attempt to enjoin any Canadian court or other Canadian governmental body from taking any action. Both the prior injunction and the present one are directed at corporate citizens of Texas' (761).

[708] *Allendale Mutual Insurance Co v Bull Data Systems Inc* (1993) 10 F 3d 425; *Kaepa Inc v Achilles Corpn* 76 3d 624 (5th Cir, 1996); *CSR Ltd v NZI Co Ltd* (1994) 36 NSWLR 138.

[709] [1987] AC 460, 465.

[710] (1990) 171 CLR 538, 565.

[711] 'Experienced international practitioners are increasingly aware of the fact that by a combination of exorbitant jurisdiction and the absence of forum non conveniens some civil-law countries have become litigation havens. Clever plaintiffs' lawyers are quick to make use of such havens when they look for a forum that is both surprising and inconvenient for the defendant': Schlesinger, Baade, Damaska and Herzog (n 114 above) 403. See also *Voth v Manildra Flour Mills Pty Ltd* (1989) 15 NSWLR 513, 525–526.

[712] See Fawcett, JJ (ed), *Declining Jurisdiction in Private International Law* (1995), 175–179, 189–195, 239, 300, and 386.

[713] *Picketts v International Playtex, Inc* 576 A 2d 518, 525 (1990).

[714] *American Dredging Co v Miller* 114 S Ct 981, 989 (1994).

In some jurisdictions, it is not possible solely to object to the jurisdiction or **4.246** apply for a stay or dismissal of the proceedings; a detailed defence on the merits together with documentary evidence will need to be filed together with any stay application, as was the case in the Greek proceedings referred to in *Continental Bank NA v Aeakos Compania Naviera SA*[715] which Aeakos Compania Naviera SA was restrained from prosecuting. The position is similar in Japan,[716] Algeria,[717] and Brazil,[718] for example. Even in jurisdictions where a stay application *simpliciter* may be made, such an application may entail discovery and depositions and/or lengthy evidence, entailing significant costs which, in countries such as the United States, will generally not be recoverable even if the stay application is successful.

In certain jurisdictions, an application for a stay of proceedings may be **4.247** conditional upon the filing of a hefty bond—a necessary price to be paid for participating in litigation in a particular forum, even when participation is only for the purposes of challenging jurisdiction; similarly, conditions may be imposed upon the granting of any stay to which the party applying for such relief would not otherwise have been subjected, for example, in the alternative forum otherwise open to it. Finally, any insistence on a party first seeking anti-suit injunctive relief exposes that party to the risk of being taken to have submitted to the foreign jurisdiction,[719] a factor which may have important ramifications at the enforcement stage of any foreign judgment.[720]

The suggested *Amchem* approach also wrongly assumes that the question **4.248** to be decided by the local forum on the anti-suit injunction is the same as the question to be decided by the foreign court on the stay motion. In fact, the questions are different. On the stay motion, the foreign court will merely be deciding whether the defendant before it has discharged the onus of establishing that there is another more appropriate forum for the resolution of the dispute (or some variant of this test). However, the local court on the anti-suit injunction will be deciding whether the conduct of the plaintiff in the foreign proceedings is a breach of a contractual or other legal right or whether it amounts to vexation or oppression in the strict sense in which those terms are used. The focus here is on equitable entitlement, whereas the focus on the stay motion in the foreign court is on jurisdictional convenience.

---

[715] [1994] 1 WLR 588, 598D.
[716] This emerges from the factual findings in *Kawasaki v 'Daeyang Honey'* (1991) 120 ALR 109, 117; *S Megga Telecommunications Ltd v Etowaru Co Ltd* [1995] 2 HKC 761.
[717] *The Eastern Trader* [1996] 2 Lloyd's Rep 585, 600.
[718] *Schiffahrtsgesellschaft Detlev von Appen v Voest Alpine Intertrading GmbH* [1997] 1 Lloyd's Rep 179.
[719] *Kuwait Airways Corporation v Iraq Airways Co* [1994] 1 Lloyd's Rep 276, 283.
[720] *Henry v Geoprosco International Ltd* [1976] QB 726.

4.249 The difference between the two remedies can be illustrated by three examples. Where the local court is not shown to be a more appropriate forum, but where the conduct of the plaintiff in bringing the foreign proceedings is in breach of a legal right or is vexatious or oppressive, the foreign court will be likely to decline the stay but the local court will be entitled to grant the anti-suit injunction. No purpose is served by the local court waiting until the foreign court has considered (and refused) the stay. Indeed, in this context, comity may well be impaired. As a second example, where the plaintiff in the foreign proceedings invokes an extraterritorial jurisdiction (for example, under an antitrust law) in a manner which the local court regards as exorbitant, the foreign court is likely to decline the stay and the only opportunity for the local court to restrain what, according to its principles, is unconscionable conduct, is via the anti-suit injunction. As a third example, in a case where the local court is plainly the more appropriate forum and where the conduct of the plaintiff in the foreign proceedings is in breach of a legal right or is vexatious or oppressive (or both), then the foreign court should, if applying like principles, grant a stay of the proceedings. However, the local court should be entitled to grant the anti-suit injunction so as to prevent the defendant in the foreign proceedings being exposed to the difficulties, inconvenience, and expense referred to earlier in prosecuting the successful stay application. Moreover, as also referred to earlier, it cannot be guaranteed that the foreign court would grant a stay.

V. NEGATIVE DECLARATORY PROCEEDINGS

4.250 The fourth technique of 'reverse' forum shopping is the action for negative declaratory relief.[721] Seeking a declaration from a domestic court that the applicant is either not, or is less, liable to the plaintiff or potential plaintiff in foreign proceedings under certain existing or envisaged causes of action (a 'declaration of non-liability' or a 'negative declaration') or alternatively seeking a declaration that a certain foreign judgment would not be entitled to recognition in the forum is an indirect technique of resisting litigation in a foreign jurisdiction. Such a course is designed to anticipate and negative the effect of foreign proceedings, as opposed to having them stayed or restrained. Paragraphs 4.251 ff below explore how this result may be achieved. The negative declaration's potential to effect the same result as the restraint of foreign proceedings by different means is illustrated by the fact that such relief is often sought in the alternative

---

[721] This topic received its first treatment in *Dicey and Morris* in the 12th edition of the text in 1993, 406–408.

to anti-suit injunctive relief.[722] Indeed *Guaranty Trust Co of New York v Hannay & Co*,[723] the very case in which the English courts embraced the conceptual possibility of a negative declaration, involved just such a strategy. English proceedings for negative declaratory relief were in essence an attempt to short-circuit American proceedings which had been commenced against the plaintiff in England.[724]

1. THE MECHANICS OF NEGATIVE DECLARATORY RELIEF

The efficacy of seeking negative declaratory relief will largely be a function of where the applicant (existing or potential defendant in the foreign proceedings) has assets. Clearly, if there are sufficient assets in the foreign jurisdiction to satisfy any judgment debt and these assets are not subject to any exchange control regulations (which would raise the possibility that the foreign plaintiff may yet wish to enforce its judgment in a third country), then seeking such relief may be a futile exercise and one in which English courts would be reluctant to participate. In *First National Bank of Boston v Union Bank of Switzerland*,[725] Sir Michael Kerr observed that: **4.251**

the Swiss action will go on whatever may happen in England, and if UBS succeed in obtaining judgment, then the sequestrated assets will be there and immediately available to satisfy the judgment. There will be no need for UBS to come to the English Courts, or to go elsewhere to enforce the judgment.[726]

This will not necessarily be the case, however, in circumstances where a declaratory judgment in favour of the foreign defendant is delivered prior to the foreign judgment and is either obliged to be recognized, as under Council Regulation 44/2001, for example, or else is subject to recognition in the foreign jurisdiction.[727] A declaratory judgment of this kind may merge with the foreign cause of action so that the matter would be *res judicata* in **4.252**

---

[722] For example, *Smith Kline & French Laboratories Ltd v Bloch* [1983] 2 All ER 72; *British Airways Board v Laker Airways Ltd* [1984] QB 142; *Midland Bank plc v Laker Airways Ltd* [1986] QB 689. See also *Ellerman Lines Ltd v Read* [1928] 2 KB 144, 154 where the application for a declaration was to the effect that a foreign judgment would not be entitled to recognition in the forum.

[723] [1915] 2 KB 536.

[724] The plaintiff in the English proceedings also sought an injunction to restrain continuance of the American proceedings. The application for a negative declaration was viewed by both Pickford and Bankes LJJ as simply an attempt to obtain indirectly what was also being sought directly by means of the injunction, namely forcing the litigation to take place in England and not America, and in these circumstances, no case for an injunction having been made out, negative declaratory relief was also refused: see [1915] 2 KB 536, esp 564, see also 550–551 and 574–575.

[725] [1990] 1 Lloyd's Rep 32.

[726] ibid 36. See also *Camilla Cotton Oil Co v Granadex SA* [1976] 2 Lloyd's Rep 10, 13–14.

[727] See, generally, Barnett, PR, *Res Judicata, Estoppel and Foreign Judgments* (2001).

that jurisdiction.[728] Alternatively, such a declaration could found a plea of issue estoppel in the foreign proceedings[729] or, at the very least, be used in the foreign court as a guide of considerable authority on the questions of the law of the forum granting the relief where such questions are subject to contention and central to the dispute in the foreign forum.[730]

4.253 Whether or not a declaratory judgment will give rise to a *res judicata* or will simply be available to be used as evidence of the foreign law may turn on whether the declaratory proceedings were *ex parte* or whether the foreign plaintiff submitted to them. This will not be the case, however, where a declaratory judgment is subject to recognition under Council Regulation 44/2001. So long as the original member state court had jurisdiction under the Regulation, then a court of another member state will be obliged to recognize it under Article 33 subject to the limited defences found in Articles 34 and 35.

4.254 Where the foreign defendant only has assets in the forum in which it seeks negative declaratory relief, such a declaration will preclude the recognition or enforcement of any subsequent foreign judgment in that forum, assuming all other requirements for an estoppel are in place. The foreign proceedings will be rendered nugatory in that forum.[731] If, however, the foreign judgment were delivered first, principle would suggest that *it* could pre-empt the hitherto incomplete domestic declaratory proceedings, assuming of course that the domestic court would grant the defendant (successful plaintiff in the foreign proceedings) leave to amend its defence or else permitted the separate recognition and enforcement of the foreign judgment. This latter course is what occurred in the *Hunt v BP Exploration Co (Libya) Ltd* litigation. The judgment given in the English proceedings[732] was held to be enforceable in Texas notwithstanding the fact that Hunt had commenced proceedings for negative declaratory relief in that State approximately one month after commencement of the

---

[728] Zamir, I and Woolf, H and J, *The Declaratory Judgment* (2nd edn, 1993) 173. Certainly the view of English law is that the effect of a declaratory judgment is to create a *res judicata* between the parties: *International General Electric Co of New York Ltd v Commissioner of Customs and Excise* [1962] 1 Ch 784, 789—'an order declaring the rights of the parties must in its nature be a final order after a hearing when the Court is in a position to declare what the rights of the parties are, and such an order must necessarily be then res judicata and bind the parties for ever, subject only, of course, to a right of appeal'.

[729] *McConnell Dowell Constructors Ltd v Lloyd's Syndicate 396* [1988] 2 NZLR 257, 273 and 277 per Somers J; *Marc Rich v Società Italiana Impianti PA* (11 November 1991) 14.

[730] *Guaranty Trust* [1915] 2 KB 536, 564; *Camilla Cotton Oil Co v Granadex SA* [1975] 1 Lloyd's Rep 470, 475 and 476–477, cf House of Lords [1976] 2 Lloyd's Rep 10, 15.

[731] Assets subsequently moved to the foreign forum or a third forum may, of course, become vulnerable to any foreign judgment against the successful applicant for negative declaratory relief.

[732] *BP Exploration Co (Libya) Ltd v Hunt (No 2)* [1983] 2 AC 352.

English proceedings. These were still pending at the time of enforcement.[733]

Whether or not an English court would apply the same analysis and **4.255** enforce a foreign judgment while 'mirror-image' declaratory proceedings were on foot in England is not completely free from doubt, however. In *The Abidin Daver*,[734] Lord Diplock, speaking of the undesirability of concurrent proceedings, said that 'novel problems relating to estoppel per rem judicatem and issue estoppel, which have not hitherto been examined by any English court, might also arise'.[735] One way to discourage multiple proceedings may be to refuse to recognize and enforce foreign judgments not given in the natural forum.

A final situation where the expedient of seeking negative declaratory **4.256** relief may avail a defendant in the battle for venue is where such a party has assets in a *third* jurisdiction against which a foreign judgment might be enforced. Assuming, again, that negative declaratory judgments are subject to recognition in this third jurisdiction, those assets may be insulated against the foreign judgment if there has been *prior* recognition of the negative declaration. The decision of the Privy Council in *Showlag v Mansour*[736] has made it clear that, where there is competition for recognition between the judgments of two foreign courts of competent jurisdiction in a third (common law) jurisdiction, the general rule is that the earlier of them in time must be recognized and given effect to the exclusion of the latter.[737] This common-sense approach also accords with the rule set down in Article 34(4) of Council Regulation 44/2001.[738]

In cases falling outside Council Regulation 44/2001 or the Brussels and **4.257** Lugano Conventions, whether or not negative declaratory judgments will be subject to recognition at all may turn on either the nature of the declaration in question or a particular jurisdiction's rules for recognition. A foreign court may refuse recognition, for example, where it does not consider the subject matter of the negative declaration justiciable in the

---

[733] *Hunt v BP Exploration Co (Libya) Ltd* 492 F Supp 885 (ND Tex, 1980). The litigation is discussed in Baade, HW (n 2 above) 202–203.

[734] [1984] AC 398.

[735] ibid 412. See for similar sentiments and a discussion of *res judicata* and issue estoppel, *Du Pont de Nemours & Co v Agnew (No 2)* [1988] 2 Lloyd's Rep 240, 248–249.

[736] [1995] 1 AC 431.

[737] Exceptions to this general rule relate to circumstances where the party seeking recognition of the prior judgment is in some way estopped from so doing: see *The Indian Grace* [1993] AC 410.

[738] This provides that a judgment shall not be recognized if it is 'irreconcilable with an earlier judgment given in a member state or in a third state involving the same cause of action and between the same parties, provided that the earlier judgment fulfils the conditions necessary for its recognition in the member state addressed'.

court providing such relief. In *Tyburn Productions Ltd v Conan Doyle*,[739] an action for a declaration in England that the defendant lacked certain intellectual property rights in the United States, Vinelott J stated that 'in the instant case there is no evidence that, if the validity of the rights claimed were justiciable in the English courts, the decision of the English courts would be treated as binding on any of the states of the United States of America and it would in my judgment be an exercise in futility to allow these claims . . . to continue'.[740]

4.258 As regards a foreign jurisdiction's rules of recognition, it was clear in *First National Bank of Boston v Union Bank of Switzerland*,[741] for example, that the Swiss courts would not recognize an English declaratory judgment in circumstances where Swiss proceedings were already on foot in relation to the same matter forming the subject of the declaration.[742] Outside the scope of Council Regulation 44/2001, Italy has (or at least had) a similar rule to Switzerland,[743] and both accord with the former common law rule which held that a foreign judgment could not be pleaded as a *res judicata* if it had been given after the *institution* as opposed to the *determination* of domestic proceedings.[744]

4.259 This section has sought to explain the somewhat detailed 'mechanics' by which an action for negative declaratory relief might be usefully employed by a party in the strategic battles that are fought over the issue of venue in transnational litigation. As to the role played by negative declarations in English law *generally*, Zamir and Woolf conclude that 'on a few occasions judges appeared to have reservations about the innovation; but on the whole they have recognised its merits'[745] and Hobhouse J has observed that it is 'not uncommon that a party to a contract comes to the court and seeks a declaration that he is not bound by the contract'.[746]

4.260 In the *specific context* of transnational litigation, Lord Wilberforce, referring to Pickford LJ's oft-quoted counsel of caution in *Guaranty Trust* to the effect

---

[739] [1991] Ch 75.   [740] ibid 89.   [741] [1990] 1 Lloyd's Rep 32.

[742] ibid 36. Switzerland's accession to the Lugano Convention means that this case would not now arise by virtue of Article 21. If concurrent proceedings did, however, proceed and recognition of any English declaratory judgment was sought prior to the rendering of a Swiss judgment, the Swiss court would be bound to recognize the earlier English judgment as Article 27(3) only appears to permit the non-recognition of a foreign judgment which is irreconcilable with a judgment already *given*.

[743] See the Jenard Report [1979] OJ C59/1, 45.

[744] *The Delta* (1876) 1 PD 393, 403. This rule was reversed, however, in *Houston v Sligo* (1885) 29 ChD 448. For a valuable, if now somewhat dated, comparative account of the effect of foreign *litispendence* on domestic proceedings, see Szászy, I, *International Civil Procedure* (1967) 541–544.

[745] Zamir, I, and Woolf, H and J (n 728 above) 167.

[746] *Gulf Bank KSC v Mitsubishi Heavy Industries Ltd* [1994] 1 Lloyd's Rep 323, 327.

that negative declarations should 'hardly ever be made',[747] observed in Gilbertian vein that ' "hardly ever" is not the same as "never" '[748] and Lord Denning has stated that 'in modern times, I think that a declaration as to non-liability can be made whenever it will serve a useful purpose. I would not limit it in any way.'[749] In *Smith Kline & French Laboratories Ltd v Bloch*,[750] Ackner LJ saw nothing intrinsically objectionable about Smith Kline's application for negative declaratory relief[751] and, in *Australian Commercial Research and Development Ltd v ANZ McCaughan Merchant Bank Ltd*,[752] Browne-Wilkinson VC expressed surprise that the plaintiffs in the English proceedings had not sought a declaration of non-liability.[753] These views, at least until very recently, have not reflected the general opposition of English and some other common law courts to the use of negative declarations in transnational litigation.

2. NEGATIVE DECLARATIONS IN THE COMMON LAW

In *Guaranty Trust*,[754] a majority of the Court of Appeal held that the Court **4.261** had power to make a declaration of rights in circumstances where the plaintiff had no independent cause of action and was not seeking to enforce any positive right. The only limitations which members of the Court placed on what was an otherwise broad discretion to give declaratory relief were that a plaintiff seeking such a declaration was not to be a 'stranger to the transaction' but had to be 'interested in the subject-matter of the declaration'[755] and that 'the relief claimed must be something which it would not be unlawful or unconstitutional or inequitable for the Court to grant'.[756] Once the power to make declarations in the absence of any further or other relief had been established,[757] the question which

---

[747] [1915] 2 KB 536, 564.

[748] *Camilla Cotton Oil Co v Granadex SA* [1976] 2 Lloyd's Rep 10, 14. See also *Finnish Insurance Corporation v Protective Insurance Corporation* [1990] 1 QB 1078, 1084.

[749] *Camilla Cotton Oil Co v Granadex SA* [1975] 1 Lloyd's Rep 470, 474–475. See also *Booker v Bell* [1989] 1 Lloyd's Rep 516, 517; and *Finnish Insurance Corporation v Protective Insurance Corporation* [1990] 1 QB 1078, 1084.

[750] [1983] 2 All ER 72.

[751] ibid 82—'Counsel for Dr Bloch accepts that the court has power to grant the two declarations sought, but he claims that they are artificial declarations which are unlikely to be granted. They provide only, he claims, a procedural hook on which to hang the claim for the injunction. I cannot accept this submission. Dr Bloch having commenced his proceedings in Philadelphia, the only declaration which the English subsidiary can then properly seek must be in the nature of a declaration of non-liability. That such a declaration is permissible is clearly established in *Guaranty Trust Co of New York v Hannay & Co*' See also *Charman v WOC Offshore BV* [1993] 1 Lloyd's Rep 378, 385; *Akai Pty Ltd v People's Insurance Company* [1998] 1 Lloyd's Rep 90, 106.

[752] [1989] 3 All ER 65.   [753] ibid 67.   [754] [1915] 2 KB 536.

[755] ibid 562.   [756] ibid 572.

[757] Lest there be any doubt, this is made plain by RSC Order 15, rule 16.

then confronted the Court was as to the propriety of granting *negative* declaratory relief.

4.262 In *Guaranty Trust*, the plaintiff sought a declaration that it was not liable to the defendant on a bill of exchange. Pickford LJ expressed the view that the power to make a negative declaration existed but, in a significant caveat, counselled against its frequent exercise. He stated that negative declarations would 'hardly ever be made' and that 'in practically every case the person asking it will be left to set up his defence in the action when it is brought'.[758] He cited in support the observation of Cozens-Hardy MR in *Dyson v Attorney-General*,[759] a case in which a declaration of non-liability was in fact granted:

> I desire to guard myself against the supposition that a person who expects to be made defendant, and who prefers to be plaintiff, can, as a matter of right, attain his object by commencing an action to obtain a declaration that his opponent has no good cause of action against him. The Court may well say: 'Wait until you are attacked and then raise your defence', and may dismiss the action with costs.[760]

4.263 Both of these dicta are concerned not to allow resort to negative declaratory relief to upset the traditional pattern of litigation, namely where a plaintiff seeks to enforce or vindicate positive rights rather than seeking a privilege or immunity. The policy justification for this caution is that, as an action may never be brought against the party seeking negative declaratory relief, the exercise may be subject to abuse, represent or impose an unnecessary expense on the defendant, and constitute a waste of judicial resources. In *Re Clay*,[761] Duke LJ apprehended:

> a great danger of needless and costly controversy fomented by parties who delight in litigation ... the grave prospect [that] if any citizen who possibly supposes he may have litigation at some future time against him is to be entitled to safeguard himself and set his affairs right by making his suppositious antagonist the defendant to an action.[762]

4.264 Why the danger of possible abuse could not be guarded against by the customary expedient of a stay of action, and 'unnecessary expense' by the sanction of a costs award, is not, however, apparent.

4.265 The dicta from *Dyson v Attorney-General*, *Guaranty Trust*, and *Re Clay* cited above betray a conservative conception of *cause of action*, certainly one which is far narrower than that articulated by the great American authority, Edwin Borchard.[763] He argued that 'so long as the courts recognize in

---

[758] [1915] 2 KB 564–565.
[760] ibid 417.
[762] ibid 78–79.
[763] *The Declaratory Judgment* (2nd edn, 1941).

[759] [1911] 1 KB 410.
[761] [1919] 1 Ch 66.

the plaintiff an interest for which they will afford him protection by means of an action and a resulting judgment, they necessarily admit that he has a "cause" of action and a "right" of action'.[764] Such an interest which is worthy of protection will exist where 'a condition of affairs is disclosed which indicates the existence of a cloud upon the plaintiff's rights, a cloud which endangers his peace of mind, his freedom, his pecuniary interests'.[765] Thus, for Borchard, there was no reason to be found in the 'natural order' of litigation for discouraging actions for negative declarations. The courts were to be used for the settlement of controversies which was a larger concept than the vindication of positive rights. In line with Borchard, one might argue that while it has been customary to speak of the 'plaintiff's cause of action', it may be more realistic to speak of the 'parties' dispute'. The clarification of a party's legal position by means of a negative declaration may be just as important as any vindication of a positive right.[766]

Resort to negative declaratory proceedings will be a particularly attrac- **4.266** tive strategy where a holder of positive rights is using the threat of litigation as a tool in negotiation. Zamir and Woolf are surely right to observe that 'such a threat, which may not be carried out for a long time, can adversely affect the plaintiff's interests. It may place his title in doubt, make his financial position uncertain, and impair the course of business as much as a threatened illegal act.'[767] In this situation, judicial reluctance to allow a 'true' defendant to test the other party's rights by having a court assess the merits of possible defences in an action for a negative declaration is unwarranted. It was seen in paragraphs 3.71 ff above that the traditional English rules for the staying of proceedings loaded the dice very much in the plaintiff's favour. The traditional reluctance of English courts to afford negative declaratory relief further reinforced this bias. In *North Eastern Marine Engineering Co v Leeds Forge Co*,[768] Joyce J reflected this pro-plaintiff orientation when he stated that:

ordinarily, an intending plaintiff may postpone his action as long as he pleases, at the risk of finding himself ultimately barred by some Statute of Limitations, and he may choose his own time for commencing proceedings. He is entitled to wait until he has collected the necessary evidence, or has made such inquiries as he thinks fit, or has obtained the requisite funds or what not.[769]

An application for a negative declaration will typically not, however, alter **4.267** the nature or character of a dispute that would otherwise have been

---

[764] ibid 21. [765] ibid 20.
[766] See Zamir, . and Woolf, H and J (n 728 above) 166–168.
[767] ibid 168. [768] [1906] 1 Ch 324.
[769] ibid 329.

commenced by a statement of claim or writ and, as the United States Supreme Court recognized as long ago as 1937, what is important from the point of view of a court's jurisdiction is 'the nature of the controversy *not the method of its presentation or the particular party who presents it'*.[770] A simple action for the rescission of a contract, which need not be accompanied by a claim for damages, is nothing more than an application for negative declaratory relief. Challenges to the validity of a patent, trade mark, or registered design may be similarly viewed: if upheld they are tantamount to a declaration that particular usage will not constitute infringement; and limitation actions in admiralty, while not declarations of non-liability, are closely akin to them.

4.268 Writing at a time when no declaratory action at all was available in England and expressing some sympathy for the vulnerable position of 'natural' defendants, Lord Brougham lamented that 'here, you must wait till a party chooses to bring you into court; here, you must wait until possibly your evidence is gone'.[771] It is submitted that in choosing both a time and venue for the resolution of a dispute, a party seeking negative declaratory relief should be no more nor less constrained than its opponent would be in bringing proceedings designed to vindicate its positive rights.

4.269 With few exceptions, prior to the Court of Appeal's decision in *Messier-Dowty v Sabena SA*,[772] the negative declaration remained unfashionable and Pickford LJ's dictum in *Guaranty Trust* that 'a declaration that a person is not liable in an existing or possible action is one that will hardly ever be made'[773] continued to be cited with approval and endorsed although frequently without any adversion to just why such relief ought to be or is so infrequent.[774] In like manner, the particularly hostile attitude towards negative declaratory relief manifested by Duke LJ in *Re Clay*[775] was similarly endorsed[776] as negative declarations continued to be depre-

---

[770] *Aetna Life Insurance Co v Haworth* 300 US 227, 244 (1937) (emphasis added).

[771] *Earl of Mansfield v Stewart* (1846) 5 Bell 139, 160.

[772] [2000] 1 WLR 2040.

[773] [1915] 2 KB 536, 564.

[774] *Camilla Cotton Oil Co v Granadex SA* [1976] 2 Lloyd's Rep 10, 14; *Du Pont de Nemours & Co v Agnew (No 2)* [1988] 2 Lloyd's Rep 240, 248; *Booker v Bell* [1989] 1 Lloyd's Rep 516, 517; *Meadows Indemnity Co Ltd v Insurance Corporation of Ireland* [1989] 2 Lloyd's Rep 298, 301–302 and 307; *First National Bank of Boston v Union Bank of Switzerland* [1990] 1 Lloyd's Rep 32, 36, and 39.

[775] [1919] 1 Ch 66, 78–79.

[776] *Midland Bank plc v Laker Airways Ltd* [1986] 1 QB 689, 700–701; *The Volvox Hollandia* [1988] 2 Lloyd's Rep 361, 371; *McConnell Dowell Constructors Ltd v Lloyd's Syndicate 396* [1988] 2 NZLR 257, 282; *The Maciej Rataj* [1991] 2 Lloyd's Rep 458, 465; *Tyburn Productions Ltd v Conan Doyle* [1991] Ch 75, 89.

cated as 'artificial'[777] and 'a somewhat unattractive form of procedure',[778] one member of the Court of Appeal observing that 'the Courts should do nothing to encourage defensive or pre-emptive proceedings'.[779]

While this last statement accords with the traditional resistance to the **4.270** 'natural' order of litigation being inverted, an additional policy concern fuels the modern antipathy to negative declarations. It is particularly pertinent in the context of considering the defensive use of negative declarations in transnational litigation. Negative declaratory relief has been perceived to run counter to considerations of comity and to lend itself to the noxious practice of forum shopping. This concern has been most clearly articulated by Kerr LJ. In *First National Bank of Boston v Union Bank of Switzerland*,[780] he stated that 'to allow FNBB's claim for a declaration of non-liability to proceed against UBS would be contrary to the spirit of comity between our Courts and the Swiss Courts. In all the circumstances I have no hesitation in concluding that it is an *abuse of the process* of our Courts.'[781] In *The Volvox Hollandia*,[782] he drew attention to 'an important wider perspective', observing that 'these claims for negative declarations are a novel type of pre-emptive forum shopping . . . Claims for declarations, and in particular negative declarations, must be viewed with great caution in all situations involving possible conflicts of jurisdictions, since they obviously lend themselves to improper attempts at forum shopping.'[783]

These criticisms require close scrutiny. They now fall to be viewed in light **4.271** of Lord Woolf MR's observation in *Messier-Dowty Ltd v Sabena SA*[784] that:

The approach is pragmatic. It is not a matter of jurisdiction. It is a matter of discretion. The deployment of negative declarations should be scrutinized and their use rejected where it would serve no useful purpose. However, where a negative declaration would help to ensure that the aims of justice are achieved the Courts should not be reluctant to grant such declarations. They can and do assist in achieving justice. For example where a patient is not in a position to consent to medical treatment declarations have an important role to play. . . . While negative declarations can perform a positive role, they are an unusual remedy insofar as

---

[777] *McConnell Dowell Constructors Ltd v Lloyd's Syndicate 396* [1988] 2 NZLR 257, 268.

[778] *Charman v WOC Offshore BV* [1993] 1 Lloyd's Rep 378, 385. See also *Banque Paribas v Cargill International SA* [1992] 1 Lloyd's Rep 96, 99; *Standard Steamship Owners' P & I Association (Bermuda) Ltd v Gann* [1992] 2 Lloyd's Rep 528, 536–537.

[779] *New Hampshire Insurance Co v Strabag Bau AG* [1992] 1 Lloyd's Rep 361, 371. See also, in a slightly different context (where such a declaration was being sought in foreign proceedings) *Sohio Supply Co v Gatoil USA Inc* [1989] 1 Lloyd's Rep 588, 593 and *The Maciej Rataj* [1991] 2 Lloyd's Rep 458, 463.

[780] [1990] 1 Lloyd's Rep 32. [781] ibid 39 (emphasis added).

[782] [1988] 2 Lloyd's Rep 361. [783] ibid 371.

[784] [2000] 1 WLR 2040, 2050–2051.

they reverse the more usual roles of the parties. The natural defendant becomes the claimant and vice versa. This can result in procedural complications and potential injustice to an 'unwilling' defendant. This in itself justifies caution in extending the circumstances in which negative declarations are granted, but subject to the exercise of appropriate circumspection, there should be no reluctance to their being granted when it is useful to do so.

Negative Declarations and Comity

4.272 Claims to the effect that negative declarations run contrary to the spirit of comity and aid and abet the concerted forum shopper in its frowned-upon enterprise must be critically examined. It is important to note from the outset that such claims are, essentially, *jurisdictional* objections rather than objections to the form of action *per se*. As has been seen throughout this book, the concept of comity is one that is regularly invoked in discussions of jurisdiction in private international law. Frequently, its mere citation is used to justify the result to which end it has been invoked without a critical examination of how the concerns of comity may be compromised. Accordingly, it is important to consider in precisely what way negative declarations may offend international comity.

4.273 Unlike the use of anti-suit injunctions, it cannot be claimed that negative declarations interfere directly with foreign proceedings.[785] Rather, they are an indirect form of relief. Further, while a negative declaration does address and determine the merits of a claim unlike an anti-suit injunction, no sanction equivalent to contempt attaches to a party continuing its foreign action. In so far as a negative declaration permits any attempt to enforce a foreign judgment in that jurisdiction to be resisted, it is local in effect and the significance of negative declaratory relief for proceedings in the foreign court or indeed a third jurisdiction, at the enforcement stage, will be a matter entirely for those courts. Nor can it be said of negative declarations, as again it might be argued with regard to anti-suit injunctions, that they offend comity because they are a jurisdictional device peculiar to the common law. That is demonstrably not the case. Borchard clearly shows that the declaratory action (including the action for a negative declaration or a declaration of non-liability) has a far longer history in civil law systems than in the common law where it was a relative latecomer.[786] Indeed the Prussian *Allgemeine Gerichtsordnung* specifically provided for negative declaratory judgments to be given as early as 1793.[787] Moreover, that countries outside the common law tradition do

---

[785] cf *Aerospatiale* [1987] AC 871, 893.   [786] Borchard, E (n 763 above) 101–125.
[787] 'When anybody knows that another is making a claim upon him which he does not wish to concede, he is privileged to appear as a plaintiff against the pretender and assert the error and invalidity of the alleged claim', cited ibid 101 n 64.

not regard negative declaratory actions as offensive to comity is evidenced by a number of multiple suit cases in recent years in which the foreign proceedings have been for negative declaratory relief.[788] Such relief is evidently also widely available in the United States.[789]

Negative declarations *can* run contrary to the spirit of comity in so far as **4.274** they may contribute to a situation where multiple suits arise from the one incident, thus raising the possibility of inconsistent judgments. It may be doubted, however, whether this particular form of relief should be held accountable for such a situation and therefore discouraged as a matter of course. As was seen more fully in paragraphs 3.84 ff above, the difficulties of multiple litigation potentially arise whenever a defendant has a cross-claim or seeks indemnification or contribution from a third party or co-defendant. Just as a party who has a cross-claim is entitled to make it in a forum of its choosing, so also a party anxious to clarify its legal position should enjoy a similar right. If it is the case that the right to initiate litigation should not be the exclusive preserve of those parties seeking to vindicate positive rights, then the problems of multiple litigation must be addressed in a way that does not simply entail the emasculation of a long-established and potentially useful form of action. There is no valid reason, in the name of comity, to penalize one prospective party and not the other in relation to matters which are as strategically critical in a transnational dispute as the timing and venue for litigation.[790]

Negative Declarations and Forum Shopping

Turning to the claim that negative declarations lend themselves to **4.275** forum shopping, it has been said that, where proceedings are threatened abroad, 'the court will watch with special caution actions commenced for declarations of non liability by parties who are not

[788] *The Stolt Marmaro* [1985] 2 Lloyd's Rep 428 (Italy); Case 144/86, *Gubisch Maschinenfabrik KG v Palumbo* [1987] ECR 4861 (Italy); *Commercial Bank of the Near East plc v A, B, C and D* [1989] 2 Lloyd's Rep 319 (Greece); *Kloekner & Co AG v Gatoil Overseas Inc* [1990] 1 Lloyd's Rep 177 (West Germany); *Marc Rich v Società Italiana Impianti PA* (11 November 1991) (Italy); *The Maciej Rataj* [1992] 2 Lloyd's Rep 552 (Netherlands); *Polly Peck International v Citibank NA* The Times, 20 October 1993 (Switzerland); *IP Metal Ltd v Ruote OZ SpA* [1993] 2 Lloyd's Rep 60 (Italy); *Kinnear v Falconfilms NV* (27 January 1994) (Spain). See also *The Daeyang Honey* (1991) 109 ALR 120 (Japan) and *China Trade & Development Corp v MV Choong Yong* 837 F 2d 33 (2nd Cir, 1987) (Korea).

[789] See, for example, *Du Pont de Nemours & Co v Agnew (No 2)* [1988] 2 Lloyd's Rep 240; *Sohio Supply Co v Gatoil (USA) Inc* [1989] 1 Lloyd's Rep 588; *Arkwright Mutual Insurance Co v Bryanston Insurance Co Ltd* [1990] 2 QB 649; *Standard Steamship Owners' P & I Association (Bermuda) Ltd v Gann* [1992] 2 Lloyd's Rep 528.

[790] *Messier-Dowty Ltd v Sabena SA* [2000] 1 WLR 2040, 2049; see also *Youell Kara Mara Shipping* [2000] 2 Lloyd's Rep 102, 124–125.

natural plaintiffs'.[791] Negative declarations have been deprecated because they are seen to be 'a method of making a pre-emptive strike so as to secure jurisdiction in the Court preferred by the plaintiff'.[792] The word 'pre-emptive' is loaded. Common sense strongly suggests that a party would not go to the trouble and expense of commencing proceedings for negative declaratory relief unless a 'live' dispute or real controversy between two or more parties existed.[793] This is especially the case when it is appreciated that, by commencing proceedings, that party assumes the burden of proof. Again it must be asked why a party under a legal cloud because of alleged claims against it should not have the same opportunity to determine the timing of and venue for the resolution of the dispute as its opponent. Moreover, the conceptual elision of negative declaratory relief with forum shopping does not necessarily follow. If forum shopping is conceived of as being, at bottom, the commencement of litigation in a forum other than the or a natural forum,[794] *the form of action of the proceedings simply does not bear on this question* and the courts must resist the temptation to treat applications for negative declaratory relief with the automatic hostility that has pervaded many of the recent cases in which such relief has been sought. Hirst J appreciated this in *The Standard Steamship Owners' Protection and Indemnity Association (Bermuda) Ltd v Gann*,[795] where he declined to discount the significance of negative declaratory proceedings which had been commenced in the United States because it was 'impossible to say that San Diego is an inappropriate forum'.[796]

4.276 There will, of course, be no occasion for the grant of negative declaratory relief when it is applied for in a forum other than the natural forum. In such circumstances, a decision to deny it is entirely appropriate, but it is important to note that such a decision will be one based on *jurisdictional* considerations rather than simple hostility to this form of action.[797] As was seen in paragraphs 3.96 ff above, not all commentators or courts accept with equanimity the proposition that, when an English court considers whether it is the natural forum, it should take into account proceedings abroad, especially where they are for negative declaratory

---

[791] *Asher v Goldman Sachs and Co* (21 October 1991), cited in Zamir, I and Woolf, H and J (n 728 above) 170, n 65.

[792] *Charman v WOC Offshore BV* [1993] 2 Lloyd's Rep 551, 558.

[793] If, of course, a court considered the dispute hypothetical or the proceedings vexatious, they could be readily struck out as an abuse of process in the court's inherent jurisdiction.

[794] *Boys v Chaplin* [1971] AC 356, 401; see also *The Albaforth* [1984] 2 Lloyd's Rep 91, 97.

[795] [1992] 2 Lloyd's Rep 528.

[796] ibid 537.

[797] This was the classical approach adopted by Lord Wilberforce in *Camilla Cotton Oil Co v Granadex SA* [1976] 2 Lloyd's Rep 10,13–14. See also *Chase v Ram Technical Services Ltd* [2000] 2 Lloyd's Rep 418.

relief. It was argued in that chapter that, in accordance with the demands of comity and in light of the strong policy in favour of minimizing the scope for inconsistent decisions, such an approach is unwarranted. Moreover, it should be appreciated that, where negative declaratory relief is sought in the natural forum, in the broadest sense of this concept, far from being a manifestation of forum shopping, such relief may in certain circumstances even provide an antidote to it and advance the desirable goal of resolving all disputes arising out of one incident in the same forum. Indeed, in spite of the majority's rhetoric to the contrary,[798] the application for a negative declaration in *The Volvox Hollandia* may be seen in this light.

The factual background to *The Volvox Hollandia*[799] was somewhat **4.277** complex. C contracted with S to carry out certain work in a North Sea oilfield. The contract included English choice of law and jurisdiction clauses and provided that any subcontracting of the work was to include such clauses. S subcontracted with V, a Dutch corporation which owned the *Volvox Hollandia*, a suction dredger, to carry out part of the work. S entered into a further contract with G to provide 'high-tech' equipment and personnel. This contract was also governed by English law and contained a London arbitration clause. In carrying out dredging operations, the *Volvox Hollandia* damaged a pipeline, said to be owned by C. In March 1985, V instituted proceedings in the District Court of Rotterdam with a view to limiting its liability as shipowners under the Brussels Convention on the Limitation of Liability of Owners of Seagoing Ships (1957). If V could establish that the damage to property had occurred without its actual fault or privity, then its maximum liability would be capped in accordance with the Dutch limitation figure which was somewhere between £290,000 and £375,000.[800] Both C and S were invited by a Judge-commissary appointed by the Rotterdam Court to participate in the limitation proceedings. C declined; S filed a claim but simultaneously contested the Rotterdam Court's jurisdiction. Both subsequently commenced proceedings in England against both V and G, seeking against V, *inter alia*, a declaration that it was not entitled to limit its liability. C claimed damages of £4.5 million. Writs in these proceedings were served out of the jurisdiction and V sought to have service of these writs set aside or, in the alternative, to have C and S's actions stayed.[801]

---

[798] It will be recalled that Kerr LJ described the application for a negative declaration in this case as a 'blatant' example of forum shopping: [1988] 2 Lloyd's Rep 361, 371.

[799] [1988] 2 Lloyd's Rep 361.

[800] [1987] 2 Lloyd's Rep 520, 523.

[801] The English actions were instituted prior to the coming into force of the Brussels Convention with the consequence that Article 21 dealing with cases of *lis alibi pendens* was not implicated.

4.278   At first instance, Staughton J refused to set aside service or stay the actions.[802] When pressed with the argument that 'it is not the practice of the English Courts to grant negative declarations', Staughton J stated that a case by case approach should be followed and that 'it is particularly relevant to consider whether there is an existing and live issue between the parties on the topic as to which a declaration is sought'.[803] He went on to say:

> The present English actions, if they stood alone, would in my view be peculiarly appropriate for the grant of negative declarations, should they be justified on the facts. As I understand the Admiralty procedure, otherwise judgment might be given in favour of Conoco or Saipem for £4.5m, apparently concluding that VO2 were liable for that amount; but VO2 could then start a limitation action. There being only one claim arising out of the accident, it seems to me appropriate that Conoco and Saipem should ask the Court to grant negative declarations, thereby *forcing* VO2 to put forward their case for limitation of liability in those actions.[804]

4.279   Of course the whole point of V's attempt to stay the English actions was that they did not 'stand alone'. An action on the very question of whether V was entitled to limit its liability had been commenced prior to the English actions and both C and S had been invited to participate, S accepting the invitation. In the final analysis, Staughton J's decision not to stay the English proceedings for negative declaratory relief was based on the fact that all four parties to the dispute had agreed to English jurisdiction clauses.[805]

4.280   It will be recalled that, when this case went on appeal, Kerr LJ described C and S's actions as a 'blatant' case of forum shopping,[806] a judgment which, on the surface at least, seems a little unfair in light of the English choice of court clauses.[807] This assessment is also a little curious when one considers that Kerr LJ stated that counsel for the shipowners 'rightly abandoned any attempt to deprive the plaintiffs of their right to pursue

---

[802] The shipowners initially attempted to have the entire English proceedings stayed, including the issues of liability and quantum, but in the Court of Appeal only sought to have service set aside in relation to the claims for negative declarations: [1988] 2 Lloyd's Rep 361, 365 and 377.

[803] [1987] 2 Lloyd's Rep 520, 528.

[804] ibid (emphasis added).

[805] ibid 529—'So far as the claim by Saipem against VO2 is concerned . . . it arises directly out of the contractual relationship which incorporated those terms. Other claims, by Conoco or against Geosite, have to be laid in tort; but they all stem from arrangements which contemplate English law and an English forum.'

[806] [1988] 2 Lloyd's Rep 361, 371.

[807] Collins, LA (n 320 above) 280 has observed that 'this judgment was somewhat harsh on the plaintiffs. The lower court had placed great emphasis on the fact that all four parties to the English litigation had expressly agreed (though not in all cases with each other) that disputes would be determined in England and by English law.'

their claims on liability and quantum in London'.[808] On this logic, the plaintiffs in the English proceedings were not forum shopping in relation to their principal claims but were severely criticized for seeking to have the same court determine whether the shipowners' liability was to be limited. The issues were seen by the majority as discrete and appropriate to be tried by different courts notwithstanding their closely related factual underpinnings.[809]

Staughton J at first instance had acknowledged that it was possible and **4.281** indeed sometimes advantageous to sever the question of the shipowner's liability from questions of actual fault or privity which affect a shipowner's right to limit liability, especially in a case where multiple claims were made against the shipowner.[810] One of the reasons for this is that a decree of limitation under the Convention is good against the world whereas if limitation is simply pleaded by way of defence, as it may be,[811] any finding will be binding only as between the parties. Where, however, there is effectively only one claim available against the shipowner, the significance of the non-conclusive nature of pleading limitation by way of defence to liability proceedings as opposed to proceeding under the Convention disappears. There need only be one hearing of all issues. Both Staughton J at first instance and Dillon and Nicholls LJJ in the Court of Appeal considered this to be a single claim case[812] and in such circumstances Dillon LJ expressed the opinion that while:

it must follow, in a multiple claims case, where there are several claims of several claimants arising out of the occurrence, and the question whether the shipowner can limit his liability must be decided in an action in rem to bind all claimants, that the shipowner who alone can start such an action can choose the forum in which to start it. But I do not see that it follows that the shipowner has an overriding or unchallengeable right to choose the forum in a single claim case where the issue of limitation and all other issues can be decided in proceedings in personam between the claimant and the shipowner. That would be to give the shipowner a special procedural privilege, of deciding the forum, which is not necessary to give effect to his right to limit in a single claim case, and which other litigants involved in litigation in personam do not have.[813]

On the facts of this case, it is clear that all the issues could have been heard **4.282** in Holland but that would have been a forum chosen by the defendant whose action to limit liability, somewhat ironically, was quite closely akin

---

[808] [1988] 2 Lloyd's Rep 360, 365.

[809] Dillon LJ in dissent stated at 377 that 'I agree with the Judge [Staughton J] in attaching importance to having all aspects of the dispute tried in the same Court at the same time.'

[810] [1987] 2 Lloyd's Rep 520, 527.

[811] See RSC Order 18, rule 22.

[812] [1987] 2 Lloyd's Rep 520, 527; [1988] 2 Lloyd's Rep 361, 376 and 378 but cf 367.

[813] ibid 376.

to an action for a negative declaration.[814] At first instance, Staughton J observed that what was described by Dillon LJ as a 'special procedural privilege' could be subject to abuse by shipowners and spoke of the possible emergence of limitation havens.[815] His reasoning, and that of Dillon LJ, seems to be that if[816] England was the natural forum for the principal proceedings as to liability and quantum, then it was inherently desirable to have all proceedings heard together, and if the claim for negative declaratory relief had the effect of forcing the shipowners to put forward their case for limitation of liability in the English proceedings, then that was in fact a consequence to be welcomed.[817] The majority decision and its refusal to countenance the grant of negative declaratory relief, predicated as it was on a perception of and aversion to 'forum shopping', had the somewhat ironic effect, on the other hand, that proceedings arising from the same underlying facts would be heard in two jurisdictions, with the possibility of inconsistent decisions. In an important respect, a decision to grant negative declaratory relief in this case would have had a virtually identical effect as the Privy Council's decision in *Aerospatiale*[818] which, as has been seen, conscious of the possibility of multiple and ongoing litigation and the unseemly possibility of inconsistent findings on central facts, restrained foreign proceedings to prevent such an outcome.[819]

4.283 One transnational context in which negative declaratory relief has been perceived to be entirely appropriate is where an insurer needs to know whether an obligation to indemnify an assured on a particular English contract of insurance arises. The provision of guidance by the courts to a

---

[814] Conversely, the negative declaration in the English proceedings was dissimilar to those sought in the other cases under discussion in this section in that it was not concerned with the applicant's own liability but rather that of the plaintiff in the Dutch proceedings.

[815] [1987] 2 Lloyd's Rep 520, 529. The facts disclosed in *The Maciej Rataj* [1991] 2 Lloyd's Rep 458 provide an illustration of how particular ports can become such havens. In this case, the liability of the owners of the *Tatry* was limited to approximately US$1.25 million in The Netherlands whereas in the United Kingdom this limit was US$4.225 million. This discrepancy arose because of the fact that, at the time of the commencement of the Dutch proceedings, The Netherlands had not but the United Kingdom had adopted the International Convention on Limitation of Liability of Maritime Claims 1976. In this context, the words of Lord Simon of Glaisdale in *The Atlantic Star* [1974] AC 436, 475 bear recollection—' "Forum-shopping" is, indeed, inescapably involved with the concept of maritime lien and the action in rem. Every port is automatically an admiralty emporium.'

[816] Which was ultimately accepted.

[817] [1987] 2 Lloyd's Rep 520, 527; [1988] 2 Lloyd's Rep 361, 377.

[818] [1987] AC 871.

[819] It was the failure to apply for just such relief that seems to have influenced Nicholls LJ in his decision to uphold the appeal in *The Volvox Hollandia*: see [1988] 2 Lloyd's Rep 361, 379. In this he reflected the approach adopted by the Court of Appeal in *Guaranty Trust*, which was to decline negative declaratory relief if a case for restraining foreign proceedings by injunction had not been made out.

plaintiff in relation to its immediate legal responsibilities will dictate whether the insurer should support the defence of any action brought against the assured.[820] In *Overseas Union Insurance Ltd v New Hampshire Insurance Co*,[821] a negative declaration was sought in a standard indemnity dispute: in the French proceedings, payments were sought under a reinsurance contract while the English proceedings were simply for declarations of non-liability. A negative declaration was given by Gatehouse J in *Booker v Bell*.[822] In granting this relief, his Honour observed that 'the declaration sought here is only one of contingent non-liability; it is not one which in any way seeks to determine the issues of fact which arise in the Californian action'.[823] Thus the twin evils of inconsistent decisions and a rush to judgment were not seen to arise in this context and no consequent threat to comity was entailed in the entertainment of proceedings for declaratory relief. Courts should exercise some caution, however, in arriving at the conclusion that an issue is so discrete that the entertainment of a suit for negative declaratory relief will not contribute to the possibility of inconsistent decisions. That is not to say that, where the jurisdiction in which such relief has been applied for is the natural forum, it should automatically be denied. That course has been criticized. It is simply to point out, as was observed in paragraphs 3.96 ff above, that the 'natural forum' may be different if an issue is seen globally, as it were, rather than hived off.

3. Negative Declarations and Council Regulation 44/2001

The burden of the examination of negative declaratory relief thus far has **4.284** been to examine and criticize the felt antagonism which was until recently ventured by English and Commonwealth courts to the negative declaration. To recapitulate, two types of objection have been isolated: the first being the 'artificial' nature of the form of action; and the second, the jurisdictional difficulties it is seen to create, specifically in the form of concurrent actions and the possibility of inconsistent decisions. The first objection is outmoded and no good reason exists for holding 'defendants' slave to the procedural tradition that they must wait to be sued and thus forfeit potentially important advantages relating to the venue and timing

---

[820] See *Insurance Corporation of Ireland v Strombus* [1985] 2 Lloyd's Rep 138, 144; see also *HIB v Guardian Insurance* [1997] 1 Lloyd's Rep 412, 416–418.

[821] Case C–351/89 [1991] ECR I–3317.

[822] [1989] 1 Lloyd's Rep 516.

[823] ibid 517. cf, for example, *Camilla Cotton Oil Co v Granadex SA* [1976] 2 Lloyd's Rep 10, 13, where Lord Wilberforce observed that the 'object of the Swiss proceedings was to establish the responsibility of the respondents for the liabilities of C & S International Ltd under the old contracts. The object of par 1 of the English writs is the exact converse. It is to establish the non-responsibility of the respondents for these same liabilities.'

of litigation. In relation to the second objection (and in light of the response to the first), it is an incomplete and inappropriate strategy to seek to address the undoubtedly difficult problems of forum shopping and concurrent transnational litigation by denying applications for negative declaratory relief in appropriate cases, that is where this form of relief is sought in the natural forum. Even if this view be doubted, where negative declaratory relief is sought in circumstances where an English court's jurisdiction is founded under the Council Regulation or the Lugano Convention, the second general objection to this form of action evaporates because the problems it is said to create are specifically addressed by the Regulation and the Convention.

4.285 As seen in paragraphs 3.49 ff above, the Regulation and the Convention eschew any use of the common law concept of the 'natural forum' in the allocation of jurisdiction among member and contracting states. While there remains *some* scope for forum shopping under the Regulation and the Convention,[824] not only are the possibilities more limited than under the individual states' traditional rules of jurisdiction but also, and more importantly, it may be doubted whether the pejorative connotations which the term 'forum shopping' typically carries under the common law tradition are appropriate or indeed legitimate in this context. The Schlosser Report states that:

> Where the courts of several states have jurisdiction, the plaintiff has deliberately been given a right of choice, which should not be weakened by the application of the doctrine of *forum conveniens*.[825]

4.286 In the face of such considerations, Collins has argued that, where an English court has jurisdiction under the Convention (and, now, the Regulation), it should nonetheless refuse to entertain proceedings for negative declaratory relief in what he describes as 'forum shopping cases'.[826] What constitutes a 'forum shopping case' in the context of the Regulation's precisely wrought scheme of jurisdictional allocation must be extremely problematic. In *First National Bank of Boston v Union Bank of Switzerland*,[827] Kerr LJ defined forum shopping as 'an attempt to persuade the Courts of one country to arrogate to themselves a jurisdiction which belongs *more properly* to Courts of another country'.[828] As neither the

---

[824] See, for example, Pearl, S, 'Forum Shopping in the EEC' (1987) 15 International Business Lawyer 391; Bogaert,PWL, 'Ius Vigilantibus: Tactics of Forum Shopping under the EEC Judgments Convention' [1988] ECLR 1; Geddes, A, 'Forum Shopping in the EEC' (1988) 138 NLJ 542.

[825] [1979] OJ C59/71, 97.

[826] (n 320 above) 287.

[827] [1990] 1 Lloyd's Rep 32.

[828] ibid 38 (emphasis added).

Regulation nor the Convention make any value judgment as between *available* forums, it is difficult to see how a plaintiff's choice of forum could ever be deprecated as illegitimate forum shopping.

In *Charman v WOC Offshore BV*,[829] Hirst J was astute to the important **4.287** difference between cases where negative declaratory relief was sought under jurisdiction prescribed by the applicable Convention, on the one hand, and under ordinary common law rules, on the other. He distinguished Kerr LJ's caustic remarks in *The Volvox Hollandia* concerning the abuse of negative declaratory applications for the purposes of forum shopping[830] as inapplicable to cases arising under the Conventions where service on the defendant was as of right.[831] This distinction was well made and it is submitted that the exercise of discretion to decline to entertain an application for negative declaratory relief based on what are essentially *jurisdictional* grounds is anathema to one of the central aspirations of the Convention. Especially conscious of the common law tradition of taking a discretionary approach to the exercise of jurisdiction, the Schlosser Report made it plain that:

States are not only entitled to exercise jurisdiction in accordance with the provisions laid down in Title 2; they are also obliged to do so. A plaintiff must be sure which court has jurisdiction. He should not have to waste his time and money risking that the court concerned may consider itself less competent than another.[832]

While an English court's refusal to grant negative declaratory relief may not amount to an assessment that it is 'less competent' than a court in which a positive right of action may be vindicated, the philosophy evident in the Schlosser Report as to the exercise of jurisdiction remains germane.

It is unclear what inherent power an English court retains to decline juris- **4.288** diction under the Conventions.[833] Section 49 of the Civil Jurisdiction and Judgments Act 1982 is not very illuminating. It provides that:

Nothing in this Act shall prevent any court in the United Kingdom from staying, sisting, striking out or dismissing any proceedings before it, on the ground of *forum non conveniens* or otherwise, where to do so is not inconsistent with the 1968 Convention.

[829] [1993] 1 Lloyd's Rep 378, reversed by the Court of Appeal on other grounds—[1993] 2 Lloyd's Rep 551.
[830] See paras 4.198 and 4.270 above.
[831] [1993] 1 Lloyd's Rep 378, 385 and [1993] 2 Lloyd's Rep 551, 558.
[832] Schlosser Report [1979] OJ C59/71, 97. See also *Aiglon SA v Gau Shan Co Ltd* [1993] 1 Lloyd's Rep 164, 174–175.
[833] This question was referred to the Court of Justice in *Re Harrods (Buenos Aires) Ltd* [1992] Ch 72 but that case has now settled.

4.289 In *Kongress Agentur Hagen GmbH v Zeehaghe BV*,[834] the European Court of Justice emphasized that it was 'necessary to draw a clear distinction between jurisdiction and the conditions governing the admissibility of an action'.[835] Matters relating to the latter consideration were for the *lex fori* as it was stated that the Brussels Convention was not intended to unify the procedural rules of Contracting States. The distinction between procedure and jurisdiction is of paramount importance in the context of a discussion of the availability of negative declaratory relief in the scheme of Council Regulation 44/2001. Building upon this distinction, it remains open to an English court to strike out proceedings for negative declaratory relief which are entirely hypothetical or of the kind apprehended by Duke LJ in *Re Clay*[836] and this is the case notwithstanding the fact that it may involve the exercise of discretion. It is only where it is proposed to exercise discretion on account of what are fundamentally *jurisdictional* objections to the form of relief sought that such discretion is improperly exercised.

4.290 In the context of Council Regulation 44/2001, the 'mechanics' of negative declaratory relief are somewhat simpler because there is very little scope for multiple proceedings arising out of the same events. As seen in paragraphs 3.25 ff above, the Regulation contains, in Article 27, a somewhat crude but undoubtedly clear-cut mechanism specifically addressed to the problem of multiple proceedings. In the words of the European Court of Justice, the very purpose of Article 21 (and, now, Article 27 of the Regulation) is 'in the interests of the proper administration of justice within the Community, to prevent parallel proceedings before the Courts of different Contracting States and to avoid conflicts between decisions which might result therefrom'.[837] What is critical is the timing of the institution of proceedings for such relief.

4.291 In this context, the strategic value to 'defendants' of seeking negative declaratory relief is clearly demonstrated by the decision of the Court of Justice in *The Tatry*.[838] In this case, the owners of the vessel *Tatry* brought an action in Rotterdam seeking a declaration that they were not liable or not fully liable to certain cargo owners for contamination of a cargo of soya bean oil. Subsequent to the commencement of this action, various cargo owners (including some of those against whom the Dutch proceedings had been brought) brought an action in England, initially *in rem*, against a sister ship of the *Tatry* (the *Maciej Rataj*), and then, as a result of

---

[834] Case C–365/88 [1990] ECR I–1845.
[835] ibid 1865.
[836] See para 4.198 above.
[837] Case 144/86, *Gubisch Maschinenfabrik KG v Palumbo* [1987] ECR 4861, 4874.
[838] Case C–406/92, [1995] 1 Lloyd's Rep 302.

acknowledgement of service of the writ, *in personam*, against the shipowners, seeking damages in relation to the contamination of the cargo. For whatever reason, strategic or substantive, the cargo owners clearly desired to have the dispute resolved in England rather than the shipowners' preferred forum, The Netherlands.

When this case came before the European Court of Justice, one of the **4.292** questions for consideration was whether an action for a negative declaration of a kind brought in the Dutch proceedings involved the same 'cause of action' within the meaning of Article 21 of the Brussels Convention[839] as an action seeking to have the defendants held liable for causing loss and claiming damages.[840] The Court had little hesitation in answering the question in the affirmative. This decision was consistent with the Court's earlier decision in *Gubisch Maschinenfabrik KG v Palumbo*,[841] a case which was the converse of *The Tatry* in that Italian proceedings for negative declaratory relief were commenced after German proceedings for breach of contract. In *Gubisch*, the Court rejected a literal interpretation of the terms of Article 21 of the Brussels Convention (the equivalent to Article 27 of the Regulation) and interpreted 'same cause of action' as meaning based on 'the same contractual [or legal] relationship'[842] rather than any narrower insistence upon *identity* of cause of action, in the sense of form of relief sought.

The effect of the decision in *The Tatry* was that the second seised (English) **4.293** court was required to decline jurisdiction. Thus, in the context of the Regulation, and assuming that the other predicate of Article 27 is made out, namely the involvement of the 'same parties' in both sets of proceedings,[843] commencement of an action for negative declaratory relief prior

---

[839] Article 21 provided that 'where proceedings involving the same cause of action and between the same parties are brought in the Courts of different Contracting States, any court other than the court first seised shall of its own motion decline jurisdiction in favour of that court'.

[840] When this question first arose in the English proceedings (*The Maciej Rataj* [1991] 2 Lloyd's Rep 458, 465), Sheen J refused to characterize the Dutch action for negative declaratory relief as involving a 'cause of action' on the basis that the applicants for such relief were not claiming any 'remedy'. He stated that 'it is a complete misuse of language to say that the shipowners have a cause of action. They have no cause to commence an action . . . In effect they are asking a court to declare that neither party has a cause of action.'

[841] Case C–144/86 [1987] ECR I–4861.

[842] ibid 4875.

[843] On the meaning of 'the same parties', another issue which the European Court was asked to determine in *The Tatry*, it was held that 'on a proper construction of Article 21 of the Convention, where two actions involve the same cause of action and some but not all of the parties to the second action are the same as the parties to the action commenced earlier in another Contracting State, the second court seised is required to decline jurisdiction only to the extent to which the parties to the proceedings before it are also parties to the action previously commenced; it does not prevent the proceedings from continuing between the other parties'.

to any action for positive relief being commenced in another member state will determine the jurisdictional battle. In the words of Lord Woolf, in the application of the Regulation, 'the correct approach is to treat negative declarations . . . in exactly the same way as claims for positive relief are treated'.[844]

VI. IGNORING FOREIGN PROCEEDINGS

4.294 The final strategy open to a party the 'victim' of a plaintiff's forum shopping is simply to ignore the foreign proceedings. Such a course will only be practicable in circumstances where the defendant does not and does not propose to have assets in the foreign jurisdiction. Otherwise, of course, execution would simply be levied against those assets based upon the default judgment. However, where a defendant has no assets in the foreign jurisdiction, orthodoxy has it that such a defendant may insulate itself from the effects of the foreign judgment by simply ignoring the foreign proceedings.[845] With the exception of Canada, such a judgment will not be enforced in a common law court if the foreign court or tribunal lacked jurisdiction in the international sense and refusal by the defendant to submit to proceedings will deprive the foreign court of such jurisdiction. As a practical matter, such a course is unlikely to be attractive to large commercial enterprises. Apart from the fact that, with the explosion of multinational business activity, such corporations are increasingly likely to have highly diversified asset portfolios which may be vulnerable to enforcement of any judgment in that jurisdiction, the existence of an outstanding foreign judgment, even if founded upon a widely criticized basis of exorbitant jurisdiction, will constitute an uninviting contingent liability for the company. The contingency in this sense is the fact that the company, or any corporate successor, may wish to transact business in the foreign state at a subsequent time and the outstanding judgment will constitute at the least an embarrassment (always capable of exploitation by an unsatisfied judgment creditor cognizant of the power of adverse publicity) and, at worst, a major financial obstacle to this course.

---

[844] *Messier-Dowty Ltd v Sabena SA* [2000] 1 WLR 2040, 2049. See also in the context of the Convention for the International Carriage of Goods by Road, *Andrew Merzario Ltd v Internationale Spedition Leitner Gesellschaft GmbH* [2001] 1 Lloyd's Rep 490.

[845] North, PM and Fawcett, JJ, *Cheshire and North's Private International Law* (13th edn, 1999) 412; see also 422–423.

1. THREATS TO THE STRATEGY—I

The first impediment to the orthodox course of ignoring foreign proceed- **4.295**
ings with impunity is presented by Council Regulation 44/2001 and the
Lugano Convention. As seen in paragraphs 3.25 ff above, these instruments do nothing less than revolutionize the method of enforcement of
judgments within the member and contracting states and while, for
parties domiciled in those states, there are essential safeguards which,
inter alia, are contained in the rules for the assumption of jurisdiction, for
non-European Union or non-EFTA domiciliaries the rules may work great
hardship.[846] An example best illustrates this. Assume a Canadian
company has a contract with a French company in relation to work to be
carried out in Canada. A dispute arises and the French company
commences proceedings in France under Article 14 of the French Civil
Code which provides that any French plaintiff may sue a foreign defendant in the French courts regardless of the fact that, apart from the plaintiff's nationality, the case lacks any connection with France. Any judgment
given by the French courts will be enforceable in all other member
states[847] so that, even if the Canadian defendant did not have any assets
in France but did have some in Germany, these would be vulnerable on
account of the French judgment. Even if the contract in question
contained an exclusive jurisdiction clause for the Canadian courts, a
French decision suggests that the French courts would still assume jurisdiction.[848] It is plain that a judgment given in these even more extreme
circumstances would also be enforceable against the defendant's assets in
other member states for Article 35 of the Regulation provides that the
jurisdiction of the court of the state in which the judgment was given may
not be reviewed at the enforcement stage in another member state and
that this state's public policy may not be invoked to object to the original
court's exercise of jurisdiction.

2. THREATS TO THE STRATEGY—II

While the perils evident in ignoring proceedings commenced in the courts **4.296**
of a member state of the European Union or a Contracting State to the

---

[846] See, for example, Pryles MC and Trindade, F (1974) 48 ALJ 185; Collins, LA (ed) (n 24
above) 49–51; North, PM and Fawcett, JJ ibid 440–442.
[847] With the exception of those which have entered into a convention with a third state
under Article 72 of the Regulation and Article 59 of the Lugano Convention, providing for
the non-recognition (and therefore non-enforcement) of judgments given by the courts of
another member or contracting state against a domiciliary of the third state based upon the
assertion of one of the exorbitant bases of jurisdiction enumerated in Article 3 of the
Regulation and Convention.
[848] *Bruno v Soc Citibank* Ct App Versailles 1991, noted 1992 Rev Crit 333 and referred to in
Collins, LA (ed) (n 24 above) 432 n 66.

Lugano Convention have been clear for some time, a more recent impediment to the traditional orthodoxy of leaving foreign proceedings to go by
default has emerged. It may be tracked indirectly to the decision of the
Supreme Court of Canada in *Morguard Investments Ltd v de Savoye*
('*Morguard*')[849] which has been taken to establish that where foreign
proceedings have been commenced in a jurisdiction having a 'real and
substantial connection' to the dispute, any judgment may be enforced in
Canada *notwithstanding* the defendant's non-appearance. This approach
has been accurately described as 'radically different'.[850]

4.297 The reason why the word 'indirectly' is used in the previous paragraph
relates to the fact that *Morguard* was a decision delivered in the context of
an attempt to enforce an Albertan judgment in British Columbia, so that
questions of Canadian constitutional law and federalism inevitably
entered the picture.[851] The decision did not involve issues of transnational
recognition and enforcement of judgments. That having been said,
however, notwithstanding the peculiarly Canadian considerations which
informed it, La Forest J in *Morguard* leaves one with the impression that
his imaginative judgment was intended for both a larger audience and a
wider application.[852]

4.298 Certainly lower courts in Canada have taken the view that *Morguard* was
not solely intended to apply to the recognition and enforcement of judgments from other Canadian provinces. In *Moses v Shore Boat Builders*,[853]
the British Columbia Court of Appeal explained its translation to the
transnational context in terms of modern requirements of comity:

> The principles of *Emanuel v Symon* are out of keeping with the modern under-
> standing of the principle of comity. Modern rules of international law must
> accommodate the flow of wealth, skills and people across state lines and promote
> international commerce.'[854]

4.299 In *Clarke v Lo Bianco*,[855] Josephson J of the Supreme Court of British
Columbia stated that 'as the foreign judgment emanates from the State of

---

[849] [1990] 3 SCR 1077.

[850] North, P and Fawcet, JJ (n 845 above) 422.

[851] 'In short, the rules of comity or private international law as they apply between the
provinces must be shaped to conform to the federal structure of the Constitution': [1990] 3
SCR 1077, 1101.

[852] He states, for example, that the 'business community operates in a world economy and
we correctly speak of a world community . . . Accommodating the flow of wealth, skills and
people across state lines has now become imperative. Under these circumstances, our
approach to the recognition and enforcement of foreign judgements would appear ripe for
reappraisal.' ibid 1098.

[853] (1993) DLR (4th) 654.   [854] ibid 667.

[855] (1991) 84 DLR (4th) 244.

California rather than a sister province, the rationale outlined in *Morguard* may be less forceful, but it is nonetheless compelling'[856] and foreign default judgments have been enforced in Canada from Alaska,[857] Arizona,[858] California,[859] Connecticut,[860] Oklahoma,[861] Florida,[862] the United States District Court for the Eastern District of Michigan,[863] and England.[864]

All courts have emphasized that the circumstances of the defendant's **4.300** contacts with the State giving judgment made it eminently fair that such judgments be recognized and enforced in Canada. In two cases, the view is adopted that the defendants impliedly submitted not (obviously) to the foreign proceedings but rather to the particular State's legal system.[865] In others, the emphasis has been more on the connection between the action and the State giving judgment, as opposed to the defendant and the State.[866] Disapproval has also been intimated at endeavours to 'shelter' behind the orthodox common law rules in order to escape liability[867] and the defendants in *Beals v Saldanha*[868] relied on advice that a Florida judgment obtained by default could not be enforced in Ontario, to their very great cost.

Perhaps the most striking example of the impact of the *Morguard* doctrine **4.301** on the enforcement of foreign default judgments is provided by *James Stoddard v Accupress Manufacturing Ltd*,[869] a case in which a Connecticut judgment for US $1,117,529 was held to be enforceable in British Columbia against a corporate defendant that had no employee nor office in Connecticut at any relevant time. Its only connection with Connecticut was that it sold and delivered a hydraulic press brake to the plaintiff's employers in that State. The plaintiff was injured while operating the

---

[856] ibid 252.

[857] *Moses v Shore Boatbuilders Ltd* [1992] 5 WWR 282; (1993) 106 DLR (4th) 654.

[858] *Minkler & Kirschbaum v Sheppard* (1991) 60 BCLR (2d) 360.

[859] *Clarke v Lo Bianco* (1991) 84 DLR (4th) 244; *McMickle v van Staaten* (1992) 93 DLR (4th) 74.

[860] *James Stoddard v Accupress Manufacturing Ltd* [1994] 1 WWR 677.

[861] *Federal Deposit v Vanstone* (1992) 88 DLR (4th) 448.

[862] *Beals v Saldanha* (2001) 202 DLR (4th) 630.

[863] *United States of America v Ivey* (1996) 139 DLR (4th) 570.

[864] *Fabrelle Wallcoverings & Textiles Ltd v North American Decorative Products Inc* [1993] I L Pr 381.

[865] *Clarke v Lo Bianco* (1991) 84 DLR (4th) 244, 253; *Minkler & Kirschbaum v Sheppard* (1991) 60 BCLR (2d) 360.

[866] *Fabrelle Wallcoverings & Textiles Ltd v North American Decorative Products Inc* [1993] I L Pr 381; *Federal Deposit v Vanstone* (1992) 88 DLR (4th) 448; *McMickle v van Staaten* (1992) 93 DLR (4th) 74. In this case, in which a Californian judgment was enforced, the defendant had never resided nor had a place of business in California (at 81).

[867] *McMickle v van Staaten* (1992) 93 DLR (4th) 74, 82.

[868] (2001) 202 DLR (4th) 630.

[869] [1994] 1 WWR 677.

brake. Of the total damages awarded, $1,020,000 was for non-economic loss and Ericco J acknowledged that the 'amount of the award in this case exceeds many times the limits to such awards in Canada by reason of the public policy decisions of the Supreme Court of Canada'.[870] He enforced the judgment on the basis that the Connecticut court acted 'through fair process with properly restrained jurisdiction and there is a real and substantial connection with the State of Connecticut'.[871]

4.302 There has been considerable academic debate as to whether the reference to 'real and substantial connection' in *Morguard* is, as one commentator has suggested,[872] akin to the 'natural forum' or whether, rather, it represents some lesser, 'due process' standard analogous to United States jurisprudence concerning judicial jurisdiction.[873] For the future, the precise ambit of the test is uncertain and it has been said that 'whether the American minimum contacts are sufficiently "real and substantial" to meet the *Morguard* test will only become clear as Canadian courts recognize and exercise their obligations under *Morguard*'.[874] Certainly the decision in *James Stoddard v Accupress Manufacturing Ltd*[875] discussed above inclines to the latter view. Whatever the exact content of the critical new touchstone for the enforcement of foreign judgments erected in *Morguard*,[876] it is clear that, as far as a party with assets in Canada is concerned, such a party named as defendant in foreign proceedings will ignore them at its peril if it has had anything more than the most fleeting connection with the foreign forum. This common law development will serve further to spark jurisdictional challenges at an early stage of litigation by one of the four methods outlined earlier in this chapter.[877]

4.303 It should be noted that Briggs has advanced an argument which in a very real sense complements that advanced by the Supreme Court in *Morguard*.[878] He argues that in the converse situation, that is where the foreign proceedings have been 'regularly' commenced on the basis of the

---

[870] [1994] 1 WWR 688.

[871] ibid.

[872] Briggs, A, 'Foreign Judgments: More Surprises' (1992) 109 LQR 449, 452.

[873] See, for example, Blom, J (1991) 70 Canadian Bar Review 733, 740–745; Black, V and Swan, J, 'New Rules for the Enforcement of Foreign Judgments: *Morguard Investments Ltd v de Savoye*' (1991) 12 Advocates' Quarterly 489, 499–505; Coakley, S, Finkle, P and Barrington, L,—'Morguard Investments Ltd: Emerging International Implications' (1992) 15 Dal LJ 629, 639. See also the papers collected in (1993) 22 Canadian Business Law Journal emanating from a symposium on *Morguard*.

[874] Coakley, S, Finkle, P and Barrington, L, ibid.

[875] [1994] 1 WWR 677.

[876] [1990] 3 SCR 1077.

[877] Glenn, HP, 'Foreign Judgments, the Common Law and the Constitution' (1992) 37 McGill LJ 537, 543.

[878] 'Which Foreign Judgments Should We Recognise Today?' (1987) 36 ICLQ 240.

defendant's temporary presence in the jurisdiction, such a judgment should not be liable to recognition or enforcement unless that jurisdiction also constituted the natural forum.[879] There is much theoretical appeal in this argument, based as it is on a more sophisticated and modern conception of jurisdiction.[880] Under it, the natural forum becomes the core concept in a de facto common law *convention double*.[881] It remains to be seen whether the courts will be receptive to this proposal. The Supreme Court of Canada's decision in *Morguard* suggests that the wells of judicial creativity are not dry in this field.

VII. CONCLUSION

This chapter has sought to provide a comprehensive picture of the range **4.304** of strategies available to a defendant embroiled in transnational litigation where the initial and frequently most important point of contention relates to the question of the venue for the resolution of the dispute. It is apparent that there is a considerable body of case law in this area of which there has been little close academic analysis. This is especially but not exclusively the case in the area of anti-suit injunctions. The explanation for this perhaps lies in the interlocutory nature of the contests involved and the view that 'procedural skirmishing' is not as deserving of scholarly appraisal as matters of substantive principle. That is clearly not a view the present writer subscribes to. The main point to emerge from this chapter is that forum shopping is by no means the exclusive preserve of plaintiffs. Just as one party's advantage is the other's disadvantage, in a context where a great deal can turn on the venue in which a particular transnational dispute is to be resolved, defendants inevitably become involved in hard-fought jurisdictional battles. The various tools available to a defendant in such contexts will vary in their efficacy both on account of the factual nature of the dispute and also according to the jurisdictions which are involved or potentially involved in its resolution. What is clear is that the nature of the battle dictates that those tools will be used to their limits by defendants and will equally be sought to be corroded and emasculated by plaintiffs in the contest for venue in transnational litigation.

---

[879] cf *Adams v Cape Industries plc* [1990] Ch 433.

[880] This conception states that jurisdiction must not be thought of in the narrow sense of simply jurisdiction *ratione personae* or *ratione materiae*; rather it should properly be seen as an amalgam of these notions and the doctrine of *forum non conveniens*. For a similar conception, see Inglis, BD, 'Forum Non Conveniens—Basis of Jurisdiction in the Commonwealth' (1964) 13 American Journal of Comparative Law 583.

[881] A complicated proposal which nevertheless amounts to much the same result as that proposed by Briggs is to be found in Teitz, LE (n 686 above).

5

Venue by Consensus — The Role of Jurisdiction and Arbitration Agreements

I.   The Nature and Importance of Jurisdiction and Arbitration
     Agreements   5.01
II. Escaping the Bargain   5.15
     1. The Existence of the Jurisdiction or Arbitration Agreement   5.16
     2. Voidability of the Agreement   5.27
     3. Overriding Effect of Mandatory Forum Law   5.37
     4. The Agreement's Continuing Efficacy   5.49
     5. The Nature of the Jurisdiction Agreement   5.54
     6. Scope and Construction of the Jurisdiction or Arbitration
        Agreement   5.61
     7. Discretion   5.72
     8. Escape at Enforcement   5.101
III. Conclusion   5.104

I. THE NATURE AND IMPORTANCE OF JURISDICTION AND ARBITRATION AGREEMENTS

Thus far, this book has been largely concerned with situations where **5.01** parties have not adverted to the question of venue for the resolution of a dispute *prior* to that dispute actually arising.[1] Failure to address this issue is, of course, not surprising in cases where the claim is one in tort where the parties will generally not have been in a prior legal relationship. The same may be said for some claims in quasi-contract or restitution, or arising under statute. Where parties to a dispute are in a contractual relationship, however, they have the opportunity to anticipate and minimize the scope for any clashes over venue in subsequent litigation by making express provision for venue or mode of dispute resolution in their

---

[1] The role of anti-suit injunctions granted in aid of an exclusive jurisdiction or arbitration agreement apart: see paras 4.146 ff above which should be read in conjunction with this chapter, as should paras 4.149–4.150 in relation to the extent of the availability of damages for breach of an exclusive jurisdiction clause. Mustill, MJ and Boyd, SC, *Commercial Arbitration* (2nd edn, 1989) 461–462 and n 17 state that there is no difference in principle between jurisdiction and agreements. To similar effect in the context of anti-suit injunctions is the observation of Millett LJ in *The Angelic Grace* [1995] 1 Lloyd's Rep 87, 96. Where there are perceived to be differences, they are drawn attention to in the text of this chapter.

contract through the expedient of a jurisdiction or arbitration agreement. An arbitration clause or agreement will also often specify the seat of the arbitration and, which may be a different matter, the place where the arbitration is to be held.[2]

5.02 Such arrangements may themselves be viewed as a form of anticipatory forum shopping[3] but with the notable difference from that practice as ordinarily understood that the chosen forum or mode and venue for dispute resolution is the product of consensual stipulation for which, especially in the case of an exclusive jurisdiction agreement, a premium will often have been paid by the party who is principally benefited by the choice. Arbitration and jurisdiction agreements or forum clauses may therefore be viewed as the anticipatory and negotiated reduction into contractual form of the inevitable self-interested jurisdictional battle which is, as has been seen throughout this book, a frequent consequence of modern jurisdictional rules. 'Forum-selection clauses reduce the international risks to which multistate contracts are exposed by reason of disparate laws, jurisdictional overlap and the conflict of laws' failure to offer certainty and predictability.'[4] This observation applies equally to arbitration agreements.

5.03 In a technical sense, 'exclusive', and in a practical sense, 'non-exclusive', jurisdiction clauses do not reduce a plaintiff's choice of jurisdiction, the doctrine of 'ouster' nowadays being little more than 'a vestigial legal fiction'.[5] In reality, however, the existence of a jurisdiction agreement between the parties should greatly reduce the scope for forum shopping in relation to any dispute which subsequently arises and which is within the agreement's scope. The position with regard to international arbitration agreements is *a fortiori* at least in those countries parties to the New York Convention on the Recognition and Enforcement of Foreign Arbitral Awards, which requires a mandatory stay of proceedings commenced in breach of an arbitration agreement to which the Convention applies so long as the dispute is one that is 'capable of settlement by arbitration' and the agreement is not null and void, inoperative, or incapable of being performed.[6]

---

[2] See *Raguz v Sullivan* (2000) 50 NSWLR 236, 254–257.

[3] In *The Cap Blanco* [1913] P 130, 135, Sir Samuel Evans P stated that 'it is conceivable that the parties agreed to that clause in the bill of lading [an exclusive jurisdiction clause in favour of the courts of Hamburg] in order expressly to avoid a trial here'. He did not comment on the propriety of this but his acceptance of it is implicit in the fact that he enforced the clause by granting a stay of English proceedings. See also *Volkswagen Canada Inc v Auto Haus Frohlich Ltd* [1986] 1 WWR 380, 381.

[4] Juenger, FK *Choice of Law and Multistate Justice* (1993) 214.

[5] *The Chaparral* 407 US 1, 12 (1972); [1972] 2 Lloyd's Rep 315, 320.

[6] In the United Kingdom, this requirement is now given effect to by s 9(4) of the

This chapter first examines the commercial significance and practical **5.04** importance of jurisdiction and arbitration agreements, considerations which it is not surprising to learn are widely appreciated. In light of the book's basic premise that 'venue matters', jurisdiction and arbitration agreements are to be viewed as a potentially valuable aspect of any contractual bargain between the parties. On the other hand, however, but related to this, the significance of venue often dictates that a party to a jurisdiction or arbitration agreement will from time to time seek to extricate itself from its contractual obligations or what, at least, on their face, appear to be contractual obligations, as regards choice of forum and/or mode of dispute resolution for various strategic reasons, some of which were examined in Chapter 2 of this book. The main part of this chapter explores the various strategies that may be pursued and arguments deployed in this endeavour, including arguments that call into question the very existence or enforceability of the jurisdiction or arbitration agreements. Those strategies and arguments need to be understood, however, in the context of a strong judicial disposition in common law countries to upholding parties' bargains, including bargains in relation to jurisdiction and arbitration.

The commercial significance of jurisdiction and arbitration agreements **5.05** was appreciated as long ago as 1913 by Lord Moulton, who said 'I always look upon these arbitration clauses as in a business point of view a substantial portion of the contract, and I think that the Courts have acted quite rightly in requiring good reason to be shewn why this part of a contract should not be strictly performed'.[7] In relation to a standard form arbitration clause contained in the Master Agreement of the International Swaps and Derivatives Association, Creswell J went so far as to say that 'if, following turmoil, now or in the future, in local markets, effect were not to be given to such an arbitration clause in such a master agreement, there is a real risk that the development and maintenance of an efficient and productive worldwide market in derivatives and swaps might be undermined'.[8] The extensive enforcement of exclusive jurisdiction agreements against Lloyd's 'Names' resident outside England following a series of disastrous losses by certain syndicates provides another context where the commercial significance of such agreements has been demonstrated.[9]

Arbitration Act 1996. In Australia, the requirement is found in s 7(2) of the International Arbitration Act 1974.

[7] *Bristol Corporation v John Aird & Co* [1913] AC 241, 257.
[8] *Bankers Trust v Jakarta International Hotels and Developments* [1999] 1 Lloyd's Rep 910, 916.
[9] See para 5.45 below.

5.06 It has been observed that 'choice of jurisdiction in an international commercial transaction is not a minor clause relating to machinery but very often a vital factor in negotiations. Every practitioner must know of cases where contracts would never have been entered into but for the choice of some particular law or jurisdiction.'[10] Ultimately, arbitration clauses and, perhaps more particularly, exclusive jurisdiction clauses must be viewed as going to the *value* of the contract in question to either party. The United States Supreme Court recognized as much in the seminal case of *The Chaparral*:[11]

> There is strong evidence that the forum clause was a vital part of the agreement, and it would be unrealistic to think that the parties did not conduct their negotiations, including fixing the monetary terms, with the consequences of the forum clause figuring prominently in their calculations.[12]

5.07 To similar effect, Delaume has said that 'in freely negotiated agreements, the selection of a forum may be the object of extensive bargaining and become one of the most significant terms of the contract, possibly determinative of the entire outcome of the negotiations'[13] and Article 17 of the Brussels Convention (and, by parity of reasoning, Article 23 of European Council Regulation 44/2001) was informed by this commercial truth.[14] A jurisdiction clause may also be negotiated to secure a neutral venue, that is to say a venue other than the respective home forums of the contracting parties.[15] The 'value' of an exclusive jurisdiction clause may extend beyond mere considerations of convenience or procedural advantage to more substantive matters. Thus, to the 'cost' of losing a jurisdiction clause battle is often to be added the fact that the 'value' of any associated choice of law clause may also be lost or at the very least jeopardized for, becoming a question of fact, the burden, expense, and risk of proving the foreign law will fall on the party who has failed to have the exclusive jurisdiction clause enforced.[16] Furthermore, a forum other than that stipulated may apply what it considers to be a mandatory law of that forum that would

---

[10] See Collins, LA, 'Forum Selection and an Anglo-American Conflict—The Sad Case of *The Chaparral*' (1971) 20 ICLQ 550, 557.

[11] 407 US 1 (1972); [1972] 2 Lloyd's Rep 315. See also *Carnival Cruise Lines, Inc v Shute* 499 US 585, 593–594 (1991).

[12] ibid 14; 320–321 of Lloyd's Rep. See also *The Benarty* [1985] QB 325, 343.

[13] *Law and Practice of Transnational Contracts* (1988) 173.

[14] See the Schlosser Report [1979] OJ C59/71, 125: 'International trade is heavily dependent on standard conditions which incorporate jurisdiction clauses. Nor are those conditions in many cases unilaterally dictated by one set of interests in the market; they have frequently been negotiated by representatives of the various interests.'

[15] See, for example, *Akai Pty Limited v People's Insurance Company* (1997) 188 CLR 418, 423; *Egon Olendorff v Libera Corporation* [1996] 1 Lloyd's Rep 388, 390.

[16] See Bissett-Johnson, 'The Efficacy of Choice of Jurisdiction Clauses in International Contracts in English and Australian Law' (1970) 19 ICLQ 541, 547.

not have applied or been given effect to in the stipulated forum.[17] In the case of an arbitration agreement, the confidentiality and perceived commerciality of that process, including the generally reduced scope for appeals, as well as the ready enforceability of awards under the New York Convention, are what is seen as valuable.

In *The Chaparral*,[18] referring to an exclusive jurisdiction clause in favour of **5.08** the English courts, Burger CJ stated that there were 'compelling reasons why a freely negotiated private international agreement . . . should be given full effect'.[19] These reasons in part bore upon the reputation and credibility of the nation's traders which were perceived to be a function of their fidelity to contractual undertakings. It has been said that the courts should do nothing to encourage 'welching' on bargains.[20] Echoing the strong internationalist and commercially conscious dissent of Wisdom J in the 5th Circuit Court of Appeals,[21] Burger CJ continued:

Manifestly much uncertainty and possibly great inconvenience to both parties could arise if a suit could be maintained in any jurisdiction in which an accident might occur or if jurisdiction were left to any place where the *Bremen* or *Unterweser* might happen to be found. The elimination of all such uncertainties by agreeing in advance on a forum acceptable to both parties is an *indispensable element in international trade, commerce and contracting.*[22]

Similar sentiments were expressed in *Northern Sales Co Ltd v Government* **5.09** *Trading Corp of Iran*[23] with regard to an Iranian jurisdiction clause, where it was observed that 'it cannot be in the commercial interest of Canada as a trading nation that it should acquire a reputation for enmeshing foreign merchants in lawsuits not grounded jurisdictionally on a footing generally accepted in the civilized world. Especially is that so when, as here, the plaintiff entered into a contract containing [an exclusive jurisdiction clause].'

In *The Eleftheria*,[24] a case concerning an exclusive jurisdiction clause in **5.10**

---

[17] The *Akai* litigation (1997) 188 CLR 418 and (1998) 1 Lloyd's Rep 90, more extensively discussed in paras 4.100, 4.140, and 4.233 above and para 5.46 below, is a classic illustration of this possibility.
[18] 407 US 1 (1972); [1972] 2 Lloyd's Rep 315.
[19] ibid 12–13; 320 of Lloyd's Rep.
[20] 446 F 2d 907, 909 (5th Cir, 1971); [1971] 2 Lloyd's Rep 348, 350 per Wisdom J.
[21] 428 F 2d 888, 896–912 (5th Cir, 1970) and 446 F 2d 907, 908–911 (5th Cir *en banc*, 1971); [1971] 2 Lloyd's Rep 348, 351.
[22] 407 US 1, 13 (1972); [1972] 2 Lloyd's Rep 315, 320 (emphasis added).
[23] (1991) 81 DLR (4th) 316, 321.
[24] [1970] P 94. This case in many respects remains the leading English authority on the attitude courts should adopt to the commencement of proceedings in England in the face of a foreign exclusive jurisdiction clause. It was approved by the Court of Appeal in *The El Amria* [1981] 2 Lloyd's Rep 119 and by the House of Lords in *The Sennar (No 2)* [1985] 1 WLR 490.

favour of the Greek courts, Brandon J stated that 'it is essential that the court should give full weight to the prima facie desirability of holding the plaintiffs to their agreement'.[25] Where parties to a commercial contract agree to the jurisdiction of the English courts, not only will such an agreement count as submission to English jurisdiction in the international sense,[26] but, once proceedings are commenced in England, it will be very difficult for the defendant to obtain a stay (or set aside an order granting leave or permission to serve out of the jurisdiction under the Civil Procedure Rules) either according to the 'natural forum' calculus of *Spiliada*[27] or by reason of a *lis alibi pendens*, even where related or identical foreign proceedings are well advanced. In *The Hida Maru*[28] notwithstanding that proceedings in Kuwait had continued for three years prior to the defendant in those proceedings instituting a claim in England, Watkins LJ said that 'an English court should hesitate long before turning [a party to a contract containing an English exclusive jurisdiction clause] away from its doors'.[29] Further, as has been seen in paragraphs 4.146–4.178 above, that same strong disposition to see exclusive jurisdiction and arbitration agreements as bargains and enforce them as such underpins the willingness to enforce exclusive jurisdiction and arbitration agreements by means of anti-suit injunctions, even in the context of proceedings commenced in a state whose jurisdictional rules are supplied by either European Council Regulation 44/2001 or the Brussels or Lugano Conventions. The importance which English courts place on upholding jurisdiction and arbitration agreements is also evidenced by statutory sanctions attached to the breach of *exclusive* jurisdiction agreements. Thus, section 32(1) of the Civil Jurisdiction and Judgments Act 1982 provides for the non-recognition and enforcement of any foreign judgment or arbitration award obtained in breach of such an agreement.[30] Similar legislation

---

[25] ibid 103.

[26] *Copin v Adamson* (1875) 1 Ex D 17; *Feyerick v Hubbard* (1902) 71 LJKB 509.

[27] In *Berisford plc v New Hampshire Insurance Co* [1990] 2 QB 631, 646, Hobhouse J observed that a non-exclusive jurisdiction agreement creates a 'strong prima facie case that the jurisdiction is an appropriate one'. The case of an exclusive jurisdiction agreement is *a fortiori*. In a service *ex juris* context, Staughton LJ suggested in *Attock Cement Co Ltd v Romanian Bank for Foreign Trade* [1989] 1 WLR 1147, 1161 that, where there is an English jurisdiction clause, factors relating to the relative convenience of the forum should not be given much if any weight. See also *British Aerospace plc v Dee Howard Co* [1993] 1 Lloyd's Rep 368; *The Rothnie* [1996] 2 Lloyd's Rep 206.

[28] [1981] 2 Lloyd's Rep 510.

[29] ibid 514. See also *British Aerospace plc v Dee Howard Co* [1993] 1 Lloyd's Rep 368, 376 but cf *Bouygues Offshore SA v Caspian Shipping Co (Nos 1, 3, 4 and 5)* [1998] 2 Lloyd's Rep 461 and *Donohue v Armco Inc* [2002] 1 Lloyd's Rep 425.

[30] See *Tracomin SA v Sudan Oil Seeds Co Ltd (Nos 1 & 2)* [1983] 1 WLR 1026. Nothing in s 32(1) affects the recognition or enforcement in the United Kingdom of a judgment required to be recognized or enforced under the Brussels or Lugano Conventions or Council Regulation 44/2001.

exists in a number of Commonwealth countries such as the Australian Foreign Judgments Act 1991.

The commercial importance of jurisdiction agreements is also acknowl-   **5.11** edged in the Official Commentary to the Brussels Convention on Jurisdiction and Judgments in Civil and Commercial Matters.[31] In that context and in apparent arguable violation of Article 21 of the Brussels Convention,[32] English courts have assumed and maintained jurisdiction under Article 17 even though second seised.[33] Article 17 of the Brussels Convention now has its equivalent in Article 23 of Council Regulation 44/2001. Moreover, amendments made to Article 17 of the Convention at the time of the United Kingdom's accession in relation to standard jurisdiction agreements in international trade contracts further deferred to their commercial significance,[34] as did amendments introduced in Article 23 of Council Regulation 44/2001.[35]

In addition to respect for sanctity of contract, the enforcement of jurisdic-   **5.12** tion and arbitration clauses has other salutary consequences. This was well appreciated by the United States Supreme Court, which observed in *Scherk v Alberto-Culver Company*[36] that 'a parochial refusal by the courts of one country to enforce an international arbitration agreement . . . would invite unseemly and mutually destructive jockeying by the parties to secure tactical litigation advantages'.[37] In other words, the more extensive the enforcement of such clauses, the less the scope for forum shopping. This consideration, when combined with the strong policy of upholding bargains, gives the impression that there is little potential for jurisdictional controversy, let alone aggressively conducted litigation, where a jurisdiction, especially of the exclusive variety, or arbitration clause has been agreed to by the parties. Indeed the very desire to avoid such battles explains the popularity of such clauses—'a clause establishing *ex ante* the

---

[31] The Jenard Report [1979] OJ C59/1, 37, commenting on Article 17, states that 'it is unnecessary to stress the importance of this jurisdiction, particularly in commercial relations'.

[32] See Case C–351/89, *Overseas Union Insurance Ltd v New Hampshire Insurance Co* [1991] ECR I–3317.

[33] *Kloeckner & Co AG v Gatoil Overseas Inc* [1990] 1 Lloyd's Rep 177; *Denby v The Hellenic Mediterranean Lines Co Ltd* [1994] 1 Lloyd's Rep 320.

[34] These amendments eliminated the strict requirement that the agreement must be in writing by permitting standard form jurisdiction clauses in international trade and commerce to be upheld when in a form which accorded with 'practice' of which the parties ought to have been aware: see the Schlosser Report [1979] OJ C59/71, 124–125. See also *Mainschiffahrts-Genossenschaft e G v Les Gravières Rhénanes SarL* [1997] ECR I–911.

[35] Briggs, A and Rees, P, *Civil Jurisdiction and Judgments* (3rd edn, 2002) 2.88.

[36] 417 US 506 (1974).

[37] ibid 516–517 (arbitration clause). See also McLeod, JG, *The Conflict of Laws* (1983) 126: 'If these clauses are too easily avoided, the courts may indirectly encourage forum shopping and assist parties in defeating justifiable contractual expectations.'

forum for dispute resolution has the salutary effect of dispelling any confusion about where suits arising from the contract must be brought and defended, sparing litigants the time and expense of pretrial motions to determine the correct forum'.[38]

5.13 Appearances are deceptive, however, and the law reports record many instances of litigation by parties 'in order to determine where they shall litigate'[39] notwithstanding the existence of an exclusive jurisdiction clause or arbitration agreement. This suggests at least four things: first, the apparent certainty yielded by exclusive jurisdiction and arbitration agreements can be overstated. As will be seen below, there are legitimate non-discretionary arguments that may be raised as reasons why a jurisdiction or arbitration clause does not apply or should not be enforced. Secondly, some first instance courts, in particular,[40] have not always been as faithful as they might have been to the rhetoric of the authoritative decisions referred to above as to the very great commercial significance of jurisdiction and arbitration agreements. Thirdly, complex multi-party transnational disputes may not always yield or lend themselves to the simplicity of the principle of enforcing two parties' agreement as to forum or mode of dispute resolution. As shall be seen, and sometimes paradoxically, that goal may serve to fracture or fragment the dispute resolution and the policy of resolving all disputes between multiple parties in one forum may trump the policy of holding a subset of those parties to their contractual bargain. Fourthly, and as a general proposition, the extent to which plaintiffs have been prepared to commence proceedings in the face of such clauses, and defendants, conversely, have strenuously resisted their institution,[41] underlines the central premise of this book, namely the proposition that venue is of vital importance in transnational litigation. It is a logical corollary of that premise that forum clauses are inserted in international commercial contracts not simply for reasons of 'neatness' and 'certainty' but also as an important function of transactional negotiation. Indeed, the very real commercial significance of arbitration and jurisdiction clauses perhaps assists in explaining why the theoretical certainty which they should afford in transnational litigation is not always evident in practice.

---

[38] *Carnival Cruise Lines, Inc v Shute* 499 US 585, 593–594 (1991). See also Delaume, GR (n 13 above) 173; Steiner, HJ and Vagts, DF, *Transnational Legal Problems* (2nd edn, 1976) 809; Pryles, MC 'Comparative Aspects of Prorogation and Arbitration Agreements' (1976) 25 ICLQ 543, 581.

[39] *Spiliada Maritime Corporation v Cansulex Ltd* [1987] AC 460, 464 per Lord Templeman.

[40] For the reason that there is little scope for successful appeal where an exercise of discretion is in play: *The Athenee* (1922) 11 Ll LR 6, 6; *The Fehmarn* [1958] 1 WLR 159, 163; *The Chaparral* [1968] 2 Lloyd's Rep 158, 163 and 164; *The Adolf Warski* [1976] 2 Lloyd's Rep 241, 248.

[41] Extreme examples are provided by *The Sennar (No 2)*, in which not only was a battle

That having been said, this chapter is not intended to be alarmist. An **5.14** accurate and representative picture of the current state of the law may not always be gleaned from the law reports, and this is perhaps especially so with respect to matters of procedure where only the unusual or extraordinary command attention.[42] It is doubtless the case that the vast majority of jurisdiction and arbitration agreements are adhered to and perform the valuable functions which have been considered above. The balance of this chapter is, however, concerned with those situations where this is not the case and where parties seek to extricate themselves from such agreements. An examination is made of the extent to which the law permits this form of forum shopping or jockeying for venue.

II. ESCAPING THE BARGAIN

The contexts in which a party wishing to extricate itself from a jurisdiction **5.15** or arbitration agreement may deploy the arguments to be considered below vary. Such arguments may be raised by a party who is a defendant in the nominated forum and relied upon as part of a challenge to that forum's jurisdiction. More likely, however, they will be deployed by a party resisting a stay application by seeking to uphold jurisdiction in a forum other than that nominated in the jurisdiction agreement, or in a court in which an anti-suit injunction in aid of an exclusive jurisdiction or arbitration agreement is being sought. There are, in essence, seven broad arguments:

- that there is no jurisdiction or arbitration agreement or that any such agreement is null and void;
- that the agreement is voidable;
- that the agreement should be overridden by the mandatory law of the forum. This may entail the consequence, in the context of an arbitration agreement, that the matter is not capable of settlement by arbitration;
- that the agreement has ceased to be binding;
- that, on its proper construction, the jurisdiction agreement is not exclusive;

---

fought all the way up to the House of Lords but also through the Dutch Courts over a five-year period: [1985] 1 WLR 490, 501; *The Chaparral*, which not only involved litigation all the way up to the US Supreme Court but also to the English Court of Appeal: [1968] 2 Lloyd's Rep 158; the *Akai* litigation, referred to in n 17 above; and, most recently, *Donohue v Armco Inc* [2002] 1 Lloyd's Rep 425.

[42] This point is well made by Kahn-Freund, 'Jurisdiction Agreements: Some Reflections' (1977) 26 ICLQ 825, 826.

- that the dispute in question falls outside the scope of the jurisdiction or arbitration agreement; and
- that the jurisdiction agreement should not be enforced (at least by means of a stay or anti-suit injunction) in the exercise of the court's discretion.[43]

It will be seen that, even in this last and, in view of the strength of the maxim *pacta sunt servanda*, least likely area, there remains considerable scope for significant jurisdictional battles in a plaintiff's quest to litigate in the most propitious forum. Finally, arguments based on the efficacy of a foreign arbitration or jurisdiction agreement which may be made at the stage of attempted enforcement of judgment or award as opposed to the initial assumption of jurisdiction will be briefly considered.

1. THE EXISTENCE OF THE JURISDICTION OR ARBITRATION AGREEMENT

5.16 A threshold argument which may be advanced by a party is that there has simply been no agreement to an exclusive jurisdiction or arbitration clause or that any such agreement is void. This may or may not form part of a broader argument that there is no contract between the parties or that any such contract is void. In either case, extremely difficult choice of law questions are raised which centre on the issue of what law governs the basic question of agreement between the parties. In common law countries, these choice of law questions are to be determined in accordance with common law conflicts principles. Where such an argument is raised in the United Kingdom, it should be noted that Article 1(2)(d) of the Rome Convention provides that the choice of law rules of that Convention have no application to choice of court or arbitration agreements. However, where it is argued in the context of Council Regulation 44/2001 that there has been no agreement to a jurisdiction clause nominating a court or the courts of a Contracting State, it may be that the existence of such an agreement is properly a matter for European law (of an as yet largely unspecified nature) rather than national conflicts principles.[44]

5.17 The leading English authority on the common law conflict of laws approach to this question, *Mackender v Feldia AG*,[45] suggests, although by

---

[43] It has already been noted that, under the New York Convention, where there is an international arbitration agreement, the matter is capable of settlement by arbitration, and the agreement is not null and void, inoperative, or incapable of being performed, a court asked to stay court proceedings commenced in breach of that agreement has no discretion and a stay is mandatory. Conditions may, however, be imposed upon the grant of a stay which may afford scope for the exercise of a measure of discretion: see, for example, *Hi-Fert Pty Ltd v Kiukiang Maritime Carriers Inc (No 5)* (1998) 90 FCR 1.

[44] See Briggs, A and Rees, P (n 35 above) 2.97.

[45] [1967] 2 QB 590.

way of obiter dictum, that English law as the *lex fori* should probably govern a plea of *non est factum*.[46] That case drew a very clear distinction between a plea which would merely render a contract voidable as opposed to void, it being evident that a plea of the former kind should be determined in accordance with the putative proper law of the contract.[47] In line with *Mackender v Feldia's* suggested application of the *lex fori* to questions of basic agreement is the High Court of Australia's decision in *Oceanic Sun Line Special Shipping Co Inc v Fay*.[48] On boarding the MS *Stella Oceanis* in Greece, Dr Fay was handed a ticket, clause 13 of which purported to provide for the exclusive jurisdiction of the Greek courts. Treating the question as one of classification, Brennan J applied Australian law as the *lex fori* in order to determine whether 'the parties [had] reached a consensus ad idem and what that consensus was'.[49] He concluded that the contract had been formed well before Dr Fay was handed his actual ticket and that 'it was too late after the original contract was made to add conditions which were not incorporated in it'.[50] Gaudron J, while agreeing with Brennan J's conclusion that the jurisdiction clause formed no part of the contract, did not see the issue as one of 'classification'. Rather, she considered that the *lex fori* should determine:

questions as to the existence, construction and validity of terms bearing on the determination of the parties' agreement as to the proper law. . . . If the question of what is the proper law is one to be answered by application of the lex fori [and it is difficult to see what other law it could be identified by], until the lex fori provides the answer to that question there is no scope for the operation of any other law.[51]

As one of the pre-eminent indicators of the proper law in the absence of **5.18** an express choice is the existence of a jurisdiction agreement,[52] then, for this to be taken into account, a court must be satisfied that there is in fact consensus between the parties as to such an agreement. On the above analysis, as this question is logically anterior to the determination of the proper law, then the only law that can be applied to test the existence of the agreement for the purposes of identifying the proper law is that of the forum.

---

[46] ibid 598 and 603.　　　　[47] ibid.　　　　[48] (1988) 165 CLR 197.
[49] ibid 225. Wilson and Toohey JJ, with whom Deane J agreed on this point (256), also applied Australian law although they did not expressly advert to the choice of law issue (202–208).
[50] ibid 228.　　　　[51] ibid 261.
[52] *Compagnie Tunisienne de Navigation SA v Compagnie d'Armement Maritime SA* [1971] AC 572.

5.19 The question of what law should govern the formation of contracts has excited considerable academic debate[53] and a variety of approaches has been suggested. In *Oceanic Sun Line Shipping*, Brennan J expressly endorsed an approach which treats the question of formation as one of classification or characterization.[54] That approach may be criticized, however, for taking an unduly expansive view of characterization. Briggs has advocated a more complex approach which, while also arguing for the law of the forum, incorporates a role for the putative proper law in the event that agreement is found sufficiently to exist according to the law of the forum.[55] This approach adopts Gaudron J's analysis in *Oceanic Sun Line Shipping* but takes it a step further by then asking whether there is a contract (or an agreement as to jurisdiction) according to the proper law as identified by the law of the forum. The simple, one stop putative proper law approach is that advocated by *Dicey & Morris*.[56]

5.20 A distinction may need to be drawn between cases where it is alleged that no contract whatsoever is in existence and cases, such as *Oceanic Sun Line Shipping*, where the contention is only that there has been no agreement to an exclusive jurisdiction clause. In the latter case, there may be fewer logical objections to applying the proper law of the contract as that will be the law which the parties have either expressly or impliedly chosen to govern their contractual relations. However, as jurisdiction clauses provide one of the key tools for ascertaining the proper law of a contract in the absence of an express choice of law, applying the putative proper law to the question of agreement must either ignore such a clause or take it into account in circumstances where its very existence is being questioned. Either approach is logically unattractive because it begs the question one way or the other. Accordingly, there is much which is attractive in the approach advocated by Briggs. It accommodates the putative proper law approach but allows full advantage to be taken of one of the most reliable tools for ascertaining the proper law of a contract.

5.21 Whatever position is preferred, it is evident that the question of what law should govern questions relating to the formation of international contracts is 'one of the more notoriously intractable problems of the modern conflict of laws'.[57] With the exception of *Oceanic Sun Line*

---

[53] See, for example, Jaffey AJE, 'Offer and Acceptance in the English Conflict of Laws' (1975) 24 ICLQ 603; Libling, DF, 'Formation of International Contracts' (1979) 42 MLR 169; Thomson, A, 'A Different Approach to Choice of Law in Contract' (1980) 43 MLR 650; Garner, M, 'Formation of International Contracts—Finding the Right Choice of Law Rule' (1989) 63 ALJ 751; Briggs, A,'The Formation of International Contracts' [1990] LMCLQ 192.
[54] (1988) 165 CLR 197, 225.
[55] (n 53 above) 197–199.
[56] Collins, LA (ed), *Dicey & Morris on the Conflict of Laws* (13th edn, 2000) 443.
[57] Briggs, A (n 53 above) 192.

Shipping, it has also not been the subject of any authoritative decision. This being the case, there is scope for much potential uncertainty in cases where a plaintiff commences litigation in the face of a foreign exclusive jurisdiction clause which it claims it never agreed to.[58] At the very least, the apparent insulation which an exclusive jurisdiction clause is ordinarily apt to provide for a defendant from potentially wearying jurisdictional battles disappears in such circumstances.

Apart from questions as to the existence of agreement, whether to the **5.22** contract as a whole or to the jurisdiction or arbitration clause in particular, another question which frequently arises in this context is whether a jurisdiction or arbitration agreement has been incorporated into a larger contract. In *Re Jogia*,[59] the plaintiff trustee in bankruptcy sought to resist a challenge to the English court's jurisdiction by arguing that an exclusive jurisdiction clause for the Commercial Court of Paris was not a term of the original contract made between the parties and therefore was not binding on the bankrupt. Browne-Wilkinson VC held that although 'there may be some doubt whether the terms of the first transaction incorporated the exclusive jurisdiction clause' the terms became part of the contract through subsequent course of dealings.[60] *The Emre II*[61] provides another straightforward example. Although the defendants pointed to a jurisdiction clause in a so-called 'Protocol' agreement, Sheen J was clear that as the action was brought upon a mortgage which contained no such agreement, it could not form the basis for any decision to stay proceedings.[62]

The relevant principles concerning the incorporation of terms should be **5.23** supplied by the proper law of the contract into which it is being sought to incorporate the jurisdiction or arbitration agreement.[63] This was the approach followed by Sheen J in *The Blue Wave*[64] and by the Court of Appeal in *The El Amria and El Minia*.[65] In the former case, the proper law was Greek but, as no evidence of Greek law on the question whether indorsees of a bill of lading were bound by its terms was presented, it was assumed to be the same as English law and section 1 of the Bills of Lading Act 1855 was applied. In the latter case, again in the absence of proof, the proper, Egyptian, law was assumed to be the same as English law.

---

[58] For a discussion of the matters germane to the existence of an agreement to arbitrate, see Mustill, MJ and Boyd, SC (n 1 above) 105–108.

[59] [1988] 2 All ER 328.   [60] ibid 335.   [61] [1989] 2 Lloyd's Rep 182.

[62] ibid 183. See also his earlier decision in *The El Amria and El Minia* [1981] 2 Lloyd's Rep 539, reversed on appeal [1982] 2 Lloyd's Rep 28.

[63] See Pryles, MC (n 38 above) 552–553.   [64] [1982] 1 Lloyd's Rep 151.

[65] [1982] 2 Lloyd's Rep 28, 31. See also *The Griesheim* (Hong Kong Court of Appeal, No 70 of 1983), referred to by Margolis, R, 'Staying an Action Because the Foreign Law is Ambiguous' [1994] LMCLQ 30, 32–33, and *Pan Lloyd Shipping Ltd v Cho Hung Bank* [1992] 1 HKLR 356, 361.

5.24 Admiralty cases provide much of the case law in this area, especially with regard to arbitration clauses. The nature of international shipping contracts is such as to encourage arguments that a jurisdiction or arbitration clause in one contract has not been incorporated down the line.[66] In *The Mahkutai*,[67] the Privy Council rejected an argument by shipowners that a Himalaya clause entitled them to the benefit of an exclusive jurisdiction clause in a bill of lading to which they were not a party. The essence of the decision rested in the fact that as the exclusive jurisdiction clause upon which the shipowners sought to rely created mutual rights and obligations, such a clause did not fall within the familiar language of 'exception, limitation, condition or liberty benefiting the carrier' in the Himalaya clause. By way of contrast, the earlier decision of the Privy Council in *The Pioneer Container*[68] was to the effect that, where goods had been sub-bailed with the authority of the owner, that authority was sufficient to bind the owner to the terms of the sub-bailment, including an exclusive jurisdiction clause contained in the contract of sub-bailment.

5.25 Where the incorporation by reference of an arbitration clause is in issue, the view traditionally taken in England, at least in shipping cases, is that, for the incorporation to be effective, the arbitration clause must be specifically referred to in the incorporation clause and that general words of incorporation will not suffice. The leading case is *TW Thomas & Co Ltd v Portsea Steamship Co Ltd*,[69] although it should be observed that later decisions have not always followed its strictures and general words of incorporation have been held to be capable of picking up an arbitration clause contained, for example, in a head contract.[70] This approach is perhaps more attractive as a matter of principle than the somewhat rigid test requiring the explicit incorporation of the arbitration clause. *TW Thomas* has not been followed in Australia.[71]

---

[66] See Tetley, W, *Marine Cargo Claims* (3rd edn, 1988) 783 and, for an example of such an argument, *Agro Co of Canada Ltd v The Regal Scout* [1984] 2 FC 851. For an English case where such an argument was unsuccessful, see *The Nerano* [1996] 1 Lloyd's Rep 1.

[67] [1996] AC 650.

[68] [1994] 2 AC 324.

[69] [1912] AC 1.

[70] See, for example, *Modern Building Wales Pty Limited v Limmer & Trinadad Co Limited* [1975] 1 WLR 1281, a decision of the Court of Appeal in which it was held that an arbitration clause was incorporated into a construction contract by general terms without any specific reference being made to the arbitration clause. Also compare *The Annefield* [1971] P 168, 173 but note that *TW Thomas* was referred to with apparent approval by the Privy Council in *The Mahkutai* [1996] AC 650, 666–667 and classically applied in *The Delos* [2001] 1 Lloyd's Rep 703.

[71] *Carob Industries Limited (In Liquidation) v Simto Pty Limited* [1997] 18 WAR 1; *Lief Investments Pty Ltd v Conagra International Fertilizer Company* [1998] NSWSC 481.

A distinction may be usefully drawn between, on the one hand, cases **5.26** where what is being incorporated is a set of standard terms and conditions, where general words of incorporation are more likely to be effective to pick up an arbitration or jurisdiction clause, as was the case in *Crédit Suisse Financial Products v Société Générale d'Enterprises*,[72] and, on the other hand, cases where what is sought to be incorporated are the terms of another contract.[73] This situation commonly arises in both shipping and reinsurance contexts. Thus it has been held that the words 'Conditions: Wording as original' contained in a reinsurance slip were insufficient to pick up an exclusive jurisdiction clause in the underlying policy of insurance both by reason of the fact that the exclusive jurisdiction clause was ancillary in nature and did nothing to define the risk being reinsured and, further, that it was unlikely that, as between reinsurer and reassured, the parties intended any disputes arising under the contract of reinsurance policy should be required to be litigated in the same forum as that specified in the underlying policy of insurance.[74]

2. VOIDABILITY OF THE AGREEMENT

Unlike the discussion in paragraphs 5.16 ff above, here there is no ques- **5.27** tion as to whether there has been agreement, either to exclusive jurisdiction, arbitration, or contractual relations as a whole. Rather, the contention is that such agreement is tainted so that the jurisdiction or arbitration clause should not be enforced. At common law, as has been seen from the references to *Mackender v Feldia AG* above, this is a question which is governed by the proper law of the agreement. In *Donohue v Armco*[75] (at first instance), Aikens J, confronted by an argument seeking, on the grounds of fraud, to impugn an exclusive jurisdiction clause upon which the plaintiff was seeking to rely for the purposes of sustaining an anti-suit injunction, said that 'for the purposes of an application for an anti-suit injunction, a court should regard an exclusive jurisdiction clause as valid unless satisfied, at the lowest, that there is credible evidence demonstrating that it is invalid or ineffective'.[76]

---

[72] [1997] CLC 168.

[73] Moore-Bick J identified this distinction in *AIG Europe SA v QBE International Insurance Ltd* [2001] 2 Lloyd's Rep 268, 273.

[74] *AIG Europe (UK) Ltd v The Ethniki* [2000] 2 All ER 566. See also *OK Petroleum AB v Vitol Energy SA* [1995] 2 Lloyd's Rep 160; *Assicurazioni Generali SpA v Ege Sigorta A/S* (31 July 2001) Colman, J.

[75] [1999] 2 Lloyd's Rep 649, 657.

[76] This point was not considered by the House of Lords which, as has been noted elsewhere, declined to enforce the exclusive jurisdiction clause by means of an anti-suit injunction: [2002] 1 Lloyd's Rep 425.

5.28 Where a court is assessing whether it has jurisdiction under Article 23 of European Council Regulation 44/2001,[77] however, the extent to which objections to validity under the proper law will be countenanced remains unclear[78] and matters of formal, as opposed to essential, validity such as writing requirements are matters for European law. The decision in *Sanicentral GmbH v Collin*[79] would tend to suggest that, for the purposes of Article 23 agreements, essential validity is also a matter for European law as opposed to national conflict of laws principles. This case established that a principle of national law that would normally invalidate an exclusive jurisdiction clause did not have this effect in the context of Article 23.[80] In *Powell Duffryn plc v Petereit*,[81] it was held that an Article 23 'agreement conferring jurisdiction' was a concept independent of national law but this decision left it very unclear as to what actual principles should be applied by national courts confronted with the argument that the jurisdiction agreement should be avoided. The view expressed in *Benincasa v Dentalkit Srl*[82] that the formal requirements of what is now Article 23 were sufficient to establish consensus, such that there was no role for the governing law to play in assessing the jurisdiction agreement's validity, has been subject to strong criticism and the view has been expressed that an autonomous European definition of 'agreement', one presumably that excludes fraud and certain other vitiating factors, will need to be developed.[83]

5.29 Returning to common law principles, it follows from the argument set out in paragraphs 5.16 ff above that, although the question of the agreement's voidability is governed by its proper law, there will also be an anterior role for the *lex fori*. This is because the validity of such an agreement must be tested before a common law court can consider whether or not to take it into account in ascertaining the contract (or agreement's) proper law. That law, as ascertained, is then to be applied to the question of whether the jurisdiction agreement should be avoided.[84] In this context, it is

---

[77] This is a task which it must undertake of its own accord: Schlosser Report [1979] OJ C59/71, 81.

[78] For example, as Article 23 specifies what may be described as the formality requirements for such agreements, additional requirements imposed under some national laws may not be used to attack an otherwise formally valid exclusive jurisdiction agreement: see Case 150/80 *Elefanten Schuh GmbH v Jacqmain* [1981] ECR 1671. See further Briggs, A and Rees, P (n 35 above) 2.97; Collins, LA (ed) (n 56 above) 12-096.

[79] Case 25/79 [1979] ECR 3423.

[80] See also *Re the Import of Italian Sports Cars* [1992] I L Pr 188.

[81] Case C–214/89 [1992] ECR I–1745.

[82] [1997] ECR I–3767.

[83] Briggs, A and Rees, P (n 35 above) 2.97; Collins, LA (ed) (n 56 above) 12-096.

[84] This includes questions of illegality: *The Amazonia* [1990] 1 Lloyd's Rep 236, 249 per Dillon LJ although, as that case illustrates, any chosen proper law may itself be illegal.

arguable that, in *Mackender v Feldia AG*,[85] having held that the voidability of the contract was a question for Belgian law, the Court of Appeal should have sought to apply Belgian law to answer that question rather than refusing to address it. If it concluded that the clause would have been avoided under Belgian law, it should then have decided whether to maintain its order for service out of the jurisdiction under the general principles applicable to such an application. If, on the other hand, it concluded that the clause would not have been avoided under Belgian law, *then* it would have been appropriate to decline to make an order for service out of the jurisdiction in the absence of exceptional circumstances.[86]

In *The Iran Vojdan*,[87] no initial reference was made to the *lex fori* although **5.30** it is clear that the agreement in that case would not have been voidable under English law. That case, however, provides a good illustration of the manner in which the validity of jurisdiction agreements should, ultimately, be tested according to the proper law. Applying German law as the proper law of the contract on the 'closest and most real connection test', Bingham J concluded that the jurisdiction clause was invalid. Expert evidence had been tendered which strongly suggested that German law would consider the exclusive jurisdiction clause to be invalid because of the small size of the printing on the clause in the bill of lading.[88]

The choice of law questions that have been considered in both this and the **5.31** previous section demonstrate that the 'security' of an exclusive jurisdiction clause may in part be dependent upon the content of the proper law of the contract in which it is contained (which will invariably supply the proper law of the jurisdiction agreement, if this is regarded as a separate or severable agreement).[89] As a consequence, it may be undermined both because the actual identity of the proper law may be somewhat problematic in the absence of an expressly chosen proper law and, perhaps more significantly, because the content of the proper law at common law is a question of fact and thus is nothing more than a function of the quality of the evidence presented. Further, as a question of fact, there is less scope for correction of errors on appeal.

The apparent position of German law as revealed in *The Iran Vojdan* no **5.32** doubt reflects a consumer-protection concern that sufficient attention be

---

[85] [1967] 2 QB 590.

[86] See *Evans Marshall & Co Ltd v Bertola SA* [1973] 1 WLR 349, 362; *Advanced Cardiovascular Systems Inc v Universal Specialties Ltd* [1997] 1 NZLR 186.

[87] [1984] 2 Lloyd's Rep 380.

[88] ibid 383–384. *The Al Battani* [1993] 2 Lloyd's Rep 219 provides another example of the application of the proper law of the contract resulting in the conclusion that the exclusive jurisdiction clause was null and void.

[89] See para 5.36 below.

drawn to any 'agreement' on jurisdiction.[90] Some legal systems take an even more absolute stance, holding all such clauses invalid.[91] Indeed the notion in common law courts that such clauses were invalid and void against public policy for 'ousting' the jurisdiction of the courts was commonly held in relatively recent times, especially in the United States, where it was only finally laid to rest in *The Chaparral*.[92] Indeed, some states have clung to the orthodoxy notwithstanding that decision.[93]

5.33 The reasons why a jurisdiction clause may be held to be invalid by a particular governing law will not always be 'at large', as it were, but may be, for example, by reference to the manner in which a particular contract was entered into. Objections of a kind which would render a contract voidable, such as fraud, undue influence, and overweening bargaining power were referred to by Burger CJ in *The Chaparral*.[94] Concepts such as overweening bargaining power and 'adhesion' contracts,[95] if not peculiarly American, are not regularly employed in other common law jurisdictions. The real significance of their employment in this context is that it suggested[96] that American courts were to apply American standards when parties sought to avoid exclusive jurisdiction clauses rather than the standards dictated by the proper law of the contract.[97] They have largely followed this course.[98] The consequence of this is that, especially where one party to a contract is American,[99] an exclusive jurisdiction clause not

[90] Section 38 of the ZPO specifies the circumstances in which jurisdiction clauses will be permitted under German law. This section is summarized in Park, WD and Cromie, S, *International Commercial Litigation* (1990) 30.

[91] Italy provides such an example in relation to agreements to which domiciled nationals are party. Article 2 of the *Codice di Procedura Civile* states that 'Italian *giurisdizione* may not be derogated by agreement in favour of a foreign *giurisdizione* or arbitrators who function abroad, unless it is in respect to a case relating to obligations between aliens, or an alien and a citizen who neither resides nor is a domiciliary of the Republic and the derogation is in a written act.' See Delaume, GR (n 13 above) 176. Spain provides another example—see Schlesinger, R, Baade, H, Damaska, M, Herzog, P, *Comparative Law: Cases-Text-Materials* (5th edn, 1988) 388 n 78.

[92] 407 US 1, 12 (1972); [1972] 2 Lloyd's Rep 315, 319; *The Fehmarn* [1958] 1 WLR 159, 161 per Lord Denning MR and 164 per Morris LJ. See also Kahn-Freund (n 42 above) 843.

[93] Solimine, ME, 'Forum-Selection Clauses and the Privatization of Procedure' (1992) 25 Cornell International Law Journal 51, 63. He cites Alabama, Georgia, Iowa, and Texas.

[94] 407 US 1, 12 (1972); [1972] 2 Lloyd's Rep 315, 321.   [95] ibid.

[96] Collins has suggested that this was perhaps more by accident than design: 'Choice of Forum and the Exercise of Judicial Discretion—The Resolution of an Anglo-American Conflict' (1973) ICLQ 332, 340. On the other hand, s 3(4) of the Model Choice of Forum Act, drafted some four years prior to the decision in *The Chaparral*, assumed application of the *lex fori* to such questions: see Reese, W, 'The Model Choice of Forum Act' (1969) 17 Am J Comp L 292. See also Juenger, FK (n 4 above) 215–220 for the view that Burger CJ's decision was based on the *lex mercatoria* and not on the law of any particular state or nation.

[97] cf Kahn-Freund (n 42 above) 827.

[98] See Born, GB, *International Civil Litigation in United States Courts* (3rd edn, 1996) 452.

[99] Because an American court will be less likely, in the alternative, to decline jurisdiction on grounds of *forum non conveniens*: *Piper Aircraft Co v Reyno* 454 US 235, 255 (1981).

in favour of American courts will be vulnerable to attack in America on general law[100] grounds which do not derive from the proper law of the agreement. The security and therefore ultimate value of such an exclusive jurisdiction clause thus turns on the scope and certainty of application of the 'vitiating' factors set out in *The Chaparral*.

Two American commentators have observed that 'in light of the parties' **5.34** purpose for including a forum clause in their agreement in order to ensure predictability in their relationship, such objective has not been obtained'[101] and the nature of the overweening bargaining power exception may not be such as to conduce certainty and predictability of outcome. It is noteworthy, therefore, that (possibly in response to such a position) the Supreme Court's decision in *Carnival Cruise Lines Inc v Shute*,[102] at first blush at least, narrowed the scope of the 'overweening bargaining power' exception. In *The Chaparral*, the Court had laid stress on the fact that the exclusive jurisdiction clause in that case had been the product of a freely negotiated arm's length agreement between international corporations.[103] In *Carnival Cruise*, it made it clear that the apparent corollary of this observation, namely that 'a non-negotiated forum selection clause in a form ticket contract [such as the clause in issue] is never enforceable',[104] did not follow.[105] However, feeling the need to provide some residual escape valve, at least in relation to forum selection clauses contained in standard form passage contracts, the Court stated that such contracts remain 'subject to judicial scrutiny for fundamental fairness'. One would not anticipate that the introduction of a concept such as 'fundamental fairness' is conducive to certainty in this area although it would appear that the Supreme Court only envisaged its application to standard form forum selection clauses.

The concern which no doubt informed the Supreme Court's 'fundamen- **5.35** tal fairness' proviso and its earlier reference to overweening bargaining power is based on the notion that, in certain types of contract, there is no realistic opportunity to negotiate and there is a great disparity between the parties in terms of legal and commercial sophistication. Kahn-Freund

---

[100] As opposed to more explicitly public policy grounds: see discussion at paras 5.37 ff below.

[101] Covey, AE and Morris, MS, 'The Enforceability of Agreements Providing for Forum and Choice of Law Selection' (1984) 61 Denver Law Journal 837, 850.

[102] 499 US 585 (1991).

[103] 407 US 1, 12 (1972); [1972] 2 Lloyd's Rep 315, 322.

[104] 499 US 585 (1991).

[105] Sturley, MF, 'Forum Selection Clauses in Cruise Line Tickets: An Update on Congressional Action "Overruling" the Supreme Court' (1993) 24 Journal of Maritime Law and Commerce 399 notes that Congress has reversed the effect of *Carnival Cruise* (but only in relation to cruise liners and not consumer contracts generally) by amending the Vessel Owners' Liability Act 46 USC App § 183c (1988).

has observed that 'the checking of an abuse of superior bargaining power through standard jurisdiction clauses is or should be essential'.[106] European Council Regulation 44/2001 adopts a rather different strategy to that of United States courts by giving extremely limited effect to jurisdiction agreements in insurance, employment, and consumer contracts. Only agreements entered into after the dispute has arisen or in favour of the assured or consumer will be given effect to.[107] The Official Commentary on the Brussels Convention, the Regulation's forebear, stated in relation to insurance contracts that 'agreements concluded before a dispute arises will have no legal force if they are contrary to the rules of jurisdiction laid down in the Convention. The purpose of this Article is to prevent the parties from limiting the choice offered by this Convention to the policy-holder, and to prevent the insurer from avoiding the restrictions imposed under Article 11.'[108] In one sense, the Regulation's strategy provides greater certainty; in another less. Greater certainty is provided in that there is no scope for jurisdictional battles over such elusive concepts as 'fundamental fairness'. On the other hand, some uncertainty is generated, at least for the 'stronger party' in such contracts, by reason of the fact that the insured, consumer, and employee respectively are afforded some latitude as to choice of forum.

5.36 The arguments considered in the preceding paragraphs assume that a direct assault is being made upon the jurisdiction or arbitration agreement in question by reference to such vitiating factors as may be able to be deployed. It is important to appreciate that the mere fact that a contract that contains a jurisdiction or arbitration clause may have been avoided *ab initio* will generally not displace a jurisdiction or arbitration clause contained in such a contract.[109] In other words, unless specifically attacked, an arbitration or exclusive jurisdiction clause will continue in existence after avoidance of the contract in which it is contained.[110] This is what is known in arbitration as the doctrine of separability or sever-

---

[106] (n 42 above) 846 n 120.

[107] Articles 13, 17, and 21. cf Unfair Terms in Consumer Contracts Regulations 1999, SI 1999/2083; and the Court of Justice's decision in C–240/98, *Oceano Grupo v Quintero* [2000], which upheld the application of Directive 93/13/EC to strike down a jurisdiction agreement in a contract for the sale of encyclopaedias in favour of the courts of Barcelona, the seller's principal place of business but where none of the Spanish purchasers lived.

[108] Jenard Report [1979] OJ C59/1, 33.

[109] *Mackender v Feldia AG* [1967] QB 590, 598 and 603–604. This is now enshrined in s 7 of the Arbitration Act 1996 (UK) in cases where the arbitration agreement is governed by English law.

[110] *Harbour Assurance Co (UK) Ltd v Kansa General International Insurance Co Ltd* [1993] QB 701. See also, in the United States, *Prima Paint Corporation v Flood & Conklin Manufacturing Co* 388 US 395 (1967). For an example of a direct assault upon an exclusive jurisdiction agreement, anticipating and bypassing the separability doctrine, see *Commonwealth Bank of Australia v White; ex parte The Society of Lloyd's* [1999] 2 VR 681.

ability. It applies equally in the context of jurisdiction clauses. By way of illustration, in *FAI General Insurance Co Ltd v Ocean Marine Mutual Protection and Indemnity Association*,[111] FAI commenced proceedings in the Supreme Court of New South Wales seeking declarations that certain policies of reinsurance had been avoided for non-disclosure. The policies were held to have contained exclusive jurisdiction clauses for the English courts. In answer to an application to stay proceedings by virtue of those clauses, FAI submitted that, as the policies had been avoided, so too had the jurisdiction clauses. This argument was rejected and the proceedings were stayed.[112]

3. Overriding Effect of Mandatory Forum Law

An important exception to the general policy in favour of the enforcement **5.37** of exclusive jurisdiction clauses arises from the occasional clash of such agreements with mandatory rules of the forum in which a plaintiff has commenced or desires to commence proceedings in prima facia breach of the clause. An English example of this principle is found in *The Hollandia*,[113] where the House of Lords refused to stay proceedings notwithstanding the existence of an exclusive jurisdiction agreement for the Dutch courts. This was for the reason that any proceedings in The Netherlands would have had the effect of lessening the carrier's liability, contrary to the Hague-Visby Rules, scheduled to the Carriage of Goods by Sea Act 1971 which, as and in the way that it implemented the United Kingdom's obligations under an international treaty, had the status of a mandatory law of the forum.[114] Proceedings were only stayed in *Pirelli v United Thai Shipping Corporation*[115] in favour of Thailand, nominated in an exclusive jurisdiction clause, in circumstances where the defendant was required to undertake not to plead a lower limit of carrier liability applicable in Thailand and not to take any limitation point.[116]

The mandatory operation of the Hague-Visby Rules has also provided the **5.38**

---

[111] (1997) 41 NSWLR 559.

[112] See also *Ash v Lloyd's Corp* (1991) 6 OR (3d) 235, 244–248; approved at (1992) 9 OR (3d) 755, 758; *Ferris v Plaister* (1994) 34 NSWLR 474; *Sonantrach Petroleum Corp v Ferrell Int Ltd* [2001] 1 All ER Comm 627.

[113] [1983] AC 565. cf *Maharani Woollen Mills Co v Anchor Line* (1927) 29 Ll LR 169.

[114] Unless a defendant in similar circumstances were to submit to the jurisdiction of the English courts within the meaning of Article 24 of Council Regulation 44/2001, this case would be decided differently today as Article 23 would give exclusive jurisdiction to the Dutch courts.

[115] [2000] 1 Lloyd's Rep 663, 669.

[116] See also *Baghlaf Al Zafer v Pakistan National Shipping Co* [1998] 2 Lloyd's Rep 229 but see the later decision in the same case reported at [2000] 1 Lloyd's Rep 1. See also *BMG Trading Limited v AS McKay Ltd* [1998] I L Pr 691.

occasion for other jurisdictions to override exclusive jurisdiction clauses in similar circumstances.[117] Other United Kingdom statutes which arguably merit the description of mandatory laws of the forum and which therefore might be invoked to subvert the operation of a foreign exclusive jurisdiction agreement include the Consumer Credit Act 1974,[118] the Law Reform (Personal Injuries) Act 1948,[119] and the Fatal Accidents Act.[120] In Australia, the Insurance Contracts Act was held to be such a mandatory law, operating to override an English exclusive jurisdiction clause, in *Akai Pty Ltd v People's Insurance Company*[121] as has the Trade Practices Act, although the position in relation to that Act can probably not be treated as settled.[122]

5.39 When considering the relationship between the operation of mandatory laws of the forum and jurisdiction agreements, it is most important to appreciate that a mandatory law will not be permitted to override a jurisdiction agreement in cases where the nominated court is in a member state of the European Union or is a contracting state to the Brussels or Lugano Convention. So much is established by the European Court of Justice's decision in *Sanicentral GmbH v Collin*.[123] In *Re the Import of Italian Sports Cars*,[124] the plaintiff sought, *inter alia*, damages under German cartel law. The defendant challenged the Stuttgart Landgericht's jurisdiction on the basis of an agreement between the parties to submit disputes exclusively to the courts of Modena and this objection was upheld. On appeal, the Oberlandesgericht, Stuttgart noted that under German cartel law, parties could not rely on a jurisdiction agreement and so evade the public law regulations of that law but emphasized that Article 17 of the

---

[117] *Compagnie des Messageries Maritimes v Wilson* (1954) 94 CLR 577; *Kim Meller Imports Pty Ltd v Eurolevant SpA* (1986) 7 NSWLR 269; *Hi-Fert Pty Ltd v United Shipping Adriatic Inc* (1998) 89 FCR 166; *Chowdhury v Mitsui OSK Lines Ltd* [1970] 2 Lloyd's Rep 272; *Union Insurance Society of Canton v SS Elikon* 642 F 2d 721 (4th Cir, 1981); *Agro Co of Canada Ltd v The Regal Scout* (1983) 148 DLR (3rd) 412; *The Epar* [1985] 2 MLJ 3; *The Andhika Samyra* [1989] 1 HKLR 198. For Dutch examples, see Verheul, JP, 'The *Forum (Non) Conveniens* in English and Dutch Law and Under Some International Conventions' (1986) 35 ICLQ 413, 419 n 32.

[118] Section 141(1).

[119] Especially s 1(3). See also Kahn-Freund (n 42 above) 844. For examples of United States statutes apart from the Carriage of Goods by Sea Act which manifest a mandatory forum policy, see Covey, AE and Morris, MS (n 101 above) 844–847.

[120] *Domansa v Derin Shipping & Trading Co Inc* [2001] 1 Lloyd's Rep 362, 368.

[121] (1997) 188 CLR 418.

[122] *Commonwealth Bank of Australia v White; ex parte The Society of Lloyd's* [1999] 2 VR 681, 704–705, considered further in para 5.45 below. cf *Leigh-Mardon Pty Ltd v PRC Inc* (1993) 44 FCR 88.

[123] Case 25/79 [1979] ECR 3423. It should be noted, however, that the social protection typically afforded by mandatory laws in the fields of employment, insurance, and consumer contracts are given jurisdictional force in ss 3, 4, and 5 of Chapter II of European Council Regulation 44/2001.

[124] [1992] I L Pr 188.

Brussels Convention (Article 23 of Council Regulation 44/2001) required qualification of this position where, as here, the nominated court was that of another Contracting State.[125]

To return to the position at common law, it should be noted that argu- **5.40** ments based on public policy cannot be taken too far in attempts to circumvent the operation of an exclusive jurisdiction clause, a point made by Lord Diplock in *The Hollandia*[126] and demonstrated by the unsuccessful argument advanced in *The Benarty*.[127] In this light, it is to be stressed that there is always a need in the conflict of laws to distinguish between laws of purely local application and mandatory laws. It is somewhat difficult, for example, to see exactly what mandatory law of the forum was being upheld in *Coast Lines Ltd v Hudig & Veder NV*,[128] where the Court of Appeal refused to enforce an exclusive jurisdiction clause in favour of the Dutch courts. Rather than advancing a mandatory policy of the forum, the Court sought to avoid the operation of a mandatory Dutch law considered to be 'contrary to the general understanding of commercial men'.[129]

Referring to mandatory laws, Juenger was surely right to observe that 'up **5.41** to now, no one has been able to delineate criteria that would tell us, with some precision, what rules qualify for the special treatment this class demands'.[130] It was either a failure sufficiently to distinguish between local and mandatory laws, or a perception that the United States doctrine[131] which refused to give effect to exclusion clauses in contracts in fact represented a mandatory law of the forum, that underpinned both the majority judgment in the 5th Circuit Court of Appeals[132] and Justice Douglas's dissent in *The Chaparral*.[133] Justice Douglas stated that:

The forum selection clause is part and parcel of the exculpatory provision in the towing agreement which . . . is not enforceable in American courts. For only by avoiding litigation in the United States could petitioner hope to evade the *Bisso* doctrine. . . . The instant stratagem of specifying a foreign forum is essentially the same as invoking a foreign law of construction except that the present circumvention also requires the American party to travel across an ocean to seek relief. Unless we are prepared to overrule *Bisso* we should not countenance devices designed solely for the purpose of evading its prohibition.[134]

---

[125] ibid 192–193.
[126] [1983] AC 565, 575.
[127] [1984] 2 Lloyd's Rep 244.
[128] [1972] 2 QB 34.
[129] ibid 44 per Lord Denning.
[130] (n 4 above) 81.
[131] As represented by the Supreme Court's decision in *Bisso v Inland Waterways Corp* 349 US 85 (1955).
[132] 428 F 2d 888, 895 (5th Cir, 1970), reported sub nom *In re Unterweser Reederi GmbH*.
[133] 407 US 1, 21 (1972); [1972] 2 Lloyd's Rep 315, 323.
[134] ibid 24; 324 of Lloyd's Rep.

The majority decision, however, was predicated on a far narrower perception of the *Bisso* doctrine's sphere of operation, noting that '*Bisso* rested on considerations with respect to the towage business strictly in American waters, and those considerations are not controlling in an international commercial agreement.'[135]

5.42 In *Oceanic Sun Line Special Shipping Co Inc v Fay*, the New South Wales Court of Appeal gave a similar and unduly expansive scope to the Contracts Review Act 1980 (NSW).[136] In the High Court, however, Brennan J correctly observed that had the exclusive jurisdiction clause been part of the contract of carriage, Greek law would probably have been held to be the proper law of the contract (and of the jurisdiction clause, if regarded as a separate agreement) which would therefore have been outside the Act's reach.[137] The temptation to characterize forum law as of a mandatory character, apart from doing damage to the conceptual integrity of the conflict of laws,[138] is also apt to create an incentive for parties bound by exclusive jurisdiction agreements to seek to justify the commencement of proceedings in breach of such a clause on the basis of a desire to take advantage of certain forum laws alleged to be of mandatory operation. It is apt to create a true conflict of laws.

5.43 Certain types of law are more likely, because of their very nature, to attract the character of a mandatory law of the forum. In the 5th Circuit Court of Appeals in *The Chaparral*,[139] in a dissenting opinion broadly supporting the use and legitimacy of exclusive jurisdiction clauses, Judge Wisdom issued an important caveat:

> In cases of bankruptcy, divorce, succession, real rights and regulation of public authorities, for example, courts cannot remit the dispute to a foreign forum lest a foreign forum render a decree conflicting with our ordering of these affairs.[140]

5.44 The same idea has been elegantly put by Graupner,[141] who stated that 'submission to a foreign Court removes only those objections which are purely personal to a particular submitting party. . . . The foreign Court will not acquire jurisdiction by submission in matters which by their nature, at common law or by statute, do not belong to it, but fall within the exclusive competence of the English Courts.'[142] Both of these observations resemble Lord Diplock's insight in a related context in *British*

---

[135] ibid 15–16; 321 of Lloyd's Rep.   [136] (1987) 8 NSWLR 242, 267.
[137] (1988) 165 CLR 197, 231.   [38] See Juenger, FK (n 4 above) 81–82.
[139] 428 F 2d 888 (5th Cir, 1970), reported sub nom *In re Unterweser Reederi GmbH*.
[140] ibid 906.
[141] 'Contractual Stipulations Conferring Exclusive Jurisdiction upon Foreign Courts in the Law of England and Scotland' (1943) 59 LQR 227.
[142] ibid 236.

Airways Board v Laker Airways Ltd[143] that certain cases—described as 'single forum' cases[144]—are only capable of being properly tried in one forum. Accordingly, it will be appropriate for courts to refuse to enforce foreign exclusive jurisdiction clauses in cases properly falling within the very limited notion of 'single forum' cases. Two New Zealand cases, concerning intellectual property rights and insolvent winding up respectively, provide interesting examples.[145]

On the other hand, the attempts of certain non-English Lloyd's 'Names' **5.45** to escape exclusive jurisdiction clauses for England in actions seeking declarations of non-liability and rescission of their membership agreements on the basis of violation of various national securities and consumer protection legislation have been successfully resisted in the United States,[146] Canada,[147] and New Zealand[148] notwithstanding the character of such legislation. In Australia, decisions have pointed in different directions. Thus, in *Williams v The Society of Lloyd's*,[149] proceedings including a claim under the Trade Practices Act were stayed by reason of an exclusive jurisdiction clause whereas in *Commonwealth Bank of Australia v White; ex parte The Society of Lloyd's*,[150] where Mr White invoked both the Trade Practices Act and the Companies Code in seeking damages and declarations that agreements he had with Lloyd's were void or unenforceable for illegality, the Court refused to give effect to an exclusive jurisdiction clause for the English courts drawn in extremely wide terms. It is significant that the proceedings contained a direct assault on the jurisdiction clause as opposed to a generalized attack on the broad contractual relationship between Mr White and Lloyd's. Byrne J regarded the exclusive jurisdiction clause as, in effect, an impermissible circumvention of both the Trade Practices Act and the Companies legislation, relief under which would not have been available in the English proceedings. He said:

It is undesirable that parties should, by entering into an exclusive jurisdiction agreement, be able to circumvent a legislative scheme established by Parliament to protect investors purchasing interests or prescribed interests. Put more positively, the statutes creating these standards of commercial behaviour for persons

---

[143] [1985] AC 58.   [144] ibid 80.
[145] *Apple Computer Inc v Apple Corps SA* [1990] 2 NZLR 598; *Air Nauru v Niue Airlines Ltd* [1993] 2 NZLR 632.
[146] *Riley v Kingsley Underwriting Agencies Ltd* 969 F 2d 953 (1992); *Roby v Corporation of Lloyd's* 996 F 2d 1353 (1993); *Bonny v Society of Lloyd's* 3 F 3d 156 (1993); *Shell v RW Sturge Ltd* 55 F 3d 1227 (1995); *Allen v Lloyd's of London* 94 F 3d 923 (1996); *Haynsworth v Corporation of Lloyd's* 121 F 3d 956 (1997); *Richards v Lloyd's of London* 135 F 3d 1289 (1998) (*en banc*).
[147] *Ash v Lloyd's Corporation* (1991) 6 OR (3d) 235; (1992) 9 OR (3d) 755.
[148] *Society of Lloyd's v Hyslop* [1993] 3 NZLR 135.
[149] [1994] 2 VR 274.   [150] [1999] 2 VR 681.

doing business in this jurisdiction do not exempt foreign corporations. Moreover, the policy behind them would not be served if exemption might be achieved by inserting stipulations as to foreign law or forum.[151]

A similar approach was taken by the three dissenting judges in the decision of the United States' Court of Appeals for the 9th Circuit in *Richards v Lloyd's of London*[152] who placed emphasis upon an observation by the United States Supreme Court in *Mitsubishi Motors Corp v Soler Chrysler-Plymouth Inc*[153] to the effect that 'in the event the choice of forum and choice of law clauses operated in tandem as a prospective waiver of a party's right to pursue statutory remedies for anti-trust violations, we would have little hesitation in condemning the agreement as against public policy'. The majority in *Richards* were content to uphold the parties' bargain in agreeing to exclusive jurisdiction in England on the basis that, notwithstanding the American statutory claims would not be available in England, they were nonetheless satisfied that English law provided 'sufficient', albeit narrower, recourse and protection for the Names.[154] In *Donohue v Armco Inc*, Lord Scott (but not the other members of the House of Lords) took the view that an English exclusive jurisdiction clause coupled with an English choice of law clause should not be interpreted as excluding a party's right to bring a RICO Act claim in the United States. He reached this conclusion as a matter of interpretation of the agreement rather than by resort to notions of mandatory law or public policy. His reasoning was simple—'it is common ground that a RICO Act claim could not be brought in an English Court. It cannot, in my opinion, be supposed that in submitting to the exclusive jurisdiction of the English courts, the parties had in mind claims which an English court had no jurisdiction to entertain.'[155]

5.46 It was the assumed 'tandem' effect of an English choice of law and English exclusive jurisdiction clause in *Akai Pty Ltd v People's Insurance Company*[156] that led a majority of the High Court of Australia to refuse to stay New South Wales proceedings commenced in apparent breach of that clause. It was considered that the dual effect of those clauses would be

---

[151] ibid 704. Note that leave to appeal from this decision was refused by the Victorian Court of Appeal and special leave to appeal was refused by the High Court of Australia. See also *Green v Australian Industrial Investment Ltd* (1989) 90 ALR 500, 512.

[152] 135 F 3d 1289 (1998) (*en banc*).

[153] 473 US 614, 637 n 19 (1985).

[154] A similar reasoning process, based upon the receipt of expert evidence as to the law of Virginia, was applied by Beazley J in *Leigh-Mardon Pty Ltd v PRC Inc* (1993) 44 FCR 88, 104–105.

[155] [2002] 1 Lloyd's Rep 425, 442. The premise to his reasoning, namely that a RICO Act claim could not be brought in England, is arguably open to question: see paras 4.98–4.99 above.

[156] (1997) 188 CLR 418.

that the otherwise applicable Insurance Contracts Act, a piece of remedial Australian legislation designed to ameliorate the rigidity of common law principles relating to insurance, would not be applied were the proceedings stayed in favour of England where English and not Australian statutory law would govern the resolution of the parties' contractual dispute. That perception proved to be correct.[157]

The role of a mandatory law of the forum may also have the consequence,   **5.47** in the context of an international arbitration agreement, that a matter is not 'capable of settlement by arbitration'. In *Tanning Research Laboratories Inc v O'Brien*,[158] Deane and Gaudron JJ observed that 'the words "capable of settlement by arbitration" indicate that the controversy must be one falling within the scope of the arbitration agreement and, *perhaps*, one relating to rights which are not required to be determined exclusively by the exercise of judicial power'.[159] Their Honours referred to Lord Mustill and Mr Boyd's observation that 'English law has never arrived at a general theory for distinguishing those disputes which may be settled by arbitration from those which may not' but that the powers of arbitrators 'are limited by considerations of public policy and by the fact that he [the arbitrator] is appointed by the parties and not by the state'.[160] By way of elaboration, Mustill and Boyd go on to observe that:

For example, he cannot impose a fine or a term of imprisonment, commit a person for contempt or issue a writ of subpoena; nor can he make an award which is binding on third parties or affects the public at large, such as a judgment in rem against a ship, an assessment of the rateable value of land, a divorce decree, a winding-up order or a decision that an agreement is exempt from the competition rules of the EEC under Article 85(3) of the Treaty of Rome.

Thus certain statutory claims may be of such a nature that a particular state requires such claims to be vindicated in public litigation. This was the issue that arose in the celebrated decision of the United States Supreme Court in *Mitsubishi Motors Corp v Soler Chrysler-Plymouth Inc*,[161] where it was held that an antitrust claim under the Sherman Act fell within the scope of an international arbitration clause and was capable of being referred to arbitration (or was arbitrable) on the footing that it would be determined in accordance with American law notwithstanding the fact that there was a Japanese choice of law clause contained in the parties' contract. Whether or not a Sherman Act claim would be arbitrable in circumstances where it fell within the scope of the arbitration clause

---

[157] [1998] 1 Lloyd's Rep 90.   [158] (1990) 169 CLR 332.
[159] ibid 351 (emphasis added).
[160] *Law and Practice of Commercial Arbitration in England* (2nd edn, 1989) 149–150.
[161] 473 US 614 (1985).

but where there was evidence that a contractual choice of law clause meant that it would never be heard on the merits because the governing law's choice of law rules would never have picked up the statutory claim is quite another matter. In such circumstances, the combined effect of an arbitration (or exclusive jurisdiction) clause and a choice of law clause may effectively result in a contracting out of a local statute. Such contracting out, even if held to be consensual, may be held to be illegitimate.

5.48 In Australia, it has been held by the New South Wales Court of Appeal that a Trade Practices Act claim founded on misleading or deceptive conduct may be the subject of a reference to arbitration in England,[162] although some doubt is arguably cast upon this conclusion by the later decision of the Full Court of the Federal Court of Australia in *Hi-Fert Pty Ltd v Kiukiang Maritime Carriers Inc (No 5)*.[163] A contrasting example is supplied by the decision in *Metrocall Inc v Electronic Tracking Systems Pty Ltd*,[164] where proceedings were commenced in the Industrial Relations Commission of New South Wales by a party to a licence agreement which contained a Texan law and arbitration clause. The licensee whose licence had been cancelled invoked the Commission's broad jurisdiction to set aside or vary contracts that were found to be harsh, unfair, or unconscionable. In making such an assessment, the Commission's constituent Act directed it to take into account matters of public interest and exercise its powers in a manner that furthered the industrial objectives set out in the Act. For this reason, the Commission concluded that Parliament intended that it exercise its functions not merely in the manner of ordinary *inter partes* litigation, but so as to assist in the achievement of industrial objectives set out in the Act. In the circumstances, the Commission reached the conclusion, notwithstanding the essentially commercial nature of the dispute, that the matter was not capable of settlement by arbitration and, accordingly, declined to grant the stay sought pursuant to the provisions of the International Arbitration Act 1974.

4. The Agreement's Continuing Efficacy

5.49 Unlike arguments already considered which claim that the jurisdiction agreement is voidable by reason of the conduct of one of the parties *at the time of* entry into the contract, the argument considered here relates to the *continuing* efficacy of the exclusive jurisdiction or arbitration clause and the question of when and how a party may lose the benefit of such a

---

[162] *Francis Travel Marketing Pty Ltd v Virgin Atlantic Airways Ltd* (1996) 39 NSWLR 160.
[163] (1998) 90 FCR 1, 23–24 and see para 5.67 below.
[164] (2000) 52 NSWLR 1.

clause. Apart from the case of frustration of the agreement,[165] this essentially involves an inquiry into the *conduct* of the parties *subsequent to* entry into the contract. Certain conduct including dilatoriness or unconscionable behaviour[166] on a defendant's part may found a conclusion that it has either waived, or is estopped from relying on, its right to enforce the exclusive jurisdiction or arbitration clause (at least by the remedy of a stay of proceedings or an anti-suit injunction). Alternatively, certain conduct may indicate a novation or contractual variation of the clause.[167]

It is clear that a party may not rely on the benefit of an exclusive jurisdic- **5.50** tion or arbitration clause where, by its own voluntary submission to the court in which the stay is sought, for example by the filing of a cross-claim or a defence on the merits, it has indicated a willingness to conduct litigation in the forum. In the context of Council Regulation 44/2001, this is enshrined in the fact that Article 23 concerning jurisdiction agreements is expressly made subject to Article 24 dealing with submission, and, where there has been a prior submission, Article 27 requires that the second seised court decline to exercise jurisdiction. Returning to the common law, where a party seeks a stay in favour of a forum other than that specified in an exclusive jurisdiction clause but on the basis of that clause, such an application is unlikely to be supported (at least on the basis of the jurisdiction clause) because the party, by its own conduct, has indicated a willingness not to be bound by it.[168] In *The Biskra*,[169] Sheen J stated that 'an application for a stay on grounds that the parties have agreed to submit the dispute to a foreign Court should be brought without delay after service of the writ'.[170] On the other hand, he also observed that there was 'no obligation on a person who may become defendant in proceedings to tell the plaintiff where to issue those proceedings'.[171] Prior to the issue of the writ, therefore, the initiative was in the hands of the plaintiff either to inquire directly as to whether the defendant would rely on the jurisdiction or arbitration clause or to force the matter by issuing proceedings.[172]

---

[165] *Carvalho v Hull, Blyth (Angola) Ltd* [1979] 1 WLR 1228, discussed more fully at para 5.71 below, although treated as a case of construction, may also be seen as a case in which the exclusive jurisdiction clause for the courts of Angola was frustrated. Schlesinger et al (n 91 above) 388–389 cite a closely analogous German decision concerning a jurisdiction clause for the Lebanese courts.

[166] *Donohue v Armco, Inc* [2002] 1 Lloyd's Rep 425, 433.

[167] *The Pia Vesta* [1984] 1 Lloyd's Rep 169 provides an example of this (originally a Danish jurisdiction clause). There may of course be an explicit novation in which case any earlier agreement will be of no effect: *The Lloydiana* [1983] 2 Lloyd's Rep 313, 319.

[168] *The Traugutt* [1985] 1 Lloyd's Rep 76.

[169] [1983] 2 Lloyd's Rep 59.

[170] ibid 62. Sheen J noted that a defendant need not (and, implicitly, should not) wait for service of the statement of claim before seeking a stay: ibid 62–63.

[171] ibid.

[172] ibid 62.

Clearly, however, inordinate delay in applying for a stay *after* the issue of the claim could justify a finding of waiver or estoppel by acquiescence.

5.51 In *The Vestris*,[173] the application for a stay on the basis of a New York exclusive jurisdiction clause was made only weeks before the scheduled hearing in circumstances where the parties had been discussing the claim for two years in contemplation of proceedings in England. A stay was refused.[174] In the converse situation, where there is an English jurisdiction or arbitration clause but where proceedings have taken place or have been pending for some time in another forum, the decision in *The Hida Maru*[175] at least suggests that English courts will be reluctant to find that the benefit of such an agreement has been waived.[176] That case would appear to be one of forum shopping *par excellence*: proceedings in England were only contemplated after a court-appointed expert had found that the defendants were not liable in delict and this report had been accepted by the Kuwaiti Court.[177] Moreover, although the plaintiffs then sought to bring a claim in contract in Kuwait, there was a possibility that the indemnity which they sought to rely on would be held to be invalid or unenforceable in that jurisdiction, a result which would not have obtained in England.[178]

5.52 None of the cases discussed above have adverted to the issue of what law should govern the question of the continuing efficacy of the jurisdiction agreement, or, in terms of the New York Convention, whether the arbitration clause has become inoperative, whether this question arises as a result of frustration, contractual novation, or where it is argued that the defendant has either waived the benefit of the agreement or should be estopped from relying on it. In all cases, the *lex fori* has simply been applied. In line with the approach to questions of validity and construction, there is much to be said for the view that the question of the continuing efficacy of a jurisdiction or arbitration clause should be governed by the proper law of the jurisdiction agreement, especially where novation and frustration are concerned. In *Recyclers of Australia Pty Ltd v Hettinga Equipment Inc*,[179] the Court proceeded on the footing that questions concerning the validity, legal effect, and interpretation of an agreement to arbitrate were governed by the proper law of the agreement. Where the

---

[173] (1932) 43 Ll L R 86.
[174] cf *The Christos* [1977] 1 Lloyd's Rep 109, where Brandon J held that the delay was not inordinate and that the enforcement of the Greek jurisdiction clause would not prejudice the plaintiffs.
[175] [1981] 2 Lloyd's Rep 510.
[176] See dictum of Watkins LJ cited at para 5.10 above.
[177] [1981] 2 Lloyd's Rep 510, 512.
[178] ibid 513.
[179] (2000) 100 FCR 420.

question of an agreement's continuing efficacy turns upon waiver or estoppel, it is arguable that these essentially equitable concepts may be governed by the law of the forum.[180]

With regard to unconscionable conduct, it has been made clear that 'it is **5.53** not open to the Court to conclude that the conduct of the defendants falls short of waiver but is so "reprehensible" that the Court will decline to enforce the contract as a matter of discretion'.[181] It is doubtful, however, to what extent this discipline has been followed in the case law. One commentator has suggested that the refusal to grant a stay in *The Fehmarn*[182] might more convincingly have been put on the basis of waiver or estoppel rather than discretion[183] and many of the discretion cases which consider 'whether the defendants genuinely desire trial in the foreign country, or are only seeking procedural advantages'[184] appear to be strongly influenced by the conduct of the defendants which presumably falls short of that sufficient to constitute waiver or estoppel.[185]

5. THE NATURE OF THE JURISDICTION AGREEMENT

Here, the argument which might be employed by a party seeking to extri- **5.54** cate itself from a jurisdiction agreement is that, on its proper construction, the agreement only confers *non-exclusive* jurisdiction on the nominated court or courts, that is, that it represents a submission to the jurisdiction and nothing more. The distinction between exclusive and non-exclusive jurisdiction clauses may be of great practical importance. A non-exclusive jurisdiction clause is technically described as a prorogation agreement and simply has the consequence that a defendant in proceedings in the nominated court is disarmed of arguments resisting the court's jurisdiction. In *Berisford plc v New Hampshire Insurance Co*,[186] it was stated that 'the fact that the parties have agreed in their contract that the English courts shall have jurisdiction (albeit a non-exclusive jurisdiction) creates a strong

---

[180] *The Amazonia* [1990] 1 Lloyd's Rep 236, 247 and 251 arguably points in this direction although Mann LJ did refer to the 'proper law of the estoppel'. See also *Man (Sugar) Ltd v Haryanto (No 2)* [1991] 1 Lloyd's Rep 429, 438. cf White, RW, 'Equitable Obligations in Private International Law: The Choice of Law' (1986) 11 Sydney Law Review 92. An argument that estoppel and waiver were either evidential or procedural would also result in the application of the *lex fori*.

[181] *The Ruben Martinez Villena* [1988] 1 Lloyd's Rep 435, 438 per Sheen J. In relation to delay, see also *The Vishva Apurva* [1992] 2 SLR 175, 185: 'Delay by the defendants is a factor in favour of the plaintiffs only if it amounts to a waiver of the defendants' rights under the exclusive jurisdiction clause'.

[182] [1957] 1 WLR 815; [1958] 1 WLR 159 discussed more extensively in paras 5.72 ff below.

[183] Webb, PRH (Note) '*The Fehmarn*' (1958) 7 ICLQ 599, 603.

[184] *The Eleftheria* [1970] P 94, 100.

[185] See, for example, *The Atlantic Song* [1983] 2 Lloyd's Rep 394, 398.

[186] [1990] 2 QB 631.

prima facie case that that jurisdiction is an appropriate one; it should in principle be a jurisdiction to which neither party to the contract can object as inappropriate; they have both implicitly agreed that it is appropriate'.[187] Conversely, where a party seeks a *Spiliada* stay in favour of the courts of the nominated (non-exclusive) jurisdiction, it will be difficult for a party resisting such an application to raise complaints or difficulties it may face were proceedings to be stayed in favour of that forum.[188]

5.55 A non-exclusive jurisdiction clause says nothing as to the parties' collective attitude to litigation in a forum other than that nominated. As such, while arguments to the effect that a jurisdiction agreement is non-exclusive will be of little moment in an application to stay proceedings *in the nominated forum* or in a challenge to the grant of leave to serve out of that jurisdiction,[189] they may be important in the context of resisting a challenge to the jurisdiction or a stay application in favour of the courts of another state. A successful argument that the jurisdiction agreement represents merely a non-exclusive submission to the nominated court's jurisdiction may also be vital in resisting an application to restrain foreign proceedings by way of an anti-suit injunction. The applicant's 'legal right' will be reduced on such an interpretation from a right to insist on litigation in the nominated forum to a right to insist that the other party may not oppose jurisdiction in that forum, a right which will by itself not warrant the restraint of proceedings commenced by the other party in another forum.

5.56 Whether a jurisdiction agreement is exclusive or non-exclusive will be a matter of construction. *Hoerter v Hanover Telegraph Works*[190] made it clear that questions of interpretation or construction of such agreements are governed by the proper law of the contract. Of course, it should be noted that, in common law countries at least, the content of the proper law will generally be taken to correspond to the law of the forum in the absence of proof otherwise, this being always a question of fact.[191] Bingham J's alternative approach to the construction of the jurisdiction clause in *The Iran Vojdan*[192] illustrates both the correct approach to be applied to questions

---

[187] [1990] 2 QB 646.

[188] *Ace Insurance SA NV v Zurich Insurance Co* [2001] 1 Lloyd's Rep 618, 630–631. See, generally, Fawcett, JJ, 'Non-exclusive Jurisdiction Agreements in Private International Law' [2001] LMCLQ 234.

[189] *The Chaparral* [1968] 2 Lloyd's Rep 158, 162 and 164; *Gulf Bank KSC v Mitsubishi Heavy Industries Ltd* [1994] 1 Lloyd's Rep 323, 329.

[190] (1893) 10 TLR 103, 104; see also *Nova (Jersey) Knit Ltd v Kammgarn Spinnerei GmbH* [1977] 1 WLR 713, 718 and 730.

[191] See, generally, Fentiman, RG, *Foreign Law in English Courts* (1999).

[192] [1984] 2 Lloyd's Rep 380. See also *Sonantrach Petroleum Corp v Ferrell Int Ltd* [2001] 1 All ER Comm 627.

of construction and the fact that propositions of English domestic law regularly perform the function of a notional foreign law. The jurisdiction clause in this case was structured in such a way that its content depended upon an election under an impermissible floating choice of law clause by one of the parties. Proceeding on the assumption that the proper law of the contract was Iranian, Bingham J stated that:

I think, as a matter of construction, that it is artificial and unreal to give effect to the ancillary provision while rejecting the main provision to which it is, as I think, parasitic. Accordingly, I reach the conclusion that this must be treated as a case in which there is no exclusive jurisdiction, applying the principles of English law on the assumption that that is the same as Iranian law.[193]

Although Article 10(1) of the Rome Convention on the Law Applicable to Contractual Obligations adopts a similar position to *Hoerter* in relation to interpretation of contracts, by Article 1(2)(d), that Convention has no application to choice of court or arbitration agreements so that the common law position continues to obtain in the United Kingdom. **5.57**

Notwithstanding what appears to be the clear textbook position and with some exceptions,[194] rather than asking what construction the proper law would place on the jurisdiction clause, English, American, and Australian courts have tended simply to construe the language used by the parties in jurisdiction clauses as though a domestic contract were involved. In this they have followed the counsel of Sir Samuel Evans in *The Cap Blanco*[195] that 'in dealing with commercial documents of this kind, effect must be given, if the terms of the contract permit it, to the obvious intention and agreement of the parties'.[196] This is an area where it is notorious that 'different persons might take different views'.[197] Each case will obviously turn on the actual terms to be found in the jurisdiction clause. It is trite that the whole of the clause, and indeed the whole of the contract in which it appears, must be construed to ascertain the proper meaning of the clause. Thus, in *FAI General Insurance Co Ltd v Ocean Marine Mutual Protection and Indemnity Association*,[198] while Giles J did not consider that the words 'subject to English jurisdiction' themselves connoted exclusivity, the composite phrase 'This Reinsurance is subject to English jurisdiction' was held to amount to an exclusive submission of all disputes **5.58**

---

[193] ibid 385.
[194] *Evans Marshall & Co v Bertola SA* [1973] 1 WLR 349, 361 (jurisdiction clause for Barcelona); *The Iran Vojdan* [1984] 2 Lloyd's Rep 380, 385.
[195] [1913] P 130.
[196] ibid 136.
[197] *Austrian Lloyd Steamship Co v Gresham Life Assurance Society Ltd* [1903] 1 KB 249, 251. For an example, compare *Street Sound Around Alecs Inc v M/V Royal Container* 30 F Supp 2d 661 (SDNY) and *The Pacific Senator* [2001] 2 Lloyd's Rep 674, 677.
[198] (1997) 41 NSWLR 117, 127.

arising under or in connection with the reinsurance contract in question. This conclusion was fortified by the existence of an express choice of English law.

5.59 The better view is that the use of the word 'exclusive' is not essential for a clause to be construed as having this effect.[199] Indeed it has been said that the contrary position would represent 'a surrender to formalism'[200] although that is the approach that appears to obtain in some United States circuits.[201] Canons of construction such as *expressio unius exclusio alterius* and *contra proferentem* may play a role in this area[202] and it has also been said that especially clear language will be required for jurisdiction clauses in certain types of contract to be held to be exclusive.[203] On the other hand, the judgment of the Court of Appeal in *Sohio Supply Co v Gatoil (USA) Inc,*[204] albeit in relation to an English jurisdiction clause, arguably introduces a presumption that, in freely negotiated and arms' length commercial contracts, any ambiguity in the jurisdiction clause should be resolved in favour of an exclusive interpretation. Staughton LJ stated that he could:

> think of no reason at all why they [the parties] should choose to go to the trouble of saying that the English Court should have non-exclusive jurisdiction. I can think of every reason why they should choose that some Court, in this case the English Court, should have exclusive jurisdiction.[205]

> Two reasons that have been suggested, however, are that such a clause may have been intended simply to put the existing jurisdiction beyond doubt or that it may have been inserted in a boilerplate fashion without either party in fact adverting to it.[206]

5.60 It suffices to note that it is not unusual for judges to take different inter-

---

[199] See, for example, *FAI General Insurance Co Ltd v Ocean Marine Mutual Protection and Indemnity Association* (1997) 41 NSWLR 117, 126.

[200] *Continental Bank NA v Aeakos Compania Naviera SA* [1994] 1 WLR 588, 594.

[201] See *The Pacific Senator* [2001] 2 Lloyd's Rep 674, 676–677.

[202] *Continental Bank NA v Aeakos Compania Naviera SA* [1994] 1 WLR 588, 594. Note, however, that an argument to the effect that a jurisdiction clause inserted for the sole benefit of one of the parties should be construed against it was rejected on the facts by Cairns, LJ in *The Makefjell* [1976] 2 Lloyd's Rep 29, 32.

[203] *Berisford plc v New Hampshire Insurance Co* [1990] 2 QB 631, 637 citing Staughton LJ in *Sohio Supply Co v Gatoil (USA) Inc* [1989] 1 Lloyd's Rep 588, 591–592 in relation to insurance contracts.

[204] [1987] 1 Lloyd's Rep 588.

[205] ibid 591. See also *British Aerospace plc v Dee Howard Co* [1993] 1 Lloyd's Rep 368, esp 374; cf *Cannon Screen Entertainment Ltd v Handmade Films (Distributors) Ltd* (11 July 1989), cited in *British Aerospace* ibid 374.

[206] *FAI General Insurance Co Ltd v Ocean Marine Mutual Protection and Indemnity Association* (1997) 41 NSWLR 117, 127.

pretations of the same clause.[207] Only the most explicit of exclusive jurisdiction clauses will be totally immune from challenge and, even then, a
perceived clarity may be lost either in translation or in a decision, by the
court seised, to examine only one of several language versions of the
contract. This was the case in *YTC Universal Ltd v Trans Europa SA,*[208]
where only the Spanish but not the English version of the contract
included an exclusive jurisdiction clause for Spain. In refusing to set aside
an order for service out of the jurisdiction, the Court of Appeal relied
upon the English version of the contract.

6. SCOPE AND CONSTRUCTION OF THE JURISDICTION OR ARBITRATION AGREEMENT

Another argument, based on the construction of a jurisdiction or arbitra- **5.61**
tion clause, is that the actual dispute before the court does not fall within
the clause's scope. Examples of cases where such arguments have been
accepted include *Trendtex Trading Corporation v Crédit Suisse,*[209] Sheen J's
decision at first instance in *The Sennar (No 2)*[210] and, in respect of two of
five claims, *Ocarina Marine Ltd v Macard Stein & Co.*[211] Other examples are
referred to below.

The most common context in which a construction argument relating to **5.62**
the scope of the jurisdiction or arbitration agreement will arise is where
the claim includes non-contractual counts, whether in tort, restitution, or
statutory. Whether or not a dispute or claim falls within the scope of a
jurisdiction or arbitration clause is properly a question for the proper law
of the contract.[212] Diplock LJ's decision in *The Sindh*[213] represents a model
application of this approach. In this case, the plaintiff sought to escape
from a French exclusive jurisdiction clause by framing its claim in
England in tort rather than contract. Diplock LJ stated that 'it being therefore now undisputed that the proper law of the contract, which included
the exclusive jurisdiction clause, was French; it being undisputed that,

---

[207] See *Austrian Lloyd Steamship Co v Gresham Life Assurance Society Ltd* [1903] 1 KB 249 and
Hoerter v Hanover Telegraph Works (1893) 10 TLR 22 and 103 where not only were the first
instance interpretations overturned on appeal but both appellate courts took a different
interpretation of what were very similar clauses.
[208] (Note) [1973] 1 Lloyd's Rep 480.
[209] [1980] QB 629, 658.
[210] [1983] 2 Lloyd's Rep 399, 401, reversed on appeal: [1984] 2 Lloyd's Rep 142 (Court of
Appeal); [1985] 1 WLR 490 (House of Lords).
[211] [1994] 2 Lloyd's Rep 524.
[212] *Recyclers of Australia Pty Ltd v Hettinga Equipment Inc* (2000) 100 FCR 420, 430–434. Apart
from authority, further arguments in favour of this approach are supplied by Briggs, A,
'Forum non Conveniens—An Update' [1985] 3 LMCLQ 360, 367–368.
[213] [1975] 1 Lloyd's Rep 372.

interpreted according to French law, the clause covered claims which the plaintiffs are seeking to put forward in the English action, no question of law . . . appears to me to arise'.[214] The English proceedings were stayed.[215]

5.63 In *The Makefjell*,[216] the plaintiffs sought to escape an exclusive jurisdiction clause for Oslo by framing at least one of their causes of action in tort. That course was supplemented by a semantic argument to the effect that the reference in the jurisdiction clause to 'any claim' was to contractual claims only and that a tort claim would only be caught by a clause referring to any or all 'disputes'. This argument was rejected[217] but it is significant to note that English cases were cited on the meaning of 'claim' and 'dispute'. In other words, there was no attempt to consider whether the proper law would have viewed a claim in negligence as falling outside the clause's scope. Commenting on these two cases, Knight[218] has observed that 'if it can be seen that a plaintiff is attempting a subtle method of forum shopping [by seeking to escape the exclusive jurisdiction clause] the court will find any way of curtailing that attempt rather than permit abuse of their policy [proper adherence to bargain]'.[219]

5.64 Debate as to the scope of a jurisdiction or arbitration clause in the sense of what type of claims the parties intended would be caught by such a clause necessarily focuses upon the width of the language of the clause in question. Such language may vary from, for example, the apparently narrow 'all disputes arising under this contract are to be submitted to arbitration' to the much broader 'all disputes arising under, out of or from, relating to or in any way whatsoever connected with this contract are to be submitted to arbitration'. On an ordinary construction of these two clauses, it may be thought that the former would not capture disputes arising out of pre-contractual representations whereas the latter did.[220]

---

[214] ibid 374. This analysis was cited with approval by Kerr LJ in *The Sennar (No 2)* [1984] 2 Lloyd's Rep 142, 148.

[215] No stay was granted in *The Forum Craftsman* [1985] 1 Lloyd's Rep 291, where the plaintiff framed its claim in tort, but this was because it was held not to be party to the bill of lading containing the jurisdiction clause, according to its proper (Japanese) law.

[216] [1975] 1 Lloyd's Rep 528; [1976] 2 Lloyd's Rep 29.

[217] As it was in *The Happy Pioneer* [1983] HKLR 43, 47, where the approach and result in *The Makefjell* was approved of.

[218] 'Avoidance of Foreign Jurisdiction Clauses in International Contracts' (1977) 26 ICLQ 664.

[219] ibid 674. This particularly comes through in the judgment of Cairns LJ in *The Makefell* [1976] 2 Lloyd's Rep 29. See also *The Sennar (No 2)* [1985] 1 WLR 490.

[220] A number of United States cases have so held: *Re Kinoshita & Co* 287 F 2d 951 (1961); *Mediterranean Enterprises Inc v Ssangyong Corporation* 708 F 2d 1458 (1983). See also *Tracer Research v National Environmental Services Co* 42 F 3d 1292 (1994); cf *Terra International Inc v Mississipi Chemical Corporation* 119 F 3d 6988 (1997).

English courts, in particular, have in recent times eschewed any particu- **5.65** larly close construction of the precise words ˌ ontained in a jurisdiction or arbitration clause and have leaned distinctly towards a broad and gener- ous interpretation of the scope of jurisdiction and arbitration agree- ments,[221] applying as part of this process a presumption in favour of 'one stop adjudication', namely the view that the parties, especially parties to a commercial contract, should not be taken to have intended that certain types of claim should be heard exclusively in one court or, as the case may be, by arbitration (those strictly falling within the scope of the clause) but that others need not be.[222] In so doing, they exhibit the strong modern prejudice noted elsewhere in this book to minimize the scope for incon- sistent decisions as a result of related concurrent proceedings or, to express it positively, to foster the goal of 'one-stop adjudication'.[223] This presumption may be particularly important in cases where the clause in question simply records that the parties submit to the exclusive jurisdic- tion of the courts of one particular forum without specifying the nature of the disputes so submitted.[224]

A leading example of the broad approach to questions of construction of **5.66** the scope of jurisdiction and arbitration clauses is supplied by *The Pioneer Container*,[225] where, in response to an argument that claims in bailment did not fall within the scope of an exclusive jurisdiction clause in relation to 'claims under the bill of lading', Lord Goff trenchantly referred to the 'extreme technicality' of such an argument and stated that such an argu- ment 'would lead to refinements and inconsistencies which are unaccept- able in a commercial context'.[226] In *The Delos*,[227] it was held that where a party agrees to submit to arbitration disputes arising under a bill of lading, that submission necessarily entails the submission of such claims as are interdependent with pure contract claims such as, in the present case, claims in bailment. In the United States, it has been said that 'accord- ing to the emerging case law, a claim would be outside the scope of the

---

[221] *Donohue v Armco Inc* [2002] 1 Lloyd's Rep 425, 430. See also Fawcett, JJ (n 188 above) 240.
[222] *The Playa Larga* [1983] 2 Lloyd's Rep 171, 183; *Ashville Investments v Elmer Contractors* [1989] 1 QB 488, 503 and 517; *Harbour Assurance Co (UK) Ltd v Kansa General International Insurance Co Ltd* [1993] 1 Lloyd's Rep 455, 470; *Continental Bank NA v Aeakos Compania Naviera SA* [1994] 1 WLR 588; *The Angelic Grace* [1994] 1 Lloyd's Rep 168, 172–174; *Pacific Resources Corporation v Credit Lyonais Rouse* (CA, 7 October 1994). cf *The Forum Craftsman* [1985] 1 Lloyd's Rep 291.
[223] *Harbour Assurance Co (UK) Ltd v Kansa General International Insurance Co Ltd* [1993] QB 701, 724; see also, for example, *The Petr Schmidt* [1995] 1 Lloyd's Rep 202, 206.
[224] See *Continental Bank NA v Aeakos Compania Naviera SA* [1994] 1 WLR 588; *Kitechnology BV v Unicor GmbH Plastmaschinen* [1995] FSR 765.
[225] [1994] 2 AC 324.   [226] ibid 343.
[227] [2001] 1 Lloyd's Rep 703.

forum-selection clause only if it arose outside of the contractual relation-ship between the parties, i.e., if it would not have arisen but for such a relationship.'[228] In the context of arbitration clauses, some United States decisions have erected a presumption in favour of coverage, requiring clear and unambiguous language if particular claims are to be excluded.[229] Canadian courts also lean towards the broad construction of the scope of jurisdiction and arbitration clauses.[230]

5.67 In Australia, while some courts have embraced the broad approach to construction and the presumption of one-stop adjudication,[231] that cannot be claimed to be a universal approach, especially in circumstances where a statutory claim has been made. In *Hi-Fert Pty Ltd v Kiukiang Maritime Carriers Inc (No 5)*,[232] the Full Court of the Federal Court of Australia held that tortious and statutory claims of misleading or deceptive conduct did not fall within the scope of a London arbitration clause which also provided that the charter party was governed by English law.[233] With regard to the statutory claims, and in a passage that is in sharp tension with the English presumption of 'one-stop adjudication', Beaumont J observed that:

> In choosing arbitrators with commercial backgrounds, the parties indicated a choice for the practical solution of disputes of the kind referred to the arbitrators. But to read cl 34 as contemplating a reference to such persons of a problem of considerable private international legal complexity, let alone the application of a foreign (Australian) law in the form of the Trade Practices legislation, would seem to contradict a desire for a practical outcome. We should not attribute such a bizarre intention to these parties. It is not likely that they intended to refer to these arbitrators in London any dispute however remotely connected with the charter party or the bill of lading and however special its legal characteristics in terms of English law.[234]

5.68 A recent decision going directly against the English trend of 'one-stop shopping' is *Domansa v Derin Shipping and Trading Co Inc*,[235] where the relevant clause provided that 'any dispute of whatever nature that may arise in relation to terms of Employment and the Employment Contract

---

[228] Scoles & Hay *Conflict of Laws* (2nd edn, 1992) 372; see also Covey, AE and Morris, MS (n 101 above) 849 n 76.

[229] *SA Mineracao da Trindade-Samitri v Utah International Inc* 745 F 2d 190 (1984).

[230] *Sarabia v 'Oceanic Mindaro'* [1997] 2 WWR 116.

[231] See, for example, *Francis Travel v Virgin Atlantic Airways* (1996) 39 NSWLR 160, 165.

[232] (1998) 90 FCR 1.

[233] See also *Paper Products Pty Ltd v Tomlinsons (Rochdale) Ltd* (1993) 43 FCR 439; *Metrocall Inc v Electronic Tracking Systems Pty Ltd* (2000) 52 NSWLR 1.

[234] (1998) 90 FCR 1, 6. The decision of Emmett J (at 23) was to similar effect. This approach bears some affinity with the judgment of Lord Scott in *Donohue v Armco Inc* [2002] 1 Lloyd's Rep 425, 442, noted at para 5.45 above.

[235] [2001] 1 Lloyd's Rep 362.

shall be resolved between the seamen and the employer directly. Should the parties not reach an agreement Cyprus should apply as a place of jurisdiction and the case should be brought before the competent Law Court in Cyprus under Cypriot law.' Proceedings had been commenced in England under the Fatal Accidents Act by relatives of a deceased Polish seaman. In response to an attempt to stay the proceedings, it was held that the jurisdiction clause did not cover claims brought in tort and that it applied only to disputes which were on foot while the employment relationship continued (the claim was one brought by relatives of the deceased seaman). The phrase 'in relation to' was seized upon as one of limitation and it was said that a submission to the exclusive jurisdiction of a Cypriot Court should be clearly spelled out as should any claim under the Fatal Accidents Act 1976, UK.

It is not surprising that arguments relating to the scope of jurisdiction **5.69** agreements have also been made in the context of Article 17 of the Brussels Convention and are likely to continue to be made in the context of Article 23 of Council Regulation 44/2001. In *Re the Import of Italian Sports Cars*,[236] the Oberlandesgericht, Stuttgart, while observing that the scope of a jurisdiction agreement must be assessed by reference to the parties' intentions, nevertheless held that claims for damages for tort and violation of cartel law in this case fell within the agreement's scope. Accordingly jurisdiction was declined in favour of the Tribunale di Modena. In *Re Missing Share Certificates*,[237] the Oberlandesgericht, Munich manifested a more absolute hostility to attempts to evade jurisdiction agreements in the context of the Brussels Convention by framing claims in delict. It concluded that:

claims in tort, in so far as they are co-extensive with a breach of contract, are also covered by the jurisdiction agreement for the purposes of Article 17. The plaintiff cannot evade the jurisdiction agreement under Article 17 on the grounds that he wishes to bring a claim for damages solely on the basis of a cause of action in tort. ... It cannot be assumed that either the party who introduced the clause or a claimant thinking reasonably would wish in the event of concurrent claims to proceed partly before the Luxembourg courts and partly before the courts of the so-called place of commission of the tort and thus submit the uniform subject-matter of the dispute to two different courts for adjudication.[238]

The Cour d'Appel, Liège has expressed a similar view.[239]

Difficult issues of construction may also arise from the fact that a juris- **5.70** diction clause, rather than identifying in specific terms the court or courts of a particular country, employs a formulaic reference such as 'any

---

[236] [1992] I L Pr 188.   [237] [1991] I L Pr 298.
[238] ibid 307.   [239] *Perfetto v Parlapiano* [1993] I L Pr 190.

dispute arising under this bill of lading shall be decided in the country where the carrier has its principal place of business'. It comes as no surprise that, in a world of multinational corporations, companies legislation that permits elaborate corporate structures, and differing revenue regimes which often dictate a corporation's official location, identifying a company's principal place of business is not always a simple exercise and, as with other questions of construction, this is an area where judicial opinions may differ. Such judicial differences are illustrated by *The Rewia*,[240] where the Court of Appeal held, with critical significance for the venue of the litigation, that the carrier's principal place of business was Hamburg and not Hong Kong, as Sheen J had held at first instance. In coming to this conclusion (which in principle should have been, but was not, governed by the proper law of the contract), Leggatt LJ remarked that the 'principal place of business is not necessarily the place where most of the business is carried out',[241] an observation that is not calculated to engender certainty in this area of law. The issue will not always be so problematic as *Coreck Maritime GmbH v Handels-veem BV*,[242] the case which established the legitimacy of this form of choice of court agreement in the context of the Brussels Convention, demonstrates, there being no issue on the facts of that case as to which party was the 'carrier' whose principal place of business was identified by the clause in question as supplying the forum for the resolution of disputes. That having been said, 'a choice of court which is given in the form of a riddle ought to be avoided like the plague, because it will risk failing to do the very thing which it is supposed to accomplish'.[243]

5.71 An unusual but interesting case which involved the construction of a jurisdiction clause was *Carvalho v Hull, Blyth (Angola) Ltd*.[244] Here the argument related neither to the question of whether or not the clause was exclusive nor to whether the claim fell within the clause's scope. Rather, the question was whether the courts to which the parties had agreed to submit their disputes still existed. It was successfully argued that the courts which existed in post-independence Angola were not the courts to which the plaintiff had agreed to submit. This qualitative difference was manifested by the absence, post-independence, of any appeal on a point of law to the Supreme Court in Lisbon[245] or by the fact that the system for judicial appointments had completely changed.[246]

[240] [1991] 1 Lloyd's Rep 69; [1991] 2 Lloyd's Rep 325 (Court of Appeal).
[241] [1991] 2 Lloyd's Rep 325, 334.
[242] [2000] ECR I–9337.
[243] Briggs, A and Rees, P (n 35 above) 2.92.
[244] [1979] 1 WLR 1228.
[245] ibid 1240.
[246] ibid 1237.

7. DISCRETION

The most likely manner in which a party may seek to subvert the opera- **5.72**
tion of an exclusive jurisdiction clause is through an appeal to the discretion of the court, more precisely, through an appeal to the court *not* to
exercise its discretion and to decline to stay proceedings.

Two important distinctions must be drawn. The first is between agree- **5.73**
ments exclusively to submit disputes to the *courts* of a foreign country, on
the one hand, and valid and binding agreements to submit disputes to
arbitration in the foreign country, on the other. In the latter case, a stay
must be granted automatically and there is no scope for retention of jurisdiction based on the court's discretion. Where there is a foreign jurisdiction as opposed to arbitration clause, a clear distinction must also be
drawn between agreements which nominate a court or the courts of a
state which is a member of the European Union or a contracting state to
the Lugano Convention or which otherwise fall within the scope of
Council Regulation 44/2001 and the Convention and those agreements
which fall to be decided according to common law principles. The former
class of case does not brook any exercise of discretion and, as such, the
Council Regulation and Convention reflect the French and German positions that, as a rule of law, a court, on finding a valid agreement for exclusive jurisdiction, must dismiss any action commenced in breach of it if the
defendant objects to the exercise of jurisdiction.[247]

Article 23 of the Council Regulation relevantly provides that: **5.74**

If the parties, one or more of whom is domiciled in a member state, have agreed
that a court or the courts of a member state are to have jurisdiction to settle any
disputes which have arisen or which may arise in connection with a particular
legal relationship, that court or those courts shall have jurisdiction. Such jurisdiction shall be exclusive unless the parties have agreed otherwise.

Courts of other member states should decline jurisdiction in such circumstances unless the defendant enters an appearance within the meaning of
Article 24.[248] Article 23 goes on to provide that 'where such an agreement
is concluded by parties, none of whom is domiciled in a member state, the
courts of other member states shall have no jurisdiction over their
disputes unless the court or courts chosen have declined jurisdiction'.

---

[247] Kahn-Freund (n 42 above) 849 n 134.
[248] See Schlosser Report [1979] OJ C59/71, Chapter 3, section II. O'Malley, S and Layton,
A, *European Civil Practice* (1989) state at 525 that 'if the agreement complies with the other
provisions of Article 17 [Article 23 of the Regulation], any court other than the court chosen
is required by Articles 18 and 19 [Articles 24 and 25 of the Regulation] to decline jurisdiction,
of its own motion, in favour of the chosen court or courts' (emphasis added).

5.75 Article 23 does not directly address the situation where an exclusive or non-exclusive jurisdiction agreement in favour of a court or the courts of a non-member state is entered into by parties, at least one of whom is domiciled in a member state, for example an exclusive jurisdiction clause for the courts of New York contained in a contract between an English and American company. Article 4 of the Regulation and the Brussels and Lugano Conventions make it plain enough that, if the English company commences proceedings in England, the common law rules (including conflicts rules)[249] apply, the defendant not being domiciled in a member or contracting state. However, when the facts are inverted, and suit is brought by the American company in England, it is less clear whether the English court may, in the exercise of its discretion, decline the jurisdiction which is conferred upon it by Article 2 of the Regulation and the Convention.[250]

5.76 Collins has suggested[251] that the answer should be in the affirmative, even in the more complex situation where both parties to the contract are domiciled in member or contracting states and the Regulation or Convention would afford jurisdiction to the courts of more than one member or contracting state.[252] Other commentators have come to the same conclusion,[253] which also appears to be in line with the Schlosser Report.[254] The argument put by Schlosser and expanded upon by Briggs and Rees on the basis of a reading of *Kongress Agentur Hagen GmbH v Zeehaghe BV*[255] seeks to rest this conclusion on the contention that a discretionary decision to stay proceedings is a procedural matter and therefore outside the scope of the Convention and Regulation. This conclusion is both attractive and consistent with the obvious importance the Regulation and Convention attach to the use of jurisdiction agreements in the allocation of jurisdiction in transnational litigation. It derives some support from the Court of Justice's observation in *Coreck Maritime*

---

[249] *Coreck Maritime GmbH v Handels-veem BV* [2000] ECR I–9337.

[250] Article 2 of the Regulation provides that 'Subject to this Regulation, persons domiciled in a member state shall, whatever their nationality, be sued in the courts of that member state.'

[251] The Civil Jurisdiction and Judgments Act 1982 (1983) 85.

[252] eg the defendant's domicile and the place of performance of the obligation in question, assuming that this is in a Contracting State which is not the defendant's domicile.

[253] Hartley, TC, *Civil Jurisdiction and Judgments* (1984) 24; O'Malley, S and Layton, A, *European Civil Practice* (1989) 557; Briggs, A and Rees, P (n 35 above) 2.94 and p 138; Collins, LA (ed) (n 56 above) 12–090.

[254] [1979] OJ C59/71, 124.

[255] Case C–365/88 [1990] ECR I–1845. This case concerned Article 6 of the Convention. *Benincasa v Dentalkit Srl* [1997] ECR 3767, which refers to jurisdiction clauses as serving a 'procedural purpose', also supports this argument.

GmbH v Handels-veem BV[256] that Article 17 of the Brussels Convention does not apply to clauses designating a court in a third country and that a court in a Contracting State that is seised under the rules of the Convention must 'assess the validity of the clause according to the applicable law, including conflict of laws rules, where it sits'.

Against this, Kahn-Freund observed that the classification of matters **5.77** arising in relation to exclusive jurisdiction clauses as procedural and therefore to be decided according to the *lex fori*, while once standard in France and Germany, has long since been rejected[257] and at least one French decision has held that no effect will be given to a jurisdiction agreement in favour of the courts of a non-member state if a defendant is domiciled in a member state.[258] Some further support for this regrettable conclusion arguably derives from passages in the Almeida Cruz Report on the San Sebastian Convention[259] and the Jenard and Möller Report on the Lugano Convention[260] in relation to litigation involving Contracting State domiciled defendants and foreign land. Essentially, both Reports contend that there is no scope for the application of what common lawyers refer to as the *Moçambique* rule[261] where the defendant in proceedings is domiciled in a Contracting State. This is notwithstanding the clear endorsement of the rule in Article 16(1) of the Conventions [Article 22 of the Regulation] with regard to proceedings concerning land situated in a contracting or member state. If consistency is not required with respect to land, it is doubtful whether it would be required for jurisdiction agreements which arguably do not present as strong a case.[262] The dicta from *Coreck Maritime* cited above, however, tend to tip the argument the other way. If this is not the intended consequence of *Coreck Maritime*, the cost of the alternative view, somewhat ironically, will be felt by member or contracting state domiciliaries who will be liable to be sued at home rather than in the forum nominated in the contract and presumably bargained for by them.

As was noted in Chapter 4, in *Re Harrods (Buenos Aires) Ltd*,[263] contrary to **5.78** the position in *Bruno v Soc Citibank*,[264] the Court of Appeal expressed the view that English courts could decline jurisdiction over a defendant

---

[256] [2000] ECR I-9337.

[257] (n 42 above) 830–831 but cf 835.

[258] *Bruno v Soc Citibank* Ct App Versailles 1991, noted 1992 Rev Crit 333 and referred to in Collins, LA (ed) (*n* 56 above) 12–090 n 66.

[259] [1989] OJ C189/35, 47.

[260] [1990] OJ C189/76, 54.

[261] *British South Africa Co v Companhia de Moçambique* [1893] AC 602.

[262] As is perhaps suggested by Article 25 of the Regulation.

[263] [1992] Ch 72.

[264] See n 258 above.

domiciled in England in circumstances where there was an exclusive jurisdiction clause for the courts of a non-Contracting State[265] and Hirst J, although not adverting to the point, proceeded on this basis in *The Nile Rhapsody*.[266] Such a position is obviously commercially desirable in view of the important role played in international trade by such clauses, is consonant with the maxim *pacta sunt servanda*, and is in line with the general policy evinced by the Conventions to jurisdiction agreements. While *Re Harrods* settled before reaching the European Court of Justice, the issue it raised was the subject of a reference in *Owusu v Jackson*.[267] It may be hoped, although the matter does not strictly arise on the facts of the case referred, that the Court of Justice takes the opportunity to make explicit what is suggested by *Coreck Maritime* and to endorse the common practice[268] found in the domestic law of member states of enforcing exclusive jurisdiction clauses in favour of the courts of non-member states by declining to exercise jurisdiction even where a member state domiciliary is sued in its country of domicile.

5.79 Returning to common law principles, there is no longer any question, as there once was, that exclusive jurisdiction clauses are invalid for 'ousting' the jurisdiction of the court. Rather the position is plain: so long as a defendant is amenable to the court's jurisdiction, such jurisdiction may be asserted over it subject only to the court's discretion to stay the action. Consonant with their stated commitment to the principle of upholding parties' bargains, dicta in both *The Eleftheria* and *The Chaparral* are to the effect that this discretion should normally be exercised where suit has been brought in breach of an agreement to refer disputes exclusively to a foreign court.[269] There must be 'strong reasons',[270] a 'strong cause',[271] or a 'strong showing'[272] why this discretion should not be exercised.[273]

---

[265] [1992] Ch 72, 97.   [266] [1992] 2 Lloyd's Rep 399.   [267] [2002] ECWA 877.

[268] See Delaume, GR (n 13 above) 175 and Pryles, MC (n 38 above) 568–571.

[269] *The Eleftheria* [1970] P 94, 99; *The Chaparral* 407 US 1, 15 (1972); [1972] 2 Lloyd's Rep 315, 321.

[270] *Donohue v Armco, Inc* [2002] 1 Lloyd's Rep 425, 433.

[271] *The Eleftheria* [1970] P 94, 99.

[272] *The Chaparral* 407 US 1 (1972). Other United States cases manifesting this approach include *Riley v Kingsley Underwriting Agencies Ltd* 969 F 2d 953 (1992); *Roby v Corporation of Lloyd's* 996 F 2d 1353 (1993); *Bonny v Society of Lloyd's* 3 F 3d 156 (1993); *Shell v RW Sturge Ltd* 55 F 3d 1227 (1995); *Allen v Lloyd's of London* 94 F 3d 923 (1996); *Haynsworth v Corporation of Lloyd's* 121 F 3d 956 (1997); *Richards v Lloyd's of London* 135 F 3d 1289 (1998) (*en banc*).

[273] Examples of application of this principle in New Zealand are supplied by *Society of Lloyd's v Hyslop* [1993] 3 NZLR 135; *Kidd v van Heeren* [1998] 1 NZLR 324; and *Advanced Cardiovascular Systems Inc v Universal Specialties Ltd* [1997] 1 NZLR 186. A similar test obtains in Australia: *Akai Pty Ltd v People's Insurance Company* (1997) 188 CLR 418, 427–428, 444–445 as well as in Canada: *G & E Auto Brokers Ltd v Toyota Canada Inc* (1980) 117 DLR (3d) 707; *Oulton Agencies Inc v Knolloffice Inc* (1988) 48 DLR (4th) 545; *Maritime Telegraph and Telephone Company v Pre Print Inc* (1996) 131 DLR (4th) 471; *Sarabia v 'Oceanic Mindaro'* [1997] 2 WWR 116.

With a keen prescience, Brandon J warned in *The Eleftheria*[274] that 'the **5.80** court must be careful not just to pay lip service to the principle involved, and then fail to give effect to it because of a mere balance of convenience'.[275] Writing in 1993, Briggs noted that, 'although courts routinely state that the party seeking to break his contract in the face of the court must make a strong case before being allowed to do so, the practice is rather different'.[276] That practice tended to elide the approach to cases involving exclusive jurisdiction clauses with the *forum non conveniens* approach enunciated in *Spiliada*.[277] Indeed, Hirst J went so far as to suggest that the only difference rendered by the presence of a choice of court clause was one of burden of proof.[278] His reference to the fact that this approach 'was recognized by both sides throughout the hearing' carried the implication that such an understanding of the effect of exclusive jurisdiction clauses was abroad in the practising profession and did not merely represent an occasional and careless elision of two discrete concepts.[279] The implicit view of exclusive jurisdiction clauses and the approach articulated by Hirst J in *The Nile Rhapsody* recalls that advocated by Lord Denning MR in *The Fehmarn*[280] which focused on the question of whether the dispute 'was a matter which properly belongs to the courts of this country'.[281]

The approach disclosed in these two cases patently operates to undermine **5.81** the certainty which an exclusive jurisdiction clause is designed to yield and exposes a party to the prospect of the very type of jurisdictional battle which the clause was designed to secure against. A significant number of cases can be cited since *The Fehmarn* in which English courts, *in the exercise of their discretion*, have refused to enforce exclusive jurisdiction clauses for other forums by staying proceedings commenced in breach of them or by declining to grant leave for service of process out of the jurisdiction[282]

---

[274] [1970] P 94. [275] ibid 103.

[276] Briggs, A, 'Jurisdiction Clauses and Judicial Attitudes' (1993) 109 LQR 382, 383.

[277] Contrary to the important point of distinction drawn attention to by Stephenson LJ in *The El Amria* [1981] 2 Lloyd's Rep 119, 129.

[278] *The Nile Rhapsody* [1992] 2 Lloyd's Rep 399, 401. Goff J (as he then was) exhibited a similar view in *Trendtex Trading Corporation v Crédit Suisse* [1980] 3 All ER 721.

[279] cf *The El Amria* [1981] 2 Lloyd's Rep 119, 129; *The Chaparral* [1971] 2 Lloyd's Rep 348, 351, 446 F 2d 907, 909 (1971): 'The forum non conveniens theory should have no bearing on this case.' See also *The Vishva Apurva* [1992] 2 SLR 175, 183 where the Singapore Court of Appeal commented adversely on the fact that 'a number of recent English authorities have moved towards an assimilation of the two tests'.

[280] [1957] 1 WLR 815; [1958] 1 WLR 159 (Court of Appeal). Noted by Webb (n 183 above).

[281] ibid 162. Lord Denning went on to state that he preferred 'to look to see with what country is the dispute most closely concerned'. Although endorsed by Edmund-Davies LJ in *Evans Marshall & Co v Bertola SA* [1973] 1 WLR 349, 383, this approach was implicitly criticized by the Court of Appeal in *The El Amria* [1981] 2 Lloyd's Rep 119, 124.

[282] *Evans Marshall & Co Ltd v Bertola SA* [1973] 1 WLR 349; *The Adolf Warski* [1976] 1 Lloyd's

although that tendency has perhaps declined in recent years, probably in recognition of the fact that the almost automatic enforcement of exclusive jurisdiction agreements nominating the English courts by means of anti-suit injunctions observed in Chapter 4 requires a similarly strict approach to the enforcement of exclusive jurisdiction clauses nominating the courts of other forums.

5.82   The appeal to discretionary considerations as a reason for the non-enforcement of exclusive jurisdiction agreements may also be observed in other common law countries and in the United States. Thus, notwithstanding Sir Owen Dixon's advice that the courts should exercise a 'strong bias in favour of maintaining the special bargain',[283] Pryles has judged that 'the record of the Australian courts, perhaps eager to provide a forum for local litigants and jealous of their jurisdiction, suggests that a somewhat lighter burden rests upon the plaintiff'.[284] The law reports provide several instances of its being discharged.[285] The Canadian experience is similarly revealing[286] and attention has been drawn to the less than rigor-

Rep 107, [1976] 2 Lloyd's Rep 241; *The Vishva Prabha* [1979] 2 Lloyd's Rep 286; *The El Amria* [1980] 1 Lloyd's Rep 390, [1981] 2 Lloyd's Rep 119; *The Panseptos* [1981] 1 Lloyd's Rep 152; *The Blue Wave* [1982] 1 Lloyd's Rep 151; *The Benarty* [1983] 2 Lloyd's Rep 50, 58–59 (alternate holding at first instance); *The Atlantic Song* [1983] 2 Lloyd's Rep 394; *The Pia Vesta* [1984] 1 Lloyd's Rep 169 (alternate holding); *The Frank Pais* [1986] 1 Lloyd's Rep 529 (Cuban jurisdiction clause); *The Al Battani* [1993] 2 Lloyd's Rep 219; *Citi-March v Neptune Orient Lines* [1997] 1 Lloyd's Rep 72; *The MC Pearl* [1997] 1 Lloyd's Rep 566; *Sinochem International Oil (London) Co Ltd v Mobil Sales & Supply Corporation* [2000] 1 Lloyd's Rep 670. For criticism of such cases, see Schuz, R, 'Controlling Forum Shopping: The Impact of *MacShannon v Rockware Glass Ltd*' (1986) 35 ICLQ 374, 405–406. See also on the topic generally, Peel, E, [1998] LMCLQ 182.

[283] *Huddart Parker Ltd v The Ship Mill Hill* (1950) 81 CLR 502, 509.

[284] (n 38 above) 560. See also Garnett, R, 'The Enforcement of Jurisdiction Clauses in Australia' (1998) 21 UNSWLJ 1.

[285] *Lewis Construction Co Pty Ltd v M Tichauer Société Anonyme* [1966] VR 341, esp 349; *Hopkins v Difrex Société Anonyme* [1966] 1 NSWR 797; *WC Thomas & Sons Pty Ltd v Bunge (Aust) Pty Ltd* [1975] VR 801 (first instance, reversed on appeal); *Lep International Pty Ltd v Atlanttrafic Express Service Inc* (1987) 10 NSWLR 614, 620; *Aldred v Australian Building Industries Pty Ltd* (1987) 48 NTR 59. Other Australian cases are collected by Garnett R (n 284 above).

[286] Canadian cases displaying what Robertson, GB, 'Jurisdiction Clauses and the Canadian Conflict of Laws' (1982) 20 Alberta Law Review 296 describes, at 302, as the '*forum non conveniens*' approach include *Polito v GENSG* [1960] Ex CR 233; *May v Reford* (1969) 6 DLR (3d) 288; *Boma Navigation Ltee v The Hansa Bay* [1975] FC 231; and *Neptune Bulk Terminals Ltd v Intertec Internationale Technische Assistenz* (1981) 127 DLR (3d) 736; and *Pirrana Small Car v Rumm* [1981] 5 WWR 79. To these may be added *Re Mithras Management Ltd* (1992) 90 DLR (4th) 726 where, although a stay was granted, *forum non conveniens* considerations were clearly elided with those which arose from the presence of an exclusive jurisdiction clause for the courts of California: see at 734 and 737–744. That this approach is not uniform emerges from *The Seapearl v Seven Seas Corp* [1983] 2 FC 161, 176–177 but note the dissent of Thurlow CJ and *Oulton Agencies Inc v Knolloffice Inc* (1988) 48 DLR (4th) 545, 547 per Carruthers CJPEI who stated that 'authorities appear to clearly state that the courts will uphold a properly framed contractual choice of forum unless the balance of convenience

ous enforcement of exclusive jurisdiction clauses in Singapore.[287] In the United States, it has been said that 'the standards for enforcement of a forum clause ... continue to vary significantly in different jurisdictions'.[288]

Writing in the aftermath of both *The Eleftheria* and *The Chaparral*, Collins's **5.83** assessment that the approach of Lord Denning and the result in *The Fehmarn* represented the 'high-water mark'[289] of what can only be described as a lax approach to the enforcement of forum clauses now seems to have been somewhat premature, at least when an English court is asked to stay English proceedings commenced in breach of an exclusive jurisdiction clause for a foreign forum.[290] The consequence is, of course, a forum shopper's delight—'plaintiffs are still prepared to breach the forum agreement and when confronted with an application for stay, gamble on the sympathy of the trial judge'[291]—especially when it is recalled that jurisdictional battles often provide the occasion, through the not inconsiderable scope for vexation,[292] for the settlement of claims.[293]

Some explanation for this unwieldy exercise of judicial discretion and the **5.84** consequent undermining of the efficacy of exclusive jurisdiction clauses lies in the veritable raft of factors which Brandon J in *The Eleftheria* suggested should govern the exercise of discretion and which still feature prominently in *Dicey & Morris's* treatment of this area.[294] They bear full quotation:

massively favours an opposite conclusion' and eschewed any application of *forum non conveniens* doctrine in such cases (552).

[287] *Amerco v Chatsworth* [1977] 2 MLJ 181; *The Maldive Importer* [1986] 1 MLJ 12; *The Vishva Apurva* [1991] 2 MLJ 440 (rev'd on appeal [1992] 2 SLR 175). The decision on appeal in this case, together with *The Asian Plutus* [1990] 2 MLJ 449 and *The Dai Yun Shan* [1992] 2 SLR 508, appear to arrest this trend, however. See the discussion by Sing, TK, 'Stay of Actions Based on Exclusive Jurisdiction Clauses under English and Singapore Law' [1991] Sing JLS 103. For a conflation of approaches in Hong Kong, see *The Frinton* [1990] 2 HKLR 700, noted by Margolis, R, 'Exclusive Jurisdiction Clauses and Multiple Plaintiffs' (1991) 21 HKLJ 240.

[288] Born, G (n 98 above) 378.

[289] 'Arbitration Clauses and Forum Selection Clauses in the Conflict of Laws: Some Recent Developments in England' (1970–1971) 2 Journal of Maritime Law and Commerce 363, 374.

[290] As was seen in Chapter 4, a strong disposition to enforce exclusive jurisdiction clauses in favour of English courts via the mechanism of anti-suit injunctions is plain in recent English decisions.

[291] Sing, TK (n 287 above) 412. See also Schuz, R (n 282 above) 405, noting that the infiltration of *forum non conveniens* principles into the area of jurisdiction clauses had led to a relaxation rather than an increase in the control of forum shopping in such cases.

[292] Although, of course, the courts cannot characterize it as such in any but the most extreme cases because such battles are the product of an extremely open-ended discretion and inconsistent case law: see on this last point especially, Sing, ibid 410–411.

[293] See paras 1.31 ff above.

[294] Collins, LA (ed) (n 56 above) 12-117.

In exercising its discretion, the court should take into account all the circumstances of the particular case. In particular, but without prejudice to [the above], the following matters, where they arise, may properly be regarded: (a) In what country the evidence on the issues of fact is situated, or more readily available, and the effect of that on the relative convenience and expense of trial as between the English and foreign courts. (b) Whether the law of the foreign court applies and, if so, whether it differs from English law in any material respects. (c) With what country either party is connected, and how closely. (d) Whether the defendants genuinely desire trial in the foreign country, or are only seeking procedural advantages. (e) Whether the plaintiffs would be prejudiced by having to sue in the foreign court because they would: (i) be deprived of security for their claim; (ii) be unable to enforce any judgment obtained; (iii) be faced with a time bar not applicable in England; or (iv) for political, racial, religious or other reasons be unlikely to get a fair trial.[295]

5.85 Perhaps the most common reason stated in those cases in Commonwealth courts in which stays of action have been refused in the exercise of the courts' discretion has related to what is seen as the superior convenience of the non-stipulated forum for the resolution of the case. Two of the five considerations enumerated by Brandon J as being relevant to the exercise of discretion can be seen to go to 'convenience' (factors (a) and (c) above). It will at once be apparent that these are also very important considerations under the *Spiliada* test[296] and this may in part explain the tendency, if not the logic, to elide the approaches taken to stay applications. In *The Makefjell*,[297] decided some five years after *The Eleftheria*, Brandon J signalled something of a retreat from the emphasis which he may have been perceived to have placed on factors of convenience. This case involved a very familiar factual scenario, a claim for damage to cargo discovered on or after discharge from the ship where contractual relations were governed by a bill of lading nominating the courts of a country other than the port of discharge (usually the shipowners' principal place of business) as having exclusive jurisdiction. Inevitably, the critical evidence in such a case will include a report prepared as soon as possible after discovery of the damage by a local surveyor and accounts of the manner of the unloading of the cargo, witnesses to which are most likely to be found in the port of discharge. The country of discharge, apart from being highly likely to be that in which the plaintiffs in any action for damages will be domiciled or otherwise resident, will obviously emerge quite clearly as presenting the most convenient forum. Aware of this, Brandon J stated that:

---

[295] [1970] P 94, 100.   [296] [1987] AC 460, 477–478.
[297] [1975] 1 Lloyd's Rep 528.

If all or most such cases are to be treated as exceptions to the general rule, there is, it seems to me, a danger that such exceptions would be so frequent as to undermine the generality of the rule; or, to put it another way, that the rule will be nearly as much honoured in the breach as in the observance. Such an outcome would, in my view, involve a departure from the basic principle that foreign jurisdiction clauses of this kind should be enforced save only in cases which can truly be described as exceptional.[298]

One might legitimately ask why any cognizance should be had of factors **5.86** of convenience. Lord Merrivale, for one, would not have agreed with Brandon J's inclusion of them in what purported to be a summary of the previous British case law in *The Eleftheria*. In *The Media*,[299] notwithstanding the fact that proceedings in Calcutta would be 'needlessly expensive and, I think, highly inconvenient', he stated that 'those are collateral considerations. It was for the goods-owners to appreciate what was the agreement that they had made.'[300] It would be unusual for the parties to an exclusive jurisdiction clause not to have had the convenience or otherwise of the nominated forum in contemplation at time of entry into the contract, especially when such clauses often bear on the ultimate contract price.[301] Even where the inconvenience of the nominated forum was not adverted to by the parties, a circumstance which Eve J thought not infrequent,[302] it is nonetheless difficult to see why the parties should not be held to their bargain, short of their being able to point to some factor vitiating or otherwise invalidating the agreement.[303] The United States Supreme Court in *The Chaparral* saw no reason to take into account factors of convenience in such circumstances.[304]

If it is said that factors of convenience go beyond the immediate *private* **5.87** interests of the parties and raise issues of *public* concern, such concern can only lead to the negative conclusion that it is against a country's public interest to tie up the courts with long and complex matters, involving the need to 'import' foreign witnesses, translate evidence, and prove foreign law. But it is not appropriate that one forum draws this conclusion on

---

[298] ibid 532. The same judge's decision to refuse a stay in a very similar fact situation in *The Adolf Warski* [1976] 1 Lloyd's Rep 107 rather undermined the cogency of this observation and only acted as a recipe to encourage further jurisdictional battles.

[299] (1931) 41 L LR 80.

[300] ibid 82. See also *The Rothnie* [1996] 2 Lloyd's Rep 206.

[301] See paras 5.05–5.07 above.

[302] *Kirchner v Gruban* [1909] 1 Ch 413, 418.

[303] For a similar view, see Granger, C, 'The Conflict of Laws and Forum Shopping: Some Recent Decisions on Jurisdiction and Free Enterprise in Litigation' (1974) 6 Ottawa Law Review 416, 428.

[304] 407 US 1, 16 (1972); [1972] 2 Lloyd's Rep 315, 321. See also *The Pacific Senator* [2001] 2 Lloyd's Rep 674; *Insurance Corporation of Hanover Inc v Latino Americana de Reasseguros SA* 868 F Supp 520, 529; *Roby v Corporation of Lloyds* 996 F 2d 1353, 1363 (1993).

another's behalf. It is properly and entirely an issue for the court nominated in the exclusive jurisdiction clause. On this view, there is no public
interest at stake for a court in which proceedings have been commenced
in breach of the exclusive jurisdiction clause.[305] An assessment that it
would in fact be convenient, both in terms of the private interests of the
parties and the public interest of the forum, should only assume any relevance if and when the court nominated in the exclusive jurisdiction clause
exercises its own discretion and declines to hear the matter.

5.88 It is a significant and desirable feature of United States jurisprudence in
this area that factors of convenience only assume relevance in the most
extreme circumstances and, where they do, their relevance in reality
pertains to the inability of the party resisting a stay to obtain justice in the
designated forum rather than any inconvenience that may be encountered
on the path to obtaining such a result. In *The Chaparral*, it was stated that
a stay would only be declined if trial in London would be 'so manifestly
and gravely inconvenient to Zapata that it will be effectively deprived of
a meaningful day in court'.[306] In that case however, the Supreme Court
drew something of a connection between 'serious inconvenience' and the
reasonableness of the exclusive jurisdiction clause,[307] having earlier noted
that a stay would not be granted if it were clearly shown that enforcement
would be 'unreasonable and unjust'.[308] In *Carnival Cruise Lines Inc v
Shute*,[309] the Supreme Court rebuked the Court of Appeals for its loose
use of unreasonableness based on inconvenience and, although there are
some United States cases which place what is considered to be an undue
emphasis on factors of convenience,[310] it appears that the general practice
is to enforce forum selection clauses notwithstanding considerable inconvenience to the resisting party.[311]

5.89 One of the most problematic of the panoply of factors set forth by
Brandon J in *The Eleftheria* is factor (d), namely 'whether the defendants
genuinely desire trial in the foreign country, or are only seeking proce-

---

[305] Unless, of course, as Fawcett has suggested, the earning of foreign exchange through
the invisible export of legal services is considered a matter of public interest: 'Forum
Shopping—Some Questions Answered' (1984) 35 NILQ 141, 146. See also Slater, AG, 'Forum
Non Conveniens: A View from the Shop Floor' (1988) 104 LQR 554, 562.

[306] 407 US 1, 19 (1972); [1972] 2 Lloyd's Rep 315, 322.

[307] Referring to a hypothetical example of an agreement between two Americans with an
exclusive jurisdiction clause for a 'remote alien forum', the Court observed that 'in such a
case, the serious inconvenience of the contractual forum to one or both of the parties might
carry greater weight in determining the reasonableness of the forum clause': ibid 17; 321 of
Lloyd's Rep.

[308] ibid 15; 321 of Lloyd's Rep.

[309] 499 US 585 (1991).

[310] eg *Copperweld Steel Co v Demag-Mannesman-Boehler* 578 F 2d 953 (3rd Cir, 1978).

[311] Born, GB (n 98 above) 406–407.

dural advantages'.[312] This factor is also, and again, quite rightly, absent from the United States jurisprudence where no focus is placed on the conduct of the parties subsequent to entry into the jurisdiction agreement. It has already been observed that subsequent conduct is not entirely without relevance[313] but that it is questionable to what extent it should be taken into account short of estoppel or waiver.[314] The notion that it is in some way illegitimate for a party to desire to exploit the procedural advantages offered by the forum which it has specifically negotiated to be the exclusive jurisdiction is perplexing if such clauses are not treated as illegitimate from the outset.[315] As it is, they are not only seen as proper but have been positively embraced as vital for international trade and commerce. The attitude to parties seeking to take advantage of their bargained for jurisdiction agreements is doubly perplexing when it is appreciated that whatever damages are available for breach of such a clause will generally only be nominal.[316] Notwithstanding these considerations, Brandon J's factor (d) has featured prominently in many of the cases where stays have been refused in the exercise of the courts' discretion.[317] It is suggested that that factor should be removed from the list of relevant concerns going to discretion. It is one thing for a party to behave so unconscionably that it should be estopped from relying on its exclusive jurisdiction clause; it is a very different thing for a party to be denied certain procedural advantages that it has specifically bargained for.

Except in circumstances where there has been an unforeseeable change in the procedure of the courts submitted to or where the general political situation of the country has altered radically,[318] the exploitation of fairly bargained for procedural advantages through the enforcement of exclusive jurisdiction clauses should be permitted, even where those advantages **5.90**

---

[312] [1970] P 94, 100.

[313] See the discussion with regard to novation, waiver, and estoppel in paras 5.49 ff above.

[314] *The Ruben Martinez Villena* [1988] 1 Lloyd's Rep 435, 438 per Sheen J, quoted at para 5.53 above.

[315] For a similar view, see Bissett-Johnson (n 16 above) 543.

[316] See *Anderson v GH Michell & Sons Ltd* (1941) 65 CLR 543, 549, where the High Court of Australia stated that a party suing in breach of an arbitration clause 'may by suing expose himself to an action for breach of his contract to refer but, having regard to the measure of damages, that is a risk which he could lightly encounter'. But see also the discussion in paras 4.149–4.150 above and Briggs, A and Rees, P (n 35 above) 4.26.

[317] eg *The Vishva Prabha* [1979] 2 Lloyd's Rep 286; *Pirrana Small Car v Rumm* [1981] 5 WWR 79; *The Atlantic Song* [1983] 2 Lloyd's Rep 394; *The Pia Vesta* [1984] 1 Lloyd's Rep 169 (alternative holding); *The Iran Vojdan* [1984] 2 Lloyd's Rep 380, 387; *The Frank Pais* [1986] 1 Lloyd's Rep 529.

[318] eg *Carvalho v Hull, Blyth (Angola) Ltd* [1979] 1 WLR 1228; *The Star of Luxor* [1981] 1 Lloyd's Rep 139. At 141, Sheen J stated that 'I have been told . . . that there are no political or other difficulties which would prevent Russian witnesses entering Egypt and giving evidence in the Egyptian proceedings. If there is hereafter any change which makes it impossible for those witnesses to enter Egypt I would regard that as grounds for lifting the stay.'

relate to the type of remedies available in the foreign jurisdiction,[319] time bars,[320] time delays,[321] exchange control restrictions,[322] and other aspects of the procedure of the foreign court such as interest on damages and cost of proceedings.[323] After all, the correlative disadvantages for the breaching plaintiff must, *ex hypothesi*, have been foreseen, or were at the very least foreseeable, at the time of entry into the contract.[324] In *The Al Battani*,[325] Sheen J considered that factors of likely delay, the non-recovery of legal costs, and the fact that interest would only be awarded on any damages as from the date of judgment were factors which made 'the financial burden of litigating in Egypt so heavy that in my judgment justice requires that a stay should not be granted'.[326] Apart from the fact that these considerations would seem to apply to every trial brought in Egypt, Sheen J's observations are all the more remarkable in light of the fact that he expressly envisaged that trial on the substantive merits would never take place.[327] The burden of the argument advanced in this paragraph is that, as has been argued above in relation to factors (a), (c), and (d), Brandon J's sub-factors (e)(ii) and (iii) should not be taken into account in the exercise of any discretion unless it is clear that such consequences were not readily foreseeable at the time of entry into the exclusive jurisdiction agreement. As for factor (e)(i)—possible prejudice to a plaintiff in the nominated forum on account of the inability to obtain security for its claim—Saville J's decision in *The Havhelt*[328] makes it clear that, as a result of section 26 of the Civil Jurisdiction and Judgments Act 1982,[329] this should no longer be a basis for refusing to enforce the foreign exclusive jurisdiction clause.

---

[319] *Law v Garett* (1878) 8 ChD 26; *Kirchner v Gruban* [1909] 1 Ch 413; *Evans Marshall & Co v Bertola SA* [1973] 1 WLR 349.

[320] *The Eleftheria* [1970] P 94, 100 but note that this is less of a consideration after the passage of the Foreign Limitation Periods Act 1984. See also *The Blue Wave* [1982] 1 Lloyd's Rep 151, where the action was not stayed because of the probable application of a time bar in Greece. This case may be decided differently on account of the Act.

[321] *The Vishva Apurva* [1992] 2 SLR 175, 188.

[322] *The Vishva Prabha* [1979] 2 Lloyd's Rep 286; cf *The Indian Fortune* [1985] 1 Lloyd's Rep 344, where, in an admirable judgment, it was said at 347: 'The current difficulties which surround the transmission of money out of India were in existence and well known at the time when the contract was made.' A stay was granted.

[323] *The Al Battani* [1993] 2 Lloyd's Rep 219; cf *The Kislovodsk* [1980] 1 Lloyd's Rep 183.

[324] *The Chaparral* 407 US 1, 16–17 (1972); [1972] 2 Lloyd's Rep 315, 322.

[325] [1993] 2 Lloyd's Rep 219.

[326] ibid 224. Note that although this conclusion was expressed in relation to a discussion under the *Spiliada* principles, he expressly adopted it as his analysis in respect of the exclusive jurisdiction in the event that it was found to be part of the bill of lading (also at 224).

[327] ibid 221, cited in paras 1.31 ff above.

[328] [1993] 1 Lloyd's Rep 523, 524–525.

[329] Allowing for the retention and application of any security obtained in England to the decision of a foreign court in favour of whose jurisdiction an English court has stayed its proceedings.

Brandon J's famous passage in *The Eleftheria*, which has become the trad- **5.91**
itional starting point in considering whether to stay proceedings in favour
of the courts nominated in a foreign exclusive jurisdiction clause, should
be reconsidered and overruled. That passage, which purported to be no
more than a summary of the then existing English case law, was formulated at a time when judicial sensitivity to the phenomenon of forum
shopping was not as acute as it is now. The factors enumerated in it,
however, provide an invitation to do just that in circumstances where the
question of the venue for any litigation should be treated as settled. A
preferable approach was articulated by Waller J in *British Aerospace plc v
Dee Howard Co.*[330] That case involved what was construed to be an exclusive jurisdiction clause in favour of the English courts but the defendant
sought a stay of proceedings on the basis that it would be more convenient for proceedings to take place in Texas where it (the defendant) had
already commenced proceedings. Rejecting this argument, Waller J stated:

It seems to me on the language of the clause that I am considering here, it simply
should not be open to DHC to start arguing about the relative merits of fighting
an action in Texas as compared with fighting an action in London, where the
factors relied on would have been eminently foreseeable at the time that they
entered into the contract . . . it seems to me that the inconvenience for witnesses,
the location of the documents, the timing of a trial, and all such like matters, are
aspects which they are simply precluded from raising.[331]

This approach has been subsequently endorsed in the context of non-
exclusive jurisdiction clauses. In *JP Morgan Securities Asia Private Ltd v
Malaysia Newsprint Industries Sdn Bhd*,[332] it was said that the adoption of
this approach 'must severely limit the normal diet of *Spiliada* circumstance
that is to be served to the judge'.[333]

The approach articulated by Waller J in *British Aerospace* accords **5.92**
precisely with that which, *mutatis mutandis*, it has been suggested should
be adopted in relation to the enforcement of *foreign* exclusive jurisdiction
clauses.[334] The history of *The Eleftheria* criteria in Commonwealth

[330] [1993] 1 Lloyd's Rep 369.
[331] ibid 376. See also *Berisford plc v New Hampshire Insurance Co* [1990] 2 QB 631, 638 per
Hobhouse J: 'it is difficult to see how there could be any discretion to stay the English
proceedings on the ground of forum non conveniens in favour of foreign proceedings in
breach of the parties' agreement [for exclusive English jurisdiction]. Neither counsel could
refer me to any case where such a power had been recognised, let alone exercised.'
[332] [2001] 2 Lloyd's Rep 41.
[333] ibid 47. See also *Mercury Communications Ltd v Communication Telesystems International*
[1999] 2 All ER 33, 41.
[334] Two Singaporean decisions, although not questioning the authority of *The Eleftheria*, in
effect deny the relevance of many of the factors set out by Brandon J in that decision: *The
Asian Plutus* [1990] 2 MLJ 449 and *The Vishva Apurva* [1992] 2 SLR 175. See also *Trendtex
Trading Corporation v Crédit Suisse* [1980] 3 All ER 721, 735.

jurisdictions is such as to suggest that the mere re-emphasis of the importance of upholding bargains may not be sufficient to arrest the unwarranted and undesirable lack of certainty in this area of the law. What is required is a clear statement that it is simply not legitimate for a court to exercise its discretion on the basis of many of the factors set out in *The Eleftheria* (and others added under its aegis) in circumstances where those factors were foreseeable at the time of entry into the jurisdiction agreement.

5.93 There are, of course, circumstances, albeit limited, where it is quite legitimate and proper for a common law court to entertain proceedings in the face of an exclusive jurisdiction clause by refusing a stay. These are essentially encapsulated in Brandon J's factor (e)(iv), namely where 'for political, racial, religious or other reasons, [the plaintiff will] be unlikely to get a fair trial'.[335] Cases such as *Ellinger v Guinness, Mahon & Co*[336] and *Carvalho v Hull, Blyth (Angola) Ltd*[337] join others in the conflict of laws, of which *Oppenheimer v Cattermole*[338] is perhaps the most notable example, where flexibility is demonstrated in order to avoid a result, either substantive or jurisdictional, which would result in the denial of a fundamental human right such as a fair trial.[339] *Ellinger v Guinness, Mahon & Co*[340] was a case where there was an exclusive jurisdiction clause in favour of the German courts which the English courts refused to enforce because of the high probability that the plaintiff's Jewish religion would deny him the opportunity of a fair trial.[341]

5.94 There remains to be considered one last and extremely important argument which a party seeking to extricate itself from the consequences of an exclusive jurisdiction clause may employ in an appeal to the court's discretion. It does not stem from the factors enumerated in *The Eleftheria*. Rather, it flows from the important decision of the Court of Appeal in *The El Amria*[342] and was most recently restated by the House of Lords in

---

[335] *The Eleftheria* [1970] P 94, 100.

[336] [1939] 4 All ER 16.

[337] [1979] 1 WLR 1228, at least in the judgment of Geoffrey Lane LJ at 1241: 'On all the evidence it seems to me that, plainly, the plaintiff was the sort of person who would be anathema to the present government in Angola . . . there was a ground for the plaintiff's fear.'

[338] [1976] AC 249.

[339] United States cases in this area have seen the refusal to enforce exclusive jurisdiction clauses in favour of Iranian courts: *McDonnell Douglas Corp v Islamic Republic of Iran* 758 F 2d 341 (8th Cir, 1985), cert denied 414 US 948; *Rasoulzadeh v Associated Press* 574 F Supp 854, 861 (SDNY 1983), aff'd 767 F 2d 908 (2nd Cir, 1985); *Harris Corp v National Iranian Radio & Television* 691 F 2d 1344, 1357 (11th Cir, 1982).

[340] [1939] 4 All ER 16.

[341] cf *The Abidin Daver* [1984] AC 398, 411; *Muduroglu v TC Ziraat Bankasi* [1986] 3 All ER 682, 698 and 714.

[342] [1981] 2 Lloyd's Rep 119.

Donohue v Armco Inc.[343] In that case, Lord Bingham stated that 'the authorities show that the English Court may well decline to grant an injunction or a stay, as the case may be, where the interests of parties other than the parties bound by the exclusive jurisdiction clause are involved or grounds of claim not the subject of the clause are part of the relevant dispute so that there is a risk of parallel proceedings and inconsistent decisions'. The decision of the Court of Appeal in *Bouygues Offshore SA v Caspian Shipping Co (Nos 1, 3, 4 and 5)*[344] is to much the same effect.

As has been seen in earlier chapters, courts are extremely sensitive to the **5.95** prospect of inconsistent judgments and have, with increasing frequency, referred to the desirability of grouping related litigation in one comprehensive set of proceedings.[345] The significance of *Donohue v Armco Inc* lies in the fact that an English court declined to give effect to an exclusive English jurisdiction clause because, in a multi-party dispute, a number of the litigants and potential litigants were not party to the jurisdiction agreement and the centre of gravity of the dispute between all parties, viewed globally, was New York. Examples of the principle of which Lord Bingham spoke have traditionally involved English courts declining to give effect to exclusive jurisdiction clauses nominating courts of another forum by refusing to stay proceedings commenced in England in breach of such a clause.

In *The El Amria*, a stay was refused despite the fact that there were **5.96** '*Eleftheria*' factors in fact pointing in favour of the nominated courts of Alexandria to bolster the prima facie case for a stay in favour of that forum. A similar approach was taken in *The Panseptos*[346] where an exclusive jurisdiction clause for Ethiopia was overridden in favour of comprehensive litigation in London and was also favoured at first instance in *The Benarty*[347] as well as in *Citi-March Ltd v Neptune Orient Lines Ltd.*[348] More recently, it has also commended itself to Rix J in both *The MC Pearl*[349] and in *Sinochem International Oil (London) Ltd v Mobil Sales & Supply*

---

[343] [2002] 1 Lloyd's Rep 425, 433.
[344] [1998] 2 Lloyd's Rep 461.
[345] *Bulk Oil (Zug) v Trans-Asiatic Oil Ltd SA* [1973] 1 Lloyd's Rep 129, 136; *Camilla Cotton Oil Co v Granadex SA* [1976] 2 Lloyd's Rep 10, 14; *The Stolt Mamaro* [1985] 2 Lloyd's Rep 428, esp 436; *McConnell Dowell Constructors Ltd v Lloyd's Syndicate 396* [1988] 2 NZLR 257, 276; *Du Pont de Nemours & Co v Agnew* [1987] 2 Lloyd's Rep 585, 589; *Meadows Indemnity Co Ltd v Insurance Corporation of Ireland plc* [1989] 1 Lloyd's Rep 181, 190, [1989] 2 Lloyd's Rep 298, 305; *FNBB v UBS* [1990] 1 Lloyd's Rep 32, 39; *New Hampshire Insurance Co v Strabag Bau AG* [1992] 1 Lloyd's Rep 361, esp 371; *Société Commerciale de Reassurance v Eras International* [1992] 1 Lloyd's Rep 570, 588.
[346] [1981] 1 Lloyd's Rep 152.
[347] [1983] 2 Lloyd's Rep 50, 58; rev'd on appeal [1985] QB 325.
[348] [1996] 1 WLR 1367.
[349] [1997] 1 Lloyd's Rep 566.

Corporation.[350] In the first of these cases, the exclusive jurisdiction clause for the courts of South Korea was overridden even though the judge accepted that 'the subject matter of these proceedings has nothing to do with England'. Such an argument will not always succeed, however, especially when the related proceedings have not yet and indeed may never commence[351] and the courts should be sensitive to the commencement of specious third party proceedings in an endeavour to undermine the operation of an exclusive jurisdiction clause for a foreign court.[352]

5.97 The tactical possibilities suggested by *The El Amria* were at play in *The Frinton*,[353] a decision of the Hong Kong Court of Appeal involving claims by cargo owners in relation to damage to goods on board The Frinton. Eighty-five of the eighty-seven plaintiffs in this case were parties to bills of lading which were in the CONLINEBILL form, clause 3 of which provided that 'Any dispute arising under this Bill of Lading shall be decided in the country where the carrier has his principal place of business.' The carrier's place of business was Greece and accordingly it applied for a stay of the Hong Kong proceedings. But the matter was complicated by the fact that two of the plaintiffs were not parties to bills of lading containing the exclusive jurisdiction clause for Greece. The plaintiffs premised their argument on the undesirability of separating the various causes of action against the carrier and then advanced the view that, as no stay should be granted against those plaintiffs not party to any jurisdiction agreement on *forum non conveniens* grounds, there should be no stay of the common proceedings. This argument was rejected but not, it would appear, on the basis that it was an unmeritorious and impermissible strategic endeavour to escape the operation of the exclusive jurisdiction clause in the vast majority of the bills of lading under which the plaintiffs' claims arose. Rather, Fuad VP, with whom Pellington JA and Barnett J agreed, granted the application to stay on the basis that Greece was in fact the natural forum. Had this happy coincidence of natural and nominated forum not been present, however, it is quite conceivable that the apparent strategy of those plaintiffs party to the exclusive jurisdiction agreements may have succeeded. The tail would very much have wagged the jurisdictional dog.

5.98 Whether for tactical or other reasons, the commencement of fifth party proceedings in Victoria by a fourth defendant in breach of an exclusive jurisdiction agreement for the courts of Charleroi (Belgium) was not

---

[350] [2000] 2 Lloyd's Rep 670, 680–681.
[351] See *The Kislovodsk* [1980] 1 Lloyd's Rep 183, 186.
[352] See *The Makefjell* [1975] 1 Lloyd's Rep 528, 533.
[353] 6 July 1990, noted by Margolis, R (n 287 above).

permitted in *Blackman & Co v Oliver Davey Glass Co.*[354] Like *The Frinton*, other parties to the litigation were not bound by this agreement. Moreover, Victoria was clearly the natural forum and it was clear that proceedings against the fourth defendant would continue there. But the Full Court held that the possibility that the fourth defendant, if found to be liable, could not seek an indemnity from the fifth defendant in Victoria because of the staying of the fifth party proceedings was a consequence it should have borne in mind at the time it entered into the agreement.[355] The consequences of an inconsistent decision on liability by the Belgian court would presumably have to be similarly borne.[356] This decision, which placed a premium on upholding parties' bargains, may be somewhat out of date with the approach manifested in more recent cases involving complex multi-party litigation.

In the shipping context, especially where the vessel has been slot char- **5.99** tered, the existence of a jurisdiction clause in a bill of lading may not yield jurisdictional certainty because where, for example, an incident occurs affecting all the cargo on board, a myriad of cargo claims may be made. Different bills of lading issued by different charterers may not all nominate the same forum. Enforcing jurisdiction clauses in those circumstances would lead to expensive fragmentation and duplication. In *The MC Pearl,* [357] Rix J observed that 'this is indeed a paradigm case for the concentration of all the relevant parties' disputes in a single jurisdiction. If in such a case a host of different jurisdiction clauses were to be observed, the casualty at the root of the action would become virtually untriable. The action would fragment and re-duplicate, at vast cost.'[358] Paradoxically, where what is provided for is arbitration rather than exclusive jurisdiction, there is no scope for the discretionary refusal to enforce the arbitration clause unless the view were adopted that a particular dispute was so entwined with a related dispute involving a party not party to the arbitration agreement that it could not be said that the 'matter' being sought to be referred to arbitration was 'capable of settlement by arbitration' with the consequence that the New York Convention is not applicable.

Each case will necessarily turn on its own facts. In *Donohue v Armco, Inc,*[359] **5.100** the House of Lords was acutely conscious of the fact that, by refusing to enforce the exclusive jurisdiction clause by anti-suit injunction, it was

---

[354] [1966] VR 570.
[355] ibid 577. See also *The Jemrix* [1981] 2 Lloyd's Rep 544.
[356] cf *Société Nationale Industrielle Aerospatiale v Lee Kui Jak* [1987] 1 AC 871, 902.
[357] [1997] 1 Lloyd's Rep 566.
[358] ibid 569.
[359] [2002] 1 Lloyd's Rep 425.

depriving the claimant of part of his bargain with the moving party in the New York proceedings. This was a matter that had to be weighed closely in the equation. Two strong policies were in tension—the wish to uphold commercial bargains, on the one hand, and the desire to avoid multiple proceedings with attendant duplication, expense, and the possibility of inconsistent decisions, on the other hand. The House was able to accommodate its concerns, in part at least, by imposing a condition upon the moving party in the New York proceedings that Mr Donohue would be protected from liability under the RICO Act in New York and by receiving an acknowledgement from that party that it could be sued, presumably in England, for damages for breach of contract.

8. ESCAPE AT ENFORCEMENT

5.101 Thus far arguments have been explored which might be deployed by a party seeking to extricate itself from the effects of an exclusive jurisdiction clause or which, at the very least, may provide a plausible basis for an unwelcome jurisdictional battle, the prospect or outcome of which may force a settlement from the party seeking to uphold the jurisdiction agreement. One last argument remains to be considered. It focuses upon attempts to resist the enforcement of a judgment given by the nominated court pursuant to a jurisdiction clause (exclusive or non-exclusive).[360] At common law, for example, many of the arguments which have been discussed in paragraphs 5.16 ff, 5.27 ff, 5.49 ff, 5.54 ff, and 5.61 ff above may also be deployed at the enforcement stage. Thus it may be argued that there was no effective agreement to the jurisdiction clause,[361] that the dispute the subject of the foreign judgment did not fall within the scope of the jurisdiction agreement, on its proper construction, or that such agreement was obtained by undue influence. Such defences are not available under Council Regulation 44/2001 or the Brussels or Lugano Conventions.

5.102 That the extent of the availability of such defences at common law may be limited, however, can be inferred from *Israel Discount Bank of New York v Hadjipateras*.[362] If the defendant did actually challenge the jurisdiction of the foreign court, although this may not amount to submission, the defendant could not resist enforcement on the basis of any argument either

---

[360] Such enforcement, of course, will only be attempted where the defendant's assets in the nominated forum are insufficient to meet the judgment debt.

[361] Such an argument was unsuccessfully made in *Copin v Adamson* (1875) LR 1 Ex D 17, where a jurisdiction agreement was held to exist in the company's articles of association.

[362] [1984] 1 WLR 137.

made or available to it in the foreign forum.[363] This is essentially an application of the rule in *Henderson v Henderson*[364] to 'issue estoppel' which the House of Lords made plain applies to jurisdiction clauses in *The Sennar (No 2)*.[365]

It may be asked why a defendant would ever effectively prefer to fight the **5.103** jurisdictional battle at the enforcement stage. Although the arguments open to a defendant will be fewer,[366] there may be some tactical advantage in this course depending upon the facts of a given case. For example, the defendant will avoid the possibility of being held to have submitted to the foreign forum by unsuccessfully contesting its jurisdiction (and thus activating a basis for enforcement). While this would not count as submission in the United Kingdom,[367] for example, it may represent the law in jurisdictions in which the defendant has assets and in which the common law position as to what constitutes submission is followed.[368] Alternatively, in a clear case, a defendant may choose to avoid the inconvenience of retaining foreign lawyers to make its case, especially in circumstances where the court purporting to exercise jurisdiction does not allow the recovery of costs by a successful party.

III. CONCLUSION

Exclusive jurisdiction agreements, if rigorously enforced, and non-exclu- **5.104** sive jurisdiction agreements, to a lesser extent, offer a considerable antidote to what is generally viewed as the undesirable practice of forum shopping. They anticipate future battles over venue and, in the vast majority of cases, are effective in preventing them. Given that a great deal can turn on success or failure in such a battle, it follows that jurisdiction clauses may in themselves constitute an important and commercially significant part of a wider contractual agreement. The strategic and commercial significance of venue, on the other hand, however, also dictates that there will often be a considerable incentive for parties to seek to escape the strictures of any jurisdiction agreement. This chapter has focused upon the various arguments which may be deployed pursuant to this strategy.

---

[363] With the possible (though illogical) exception that the jurisdiction agreement had been procured by fraud: see *Owens Bank v Bracco* [1992] 2 AC 443.

[364] (1843) 3 Hare 100.

[365] [1985] 1 WLR 490. See Barnett, PR, *Res Judicata, Estoppel and Foreign Judgments* (2001) paras 5.35–5.48.

[366] There is no equivalent discretionary basis available at the enforcement stage, for example.

[367] Section 33 of the Civil Jurisdiction and Judgments Act 1982.

[368] See the Court of Appeal's judgment in *Henry v Geoprosco International Ltd* [1976] QB 726.

5.105 An examination of English and Commonwealth decisions in this area discloses some unevenness in approach towards the enforcement of jurisdiction agreements depending upon whether the court nominated is foreign or that of the forum state. There would appear to be more scope for a party seeking to extricate itself from such jurisdictional arrangements in the former case. Matters of discretion aside, it has also been seen that there are several further arguments which may be deployed by a party seeking to escape the effects of an exclusive jurisdiction clause. When the choice of law questions which underpin such arguments are fully appreciated, the certainty yielded by the exercise of formalizing jurisdictional arrangements at the time of entry into contractual relations may be somewhat illusory. Even in this least likely of areas, one theme recurs. That is that the venue in which it is decided a transnational dispute should be fought out is of paramount importance in modern transnational litigation. And this is the case even if substantive proceedings never come on foot.

6

Conclusion

'Forum shopping' is a phrase which has entered into the common **6.01**
parlance of courts dealing with transnational disputes in the last three
decades. As a practice, it is undoubtedly older than that, for it constitutes
a totally rational response to a situation where a range of forums is available for the resolution of a given transnational dispute. In these circumstances it is not surprising that plaintiffs, or their legal advisers, will be
astute to differences between litigating in particular forums and will
select that forum which offers the best prospects for the most favourable
outcome from the plaintiff's perspective.

What perhaps accounts for the increased judicial and academic awareness **6.02**
of forum shopping is the coincident emergence of a global economy, a
factor which has been apt to generate an increased number of disputes
with a transnational dimension and, as a related consequence, to offer a
range of potential forums in which these disputes may be litigated. Not to
be underestimated in this context is the significance of the growth of international law firms, whether organized on a formal basis or de facto
through the development of strong agency relationships between national
firms in different jurisdictions. Such firms are not only able to co-ordinate
complex transnational litigation but, through their pooled resources and
expertise, are in a position to identify in which forum a plaintiff would be
well advised to commence litigation. According to the potential forums
available on the facts of any given case, this decision may be affected by
differences in procedure as between forums such as the level and mode of
damages available or the attitude of the respective forums to documentary discovery. Alternatively, it may be conditioned by an assessment of
what law a particular forum would apply to the dispute. This assessment
will go beyond simply identifying each forum's particular domestic law
for, *ex hypothesi*, choice of law issues will arise in the type of transnational
disputes under consideration.

The foregoing description of the practice of forum shopping suggests that **6.03**
the venue in which a transnational dispute is to be resolved may be of
vital importance for the ultimate outcome of the dispute. This will especially be so the greater the differences, whether in matters of procedure,
substantive principles of law, or conflict of law rules, between potentially
available forums. Many of these differences, which are the root cause of
forum shopping, were explored in Chapter 2. It was there seen, at least in

relation to various aspects of procedure, that the United States provides a particularly attractive destination for the concerted forum shopper. But it should not be thought that the United States is the only forum (or, more accurately, collection of forums) to which a plaintiff will look in considering potential venues in which to litigate a transnational dispute. So much emerges from the large body of case law that has been considered in this book. Certainly much of it has involved clashes over the question whether litigation should occur in a particular forum or the United Sates but that is by no means exclusively the case. Depending on the facts of any given dispute, other forums may also yield attractions for plaintiffs. And it would seem to follow as a consequence not only of increased international trade but also increasing familiarity with the legal systems of different countries that, left unchecked, forum shopping is a practice that is likely to grow.

6.04 Judicial responses to forum shopping have been almost entirely negative and the phrase generally carries pejorative connotations when found in judgments. It has not yet been elevated to formal juridical status, that is to say, the identification and classification of a case as a 'forum shopping case' does not result in automatic legal consequences. Nevertheless it is clear that antipathy towards forum shopping has fuelled various responses to this practice. Two such responses were examined in Chapter 3. The first, embodied in the model provided by the Brussels Convention and now in Council Regulation 44/2001, does not eradicate the potential for forum shopping in the sense of only ever allocating one forum in which any given dispute may be resolved. Rather, it seeks to restrict a plaintiff's choice of forum to what are deemed to be acceptable and jurisdictionally appropriate limits. It was argued that, for this reason, it is not appropriate to characterize litigation commenced pursuant to a choice provided by the Regulation or Conventions as 'forum shopping', at least in the traditional and negative sense in which that phrase is used and understood in the common law.

6.05 While those instruments seek to provide the parties to a transnational dispute with some certainty as to the forum(s) available for its resolution, the common law's response to forum shopping or jockeying for venue, on the other hand, places increased emphasis on judicial discretion mediated (other than in Australia) through the concept of the 'natural forum'. The emergence of that concept was in response not only to the perceived evil of forum shopping but also to the more general problems of concurrent litigation. The theoretical foundation underscoring the concept of the natural forum is one that equates to procedural fairness in a transnational context. The notion of the natural forum responds to a perception that it is fundamentally unfair to permit the plaintiff to make a unilateral decision as to the venue in which a piece of transnational litigation will be resolved. Cognate with this is a recognition of the potential significance of choice of forum for the ultimate outcome of a given piece of transnational litigation.

Consideration of the natural forum, which typically only becomes of **6.06** importance when there is an actual contest over venue, requires a court to identify, according to objective connecting factors, that forum with which the dispute has the closest and most real connection. Unless the parties have made special provision otherwise in the form of a jurisdiction or arbitration agreement, this forum is the one in which it is considered the parties would reasonably expect any disputes to be tried and the forum whose laws (including conflicts rules) would determine the content of their respective rights and liabilities. A defendant's right to insist that proceedings be stayed in favour of the natural forum provides both an antidote to, and a disincentive for a plaintiff to engage in, forum shopping. The natural forum, moreover, acts as something of a unifying concept in the broader area of the common law dealing with questions of venue in transnational litigation, being of importance in the exercise of jurisdiction against parties outside the forum, forming an element of what is required to be shown before anti-suit injunctive relief will be granted, and having an incipient role to play in the recognition and enforcement of foreign judgments.

Apart from forum shopping in the narrow sense of the term, this book has **6.07** also illustrated the fact that modern transnational litigation frequently involves several parties which may have a complex array of claims and cross-claims against each other. Such a factual scenario produces dilemmas which must be considered in any study of venue in transnational litigation, for parties will seek to exploit all jurisdictional possibilities in an endeavour either to maximize their chances of success or else minimize their liability. This may involve the initiation of litigation in several forums, either by the same or different parties. Such tactical manoeuvrings may also be considered to be a type of forum shopping in the sense that they represent the deliberate exploitation of broadly drawn jurisdictional rules. It has been seen that the Council Regulation and Brussels and Lugano Conventions address this difficulty by providing various mechanisms designed to forestall concurrent litigation and channel all related litigation into one forum. Ironically, however, it has been seen that the rigidity of certain aspects of those schemes may sometimes promote fractured or fragmented litigation.

Common law courts have also been sensitive to the desideratum of mini- **6.08** mizing the scope for concurrent litigation. This concern is fuelled by a justifiable dislike for inconsistent decisions and the entanglement of the courts in a 'race' for judgment. Moreover, such multiplication of litigation represents a waste of resources. It has been argued that the natural forum is, within the limits on certainty implicit in any discretionary jurisdiction, a sufficiently sophisticated and sensitive tool to respond to the frequent complexities of modern transnational litigation. Courts applying the calculus of the natural forum have on the whole placed emphasis on the need and importance of identifying the natural forum in the context of the overall dispute, that is to say, they have taken an appropriately global perspective.

6.09 In the battle over venue in transnational litigation, the defendant is far from impotent. In this context, Chapter 4 sought to show that forum shopping is by no means the sole domain of plaintiffs for while, with the exception of cases in which negative declaratory relief is sought by a party which would normally be a defendant, plaintiffs enjoy the initial choice as to venue, there are various strategies which a defendant may employ to thwart this choice and thereby affect the central question of venue for the resolution of the dispute. None of these strategies, it must be said, however, provides a total panacea for defendants engaged in litigation with a forum shopping plaintiff. Apart from the fact that not all strategies will be available on the facts or in the circumstances of a given case, many of them have limitations which may work to insulate the plaintiff's choice of forum. Thus it was seen that the strength of a case which a plaintiff is required to establish in seeking leave to serve a defendant outside the forum has been diluted in England, while in Australia a plaintiff need not establish that the relevant state or federal jurisdiction is *forum conveniens*, merely that it is 'not clearly inappropriate'. In the United States, it will be difficult to obtain a stay of proceedings commenced by a United States national. It was also seen that the doctrinal integrity of concept of the natural forum has been partially emasculated through the use of the so-called 'justice' exception in cases where the individual demands of often injured and/or impoverished plaintiffs confront the courts. While the existence of the exception is not questioned, nor the need for its residual role doubted, it has been seen that parochial notions of justice have in some cases resulted in defendants being denied the opportunity to argue cases in what is accepted to be the natural forum.

6.10 When one turns to the third 'reverse forum shopping' strategy, the anti-suit injunction, apart from technical jurisdictional obstacles which may stand in the way of this form of relief from the outset, an understandable judicial reluctance to restrain foreign proceedings on the basis that so to do would run counter to concerns of international comity may mean that this tool is of limited utility. On the other hand, it has been argued that the claims of comity should be considered according to the precise context in which the anti-suit relief is sought and that, in this light, the bland invocation of comity should not suffice to convince a judge to refrain from restraining foreign proceedings in appropriate circumstances. If the courts are genuinely concerned to police forum shopping, then the anti-suit injunction will be an important part of their weaponry. In certain circumstances, for example, directing an applicant for anti-suit relief to seek a stay in the foreign forum may be to consign it to the very kind of vexation and oppression that the equitable jurisdiction is designed to protect parties against. An order restraining such proceedings may not only be more expeditious but a surer way of ensuring that a forum shopping plaintiff does not gain an improper advantage in the battle for venue in transnational litigation.

It has also been seen and suggested that anti-suit injunctions may be **6.11** deployed to effectuate another important policy goal about which courts have been increasingly vocal, namely the desirability, so far as is possible, of grouping or consolidating litigation in order to avoid the prospect of inconsistent decisions emanating from the courts of different countries. The anti-suit injunction may be used proactively in this context to ensure that all aspects of a particular dispute are resolved in one forum.

The fourth reverse forum shopping strategy, the application for negative **6.12** declaratory relief, is one which, traditionally at least, has been the least efficacious for defendants in common law jurisdictions other than the United States. That circumstance, as has been seen, has undergone a recent change in a manner that is potentially advantageous to putative defendants. So long as proceedings are not hypothetical, permitting a defendant at least the opportunity of seeking negative declaratory relief is one very obvious and direct way of ensuring that plaintiffs are not always the parties with control over the venue and timing of litigation. The past and occasionally lingering deprecation of negative declaratory relief on the footing that it lends itself to forum shopping is somewhat ironic as it is qualitatively no different from any case in which a plaintiff chooses when and where to commence proceedings. There is nothing peculiar about the form of relief per se which warrants the adverse attitude traditionally taken towards it by common law courts. On this basis, and again not without an element of irony, the opportunity to seek negative declaratory relief may yet prove a highly effective reverse forum shopping strategy.

The final course open to a defendant in the battle over venue in transna- **6.13** tional litigation was seen to be the simple expedient of ignoring foreign proceedings in circumstances where the defendant lacked assets in that forum. This strategy, however, is likely to be of diminished practical value for the reason that, as was seen in Chapter 1, one of the characteristics of the modern economy and the multinational business enterprise is the diversification of assets and the mobility of capital. On a doctrinal level, also, the efficacy of this strategy is undermined for defendants to proceedings in Europe or, in circumstances where a defendant has assets in Canada at least, as a result of a most significant common law development in relation to the recognition and enforcement of foreign judgments in that country.

6.14 The difficulties posed by the combination of concurrent jurisdiction and the lack of uniformity at all levels of the law between different countries, and the clashes over venue which are the product of these circumstances, may of course be resolved consensually. In commercial transactions, in particular, parties commonly anticipate such potential clashes by agreeing as part of the contractual terms that a particular forum may have jurisdiction for the purposes of any future legal disputes between the parties. Such agreements not only minimize the scope for interlocutory litigation battles over the question of venue, but they also, it has been argued, recognize the commercial value and significance of the forum in which a particular dispute is to be resolved. That value represents the projected difference between the possible outcome in the nominated forum and that in other potentially available jurisdictions based on differences in procedure, substantive principles of law, and the conflict of laws rules in the respective forums. The proposition underlying this analysis, and the fundamental premise of this book, namely that venue can matter a great deal in transnational litigation, is confirmed by the number and variety of arguments which the cases record as having been deployed by parties in an endeavour to extricate themselves from jurisdiction agreements. These arguments formed the principal focus of Chapter 5 and the unmistakable inference is that the significance of venue is such that parties are prepared to engage in interlocutory litigation, often to an appellate level, in an endeavour to avoid the projected consequences of suing or being sued in the nominated forum.

6.15 This allows a more general point to be made in conclusion. That is that the vast bulk of material upon which this book has drawn emanates from the law reports of the last two decades. That is perhaps hardly surprising in a work of this nature but it does tend to illustrate not only the growth in transnational litigation in recent years but also the central significance of the question of venue. The law reports do not reflect a similar concern with questions of choice of law, the traditional domain of academic scholarship in the conflict of laws. One explanation for this disparity undoubtedly lies in the fact that the vast majority of transnational disputes settle.

While this is no doubt also true in the case of purely domestic legal disputes, a peculiar consequence of transnational disputes is that there is a range of parameters against which settlement may take place, namely the different forums which are potentially available for the resolution of the substantive issues and the enforcement of any judgments or awards. Given likely and important differences at all levels of the law between such forums, the question of in what venue the dispute will ultimately be tried may become a crucially significant contingency in settlement negotiations. This book has explored the law surrounding the battle that frequently attends the identification of that venue.

Index

Anti-deposition injunction 4.126–4.128
Anti-suit injunctions
  Anti-Anti-Anti-suit injunctions
    4.142
  Anti-Anti-suit injunctions 4.136–4.141
  Brussels Convention and Council
    Regulation 44/2001 3.28, 3.33,
    4.166–4.178
  Comity, and 4.86, 4.114, 4.120, 4.186,
    4.223–4.249
  Development of 4.107–4.124
  Generally 4.79–4.249
  Historical origins of 4.85–4.86
  Inconvenience, and 4.200–4.203
  Jurisdiction and arbitration agreements,
    in aid of 4.146–4.178
  Jurisdiction, to protect 4.125–4.144
  Multiple proceedings, and 4.204–4.216
  Natural forum, and 3.147–3.148
  Personal jurisdiction over defendant,
    requirement for 4.88–4.93
  Reasons for seeking 4.79–4.82
  Single forum cases, and 4.96–4.102
  Terminology 4.83
  United States, in the 4.118–4.122, 4.209,
    4.213
  Vexatious and oppressive conduct, to
    restrain 4.179–4.222
Arbitration Agreements
  Anti-suit injunctions and 4.146–4.178
  Arbitration agreements, reasons for
    1.28–1.29
  Bills of lading, and 5.24
  Existence of 5.16–5.26
  Generally Chapter 5 *passim*
  Mandatory law, and 5.47–5.48
  Matter to be 'capable of settlement by
    arbitration' 5.47–5.48
  Multi-party proceedings, and 3.137
  New York Convention 3.137, 5.03, 5.15,
    5.99
  Scope of 5.61–5.71
  Separability, doctrine of 5.36
  Voidability 5.27–5.36
Australia
  Akai litigation 4.100, 4.140, 4.233, 5.46
  Anti-suit injunctions 4.117, 4.134
  Forum non conveniens 3.94, 4.67–4.73
  Forum shopping within 4.09
  Insurance Contracts Act 2.50–2.51, 3.108,
    5.38
  Jurisdiction agreements 5.67, 5.82
  Jurisdictional rules 1.21, 4.18, 4.26

  Multiple proceedings, attitude towards
    3.103
  Substance and procedure 2.11–2.13
  Trade Practices Act 3.109, 3.111, 4.71,
    5.38, 5.45, 5.48, 5.67

**Brussels Convention (see European
    Council Regulation 44/2001)**
  Origins of 3.06–3.09

Canada
  Anti-suit injunctions 3.148, 4.116
  Comity 3.148, 4.116
  Enforcement of judgments 3.148,
    4.296–4.303
  Jurisdiction agreements 5.66, 5.82
  Jurisdictional rules 1.22
  Natural forum, and 3.148
  Stay of proceedings 3.134
Choice of law rules
  Characterization, and 2.42
  Continuing efficacy of jurisdiction
    agreement, and 5.52
  Equity 2.38
  Existence of jurisdiction or arbitration
    agreement, and 5.16–5.21
  Family law 2.38, 2.59
  Forum shopping, and 1.42, 2.02,
    2.40–2.44, 2.48
  Lex fori 2.38–2.39
  Mandatory laws, and 2.48–2.54
  Personal law 2.41
  'Proper law' rules 2.43–2.44
  Scope of jurisdiction and arbitration
    agreements 5.62
  Shift away from 1.31, 6.15
  Significance for forum shopping 1.34,
    2.37–2.44, 4.57–4.58
Comity
  Anti-suit injunctions, and 4.86, 4.114,
    4.120, 4.186, 4.223–4.249
  Exorbitant jurisdiction, and 4.16–4.20
  Multiple proceedings, and 3.96–3.98,
    3.102, 3.120
  Negative declarations and 4.272–4.274
  Significance of 1.27
Comparative procedural law 1.02
**Concurrent proceedings (see Multiple
    Proceedings)**
Convention *double* 3.08–3.09, 3.51–3.55,
    3.66, 3.171
Convention *simple* 3.07

Corporations 1.13–1.15
    One-ship companies 1.13
Costs
    Contingency fees, and 2.15, 2.21, 2.28
    Relevance to forum selection 4.55
    United States, in the 2.15, 2.16, 2.21
Damages
    Differences between jurisdictions 1.36,
        2.17–2.22, 2.29, 2.48
    Jurisdiction and arbitration agreements,
        for breach of 4.149–4.151
    Multiple damages 2.22
    United States, in the 2.17–2.22,
        4.190
Defamation (see **Libel**)
Disclosure (see **Discovery**)
Discovery
    Anti-suit injunctions, and 4.130–4.133,
        4.187–4.190
    Civilian attitudes towards 2.23–2.24
    Product liability, and 2.24
    Significance of in transnational
        litigation 2.23–2.27
    United States, in the 2.16, 2.23,
        2.26–2.27

European Council Regulation 44/2001
    Anti-suit injunctions, and 3.28, 3.33,
        4.166–4.178
    Concurrent proceedings 3.22–3.40
    Forum non conveniens, and 4.62–4.66
    Forum Shopping under 2.29
    Generally 3.03–3.49
    Jurisdiction agreements, and 5.28, 5.39,
        5.50, 5.69, 5.72–5.78
    Jurisdiction, challenging 4.34–4.37
    Recognition and enforcement of judg-
        ments under 3.45–3.48, 4.295
    Related proceedings 3.41–3.44
    Reverse forum shopping, and 4.07
    Significance of defendant's domicile
        3.17–3.18, 3.58
    Special jurisdiction 3.20–3.23

Family law
    Choice of law for property settlements
        2.59
    Choice of law rule for divorce 2.38
Foreign Law
    Natural forum, and 3.94, 3.163
    Need to prove 2.46–2.47
Forum non conveniens (see also **Natural
        forum, Stays of proceedings**)
    Australia 4.67–4.73
    Canada 4.39, 4.42
    European Council Regulation 44/2001,
        and 3.58, 4,62–4.66

Hong Kong 4.39, 4.58
New Zealand 4.41
United Kingdom 3.71–3.102,
    3.104–3.107
United States, in 3.164, 4.74–4.78
Forum Shopping
    Choice of law, and 1.42, 2.02, 2.40–2.44
    Council Regulation 44/2001, and 3.23
    Fairness, and 3.85–3.89
    Generally 1.34–1.43, 2.07, 4.77, Chapter
        6 *passim*
    Multi-party cases, in 3.117–3.118
    Negative declarations, and 4.270,
        4.275–4.283, 4.286–4.287
    Propriety of 1.40–1.42, 2.05, 2.18,
        3.79–3.80, 3.85–3.89
    Reasons for 1.33, 1.41, 2.01–2.07
    Reverse forum, shopping Chapter 4
        passim
    Rule of law, and 1.27, 1.41, 3.152
    Settlement, and 1.35–1.39
    Traditional encouragement in England
        3.74, 3.78
    Undertakings, role of 4.05

Hague Conference 2.40
    Multilateral jurisdiction and judgments
        convention 3.52, 3.56–3.57,
        3.172
Human Rights 4.52, 4.158

Insolvency
    Anti-suit injunctions and 4.143–4.144,
        4.220
    Jurisdiction agreements, and 5.43–5.44
Insurance
    Akai litigation 4.100, 4.140, 4.233,
        5.46
    Incorporation of jurisdiction/arbitration
        agreements in 5.26
    Jurisdiction agreements and Council
        Regulation 44/2001 5.35
    Lloyd's 5.05, 5.45
    Mandatory laws, and 2.50
    Multi-party proceedings, and
        3.123–3.134, 3.138–3.139
    Public policy, and 2.56
Intellectual Property
    Jurisdiction 2.36, 5.43–5.44
    Patents 2.29, 2.34
    Single forum cases, and 3.108,
        4.100–101
    Source of mandatory forum law,
        as a 2.53
Internet 2.54
International travel 1.06, 1.16

Judgments
  Canadian approach towards 3.148,
     4.296–4.303
  Council Regulation 44/2001, and
     3.45–3.48, 4.295
  Enforceability, significance of 1.15, 2.32
  Natural forum, role in 3.148
  'Race to' 1.27
Jurisdiction
  Challenges to 4.13–4.37
  Civil law, under 1.20
  Common law, under 3.68–3.70
  Council Regulation 44/2001 3.13–3.48,
     4.34–4.37
  'Effects' jurisdiction 1.23
  'Exorbitant' or 'long arm' 1.10,
     1.19–1.25
  Extraterritoria 1.23
  International conventions as source of
     3.03–3.06
  'Tag' jurisdiction 1.14, 1.16
  United States, in the 4.28–4.33
Jurisdiction Agreements
  Anti-suit injunctions and 4.146–4.178
  Bills of lading, and 5.24, 5.66, 5.97, 5.99
  Council Regulation 44/2001 3.15–3.16,
     5.28, 5.39, 5.50, 5.69, 5.72–5.78
  Discretion, and 5.72–5.100
  Existence of 5.16–5.26
  Generally Chapter 5 *passim*
  Incorporation of 5.22–5.26
  Insurance and consumer contracts 3.16
  Mandatory law, and 5.47–5.48
  Multi-party proceedings, and 3.136,
     5.94–5.100
  Neutral venue, as providing a 5.07
  Non-exclusive jurisdiction agreements
     5.54–5.60
  Reasons for 1.28–1.29
  Scope of 5.61–5.71
  Separability, doctrine of 5.36
  Voidability 5.27–5.36

Law Firms 1.07, 6.02
Legal Aid 2.31, 4.52
Libel 1.26
Lis Pendens (see **Multiple Proceedings**)

Mandatory Law
  Anti-suit injunctions, and 4.141
  Articulation of 5.41
  Incentive for forum shopping, as an
     2.48–2.54
  Overriding jurisdiction and arbitration
     agreements 5.37–5.48
Multi-party Proceedings
  Complex litigation 3.114–3.144

  Jurisdiction and arbitration agreements
     5.94–5.100
Multiple Proceedings
  Anti-suit injunctions and 4.163–4.165;
     4.196, 4.203–4.216
  Australian attitude towards 3.103
  Complex litigation 3.114–3.144
  Council Regulation 44/2001 and 3.09,
     3.25–3.44
  First filed rule 3.27, 3.31–3.32
  Jurisdiction agreements, and 5.94–5.100
  Natural forum, and 3.96–3.113
  Related proceedings 3.41–3.44
  Traditional English attitude towards
     3.76
  United States attitude towards
     3.141–3.142

Natural Forum (see also *Forum non
     conveniens*, **Stays of proceedings**)
  Abuse of process, and 3.165–3.169
  Anti-suit injunctions, and 3.147–3.148
  Australian attitude towards 4.67–4.73
  Cambridgeshire factor 3.93, 3.114
  Complex litigation 3.114–3.144
  Concurrent litigation 3.96–3.113
  Connecting factors 3.91–3.92, 3.163,
     4.73
  Convenience, and 3.90–3.95
  Criticism of the concept 3.149–3.169
  Derogations from in interests of justice
     4.47–4.61
  Development of the concept 3.78–3.83
  Enforcement of judgments, and 3.148
  Fairness, and 3.85–3.89
  Forum shopping, and 1.47, 3.84–3.148
  Human rights, and 4.52
  Interests of justice, and the 4.47–4.61
  Juridical advantages 3.158–3.159
  Multiple parties, and 3.114–3.144
  Multiple proceedings, and 3.100–3.113
  Negative declarations 3.106–3.107,
     3.139
  Rule of law, and 3.151–3.155
  Service out of jurisdiction, and
     4.23–4.25
  Single forum cases, and 3.108
Negative declarations
  Anti-suit injunctions and 4.198–4.199
  Comity, and 4.272–4.274
  Council Regulation 44/2001 and
     4.284–4.293
  Forum shopping, and 4.275–4.283
  Generally 4.250–4.293
  Natural forum, and 3.106–3.107

Personal Injury 1.21–1.22, 2.11, 2.17

Product Liability
  Damages, and 2.29
  Discovery, and 2.24, 2.29
  Forum shopping, and 2.34
  Jurisdiction, and 2.35–2.36
Provisional measures 1.27, 1.28
  Forum shopping, as a reason for 2.31
Public Policy (see also **Mandatory Law**)
  Anti-suit injunctions in aid of
    4.143–4.144
  Articulation of 2.57
  Incentive for forum shopping, as an
    2.55

Res judicata 1.27
**Rome Convention on Law Applicable to
    Contractual Obligations** 2.40,
    5.16

Service of Process
  Common law rules, and 4.13–4.26
  Natural forum, and 3.145–3.146
Settlement 1.35–1.39, 2.27, 2.58, 3.99, 3.169,
    4.03, 5.83, 6.15
Shipping
  Arrest jurisdiction 1.17
  Choice of law on high seas 2.39
  Collision Convention 2.52
  Hague-Visby rules 5.37–5.38
  Jurisdiction and arbitration clauses, and
    5.24–5.25, 5.66, 5.97, 5.99
  Limitation funds 2.52, 2.56
  Multi-party disputes 3.35–3.136, 5.97,
    5.99
  Multiple proceedings 3.101, 3.112
  One ship companies 1.13
  Stays of action 3.81, 4.58
Single forum cases 3.108–3.109, 4.96–4.102,
    5.44
Stays of proceedings (see also *Forum non
    conveniens*, **Natural forum**)

Approach pre-*Spiliada* 3.71–3.83
  Arbitration agreement, by reason of
    5.73
  Australia, in 3.103. 4.67–4.78
  European Council Regulation 44/2001,
    and 4.62–4.66
  Forum non conveniens, and 4.38
  Human rights, and 4.52
  Interests of justice, and the 4.47–4.61
  Jurisdiction agreement, by reason of
    5.72
  Limitation periods, and 4.50, 4.58
  Submission to jurisdiction, and 4.43
  Temporary stays 3.140
  United States, in the 4.74–4.78
Substance and Procedure 1.43, 2.09–2.13
  Limitation periods, and 2.13, 2.31

United States of America
  Alter ego doctrine 1.13
  Anti-suit injunctions 4.118–4.122, 4.209,
    4.213
  Constitution 3.10, 4.28–4.34
  Costs 2.15–2.16, 2.21
  Damages 2.17–2.22, 3.52
  Discovery 2.16, 2.23, 2.26–2.27
  Effects doctrine 1.23, 3.52
  First-filed rule 3.27
  Forum non conveniens 4.42, 4.74–4.78
  Forum shopping and 2.14–2.22
  Forum shopping within 4.09
  Full faith and credit 3.10–3.11
  Juries 2.19–2.21, 3.52
  Jurisdiction agreements, and 5.06, 5.08,
    5.12, 5.33–5.34, 5.82, 5.88
  Jurisdictional rules in 1.24, 4.28–4.34
  Multi-party proceedings 3.141–3.142
  'Proper law' choice of law rules, and
    2.44
  Sherman Act 3.111, 4.217–4.219,
    4.187–4.188, 4.222, 5.47